The Rorschach: A Comprehensive System, in two volumes
by John E. Exner, Jr.

Theory and Practice in Behavior Therapy
by Aubrey J. Yates

Principles of Psychotherapy
by Irving B. Weiner

Psychoactive Drugs and Social Judgment: Theory and Research
edited by Kenneth Hammond and C. R. B. Joyce

Clinical Methods in Psychology
edited by Irving B. Weiner

Human Resources for Troubled Children
by Werner I. Halpern and Stanley Kissel

Hyperactivity
by Dorothea M. Ross and Sheila A. Ross

Heroin Addiction: Theory, Research and Treatment
by Jerome J. Platt and Christina Labate

Children's Rights and the Mental Health Profession
edited by Gerald P. Koocher

The Role of the Father in Child Development
edited by Michael E. Lamb

Handbook of Behavioral Assessment
edited by Anthony R. Ciminero, Karen S. Calhoun, and Henry E. Adams

Counseling and Psychotherapy: A Behavioral Approach
by E. Lakin Phillips

Dimensions of Personality
edited by Harvey London and John E. Exner, Jr.

The Mental Health Industry: A Cultural Phenomenon
by Peter A. Magaro, Robert Gripp, David McDowell, and Ivan W. Miller III

Nonverbal Communication: The State of the Art
by Robert G. Harper, Arthur N. Wiens, and Joseph D. Matarazzo

Alcoholism and Treatment
by David J. Armor, J. Michael Polich, and Harriet B. Stambul

A Biodevelopmental Approach to Clinical Child Psychology: Cognitive Controls and Cognitive Control Theory
by Sebastiano Santostefano

Handbook of Infant Development
edited by Joy D. Osofsky

Understanding the Rape Victim: A Synthesis of Research Findings
by Sedelle Katz and Mary Ann Mazur

Childhood Pathology and Later Adjustment: The Question of Prediction
by Loretta K. Cass and Carolyn B. Thomas

Intelligent Testing with the WISC-R
by Alan S. Kaufman

Adaptation in Schizophrenia: The Theory of Segmental Set
by David Shakow

Psychotherapy: An Eclectic Approach
by Sol L. Garfield

Handbook of Minimal Brain Dysfunctions
edited by Herbert E. Rie and Ellen D. Rie

Handbook of Behavioral Interventions: A Clinical Guide
edited by Alan Goldstein and Edna B. Foa

Art Psychotherapy
by Harriet Wadeson

Handbook of Adolescent Psychology
edited by Joseph Adelson

Psychotherapy Supervision: Theory, Research and Practice
edited by Allen K. Hess

Continued on back

BEHAVIORAL MEDICINE

BEHAVIORAL MEDICINE
CLINICAL APPLICATIONS

SUSAN S. PINKERTON

Presbyterian Hospital
Dallas, Texas

HOWARD HUGHES

North Texas State University
Denton, Texas

W.W. WENRICH

North Texas State University
Denton, Texas

1807 1982

A WILEY-INTERSCIENCE PUBLICATION
JOHN WILEY & SONS
New York • Chichester • Brisbane • Toronto • Singapore

Copyright © 1982 by John Wiley & Sons, Inc.

Library of Congress Cataloging in Publication Data:

Pinkerton, Susan S.
  Behavioral medicine.

  (Wiley series on personality processes, ISSN 0195-4008)
  "A Wiley-Interscience publication."
  Includes index.
  Bibliography: p.
  1. Medicine and psychology. 2. Behavior therapy.
I. Hughes, Howard, 1937–   . II. Wenrich, W.W.,
1932–   . III. Title. IV. Series. [DNLM:
1. Behavior therapy. WM 425 P655b]

R726.5.P56   615.8′51   81-11417
ISBN 0-471-05619-7   AACR2

Printed in the United States of America

10 9 8 7 6 5 4 3 2 1

To the Pennsylvania Dutchman and my two "liebchen," Jody and Cissy.

S.S.P.

To Anita, whose love brings out the best in me.
To my father, who set the best of examples.
To my mother, who bolstered the confidence for independence of thought.
To Howard II, Jennifer, Halane, and Hillary, for their belief in and worth to me.

H.H.H.

To "Alice" and similar vicissitudes of life.

W.W.W.

Series Preface

This series of books is addressed to behavioral scientists interested in the nature of human personality. Its scope should prove pertinent to personality theorists and researchers as well as to clinicians concerned with applying an understanding of personality processes to the amelioration of emotional difficulties in living. To this end, the series provides a scholarly integration of theoretical formulations, empirical data, and practical recommendations.

Six major aspects of studying and learning about human personality can be designated: personality theory, personality structure and dynamics, personality development, personality assessment, personality change, and personality adjustment. In exploring these aspects of personality, the books in the series discuss a number of distinct but related subject areas: the nature and implications of various theories of personality: personality characteristics that account for consistencies and variations in human behavior; the emergence of personality processes in children and adolescents; the use of interviewing and testing procedures to evaluate individual differences in personality; efforts to modify personality styles through psychotherapy, counseling, behavior therapy, and other methods of influence; and patterns of abnormal personality functioning that impair individual competence.

IRVING B. WEINER

University of Denver
Denver, Colorado

Preface

In view of the prolific amount of behavioral research bearing on the treatment of problems heretofore regarded as unique to the medical profession, the development of interest groups, journals, and, recently, the Health Care Division of the American Psychological Association, as well as the appearance of a plethora of edited books germane to behavioral medicine, it appears that the concept and practice of behavioral medicine is well enmeshed in the Zeitgeist. With this observation, we contracted with our publisher over two years ago to write the first authored text in this domain. Our intent was to provide a comprehensive volume, helpful to professionals and paraprofessionals in both psychology and medicine.

The book is divided into two parts. The focus in Part I is to give the reader practical knowledge in the operation of basic behavioral principles and techniques as they relate to the treatment of maladies which in the past were seen as provinces of the physician. In Part II we attempt to demonstrate the manner in which these principles and techniques are brought to bear on the amelioration of specific medical and medically related problems through direct service applications.

It is hoped that this developing alliance between behavioral psychology and medicine will provide a format and practice that benefits both professions through more comprehensive and efficacious treatment interventions and increased effectiveness in reducing illness and enhancing health. While the introduction is not embedded within the chapters, the reader is strongly encouraged to read it prior to a review of any succeeding material. The introduction provides the point-of-view taken by the authors as well as an orientation to the book as a whole.

In conclusion, a comment must be made with regard to the sequencing of authors. Upon assuming contractual arrangements with John Wiley and Sons it was clearly recognized that at some point in time a decision would have to be made regarding the ordering of the authors' names. For one reason or another we did not attend to this matter until the book was in production. Finally, when the decision could no longer be forestalled, and upon urging by our editor, we decided to entrust the outcome to a game of chance.The resulting sequence of authors reflects nothing more than the fact that some were luckier at "odd man out" than others.

SUSAN S. PINKERTON
HOWARD HUGHES
W.W. WENRICH

September 1981

Contents

Introduction: A Synopsis of Behavioral Medicine, 1

Overview, 1
Treatment Interventions, 4
Applications, 5
Summary, 7
References, 8

PART I   TREATMENT INTERVENTIONS

CHAPTER

1   Assessment in Behavioral Medicine, 11

Overview, 11
Interview, 12
Questionnaires, 14
Self-Monitoring, 16
Behavioral Observation, 18
Psychophysiological Measurement, 22
Summary, 28
References, 28

2   Basic Respondent and Operant Techniques, 33

Overview, 33
Respondent Techniques, 33
Operant Techniques, 38
Summary, 48
References, 48

3   Biofeedback, 51

Overview, 48
Instrumentation, 53
Clinical Biofeedback Procedures, 53
Summary, 83
References, 84

4   Relaxation Training, 90

Overview, 90
Instrumentation, 91
Relaxation Procedures, 92
Summary, 102
References, 103

5   Cognitive Strategies, 107

Overview, 107
Cognitive Procedures, 112
Summary, 120
References, 122

6   Self-Management Techniques, 126

Overview, 126
Self-Management Procedures, 129
Summary, 135
References, 137

PART II   DIRECT APPLICATIONS

7   Cardiovascular Disorders, 145

Overview, 145
Hypertension, 146
Cardiac Arrhythmias, 157
Raynaud's Disease, 162
References, 165

8   Gastrointestinal Disorders, 174

Overview, 174
Anorexia Nervosa, 174
Chronic Vomiting, 174
Encopresis/Fecal Incontinence, 181
Ulcers, 185
Irritable Bowel Syndrome, 188
References, 190

9   Musculoskeletal Disorders, 196

Overview, 196
Spasmodic Torticollis, 196
Tics, 200

Cerebral Palsy, 203
Cerebrovascular Accidents, 205
Spinal Cord Injuries, 208
References, 210

10   Nervous System Disorder, 215

Overview, 215
Epilepsy, 216
References, 229

11   Respiratory Disorder, 233

Overview, 233
Asthma, 233
References, 244

12   Skin Disorders, 248

Overview, 248
Neurodermatitis, 249
Urticaria, 252
Psoriasis, 254
Prurigo Nodularis, 255
Hyperhidrosis, 256
Summary, 256
References, 258

13   Pain, 261

Overview, 261
Chronic Pain, 264
Headaches, 274
References, 286

14   Other Disorders, 293

Overview, 293
Insomnia, 293
Diabetes, 299
Dysmenorrhea, 303
Dental Disorders, 306
Cancer, 309
References, 313

Concluding Remarks, 322

Appendix, 323
   Biofeedback Instrumentation, 323
   Relaxation Training Instructions, 341
   Autogenic Training, 342
   References, 346

AUTHOR INDEX, 351

SUBJECT INDEX, 365

BEHAVIORAL MEDICINE

A Synopsis of Behavioral Medicine

OVERVIEW

The term "behavioral medicine" is being used with increasing frequency within the disciplines of psychology, medicine, and the allied health professions. Its employment focuses upon particular techniques of behavioral psychology in the therapeutic intervention and amelioration of problems heretofore regarded as unique to the practice and domain of the medical profession.

It has become apparent among a variety of professionals that problems of health and illness are not only related to physical factors, but to behavioral and environmental factors as well. Each of these factors contributes to the maladies and problems encountered in medical treatment. When a patient presents a physician with a physical complaint, the physical problem is often related to the behavior of the patient, his life style and general interaction with his environment. In many cases, the presenting complaint is only partially resolved, or not resolved at all by direct application of a medical regime. The utilization of behavioral techniques to deal with these physical symptoms is gaining in viability and validity.

Interest in the interrelationship of behavior and disease dates back to the development of medicine as science and practice. However, systematic empirically supported behavioral approaches in medicine have become credible only recently. In this context, an integrated model of health care that combines medical and behavioral science holds considerable promise.

It is important to differentiate behavioral medicine from other related areas, such as psychosomatic medicine and medical psychology, in order to have a clear conceptualization of this particular approach. Practitioners of psychosomatic medicine are primarily interested in the interaction of emotion and disease, and emphasize a "biopsychosocial" model in explanation of this interaction (Weiner, 1977). This focus has primarily involved the etiology and pathogenesis of physical disease, with therapy directed towards the amelioration of presumed emotional causes or precipitators of disease.

Associated with the above orientation, medical psychology was originally coined to describe the use of psychological principles in the diagnosis and assessment of physical illness, and referred to a broad range of techniques, including psychometric assessment, projective testing, and personality theory in the evaluation of treatment. Emphasis, however, was still on viewing medical illness in the psychosomatic context, and medical psychology remained, for the most part, restricted to the field of medical art, to tact and intuition in dealing with the patient. Often, for instance, with a patient suffering from essential hypertension, the physician could only advise him to relax, take life less seriously, and avoid overwork. His basic stratagem was to try to convince the patient that an overactive, overambitious attitude was functionally related to high blood pressure. If advisement proved unsuccessful, referral to a psychiatrist was another, although infrequently used, alternative. While more expertly able to delve into the "why" of the behavior than the physician, the psychiatrist often did not address himself principally to alleviating the problem behavior itself.

One of the reasons for the lack of emphasis on the importance of behavior and the application of behavioral sciences in medicine was the paucity of clinically useful principles and procedures in effecting changes in behavior. With the advent of an objective, behaviorally oriented approach, the ability to develop a technology for empirically validated treatment techniques in the alleviation of a specific problem emerged. This approach came to be known as behavior therapy or behavior modification, and it conveyed a unique therapeutic position, which was reflected in its theory, research and practice. Behavior therapy may be defined as:

> The application of experimentally derived principles such as conditioning procedures to bring about behavior change in an applied situation. This includes the relatively continuous measurement of behaviors of a given individual for the purpose of an ongoing evaluation of the specific operationalized and replicable behavior change procedures utilized.

Behavior therapy has used principles of learning and conditioning in a wide variety of situations to modify maladaptive behavior or to increase more adaptive patterns (Risley & Baer, 1973). One of the more notable features of behavior therapy is the control and specificity it gives the therapist, both in the general planning of therapeutic strategy and in the modification of strategy as dictated by the progress of therapy (Wolpe, 1969). When a particular maneuver fails to accomplish change, or meet therapeutic criteria, other intervention techniques are employed until the therapeutic goals are met. The behavior therapist's ability to intervene and promote a specific predetermined therapeutic outcome is in striking contrast to the vagaries and highly abstract goals designated by the nonbehavioral therapist.

The behavioral view of physical disorders emphasizes the combination of physiological, behavioral, and environmental factors in the etiology and maintenence of the disorders. Mere identification of organic etiology is no longer sufficient as a basis for the treatment of health related problems. With its emphasis on the careful analysis of all factors involved in health care problems, behavioral medicine has provided the necessary technology for comprehensive treatment.

So then, just what is behavioral medicine? Defining the boundaries of a new field always poses difficulties. If the definition is too broad, there may be a lack of sufficient identity to direct appropriate movement and focus. On the other hand, if the definition is too narrow and specific, future activity and experimentation may be curtailed. Certainly any definition will alienate some professionals who identify with a given discipline while it pleases others. Already there are diverse ''camps'' in behavioral medicine.

One point of view (Schwartz & Weiss, 1978) defines this specialty as ''the field concerned with the development and integration of behavioral and biomedical science knowledge and techniques relevant to health and illness, and the application of this knowledge and these techniques to prevention, diagnosis, treatment, and rehabilitation.'' One major drawback to this definition is that it does not emphasize its origins in modern behaviorism. It implies that behavioral medicine is derived from a variety of disciplines subsumed under the term ''behavioral sciences.'' Although significant contributions have come from the social and biological sciences, these and related disciplines have constituted a necessary but not sufficient condition for the development of behavioral medicine (Pomerleau, 1978).

Another point of view more closely aligned with the one espoused in this book defines behavioral medicine as ''the clinical use of techniques derived from the experimental analysis of behavior—behavior therapy and behavior modification—for the evaluation, prevention, management, and treatment of physical disease or physiological dysfunction; and the conduct of research contributing to the functional analysis and understanding of behavior associated with medical disorders and problems in health care'' (Pomerleau & Brady, 1979).

Although acknowledging that there are differing points of view regarding the definition of behavioral medicine, a definition will be offered here which parallels the one given by Pomerleau and Brady (1979), and which we believe is most consistent with current practice. Consequently, behavioral medicine is herein defined as:

> The clinical application of principles, techniques, and procedures of behavior therapy in the assessment, treatment, management, rehabilitation, and prevention of physical disease or concomitant behavioral reactions to physical dysfunction; and the validation and refinement of such treatment techniques as applied to medical problems and health related issues through systematic investigations and research.

It may be diplomatic to repeat that at this stage in the development of behavioral medicine any definition should be regarded as preliminary and tentative. A scientific field is frequently conceptualized by what it does. If conditions change, the definition of behavioral medicine should be modified. As new viewpoints and problems are attended, improved methods and approaches may be required, eventuating in a modified conceptualization of the subject domain.

TREATMENT INTERVENTIONS

As has been stated, behavioral medicine as a technology has been influenced by developments in certain basic principles of behavior and represents the vanguard of the continuing expansion of applied behavioral psychology.

The first task in behavioral medicine is to delineate a patient's problems in terms of measurable behaviors. In this regard, the behavioral medicine practitioner looks at the data bearing on the present problem. This includes a comprehensive, objective, behavioral assessment of all of the relevant physical, behavioral, and environmental variables affecting the problem under consideration.

Behavioral intervention strategies depend directly upon data derived from the assessment procedures, and are selected and individually tailored for each individual, group, or institution. Because behavioral intervention programs are usually idiosyncratic with individual cases, behavioral assessment is an extremely important component of the treatment plan (Kanfer, 1972). Data concerning characteristics of the client, the behavioral problems or reasons for needing help, and relevant environmental factors must be gathered and evaluated to determine which procedure to employ and upon what aspects of the behavior and environment therapeutic focus should be placed.

The goals of behavioral assessment and the various assessment methods typically used in the practice of behavioral medicine will be presented in Part 1, Chapter 1. The assessment methods to be discussed include: interviews, questionnaires, self-monitoring, behavioral observation, and psychophysiological measurement.

After accurate assessment of the behavioral problem and the selection of specific intervention procedures, the overall design of the intervention program must be set up. The treatment techniques used most frequently in behavioral medicine will be given in detail in Part 1, Chapters 2 through 6, and should facilitate appreciation of the direct service aspect of behavioral medicine emphasized in this book. A number of relatively specific, behavior change procedures will be considered, and basic behavior therapy procedures will be explained with numerous references provided for readers not grounded in such techniques. These basic procedures include respondent conditioning with specific emphasis on systematic desensitization, flooding, and aversive conditioning, as well as operant conditioning procedures including contingency management, assertion, and social-skills training. Several behavioral treatment techniques shall be presented in more detail since they appear to have particular application to behavioral medicine. Included are the techniques of biofeedback, relaxation training, cognitive therapy, and self-management training.

APPLICATIONS

There are three principal areas of emphasis in the application of behavioral techniques in contemporary behavioral medicine: (1) direct patient service, or the application of behavioral programming to the patient himself, or more specifically to his problem behavior; (2) adherence, or the use of behavioral techniques to improve the patient's adherence to the medical regime and, (3) prevention, or behavioral intervention to modify behaviors that constitute risk factors for disease.

In direct patient service, behavioral techniques are being applied in the treatment of problems that have traditionally been considered almost exclusively medical. Relevant examples of applications, which are discussed in detail in Part 2, Chapters 7 through 14, are seen in the use of biofeedback and progressive relaxation for the treatment of hypertension, migraine and tension headaches, epilepsy, gastrointestinal disorders, fecal incontinence, neuromuscular rehabilitation, asthma, and spasmodic torticollis. These diseases have traditionally been considered medical problems and, in most cases, there is definite pathophysiological involvement.

The area of direct patient service not only includes treating the physiological disorder directly but also applying behavioral techniques in changing concomitant behavioral reactions associated with the physiological disorder. Many practitioners realize that the patient's behavior plays a part in much of disease and that changes in behavior are desirable as an intergral part of the treatment program. Relevant examples would include the use of covert positive reinforcement, covert punishment, and operant conditioning, in treating maladaptive chronic pain behavior resulting from reinforcement of such behavior by the social environment.

It should be clear that behavioral medicine treatment strategies may be applied independently, or in combination, in the treatment of a singular disorder. These treatment strategies are also most amenable to inclusion in multifaceted approaches which include more traditional pharmacological, medical, or surgical interventions. The unique contribution of behavioral medicine to this area is its delineation of the "nonmedical" or behavioral factors operating in health problems, and its effectiveness in the modification of these factors in the alleviation of distress.

The second focus of behavioral medicine is the use of behavioral techniques to improve the patient's adherence to the prescribed medical regime, whether it be diet alteration, life style alteration, or taking prescribed medication in the proper dosage and schedule. Adherence has been a particularly frustrating and difficult problem in medical practice, as seen in cases of diabetes, renal disease, ulcerative colitis, allergies, gastrointestinal carcinoma, and physical rehabilitation. There has been a growing awareness that the failure of patients to adhere to prescribed medical regimes is probably the single greatest problem in achieving effective medical care (Dunbar & Stunkard, 1977).

Adherence is, in fact, a behavioral problem since one of the goals in behavioral medicine is to alter the patient's health-related behaviors that interfere with successful treatment outcome. Clearly, the social context in which the patient lives, and the context in which he is treated, must be studied to identify the environmental variables that influence adherence behavior. Examples of behavioral techniques useful for increasing adherence are: educating the patient concerning the regime, self-monitoring techniques, tailoring the regime to fit the patient's daily routine, shaping the desired performance, and making use of social support for adherence from the family and co-workers.

The third focus in behavioral medicine is in the area of prevention of disease. The behavior to be changed is clinically important because it leads to or exacerbates a medical condition or disease. Coronary artery disease, cerebrovascular disease, chronic obstructive pulmonary disease, lung cancer, and accidents constitute the leading causes of death in adults (U.S. Department of Health, Education, and Welfare, 1973). For years it has been proposed that specific aspects of life style, such as diet, physical activity, cigarette smoking, and consumption of alcohol influence morbidity and mortality. Excessive eating increases the risk of cardiovascular disease; hard-driving overexertion of physical activity links up with increased coronary artery disease; cigarette smoking contributes to pulmonary diseases, such as lung cancer, bronchitis, and emphysema; and chronic excessive alcohol use leads to cirrhosis of the liver as well as increased risk of accidental death. To the extent that health practices can be modified, the occurrence of such diseases can be greatly reduced.

Examples of behavioral techniques used in prevention are: behavior modification sessions using self-control techniques for overeating, smoking, and alcohol consumption, modification of individual risk factors for hypertension and cardiovascular disease, and education of the public by physicians and health educators of risk factors in disease.

While adherence and prevention are important aspects in the practice of contemporary health care psychology, they are sufficiently extensive to require a second volume, which will be undertaken at a later date. The primary focus of this bcok about behavioral medicine is direct patient service. It is in this sense that Part 2 represents the *raison d'être* of our efforts. All of the concerns presented in Part 1 subserve our intent to guide the reader in the effective, direct application of behavioral techniques in the amelioration of medical or health related problems.

SUMMARY

The objective of any treatment modality is amelioration of the malady being treated, and this objective implies control of the variables of which the malady is a function. In this context, there is little difference between the goals of behavioral medicine and those of traditional medical treatments used by physicians. It must be stressed, however, that caution should be exercised in extending behavioral technology to all medical problems. Although behavioral therapy does not specifically address itself to the underlying etiology of a disease, that is not to say the etiology need not be taken into account. When a great deal is known about the antecedent pathophysiology of the problem, such as in myocardial disease, the treatment goal of modifying the aberrant response must take into account the limits set by the existing pathology (Schneiderman, Weiss, & Engel, 1978). In such cases, a thorough medical evaluation and periodic reassessment of the disease state should be part of a comprehensive behavioral treatment plan.

This general overview suggests that the domain of behavioral medicine is rather comprehensive, and includes nearly every aspect of human pathology and behavior maladaptation. The emphasis that unites most of the diverse treatment strategies reviewed is the behavioral orientation of the procedures. To date, the most important contributions made by behavioral medicine relate not only to specific behavior recommendations for treatment, but also to an emphasis on behavioral technology for ameliorating problems in medical care (Pomerleau & Brady, 1979). It is this attitude which permeates every aspect of treatment from initial assessment through direct treatment and follow-up. It incorporates the position that people are not self-contained, rather, they are integrally related to a larger bioecological system, the environment.

In the following pages, the multivariate factors that comprise the clinical practice of behavioral medicine will be examined and discussed. The text is divided into two basic parts. Part 1 presents treatment interventions including assessment techniques and behavioral strategies used in treating behavioral aspects of medical problems. Part 2 involves the direct application of these behavioral techniques in the amelioration of medical and related behavioral problems.

The book is clinically oriented and offers a ''how-to-do-it'' approach as well as a ''review of the literature–what has been done'' presentation. Upon completion of this book, it is intended that the reader will have become acquainted with most of the practical clinical skills in behavioral medicine, and will, with appropriate guidance, become adept in the application of these skills as a practitioner of behavioral medicine.

REFERENCES

Dunbar, J. & Stunkard, A.J. Adherence to diet and drug regime. In R. Levey, B. Rifkine, B. Dennis, & N. Ernst (Eds.) *Nutrition, lipids, and coronary heart disease.* New York: Raven Press, 1977.

Kanfer, F.H. Assessment for behavior modification. *Journal of Personality Assessment,* 1972, **36,** 418–423.

Pomerleau, O.F. On behaviorism in behavioral medicine (Editorial). *Behavior Medicine Newsletter* 1978, **1** (3), 2.

Pomerleau, O.F. & Brady, J.P. Introduction: The scope and promise of behavioral medicine. In O.F. Pomerleau & J.P. Brady (Eds.) *Behavioral medicine: Theory and practice.* Baltimore: Williams & Wilkins, 1979.

Risley, T. & Baer, D. Operant behavior modification: The deliberate development of behavior. In B. Caldwell & H. Ricciuti (Eds.) *Review of child development research,* Vol. 3. Chicago: University of Chicago Press, 1973.

Schneiderman, N., Weiss, T., & Engel, B. Modification of psychosomatic behaviors. In R.S. Davidson (Ed.) *Experimental analysis of clinical phenomena.* New York: Gardner Press, 1978.

Schwartz, G. & Weiss, S. What is behavioral medicine. *Journal of Behavioral Medicine,* 1978, **1,** 249–251.

U.S. Department of Health, Education, and Welfare. Vital Statistics Report for 1972, **21,** (13), HSM 73-1121. Washington D.C.: U.S. Government Printing Office, 1973.

Weiner, H. *Psychobiology and human disease.* New York: Elsevier, 1977.

Wolpe, J. *The practice of behavior therapy.* New York: Pergamon Press, 1969.

PART ONE

Treatment Interventions

Part 1 presents an overview of the treatment interventions used by the behavioral medicine practitioner in the amelioration of specific maladies heretofore regarded as unique to the medical profession. The first chapter in this section is intended to provide the reader with an understanding of the basic assessment procedures used in developing a treatment plan for a particular client or group of clients. Chapter 2 offers a review of fundamental conditioning principles and behavior therapy interventions. The four chapters that follow present treatment techniques particularly germane to behavioral medicine. These latter chapters emphasize procedures that allow some degree of self-direction appropriate to many behavioral medicine clients, especially those seen on an outpatient basis.

The treatment intervention section is arranged in such a manner that it may serve as a book within a book. That is, it is acknowledged that readers will have had varying amounts of training in behavioral treatment techniques. Accordingly, it is suggested that those who are currently proficient in these techniques either do not read this section of the book, or read it only for review and orientation. Finally, readers not familiar or proficient with a behavioral orientation to treatment should read all of this section, including the material in the appendix.

Some redundancy across the latter four chapters will be noticed, but this repetition should facilitate rapid development of proficiency in learning the techniques. It is hoped that the format utilized will make the book appropriate for most readers including those with little or no training in behavioral techniques.

CHAPTER 1

Assessment in Behavioral Medicine

OVERVIEW

In a behavioral medicine treatment program, the statement "If you don't know where you are going, you won't know when you get there" is quite appropriate. In this regard, the primary intervention strategy is the delineation of the patient's problems in terms of objective measurable behavior. This delineation should accomplish two things: it should specify the parameters of the malady and perhaps, more important, it should clearly indicate the conditions that constitute resolution of that malady. In this regard there are several functions central to behavioral medicine assessment.

The first function is to determine exactly, preferably in observable terms, the behavior problems or complaints of the patient. These behavioral problems are referred to as target behaviors and must be grounded in specific behavioral referents before intervention can proceed.

A second function of assessment pertains to the identification of all the variables that currently influence the target behavior. These variables may include antecedent events, which elicit or precipitate the patient's discomfort, or consequent events, which reinforce or maintain the disorder under consideration. Next, whenever possible, the target behavior and the variables pertinent to the target behavior should be quantified. That is, they should be stated in terms of measures, such as rate, frequency, and duration of occurrence.

The above information will provide a relatively clear picture of the current status of the patient's disturbance. Finally, an intervention program is established which should specify in quantitative terms the desired goal and outcome of intervention. Quantitative specification of the goal provides for "where you are going," and the specified intervention program tells you "how you are going to get there."

Perhaps one other point in regard to assessment should be made. In contrast to many nonbehavioral intervention strategies, a behavioral strategy requires continual assessment of the effectiveness of the strategy per se. In other words, if your behavioral medicine program is not maintaining the course leading to resolution of the patient's discomfort or disturbance, the program must be changed. In fact, the credibility of a given program is determined singularly by its efficacy in reaching the goal you have specified.

Information used in behavioral medicine comes from a wide variety of sources. These sources may include interviews, questionnaires, self-monitoring, direct observation of a patient in a natural environment, observation in a structured situation, and psychophysiological measurement. In the pages that follow, the sources of information employed in behavioral medicine assessment along with related methodology will be discussed in detail. Attention will also be given to the applicability of information to particular target behaviors, and the more empirical criteria of reactivity, sensitivity, reliability, and validity will be considered.

INTERVIEW

The interview is probably the oldest, most frequently used of the behavioral assessment procedures. Since it typically occurs during the initial meeting between patient and practitioner, the interview has significant influence on the patient's expectations as well as on the outcome of subsequent assessment and intervention. Unlike other behavioral assessment procedures, the interview is an indispensable part of every assessment.

The purpose of the interview is to obtain preliminary information pertinent to the conceptualization of the target behavior and variables of which the target behavior is a function. This preliminary information, in addition to providing an overview of the patient's problem, should also suggest areas in which more rigorous assessment procedures will be appropriate, as well as suggest some of the major variables germane to the patient's presenting complaints.

The behavioral medicine practitioner must consider how to structure the interview within the framework of the goals described. In a behavioral medicine assessment, interview structure can vary from being very structured to flexible and open. In structured interviews the topics discussed follow a prearranged format. They are more likely to be employed in conjunction with intervention programs designed around specific psychophysiological problems such as cardiovascular, gastrointestinal or pain disorders, or in situations when the interviewer has been informed of the nature of the referral problem prior to initial interview. The following interview format (used by Haynes et al., 1975) provides for a fairly clear delineation of the target behavior, in this case recurrent headaches:

1. Descriptive statistics (age, sex, marital status, occupation, education, address, phone).
2. Handedness (right or left).
3. Headache history (age when started, progress, cyclicity).
4. Historical precipitating conditions.

5. Average maximum intensity.
6. Average frequency/week.
7. Average duration.
8. Localization (neck, frontal, temporal, eyes).
9. Typical onset and progression.
10. Associated symptoms (rating intensity 0 = never, 3 = always).
11. Relatives with headaches and their diagnosis.
12. Physician's name and address.
13. Medication history and current status.
14. Previous diagnostic workups (place and procedures).
15. Reaction of social environment to the headaches.
16. Perception of different headache types.
17. How headaches affect behavior.
18. General medical history.
19. Current medical status.

A flexible or unstructured interview is one which imposes minimum constraints on the topics discussed by the patient. The interviewer follows cues provided by the patient and does not restrict questioning to a specific sequence of topics. Unstructured interviews are more likely to be used when patients have multiple behavioral problems or when the problems have not been indicated prior to initial contact with the patient. In many cases, the practitioner uses the unstructured interview as a follow-up to the structured interview to obtain additional information pertinent to accurate identification of the target behavior.

The following excerpt is an oversimplified example of the interviewer (I) attempting to focus on target behaviors and the variables supporting the target behaviors of the client (C):

I. Is there any specific time of the day when your headaches usually occur?
C. Most of the time it's mid-afternoon when the children return from school. They come in yelling and turn on the TV and want something to eat.
I. What happens to you when you feel a headache beginning?
C. I get very tense and irritable.
I. What do you mean by irritable?
C. I yell at my husband or children or anyone else who is around.
I. How does your husband react?
C. He sometimes leaves the house completely for a few hours until it, the headache, goes away.
I. What occurs when he returns?
C. He usually brings me iced tea and crackers while I'm in bed. He also

takes care of the kids for me and makes sure everyone is quiet. Sometimes he will come in and rub my neck for awhile.

I.   Does that help?

C.   Oh yes, I relax quite a bit. When my headache is not so severe, we will have a nice talk while he is rubbing my neck.

It appears that the target behavior identified as tension headaches, is precipitated by a particular antecedent event, her children returning home from school, and is supported by a particular chain of consequent events, including the patient reacting by yelling, and the husband leaving and later returning to provide food and attention. By recognizing a possible area of concern in a structured interview and skillfully questioning the patient, additional information was obtained which further aided in the delineation of the problem and in selection of the intervention strategy to be used in treatment.

Therefore, the reader is urged to review both interview formats remembering the stated goals of the interview: identification of the target behavior, and the variables of which the target behavior is a function. It should then be apparent that the examples given, though briefly, did begin to identify and isolate the behavior to be targeted and the variables to be attended through additional assessment. One final point, by identifying those variables, which at least in part influence the onset and maintenence of the problematic headaches, stratagem to be used in the resolution of the headache problem is implicit.

QUESTIONNAIRES

While questionnaires may be used in a behavioral medicine assessment they are one of the less frequently employed techniques. However, dependent upon the kinds of information obtained in the initial interview, the use of a questionnaire is sometimes indicated. For instance, questionnaires are often used in the assessment of psychophysiological disorders, chronic pain behavior, social behavior, depression, and as an indicator of potential reinforcers to be used in a specific treatment program designed for a given patient.

The general functions of a questionnaire are consistent with those of the other behavioral assessment techniques. The function most unique to questionnaires, however, is expediency. They can be self-administered, require relatively little time to interpret, and yield quantitative data relevant to the problem behavior. In fact, when the more direct methods of assessment are not feasible, questionnaires may be the assessment procedure of choice.

Questionnaires are used most frequently with patients whose behavior is not part of a readily observable social system, for example, an unmarried outpatient who works in the field or is out of town much of the time. Although social environmental factors are important determinants of behavioral problems such as depression, chronic pain behavior, and psychophysiological disorders, it is sometimes difficult to observe the patient in the natural environment. In the case of patients in this category, questionnaires along with interviews and self-monitoring, are the primary source of assessment data.

Practitioners are often hesitant to use questionnaires because of the notoriously low validity that characterizes these instruments. Another consideration that lends itself to a depreciation of questionnaires by behavioral medicine practitioners is the emphasis by practitioners on the importance of direct observation of the patient's problems and the variables associated with these problems.

Further, most of the available questionnaires do not deal directly with the assessment of specific physiological dysfunctions, such as hypertension or headaches, but may be useful in determining certain components of the problem, such as level of stress and anxiety. Information pertaining to certain behavioral components secondary to the physical dysfunction may also be assessed through certain questionnaires measuring assertiveness, depression, and sources of reinforcement for the patient.

For the purpose of informing the reader with some of the more frequently used inventories, a partial list will be presented. In regard to the measurement of anxiety and stress, questionnaires used include: The S–R Inventory of Anxiousness (Ender, Hunt, & Rosenstein, 1962); The State Trait Anxiety Inventory (Speilberger *et al.*, 1970); The Multiple Affect Adjective Checklist (Zuckerman & Lubin, 1965); and The Pleasant Events Schedule (Lewinsohn, 1975).

The Assertion Inventory (Gambrill & Richey, 1975) and The Rathus Assertiveness Inventory (Rathus, 1973) measure degree of assertiveness and discomfort in a variety of situations. The Beck Depression Inventory (Beck 1967) and Depression Experiences (Blatt *et al.*, 1976) assess depressed mood, feelings, affect, and behavior. Questionnaires measuring sources, or perceived sources, of reinforcement are: The Reinforcement Survey Schedule (Cautela & Kastenbaum, 1967), The Reinforcement Menu (Homme *et al.*, 1969) and the Rotter I-E Scale (Rotter, 1966).

Even though not empirically validated, questionnaires devised by the behavioral medicine practitioner to identify specific target behaviors, antecedent and consequent events, quantitative data and potential reinforcers of the components of a medical problem can be useful and efficient. Similar information obtained in a structured interview situation can also be obtained from a questionnaire. The example used earlier of an interview format used by Haynes *et al.* (1975) for individuals seeking assistance for recurrent headaches could easily be converted to questionaire form. It would simply entail devising a form with specific questions and appropriate space for the patient's responses.

The potential validity of questionnaires has probably been underestimated by behaviorally oriented interventionists. There is an increasing amount of research data which supports the hypothesis, that under some conditions, (with specific populations, specific behaviors, or with specific questionnaires) questionnaires can accurately predict or covary, with behavior measured by other instruments and in other situations. If observed covariations between questionnaire and observation derived data are found, there is little doubt that in many cases questionnaires would be the measurement instrument of choice because of the ease with which relevant data can be obtained.

SELF-MONITORING

In contrast to the questionnaire, self-monitoring is one of the more frequently used behavioral assessment procedures. One of the reasons for its frequency of use is that it meshes very clearly with the behavioral practitioner's inclination to precisely quantify behavior that can be directly observed. The procedure itself involves a patient's self-observation and his systematic recording of these observations. The observations usually focus on the patient's rate and topography of problem behavior as well as the antecedents and consequents of his behavior. It is also used as a means to educate the patient, as an intervention strategy to facilitate behavior change, and as a means to assess the effectiveness of intervention.

In the evaluation of self-monitoring assessment, several considerations will be made. These considerations focus on the questions of applicability, methods of recording self-monitored behavior, reactive effects, and validity.

Applicability

Self-monitoring has been used with a wide range of target behaviors. These include overt behaviors such as frequency, duration, and intensity of asthmatic, epileptic, or headache attacks; pain and pain tolerance; scratching associated with skin disorders; medication intake; and marital and family interactions. Additionally, covert behavior, such as thoughts or fatigue, have been self-monitored. This technique may be a more efficient assessment method than other procedures when behaviors that do not occur frequently are the targets of assessment, for example, epileptic or asthmatic attacks and drug ingestion. Also, covert behaviors can frequently be more validly assessed through self-monitoring than through other assessment procedures, since behaviors such as headaches, obsessive thoughts, feelings of inadequacy or helplessness, and covert reinforcers and punishers cannot be observed by others, and their assessment through other self-report measures, such as interviews and questionnaires, are often suspect.

Finally, self-monitoring may be particularly useful when other methods of observation are patently ineffective, produce reactive effects, require an excessive amount of observation time, or are simply invalid.

Methods of Recording

As with other methods of assessment, a preliminary step in self-monitoring involves identification and specification of the target behaviors to be monitored. The behavioral medicine practitioner can increase the probability that the resultant data will be an accurate representation of what actually occured if time is taken to insure that the patient can identify the target behavior, understands the recording methods, and comprehends the importance of reliable and accurate monitoring.

There are numerous methods by which an individual can record the occurrence of self-monitored behaviors. Use of a wrist counter is an efficient method of recording self-observed events (Lindsley, 1968; McFall & Hammer, 1971; Hannum, Thoreson, & Hubbard, 1974). Although wrist counters are a particularly useful method of recording self-monitored data, any method that allows easy recording of responses can be used. Often, responses are recorded on index cards kept in the pocket or purse, data recording forms, or slips of paper. As contiguity between the occurrence of the behavior and its recording seem to affect the accuracy of self-monitoring (Bellack et al., 1974), the recording device should be easily accessible to the patient, and the patient should be instructed to record immediately after the occurence of the behavior.

Reactive Effects

The act of self-monitoring itself, like other procedures such as observation, may effect changes in the rate or topography of the monitored behavior. Numerous studies have supported the assumption that, under some conditions, self-monitoring has behavior-change qualities (Kunzelman, 1970: Mahoney et al., 1974; Nelson, Lipinski, & Black, 1976; Zimmerman, 1975; Layne et al., 1976; Kazdin, 1974; & Bellack et al., 1974). Other studies, however, have shown reactive effects to be absent or minimal, or to endure only temporarily (Maletzky, 1974; Romanczyk, 1974; Broden et al., 1971).

Several variables affect the degree of reactivity to self-monitoring. These include recording the data prior to or following emission of the behavior, monitoring, and recording either occurrence or nonoccurrences, the contiguity between the behavior and its recording, the schedule of self-monitoring, social contingencies associated with self-monitoring, self-evaluative or self-delivered contingencies associated with self-monitoring, and the valence, or personal and social value associated with the monitored behavior.

The effects of self-monitoring on other, perhaps related, nonmonitored behavior has also been investigated. The response generalization of self-monitoring would enhance the utility of self-monitoring as an intervention modality if nonmonitored behaviors showed desirable changes in rate concomitant to that observed with monitored behavior. However, studies are inconclusive and suggest many variables are involved which contribute to the variance in results (Haynes, 1978).

Validity

The issue of validity is particularly important in self-monitoring because of the strong reactive effects sometimes observed. Self-monitoring may be associated with a modification in the rate of the behavior sufficient to render resultant data useless for assessment purposes. Data derived from self-monitoring may be an accurate reflection of the current behavior rate, but not of the rate prior to self-monitoring, or when self-monitoring is not occurring.

In summary, self-monitoring does offer some strengths as an assessment procedure, particularly when compared with questionnaires. However, as indicated, there also are some weaknesses in this procedure related to reactivity and accuracy.

BEHAVIORAL OBSERVATION

Behavioral observation plays one of the most significant roles in behavioral medicine assessment. Of the assessment procedures available, practitioners are more likely to emphasize behavioral observation than any other procedure, since confidence in the validity of the resultant data is usually appreciably greater than with data derived from other procedures (Haynes, 1978).

Behavioral observation, like the other assessment procedures, is used primarily in the identification and quantification of the target behaviors, the determinants and covariates of that behavior, its reinforcers as well as assessment of the intervention outcome. There are many factors that influence selection of target behaviors to be observed, the setting in which to observe them, who should observe them, and for how long they should be observed. These and related considerations will be reviewed in the following subsections, which deal with observation in the natural environment and observation in structured settings.

Observation in the Natural Environment

In behavioral medicine, emphasis is clearly on the assessment and modification of behavior as it occurs in the patient's natural environment. In many cases, direct observation of the target behavior as it occurs will yield reliable, valid indices of that behavior and the variables of which it is a function.

Selection of Target Behavior

With any particular individual, there are specific target behaviors that could be observed, and those which are most conducive to observation must be selected. Some behaviors may be more readily or validly assessed through nonobservational methods, such as interviews or questionnaires, while other behaviors are less reactive, more observable, and therefore, more amenable to assessment through observation.

There are several characteristics of target behaviors that may affect amenability to observation in the natural environment. These include the rate of the behavior, situations in which it is likely to occur, the social value of the behavior, and the cost of the observation. It is impractical and expensive to observe behaviors that do not occur frequently, such as seizures or migraine headaches, in the natural environment unless the observation is carried out by the client himself or by someone normally in the company of the client during the occurrence of the behavior. Some behaviors occur in situations that do not lend themselves to direct observation; for example, at work or in a doctor's office. In addition, because of their negative social value, many behaviors, such as moaning and limping associated with chronic pain, or intake of addictive substances, are not readily amenable to observation other than through self-monitoring. With the above considerations in mind, those behaviors most conducive to direct observation are behaviors which occur with a relatively high frequency in a situation conducive to observation.

Selection of Observation Situation

Another consideration in direct observation assessment is the selection of the environment or setting in which to observe the patient. As with target behaviors, the primary factor affecting the applicability of observation procedures is reactivity. For instance, in many situations, the presence of an observer or observational equipment would alter the stimulus properties of the environment and yield data of questionable reliability. In such cases, the use of self-observation or hidden equipment may be considered so as to minimize disruption or the effects of reactivity. To the extent that reactivity is in effect during an observation period, the observation should be continued until reactivity is minimized or eliminated.

The setting in which the patient is observed will, in large measure, be dependent upon the goals of a particular assessment. Typically, patients are observed in situations in which the probability of occurrence of the targeted behavior is high; in other words, in a situation in which the problematic behavior occurs. This permits the practitioner to most efficiently identify and analyze the factors which influence the behavior.

Selection of Observers

The selection of observers is often a function of the particular patient, the behavior under consideration and the situation in which the behavior occurs. Nonprofessional observers, such as family members or friends, may be used to gather data in a more economical and less reactive manner. Disorders in which the targeted behavior occurs infrequently, such as low frequency seizures, asthmatic attacks, and migraine headaches, can more efficiently be monitored by individuals in the environment of the patient than by professional observers. In cases in which the behavior occurs frequently, however, it may be more desirable to use professionally trained outside observers, or to audio- or video-tape the patient so as to insure objectivity.

Time Sampling

Following selection of the target behavior to be observed, the situation in which to observe, and observers, temporal structuring of the observational sessions must be determined. The amount of time necessary to adequately monitor a particular target behavior often varies inversely with the magnitude and variability of the behavior. In other words, when the rate of behavior varies a great deal between observational sessions or occurs infrequently, more observation time is required to derive a reliable estimate of the typical rate.

Usually, a session is divided into small intervals. This is done to enhance the consistency of data gathering between observers and to provide a means of determining interobserver agreement. For example, a 30-minute observation period may be divided into 120 15-second periods in which observed events are recorded every 15 seconds. In any event, the idea behind the division of a session into intervals is to increase the likelihood that data obtained will be a valid and reliable index of the parameters of a problem behavior and the factors which influence that problem.

Interpretation of Resultant Data

Following the observation sessions, the data gathered is then interpreted. One of the more common methods of analysis involves graphical or tabular presentation of rates and frequencies of the behavior observed. Visual inspection of the data may then provide hypotheses relating to variables affecting variability, and changes across time of the problem behavior. Where appropriate, the data may also be subjected to statistical analysis.

Therefore, there are many variables to consider when using observation in the natural setting as an assessment technique. This method of assessment is sometimes time-consuming and economically unfeasible, particularly when professional observers are employed. Also, biases or errors of nonprofessional observers and excessive reactivity can sometimes reduce the validity of the information obtained. However, when these variables prove conducive to observing the patient in his natural environment, this technique should clearly be a part of the assessment.

Observation in Structured Settings

Another method of observing target behaviors is to structure an environment specifically with a view towards obtaining certain kinds of information. A given structure is established for several reasons: (1) to promote the efficiency of observation methods by increasing the probability of the occurrence of certain target behaviors; (2) to facilitate the observation of a behavior that might not occur if observation was conducted in the natural environment; (3) to reduce the variability of observation-derived data; and (4) to provide an efficient and sensitive behavioral measure of the effects of particular intervention programs. The type of structure employed in the assessment of a target behavior will be, in part, a function of the goals of the observation, characteristics of the patient and the behavior being investigated, and the hypotheses under investigation. Structured situations can involve use of minimal structure in the natural environment as well as use of a highly structured setting, such as a laboratory or clinic. While there are other kinds of structured situations, these are the ones to be considered, since they are particularly germane to application in behavioral medicine.

Minimal Structure of Natural Environment

In some situations it is helpful to impose structure upon the behavior of patients; for instance, in the home when observing family interaction, or on a hospital ward when observing interaction of patient and hospital staff. This structure is sometimes necessary to mitigate interference with the observation process by events that might interfere with the observation, to eliminate some of the reactive consequences that may be imposed inadvertently by observers, and to increase the general efficiency of the observation process.

Observations of family interactions in the home are sometimes interrupted by events, such as telephone calls, the television, or the intrusion of visitors. Therefore, to make the data obtained from the observation more reliable, constraints may be placed on the family members when observers are present. The most frequent structures imposed involve limiting the family to a few rooms, restricting phone calls, and visitors, and keeping the television turned off. Similarly, in a hospital milieu, routine interruptions such as taking of vital signs and visitation may be controlled during the observation period. In each instance, these kinds of restrictions simply make it more likely that the data obtained in regard to the target behavior, as well as the interactions affecting those behaviors, will be valid.

Structured Laboratory Observation

The most frequently used structured observation procedure in a behavioral medicine program involves a laboratory setting such as a clinic or hospital. The clinic or hospital is used for the obvious reason that this is the situation in which direct service applications in behavioral medicine often take place. While physically dissimilar to the natural environment, particular care is taken to employ as many familiar people and circumstances as possible, in order that the observed behavior may occur in a setting that approximates the environment in which it is usually displayed. Consequently, the social stimuli are usually provided by individuals normally found in the natural environment, such as spouse, parent, or child. In this context, the patient alone, or conjointly with a family member, is asked to do certain tasks, and as before, relevant data is recorded.

Thus, whether minimally structuring the natural environment or using a highly structured laboratory setting, observation in a structured setting can be an efficient and valid means by which to observe behavior which is not conducive to observation in the natural environment.

While this overview of behavioral observation should provide the reader with most of the general essentials of this assessment technique, more specific information pertaining to methods of recording and analyzing data may be obtained from a variety of supplementary readings that will be provided at the end of this chapter.

PSYCHOPHYSIOLOGICAL MEASUREMENT

In behavioral medicine, many of the problems or target behaviors involve physiological events, and in these instances, psychophysiological measurement is usually both desirable and necessary as part of the assessment process. It may also be noted that many behavioral intervention strategies are often designed specifically in order to modify a patient's physiological functions, those which are problematic. Therefore, in order to adequately assess physiological target behaviors and to monitor the progress and effectiveness of certain physiological intervention procedures, the behavioral medicine practitioner will most often employ psychophysiological measurement procedures.

Psychophysiological measurement is an assessment technique involving the surface recording of physiological events, which are mainly, although not exclusively, controlled by the autonomic nervous system. As stated earlier, there are a number of target behaviors and intervention procedures for which physiological events are important and for which psychophysiological measurement procedures may be applicable. Examples of applicability would include the amelioration of essential hypertension, cardiac arrhythmias, tension or migraine headaches, dental disorders, and neuromuscular spacticity or flaccidity. Other disorders, for example, epilepsy, asthma, insomnia, chronic pain, and addictive disorders, also have important physiological components involved in contributing to the disorder. With psychophysiological disorders such as hypertension, the targeted physiological events define the disorder. In other disorders, such as chronic pain, physiological events are assumed to sometimes play a mediating role in the occurrence of the target behavior.

Essential hypertension, for example, is defined as elevated blood pressure in the absence of identified organic factors. Because the disorder is defined by a physiological event (elevated blood pressure), assessment of essential hypertension must involve assessment of that event. Thus, evaluation of an intervention program with an essential hypertensive patient involves both pre- and postintervention assessment of blood pressure levels.

In other cases, psychophysiological assessment may serve as a preintervention diagnostic device for identification of a particular disorder or to suggest appropriate intervention strategies to be used. If the patient reports the occurrence of headaches, for example, the behavioral medicine practitioner may use psychophysiological measurement procedures to facilitate the identification of etiological factors. By measuring frontalis muscle tension levels and temporal artery blood flow when the patient is at rest as well as when the patient is under stress, an attempt is made to delineate the headache as either primarily of a muscle contraction or vascular etiology. Then, if the muscle contraction is identified as the etiological factor in the production of the headache, electromyographic (EMG) biofeedback or relaxation training might be selected as the intervention strategy. On the other hand, if vascular factors are suggested as the etiologic base, temporal artery, peripheral skin temperature and/or EMG feedback and relaxation training might be the most effective behavioral intervention.

It may also be noted that many behavior therapy procedures, such as classical aversion conditioning, systematic desensitization, covert sensitization, biofeedback, and relaxation training involve either direct or indirect control of physiological variables. The modification of these variables may in some instances be the primary goal of the intervention strategy. For instance, this would apply with intervention procedures designed to produce a decrease in blood pressure, muscle tension, or rate of cardiac arrhythmias. In other cases, the intervention may be conceptualized as involving the modification of a mediating variable, such as reducing anxiety with the supposition that reduction in seizures or asthmatic attacks will follow. Because of the importance of physiological variables and the physiological nature of many target behaviors, valid assessment of these factors is extremely important.

Psychophysiological assessment most often occurs within a laboratory setting. Typically, a patient is seated in an environmentally controlled room with electrodes and transducers attached to those areas of the body which most effectively permit monitoring of the physiological event under consideration. An adaptation period is provided and is intended to decrease the likelihood that the obtained physiological data are confounded. After adaptation, the patient is then presented with the various audio or video stimuli, exposed to intervention procedures, or instructed to engage in various activities while being monitored. Although often preferable, assessment is not necessarily confined to highly controlled laboratory settings. Sometimes physiological responses are monitored during interviews, as well as through the use of telemetric devices remotely stationed in more natural environments. With this general background regarding psychophysiological assessment, the remaining pages of this section will attend specifically to the measurement procedures most currently employed in behavioral medicine.

Measurement Procedures

Numerous psychophysiological response systems have been monitored in behavioral medicine assessment. Some of the more commonly utilized response systems include electrical activity of muscles (EMG), cardiovascular measures such as heart rate, blood pressure, and peripheral temperature, and electrodermal activity.

EMG

Electromyography involves the measurement of the electrical activity generated when muscles contract. Placement of surface electrodes along a muscle fiber allows the changes in muscle action potential to be monitored. As a function of monitoring electrical activity generated from a muscle or muscle group, it is possible to infer the level of muscle tension.

There are several ways in which EMG may be useful in behavioral medicine assessment. It may be used to assess the presence, severity, and covariates of physiological disorders and to assess the effectiveness of the behavioral intervention strategies used in treatment. Most psychophysiological disorders are assumed to be characterized by prolonged or excessive arousal of the sympathetic division of the autonomic nervous system (ANS), either during or before symptom onset. Inferences that ANS-mediated arousal may be a precipitating or concomitant factor in psychophysiological disorders, and that EMG measures can provide a sensitive index of general physiological arousal, suggest that monitoring EMG levels of patients with psychophysiological disorders may provide useful information about etiological factors and thus affect the design of the intervention program.

Researchers and practitioners have used EMG measures, specifically frontalis EMG levels, as a diagnostic tool with persons having muscle-contraction headaches. Haynes, Griffin, Mooney, and Parise (1975) found that patients reporting frequent muscle-contraction headaches had higher frontalis EMG levels than patients having few or no muscle-contraction headaches. It was also found that some patients with frequent muscle-contraction headaches had relatively low resting levels of EMG, and some patients with no muscle-contraction headaches had relatively high resting levels of EMG. To further complicate etiological issues, Vaughn, Pall, and Haynes (1976) found that patients with infrequent headaches demonstrated greater response to stress than patients with frequent headaches. These findings suggest that the occurrence of muscle-contraction headaches may be only partly a function of muscle tension levels about the head and neck, and that other variables may influence their occurrence. It seems likely that social factors, such as reinforcement for the report of muscle-contraction headaches, may play an etiological or maintaining role and that the role of these social factors may be more significant in headache patients with low EMG levels compared to those with high EMG levels.

This initial assessment of frontalis EMG levels may suggest whether or not assessment of socioenvironmental factors is important and may influence the design of the intervention program. For a patient in which elevated EMG levels seem to be an etiological factor, biofeedback or relaxation training might be most effective. In contrast, alleviation of headaches with patients not demonstrating elevated EMG levels might more effectively be treated with marital or family therapeutic intervention, self-control programs, or cognitive skills training.

EMG is also used as a diagnostic aid with patients having essential hypertension (EHT). EHT may, among other things, be a function of excessive and prolonged activation of the sympathetic division of the ANS. Assuming that EMG levels are indicative of sympathetic division activation, monitoring frontalis EMG levels may provide information of etiological significance. Low levels of EMG without other signs of Sympathetic Nervous System (SNS) arousal in the presence of elevated blood pressure suggests that etiological factors other than the ANS activity should be investigated. The diagnosis of EHT, usually defined as a diastolic blood pressure above 90 mm Hg and systolic blood pressure above 140 mm Hg, is often difficult because it is based on the rejection of organic causes, which is a tenuous diagnostic process. EHT in the absence of elevated EMG levels or other signs of SNS arousal indicates that relaxation training or EMG biofeedback might not be the intervention modality of choice, and that potential involvement of organic factors should be considered further. Elevated EMG levels, however, do not preclude organic etiology, and thorough physical examinations are recommended with all psychophysiological disorders.

EMG is also useful in monitoring the effectiveness of intervention procedures such as biofeedback, relaxation training, systematic desensitization, and covert conditioning techniques. Monitoring frontalis EMG levels, for example, during relaxation training or systematic desensitization, provides feedback for the behavioral medicine practitioner concerning levels of arousal during the program and indicates attainment of sufficient levels of relaxation, and thus the length of relaxation training needed. It is also helpful in identifying stimuli which impede relaxation. This information helps the practitioner in planning, monitoring, and reformulating intervention procedures.

Level of relaxation as measured by frontalis EMG levels may also facilitate prediction of differential patient responses to intervention procedures. Some patients may demonstrate greater reduction in EMG levels to passive relaxation instructions, others to autogenic training, Jacobson's relaxation procedures, or EMG biofeedback. Other patients may demonstrate inability to relax across several relaxation-induction procedures. EMG and other physiological indices of arousal can provide useful information and may improve the selection and efficiency of behavioral intervention procedures.

Cardiovascular Measures

Measures of cardiovascular activity, such as heart rate, blood pressure, and blood flow play important roles in psychophysiological assessment.

In assessing heart rate, the characteristics of the heart beat, such as wave forms, and rate and its dysfunctions, such as arrhythmias, are most often monitored by an electrocardiogram (EKG). The measure most frequently used in applied psychophysiology and behavioral medicine assessment is heart rate, as measured by a cardiotachometer, which measures the time between successive beats. Increases in rate are generally assumed to be indicative of relative dominance of the sympathetic division of the ANS, and heart rate decreases are generally assumed to be indicative of relative dominance of the parasympathetic division of the ANS. Electrocardiograms may be recorded from many sites, but heart rate is most frequently recorded from electrodes placed on the right wrist and left leg, with the right leg serving as a ground.

In behavioral medicine assessment, heart rate, like EMG, has been used most frequently as a measure for assessing essential hypertension and cardiac arrhythmias, and to assess patients' response to intervention procedures such as relaxation training and biofeedback. Research involving heart rate has focused on the orienting response (Graham & Clifton, 1966), classical conditioning of heart beat characteristics (Bykov, 1957; Dykman, & Gantt, 1956), and the parameters of biofeedback (Lang & Twentyman, 1974). Heart rate is one of the most error-free measurement procedures because it is fairly resistent to artifacts from movement, electrical interference, electrode polarization, and interference from other electrophysiological measurement procedures.

Blood pressure is another frequently monitored cardiovascular variable completely controlled by baroreceptors, cardiac output, hormones and other biochemical factors, by resistance in arteries and arterioles, and by fluid retention. Blood pressure is used in psychophysiological assessment as one indicator of sympathetic activity and involves measurement of systolic and diastolic pressures.

Systolic and diastolic blood pressure differ in sensitivity to transient stimuli. Diastolic blood pressure is less sensitive than systolic blood pressure to transient stimuli, and provides, therefore, a measure of general systemic conditions. Systolic blood pressure is more reactive to the effects of immediate environmental manipulations, such as exposure to feared stimuli, or relaxation and/or biofeedback training. Systolic blood pressure, therefore, sometimes provides a better index of immediate cardiovascular response to environmental stimuli. Diastolic blood pressure may be more useful in detecting long-term, overall changes in cardiovascular tone (Gunn et al., 1972).

Blood pressure is frequently monitored during the course of behavioral intervention strategies, such as relaxation and biofeedback training, with persons having EHT in order to measure the effects of the treatment on blood pressure reduction.

Peripheral blood flow, or the amount of blood flow through the peripheral arterioles has been assumed to reflect sympathetic, ANS division activity. Contraction of the arterioles results in decreased blood flow and may be affected by autonomic nervous system activity, hormones, or other biochemical factors. Peripheral blood flow, particularly within areas rich in vasculature, such as finger tips and ear lobes, is assumed to be affected by environmental and psychological stimuli. Peripheral blood flow can be inferred from measurement of temperature at those sites rich in vasculature.

Increases in temperature may be indicative of decreased sympathetic activation, decreased arteriole construction, and increased blood flow. In addition to utilizing temperature as a measure, blood flow can be measured by pressure plethysmography and photoplethysmography.

Measures of blood flow have been used most frequently in the assessment of vascular changes in disorders such as migraine headaches, Raynaud's disease, and essential hypertension. These measures are particularly relevant in the assessment of essential hypertension because of the assumption that elevated blood pressure may result from constriction of peripheral arterioles. Monitoring blood flow during relaxation and stress, and comparing the responses of essential hypertensives with normotensives, suggests the likelihood of etiological or concomitant vascular changes with essential hypertension.

Electrodermal Activity

There are many measures of electrodermal activity (Edelberg, 1972) including skin resistance, skin conduction, skin potential, and skin impedance responses. The most frequently used measures for assessing electrodermal responding are the Galvanic Skin Response (GSR) which measures changes in resistance of the skin, and the Skin Potential Response (SPR) which measures changes in electrical potential of the skin.

Although the physiological etiology of skin resistance and skin potential is a subject of debate, it is evident that these electrodermal responses, when measured from palmar areas, change as a function of cognitive activity and stress. In general, decreased skin resistance and increased skin potential is a reflection of increased sympathetic arousal or stress. Use of this general interpretation of electrodermal responses is complicated by the finding that the various measures often show low intercorrelations (Edelberg, 1972; Gaviria, Coyne, & Thetford, 1969), and by the fact that artifacts such as spurious auditory sounds (the slamming of a door) may alter results.

Other Psychophysiological Measures

There are many other response modalities that have been used in psychophysiological assessment, including electroencephalography, gastrointestinal activity, pupillometry, and several other measurements. Electroencephalography (EEG) has been used in the assessment of neurological disorders, such as tumors and epilepsy. The measurement of gastric activity may be useful in the assessment of patients with psychophysiological gastrointestinal disorders, such as ulcers. The use of pupillometry involves monitoring pupil variations which may reflect general physiological or cognitive arousal. Pressure transducers utilized to measure contraction of the rectal sphincters have been used to assess and treat fecal incontinence, and an electronic stethoscope has been used to amplify bowel sounds used in the assessment and treatment of irritable bowel syndrome.

Therefore, psychophysiological measurement is both desirable and necessary as part of the assessment process, particularly when the target behaviors involve physiological events. Undoubtedly psychophysiological measurement procedures will become more valid and useful with increased technological developments and increased sophistication in behavioral conceptualization of psychophysiological variables. As the field of behavioral medicine progresses and technological advances are evidenced, the area of psychophysiological assessment may become one of the more useful forms of assessment with physiological disorders.

SUMMARY

This chapter has presented most of the principles, functions, and uses of assessment in behavioral medicine intervention. Assessment is important not only because it identifies the patient's problems, but it also aids in the delineation of a specific type or types of intervention techniques to be used in treatment as well as providing the behavioral medicine practitioner with a means by which to assess the intervention outcome.

Behavioral medicine assessment is a necessary component of the intervention process because this general process is tailored to the individual and the individual's unique problems. In this regard, the functions of behavioral assessment vary across different assessment methods, but generally include specification and selection of target behaviors, delineation of antecedent and consequent events relating to the target behaviors, and collection of quantitative data relevant to the target behavior as well as the variables which bear upon the target behavior itself. It is this multipurposed enterprise that characterizes nearly all initial intervention in a behavioral medicine regime, irrespective of the particular assessment procedures employed.

Each of the assessment methods, interviews, questionnaires, self-monitoring, behavioral observation, and psychophysiological measurement, was discussed in light of its applicability to certain patients and target behaviors. Finally, as indicated earlier, there are a variety of readings which may be regarded as helpful supplements to this chapter. Among the readings available, one or more of the following are recommended: S.N. Haynes' *Principles of Behavioral Assessment* (1978), M. Terdall's *Behavior Therapy Assessment* (1976), M. Hersen and A. Bellack's *Behavioral Assessment; A Practical Handbook* (1976), and Keefe, Kopel, and Gordon's *Practical Guide to Behavioral Assessment* (1978).

REFERENCES

Beck, A.T. *Depression: Clinical, experimental and therapeutic aspects.* New York: Harper and Row, 1967.

Bellack, A.S., Rozensky, R., & Swartz, J. A comparison of two forms of self-monitoring in a behavioral weight reduction program. *Behavior Therapy*, 1974, **5**, 523–530.

Blatt, S.J., D'Afflitti, J.P., & Quinlan, D.M. Experiences of depression in normal young adults. *Journal of Abnormal Psychology*, 1976, **85**, 383–389.

Broden, M., Hall, R.V., & Mitts, B. The effect of self-recording on the classroom behavior of two eighth-grade students. *Journal of Applied Behavior Analysis*, 1971, **4**, 191–199.

Bykov, K.M. *The cerebral cortex and the internal organs.* Translated by W. Gantt, New York : Chemical Publishing, 1957.

Cahalan, D., Cisin, E.H., & Crossley, H.M. *American drinking practices.* (Monograph No. 6) New Brunswick, N.J.: Rutgers Center of Alcohol Studies, 1969.

Cautela, J.R. & Kastenbaum, R.A. A reinforcement survey schedule for use in therapy, training and research. *Psychological Reports*, 1967, **20**, 1115–1130.

Coleman, R.E. Manipulation of self-esteem as a determinant of mood of elated and depressed women. *Journal of Abnormal Psychology*, 1975, **84**, 693–700.

Conger, J.C., Conger, A.J. & Brehm, S.S. Fear level as a moderator of false feedback effects in snake phobics. *Journal of Consulting and Clinical Psychology*, 1976, **40**, 135–141.

Curran, J.P. & Gilbert, F.S. A test of the relative effectiveness of a systematic desensitization program and an interpersonal skills training program with date anxious subjects. *Behavior Therapy*. 1975, **6**, 510-552.

Dykman, R.A. & Gantt, W.H. Relation of experimental tachycardia to amplitude of motor activity and intensity of motivating stimulus. *American Journal of Physiology*, 1956, **185**, 495–498.

Edelberg, R. Electrical activity of the skin. In N.S. Greenfield & R.A. Sternback (Eds.) *Handbook of psychophysiology.* New York: Holt, 1972.

Endler, N.S., Hunt, J.McV., & Rosenstein, A.J. An S-R inventory of anxiousness. *Psychological Monographs*, 1962, **76**(17, whole No. 536).

Forrest, M.S. & Hokanson, J.E. Depression and autonomic arousal reduction accompanying self-punitive behavior. *Journal of Abnormal Psychology*, 1975, **84**, 346–357.

Gambrill, E.D. & Richey, C.A. An assertion inventory for use in assessment and research. *Behavior Therapy*, 1975 **6**, 550–561.

Gavira, B., Coyne, L., & Thetford, P.E. Correlation of skin potential and skin resistance measures. *Psychophysiology*, 1969, **5**, 465–477.

Graham, F.K. & Clifton, R.K. Heart rate changes as a component of the orienting response. *Psychological Bulletin*, 1966, **65**, 305–320.

Gunn, C.G., Wolf, S., Block, R.J., & Person, R.J. Psychophysiology of the cardiovascular system. In N.S. Greenfield & R.A. Sternbach (Eds.) *Handbook of psychophysiology.* New York: Holt, 1972.

Hannum, J.W., Thoreson, C.E., & Hubbard, D.R. Jr. A behavioral study of self-esteem with elementary teachers. In M.J. Mahoney & C.E. Thoreson (Eds.) *Self-control: Power to the person.* Monterey, Ca: Brooks/Cole, 1974.

Haynes, S.N. *Principles of behavioral assessment.* New York: Gardner Press, 1978.

Haynes, S.N., Griffin, P., Mooney, D., & Parise, M. Electromographic biofeedback and relaxation instructions in the treatment of muscle contraction headaches. *Behavior Therapy*, 1975, **6**, 672–678.

Haynes, S.N. & Wachwitz, J.H. Digital coding and computer analysis of behavior observation data. *Journal of Applied Behavior Analysis*, 1975, **8**, 475–477.

Hersen, M. & Bellack, A. *Behavioral assessment: A practical handbook*. New York: Pergamon Press, 1976.

Higgins R.L. & Marlatt, G.A. Fear of interpersonal evaluation as a determinant of alcohol consumption in male social drinkers. *Journal of Abnormal Psychology*, 1975, **84**, 644–651.

Homme, L.E., Csaneji, A.P., Gonzales, M.A., & Rchs, J.R. *How to use contingency management in the classroom*, Champaign, Ill. Research Press, 1969.

Katkin, E.S. Electrodermal lability: A psychophysiological analysis of individual differences in response to stress. In I.G. Sarason & C.D. Speilberger (Eds.) *Stress and anxiety*, Washington, D.C.: Hemisphere, 1975.

Kazdin, A.E. Reactive self-monitoring: The effects of response desirability, goal setting, and feedback. *Journal of Consulting and Clinical Psychology*. 1974, **42**, 704–716.

Keefe, F.J., Kopel, S.A., & Gordon, S.B. *A practical guide to behavioral assessment*. New York: Springer, 1978.

Kendall, P.C., Finch, A.J., Fr., Auerbach, S.M., Hooke, J.F., & Mikulka, P.J. The strait-trait anxiety inventory: A systematic evaluation. *Journal of Consulting and Clinical Psychology*, 1976, **44**, 406–412.

Klein, D.C. & Seligman, E.P. Reversal of performance deficits and perceptual deficits in learned helplessness and depression. *Journal of Abnormal Psychology*, 1976, **85**, 11–26.

Kleinknecht, R.A., McCormick, C.E., & Thorndike, R.M. Stability of stated reinforcers as measured by the reinforcement survey schedule. *Behavior Therapy*, 1973, **4**, 407–413.

Kunzelmann, H.D. (Ed.) *Precision Teaching*, Seattle: Special Child Publications, 1970.

Lang, P.J. & Twentyman, C.T. Learning to control heart rate; Binary vs. analogue feedback. *Psychophysiology*, 1974, **11**, 616–629.

Layne, C.C., Richard, H.C., Jones, M.T., & Lyman, R.D. Accuracy of self-monitoring on a variable ratio schedule of observer varification. *Behavior Therapy*, 1976, **7**, 418–488.

Lewinsohn, P.M., Munoz, R.F., Youngren, M.A., & Zeiss, A.M. *Control your depression*. Englewood Cliffs, N.J.: Prentice-Hall, 1978.

Lindsley, O. A reliable wrist counter for recording behavior rates. *Journal of Applied Behavior Analysis*, 1968, **1**, 77–78.

Mahoney, M.J., Moore, B.S., Wade, T.C., & Moura, N.G. Effects of continuous and intermittent self-monitoring on academic behavior. *Journal of Consulting and Clinical Psychology*, 1974, **42**, 118–123.

Maletzky, B.M. "Assisted" covert sensitization in the treatment of exhibitionism. *Journal of Consulting and Clinical Psychology*, 1974, **42**, 34–40.

Marlatt, G.A. Behavioral assessment of social drinking and alcoholism. In G.A. Marlatt & P.E. Nathan (Eds.) *Behavioral approaches to the assessment and treatment of alcoholism.* New Brunswick, N.J.: Center of Alcohol Studies, Rutgers University, 1976.

Matarazzo, J.D. & Weins, A.N. *The interview: Research on its anatomy and structure.* Chicago: Aldine-Atherton, 1972.

McFall, R.M. & Hammer, C.L. Motivation structure and self-monitoring: The role of nonspecific factors in smoking reduction. *Journal of Consulting and Clinical Psychology,* 1971, **37,** 80–86.

Nelson, R.O., Lipinsky, D.P., & Black, J.L. The relative reactivity of external observations and self-monitoring. *Behavior Therapy,* 1976, **4,** 80–86.

Olmsted, F. Measurement of blood flow and blood pressure. In C.C. Brown (Ed.) *Methods in psychophysiology.* Baltimore: Waverly Press, 1967.

Rathus, S.A. A 30-item schedule for assessing assertive behavior. *Behavior Therapy,* 1973, **4,** 398–406.

Romanczyk, R.G. Self-monitoring in the treatment of obesity: Parameters of reactivity. *Behavior Therapy,* 1974, **5,** 531–540.

Rotter, J.B. Generalized expectancies for internal vs. external control of reinforcement. *Psychological Monographs,* 1966, **80** (1, Whole No. 609).

Ryan, V.L., Drall, C.A., & Hodges, W.F. Self-concept change in behavior modification. *Journal of Consulting and Clinical Psychology,* 1976, **44,** 638–645.

Schroeder, H.E. & Rich, A.R. The process of fear reduction through systematic desensitization. *Journal of Consulting and Clinical Psychology,* 1976, **44,** 191–199.

Sobell, M.B., Schaefer, H.H., & Mills, K.C. Differences in baseline drinking behavior between alcoholics and normal drinkers. *Behavior Research and Therapy,* 1972, **10,** 257–267.

Spielberger, C.D., Gorsuch, R.L., & Lushene, R.E. *STAI Manual.* Palo Alto, Calif.: Consulting Psychologists Press, 1970.

Terdall, L.G. & Mash, E.J. *Behavior therapy assessment.* New York: Springer, 1976.

Thomas, E.J. Bias and therapist influence in behavioral assessment. *Behavior Therapy and Experimental Psychiatry,* 1973, **4,** 107–111.

Thorndike, R.M. & Kleinknecht, R.A. Reliability of homogeneous scales of reinforcers: A cluster analysis of the reinforcement survey schedule. *Behavior Therapy,* 1974, **5,** 58–63.

Vaal, J.J. The Rathus assertiveness schedule: Reliability at the junior high school level. *Behavior Therapy,* 1975, **6,** 566–567.

Vaughn, R., Pall, M., & Haynes, S.N. Frontalis EMG response to stress in subjects with frequent muscle-contraction headaches. *Headache,* 1977, **16,** 313–317.

Wein, K.S., Nelson, R.O., & Odom, J.V. The relative contributions of reattribution and verbal extinction to the effectiveness of cognitive restructuring. *Behavior Therapy,* 1975, **6,** 459–474.

Wener, A.E. & Rehon, L. Depressive affect: A test of behavioral hypotheses. *Journal of Abnormal Psychology,* 1975, **84,** 221–227.

Wollersheim, J.P. Effectiveness of group therapy based upon learning principles in the treatment of overweight women. *Journal of Abnormal Psychology,* 1970, **76,** 462–474.

Zemore, R. Systematic desensitization as a method of teaching a general anxiety-reducing skill. *Journal of Consulting and Clinical Psychology*, 1975, **43**, 157–161.

Zimmerman, J. If it's what's inside that counts, why not count it? I: Self-recording of feelings and treatment by self-implosion. *The Psychological Record*, 1975, **25**, 3–16.

Zuckerman, M. & Lubin, B. *Manual for the multiple affect adjective check list*. San Diego: Educational and Industrial Testing Service, 1965.

CHAPTER 2

Basic Respondent and Operant Techniques

OVERVIEW

One point central to the concept of behavioral medicine is that people are not self-contained, but integrally related to a larger bioecological system, the environment. People always act within the context of environmental surroundings, with these environmental factors playing a major role in influencing behavior through learning and conditioning. Many physical disorders treated within a medical regime are often precipitated by environmental causes or stimuli and maintained by environmental events.

Just as medical science is concerned with acquiring knowledge to prevent, alleviate, or cure disease, behavioral science seeks to attain this goal by analyzing and describing relationships between environmental stimuli and problematic physical symptoms. The basic behavior therapy techniques of respondent and operant conditioning deal directly with environmental influences, which promote or maintain physical symptoms, and provide a scientifically useful basis for understanding and treating increasingly more complex organism-environment interactions of direct relevance to behavioral medicine.

It is important at this point to discuss some of the basic principles of respondent and operant conditioning and the treatment strategies associated with them. This discussion is not comprehensive and will not delineate all of the conditioning principles and stratagems of the behavioral literature. Rather, the presentation is intended to provide an understanding of conditioning principles and stratagems as they are applied in the practice of contemporary behavioral medicine.

RESPONDENT TECHNIQUES

As has been stated, environmental stimuli can either establish or maintain physiological symptoms or associated behavioral responses. Respondent behavior is elicited by preceding stimuli, and involves an involuntary or automatic response, a reflex, that is primarily mediated by the smooth muscles and glands of the autonomic nervous system. The unconditioned reflex describes a relationship between stimulus and response that is usually present at birth and determined by the organism's inherited physiology. Examples of respondent behaviors that are elicited by specific stimuli include perspiration in response to warmth, salivation in response to food, vomiting in response to esophageal stimulation, and the startle reaction in response to sudden noise. Examples of respondent behaviors that are more directly relevant to the area of behavioral medicine, include heart rate, blood pressure, air flow from the lungs, and bladder and bowel functions.

Because most of the behavior which comprises emotion is elicited by antecedent stimuli, emotional behavior is also generally classified as respondent. These respondents include all of the uncomfortable and occasionally incapacitating emotional reactions such as anger, guilt, fear, and anxiety which provides the substructure for a wide variety of psychophysiological disorders. Consideration of these respondents is important in understanding behavior and its relationship to the environment, and such consideration also serves as a point of reference for the introduction of operant behavior and the interrelationship of respondents and operants as they apply to behavioral medicine.

Respondent Conditioning

Respondent conditioning refers to the fact that a neutral stimulus, after being paired with an eliciting stimulus, may itself become an eliciting stimulus. For instance, a tone after being paired with a lemon drop, a stimulus which elicits salivation when placed in the mouth, will itself become an elicitor of salivation. After such an arrangement, the tone is called a *conditioned stimulus* and salivation is called a *conditioned response*.

One example of the application of respondent conditioning is seen in Efron's (1957) report of treating an epileptic. Most epileptics can detect the onset of a seizure by a subjective aura that precedes the seizure. Efron found that one of his female clients could inhibit her seizures by inhaling the odor of jasmine during the early stages of the aura. Presumably the odor of jasmine functioned as a stimulus, eliciting an inhibitory response of a seizure. Efron then respondently conditioned the smell of jasmine to the sight of a bracelet. After a number of pairings of the smell of jasmine with the sight of the bracelet, the bracelet became a conditioned stimulus and the client was able to inhibit a seizure by simply looking at the bracelet. Eventually, just thinking about the bracelet would inhibit the seizure.

Although there are situations, such as the one above, in which a new effective stimulus needs to be established by respondent conditioning, it is also important to change or eliminate undesired behaviors, such as maladaptive emotional responses. Emotional states such as anger, guilt, fear, or anxiety usually involve alterations in the form and frequency of several behaviors simultaneously. Many of these altered behaviors are directly observable and include changes in facial or vocal expression, blushing, loco-motor activity, postural orientation, and gestural reactions. Conversely, others are experienced internally, such as increases in heart rate, blood pressure, stomach contractions, and perspiration.

Painful stimuli are capable of producing emotional behavior independent of prior learning. Through conditioning, however, emotional behavior may also occur in response to innocuous, or formerly neutral, stimuli, producing a conditioned emotional reaction, though no real threat of danger is present. It has generally been concluded that prolonged or excessive conditioned emotional responses, with accompanying physiological arousal, may produce enduring structural changes, such as duodenal ulcers, ulcerative colitis, neurodermatitis, essential hypertension, and cardiac arrhythmias (Lachman, 1972). It is important to determine ways in which to eliminate or alter these conditioned emotional reactions. In the instance of conditioned respondent behavior, this is accomplished, typically, through either extinction or counterconditioning.

Extinction

Extinction is a process by which a conditioned emotional reaction is eliminated when the conditioned stimuli are no longer paired with the environmental stimuli that had previously evoked the occurrence of that behavior. A young child who becomes afraid when first exposed to friendly strangers will usually show less fear with subsequent exposure. In this case, the response, fear, undergoes extinction.

There are basically two ways of carrying out extinction, gradual and nongradual. The gradual approach consists of moving through a sequence of steps, called a hierarchy, toward the object or situation that elicits the maladaptive response. The nongradual approach involves bypassing most of the intermediate steps by confronting the final situation immediately. An example of extinction pertinent to the field of behavioral medicine would be to extinguish the fear response in a child about to undergo surgery. The gradual approach would involve taking the child to the hospital, meeting the nurses, seeing his hospital room, meeting other children recovering from surgery, and finally visiting the operating room. A good variation used in treatment would be to have the person go through the hierarchy of steps in his imagination first, and then in real life, the latter being called "*in vivo*."

The nongradual approach might involve taking the child directly to the operating room and remaining in that situation until the fear response is extinguished. This procedure is called *flooding*, which involves bombarding the person with the anxiety-producing stimuli or keeping the person in the anxiety-arousing situation without escape.

Overall, the gradual approach is usually preferable to the nongradual approach, as it is generally more acceptable to the patient, and there may be less likelihood of premature termination of treatment. The use of classical respondent conditioning and extinction has practical applications in the field of behavioral medicine, as will be seen in later chapters on direct applications.

Counterconditioning

Counterconditioning is another way in which to alter undesirable or problematic behaviors. The first step is to determine the situations that elicit the maladaptive physical or emotional reaction. The next step is to determine or establish ways to elicit a response incompatible with the maladaptive response. Finally, the incompatible response is respondently conditioned to the stimuli eliciting the maladaptive response. This counterconditioning procedure is continued until the maladaptive response has been effectively reduced, or eliminated.

It is important in counterconditioning that the incompatible response is dominant to the undesired response. The way to insure this is through the use of a hierarchy, similar to the gradual approach described earlier. Counterconditioning is, therefore, not simply replacing the maladaptive response with the incompatible response. Rather, it is a matter of moving along a continuum from the undesired response toward the incompatible response, with extinction and counterconditioning occurring at each step of the way.

Relaxation is the most commonly used technique for counterconditioning various maladaptive emotional responses, such as anxiety, and various physiological responses, such as blood pressure and heart rate. Since relaxation training is one of the most widely used procedures in the practice of behavioral medicine, it will be discussed at length in Chapter 4.

Another major counterconditioning treatment procedure used in behavioral medicine is *systematic desensitization*. This procedure involves the counterconditioning of anxiety using relaxation as the incompatible response. As described by Wolpe (1969, 1973), systematic desensitization is based on the premise that anxiety and relaxation are physiologically incompatible responses that cannot occur simultaneously in the presence of the same stimulus. When used as a therapeutic procedure, desensitization literally involves training the patient to relax in the presence of stimuli that previously elicited anxiety. Desensitization has three basic components: training in relaxation, construction of anxiety hierarchies, and counterconditioning, or counterposing relaxation and anxiety-arousing stimuli from the hierarchies.

Since relaxation is to be used as the incompatible response in counterconditioning, the patient is first taught how to relax, usually using a shortened version of Jacobson's (1938) deep muscle relaxation method. Following relaxation training, anxiety producing stimuli are carefully identified and arranged hierarchically from least to most fear evoking. Physiological measures are useful in ranking the stimuli, but usually the patient's subjective estimate as to the amount of anxiety experienced in each situation is considered sufficient.

After the appropriate hierarchies have been constructed and the patient has learned relaxation procedures, counterconditioning begins. Hierarchy items that elicit the least anxiety are presented individually while the patient is completely relaxed. This is accomplished by instructing the patient to imagine approximations to the feared stimulus, or *in vivo* by graded exposure to real stimuli. In both cases, however, progression through the hierarchy is usually gradual and dependent upon complete extinction of anxiety responses to subordinate items before succeeding items are presented. Through a series of gradual steps, the patient eventually experiences the anxiety producing stimulus with minimal subjective disturbance. As evidenced in a later chapter, systematic desensitization and relaxation training have direct application to a wide variety of clinical disorders, including psychophysiological disturbances as well as concomitant emotional disturbances relating to the physiological symptoms. Desensitization has proven to be a useful tool in reducing the intensity of an epileptic seizure or an asthmatic attack by reducing the fear or anxiety aroused by onset of the attack.

While desensitization uses counterconditioning to reduce aversive-avoidance reactions to certain situations, *aversive counterconditioning* uses counterconditioning to reduce unwanted positive-approach reactions of the patient. In this procedure, the unwanted positive reactions are counterconditioned using the response to an aversive or unpleasant stimulus as the incompatible response. The rationale is to pair stimuli that elicit the undesired positive response, such as relief obtained from scratching behavior associated with some skin disorders, with stimuli that elicit a dominant, incompatible, aversive response, such as the reaction to electric shock.

Aversive counterconditioning follows the general approach of counterconditioning previously described. First, those stimuli that elicit the undesired response are identified. Then an aversive stimulus, usually electric shock, is gradually applied, using a hierarchy to control response dominance. A hierarchy is often unnecessary since the aversive stimulus is usually dominant to the undesired response. However, this is not always the case, and practitioners sometimes overlook the importance of a hierarchy in aversive counterconditioning.

Aversive counterconditioning, as applied by the behavioral medicine practitioner, is primarily used with self-reinforcing behaviors. In addition, it is also used with less frequency, though with success, in life threatening situations; for example, with children exhibiting chronic vomiting.

Therefore, there are many psychophysiological disorders that are influenced by certain antecedent events that evoke some degree of undesired behavior or maladaptive response. In these cases, the respondent conditioning procedures can prove to be very effective techniques for the amelioration of these maladies. Specific disorders treated with these techniques will be further elaborated upon in Part 2, Direct Applications.

OPERANT TECHNIQUES

Elicited respondents of the type that have provided the primary focus for such basic and important classical conditioning analyses must be seen to represent only a relatively small proportion of the behavioral interactions of higher organisms. The most prominent aspects of such advanced repertoires are represented by the operant paradigm. This paradigm addresses behavior for which there is no environmental eliciting stimulus and which is generally described as "voluntary" or emitted. The frequency of occurrence of an operant is chiefly determined by the environmental consequences that follow the emitted response. Buying a car, calling for help, walking, reading a book, and solving a problem are all examples of operants that occur because they alter the environment to produce specific outcomes. Most of one's interpersonal behavior is operant in nature.

Unlike respondent behavior, operant behavior is not automatically evoked by antecedent stimuli. Because it is often impossible to identify the specific stimuli that produce operants, they are referred to as emitted behaviors to distinguish them from the elicited nature of respondents. Other features distinguish operant from respondent behavior. Operants are generally "voluntary" behaviors involving striated musculature and mediation by the central nervous system. Respondents more commonly entail mediation by the autonomic nervous system, involving the activity of smooth muscles and glands which are considered reflexive or "involuntary."

However, preliminary evidence from recently conducted laboratory research (Kimbel, 1967; Miller, 1969; Shapiro & Schwartz, 1972) suggests that under certain conditions this voluntary-involuntary distinction may be more artificial than real. By providing discriminable information about specific autonomic processes, using a technique called biofeedback, organisms can learn to regulate some internal activities, such as galvanic skin response, blood pressure, heart rate, and brain alpha rhythm, which were previously believed to be beyond selective, voluntary control. Clinical applications of biofeedback are discussed at length in Chapter 3.

One of the most crucial distinctions between operants and respondents is that respondents are phylogenetically determined and require only the proper stimulus to evoke them, while operants are acquired behaviors that may take any form the environment dictates within the neuroanatomical potential of the organism. Consider responses to pain inducing stimuli. Pain is an unconditioned stimulus that elicits similar physiological responses in most people; for example, increased blood pressure, rapid respiration, and sweating. However, activities subsequently performed to relieve pain are operants that may or may not occur depending upon the person's unique conditioning history. Examples would include verbally requesting medical assistance, consuming an aspirin, resting in bed, complaining, crying, or showing casual indifference.

Although operants and respondents differ along many dimensions, in day-to-day living they interact to influence the ongoing activity of the behaving organism. In humans, for example, emotional states are usually elicited by conditioned or unconditioned stimuli. When these emotional states occur, they alter the probability that selected operant behaviors will also occur. Crying in a young child may begin as a respondent behavior, elicited in response to pain or discomfort. However, crying also produces environmental consequences, such as parental attention, food, or a diaper change. Depending on the nature of the consequences, crying may become an operant behavior as evidenced by changes in the form of frequency with which it occurs. The significance of the interaction between operants and respondents will become apparent as the concepts of positive reinforcement and punishment are discussed.

In a behavioral medicine treatment program, there are two primary ways in which operant conditioning is useful in treating psychophysiological disorders. The first application relates to procedures intended to increase desirable, "healthy," behavior, and the second relates to decreasing undesirable, potentially pathological behavior.

Techniques for Increasing Desirable Behavior

Positive Reinforcement

The most commonly used operant approach for increasing desired behavior consists of simply reinforcing the desirable behaviors. This technique is simple, and should generally be a component of all behavioral medicine treatment programs, even when emphasis is on some other approach. The premise upon which positive reinforcement works is that events which function as reinforcers for a particular patient are identified and used to alter the problematic behavior.

Identification of reinforcers is an important aspect of this treatment technique. A sometimes overlooked point is that identification of what is actually reinforcing desirable behavior must be derived empirically. Practitioner expectations may or may not function as reinforcers for a given patient. Similarly, events that the practitioner may not consider to be reinforcing may, in fact, function as reinforcers. A useful approach in determining reinforcers for a given person is to ask the person what is reinforcing, perhaps using a Reinforcement Survey Schedule (Cautela & Kastenbaum, 1967).

There are several reinforcers relatively common to all patients that may easily be incorporated into a behavioral medicine program when operant conditioning is being used to treat a specific disorder. Praise is often a common and powerful reinforcer. Money, for most people, is another powerful reinforcer. Positive reinforcement need not be limited to material or social events, but rather may consist of opportunities to engage in certain behaviors. Using a relatively high-probability behavior to increase less frequent behavior can be very effective. This procedure is called the *Premack Principle* (Premack, 1959) or "Grandma's Rule," since grandmothers and others have been using this approach for a long time: eat your potatoes (low probability behavior) and then you can go out and play (high probability behavior). A more useful example pertaining to behavioral medicine would be the case of a sports-minded patient who is allowed to participate in recreation therapy (high probability behavior) only after compliance with required and perhaps, unpleasant diagnostic and treatment procedures (low probability behavior).

There are several variations of reinforcement including covert reinforcement and self-reinforcement. Covert reinforcement (Cautela, 1970) involves the patient imagining a pleasant scene, such as going home from the hospital, as the reinforcement. Self-reinforcement is reinforcement one gives oneself, such as self-praise. Further, a number of procedures exist which may serve to enhance the effectiveness of positive reinforcement. Those most applicable to the practice of behavioral medicine include shaping, prompting, modeling, assertiveness training, and contingency contracting.

Shaping, also called successive approximation, is the reinforcement of behaviors that gradually approximate the desired behavior. The key to shaping is to differentially apply reinforcent to those responses that constitute a closer and closer approximation to the ultimate response desired. For example, in teaching a patient to walk using an artificial leg, reinforcement should not be postponed until he is actually walking. Results would be attained more readily by making reinforcement contingent upon a more easily reached criterion, such as applying the prosthesis. After this behavior is mastered, the criterion for reinforcement could gradually be increased to include standing, balancing, or taking a single step. Shaping is based on the premise that a terminal response can be broken down into its component parts, which may then be reinforced as approximations to the final goal. This insures that the individual meets with early and continued success rather than with repeated failure (Katz & Zlutnick, 1975).

Prompting is another means by which new behavior may be initiated, and this may be carried out either verbally or by physical guidance. In its verbal form, prompting is often used to establish new motor responses, as in the case of teaching a quadriplegic to feed himself. Initially the nurse might place the patient's fingers around the base of the spoon and physically help him move the spoon toward his mouth. Gradually the nurse would eliminate the prompting until he is able to feed himself. The gradual elimination of prompting is called *fading* and will be described in more detail later in this chapter.

Modeling is another useful technique used to increase the likelihood of desired behavior. Modeling, or imitation, is a technique whereby the patient observes the behavior and behavioral consequences of others and imitates the observed performance. Several variables have been shown to influence the extent to which a model is imitated. These variables include sex, power, social attractiveness of the model, and whether reinforcing outcomes are provided for the imitated behavior (Bandura, 1969). Using modeling procedures, it is possible to initiate new behavior quickly by first demonstrating the response and then reinforcing the observer for successful imitation. This is an expeditious alternative to shaping and an extremely useful means of facilitating new behavior. For example, a nurse in a physician's office might have an older nonfearful child receive an innoculation in the presence of a younger, more anxious child in order to reduce the second child's fear.

Assertiveness training can be taught via modeling. Patients not standing up for their rights, or openly expressing their feelings tend to be concerned about feelings of inadequacy and experience various anxieties. Assertiveness training involves teaching the patient appropriate assertive behaviors for various situations (Dawley & Wenrich, 1976; Lange & Jakubowski, 1976). Much of assertiveness training is discrimination learning, for the patient generally does not know appropriate assertive behavior, or is ineffective in acting assertively in certain situations. Thus, modeling is often used to demonstrate the desired behavior.

The practitioner ordinarily begins this procedure by discussing the patient's rights to be assertive. The next step involves the training of the patient in assertive behavior. This includes nonverbal behaviors such as eye contact, posture, gestures, facial expressions, as well as verbal behaviors, such as tone, inflection, and volume of the voice. Focus is usually on the speaker's content, including basic communication skills, expression of feelings, and verbalizations appropriate to specific situations. Most of the training centers around simulations of actual situations with the practitioner modeling the appropriate behavior. After observing the model, the patient engages in behavioral rehearsal, practicing the modeled behavior. He is then gradually phased into a real situation through a series of behavioral tasks.

It is necessary that the patient learn behavior that will insure against eliciting punishment, be reinforcing, and supportive. Patients, particularly if they are in a hospital, may have a strong fear concerning the consequences of becoming more assertive. For example, a patient may want to ask his physician for more information concerning his illness, diagnostic procedures, or upcoming surgery, but may be fearful that there will be repercussions from the physician. Learning assertive skills will help him to be able to ask the physician in a manner that will elicit reinforcement and support from the physician rather than anger. Mastery of this skill by patients will often alleviate much of the anxiety contributing to their physiological disorder or general emotional status as a consequence of their illness.

Operant reinforcement strategies are some of the most powerful behavior change approaches available, and it is in this context that contingency contracting and token economies are ways of formalizing these approaches which will often increase their effectiveness.

Contingency contracting is a program in which the operant contingencies are clearly specified and understood by everyone involved. These contingencies, including reinforcements and punishments that can be expected for different behaviors, are formalized into a written contract. Sometimes the contract is imposed on a patient, but the most effective approach involves negotiating as much as possible with all involved concerning the nature of the contract. In most cases, the contract will need to be altered over time, new provisions added, loopholes plugged up, or otherwise some aspects of the contract renegotiated. Contracts should not be changed retroactively, but for future use only. Contracts often need to be altered to find an effective balance between behaviors and reinforcement. If too little reinforcement is given for a behavior, the behavior may not occur; if too much reinforcement is given, the system is ineffective and perhaps wasteful. Contracting is most effective when accompanied by graphs, signs, and checklists posted in conspicuous places. All aspects of the contract should be written, and upon completion of some part of the contract, it should be marked off or indicated in some written manner.

Contracting is used with individuals or in clinic and hospital ward settings. It is the major technique used in treating scratching behavior associated with some skin disorders, and in most inpatient chronic pain units (Mann, 1972; Fordyce, 1976). In some contingency contracting programs, the patient is reinforced with tokens, such as poker chips, marks on a chart, or paper stars, that can later be exchanged for one's choice of reinforcers. Contingency contracting programs using tokens are called *token economies*. One of the primary strengths of token systems is that tokens are easily dispensed and can be given immediately after the desired behavior has been exhibited. For example, on a chronic pain inpatient unit, patients can gradually be shaped to do such things as taking care of themselves, attending and participating in physical or psychological therapy, reducing offensive whining or complaining behavior, and generally taking control of their lives. With their tokens, they may buy recreational opportunities, commissary items, or weekend passes.

One final area of concern in setting up a positive reinforcement program as part of a behavioral medicine treatment plan involves the practitioner being aware of certain variables of reinforcement. The amount of reinforcement given is extremely important and refers to both quality and quantity. Within limits, as the amount of reinforcement is increased, the effectiveness increases. It is necessary to determine how much reinforcement is needed for a given patient to insure the likelihood that the patient will engage in the desired behavior. In addition to the amount of reinforcement, it is advisable to give the reinforcement as close in time to the desired behavior as possible. As the delay of reinforcement increases, the effectiveness decreases.

Another variable which affects the effectiveness of the reinforcement program is the schedule or pattern by which reinforcers are related to responses. The fastest way to strengthen behavior is to reinforce it continuously each time it occurs. In shaping, for example, continuous reinforcement is required to move from one approximation to the next. However, once behavior occurs at an acceptable level, maintaining it at that level requires a different kind of reinforcement schedule. When reinforcement does not occur after every response, the relationship between response and reinforcement is called an intermittent schedule of reinforcement. Learning is faster with continuous reinforcement than with intermittent reinforcement, but time to extinction is longer with intermittent reinforcement. Therefore, it is often strategic to teach the behavior desired under continuous reinforcement, and gradually change to intermittent schedules of reinforcement if maintaining behavior is regarded as a desirable goal (Mikulas, 1972).

In summary, positive reinforcement and the procedures used to enhance positive reinforcement can be one of the most effective means by which to obtain and maintain desired behaviors. It is also important to reiterate that positive reinforcement of desired behavior should be included as a part of most behavioral medicine treatment programs.

Techniques for Decreasing Undesirable Behavior

While positive reinforcement involves increasing desirable behavior by rewarding that behavior, techniques for decreasing undesirable behaviors, which often are contributory in maintaining the problematic behavior, are important to consider in a behavioral medicine treatment program. There are several ways in which the behavioral medicine practitioner can insure the likelihood that these undesirable behaviors will be reduced or eliminated.

Punishment

Punishment refers to the application of an aversive stimulus after an undesired response, in order to decrease the occurrence of that response. To be appropriately referred to as punishment, a stimulus presented contingent upon a response must suppress the frequency of that response (Azrin & Holz, 1966). Disapproval, criticism, fines, and pain are common forms of punishment.

The effects of punishment are related to the immediacy and frequency of the punishing stimulus as well as the availability of alternate responses. As with positive reinforcement, punishment is more effective when the aversive stimulus occurs immediately after the behavior. As punishment is delayed, its effectiveness is reduced. In addition, greater suppression of the undesired behavior is achieved when punishment occurs after each response rather than on an intermittent basis. To the extent that punishment occurs inconsistently, its utility in suppressing behavior is reduced.

Since many behaviors are maintained by reinforcement, reinforcement variables interact with punishment to determine punishment effectiveness. More suppression occurs when punishment is used in conjunction with positive reinforcement for other desirable behavior than when competing behaviors are not concurrently reinforced (Herman & Azrin, 1963; Katz, 1973). In practice this principle involves simultaneously informing the person of what to do and what not to do. Administering punishment only for retribution does not produce new and appropriate behavior. The latter task requires positive reinforcement.

Even though punishment can be a useful means by which to suppress undesirable behavior when carefully administered and used in conjunction with other techniques, the desirability of using this technique has been criticized for both ethical and practical reasons. On ethical grounds, it is commonly argued that to intentionally inflict pain is contrary to fundamental humanitarian values. Practical objections have centered around the often transitory effectiveness of punishment as well as its potential for eliciting undesirable behavioral by-products (Bandura, 1962). For example, unless the punishing stimulus is severe, behavior is suppressed temporarily rather than eliminated altogether.

It is for these reasons that the use of punishment is probably best restricted to behaviors that require immediate suppression, as in the case of life-threatening situations, such as chronic vomiting. For example, Lang and Melamed (1969) worked with a 9-month-old child weighing 12 pounds whose persistent vomiting prevented weight gain. Various types of treatment, such as dietary changes, use of antinauseants, small feedings, and establishing a warm secure feeling for the child had been ineffective, and there was a chance the child would die. Electromyogram (EMG) was used to determine the onset of vomiting by measuring muscle activity. The child received a shock to the leg when the EMG showed the onset of vomiting, and the shock was terminated when the vomiting stopped. A total of nine punishment sessions ended the problem, and one month later the child weighed 21 pounds. Similar cases are cited in Chapter 8.

In addition to being used in life threatening situations, punishment is also effective as used in self-management programs when a patient is punishing himself for his own undesired behaviors. This technique works particularly well when coupled with positive reinforcement in the case of scratching behavior associated with some skin disorders.

Extinction

Another means by which to decrease undesirable behavior is by extinction. While punishment reduces the behavior by presenting an aversive stimulus, extinction reduces the undesirable behavior by withdrawing all reinforcement for sustaining the behavior. Extinction is based on the principle that behavior which fails to produce reinforcements is usually not repeated for very long. Referring to the example of the pain patient that cries and complains, the crying and complaining might be extinguished by instructing the family members to completely ignore the crying or complaining behavior whenever it occurs. By removing the reinforcing consequence, attention, the frequency of the behavior will gradually decrease.

Problems associated with inpatients who make recurrent unreasonable demands on staff members may be handled in a similar manner. With the staff ignoring the patient and withholding reinforcement, unreasonable demands should eventually decrease in stridency and rate of occurrence. Extinction does not mean to deny the patient all reinforcement, but only to withhold it consistently for certain activities deemed undesirable. As is the case with punishment, if extinction is to be properly applied, it must be carried out in combination with reinforcement for appropriate behavior.

It is important to be aware of the fact that the introduction of extinction results in a temporary increase in negative behavior before a decline in such responses is observed. For example, the pain patient will initially complain more in an effort to receive the attention he is now not receiving. Because of these extinction "bursts," and since the majority of human activities are maintained according to intermittent schedules of reinforcement, the use of extinction to decrease behavior can be slow and frustrating. Unlike punishment, however, extinction is a means of eliminating behavior completely without the introduction of aversive stimuli.

Since extinction can be slow and frustrating, two variations of this technique can be useful in promoting behavior change more rapidly. These variations are termed "time-out from positive reinforcement" and "response cost." *Time-out from positive reinforcement* is a procedure which eliminates all opportunities to earn positive reinforcement, and functions as an aversive stimulus to weaken the behavior it follows. Time-out involves removing the individual from a reinforcing environment for a brief period of time contingent upon some specified behavior. This may be accomplished by physically transferring the person from one area to another. Although time-out is distinguishable from extinction, in which consequences that follow behavior are discontinued, both decrease behavior by removing reinforcement. Time-out ordinarily suppresses behavior quickly, especially when used in conjunction with reinforcement for other desired behavior because the patient discriminates extinction more rapidly (Holz, Azrin, & Ayllon, 1963). Thus, termination of time-out should be made contingent upon desirable behavior. This technique is used successfully with asthmatic or epileptic children engaging in disruptive or avoidance behavior on a hospital ward or in school.

Another variation is the use of *response cost*. Response cost is the forfeiture of positive reinforcers contingent upon the undesired behavior. Because the loss of reinforcers usually functions as an aversive stimulus, response cost decreases the behavior it follows. It commonly involves withdrawal of money, tokens or the privilege of watching television. Response cost is differentiated from extinction in that it is discontinued for a specific behavior, as well as from time-out from reinforcement where the availability of all reinforcement is temporarily interrupted. In common with these procedures, however, response cost entails removing reinforcing stimuli, and is best used in combination with positive reinforcement for alternative behavior (Kazdin, 1972).

Differential Reinforcement of Other Behavior

In addition to punishing and extinguishing undesirable behavior, it is also possible to achieve reduction of undesired behavior by positively reinforcing other incompatible behaviors. Since most gross motor behaviors cannot occur simultaneously, the relative strength of different behaviors will be determined by their respective success in producing reinforcement. If appropriate behavior produces more reinforcement than inappropriate behavior, it will predominate. The procedure of differentially reinforcing other behavior can be used alone to affect behavior change, or in combination with alternative methods of weakening behavior. One of the most efficient ways to keep a restless cardiac patient from constantly leaving his bed, is to reinforce him when he remains in it.

Stimulus Control

The techniques thus far discussed have dealt with the control of operant behavior by its consequences. In some cases, stimuli that precede the behavior may also acquire appreciable control over responding. It is important to look at this issue in addition, as it has particular relevance to the treatment of insomnia discussed in Chapter 14.

Stimulus control deals with the antecedent side of operant behavior as opposed to the consequent side. When antecedent events control behavior because of consequences delivered in their presence, this is referred to as stimulus control of behavior. These stimuli are called *discriminative stimuli*, since people learn to discriminate behavior of stimulus events according to consequences associated with them. Discriminative stimuli do not elicit the behavior, but rather set the occasion for the behavior, making it more or less probable the behavior will occur. For example, the presence of a police officer's car affects people's driving. One often slows down when a patrol car is in the vicinity and accelerates once the patrol car has passed. However, the patrol car would not affect driving without differential consequences, such as the possibility of a traffic ticket.

In considering antecedent stimuli, discrimination conditioning involves setting the occasion for the availability of reinforcement. The other involves setting the occasion for the absence of reinforcement. For example, seeing a friendly smile on the face of a passerby usually sets the occasion for the remark "hello," because one is usually reinforced for saying it under these conditions. On the other hand, a frown or look of indifference signals lack of reinforcement, and the person is less likely to say hello.

The stimulus control of behavior assumes great importance when it is considered that most behaviors are specific to certain settings; they do not occur all of the time. However, whether or not behavior occurs usually depends on the presence of discriminative stimuli that have acquired control over responding. In some psychophysiological disorders, stimulus control variables can play a major role. Stimuli associated with hospital environments exert control over a wide variety of patient behaviors, such as statements reflecting somatic or psysiological complaints and diverse forms of help-seeking activity. These behaviors occur in medical settings because it is here that they are most commonly followed by some form of desired attention. The solution to the problem does not entail changing the basic response, but the conditions under which it occurs.

A phenomenon related to stimulus control is *stimulus generalization.* This refers to the control of a response by events that resemble the stimulus to which the response was first acquired. For example, a patient who has had a heart attack may later overreact to any chest pain regardless of etiology. In this case generalization occurs across the dimension of chest pain, and consequently the patient assumes that all chest pain is the result of a serious coronary problem. Similarly, a patient who has had an unpleasant experience with a particular diagnostic procedure involving needle injection may generalize his fear to similar diagnostic or laboratory procedures. Stimulus generalization and discrimination learning are reciprocal processes, for generalization implies the absence of well-defined discriminative control of behavior.

Aspects of stimulus generalization may be used to therapeutic advantage. A procedure for accomplishing this is known as *fading*, which refers to the gradual changing of stimulus conditions under which a response occurs. Fading does not involve the manipulation of behavioral consequences, but rather the alteration of antecedent stimulus events. A pertinent example would be a child on a pediatric ward who screams the moment his mother attempts to leave. In her presence he appears calm and able to accept the hospital routine. "Good patient behavior" is discriminated during mother's presence, while crying is discriminated in her absence. One therapeutic plan might be to have the mother initially leave for a very brief period of time and quickly return before crying begins. Gradually the duration of her time away from the child could be increased until the child continues to behave appropriately in her absence. Under these conditions, stimulus control would have been faded by changing the stimulus conditions (mother's presence) under which a desired response (behaving calmly and cooperatively) occurs. Stimulus control and stimulus generalization are also used successfully in the treatment of insomnia.

In conclusion, there are many psychophysiological disorders which are in part influenced or maintained by the environmental consequences that occur as a result of having the disorder. In these cases, the operant conditioning procedures can be very effective techniques for both increasing desired behavior and decreasing undesired behavior associated with the illness. Specific disorders treated with these techniques will be further elaborated upon in Part 2, Direct Applications.

SUMMARY

The principles of respondent and operant conditioning, as they pertain to the practice of contemporary behavioral medicine, and their major treatment techniques have been discussed in this chapter. There are many extensions of the principles offered in this overview, and more detail is actually involved in carrying out the treatment procedures than was described. Nevertheless, the treatment approaches covered appear to be the ones most widely used in direct application.

A point that is central to this chapter is that many psychophysiological disorders are influenced by environmental stimuli. These stimuli may relate to the precipitation of a disorder or to the maintenance of its symptoms. Generally speaking, respondent conditioning techniques focus on amelioration of problematic behavior as it relates to influences by eliciting stimuli. Operant conditioning techniques focus on amelioration of problematic behavior as it relates to influences by consequent environmental stimuli which may be involved in the development and maintenance of symptoms.

Of relevance to behavioral medicine is the necessity of frequently having to combine respondent and operant procedures. In considering the behavior of a person with a psychophysiological disorder, part of the patient's behavior may be based on conditioned reactions, such as anxiety or anger, which can be altered respondently. Similarly, the patient's response to the disorder may be in part a function of a reinforcement milieu, which can be altered operantly.

With this general introduction to respondent and operant techniques, we now turn to the extensions of these techniques as they apply to biofeedback, relaxation training, cognitive strategies, and self-management procedures.

REFERENCES

Ayllon, T. & Azrin, N. Reinforcement and instructions with mental patients. *Journal of the Experimental Analysis of Behavior*, 1964, **7**, 327–331.

Ayllon, T. & Azrin, N. *The token economy: A motivational system for therapy and rehabilitation.* New York: Appleton-Century-Crofts, 1968.

Azrin, N. & Holz, W. Punishment. In W. Honig (Ed.) *Operant behavior: Areas of research and application.* New York: Appleton-Century-Crofts, 1966, 380–447.

Bandura, A. Punishment revisited. *Journal of Consulting Psychology.* 1962, **26**, 298–301.

Bandura, A. *Principles of behavior modification.* New York: Holt, Rinehart, and Winston, 1969.

Cautela, J.R. Covert reinforcement. *Behavior Therapy*, 1970, **1**, 33–50.

Cautela, J.R. & Kastenbaum, P. A reinforcement survey schedule for use in therapy, training, and research. *Psychological Reports*, 1967, **20**, 1115–1130.

Dawley, Jr., H.H. & Wenrich, W.W. *Achieving Assertive Behavior.* Monterey, Calif.: Brooks/Cole, 1976.

Efron, R. The conditioned inhibition of uncinate fits. *Brain*, 1957, **80**, 251–262.

Fordyce, Wilbert E. *Behavioral methods for chronic pain and illness.* St. Louis: Mosby, 1976.

Herman, R. & Azrin, N. Punishment by noise in an alternative response situation. *Journal of the Experimental Analysis of Behavior*, 1964, **7**, 185–188.

Holz, W., Azrin, N., & Ayllon, T. Elimination of behavior of mental patients by response produced extinction. *Journal of the Experimental Analysis of Behavior*, 1963, **6**, 407–412.

Jacobson, E. *Progressive relaxation.* Chicago: University of Chicago Press, 1938.

Katz, R. Effects of punishment in an alternative response context as a function of relative reinforcement density. *Psychological Record* 1973, **23**, 65–74.

Katz, R., Johnson, C., & Gelfand, S. Modifying the dispensing of reinforcers: some implications for behavior modification with hospitalized patients. *Behavior Therapy*, 1972, **3**, 579–588.

Kazdin, A. Response cost: The removal of conditioned reinforcers for therapeutic change. *Behavior Therapy*, 1972, **3**, 533–546.

Kimble, G. *Hilgard and Marquis' conditioning and learning.* New York: Appleton-Century-Crofts, 1967.

Lachman, S. *Psychosomatic disorders: A behavioristic interpretation.* New York: Wiley, 1972.

Lando, H.A. A comparison of excessive and rapid smoking in the modification of chronic smoking behavior. *Journal of Consulting and Clinical Psychology*, 1975, **43**, 350–355.

Lang, P.J. & Melamed, B.G. Case report: Avoidance conditioning therapy of an infant with chronic ruminative vomiting. *Journal of Abnormal Psychology*, 1969, **74**, 1–8.

Lange, A.J. & Jakubowski, P. *Responsible assertive behavior: Cognitive/behavioral procedures for trainers.* Champaign, Ill.: Research Press, 1976.

Lichtenstein, E., Harris, D.E., Birchler, G.R., Wahl, J.M., & Schmahl, D.P. Comparison of rapid smoking, warm smoky air, and attention placebo in the modification of smoking behavior. *Journal of Consulting and Clinical Psychology*, 1973, **40**, 92–98.

Mann, R.A. The behavior-therapeutic use of contingency contracting to control an adult behavior problem: weight control. *Journal of Applied Behavior Analysis*, 1972, **5**, 99–109.

Mikulas, W.L. *Behavior modification.* New York: Harper and Row, 1972.

Miller, N. Learning of visceral and glandular responses. *Science*, 1969, **163**, 434–445.

Patterson, G. & Reid, J. Reciprocity and coercion: Two facets of social systems. In C. Neuringer & J. Michael (Eds.) *Behavior modification in clinical psychology.* New York: Appleton-Century-Crofts, 1970, pp. 133–177.

Pavlov, I. *Conditioned reflexes.* London: Oxford University Press, 1927.

Premack, D. Toward empirical behavioral laws: I. positive reinforcement. *Psychological Review*, 1959, **66**, 219–233.

Razran, G. The observable unconscious and the inferable conscious in current Soviet psychophysiology: Interoception conditioning, semantic conditioning, and the orienting reflex. *Psychological Review,* 1961, **68,** 81–147.

Resnick, J.H. Effects of stimulus satiation on the over-learned maladaptive response of cigarette smoking. *Journal of Consulting and Clinical Psychology,* 1968, **32,** 501–505.

Sajwaj, T., Libet, J., & Agras, S. Lemon-juice therapy: The control of life-threatening rumination in a six-month old infant. *Journal of Applied Behavior Analysis,* 1974, **7,** 557–563.

Shapiro, D. & Schwartz, G. Biofeedback and visceral learning: Clinical applications. *Seminars in Psychiatry,* 1972, **4,** 171–183.

Ulrich, R. & Azrin, N. Reflexive fighting in response to aversive stimulation. *Journal of the Experimental Analysis of Behavior,* 1962, **5,** 511–520.

Wenrich, W.W. *A primer of behavior modification.* Monterey, Calif.: Brooks/Cole, 1970.

Wenrich, W.W., Dawley, H.H., & General, D. *Self-directed systematic desensitization.* Kalamazoo, Mich.: Behaviordelia, 1976.

Wolpe, J. *Psychotherapy by reciprocal inhibition.* Stanford, Calif.: Stanford University Press, 1958.

Wolpe, J. *The practice of behavior therapy.* Elmsford, N.Y.: Pergamon Press, 1969.

CHAPTER 3

Biofeedback

OVERVIEW

Biofeedback is a therapeutic procedure utilized to bring about behavior change. It is a type of self-regulation, an approach wherein one learns to modify one's own autonomic responsivity. In clinical application, biofeedback includes the assessment and treatment of behavioral and physical disorders. Biofeedback treatment is not administered singularly; rather it is typically part of a larger therapy program that very often includes a broad behavior therapy strategem, such as cognitive therapy, social skills training, and progressive relaxation. For this reason it is highly desirable that one who intends to practice biofeedback should have expertise in other, concomitant, behavior therapy skills.

Biofeedback has been defined as a process in which a person learns to reliably influence physiological responses that are not ordinarily under voluntary control or responses which are ordinarily easily regulated but for which regulation has broken down due to trauma of disease (Blanchard & Epstein, 1978). The biofeedback procedure involves detection and amplification of the biological response, conversion of the amplified signal to an easily processed form, for instance proportional auditory or visual signals and the feeding back of these signals to the person on a relatively immediate basis. The recording of this quantified information concerning physiological responses can also be considered as an essential part of this process. Generally speaking, the operant conditioning paradigm has been utilized as an appropriate model for biofeedback phenomena. This may be exemplified by the following:

> The importance of feedback is clear. The organism must be stimulated by the consequences of its behavior if conditioning is to take place. In learning to wiggle ears, for example, it is necessary to know when the ears move if responses which produce movement are to be strengthened in comparison with responses which do not. In reeducating the patient in the use of a partially paralysed limb, it may be of help to amplify the feedback from slight movements, either with instruments or through the report of an instructor. (Skinner, 1953)

During the 1970s there was a great proliferation of activity in the domain of biofeedback, including somewhat astronomical promises as to its utility. Fortunately, there also evolved a foundation of research that is ever accumulating and which serves as a basis for current biofeedback applications. The biofeedback applications most relevant to behavioral medicine will be considered at a later point in this chapter. At this point, however, attention will be directed to a basic question: Why would one utilize biofeedback?

It would appear that biofeedback has been established as an effective method for obtaining lowered physiological arousal, which in turn has been shown to be effective in the treatment of many stress-related disorders. Yet other procedures, such as relaxation training have in many cases been shown to be equally effective and have the advantage of not necessitating expensive equipment (Silver & Blanchard, 1978). The basic rationale for employing biofeedback is not one that directly supports the efficacy of biofeedback per se; but, rather, pertains to the utilization of specialized equipment for accurate data acquisition. One of the crucial aspects of a science, and the development of a corresponding applied technology, is empirically derived, quantifiable data. The "numbers" that emanate from biofeedback apparatus expand the domain of behavioral medicine to include relatively immediate and continuous objectively quantified information concerning physiological responses. In this sense quantitative data as to a physiological response, such as EMG or blood pressure, could be utilized to assess the effectiveness of a given lowered arousal technique, whether it be biofeedback or another procedure such as relaxation.

Biofeedback training itself may also provide advantages over other procedures apart from the capacity to quantify. For example, it would appear that biofeedback is the treatment of choice for fecal incontinence (Engel, Nikoomanesh, & Schuster, 1974) in that effective alternatives are not available. In addition, it would seem probable that because of individual differences some clients would be able to attain lowered arousal more effectively utilizing biofeedback training than another procedure, such as relaxation training even though the reverse may be the case for another client.

Finally, biofeedback may also engender an increased capacity over other techniques for standardization of therapy procedures. Assuming that biofeedback procedures effectively ameliorate a variety of maladies, then increased standardization should facilitate effective training of practioners, enhance client self-directed therapy regimens, and generally promote its practical applicability.

Biofeedback training would appear to offer the greatest application in behavioral medicine to stress-related physical disorders. Biofeedback techniques may be utilized in the assessment of stress and the remediation and prevention of maladaptive physiological arousal. Indications for these procedures will be covered later in this chapter and in later chapters concerning direct applications.

INSTRUMENTATION

Instrumentation is important in biofeedback as the detection, amplification, quantification, and feedback of biological responses which typically involve utilization of electronic equipment. The physiological responses most frequently used in biofeedback are muscle contraction and relaxation (electromyograph), peripheral vasomotor response or blood flow (photoplethysmograph or skin temperature), blood pressure (sphygmomanometer), heart rate (cardiotachometer, electrocardiogram), electrodermal response (galvanic skin response, skin potential response), and electrochemical activity of brain cells (electroencephalogram). Other physiological responses that have been utilized for biofeedback are stomach acid pH, sphincter activity, bowel sounds and gastrointestinal motility, respiration, sexual arousal, and blood alcohol level.

In general it is necessary to know the physiological basis of the response being utilized, transducer characteristics, transducer placement site and attachment methods, and characteristics and operation of the amplification, quantification, and feedback equipment. An overview of psychophysiological instrumentation is presented in the appendix.

CLINICAL BIOFEEDBACK PROCEDURES

It is assumed that the reader has undergone some relevant professional training and is familiar with general clinical procedures utilized with mental health and/or physical health problems since biofeedback techniques are utilized within the context of these general clinical procedures. The relative predominance of one or the other sets of procedures varies from case to case, therapist to therapist, and problem to problem. Concomitantly, assessment procedures should be broad enough to assess the major areas of life functioning. The particular model of assessment would depend upon the therapist's conceptual predilections. One may wish to consider the major areas of interpersonal, physiological, and cognitive behavior as well as the environmental variables bearing on a particular case.

Conceptualization Training

In most forms of behavior therapy, the client learns the concepts relevant to the therapy. Frequently, this learning is implicit, that is, it is embedded in the total procedure. The authors believe that in biofeedback training it is desirable to present the basic foundations of a conceptual model in an explicit manner early in the training program. These concepts are then elaborated upon and extended in an explicit and implicit manner as training progresses. Conceptualization training may begin during the first interview or during any session thereafter; however, it is desirable to have it occur before self-monitoring training.

The objective of conceptualization is to begin teaching the client the basic concepts relevant to understanding the therapy process and its relation to the target symptoms. The specifics of this training should take into account the orientation of the therapist and client, and a major result of the training should be facilitation of client-therapist communication. The concepts presented should, as much as possible, rest upon empirical findings. How extensive this training should be is to some extent a function of the particular client. Some clients prefer an extensive orientation with supplementary reading, others prefer the minimum. The conceptual training model that follows is presented as an example. It is relatively brief, but hopefully will assist a therapist to develop a conceptual training procedure. The concepts may be presented in whole or in part to the client in oral and/or written form. The therapist then responds to the client's questions and elicits questions from the client when none is forthcoming. An attempt is made to foster an interactive discussion with both parties giving examples of how the concept might apply to the client or someone else with a physical symptom. The model to be presented here is relatively general and does not focus on biofeedback per se, but rather upon a more generic model of stress and stress management, which may be utilized in conceptualization training for biofeedback, relaxation, self-management, and cognitive behavior therapy applications.

Life Stress and Physical Disorders: An Outline for the Client

1. Many physical disorders are initiated, exacerbated and/or maintained by life stress through the elicitation of physiological hyperarousal above that which is adaptive. The probability of stress-related physical disorders is great today as a result of medical advances in preventing disorders due to infections and treating disorders of structural abnormalities. In other words, the prevalence of stress-related disorders is greater as a result of an increase in life span.
2. The probability that a physical disorder will develop in response to life stress events, and the particular disorder that results, is related to the biological condition of body structures that is determined by one's genetic characteristics as well as one's environmental experiences which may include injury, infection, toxin, nutritional deficiency, and life style.
3. Physiological hyperarousal is directly related to conditioning, that is, a person's life history may include learning experiences whereby environmental stimuli have acquired some control over his/her human electrochemical system. These stress stimuli may be both overt and covert, and may evidence a "vicious circle" characteristic, whereby the elicited arousal pattern includes new responses (e.g., worry) that serve as stimuli which reelicit arousal.
4. Physiological hyperarousal is more likely to be learned in modern

society because the basic "flight or fight" response pattern, which historically functioned to terminate stress induced arousal, is not generally possible. However, socially accepted delayed escape and avoidances responses increase as the frequency of arousal increases, thereby inhibiting and preventing the learning of effective coping behaviors in the stress situation.

5. Through conditioning, a great variety of stimuli may come to elicit a complex, relatively stereotyped reaction pattern. This pattern becomes overlearned and is, thus, persistent and resistant to change. The eliciting stimuli, and to some extent the response pattern, through habituation, have receded from awareness and are habitual and automatic. Thus, a person would generally be unable to identify many of the stress stimuli in his environment.

6. Stress arousal patterns are characterized by one or more of the following responses: increased behavioral activity characterized by attempts to escape, avoid, attack, or otherwise terminate the stress stimuli; subjective thoughts and feelings of apprehension and distress which may or may not include specific awareness of the stress stimuli; and electrochemical physiological arousal characterized by changes in the endocrine, hormonal, and autonomic nervous system resulting in individualized patterns of responses, such as increases in heart rate, sweat gland activity, blood sugar, muscle tension, and/or respiratory rate, as well as decreases in blood flow, salivation, and/or respiratory regularity.

7. Even though there are large individual differences in stress arousal patterns, there tends to be specificity in response for a given person. That is, a given individual generally reacts to a variety of stress stimuli with a consistent arousal response pattern.

8. Stress stimuli are identifiable, not only by the arousal responses elicited in a given individual, but also by their persistent and self-sustaining quality. Stress stimuli are also functionally associated with the occurence of the physical symptoms.

9. In addition to the conditioning previously mentioned, in which many stimuli take on the capacity to elicit arousal, both the arousal response and the physical symptoms are functionally related to their environmental consequences. That is, to a greater or lesser extent, the arousal pattern and the symptoms are further maintained by associated reinforcing consequences.

10. An individual's stress related physical symptoms may be alleviated by reducing stress through environmental manipulation, or conditioning therapy whereby one learns alternative responses (i.e., low arousal) to environmental stress stimuli. When these alternative responses are learned, former stress stimuli and the contingencies are altered in such a manner that they no longer maintain physical symptoms.

A similar outline that presents the concepts specifically focused on biofeedback could be included in the orientation procedures of each phase of biofeedback training. Finally, an outline of what the physiological disorder is, including some detail concerning the major physiological mechanisms involved should be presented. This kind of information is presented in later parts of this book for the various physical disorders to which behavioral medicine approaches are directly applicable. Additional information of this type may be found in Guyton (1976).

Psychophysiological Assessment

While assessment was presented in some detail in Chapter 1, its centrality in behavioral medicine cannot be overemphasized. Within this context, while acknowledging some repetition, we will again review some aspects of assessment, particularly as it pertains to biofeedback. The objective of a psychophysiological assessment is to identify the specific physiological response(s) that change in response to the presentation of stimuli intended to elicit low, neutral, and high arousal responses. There is no standard methodology for conducting such an assessment; however, procedures similar to those presented here have been suggested by Gaarder and Montgomery (1977), Fuller, (1977), Kallman and Feuerstein, (1977), Stoyva, (1979), and Budzynski, (1979). This approach is based on earlier work by Wenger (1966), and Lacey (1967).

Ideally, the assessment procedure should begin approximately 30 minutes after the client arrives in the office during which time a portion of the biofeedback interview is conducted. Such an adaptation period facilitates stability of the initial recordings by mitigating the effects of other variables, such as outside temperature, preceding activity, and so forth. Further, the situation is set up to simultaneously record a number of physiological responses.

A decision must be made as to which physiological responses to record and at what intervals; ideally, the more responses recorded, the better the results. At a more practical level, the following guidelines are offered. Always utilize frontal EMG and record at 60, 100, or 120 second intervals. Generally, utilize finger skin temperature or vasomotor response recorded at intervals of one to 5 minutes. If possible, utilize heart (or pulse) rate recorded at 1 minute intervals or blood pressure recorded at approximately one to five minute intervals. Employ GSR and EEG less frequently pending additional research substantiating the more general utility of each. Finally, always select the response or responses that are indicated by reviewing the literature on treatment of the presenting symptom. Table 3.1 presents a guide for selection of responses for psychophysiological assessment based on literature reviews. It is apparent at this point that the practicality of this approach is limited by the availability of the various instruments that are indicated. Even if they are all available, the number and combination that can be utilized simultaneously and the frequency with which data is recorded

TABLE 3.1.   Physiological Responses Indicated for the Psychophysiological Assessment of Clients with Given Presenting Symptoms Based on a Review of Treatment Research

Symptom	Physiological Responses Most Indicated
Arthritis	Finger temperature, frontal EMG
Asthma	Airway resistance, frontal EMG
Anginal pain	Finger temperature
Bruxism	Frontal, masseter and temporalis EMG
Cardiac arrhythmias	Heart rate
Causalgia	Finger temperature
Childbirth pain	Frontal and wrist EMG, GSR
Colitis (irritable bowel syndrome)	Rectosigmoid and rectum pressure, bowel sounds
Dermatitis	Frontal EMG
Diabetes	Frontal EMG
Dysmenorrhea	Finger and vaginal temperature, frontal EMG
Fecal incontinence	Anal sphincter pressure
Homosexuality	Penile pressure or vasomotor response
Hyperactivity	Frontal EMG, SMR EEG
Hypertension	Blood pressure, frontal EMG, finger temperature, GSR
Impotence (sexual)	Penile pressure or vasomotor response
Insomnia	Frontal EMG, theta EEG
Low back pain	Frontal EMG
Migraine	Frontal EMG, finger temperature, temporal artery vasomotor response
Pedophilia	Penile vasomotor response
Psoriasis	Temperature of psoriatic site
Prurigo nodularis (skin disorder)	Frontal EMG
Raynaud's Disease	Toe and finger temperature or vasomotor response
Seizures	SMR EMG
Stuttering	Frontal EMG, finger temperature
Tardive Dyskinesia	Masseter EMG
Tempomandibular joint/ Myofascial pain-dysfunction	Masseter EMG
Tension/muscle contraction headache	Frontal and trapezius EMG
Tinnitus	Frontal EMG
Torticollis	Left and right sternocleidomastoid EMG
Ulcers	Frontal EMG, stomach acid pH
Urticaria (hives)	GSR

are a function of the availability of automated recording devices. Thus, monetary and technological limitations are present, and one must do the best he/she can with what one can afford. In other words, within practical limitations, record as many responses as you can.

In addition to instrument-recorded physiological responses, other responses should be self-recorded simultaneously at approximately 5-minute intervals. The client verbally gives a numerical rating upon presentation of a prearranged auditory stimulus, such as a tone or the therapists saying "now." Again the therapist must determine what is to be self-rated. Generally, some "level of arousal" rating is utilized. The specific rating utilized may be, among other things, a function of the presenting symptom(s), the client's perception of the causes of the symptom(s), the therapist's rationale for treatment, and the physiological responses to be utilized. Thus, a client with muscle contraction headaches may give ratings of both muscle tension or relaxation and level of headache pain. A hypertensive patient may rate mental relaxation or tension and estimate whether his/her blood pressure is normal, borderline, or abnormal. The following are examples of self-ratings that may be utilized directly or as a basis to construct rating systems for individual clients: subjective units of disturbance ratings (Wolpe & Lazarus, 1966), fear/anxiety thermometer ratings (Walk, 1956; Davis & Hughes, 1979); and mental and physical relaxation ratings (Mitchell & White, 1977).

Psychophysiological assessment typically begins by orienting the client concerning the rationale for the procedure. Since it follows the more general orientation given during the biofeedback interview, it may be relatively brief. The essential communication to the clients is that you are assessing their physiological responsivity and response patterning at a variety of arousal levels. Further, it should be made clear that the assessment information obtained will be utilized to develop an individualized biofeedback training program for them. Relevant client questions should be elicited and answered. During this orientation, the therapist should be attaching the transducers of the physiological recording devices and setting them into operation. In addition, the client is familiarized with the self-rating procedure, and the entire recording procedure is then put into effect for a brief pilot-period to insure that everything is operating properly.

In the second session of the psychophysiological assessment procedure, baseline is begun by giving the client instructions. Either or both of two baseline conditions may be utilized. Our preference is to use an estimated baseline arousal condition wherein the client is instructed to engage in some relatively nonarousing activity, an activity he may pursue during periods of nonarousal in his "natural" environment, while data is collected. Reading a newspaper, news magazine, or biofeedback book, are activities that may be utilized for most clients. Work sample activities that do not involve excessive motor responses, such as doing arithmetic problems, or other repetitive tasks, may also be utilized. The second baseline procedure may be referred to as a sensory restriction baseline arousal condition (Wickramasekera, 1970). In this approach, the client is instructed to adjust the chair to a reclining position and to close his/her eyes, minimize movements, and refrain from talking while initial recordings are made. Although, ideally, the baseline period should continue until the various physiological responses have stabilized, in practice this and subsequent periods may be limited to 10 minutes.

The third period involves a self-directed relaxation training that is intended to lower general arousal. During this period, the client is instructed to relax anyway he/she knows how while sitting or reclining with eyes closed. The stress arousal assessment period is the fourth period. Although the stress stimuli utilized are usually considered to be mild and comparable to those encountered in daily living, precaution should be taken, that is the client should be informed as to the nature of the stimuli, and if either the client or the therapist has doubts as to the safety of the procedure, the client's physician should be consulted. Clients with cardiac arrhythmias, prior myocardial infarction, and other serious maladies may require careful and extraordinary supervision. In any event, the client should be informed and reminded that he/she may terminate the procedure at any time. Conversely, one should attempt to avoid unduly alarming the client or physician in view of the fact that, to the author's knowledge, such procedures have been utilized innumerable times without reported harmful effects. Nevertheless, the client should be informed that stress stimuli will be presented in order to assess his/her physiological responsivity. The exact nature of the stress stimuli should be disclosed and questions should be elicited and answered.

The client is then instructed to remain as calm as possible, and the stimuli are presented on a continuous or intermittent basis. The more aversive stimuli, such as electric shock, are generally presented intermittently, while the less aversive stimuli, such as imagery, are presented continuously. Generally, one stress stimulus is utilized during one 10 minute period. However, if increased arousal does not occur upon presentation, another type of stimuli may be employed. Likewise, during a subsequent session or the same session, after the client has returned to baseline levels of arousal, additional stress stimuli may be employed. The objective in this procedure is to elicit increased arousal to the most relevant stress stimuli available.

The selection of which stimuli to utilize in the assessment is based on their availability, and their reported or hypothesized ability to elicit the target symptoms and/or physiological arousal or anxiety. Although the categories somewhat overlap, it may be useful to consider these types of stressors: environmental, psychosocial, and cognitive. Environmental stressors would include such stimuli as the cold pressor procedure (Hilgard, Morgan, Lange, Lenox, MacDonald, Marshall, & Sachs, 1974), cold room temperature (Surwit, Pilon & Fenton, 1978), aversive films (McCutcheon & Adams, 1975), electric shock (Ewing & Hughes, 1978), sublingual substance (food, chemicals) test (Dickey, 1976), a sudden hand-clap or pinch (Fuller, 1977), a strike of a rubber band (Rinn, 1975), noxious odors (Tanner & Zeiler, 1975) and the holding of one's breath. Psychosocial stressors include such procedures as the therapist placing his hand on some portion (shoulder, for example) of the client's body after requesting to do so (Russell, 1978), or the therapist confronting the client in a verbally aggressive manner.

Cognitive stressors include such stimuli as a serial 7 task starting with a number, such as 115 and subtracting 7 from the result, then 7 from that result, continuing down the series with each response timed and checked for accuracy (Budzynski, 1979; Stoyva, 1979); free association concerning life problems (Wilson & Smith, 1968); instructions to think, image, or relive difficult life situations previously found to be upsetting (Fuller, 1977; Goldstein, Grinker, Heath, Olsen, & Shipman, 1964); instructions to self-talk in the manner that the client utilizes frequently on a daily basis (this generally requires prior assessment as to what such specific talk is to be so utilized).

The fifth period in the psychophysiological assessment may involve a recovery phase. The stress stimuli are withdrawn and latency to recovery to baseline levels of responding is evaluated. Shorter recovery times are considered to be more adaptive than longer ones.

The sixth and final period involves presentation of brief taped or live samples of lowered arousal exercises, such as progressive physical tension/relaxation (Jacobson, 1938: Wolpe, 1958; Wolpe & Lazarus, 1966; Bernstein & Borkovec, 1973); meditation and passive mental relaxation, such as transcendental meditation (Benson, Rosser, Marzetta, & Klemchuck, 1974) and the relaxation response (Bensen, Beary, & Carol, 1974; Benson, 1975); yoga exercises (Datey, Deshmukh, Dalvi, & Vinekar, 1969; Patel, 1973 & 1975; Patel & North, 1975); cue-controlled relaxation (Paul, 1966; Bernstein & Borkovec, 1973; Russell & Sipich, 1974; Reeves & Mealiea, 1975; Cox, Freundlich, & Meyer, 1975); breathing exercises, such as abdominal breathing and controlled rebreathing (Avenci & Cutter, 1977); autogenic training (Schultz & Luthe, 1959, 1969; Luthe, 1977); metronome-conditioned relaxation (Brady, 1973; Brady, Luborsky, & Kron, 1974); hypnosis (Barber & Hahn, 1963; Borkovec & Fowles, 1973; Spiegel, 1970; Spiegel & Spiegel, 1978; Paul, 1969); imagery (Achterberg & Lawlis, 1979); imagery of biofeedback modeled relaxation (Gibb, Stephan, & Rohm, 1975); pink noice (Tentoni, 1978); and, to conclude this list, physical exercise (Driscoll, 1976).

The number of types and duration of lowered arousal exercises must be determined by the presenting symptoms, client preferences, and therapist preferences. For example, it may be desirable to avoid using progressive relaxation initially with clients having symptoms of muscle spasms, such as torticollis. The tensing portion of these relaxation exercises may elicit muscle spasms, and thereby increase this symptom. It might be useful to reserve hypnotic procedures for subjects scoring high on hypnotic susceptibility scales, thereby expressing positive attitudes toward hypnosis. Autogenic training might be included for clients with problems related to peripheral bloodflow, such as Raynaud's disease (Surwit, Pilon & Fenton, 1978). Procedures requested by the client should generally be utilized. Such a screening procedure may sometimes be completed in a relatively short time period and still yield useful information that can be utilized in selecting optimal relaxation procedures to be used during transfer training.

The data from the psychophysiological assessment may be utilized in a number of ways. It serves to partially verify whether or not the client is evidencing a hyperarousal stress reactivity syndrome, an identified relationship between stress, physiological responsiveness, and symptoms of a disorder. It is valuable information to use in determining whether biofeedback is indicated, with which physiological response to begin the biofeedback training, and which responses should be included in the total training program. The data is also useful as a baseline reference in setting treatment objectives, assessing the progression of biofeedback training, determining when to terminate training, and ascertaining whether learned self-control is maintained during post treatment and after. This necessitates that all or specific portions of the psychophysiological assessment procedure are repeated prior to training, during training, post training, and follow-up.

In addition to within-subject comparisons, across-subject comparisons are desirable. However, such comparisons are somewhat tentative at the present time due to the paucity of standardized normative data. Despite enormous difficulties involved, such data is likely to emerge even if slowly. It is difficult to compare EMG data across instruments as there is no standardization of measurement characteristics, such as units of measure (microvolts-root mean square vs peak to peak vs average) and band pass characteristics (utilization of a 60-hertz filter, level of upper and lower frequency cutoff). Skin temperature measures would appear to be relatively comparable across instruments. However, the question of calibration of each apparatus does arise. Other difficulties arise also, such as habituation to the measurement site, maintenance of a constant known room temperature, and the effect of variation in clothing and outside temperature. In addition, many other variables must be controlled; overt and covert activities in which the subject is engaged (resting, reading, sleeping, working, or worrying). Furthermore, such variables as age (BP ranges vary) and sex (peripheral bloodflow varies) must be considered. Some of the literature presented in Part 2 will serve as references from which the reader may obtain tentative, normative data for the various physiological measures.

Setting Goals

The specification of treatment goals is a continuous process. It begins during the first contact with the client. Initially, it may involve an implicit understanding that biofeedback training will probably be efficacious in alleviating the client's symptoms. The rapidity with which this general understanding evolves to a more specific delineation of multiple objectives and treatment procedures is a function of the propensities of the particular therapist-client combination. Generally, specific objectives are agreed upon just prior to initiation of the corresponding training phase. These objectives are based upon all available information gathered up to that point. Thus, objectives would be specified for self-monitoring skills, conceptual skills (concerning stress management), discrimination (of physiological arousal) skills, physiological control skills, and transfer of training skills. These will be considered in conjunction with each skills training phase.

The establishment of specific objectives for any given phase of training involves sensitive clinical judgments. However, general guidelines may be offered. The therapist should strive to establish relatively specific objectives that are attainable on a short-term basis. Objectives can then be increased in small successive increments of approximation. It is important to arrange contingencies so the client is experiencing a high rate of success (70 to 90% but not 100%) at any given time. The therapist should give the client a liberal amount of positive feedback for success and moderate positive feedback for appropriate striving even when success (below 50%) is not achieved. Many times an attentive but passive striving should be shaped rather than an overstriving.

Self-Monitoring Training

Although self-monitoring was included in the chapter on assessment, it will be considered again in each therapy chapter as it is crucial to the success of biofeedback training and other self-regulation therapies. It is the basis from which data is obtained concerning the target symptoms and accompanying responses, the antecedent daily life stress stimuli, and the consequent events. Initial training focuses primarily on methods of recording the target symptoms and medication intake that is necessary before baseline can begin. Self-monitoring through self-detection is the most frequently employed approach. Figure 3.1 presents a sample form that illustrates a data system for hourly recording of migraine and tension headaches, similar to that utilized by Budzynski, Stoyva, Adler, and Mullhaney (1973). This type of recording system may be utilized for subjective ratings of symptoms, such as back pain, arthritic pain, Raynaud's discomfort, dysmenorrhea discomfort, psoriasis itching, perspiration (hyperhidrosis), stomach discomfort, obstruction of nasal breathing due to rhinitis, or frequency recording of symptoms, such as tics, constipation, diarrhea, blepharospasm, seizures, and acne.

Self-monitoring based on the utilization of a measurement device is another useful procedure. Blood pressure cuff recordings have been utilized for hypertension (Kleinman, Goldman, Snow, & Korol, 1977; Beiman, Graham, & Ciminero, 1978; Bradley & Hughes, 1979; Hughes & Cunningham, 1980; Kristt & Engel, 1975; Pollack & Zeiner, 1977); EMG recordings have been employed for bruxism (Rugh & Solberg, 1975; Rugh & Schwitzgabel, 1976), and childbirth pain (Gregg, 1978; Gregg, 1979); actometer motoric movement recordings have been used for hyperactivity (Rogers & Hughes, 1981) and thermometer skin temperature recordings have been utilized for Raynaud's disease (Surwit, Pilon, & Fenton, 1978) and childbirth pain (Gregg, Frazier, & Nesbit, 1976; Gregg, 1979). Other measurement devices could be utilized. For example, a camera may be employed to take pictures of psoriasis (Hughes, England, & Goldsmith, 1981), atopic dermatitis (Haynes, Wilson, Jaffe, & Britton, 1979), or other skin disorders. The pictures may be quantified at a later time using objective rating procedures (Hughes, England, & Goldsmith, 1981).

An additional concern is the setting in which the self-monitoring is to occur. Some self-monitoring may be employed in the therapy or laboratory setting. This is particularly the case for those aspects of symptoms which can be monitored through self-ratings, such as those mentioned earlier: pain,

WEEKLY SUMMARY

INSTRUCTIONS:
1. *Enter date under "DAY" columns*
2. *See "DIRECTIONS" below*

NAME _____ NUMBER _____ MONTH-YEAR _____

DAY →	MON.				TUE.				WED.				THU.				FRI.				SAT.				SUN.			
DATE →																												
COL. NO. →	1	2	3	4	1	2	3	4	1	2	3	4	1	2	3	4	1	2	3	4	1	2	3	4	1	2	3	4
5 A.M.																												
6 A.M.																												
7 A.M.																												
8 A.M.																												
9 A.M.																												
10 A.M.																												
11 A.M.																												
12 NOON																												
1 P.M.																												
2 P.M.																												
3 P.M.																												
4 P.M.																												
5 P.M.																												
6 P.M.																												
7 P.M.																												
8 P.M.																												
9 P.M.																												
10 P.M.																												
11 P.M.																												
12 MID-NITE																												
1 A.M.																												
2 A.M.																												

DIRECTIONS *(make entries for each hour)*

COL. 1: TYPE OF HEADACHE   *"M" = migraine*   *"T" = tension*
Migraine: Nausea before and during headache state; sensory, motory and mood disturbances; unilateral, pulsating or throbbing
Tension: Tight , band-like pain located bilaterally on the occipital and/or forehead

COL. 2: DEGREE OF HEADACHE   *"S" = Sleeping*   *"0" thru "5" = Awake*
"0" = No headache symptoms
"1" = Pre-headache symptoms barely noticeable
"2" = Pre-headache symptoms increased but able to ignore
"3" = Headache symptoms painful, conscious of presence most of time, but able to ignore
"4" = Headache symptoms severe, concentration difficult, able to perform tasks of undemanding nature
"5" = Headache symptoms incapacitating, intense pain, unable to perform any tasks, bedridden

COL. 3: MEDICATION   *List type of medication, using following abbreviations; enter amount of medication showing quantity (number amount in milligrams). Use blank spaces to formulate abbreviations as needed.*
"A" = Aspirin   "B" = Bufferin   "DIL" = Dilantin   "VAL" = Valium   "AN" = Anacin
"DAR" = Darvon   "LIB" = Librium   ____ = ____   ____ = ____   ____ = ____

COL. 4: RESPONSE   *List response to headache or anticipated onset of headache; combinations such as "TR", "RB", "TRS", etc. may be used.*
"T" = Played relaxation   "R" = Self-directed attempt to relax without use of tape
"B" = Self-directed attempt to reduce tension thru biofeedback without apparatus
'S" = Spontaneous or intended sleep

RETURN TO: Howard Hughes, Ph.D.
Department of Psychology   Phone: 817–788–2631
NTSU   788–2632
Denton, Texas   76201   (Home)   817–387–7641

Figure 3.1   Headache Self-Monitoring Form

discomfort, and itching. Usually those detected by measurement devices are, in the laboratory situation, monitored by the therapist. In general, it is desirable to utilize self-monitoring in the client's environment since there are limited alternative means of data collection, and the client's environment includes by definition the site of occurrence of the target behaviors. The target site, whether it be at home, at work, at the physician's office, or other public places, is the primary focus of self-monitoring. A target site could be even more specific, for example, at home during sleep, at home when the spouse is present, at the therapist's office during social confrontation rehearsal, or at work when the supervisor is present. Self-monitoring of symptoms and medication should begin as soon as possible and continue through baseline, treatment, transfer training, and follow up.

Information other than target symptoms, medication, and site of recordings may be obtained by self-monitoring. However, problems in compliance are probably exacerbated by the increased time and effort required for completion of the procedures. For this reason, the data to be collected throughout the course of the biofeedback program should be held to a minimum.

Additional information may be collected through self-monitoring during specific intervals of time. For example, relatively brief self-monitoring assessments: one-occasion, one-day, or one-week periods may be utilized during the baseline phase and subsequent phases of the biofeedback program. This procedure is similar to the psychophysiological assessment procedure that is conducted in the laboratory setting. The objective is to identify eliciting life stress stimuli antecedent to symptoms; symptom-related cognitive, physiological, or behavioral responses, and consequent events related to symptom maintenance. This can be done with direct measures, such as skin temperature, blood pressure, muscle tension, and indirect measures, such as analysis of blood, urine, feces, or hair. Antecedent stimuli and concurrent responses may be identified in terms of geographic location, persons present, overt and covert activity, or emotional state. Consequent events can be coded as changes in the stimulus response matrix. This is seen in activities that have stopped, such as work, and in activities that have been initiated, such as drinking, eating, sleeping, or changes in location and changes of persons present. Figure 3.2 illustrates a form that could be utilized in such a self-monitoring procedure. This assessment procedure is facilitated by the utilization of measurement devices. An excellent illustration of self-monitoring assessment may be seen in the work of Rugh and Solberg (1975).

The development of stress detection skills through self-monitoring assessment is extremely important. These detector skills result from the discovery of contiguity between environmental stimuli and behavioral, cognitive, or physiological arousal. These skills enable the client to experience the stress hyperarousal sequence, and this experience could increase his/her motivation to continue treatment and comply with the treatment procedures. In addition, during transfer training, stress detection may be utilized to self-initiate home practice self-control exercises.

DAILY RECORD

YOUR NAME

DATE

INSTRUCTIONS
1. Fill out one report for each day (use second sheet if necessary).
2. Enter time each activity initiated in "Hour" column beginning with the time you awoke.

HOUR A.M./P.M.	ACTIVITY	TIME SPENT	INTERACTION DURING ACTIVITY	THOUGHTS AND FEELINGS ASSOCIATED WITH ACTIVITY	PRESENTING PROBLEMS - CRITICAL INCIDENTS	OTHER PROBLEMS - CRITICAL INCIDENTS

Figure 3.2 Activity Self-Monitoring Form

65

Additional self-monitoring is also desirable during transfer training and follow up. In particular, it is important to collect data concerning home practice of self-control exercises. You may note that provision for such recording is provided on the form shown in Figure 3.2. The data gathered during self-monitoring similarly to the data obtained from the psychophysiological assessment is used not only to determine whether biofeedback is indicated, but also to assess whether a hyperarousal stress reactivity syndrome is present. In addition, the data is useful in making decisions in individualizing the treatment process; for example, the inclusion of specific physiological responses and determination of when to terminate biofeedback training. Other relevant uses of the data include assessment of occurrence of transfer of training and maintenance at follow up.

Once the therapist arrives at a specification of the various aspects of a client's self-monitoring, the specifics should be presented to the client as training objectives. A client may be told that the initial training objective is learning to take and record his own blood pressure accurately five times daily at specified place/time situations. Appropriate rationales are also presented or reviewed if presented earlier. The specifics of self-monitoring training vary among clients, but if clients have the same or similar presenting symptoms or need to utilize the same measurement devices, a group self-monitoring training approach may be more efficient. Further written procedural handbooks may be developed for the various symptoms and measurement devices and be utilized in lieu of or in conjunction with verbal instructions.

It is generally desirable to have the client practice the self-monitoring procedure(s) until a skills mastery is attained. This is usually done in the laboratory setting with appropriate supervisory feedback. For example, the client may practice self-rating of headache activity and self-recording of medication intake on the appropriate form. He does this by utilizing his memory of the waking hours of the last seven days as a simulated situation. Additionally, the client and another person may practice self-recording their skin temperature and blood pressure until an acceptable level of interobserver reliability is obtained. Ideally, self-monitoring by the client doesn't begin until sufficient training has been completed.

Additional decisions relating to time and place of self-monitoring must be made. Self-monitoring may be programmed to occur wherever the client is, be it at home, at work, in the client's automobile, in the physician's office, or in the therapist's office. For a given situation, self-monitoring generally occurs at a specified time. This can be at the time of occurrence of the symptom, at the end of each hour, at the time of specified daily events (such as getting up, eating, going to the bathroom, getting home from work, or going to bed) or upon the occurrence of an electronically-programmed auditory stimulus.

Finally, a decision must be made concerning the frequency at which the self-monitored data is presented to the therapist. The data usually is given to the therapist at the beginning of each appointment. However, it may be recorded on a postcard and mailed to the therapist daily. There are advantages to the latter procedure in that recording at the designated intervals minimizes recording based on memory. Reinforcement for attainment and compliance is imperative. Thus, at the beginning of each session, the therapist receives the data from the client and verbally reinforces the client as the data form is checked. Additional reinforcement can be arranged by utilizing a contractual procedure wherein the client is presented with previously arranged reinforcers, such as money or personal valuables. The importance of reinforcement for self-monitoring cannot be overemphasized.

Once the data is received and checked by the therapist, it is necessary to transform it into a meaningful form. Self-reported headache ratings are utilized to derive figures of the weekly average headache frequency and duration, and the average intensity per waking hour, and per headache. The data is generally plotted in graph form.

A symptom measurement baseline is obtained from the time of monitoring procedures, before biofeedback control training begins. Ideally, this phase continues for a period long enough to demonstrate a relatively stable level of symptomatic behavior. This varies greatly with the type of measurements taken, and the specific characteristics of the client. Generally, 2 to 3 weeks is allowed. However, shorter periods of time may be sufficient, based upon available research data, such as 5 to 8 days, for blood pressure measurements, (Clark, Schwitzer, Glock, & Vought, 1956; Luborsky, Brady, McClintock, Kron, Bortnichak, & Levitz, 1976). During this period, sessions occur weekly and may include brief periodic collection of more detailed data as to antecedent events, accompanying responses, and consequent events; conceptualization training; and discrimination training. During these sessions, it is desirable to collect baseline data on the client's attempts to self-control the physiological responses that are likely to be the major parameter of biofeedback control training. The same procedures utilized in the second, third, and possibly fourth segments of the psychophysiological assessment are repeated here, for example, a 10-minute session baseline, and a 10-minute self-directed relaxation period. A 10-minute stress arousal phase could follow if time permits. This approach provides repeated measures of the presence or absence of physiological self-control skills.

During the symptom measurement baseline phase, the issue of medication should be considered. If the client is taking prescribed medications, communication with the physician either directly or through the client is recommended. Medication alteration may be carried out in a number of ways. One approach is to evaluate the effects of the medication by having the client discontinue medication intake. This is done only if it is not considered hazardous to the client's health, as verified by his/her physician. Withdrawal of medication is the only possible approach other than not utilizing biofeedback, if effects of the medication prevent or significantly inhibit learned control. In other words, intake of a medication that vasodilates the cranial arteries is likely to interfere with discrimination and biofeedback control training of blood flow (vasomotor) of the temporal arteries. Furthermore, an increase in symptoms, due to discontinued medication, may increase motivation and compliance with the treatment program.

A second approach involves the continuation of medication using procedures to insure that intake is held constant. If the medication is held constant, it may be ruled out as a causative factor in any change in the dependent measure. Medication is frequently held constant in biofeedback treatment of essential hypertension.

A third approach permits medication to vary with continued intake monitoring. The most frequent example of this is when medication is taken on an as needed (prn) basis. This is generally an undesirable procedure as it is a source of uncontrolled variation, as in the case of analgesic intake of pain clients. An alternate procedure is for the therapist to control medication intake. A good example is the pain cocktail procedure (Fordyce, 1976) in which the client takes the same substance at specific times with the amount of medication contained therein being determined by the therapist. Another possibility is to make medication intake a function of a relatively objective event. Therefore, the level of insulin a diabetic takes could be dependent upon a minimum detectable spillage of sugars into the urine as ascertained by daily urine tests. Likewise, analgesic intake can be a function of the presence of a pain rating of 5 (incapacitating, unable to perform any tasks, bedridden) on a five point scale.

In addition to making a determination as to a medication intake procedure, the physiological responses to be trained must be selected. The approaches used are diverse and varied; however, the following considerations may be used as guidelines. From a practical standpoint, the first consideration relates to the availability of functioning equipment. It is suggested that EMG and photoplethysmograph bloodflow biofeedback equipment should be acquired and utilized as basic response measures. In addition, a relatively inexpensive blood pressure cuff with combination light and tone indicators of Korotkoff sounds (partially occluded pulse) and an inexpensive thermometer to measure skin temperature are desirable. A second consideration is the selection of responses that are indicated by reviewing the literature on treatment of the presenting symptoms. A third consideration relates to assessing the extent to which the client associates or is able to learn to associate a physiological response with his symptom. For example, it may be more acceptable to a migraine client to work with bloodflow in the temporal arteries as opposed to finger skin temperature. This is seen in light of the hypothesized physiological mechanism of migraine pain as caused by excessive dilation of the cranial arteries. A fourth consideration has to do with which physiological response is most closely associated with the presentation and withdrawal of stress and relaxation stimuli during the psychophysiological assessments. For example, if a client consistently responds to stress conditions by increasing muscle tension and responds to low arousal conditions by decreasing muscle tension, EMG is indicated. A fifth consideration involves the percentage of time the response is outside normal limits. The more the response exceeds normal limits the more it should be considered as a training response. Although this is frequently difficult to ascertain since normative data is not usually available, some determinations can be made by reviewing the treatment literature. Additional information is likely to become available in the future. For example, there are usable norms for obtaining blood pressure in a medical situation. Published skin temperature data are relatively useful since the various measurement devices utilize the same scale. Although the variability of measurement devices limit the utility of published EMG data, extreme scores (above $30\mu V$) during usual or low arousal conditions are considered to be outside normal limits. A sixth consideration involves determining the likelihood that a particular response can be trained successfully. Budzynski (1973) suggests that when EMG is indicated, it is desirable to start with forearm and shift to frontal training. Gaarder and Montgomery (1977) suggest beginning training with the response that is most labile during the psychophysiological assessment. Finally, other things being equal, it is desirable to select a response that can be monitored in the client's environment so that transfer of training may be more easily evaluated.

After selection of the physiological response(s) to be trained, at some point it may be necessary to switch to another response or train an additional response successively. The above guidelines and additional accumulating data are utilized during the subsequent training phases to assess the feasibility of continuation of the original and subsequent physiological responses to be trained. The basic objectives are to insure success in discrimination and control training and to observe concurrent change in symptom target behaviors.

Discrimination Training

Discrimination training can not be explicitly considered as a necessary part of biofeedback, but is important nonetheless because it attempts to train the client in the self-detection of symptom occurrence and/or hyperarousal of an associated physiological response. The necessity of the client's learning such skills may be obviated under certain circumstances. One such circumstance is if the objective of biofeedback training of a specific physiological response is to produce relatively permanent tonic changes. In other words, the changes are maintained automatically once the biofeedback is discontinued (Blanchard & Epstein, 1978). This may be the case with certain individuals, or with certain physiological responses; possibly with persons receiving sensory-motor rhythm EEG biofeedback training for the treatment of seizure disorders (Sterman, 1973). In contrast, it would appear that a self-control model (Blanchard & Epstein, 1977, 1978) is more widely applicable to most biofeedback training. In the self-control model the control of physiological responding established by biofeedback training does not automatically transfer to the nonlaboratory environment. Therefore, optimal utilization of the learned physiological control skills requires that the client is able to self-detect the presence of the symptoms, and the associated physiological responses which are outside normal limits. It follows that prevention and abortion of symptoms become possible. For example, if sustained contraction of face and neck muscles is associated with the occurrence of tension headaches, the detection of excessive muscle tension may serve as a discriminative stimulus to utilize the muscle relaxation skills learned through frontal EMG biofeedback. This action can then facilitate transfer of training to the environmental setting.

The necessity of discrimination training could also be circumvented if the self-control skills learned in biofeedback training were practiced sufficiently on a daily basis independent of symptom occurrence and deviation of the associated physiological responses from an acceptable level. A number of studies support the contention that beneficial effects of biofeedback training are maintained after such training is discontinued only to the extent that daily home practice is continued (Blanchard, Theobald, Williamson, Silver, & Brown, 1978; Budzynski, Stoyva, Adler, & Mullhaney, 1973).

The necessity of discrimination training is also obviated if the client shows mastery of such skills as becomes apparent during the baseline assessment portion of the discrimination training procedure. The probability of previous mastery of skills may be increased if biofeedback control training occurs before discrimination training. Even though prior biofeedback control training may not result in adequate discrimination skills, it may facilitate the rapidity of subsequent discrimination training (Gainer, 1978).

On the other hand, there may be advantages to having discrimination training precede biofeedback training. For instance, the naive client cannot artificially increase his percentage of correct discriminations by using self-control skills to increase or decrease the response level. At the present time, there appears to be no information available to determine whether discrimination should precede, follow, or be carried out concurrently with biofeedback control training as a general procedure for all clients, or as a specific procedure based on prediction utilizing client characteristics. However, at present, it would appear that discrimination training should precede biofeedback training. One advantage is that it may facilitate acceptance by the client of an adequate symptom measurement baseline period as he/she may be constructively occupied with discrimination training. This position is also based on the Premack principle. The client's primary choice is generally to start the biofeedback training as soon as possible, and discrimination training is facilitated by making the onset of biofeedback contingent upon the completion of discrimination training. It may be that prior discrimination training facilitates subsequent biofeedback control training. Furthermore, if the client learns discrimination training, it is possible that he/she may learn self-control skills based on trial and error in the environment without a biofeedback device. This would essentially be biofeedback based on the client's discrimination skill and would obviate or shorten biofeedback training (Blanchard & Epstein, 1978).

Symptom detection is to a large extent the focus of self-monitor training whereas detection of a physiological response associated with the symptom is the focus of discrimination training. In some cases, the symptom and an abnormal level of the physiological response are the same or highly correlated. For example, essential hypertension is elevated blood pressure and the discomfort of Raynaud's disease is correlated with low skin temperature. Some physiological responses, such as heart (pulse) rate and respiration, are easily detectable by their natural sensory consequences. Others, such as EMG, and skin temperature, appear to be moderately detectable. Finally, others, such as EEG, GSR, and blood pressure, appear to be difficult to discriminate. Selection of the response to be utilized in discrimination training is based on prior information from the psychophysiological and self-monitoring assessments.

The training procedure outlined here is similar to the outline presented by Blanchard and Epstein (1978). First, an objective measure of the physiological response is needed, and whenever possible, it is desirable to have a measurement device available for both laboratory and home settings. In the latter case, portable instruments may be necessary. Second, a response system must be developed and presented to the client in communicating the level of the physiological response to the therapist. This is accomplished by taking baseline measurements of the response under the same conditions that will be present during discrimination training. Next, the mean or median measure is calculated over the selected baseline period. A two-, three- or five-point scale is then derived. For example, a two-point would involve a rating of "high" if the response is currently above the median of the previous week or "low" if it is currently below the median. A three-point scale might designate high as being greater than one standard deviation above the mean, low as being greater than one standard deviation below, and average as being within one standard deviation above or below the mean. Third, prior to onset of discrimination training, the therapist should present the rationale for the training and specify the training objectives to the client. The objective may be for the client to reliably detect when his/her blood pressure has increased to the point of being outside normal limits. Fourth, the training involves the client recording his rating of the physiological response at specified intervals concurrently or after the therapist has obtained an objective measure of the same response. It is, however, necessary to control activities in which the client has participated prior to measurement; running or resting, for instance and control other conditions that may affect the response in question, such as temperature or noise level. Finally, it may be necessary to switch from the rating system previously mentioned to a rating system based on health-related issues. For example, a useful scale for hypertensive clients would include normal, borderline, and abnormal blood pressure ratings as indicated by prior research documenting the relationship between blood pressure levels and mortality rates.

Regardless of the rating system used, training should continue until the client achieves an acceptable level of correct discriminations with a rough guideline of 75% correct. Exactly what is correct must be operationally defined in relation to the measurement system and the variation in objective measurements taken over an equivalent time interval. For example, the mean variation of ±5.8 mm Hg for systolic blood pressure measurements taken from one minute to the next may serve as a reference to compare the mean error of subject estimates ±7.4 mm Hg (during blood pressure discrimination training) given within 10 seconds to 2 minutes 10 seconds prior to the measurements (Luborsky, Brady, McClintock, Kron, Bortnichak, & Levitz, 1976). In other words, the accuracy of the client's discriminations can be no better than the accuracy of the response measurement system.

The discrimination training procedure presented focuses on the range of the physiological response present in the training setting. Prior to or after this type of training, a different approach may be utilized. Essentially, the same procedures may be employed, but the physiological response may be manipulated periodically by the experimenter thereby altering the magnitude of difference between successive discriminations. Vidergar, Lee, and Goldman (1978) utilized cold pressor, heat, and vigilance task conditions to manipulate blood pressure during discrimination training.

Another possible variable in discrimination training procedures is the distribution of the discrimination learning trials. At one extreme, the procedure may involve one trial per session. At the other extreme, the procedure may involve a large number of trials, for example one per minute over a 50-minute session. One may combine massed and distributed trials either simultaneously or successively. Distributed trials may be used for home practice periods and massed trials for the therapist's office sessions. Comparative data being unavailable, it is suggested that after an initial introductory session or two of massed trials, distributed trials are instituted so as to reserve a large portion of the therapy session for the other components of the biofeedback program.

Discrimination training procedures may differ with respect to the nature of the client's response. The basic procedure previously presented utilizes a verbal or written overt response system which the client employs to communicate information to the therapist concerning his/her judgments or estimates of the physiological response of interest. Such an overt response system is necessary in assessing the client's ability to make accurate discriminations. This assessment should be utilized prior to training to ascertain if training is needed and after training to assess the success of the training. During discrimination training, either a covert and/or overt response system may be employed. Gainer (1978) uses a covert response system procedure for skin temperature discrimination training. Although generalizations from this study are limited since it involves a single case, the results demonstrate that an improvement in discrimination accuracy from 47 to 79% was sufficient to be associated with clinical improvement in migraine headache activity.

A discrimination training procedure may also vary with respect to the setting in which the training trials are conducted, either in the client's environment or in the therapist's office. It would be desirable to have the initial training occur in the therapist's office to insure sufficient learning of the procedure in order to conduct it in a standardized manner in the natural environment. It would further appear to be desirable to conduct at least a single discrimination trial during all subsequent sessions in the therapist's office in order to assess the accuracy of the client's discriminations. Practically speaking, trials can be conducted in the client's environment only if a self-directed objective measurement system is available. Ultimately, it is anticipated that advancing technology will make such measurement systems available for most physiological responses. At this time, home measurement appears to be relatively possible for blood pressure (Beiman, Graham, & Ciminero, 1978; Bradley & Hughes, 1979; Hughes & Cunningham, 1980; Kristt & Engel, 1975) and skin temperature (Roberts, Hughes, & Goldstrich, 1981; Surwit, Pilon, & Fenton, 1978), using conventional methods and with more sophisticated and costly approaches for a 24-hour recording of blood pressure (Pollock & Zeiner, 1977), and nighttime recording of EMG (Rugh & Solberg, 1975; Rugh & Sohwitzgebel, 1976).

Assuming objective home measurement is possible, it would be desirable to utilize home discrimination training after some initial training in the therapist's office. Training in the client's natural environment is covered more completely under the topic of transfer training. A number of additional studies have demonstrated discrimination of physiological responses. Brener and Jones (1974), Cinciripini, Epstein, and Martin (1979), Epstein, Cinciripini, McCoy, and Marshall (1977), and Epstein and Stein (1974) have shown discrimination with heart rate; Shapiro, Redmond, McDonald, & Gaylor (1975) with blood pressure; and Lansky, Nathan, & Lawson (1978) and Maisto & Adesso (1977) with blood alcohol level. It should be noted that if discrimination training is utilized prior to biofeedback control training, the training can be repeated after control training profitably if the range of the physiological response has been appreciably altered.

Biofeedback Control Training

The purpose of biofeedback training is to learn to control physiological responses. Prior to initiation of biofeedback training, the physiological response(s) to be utilized in control training has been identified. The data collected during the symptom measurement baseline pertaining to the client's attempts at self-control of the physiological response(s) most likely has established that self-control is not present. If these data suggest that adequate self-control is present, the biofeedback control training is unnecessary and transfer training should begin. Although they appear to be infrequent, there are clients who have such self-control skills but do not effectively utilize them. They essentially see their disorder as a physical problem to be solved by a doctor, and do not relate the symptoms to either stress, hyperarousal to stress, or their ability to achieve lowered arousal. In such cases, the stress management learned through self-monitoring, conceptualization, discrimination, and transfer training would appear to be sufficient without biofeedback control training.

Although the physiological response(s) to be trained is selected during the self-monitoring and discrimination training phases, the choice should be reevaluated prior to control training. In addition, a decision must be made as to the type of control training to be used. Generally, training is unidirectional and limited to altering the physiological response in the direction of lowered arousal, such as in lowering muscle tension, heart rate, blood pressure, or raising skin temperature. In some cases, the indicated change may be in the opposite direction, and the objective may be to increase muscular activity as during neuromuscular retraining. Training may also be bidirectional wherein the objective is to learn to alternately raise and lower arousal (Kristt & Engel, 1975). A third training strategy involves learning to control the variability of a response (Lang, Stroufe, & Hastings, 1967). It is possible for training to include all three strategies. The complete training involving increase, decrease, and variability control training would appear to be desirable. However, adequate information is not available at this time to determine whether such training is more effective than unidirectional training. The type of training is likely to be a function of the therapist's preferences and practical considerations until such information is available. Decisions concerning medication intake should also be reviewed. Medication that prevents learning control of the physiological response should be discontinued as previously discussed in the section on self-monitoring training.

Biofeedback control training is preceded by an orientation. In most cases, the client has previously been introduced to the equipment. It may be desirable to review this again. The client is informed of the objective of this training phase: to learn to decrease muscle tension in response to everyday events. He/she is then educated as to the mechanisms of biofeedback. An example of what is said to the client is as follows:

> An electromyograph detects electrical signals emanating from the muscles in the area where the electrodes are placed. An EMG then amplifies these signals and transforms them into usable, visual, or auditory stimuli that vary in proportion to the muscle activity. The availability of biofeedback information then facilitates learned control of muscle activity, much like the availability of visual information facilitates learning to thread a needle. The signal does not control you, rather it enables you to control your behavior.

After an initial period of experiencing the feedback stimulus, the client is told:

> The task is to lower the level of the auditory or visual stimulus. Even people who have learned to do this can not explain satisfactorily how

they did it. What works best for one person will not necessarily work best for another. The important fact is that practice facilitates learned control. This probably involves a trial and error procedure, so experiment with different responses and keep those that produce the desired biofeedback information. Some of the things you may want to try are self-guided: imagery (auditory, visual, tactile, gustatory, olfactory, i.e., seeing oats slowly spilling out of a bag and piling up from the floor), thoughts and subvocalizations (self statements), vocalizations (chanting, singing), movements (deep breathing, and isometric tensing and relaxing, rocking), and other possibilities (Budzynski, 1979). These strategies may focus on the memory of past events or fantasy of future events. They may be concerned with specific times, places, people, and activities. Various meditative approaches may be used: for example, narrowing of attention on a repetitive experience, such as continually saying a word, or an expansion of attention to a continuous passive acceptance of events as they happen. It is particularly important to assume a passive volition; that is, to be attentive but just allow it to happen naturally even though you have experienced success in other tasks using active volition which involves making things happen now with time and performance pressure (Taub & Emurian, 1976; Stoyva, 1979). Maintain a perspective and try not to be unduly anxious, discouraged or encouraged, since learning may seem painfully slow both initially and after rapid gains have occurred.

It would probably be desirable to utilize an audio or videotape presentation of all or part of this orientation. This could be done in the context of a successful case study to facilitate positive expectancies. After completion of the orientation period, biofeedback control training begins a typical biofeedback training session of 50 minutes. At the beginning of the session, the client gives the data that has been collected to the therapist. The therapist briefly examines it to insure compliance, then instructs and reinforces the client accordingly. Past data in graphic form may be briefly reviewed with the client. During this time, the appropriate transducers are attached to the client, and physiological recording is initiated. During the next 10 minutes, a session baseline is established. This is done either under simulated activity or sensory restricted arousal conditions depending on the therapist's preference after observing the client's responses under both conditions during the psychophysiological assessment. If 10 minutes is not enough time to establish a stable session baseline, it may be necessary to have the client arrive 15 to 30 minutes early and remain in the waiting room prior to the session. This modulates the effects of previous arousing activities, such as exercise, and environmental conditions, such as outside temperature extremes.

The next 20 to 30 minutes are utilized for biofeedback training. Essentially, the client is practicing a new skill, and the therapist assumes the role of coach or mentor. The therapist should observe the client periodically to correct any behaviors or conditions that might interfere with learning; for instance, sleeping or equipment malfunction. If the physiological data is automatically recorded, the therapist may occupy himself with other activities until the end of the practice period. Some therapists prefer to hire technicians to carry out these portions of the training procedure. At the end of the practice session, the transducers are disconnected. The therapist has 5 to 15 minutes to briefly review the data from this and prior sessions. He also may ask and answer questions and make appropriate comments to the client. A longer period of time may be desirable for concurrent psychotherapy or behavior therapy. Enough time is allowed to maintain the therapeutic relationship and to adequately monitor the client's progress both during the session and at home.

The primary responsibility of the therapist is to maintain conditions suitable for learning the biofeedback task. This involves helping the client maintain a passive orientation. Additional verbal and/or graphic feedback may be given in such a manner as to allow the client to maintain a positive perspective and thereby facilitate continued practive and acceptance of the rate of learning that occurs. During periods when learning is relatively slow, the therapist focuses on and reinforces appropriate client behaviors, such as maintaining effort and positive attitude, and minimizes the lack of instant progress in altering the physiological response. Likewise, during periods when learning is relatively accelerated, a perspective is maintained by combining positive feedback with some discussion of future objectives and the continued practice that will be necessary.

Numerous issues may arise in conjunction with attempts to develop control skills. Stoyva (1979) has considered a number of the more typical concerns and problems that arise and suggests how the therapist could most appropriately deal with them. Falling asleep may necessitate taking measures to insure that the client has a sufficient amount of sleep daily, scheduling the practice session at a different time of day, or changing the sitting position used during the session. Conditions may also be altered in the direction of increasing arousal by brightening the lights, increasing noise level, and encouraging the client to keep his eyes open. A client may experience strange sensations, images, or intense thoughts during the training. It is helpful to reassure him/her that such phenomena are not uncommon and will typically dissipate over time. It may also be desirable to suggest that the client not concern himself with banishing such thoughts. Other possibilities involve allowing the thoughts to dissipate naturally; engaging in repetitive relaxing behaviors, such as scanning for muscle tension around the face, eyes, and throat regions and relaxing these areas; humming softly; and repeating words or phrases. Another problem that may be incurred is the client's persistance in a wrong strategy; for example, utilizing breathing responses without success. Through behavioral observation and inquiry, the therapist should detect the persevered strategy and counsel the client to use different strategies. If the client does not appear to be learning to control a given physiological response after sufficient effort and practice, it may be desirable to switch temporarily to another physiological response in order to attain successful experiences. One way, for example, is to switch from skin temperature training to EMG training, or from frontal EMG to forearm EMG.

When working with young children, additional procedures are generally desirable. An overt reinforcement procedure is established typically in the form of a token system. The procedure may be manual wherein tokens are dropped into a can, or an automated programmed reinforcer or token dispenser may be used. At the conclusion of each session, tokens are exchanged for reinforcers. The procedure includes a shaping paradigm established by the therapist. Employing the baseline data as a frame of reference, a response change criterion is selected that is likely to result in the client's attaining success 70 to 90% of time. The successive criterion gradually approximates the terminal response, which is the objective of the training. A child would receive verbal praise and one token for attaining a reduction of $1\mu V$ when the previous reading was 10 μV or above, a reduction of 0.5 μV when the previous reading was between 6 and 9.9 μV, a reduction of .2 μV when the previous reading was between 3.1 and 5.9 μV, or any reading of 3 μV, or lower (Hughes, Henry, & Hughes, 1980).

Scheduling two biofeedback training sessions per week appears to be optimal and allows for the possible facilitation of massed trials. In certain circumstances, such as direct blood pressure biofeedback training, trials are massed to the extent of two to three sessions per day (Bradley & Hughes, 1979; Elder, Ruiz, Deabler, & Dillenkoffer, 1973; Kristt & Engel, 1975). However, additional research is necessary to clarify this issue. Sometimes, sessions are scheduled at a frequency of one per week, and if given enough instruments, group biofeedback control training is possible. Bradley and Hughes (1979) utilized a group training format for blood pressure biofeedback. These authors have also shown that the greater portion of biofeedback control training may occur in the client's home environment rather than in the therapist's office.

Biofeedback control training for a particular physiological response is considered to be complete when the terminal specified objective for control training has been attained. An example would be attainment and maintenance of 2 μV forearm or 3 μV frontal EMG levels as the terminal specified objective for a client receiving frontal EMG biofeedback training (Budzynski, 1973; Ewing & Hughes, 1978; Hughes, Henry, & Hughes, 1980; Stoyva, 1979). Likewise, attainment and maintenance of blood pressure readings of 140/90 mm Hg or lower may be the terminal specified objective for a middle-aged hypertensive client. Other possible terminal specified objectives are 90°F or greater finger temperature (Stoyva, 1979) and two or fewer spontaneous GSRs per minute. In any event, the total number of biofeedback control training sessions for one physiological response generally falls within the range of 4 to 16 sessions. If one chooses to learn control of other physiological responses, additional trials are necessary.

Transfer Training

The objective of transfer training is to facilitate generalization of the skills learned during discrimination and/or biofeedback control training. There is no sharp delineation between biofeedback training and the initial portion of transfer training, and they may occur simultaneously. That is, biofeedback control training of a second physiological response may be alternated with transfer training of the initial trained response. Transfer training begins as soon as the terminal objective of biofeedback control training has been attained.

The client receives a general orientation to transfer training. The presentation includes such statements as:

> The discrimination and control of physiological responses learned in the office setting under optimal conditions with biofeedback equipment will not necessarily transfer to your home environment. Transfer training will facilitate generalization, and it involves practice exercises in the office and at home. The general idea is to practice the skills under conditions that are successively more similar to the conditions in the environment in which they will be used.

The therapist arranges the treatment sessions in such a manner that the client's discrimination and/or control skills are assessed under conditions more or less similar to the client's actual environment. Biofeedback discrimination and control training take place in the office under conditions of sensory restriction (Wickramaskera, 1970). The typical therapist's office offers a relatively low noise level; there is seldom more than one person other than the client present, and verbal sounds are minimally present. Visual stimulation is reduced markedly, not only by the constancy of the office environment and the client's location therein but by the fact that his/her eyes are closed. Finally, sensory reduction occurs from the marked restriction of activity associated with remaining relatively still in a reclining position. The possible number of graduated steps from sensory reduced training to the client's life environment is astronomically large. The therapist's task is to engineer this transition to minimize the number of steps and time required while maintaining the learned skills. Although this process must be individualized for each client, an approximation of the typical procedures will be set forth here. Additional information concerning these procedures is presented by Budzynski (1973), Fuller (1977), and Gaarder and Montgomery (1977).

The client is given a brief orientation of each step in transfer training prior to its occurrence. The first step typically involves the therapist terminating the biofeedback signal during a training session when the client has attained the terminal objective, 3 μV or less EMG level for 10 minutes (Budzynski, 1979). The client's task is to maintain the response criterion without further reliance on the biofeedback signal. It may be desirable to have the client demonstrate this maintenance skill over two or three sessions before proceeding to the next transfer task. The second transfer task is for the client to obtain the response criterion without the assistance of the biofeedback signal. The client attempts self-directed low arousal after the session baseline is established and before biofeedback is initiated. Essentially, the self-directed low arousal instruction now precedes rather than follows the biofeedback control training.

The transition from attaining low arousal with biofeedback signals to attaining this condition without assistance frequently occurs with graduated fading of the biofeedback signals. There are advantages, however, to utilizing a specific procedure, such as cue-controlled training, to accomplish the transition. Cue-control training further emphasizes the self-control set already inherent to biofeedback training. The cue-controlled procedure has been demonstrated as more effective than biofeedback alone in facilitating transfer of lower frontal EMG responses from feedback to no feedback conditions (Ewing & Hughes, 1978). The major limitation of cue-controlled training applications with biofeedback is that it has only been utilized with EMG biofeedback. Hughes (1978) has advocated its use with other biofeedback trained responses, and Goldman and Hughes (1979) are currently investigating its effectiveness with finger temperature biofeedback.

The training procedure is relatively brief and is initiated at anytime during biofeedback that low arousal criterion of 3 μV EMG or less has been attained by the client. This procedure is similar to that used by Russell & Sipich (1973), Reeves & Mealiea (1975), and Ewing & Hughes (1978). At this time, the biofeedback signal is generally terminated. The therapist instructs the client to focus attention on breathing; to take slow deep breaths, and to subvocalize, or say to himself/herself the word "relax" at the onset or during each of the next 20 exhalations. With each of the client's next five exhalations, the therapist vocalizes the cue-word. The client then continues subvocalizing for 15 more pairings. The therapist then instructs the client to stop subvocalizing but to continue focusing on his/her general body sensations of relaxation or warmth. If the measured physiological response, EMG, is not within the criterion range, the biofeedback signal is reinstated until the criterion is achieved. If it is within criterion range, the procedure continues after 1 minute and the therapist instructs the client to subvocalize the stimulus word 20 more times in the previous manner without therapist vocalizations. Cue-controlled training is repeated during subsequent training sessions until the client can achieve the low arousal criterion under self-directed instructions without biofeedback. The client then is instructed to utilize cue-control skills during subsequent home practice exercises. Additional cue-controlled training trials may be utilized as part of subsequent transfer training steps involving conditions other than sensory restriction.

When low arousal attainment and maintenance has been reliably demonstrated under conditions of sensory restriction in the therapist's office, instructions for the second transfer task, cue-controlled practice under sensory restriction in the client's natural environment, should begin. Home practice is probably the single most important element in the total biofeedback training program. The extent to which the client engages in home practice and maintains it over time is a good indicator of maintenance of therapeutic gains at the time of follow up (Blanchard, Theobald, Williamson, Silver, & Brown, 1978, Budzynski, Stoyva, Adler, & Mullhaney, 1973, Reinking, 1976).

Orientation toward home practice should be particularly thorough. The procedure includes having the client record a subjective rating of the level of arousal attained during practice, also when, where, how long. The client may record this information on the same form that is used for symptom recording. Whenever possible, particularly if discrimination has been employed, objective measurements of the target response in the client's environment should be taken just before and after home practice (Beiman, Graham, & Ciminero, 1978; Bradley & Hughes, 1979; Hughes & Cunningham, 1980; Fowler, Budzynski, & Vandenbergh, 1976; Pollack & Zeiner, 1977; Kristt & Engel, 1975; Rugh & Solberg, 1975; Rugh & Schwitzgebel, 1976; Rogers & Hughes, 1981; Schneider, 1968, Surwit, Pilon, & Fenton, 1978). It is desirable to meticulously formulate with the client an environmental practice schedule that is practical and can be incorporated into the client's life style behaviors in a manner similar to brushing one's teeth twice a day. Upon awakening in the morning and arrival home from work are optimal practice times. Other times frequently employed are prior to a meal; prior to a coffee break; upon encountering a traffic light; and after going to the bathroom, which generally assures privacy and restricted sensory conditions, even at work or in public places. Other discriminative stimuli used to begin practice include auditory beepers programmed to sound at given intervals and stars placed on mirrors or on cars. It is generally desirable to start with a practice schedule of one time per day and gradually increase the frequency to three, five, or more times daily. During maintenance, frequency may be reduced to one time daily.

The therapist should arrange for reinforcement of home practice in a manner similar to that utilized to insure consistent daily self-monitoring of symptoms. If necessary, this may be arranged with contingency contracting of environmental reinforcers. The duration of each practice time may vary. However, it should not be so long as to be aversive or impractical considering the client's typical daily activities. Initially, when the frequency of practice is low, the client may gradually increase practice duration from 10 minutes to 15 or 30 minutes. This should be 5 to 10 minutes longer than the average time it takes the client to attain criterion under sensory-restricted conditions. The client's latency to criterion should decrease with continued training and practice if cue-controlled training is employed. As the latency decreases, practice duration may be reduced to 10, 5, or 2 minutes with a corresponding increase in practice frequency so the total daily practice time approximates 30 to 45 minutes. When subjective arousal ratings and/or the objective target response measurements are taken in the client's life environment after practice indicates successful attainment of low arousal, the client should be instructed to practice on an as needed basis prior to encountering any known predictable stress conditions.

Before proceeding, it should be noted that during the initiation of home practice, it is frequently necessary to shift the focus of therapy from biofeedback training to altering the client's "life-style" behaviors to allow for sufficient home practice. This is particularly the case for those clients claiming to have limited time in their daily routine or who are unwilling to attempt such practice. It is also the case for those who are unsuccessful after a couple of weeks of practice, or who stop practicing after a period of successful home practice which produced symptom relief. It may be necessary and desirable to suspend training sessions while maintaining self-monitoring of target symptoms. In this case, an explicit appointment should be set 3 to 6 months hence to reassess the client's commitment to treatment.

At this time, the third step in transfer training should begin. This involves a gradual fading of the sensory restriction conditions in the therapist's office to an average level of stimulation (Budzynski, 1973; Hughes, Henry, & Hughes, 1980; Hughes, Jackson, DuBois, & Erwin, 1979). First, attempts to maintain low arousal attained under sensory restriction conditions are made. Then attempts to attain low arousal under graduated increases in sensory levels are made. Some of the possible procedures for fading sensory restriction are: opening of the eyes, increasing intensity of office lights, sitting up, standing, engaging in an activity, such as working math problems, talking to the therapist, reading, or watching TV, and introducing audio-tape recordings of normal environmental sounds. Cue-controlled training would also facilitate successful fading of the sensory restriction conditions. Once the client is able to reliably attain and maintain low arousal under levels of stimulation in the therapist's office that approximate non-stress levels of stimulation in the client's environment, the next training step is initiated.

The fourth step involves the client engaging in home practice in the natural environment during average levels of stimulation. Most of the considerations presented earlier concerning home practice for step two of transfer training should be included in the subsequent steps. It is generally necessary for these home practice regimens to include some brief-duration, relatively non-intrusive exercises to increase their social acceptability. For example, during the commercial of a TV program or in a restaurant, the client may rest his/her chin on his/her hand and appear to be in deep thought while practicing low arousal exercises for 2 minutes. Similarly to prior transfer tasks, this and subsequent tasks are likely to be facilitated by cue-controlled training.

The fifth step in training involves a gradual introduction of stressful sensory conditions in the therapist's office (Budzynski, 1973, 1979). Again, the client attempts to maintain low arousal attained under sensory restriction and/or average stimulation conditions and attempts to attain low arousal under graduated increases in stress stimulation. Any of the stress stimuli previously used during psychophysiological assessment may be utilized, but audio recordings from the client's environment should be introduced in a graduated presentation.

Finally, once the client is able to reliably attain and maintain low arousal under levels of stress stimulation in the therapist's office that approximate levels of stress stimulation in the client's environment, the sixth training step begins. In this procedure, home practice exercises are expanded to occur during identified high arousal periods that are associated with stress stimulation conditions. When the client is able to reliably attain and maintain low arousal under conditions of stress in the natural environment, transfer training skills are attained.

The major task of daily utilization of the low arousal skills remains. The skills should be practiced often enough to insure skill maintenance. This is done to insure availability of the skills should the same or other hyperarousal-based symptoms occur at a later time. More typically, some determination is made concerning when and where continued practice of the low arousal exercises is to occur. It is generally concluded that the amount of practice effective in reducing the target symptoms to their minimum is desirable. This may be accomplished empirically through continued self-monitoring of symptoms and practice. The practice exercises are gradually reduced until the symptoms increase or the schedule is the minimum necessary for skill maintenance. As symptoms appear, practice is increased to a level correlated with symptom reduction.

The biofeedback program presented requires a great deal of activity on the part of the client but still maintains the basic outpatient model with a considerable portion of the treatment occurring in the therapist's office. An alternative approach would shift an even larger portion of the treatment into the client's life environment. The therapist would conduct office training to teach the client to utilize portable biofeedback equipment for self-directed data collection and self-directed biofeedback training. Discrimination, control, and transfer training would be carried out in the client's home. In fact, he would be his own biofeedback technician. This approach requires an intelligent, well-motivated client. The idea would be to get the same job done utilizing less of the therapist's time. Client savings by way of therapist's cost would be mitigated to some extent in terms of added costs for equipment rental or purchase. However, some equipment is relatively inexpensive, such as devices for blood pressure and skin temperature recording and feedback (Bradley & Hughes, 1979; Hughes & Cunningham, 1980; Kristt & Engel, 1975; Surwit, Pilon, & Fenton, 1978). It is a major advantage if the client has long-term access to such equipment because a given physiological response can be monitored with the data available on an empirical basis for decision making. This is of great value in treating a disorder in which the main symptom is otherwise "silent," such as essential hypertension.

The transfer training procedures are relatively detailed. In practice, all of the steps may not be meticulously observed, but treatment may continue anyway if one or more steps are skipped, and transfer of the skill does still occur. However, if transfer does not occur, the procedures that were skipped may then be appropriately utilized. It is suggested that self-directed low arousal skills be assessed under the various conditions to insure that transfer has occurred.

Finally, it is common practice to utilize low arousal procedures other than biofeedback as part of the treatment program. These procedures are usually put into effect after biofeedback control training. If control training is not successful, the procedures are in effect treatment alternatives. If control training is successful, the procedures may be utilized as treatment combinations during or after transfer training. These low arousal procedures include the various types of training covered in the chapter on relaxation (progressive relaxation, passive relaxation, autogenic training, meditation, yoga, breathing, rebreathing, visualization, imagery, hypnosis) and other approaches, such as concentration exercises (Gaarder & Montgomery, 1977), manipulation therapy, physical therapy, exercise physiology, and possibly, assertive/social skills training.

SUMMARY

Biofeedback procedures have been presented in considerable detail in order to benefit the large number of practitioners and students interested in behavioral medicine who have had little or no training in biofeedback methods. Biofeedback is a process wherein one learns to reliably self-regulate physiological responses not ordinarily or currently under voluntary control. The procedure involves detection, amplification, quantification, and feedback of biological responses. Biofeedback is not used in isolation, rather it is imbedded in a larger therapeutic paradigm such as behavior therapy. An overview of biofeedback instrumentation utilized to measure EMG and other physiological responses is presented. Conceptualization is the first phase of biofeedback training and involves an explicit presentation of a conceptual model of the behavioral and physiological basis of the client's symptoms, of the biofeedback treatment, and of the means through which each stage of biofeedback training alters the symptoms.

Psychophysiological assessment attempts to identify the specific physiological responses that are outside normal limits and/or that change in response to stimuli intended to elicit varying arousal levels. The stimulus conditions frequently utilized during this assessment are sensory restriction baseline, nonarousing activity baseline, self-directed relaxation, stress stimuli, relaxation recovery, and relaxation training samples. Data from a psychophysiological assessment may be utilized to identify a hyperarousal stress reactivity pattern, to specify relationships among stress, physiological responsiveness, and symptoms, to determine whether biofeedback is indicated, to determine which physiological responses to utilize in biofeedback training and, to serve as a baseline reference for setting treatment objectives and assessing training progress.

Goal setting is a continuous process that is related to accumulating treatment data and involves increasing specificity of multiple objectives for attainment of skills for each biofeedback training phase and alleviation of symptoms. Self-monitoring training results in the attainment of data concerning symptoms and associated antecedent stimuli and consequent responses. This may include recording associated events, such as physiological responses for which portable measurement devices are available, medication intake, and frequency and durations of home practice. The shaping and reinforcement of compliance to the self-monitoring program is crucial for successful biofeedback training. Discrimination training focuses on the clients learning to detect (without measurement devices) when a physiological response is outside normal limits or is changing appreciably. It is an important component in the development of a self-control program that does not necessitate daily scheduled home practice.

The purpose of biofeedback control training is to learn to control specific physiological responses. Generally this involves altering the response in the direction of homeostatic normalcy. Control is facilitated by attaining a passive mode of attention and utilizing the feedback with a trial and error paradigm. Massed training of two to three sessions in the therapist's office per week for 4 to 16 sessions is often required to attain control. Transfer training is to insure generalization of learned discrimination and control skills from the training setting to the client's life environment. The client practices these skills in the therapist's office, which is gradually altered so that it is successively more similar to the client's environment. In addition, successful self-directed home practice is shaped and established within a self-control paradigm.

REFERENCES

Avenci, C.A. & Cutter, H.S.G. Controlled rebreathing. *Behavioral Engineering,* 1977, **4,** 17–21.

Barber, T.X. & Hahn, K.W. Hypnotic induction and "relaxation": An experimental study. *Archives of General Psychiatry,* 1963, **33,** 295–300.

Beiman, I., Graham, L.E., & Ciminero, A.R. Setting generality of blood pressure reductions and the psychological treatment of reactive hypertension. *Journal of Behavioral Medicine,* 1978, **1,** 445–453.

Benson, H. *The relaxation response.* New York: William Morrow, 1975.

Bensen, H., Beary, J.F., & Carol, M.P. The relaxation response. *Psychiatry,* 1974, **37,** 37–46.

Benson, H., Rosser, B.A., Marzetta, B.R., & Klemchuck, H.M. Decreased blood pressure in pharmacologically treated hypertensive patients who regularly elicited the relaxation response. *Lancet,* 1974, **1,** 289–291.

Bernstein, D.A. & Borkovec, T.D. *Progressive relaxation training: A manual for helping professionals.* Champaign, Ill: Research Press, 1973.

Blanchard, E.B. & Epstein, L.H. The clinical usefulness of biofeedback. In M. Hersen, R.M. Eisler, and P.M. Miller (Eds) *Progress in behavior modification.* New York: Academic Press, 1977.

Blanchard, E.B. & Epstein, L.H. *A biofeedback primer.* Reading, Mass.: Addison-Wesley, 1978.

Blanchard, E.B., Theobald, D., Williamson, D., Silver, B., & Brown, B. Temperature feedback in the treatment of migraine headaches. *Archives of General Psychiatry,* 1978, **35,** 581–588.

Borkovec, T.D. & Fowles, D.C. Controlled investigation of the effects of progressive and hypnotic relaxation on insommia. *Journal of Abnormal Psychology,* 1973, **82,** 153–158.

Bradley, R.W. & Hughes, H. Blood pressure biofeedback and relaxation training: The effects of home practice on reduction of blood pressure in persons with essential hypertension. Unpublished manuscript, 1979.

Brady, J.P. Metronome-conditioned relaxation: A new behavioral procedure. *British Journal of Psychiatry,* 1973, **122,** 729–730.

Brady, J.P., Luborsky, L., & Kron, R.E. Blood pressure reduction in patients with essential hypertension through metronome-conditioned relaxation: A preliminary report. *Behavior Therapy,* 1974, **5,** 203–209.

Brener, J. & Jones, J.M. Interoceptive discrimination in intact humans: Detection of cardiac activity. *Physiology and Behavior,* 1974, **13,** 763–767.

Budzynski, T.H. Biofeedback procedures in the clinic. *Seminars in Psychiatry,* 1973, **5,** 537–547.

Budzynski, T.H. Biofeedback strategies in headache treatment. In J.V. Basmajian (Ed.) *Biofeedback – Principles and practice for clinicians.* Baltimore: Williams & Wilkins, 1979.

Budzynski, T.H., Stoyva, J.M., Adler, C.S., & Mullhaney, D. EMG biofeedback and tension headache: A controlled-outcome study. *Psychosomatic Medicine,* 1973, **35,** 484–496.

Cinciripini, P.M., Epstein, L.H., & Martin, J.E. The effects of feedback on blood pressure discrimination. *Journal of Applied Behavioral Analysis,* 1979, **12,** 345–353.

Clark, E.G., Schwitzer, M.D., Glock, C.Y., & Vought, R. L. Studies in hypertension III. Analyses of individual blood pressure changes. *Journal of Chronic Diseases,* 1956, **4,** 477–489.

Cox, D.J., Freundlich, A., & Meyer, R.G. Differential effectiveness of electromyograph feedback, verbal relaxation instructions, and medication placebo with tension headaches. *Journal of Consulting and Clinical Psychology,* 1975, **45,** 892–898.

Datey, K.K. Biofeedback training and shavasan in the management of hypertension. *Biofeedback and Self-Regulation,* 1977, **2,** 303.

Datey, K.K., Deshmukh, S.N., Dalvi, C.P., & Vinekar, S.L. "Shavasan": A yogic exercise in the management of hypertension. *Angiology,* 1969, **20,** 325–333.

Davis, R. & Hughes, H. The effect of EMG biofeedback-induced physiological arousal on test anxiety and test performance. Paper presented at the meeting of the Southwestern Psychological Association, San Antonio, April 1979.

Dickey, L.D. (Ed.) *Clinical Ecology.* Springfield, Ill. Charles C Thomas, 1976.

Driscoll, R. Anxiety reduction using physical exertion and positive images. *Psychological Record,* 1976, **26,** 87.

Elder, S.T., Ruiz, R.Z., Deabler, H.J., & Dillenkoffer, R. L. Instrumental conditioning of diastolic blood pressure in essential hypertensive patients. *Journal of Applied Behavioral Analysis,* 1973, **6,** 377–382.

Engel, B.T., Nikoomanesh, P., & Schuster, M.M. Operant conditioning of rectosphincteric responses in the treatment of fecal incontinence. *New England Journal of Medicine,* 1974, **290,** 646–649.

Epstein, L.H. & Stein, D.B. Feedback-influenced heart rate discrimination. *Journal of Abnormal Psychology,* 1974, **83,** 585–588.

Epstein, L.H., Cinciripini, P.M., McCoy, J.F., & Marshall, W.R. Heart rate as a discriminative stimulus. *Psychophysiology,* 1977, **14,** 143–149.

Ewing, J. & Hughes, H. Cue-controlled relaxation: A technique to reduce and maintain low EMG levels during aversive stimulation. *Journal of Behavior Therapy and Experimental Psychiatry,* 1978, **9,** 39–44.

Fordyce, W.E. *Behavioral methods for chronic pain and illness.* Saint Louis: C.V. Mosby, 1976.

Fowler, J.E., Budzynski, T.H., & Vandenbergh, R.L. Effects of an EMG biofeedback relaxation program on the control of diabetes. *Biofeedback and Self-Regulation,* 1976, **1,** 105–112.

Fuller, G.D. *Biofeedback: Methods and procedures in clinical practice.* San Francisco: Biofeedback Press, 1977.

Gaarder, K.R. & Montgomery, P.S. *Clinical biofeedback.* Baltimore: Williams & Wilkins, 1977.

Gainer, J.C. Temperature discrimination training in the biofeedback treatment of migraine headaches. *Journal of Behavior Therapy and Experimental Psychiatry,* 1978, **9,** 185–188.

Gibb, J.D., Stephan, E., & Rohm, C.E.T., Jr. Belief in biofeedback for the control of short term stress. *Behavioral Engineering,* 1975, **3,** 79–84.

Goldman, M.P. & Hughes, H. Effectiveness of skin temperature biofeedback with versus without cue-controlled training in Raynaud's disease and "cold hands" clients. Unpublished manuscript, 1979.

Goldstein, I.B., Grinker, R.R., Heath, H.A., Olsen, D., & Shipman, W.G. Study in psychophysiology of muscle tension: I. Response specificity. *Archives of General Psychiatry,* 1964, **11,** 322–330.

Green, E.E. & Green, A. General and specific application of thermal biofeedback. In J.V. Basmajian (Ed.) *Biofeedback – Principles and practice for clinicians.* Baltimore: Williams & Wilkins, 1979.

Gregg, R.H. Biofeedback and biophysical monitoring during pregnancy and labor. In J.V. Basmajian (Ed.) *Biofeedback – Principles and practice for clinicians.* Baltimore: Williams & Wilkins, 1979.

Gregg, R.H., Frazier, L.M., & Nesbit, R.A. Effects of techniques of biofeedback on relaxation during childbirth. Paper presented at the meeting of the Biofeedback Research Society, Colorado Springs, February 1976.

Guyton, A.C. *Textbook of medical physiology*. Philadelphia: Saunders, 1976.

Haynes, S.N., Wilson, C.C., Jaffe, P.G., & Britton, B.T. Biofeedback treatment of atopic dermatitis. *Biofeedback and Self-Regulation*, 1979, **4**, 195–209.

Hilgard, E.R., Morgan, A.H., Lange, A.F., Lenox, J.R., MacDonald, H., Marshall, G.D., & Sachs, L.B. Heart rate changes in pain and hypnosis. *Psychophysiology*, 1974, **11**, 692–702.

Hughes, H. *Cue-controlled Biofeedback Training*. Faculty research grant proposal. Denton: North Texas State University, April 1976.

Hughes, H. & Cunningham, D.P. Behavioral treatment of Essential Hypertension: Effect of multi-element and cognitive behavior self-regulation therapies. Unpublished manuscript, 1980.

Hughes, H., England, R. & Goldsmith, D.A. Biofeedback and psychotherapy treatment of psoriasis: A brief report. *Psychological Reports*, 1981, in press.

Hughes, H., Henry, D., & Hughes, A. The effect of EMG biofeedback training on the behavior of children with activity level problems. *Biofeedback and Self-Regulation*, 1980, **5**, 207–219.

Hughes, H., Jackson, K., DuBois, K.E., & Erwin, R. Treatment of cursive handwriting problems: The effect of EMG biofeedback training. *Perceptual and Motor Skills*, 1979, **49**, 603–606.

Jacobson, E. *Progressive relaxation*. Chicago: University of Chicago Press, 1938.

Kallman, N.N. & Feuerstein, M. Psychophysiological procedures. In A.R. Cimenero, K.S. Calhoun, & H.E. Adams (Eds.) *Handbook of behavioral assessment*. New York: Wiley 1977.

Kleinman, K.M., Goldman, H., Snow, M.Y., & Korol, B. Relationship between essential hypertension and cognitive functioning II: Effects of biofeedback training generalize to nonlaboratory environment. *Psychophysiology*, 1977, **14**, 192–197.

Kristt, D.A. & Engel, B.T. Learned control of blood pressure in patients with high blood pressure. *Circulation*, 1975, **51**, 370–378.

Lacey, J.I. Somatic response patterning and stress: Some revisions of activation theory. In M.H. Appley, & R. Trumball (Eds.) *Psychological stress: Issues in research*. New York: Appleton-Century Crofts, 1967.

Lang, P.J., Sroufe, L.A., & Hastings, J.E. Effects of feedback and instructional set on the control of cardiac rate variability. *Journal of Experimental Psychology*, 1967, **75**, 425–431.

Lansky, D., Nathan, P.E., & Lawson, D.M. Blood alcohol level discrimination by alcoholics: The role of internal and external cues. *Journal of Consulting and Clinical Psychology*, 1978, **46**, 953–960.

Luborsky, L., Brady, J.P., McClintock, M., Kron, R.E., Bortnichak, E., & Levitz, L. Estimating one's own systolic blood pressure: Effects of feedback training. *Psychosomatic Medicine*, 1976, **38**, 426–438.

Luthe, W. Introduction to the methods of Autogenic therapy: Manual for a workshop. Denver: Biofeedback Society of America, 1977.

Maisto, A. & Adesso, V.J. Effect of instructions and feedback on blood alcohol level discrimination training in nonalcoholic drinkers. *Journal of Consulting and Clinical Psychology*, 1977, **45**, 625–636.

Mitchell, K.R. & White, R.G. Behavioral self-management: An application to the problem of migraine headaches. *Behavior Therapy,* 1977, **8,** 213–221.

McCutcheon, B.A. & Adams, H.E. The physiological basis of implosive therapy. *Behavior Research and Therapy,* 1975, **13,** 93–100.

Patel, C.H. Yoga and biofeedback in the management of hypertension. *Lancet,* 1973, **2,** 1053–1055.

Patel, C. Yoga and biofeedback in the management of hypertension. *Journal of Psychosomatic Research,* 1975, **19,** 355–360.

Patel, C.H. & North, W.R. Randomized control of yoga and biofeedback in management of hypertension. *Lancet,* 1975, **2,** 93–95.

Paul, G.L. *Insight vs. desensitization in psychotherapy.* Stanford, Calif.: Stanford University Press, 1966.

Paul, G.L. Physiological effects of relaxation training and hypnotic suggestion. *Journal of Abnormal Psychology,* 1969, **74,** 425–437.

Pollack, M.H. & Zeiner, A.R. Effects of relaxation training on daily ambulatory blood pressure. Paper presented at the meeting of the Southwestern Psychological Association, Fort Worth, April 1977.

Reeves, J.L. & Mealiea, W.L. Biofeedback-assisted cue-controlled relaxation for the treatment of flight phobias. *Journal of Behavior Therapy and Experimental Psychiatry,* 1975, **6,** 105–109.

Reinking, R. Follow-up and extension of "tension headache" – What method is the most effective? *Biofeedback and Self-Regulation,* 1976, **1,** 350.

Rinn, R.C. An inexpensive portable self-administered source for aversive stimulation: The rubber band. *Behavioral Engineering,* 1975, **3,** 39.

Roberts, D., Hughes, H., & Goldstrich, J.D. Effect of autogenic relaxation training on *angina pectoris:* An N-1 design with a placebo control condition. Unpublished manuscript, 1981.

Rogers, G.S. & Hughes, H. Dietary treatment of children with activity level problems. *Psychological Reports,* 1981, in press.

Rugh, J.D. & Schwitzgabel, R.L. Instrumentation for behavioral assessment. In A.R. Ciminero, K.S. Calhoun, & H.E. Adams, (Eds.) *Handbook of behavioral assessment.* New York: Wiley, 1977.

Rugh, J.D. & Solberg, W.K. Electromyographic studies of bruxist behavior before and during treatment. *Journal of California Dental Association,* 1975, **3,** 56–59.

Russell, H.L. A discussion of clinical biofeedback. Presentation at the meeting of the Biofeedback Society of Texas, Dallas, October 1978.

Russell, R.K. & Sipich, J.R. Cue-controlled relaxation in the treatment of test anxiety. *Journal of Behavior Therapy and Experimental Psychiatry,* 1973, **4,** 47–49.

Schneider, R.A. A fully automated portable blood pressure recorder. *Journal of Applied Physiology,* 1968, **24,** 115–118.

Schultz, J. & Luthe, W. *Autogenic training: A psychophysiologic approach in psychotherapy.* New York: Grune and Stratton, 1959.

Schultz, J.H. & Luthe, W. *Autogenic therapy: Autogenic methods.* New York: Grune and Stratton, 1969.

Shapiro, A.P., Redmond, D.P., McDonald, R.H., & Gaylor, M. Relationships of perception, cognition, suggestion, and operant conditioning in essential hypertension. *Progress in Brain Research,* 1975, **42**, 299–312.

Silver, B.V. & Blanchard, E.B. Biofeedback and relaxation training in the treatment of psychophysiological disorders: Or are the machines really necessary? *Journal of Behavioral Medicine,* 1978, **1**, 217–239.

Sobell, L.C. & Sobell, M.B. A self-feedback technique to monitor drinking behavior in alcoholics. *Behavior Research and Therapy,* 1973, **11**, 37–38.

Spiegel, H. A single-treatment method to stop smoking using ancillary self-hypnosis. *International Journal of Clinical and Experimental Hypnosis,* 1970, **18**, 235–250.

Spiegel, H. & Spiegel, D. *Trance and treatment.* New York: Basic Books, 1978.

Sterman, M.B. Neurophysiologic and clinical studies of sensorimotor EEG biofeedback training: Some effects on epilepsy. *Seminars in Psychiatry,* 1973, **5**, 507–524.

Stoyva, J.M. Guidelines in the training of general relaxation. In J.V. Basmajian (Ed.) *Biofeedback–Principles and practice for clinicians.* Baltimore: Williams & Wilkins, 1979.

Surwit, R., Pilon, R., & Fenton, C. Behavioral treatment of Raynaud's disease. *Journal of Behavioral Medicine,* 1978, **1**, 323–335.

Tanner, B.A. & Zeiler, M. Punishment of self-injurious behavior using aromatic ammonia as the aversive stimulus. *Journal of Applied Behavior Analysis,* 1975, **8**, 53–57.

Taub, E. & Emurian, C.S. Feedback aided self-regulation of skin temperature with a single feedback locus: I. Acquisition and reversal training. *Biofeedback and Self-Regulation,* 1976, **1**, 147–148.

Tentoni, S.C. Reduction of physiological correlates of stress using pink noise. *Behavioral Engineering,* 1978, **5**, 5–11.

Vidergar, L.J., Lee, R.M., & Goldman, M.S. Discrimination of systolic blood pressure. Paper presented at the annual meeting of the American Psychological Association, Toronto, 1978.

Walk, R.D. Self-ratings of fear in a fear envolking situation. *Journal of Abnormal and Social Psychology,* 1956, **52**, 171–178.

Wenger, M.A. *Psychophysiology,* 1966, **2**, 173–186.

Wickramasekera, I. Effects of sensory restriction on susceptibility to hypnosis: A hypothesis and more preliminary data. *Journal of Abnormal Psychology,* 1970, **76**, 69–75.

Wilson, A.E. & Smith, F.J. Counterconditioning therapy using free association: A case study. Proceedings of the 76th Annual Convention of the American Psychological Association, 1968, **3**, 529–530.

Wolpe, J. Psychotherapy by reciprocal inhibition. Stanford, Calif.: Stanford University Press, 1958.

Wolpe, J. & Lazarus, A.A. *Behavior therapy techniques.* London: Pergamon Press, 1966.

CHAPTER 4

Relaxation Training

OVERVIEW

There are many similarities between relaxation and biofeedback training. They are both therapeutic behavior change procedures that are generally utilized to achieve a state of lowered arousal. Both emphasize self-regulation and are part of a more general behavior therapy matrix. There appear, however, to be three major differences. First, equipment is a requisite of biofeedback, but not relaxation training. There is, then, an associated increase in cost associated with the purchase and maintenance of this apparatus. Second, biofeedback lends itself to more comprehensive assessment than relaxation does, which does not include relatively immediate and continuous objective quantified data concerning physiological responses. Third, relaxation is generally limited to a focus on the reduction of muscle tension, and possibly respiratory and pulse rate; whereas biofeedback may focus on any number of measurable physiological parameters such as muscle tension, heart rate, blood pressure, and stomach acidity. Of course, if biofeedback equipment is utilized for data collection purposes in conjunction with relaxation training, differences are minimized. Furthermore, the two procedures may be utilized in combination in such a manner as to compliment one another.

Relaxation training has been defined as a procedure aimed at achieving muscle and "mental" relaxation (Taylor, 1978). Thus, EMG biofeedback training could be considered to be a type of relaxation training. Progressive relaxation (Bernstein & Borkovec, 1973; Jacobson, 1938; Wolpe, 1958; Wolpe & Lazarus, 1966) is probably the most widely used procedure in the United States, whereas autogenic training (Luthe, 1977; Schultz & Luthe, 1959) is more popular in Europe. Eastern approaches such as yoga (Datey, 1969, 1977; Patel, 1973, 1975; and Patel & North, 1975) and transcendental meditation (Benson, Rosser, Marzetta, & Klemchuck, 1974) have been evaluated more recently. Some of the numerous other approaches to relaxation are hypnosis (Barber & Hahn, 1963; Borkovec & Fowles, 1973); the relaxation response (Benson, 1975; Benson, Beary, & Carol, 1974); cue-controlled relaxation (Berstein & Borkovec, 1973; Cox, Freundlich, & Meyer, 1975; Paul, 1966; Reeves & Mealiea, 1975; Russell & Sipich, 1973); metranome-conditioned relaxation (Brady, 1973; Brady, Luborsky, & Kron,

1974); physical exercise (Driscoll, 1976); autogenic training instruction (Surwit, 1978; Surwit, Pilon, & Fenton, 1978); relaxation as an active coping skill (Goldfried & Trier, 1974); self-managed relaxation (Epstein, Abel & Webster, 1974); video-tape relaxation (Weiher & Striefel, 1979); passive relaxation (Haynes, Moseley, & McCowan, 1975); differential relaxation (Bernstein & Borkovec, 1973; Deffenbacher, 1976; Deffenbacher & Michaels, 1978; Jacobson, 1938); rapid relaxation (Chesney & Shelton, 1976); mini-relaxation (Stroebel, 1980); imagery (Achterberg & Lawlis, 1978); controlled rebreathing (Aveni & Cutter, 1977); and pink noise (Tentoni, 1978).

Although it would appear that relaxation training is in need of a great deal of procedural standardization, there is no definitive evidence that one type of relaxation training is more effective than another. After reviewing the relevant literature, Taylor (1978) concluded, "No advantage has been demonstrated for one method of relaxation training over another . . . . In most cases, the simplest training procedure seems to produce as much benefit as the more complex." Taylor stated that in some cases, for instance, tension headache and insomnia, a combination of relaxation procedures including EMG biofeedback may be more effective than a given technique used alone. In any event, there is an accumulating body of research suggesting that relaxation training may be effective when applied to disorders considered to be under the province of behavioral medicine. This literature will be considered at a later point in this chapter. Like biofeedback, relaxation training appears to offer its primary behavioral medicine application in stress-related physical disorders leading to the remediation and prevention of maladaptive physiological arousal.

INSTRUMENTATION

Although relaxation training can be carried out with little or no apparatus, the availability of some accoutrements and instrumentation is a definite advantage. A comfortable reclining chair that offers support to all parts of the body including the neck and head is desirable. It is useful for the client as well as the therapist to have an audio-tape recorder available. An EMG with a time period integrator and, if possible, automated data recording features, such as a printer, is an asset. Used EMGs that are adequate for monitoring relaxation should be available at reduced prices, as technological advances make the current biofeedback equipment relatively obsolete. More sophisticated apparatus would, of course, offer some advantages. For example, a multichannel EMG or an EMG with multiple sets of electrodes, and a microprocessor that successively switches to different electrodes, would make multiple recording sites available, which would be useful in assessing muscle tension/relaxation levels across body sites. Portable EMGs are available that may be utilized for assessment purposes in the clients' life environment (Rugh & Schwitzgebel, 1977; Rugh & Solberg, 1975). Pneumographs and skin temperature thermometers may be employed to record breathing responses (Gunderson, 1971). In addition, other apparatus may be useful in gathering data on other physiological responses (i.e., vasomotor, blood pressure, heart rate, electrodermal, and EEG), which may be good indices of a particular client's arousal level, or which may be a good index of the target symptom. An overview of psychophysiological instrumentation is presented in the appendix.

RELAXATION PROCEDURES

Conceptualization Training

It is assumed that the reader has had some professional training and that relaxation training will be utilized within the context of some more general clinical method, such as behavior therapy. Conceptualization training focuses upon explicitly teaching the client the basic concepts relevant to understanding the therapy process and its relation to the target symptoms. Conceptualization training is an important part of relaxation training and may be conducted in a manner almost identical to that presented in the chapter on biofeedback training. See also relaxation rationale presented by Bernstein and Borkovec (1973), Patel and North (1975), and Taylor, Farquhar, Nelson, and Agras (1977).

Psychophysiological Assessment

If the therapist has the appropriate instruments available, it is advisable to conduct a thorough psychophysiological assessment. The procedures for a psychophysiological assessment have been given in considerable detail in the chapter on biofeedback. If the appropriate instruments are not available certain portions of a complete assessment procedure may be utilized as a relaxation assessment procedure.

The data for noninstrumented relaxation assessment should include client self-ratings of arousal level or muscle tension/relaxation, given at approximately 5-minute intervals, in addition to the therapist's behavioral observation of arousal level. Client self-ratings, previously presented, might utilize separate scales for physical and cognitive relaxation (Mitchell & White, 1977). Some indices that could be utilized for behavioral observation are trembling and tremors, facial tension, perspiration, extraneous movements (Paul, 1966), facial rigidity or relaxation, rate and sound of breathing, twitching of eyelids, and fidgeting movements (Gaarder & Montgomery, 1977); coughs, squirming, eye twitching, regularity of breathing (Fuller, 1977); feet parallel, lips tight and closed, fidgeting, absence of slow regular breathing, opening eyes, attempting to talk (Bernstein & Borkovec, 1973); muscle tension and pulse rate monitored by holding the client's wrist (Sipprelle, 1967);

and forehead wrinkles smoothing out, jaws falling slightly open, head falling forward against chest and slow regular breathing (Taylor, 1978). Luiselli, Steinman, Marholin, and Steinman (1978) employed a relatively comprehensive relaxation checklist to assess muscle relaxation that utilized behavioral observation.

Relaxation assessment is introduced during an initial period orienting the client to the rationale for the procedure. An attempt should be made to communicate to the client that you are assessing his tension/relaxation response to a variety of stimuli at a number of levels of arousal. The client should be further informed that the data will be utilized to develop an individualized relaxation training program. The data collection procedure is then initiated for approximately 10 minutes (or until the data has stabilized) under baseline conditions. During this second period the client is instructed to engage in some relatively nonarousing activity, such as reading, while data is being collected. During the third period, self-directed relaxation, the client is instructed to relax anyway he knows how while reclining with eyes closed. These second and third periods are extremely important for assessing the client's relaxation skills before, during, and after training. Information from these periods is initially used to determine whether there is a need for relaxation training per se or for training in the utilization of relaxation skills already present. Assessing relaxation skills during training and followup employs data from periods two and three to address issues, such as deciding if the initial state of relaxation training is complete and considering whether or not it is time to initiate home practice instructions. Stress arousal assessment is the focus of period four and appropriate mild stress stimuli are presented. A fifth period involves removal of the stress stimuli and the recording of latency of recovery to baseline levels of tension/relaxation. Periods four and five are utilized to detect and evaluate a hyperarousal syndrome. The final period (sixth) includes brief taped or live samples of different types of relaxation training and is oriented toward generating information as to which type of training will be optimal for a particular client.

Self-Monitoring Training

Self-monitoring training for a relaxation training program is not essentially different from that presented for a biofeedback paradigm. The primary focus of this training is detection and quantification of the target symptom. The client is initially given training on how and when to record target symptoms; for instance, headaches, and medication usage, with the data typically being collected during baseline, treatment, and specified follow-up periods. In some cases, the data may be acquired with portable measurement devices (i.e., blood pressure cuff, EMG, skin temperature thermometer). However the bulk of information is generally based on self-recording. The collection of additional data as to antecedent daily life stress stimuli, responses accompanying the target symptoms and consequent events are usually limited to specific, relatively brief periods of 1 to 7 days. In this manner, comprehensive data may be collected while minimizing the time and effort required of the client. In particular, it is crucial to collect data concerning home practice of self-relaxation during later training phases.

Particular attention should be paid to informing the client as to relevance of the information to be collected, seeing that he is provided with adequate instructions, materials and training, reinforcing self-monitoring responses (compliance), and transformation of the data into a utilizable form. If the client is currently taking medication, then a decision must be made as to whether the medication is to be withdrawn, held as constant as possible, or continued and varied independent of the relaxation training. It is advisable that this decision should be made conjointly by the client and the client's physician, and, when medication is indicated, the frequency, amount, and kind of medication should be carefully self-monitored. A more complete discussion of the medication issue is found in the preceding chapter.

Information collected by self-monitoring is of the utmost importance as therapeutic objectives are almost always made within the context of bringing about behavior change in the client's life environment. Self-monitoring data is germane to therapeutic decision-making and is thus related to considerations, such as whether a hyperarousal stress reactivity syndrome is present and relaxation training is indicated, and the individualization of the treatment process. Self-monitoring training usually occurs concomitantly with conceptualization training, psychophysiological assessment procedures, and a symptom baseline measurement phase.

Discrimination Training

The focus of discrimination training is the detection of physiological arousal, particularly muscle tension that is presumably associated with the target symptom. A basic question exists as to whether discrimination training is necessary and if so, when it should occur. Within the context of a self-control model, optimal utilization of learned relaxation skills necessitates self-detection of states of elevated tension as well as the associated target symptoms. This facilitates prevention and obviation of such symptoms. For example, the detection of sustained contraction of neck and face muscles associated with tension headaches may serve as a discriminative stimulus for the initiation of relaxation exercises. Discrimination may be particularly important for certain disorders such as hypertension which initially have few aversive symptoms. The necessity of discrimination is reduced or eliminated if the client already possesses these skills or if the learned relaxation skills are practiced on a daily basis independent of the occurrence of hyperarousal and target symptoms. Daily practice may be adequate in most cases provided long-term maintenance of practice is arranged.

Whether discrimination training should occur before or after relaxation control taining is an open question, but it may be noted that whichever type of training occurs first is likely to facilitate the one that occurs second. The authors have found it convenient to program discrimination to precede relaxation control training. Keeping the client constructively occupied with discrimination training facilitates the acceptance of an adequate symptom measurement baseline. Also, based on the Premack principle, the onset of relaxation control training serves as a contingent reinforcer for learning discrimination skills. Furthermore, it is rather likely that once the client possesses adequate discrimination skills, it becomes possible for him to learn relaxation control skills based on trial and error experiences in the life environment.

Ideally, discrimination training for muscle tension/relaxation utilizes EMG recordings as a criterion measure. The recording site's selection should be based on the data from a psychophysiological assessment. A response system is then developed which enables the client to communicate and quantify his muscle tension/relaxation level. Thus, the client may be directed to a three point scale of high, average, and low to report his tension/relaxation level. EMG recordings could be quantified utilizing an analogue three point rating scale. Accordingly EMG levels greater than one standard deviation above the mean would be designated as high, EMG levels more than one standard deviation below the mean would be designated to be low, and EMG levels within one standard deviation above or below the mean would be designated as average. The discrimination training procedure would then include simultaneous recording of muscle tension/relaxation levels based upon the client's personal report and EMG measurement. Training would continue until the client's muscle tension/relaxation discriminations stabilize at 75% or greater correct as defined by concurrence with the EMG based rating scale. A discrimination training procedure may vary on a number of dimensions such as the behavior activity in which the client engages, the range within which muscle tension varies, distribution of trials, whether the discrimination response is overt or covert, and whether the training occurs in the office or home setting. Finally, discrimination assessment trials are generally utilized periodically after training is complete to monitor the maintenance of the learned skill.

Since muscle tension/relaxation is to some extent detectable by its natural sensory consequences, especially at the extremes of the tension/relaxation continuum, with tension extremes being relatively attainable voluntarily, discrimination training is possible without EMG recordings. This type of discrimination training is embedded in the comprehensive progressive relaxation exercises advocated by Jacobson (1938). However, Jacobson's approach is not widely used, as a relatively large number of training sessions (56 or more) are required. To an appreciable extent, discrimination training is incorporated into the more abbreviated forms of progressive relaxation (Bernstein & Borkovec, 1973; Wolpe, 1958; Wolpe & Lazarus, 1966). Discrimination training appears to be most accented in the differential relaxation portion of comprehensive progressive relaxation (Bernstein & Borkovec,

1973; Deffenbacher, 1976; Deffenbacher & Payne, 1977; Deffenbacher & Snyder, 1976; and Jacobson, 1938). A direct comparison of the relative effectiveness of EMG-aided discrimination training and discrimination skills that result as a consequence of differential relaxation training without the assistance of EMG measurements does not appear to be available at this time.

Relaxation Control Training

Since the objective of relaxation training is to learn to control cognitive and muscle relaxation, prior assessment should have established whether or not self-control relaxation skills are present. If the client is proficient at self-directed relaxation, then relaxation control training may be omitted or abbreviated, and transfer training initiated. Some clients essentially see no relationship between hyperarousal to stress, their ability to achieve relaxation and their physical disorder, which they usually believe can be resolved only by a physician's intervention. In these cases, stress management skills learned through self-monitoring, conceptualization training, as well as discrimination and transfer training, appear to be effective.

The therapist must decide on the specific type of control training to be utilized. Training, with few exceptions, focuses on lowering cognitive and muscle tension with possible concomitant reduction of other physiological responses, such as blood pressure. However, more comprehensive training objectives such as bidirectional control, which involves maintenance within a specified range, may be incorporated. In the absence of research as to the relative effectiveness of these types of training, the therapist's decision in this matter would relate to such consideration as his own therapeutic proclivities, client preferences, and cost. Medication intake should be reviewed to insure it does not interfere with learning relaxation skills.

At this point the client may be briefly oriented to the nature and purpose of relaxation control training with respect to specified symptoms. The client is then informed that the objective of this training is to learn self-directed muscle and cognitive relaxation. The therapist collects and briefly examines the self-monitored data, instructs and reinforces the client, and reviews accumulated data, which is usually presented in graphic form. Next, a session baseline of approximately 10 minutes is initiated utilizing simulated activity or sensory restricted conditions as indicated by psychophysiological assessment. Self-report and behavioral observation indices of level of relaxation/tension are generally collected during this time, and during the last 10 minutes of the 20 to 30 minute relaxation instruction phase that follows. The final 5 to 15 minutes of the session may be utilized to review data, ask and answer questions, and maintain the therapeutic relationship. Initially, relaxation training sessions are approximately 50 minutes in duration. Later, as the skills are acquired, 20 or 30 minutes is sufficient and thus additional time is available for concurrent psychotherapy or behavior therapy.

A question arises as to exactly what should occur during the relaxation instruction portion of the training. A large number of approaches to relaxation training have been enumerated and it is likely that additional approaches will be developed and advocated. Which is best? Which is best for you as a therapist? Which is best for a specific client? It is suggested that the therapist learn many different training procedures, and utilize the psychophysiological assessment results, therapist's preference, and client's preference, while remaining alert to future research findings that might shed additional light on this matter. As indicated earlier, one method of training appears to be as good as the other in terms of effectiveness (Taylor, 1978).

Relaxation training methods appear to have certain commonalities (Benson, 1975; Jacob, Kraemer, & Agras, 1977; and Taylor, 1978). A task awareness or instructional set component is an ever present aspect of the clinical application of relaxation training. That is, instructions are given that facilitate therapeutic expectance as to the positive effects learning relaxation will have on symptom reduction. A second component involves muscle quietude or physiological relaxation, a face validity component. Interestingly enough, one can not be sure that this is a necessary component in and of itself or whether it is of primary importance in promoting cognitive relaxation (Taylor, 1978). A third element involves narrowing of attention or cognitive focusing. This component could better be considered the attainment of cognitive quietude or relaxation. In this context, cognitive focusing could be seen as a procedure aimed at attaining cognitive relaxation. Thus, cognitive content may be narrowed by covert repetition of sounds and images (Jacob, Kraemer, & Agras, 1977). A fourth component is regular practice and there appears to be nearly universal agreement that it is a necessary element for the attainment and maintenance of clinical-therapeutic effects.

At this point we will focus on an overview of the procedures that influence the presence of the four components of relaxation. The instructional set component of relaxation training is directly related to conceptualization and the therapeutic contract implied in the client coming to the therapist and the therapist accepting the client into training. The muscle relaxation component of training is primarily related to assuming a comfortable position in nonbinding clothing (assuming an acceptable, ambient temperature) with instructions to minimize or eliminate movements. Muscle relaxation is at least secondarily related to the procedures that facilitate the cognitive relaxation. The cognitive relaxation component of training includes provision for a quiet environment, which generally includes closing one's eyes. "Quiet" in this case is used in the relative mode, that is, quiet, with respect to the environment in which the client is not relaxing. During relaxation control training, this usually involves an office that is relatively free of noise and other sensory obtrusions. Later during transfer training, quiet may refer to closing one's eyes in a relatively noisy work setting. A second procedure related primarily to cognitive relaxation involves instructions to assume a passive attitude. Benson (1975) has discussed this procedure at great length, and the essential idea is not to be overly concerned about how well one is performing. Thus, one does not attempt to make relaxation occur, rather they let it occur. This procedure is somewhat related to instructions to use a cognitive device that is also related to cognitive relaxation. Use of a cognitive device, for instance, may involve self-directed repetition of words, sounds, and images or repetitive attention to one's own proprioceptive stimuli, such as breathing, specific muscle groups, or heart rate. A passive attitude may also be induced through instructions not to worry about distracting thoughts when they occur, and to return to the repetition of the cognitive device (Benson, 1975). The regular practice component of relaxation training is related to scheduling of sessions during relaxation control training and to attaining home practice of relaxation during transfer training.

It is suggested that the relaxation response (Benson, 1975), progressive relaxation (Bernstein & Borkovec, 1973; Jacobson, 1938; Wolpe & Lazarus, 1966), and autogenic training (Luthe, 1977, Surwit, 1978, Surwit, Pilon, & Fenton, 1978) would serve as three basic procedures for psychophysiological assessment and relaxation control training to which other procedures could be added. Specific instructions for the relaxation response (Bradley & Hughes, 1979; Hughes & Cunningham, 1980) and autogenic relaxation (Surwit, 1978) are given in the appendix. It is suggested that the instruction presented by Bernstein and Borkovec (1973) and Rosen (1977) be employed for progressive relaxation training. Finally instruction for other relaxation procedures may be obtained from the sources cited in the references. The therapist's primary responsibility is to maintain conditions wherein the client may learn relaxation skills regardless of which type of training is utilized. This includes verbal feedback and reinforcement to facilitate the client's maintenance of a positive perspective, in addition to continued practice and acceptance of the rate of learning that occurs. Thus, at times the therapist focuses on what the client is doing right (maintaining effort, a positive attitude) while minimizing the lack of instant progress. When learning is accelerated, positive feedback is tempered with consideration of future objectives and the continued practice that is required. Falling asleep, and experiencing strange sensations or intrusive thoughts are problems typical of those which arise during relaxation training. Falling asleep is handled by altering the practice conditions in the direction of increased arousal. This could involve changing posture from reclining to sitting, to sitting more erect, opening one's eyes, brightening the light, increasing the noise level, practicing at a different time of day or getting a sufficient amount of sleep daily. Intrusive sensations and thoughts call for therapist reassurance that such phenomena are common and usually dissipate over time. It may be wise to counsel the client not to attempt to make the thoughts go away, but, rather, to let them run their course as skill is gained in the utilization of a cognitive device. A more detailed discussion of these types of problems is presented by Bernstein and Borkovec (1973) and Stoyva (1979).

The optimal distribution of relaxation training sessions is open to question.

There is some suggestion that massed practice is desirable, according to Lowenstein (1979) who feels eight, 1-hour sessions over a 1-week period produces the best results. Nevertheless, two sessions per week would appear to be a compromise, with one session per week being acceptable.

Relaxation training can also be conducted in a group format (Lowenstein, 1979). Losses in individualization of training would be to some extent offset by the reduction in costs (fees or professional time). Furthermore, both group and individual sessions could be employed. Such a combined approach might result in a training program superior to either alone. Relaxation training can also be conducted utilizing audio tapes. This approach appears to be adequate in some cases, however, live therapist relaxation training was found to be superior to audio-taped relaxation in the reduction of physiological indices of arousal (Borkovec & Sides, 1979; Paul & Trimble, 1970). Recently, a video-tape relaxation procedure has been developed with initial results being impressive (Weiher & Streifel, 1979), however, further research is indicated to adequately evaluate its clinical potential.

Relaxation control training is complete when the client is able to attain a relaxed state rapidly during ten minute self-directed relaxation tests. If an EMG is available, then a level of two microvolts for forearm electrode placement and three microvolts for frontalis electrode placement may be utilized as a criterion for attainment of relaxation. Otherwise self-ratings and therapist observations are utilized in evaluating the presence or absence of relaxation.

Transfer Training

Promotion of the generalization of the skills learned during discrimination and/or relaxation control training to the client's life environment is the objective of transfer training. There is no sharp demarcation between control training and the initial portion of transfer training and they may overlap and thus occur simultaneously. Furthermore, relaxation control training may take place primarily in the client's home environment (Bradley & Hughes, 1979, Mitchell & White, 1977). Under such circumstances the distinction between these two training phases all but disappears.

The client is given a general orientation to transfer training. The focus is on facilitating generalization of the discrimination and control skills learned in the office. This involves practicing these skills under conditions successively more similar to the conditions in the target environment. The therapist must promote this transition so as to minimize the number of graded steps and amount of time required. The initial step involves terminating the relaxation instructions (the therapist's verbalization of a relaxation script) after the client has attained a relaxed state. The client then attempts to maintain the relaxation response. Following successful maintenance over two or three sessions, the client attempts self-directed relaxation after the session baseline with no therapist instructions. The essential element is then a graduated fading of therapist instructions. This process may be facilitated by utilizing a specific procedure such as relaxation by recall or counting (Bernstein & Borkovec, 1973), metranome-conditioned relaxation (Brady, 1973; Brady, Luborsky, & Kron, 1974) or cue-controlled relaxation (Dial & Hughes, 1979, Paul, 1966, Russell & Sipich, 1973). The authors frequently utilize cue-controlled procedures that emphasize a self-control set. The training procedure is relatively brief and may be initiated at any time during control training in which the relaxation criterion is attained. The procedure is given in detail in the chapter on biofeedback training.

When self-directed attainment and maintenance of the relaxation response under the sensory restricted conditions of the therapists's office is reliably demonstrated, home practice under similar conditions in the client's life environment is initiated. This, and subsequent home practice is the critical element in the total relaxation training program. Maintenance of home practice over time is the best index of therapeutic success at follow up. Orientation should be thorough and self-monitoring data are crucial. The time, place, and duration of the practice should be recorded on a "symptom" recording form. Additional data should include self-rating of level of relaxation before and after the practice. If possible, objective measurements of the target responses (i.e., EMG, blood pressure, skin temperature) should also be taken before and after practice.

It is important to engineer home practice as a relatively permanent modification in the client's life style (i.e., like brushing one's teeth twice a day for a lifetime). The following are examples of discriminative stimuli used to initiate the practice of relaxation: awakening in the morning, getting home from work, retiring at night, just prior to meals or coffee breaks, encountering a traffic light, going to the bathroom, reminders such as gold stars pasted on wrist watches, mirrors and other environmental locations, and timed auditory alarms. It is necessary to arrange for adequate reinforcement for practice including therapist reinforcement during sessions and self-administered reinforcement (contingency contracting may be necessary) in the environment.

It is generally wise to begin with a practice schedule of once per day and increase gradually to about five times per day during treatment. Later, during maintenance, this may be reduced to one to three times daily. The frequency of practice is not independent of its duration. Generally the greater the frequency the shorter the duration and vice versa. The duration of practice has generally varied from approximately 5 minutes to 30 minutes; however, Strobels (1980) advocates practice of even briefer duration. A good guideline is to continue practice 5 to 10 minutes longer than it takes the client to attain the relaxation criterion. Thus, as the client's latency to relaxation decreases with continued practice, frequency of practice should be increased with the total daily duration of practice being at minimum 30 to 45 minutes. If for any reason the client is not practicing, the focus of therapy should be shifted to overcoming this problem. This would necessitate reducing or temporarily eliminating relaxation training during therapy sessions. In extreme cases, it could involve scheduling a vacation from therapy (i.e., 3 months of symptom self-monitoring) to evaluate the client's commitment to treatment. On the other hand, as soon as successful home practice is attained, the client should be instructed to utilize this practice (under sensory restricted conditions) on an as-needed basis just prior to encountering any predictable stress situation.

The third transfer training step focuses on a gradual fading of sensory restriction conditions of the therapist's office until self-directed relaxation is achieved under an average level of stimulation (Budzynski, 1973; Hughes, Henry, & Hughes, 1980; Stoyva, 1979). Initially, the client achieves relaxation, then he learns to maintain low arousal under increases in sensory levels and finally he attempts to attain and maintain relaxation under these increased sensory levels. The following are examples of procedures to gradually increase sensory stimulation during relaxation training: opening of the eyes, increasing lights to normal levels, sitting up, standing, engaging in an activity such as working math problems, talking, reading, watching TV, and audio-tape recordings of normal environmental sounds.

The fourth step of transfer training includes home practice in the client's environment during average levels of stimulation. Generally, this should include some brief duration, relatively nonintrusive (minimal disruption of ongoing social activities) exercises. For example, the client may practice relaxation during TV commercials, and in public places while appearing to be in deep thought with eyes closed.

The fifth and sixth steps of training are analogous to the third and fourth but involve fading in stressful sensory conditions rather than average sensory levels. First, this is done during an already attained relaxed state, and then during attempts to attain relaxation. The stress stimuli mentioned in the section on psychophysiological assessment and client recall, as well as audio recordings of stress situations from the client's environment, may be utilized in the therapist's office. In the client's life environment practice is scheduled, as needed, during conditions of high stress stimulation.

The transfer training procedures presented are relatively comprehensive and in practice every step may not be followed. Nevertheless, relaxation skills should be assessed periodically under the various conditions. If the relaxation response is generalized, then the process is likely to move rapidly; however, if the skills do not generalize, then the procedures in the omitted steps can be appropriately utilized.

When the client has successfully negotiated all these steps, the relaxation response under life environment conditions should have been acquired. However, the primary task of daily utilization of these relaxation skills remains. Relaxation should be practiced often enough to insure skill maintenance, and often enough to effectively maintain reduction of the target symptoms. Thus, self-monitoring of symptoms and relaxation practice is maintained while frequency and duration of practice is varied to ascertain the optimal practice regime for the particular client.

The relaxation training program presented maintains a basic outpatient model wherein much of the treatment occurs in the therapist's office. However, it is possible to conduct a larger portion of the training in the client's life environment. Relaxation discrimination, control, and transfer training can be carried out in a self-directed manner in the client's home. In this type of approach, the therapist helps the client develop such a program and utilizes office assessments and self-monitoring data as a basis for periodic consultation sessions. A predominantly home practice training method would be easier if portable instrumentation was available for additional data collection in the home situation. The home training model may necessitate an intelligent, well-motivated client. However, it may offer advantages in terms of reduced cost and facilitation of maintenance of treatment effects after therapy is terminated.

SUMMARY

Relaxation and biofeedback training are similar as both focus on attaining a state of lowered arousal within a self-regulation context. Relaxation differs from biofeedback training because it is primarily oriented toward attaining reduction of muscle tension, and it does not necessitate equipment, and accordingly, offers less comprehensive assessment data. These differences are minimized because physiological recording equipment can be utilized in conjunction with relaxation training and both biofeedback and relaxation can be employed in combination to compliment one another.

Relaxation training is a procedure aimed at achieving muscle and "mental" relaxation. There are a large number of different relaxation procedures that have been developed; for instance, progressive relaxation, the relaxation response, autogenic training, and deep breathing are some of the better known procedures. These procedures may be used in combination. Further, there is no definite evidence that one type of relaxation is more effective than another. Although any of the biofeedback instruments may be utilized in assessing the physiological effects of relaxation, an EMG for recording muscle tension, and a pneumograph or a skin temperature device for recording breathing are most likely to be used in relaxation training.

The first phase of learning relaxation is conceptualization training. Here, the client is exposed to the concepts concerning the behavioral and physiological basis of the symptoms, the relaxation training, and the means by which the latter alters the former. Psychophysiological assessment for relaxation training typically includes EMG, self-ratings and therapist's behavioral observation of muscle tension/relaxation during conditions of sensory restriction baseline, nonarousing activity baseline, self-directed relaxation, stress stimuli, relaxation recovery, and relaxation training samples.

Self-monitoring training focuses primarily on the detection and quantification of target symptoms and secondarily on the identification of related antecedent stimuli and consequent responses. Particular attention is focused on attaining compliance with the self-monitoring program by informing the client about the relevance of the information to be collected, providing adequate instructions, materials and training, reinforcing compliance, and transforming the data into a utilizable form. Discrimination training involves learning to detect excessive muscle tension that is presumably associated with maintenance of the target symptom.

Relaxation control training is aimed at attaining muscle and cognitive relaxation. It is suggested that client and therapist preference be utilized to select several different types of relaxation instruction for training. Attention should be focused on insuring that the four major components of relaxation are included. First, an instructional set providing an expectancy for positive change is utilized within the context of conceptualization training. Second, muscle quietude is enhanced by assuming a comfortable position, wearing nonbinding clothing, and giving instructions to minimize movement in an environment maintained at an acceptable ambient temperature and lighting. Third, cognitive relaxation is facilitated by providing a relatively quiet environment with instructions to assume a passive attitude toward one's performance by employing a cognitive device, such as the covert repetition of words, sounds, and images; or attending repetitively to one's breathing or proprioceptive sensations from specific muscles. Fourth, regular practice in the therapist's office is arranged. Transfer training focuses on facilitating generalization of learned skills to the client's life environment utilizing fading techniques and self-directed home practice.

REFERENCES

Achterberg, J. & Lawlis, G.F. *Imagery of cancer.* Champaign, Ill.: Institute for Personality and Ability Testing, 1978.

Aveni, C.A. & Cutter, H.S.G. Controlled rebreathing. *Behavioral Engineering,* 1977, **4**, 17–21.

Barber, T.X. & Hahn, K.W. Hypnotic induction and "relaxation": An experimental study. *Archives of General Psychiatry,* 1963, **33**, 295–300.

Benson, H. *The relaxation response.* New York: William Morrow, 1975.

Bensen, H., Berry, J.F., & Carol, M.P. The relaxation response. *Psychiatry,* 1974, **37**, 37–46.

Benson, H., Rosser, B.A., Marzetta, B.R., & Klemchuck, H.M. Decreased blood pressure in pharmacologically treated hypertensive patients who regularly elicited the relaxation response. *Lancet,* 1974, **1**, 289–291.

Bernstein, D.A. & Borkovec, T.D. *Progressive relaxation training: A manual for helping professionals.* Champaign, Ill.: Research Press, 1973.

Borkovec, T.D. & Fowles, D.C. Controlled investigation of the effects of progressive and hypnotic relaxation on insomnia. *Journal of Abnormal Psychology,* 1973, **82**, 153–158.

Borkovec, T.D. & Sides, J.K. Critical procedural variables related to the physiological effects of progressive relaxation: A review. *Behavior Research and Therapy,* 1979, **17,** 119–125.

Bradley R.W. & Hughes, H. Blood pressure biofeedback and relaxation training: The effects of home practice on reduction of blood pressure in persons with essential hypertension. Unpublished manuscript, 1979.

Brady, J.P. Metronome-conditioned relaxation: A new behavioral procedure. *British Journal of Psychiatry,* 1973, **122,** 729–730.

Brady, J.P., Luborsky, L., & Kron, R.E. Blood pressure reduction in patients with essential hypertension through metromone-conditioned relaxation: A preliminary report. *Behavior Therapy,* 1974, **5,** 203–209.

Budzynski, T.H. Biofeedback procedures in the clinic. *Seminars in Psychiatry,* 1973, **5,** 537–547.

Chesney, M.A. & Shelton, J.L. A comparison of muscle relaxation and electromyogram biofeedback treatment for muscle contraction headache. *Journal of Behavior Therapy and Experimental Psychiatry,* 1976, **7,** 221–225.

Cox, D.J., Freundlich, A., & Meyer, R.G. Differential effectiveness of electromyograph feedback, verbal relaxation instructions, and medication placebo with tension headaches. *Journal of Consulting and Clinical Psychology,* 1975, **43,** 892–898.

Datey, K.K., Deshmukh, S.N., Dalvi, C.P., & Vinekar, S.L. "Shavasan": A yogic exercise in the management of hypertension. *Angiology,* 1969, **20,** 325–333.

Datey, K.K. Biofeedback training and shavasan in the management of hypertension. *Biofeedback and Self-Regulation,* 1977, **2,** 303.

Deffenbacher, J.L. Relaxation *in vivo* in the treatment of test anxiety. *Journal of Behavior Therapy and Experimental Psychiatry,* 1976, **7,** 289–292.

Deffenbacher, J.L. & Michaels, A.C., Two self-control procedures in the reduction of targeted and nontargeted anxieties—A year later. Paper presented at the meeting of the Association for Advancement of Behavior Therapy. San Francisco, December 1979.

Deffenbacher, J.L. & Payne, D.M. Two procedures for relaxation as self-control in the treatment of communication apprehension. *Journal of Counseling Psychology,* 1977, **24,** 255–258.

Deffenbacher, J.L. & Snyder, A.L. Relaxation as self-control in the treatment of test and other anxieties. *Psychological Reports,* 1976, **39,** 379–385.

Dial, M.H. & Hughes, H. Cue-controlled relaxation: Muscle tension reduction using covertly versus overtly produced cues under stress and no stress conditions. Unpublished manuscript, 1979.

Driscoll, R. Anxiety reduction using physical exertion and positive images. *Psychological Record,* 1976, **26,** 87.

Epstein, L.H., Abel, G.G., & Webster, J.S. Feedback assisted control and discrimination of EMG activity in the treatment of tension headaches. Paper presented at the meeting of the Association for Advancement of Behavior, Therapy, Chicago, December 1974.

Fuller, G.D. *Biofeedback: Methods and procedures in clinical practice.* San Francisco: Biofeedback Press, 1977.

Gaarder, K.R. & Montgomery, P.S. *Clinical biofeedback.* Baltimore: Williams & Wilkins, 1977.

Goldfried, M.R. & Trier, C. Effectiveness of relaxation as an active coping skill. *Journal of Abnormal Psychology,* 1974, **83,** 348–355.

Gunderson, J. Graphic recording of breathing rate using a simple thermocouple system. *Biomedical Engineering* 1971, **6,** 208–210.

Haynes, S.N., Moseley, D., & McCowan, W.T. Relaxation training and biofeedback in the reduction of frontalis and muscle tension. *Psychophysiology,* 1975, **12,** 247–252.

Hughes, H., Henry, D., & Hughes A. The effect of EMG biofeedback training on the behavior of children with activity level problems. *Biofeedback and Self-Regulation,* 1980, **5,** 207–219.

Jacob, R.G., Kraemer, H.C., & Agras, W.S. Relaxation therapy in the treatment of hypertension: A review. *Archives of General Psychiatry,* 1977, **34,** 1417–1427.

Jacobson, E. *Progressive relaxation.* Chicago: University of Chicago Press, 1938.

Lowenstein, T.J. A health-oriented multilevel university community based biofeedback/relaxation training program. *Proceedings of the Biofeedback Society of America,* 1979, **10,** 261.

Luiselli, J.K., Steinman, D., Marholin, D., & Steinman, W.M. The setting function of progressive muscle relaxation: An experimental analysis. Paper presented at the meeting of the American Psychological Association, Toronto, 1978.

Luthe, W. *Introduction to the methods of autogenic therapy: Manual for a workshop.* Denver: Biofeedback Society of America, 1977.

Mitchell, K.R. & White, R.G. Behavioral self-management: An application to the problem of migraine headaches. *Behavior Therapy,* 1977, **8,** 213–221.

Patel, C.H. Yoga and biofeedback in the management of hypertension. *Lancet,* 1973, **2,** 1053–1055.

Patel, C. Yoga and biofeedback in the management of hypertension. *Journal of Psychosomatic Research,* 1975, **19,** 355–360.

Patel, C.H. & North, W.R. Randomized control of yoga and biofeedback in management of hypertension. *Lancet,* 1975, **2,** 93–95.

Paul, G.L. *Insight* vs. *desensitization* in *psychotherapy.* Stanford, Calif.: Stanford University Press, 1966.

Paul, G.L. & Trimble, R.W. Recorded vs. "live" relaxation training and hypnotic suggestion: Comparative effectiveness for reducing physiological arousal and inhibiting stress response. *Behavior Therapy,* 1970, **1,** 285–302.

Reeves, J.L. & Mealiea, W.L. Biofeedback-assisted cue-controlled relaxation for the treatment of flight phobias. *Journal of Behavior Therapy and Experimental Psychiatry,* 1975, **6,** 105–109.

Rosen, G.M. *The relaxation book.* Englewood Cliffs, N.J.: Prentice-Hall, 1977.

Rugh, J.D. & Schwitzgebel, R.L. Instrumentation for behavioral assessments. In A.R. Ciminero, K.S. Calhoun, & H.E. Adams (Eds.) *Handbook of Behavioral Assessments.* New York: Wiley, 1977.

Rugh, J.D. & Solberg, W.K. Electromyographic studies of bruxist behavior before and during treatment. *Journal of California Dental Association,* 1975, **3,** 56–59.

Russell, R.K. & Sipich, J.F. Cue-controlled relaxation in the treatment of test anxiety. *Journal of Behavior Therapy and Experimental Psychiatry*, 1973, **4**, 47–49.

Schultz, J. & Luthe, W. *Autogenic training: A psychophysiologic approach in psychotherapy*. New York: Grune and Stratton, 1959.

Schultz, J.H. & Luthe, W., *Autogenic therapy: Autogenic methods*. New York: Grune and Stratton, 1969.

Sipprelle, C.N. Induced anxiety. *Psychotherapy: Theory, Research and Practice*, 1967, **4**, 36–40.

Stoyva, J.M. Guidelines in the training of general relaxation. In J.V. Basmajian (Ed.) *Biofeedback principles and practice for clinicians*. Baltimore: Williams & Wilkins, 1979.

Stroebel, C.F. *Quieting response training*. New York: BMA Audio Cassette Publication, 1980.

Surwit, R. Autogenic training manual. Unpublished manuscript, 1978.

Surwit, P., Pilon, R., & Fenton, C. Behavioral treatment of Raynaud's disease. *Journal of Behavior Medicine*, 1978, **1**, 323–335.

Taylor, C.B. Relaxation training and related techniques. In W.S. Agras (Ed.) *Behavior modification: Principles and clinical applications*. Boston: Little, Brown, 1978.

Taylor, C.B., Farquhar, J.W., Nelson, E., & Agras, W.S. Relaxation therapy and high blood pressure. *Archives of General Psychiatry*, 1977, **34**, 339–342.

Tentoni, S.C. Reduction of physiological correlates of stress using pink noise. *Behavioral Engineering*, 1978, **5**, 5–11.

Weiher, R.G., & Streifel, S. Effects of EMG feedback and video-tape relaxation on frontalis activity. Paper presented at the meeting of the Association for Advancement of Behavior Therapy, Chicago, December 1979.

Wolpe, J. *Psychotherapy by reciprocal inhibition*. Stanford, Calif.: Stanford University Press, 1958.

Wolpe, J. & Lazarus, A.A. *Behavior therapy techniques*. London: Pergamon Press, 1966.

CHAPTER 5

Cognitive Strategies

OVERVIEW

Behavior therapy was founded on a commitment to empiricism and consequently focused almost exclusively on the therapeutic utilization of overt environmental stimuli and overt behavioral responses. The inclusion of data concerning measured physiological responses has more recently become practical with the increased availability of recording equipment associated with the biofeedback movement. Physiological responses, overt stimuli, and overt responses may be directly observed by other persons and/or instruments and thus, serve as an empirical data base for behavior change procedures. There remains the subjective report, which has been one of the major sources of data in general psychotherapeutics. In behavior therapy, this information source has been utilized by operationally defining covert events in terms of overt therapists instructions, overt self-instructions, and overt self-reports. Thus, a covert stimulus may be defined as the therapist instructing the client to imagine a pink elephant or imagine being at a beach. Likewise, while at home the client could instruct himself/herself in a similar manner. The client's covert responses are defined by subjective report. These subjective responses may be defined with operational referents, such as the experience of head-pain at an intensity that interferes with attention to other activities. Further, it may be noted that behavior therapists generally assume that covert events may be subsumed under the same conditioning principles as overt events.

Cognitive behavior therapy is, then, those behavior change procedures wherein operationally defined covert events—stimuli and responses—are manipulated in an attempt to alter covert and overt target behaviors. Behavior therapy and cognitive behavior therapy may be differentiated along a continuum of relative emphasis of cognitive events, as both covert and overt events are to some extent part and parcel of both approaches. In general, cognitive behavior therapy would include an appreciable, but not primary, focus on overt events with behavior therapy (i.e., systematic desensitization) being less inclusive of covert events.

A number of different types of cognitive behavior therapies have been developed. The most notable are cognitive restructuring (rational-emotive therapy, Ellis, 1962; cognitive therapy, Beck, 1970; Beck & Emery, 1979) and self-instructional training (Meichenbaum, 1977). Cognitive restructuring places emphasis on altering the client's irrational beliefs through Socratic dialogue and rational self-examination of cognitive responses. In this manner, one learns to discriminate irrational self-defeating thoughts from rational alternatives. Also, attempts may be made to alter not only the content of a client's irrational belief system but also illogical thought processes. Through this procedure, the client begins to generate more rational cognitive responses. In contrast, self-instructional training appears to focus primarily on the covert responses per se rather than hypothesized belief systems and thought processes, and the client gradually learns to utilize self-instructions and replace maladaptive self-statements with adaptive coping self-statements.

These two types of cognitive behavior therapy have a number of common characteristics. Both employ conceptualization training wherein the rationale for cognitive therapy is presented and the influence of cognitive responses on overt behavior is demonstrated. Each approach then includes an awareness-training phase. Self-monitoring of covert responses is utilized to identify self-defeating cognitions occuring just before, during, and after the occurrence of the target behaviors. These cognitive responses are considered to be so habitual and overlearned that they occur "automatically" and are not typically within the client's awareness. Another common characteristic is that both types of cognitive behavior therapy utilize a coping skills training phase wherein the client learns adaptive self-statements. This is accomplished through modeling, and overt and covert rehearsal of self-statements. Finally in the concluding training phase both cognitive approaches include home practice and *in vivo* utilization of the newly learned cognitive coping responses. Identified stress situations, distress responses (i.e., negative thoughts, emotional responses), and target symptoms are employed as cues to initiate and utilize the coping skills. It should be noted that these techniques involve the manipulation of overt stimuli and overt responses in an attempt to manipulate covert events.

Cognitive behavior therapy procedures have also been conceptually organized within a conditioning framework which could be viewed as a third major type of cognitive therapy (Kazdin & Smith, 1979). This covert conditioning model assumes, as stated earlier, that cognitive stimuli and responses follow essentially the same principles as overt operants (Homme, 1965). The idea is that covert responses may be altered utilizing conditioning procedures. It then follows that covert conditioning may be utilized to alter those cognitive responses that are efficacious in changing covert and overt target behaviors. Within this framework covert conditioning procedures are analogous to operant conditioning procedures.

Covert Positive Reinforcement

In the employment of covert positive reinforcement, the client is instructed (by the therapist or autogenically) to imagine performing a specified adaptive response in a specified situation and then immediately to imagine a specified positively reinforcing event. For instance, the client might imagine having just received notice of a pending physical exam by the airline where he is employed as a pilot. This might be followed by an imagined discussion about the exam with someone while he expresses confidence that his blood pressure will be within normal limits during the exam. He may then immediately imagine himself on a beautiful beach in Hawaii with the successfully completed exam behind him. It should be noted that, as with overt techniques, covert procedures also use shaping of a response in order to arrange for the gradual approximation of the desired adaptive behavior. This as well as most overt operant principles, such as the importance of the immediacy of reinforcement, are applicable in covert conditioning (Kazdin & Smith, 1979). In closing this section, it should be observed that in covert positive reinforcement, and other covert applications, it is of importance that the imagery be very vivid (Kroger & Fezler, 1976). This suggests that imagery should be practiced until it is quite clear, as well as mediated, by as many of the sensoria as is possible with a given client. Imagery instructions should include referents to all five senses (Kroger and Fezler, 1976) and to both stimulus and response aspects of the imaged situations (Glenn & Hughes, 1979).

Covert Negative Reinforcement

In this procedure the client is instructed to imagine experiencing a specified aversive situation and then to terminate this image immediately upon picturing the performance of a specified adaptive response in the specified situation. As an example, a client who fears flying might imagine being trapped in a burning building. Next, it is imagined that a helicopter suddenly appears at the window and that he/she climbs aboard and is carried away from the burning building into the clear blue sky (Kroger & Fezler, 1976). This procedure would generally be utilized when clients do not respond to covert positive reinforcement, possibly because there is little that is positively reinforcing in their lives or they are unable to imagine positive experiences.

Covert Extinction

Covert extinction involves instructing the client to imagine performing a specified maladaptive response in a specified situation without experiencing the positive consequences that typically follow. For example, a client might imagine the spouse is leaving to go jogging, pleading with the spouse not to go because of a terrible headache, the spouse says that it will be all right and leaves (Kroger & Fezler, 1976). This technique is most appropriate for undesirable behaviors that ordinarily have positively reinforcing consequences such as excessive eating or drinking, sexual deviation, and responses maintained by secondary gain in the form of attention or avoidance.

It is desirable to utilize scenes of maladaptive behavior that are typical of the client's response repertoire.

Covert Punishment

Covert punishment was initially referred to as covert sensitization (Cautela, 1966, 1967). Like covert extinction, it has been utilized with maladaptive behaviors that ordinarily have positively reinforcing consequences. The client is instructed to imagine performing a specified maladaptive response in a specified situation and then immediately producing, in imagery, a specified aversive event. The client might begin by imagining eating an excessive amount of food, experiencing nausea at the sight of more food, and then gags and vomits. *Covert response cost* is a particular type of covert punishment wherein the aversive event involves the loss of positive reinforcement. Covert response cost may be conceptualized as a combination of covert positive reinforcement and covert extinction wherein the imagined occurrence of adaptive responses followed by positive consequences is interrupted by maladaptive responses followed by the absence of positive consequences. In addition, *thought stopping* (Wolpe, 1969) is a particular technique that fits within the covert punishment paradigm in that a thought is consequated with a covert image of the word "stop." In the initial phases of this technique, the thought is consequated by the therapist overtly shouting "stop" and later the client is instructed to covertly shout "stop" at the first intrusion of undesirable thoughts.

Combinations

Of course, there are many possible combinations of the covert conditioning procedures. For example, covert punishment is typically combined sequentially with covert negative reinforcement and covert positive reinforcement. Thus, a client might imagine engaging in a deviant sexual behavior and then experiencing negative consequences, which are terminated with the onset of an adaptive response. This adaptive response is then imagined to have a positive consequence. Over practice trials this sequence is shortened as in an avoidance conditioning paradigm. Thus, the initial imagined situation is now followed by the adaptive response before the onset of the aversive event, thus, resulting in avoidance of the aversive event. The adaptive (avoidance) response may then be followed by a positive consequence.

    Some authors (Cautela, 1967; Kazdin & Smith, 1979) consider *covert modeling* to be a separate covert conditioning procedure. Covert modeling involves the client's imagining that models perform the behavior rather than oneself. From the standpoint of practical application of covert conditioning procedures this would not appear to be an important distinction to make at this time. Pending research findings to the contrary, it is suggested that each of the covert procedures previously defined could be conducted with the client imagining both himself performing the behavior and a model performing the behavior. It may be particularly efficacious to have the client imagine a model performing the behavior in the early conditioning trials, especially if the client has initial difficulties producing imagery concerning himself performing the behavior.

Upon reflection it may be seen that the covert conditioning procedures just described involve mainly the systematic manipulation of covert stimuli and covert responses to alter covert and overt target behaviors. These procedures may be utilized in such a relatively pure form as therapy per se or as a therapeutic component. However, these basic procedures may also be utilized in various combinations with simultaneous manipulation of both overt and covert stimuli and responses. As previously mentioned, behavior therapies may be conceptualized along a continuum of relative emphasis on covert versus overt events. Thus, covert conditioning procedure may be viewed as primarily covert whereas contingency management may be primarily overt. Then, also, combination procedures, such as cognitive restructuring and self-instructional training would seem to place emphasis on covert events; whereas combination procedures, such as systematic desensitization and assertive training would place emphasis on overt events. We would recommend that, whenever possible, it is better to use overt events in conjunction with the covert events employed in the various conditioning procedures, rather than to use covert events singularly.

The question as to why one should use cognitive behavior therapy may be addressed here. At first glance, one might assume that a behavior therapy orientation would mitigate against the utilization of covert events due to the difficulties inherent in operationally defining them. However, it is our opinion that another premise of behavior therapy takes precedence. That is, one should utilize the most parsimonious set of operationally defined events that are therapeutically effective in the modification of the behavior under the therapist's consideration. In this sense, the "jury is still out" and the burden of proof lies on those who wish to place greater emphasis on covert events. Furthermore, one may be wise not to consider this an all or nothing issue. Rather, it may be efficacious to emphasize covert events with certain maladaptive conditions, or with certain individuals and not with others. Finally, it is likely that it is impossible to carry out pure covert or pure overt procedures in verbal homo sapiens.

One may also consider the potential advantages associated with the utilization of cognitive behavioral procedures. These procedures would appear to offer increased standardization of "talking therapies"; a more specific behavior therapy or psychotherapy. This increased operationalism should facilitate the training of therapists, the training of clients in self-management, and the evaluation of treatment outcome. Cognitive behavioral procedures are also likely to be relatively congruent with the typical client's conceptualization of his behavior, which may affect his acceptance of treatment and motivation for continuing in treatment.

Apart from consideration of why one should use cognitive behavioral procedures and what advantages accrue, the fact is that these procedures have been used successfully in the treatment of the following behavioral medicine disorders: cancer (Sobel, 1978; Weisman & Sobel, 1979), chronic abdominal pain (Levendusky & Pankratz, 1975), chronic back pain (Bowen & Turk, 1979; Follick, 1979; Follick, Zitter, & Kulich, 1979), insomnia (Lowery, Denny, & Storms, 1979; Mitchell, 1979; Mitchell & White 1977a), irritable colon syndrome (Bowen & Turk, 1979; Harrell & Beiman, 1978), migraine headache (Huber & Huber, 1979; Lake, Rainey, & Papsdorf, 1979; Mitchell & White, 1977b), myofacial pain syndrome (Stenn, Mothersill, & Brooke, 1979), tension headache (Anderson, Lawrence, & Waldruff, 1979; Bowen & Turk, 1979; Holroyd & Andrasik, 1978; Holroyd, Andrasik, & Westbrook, 1977; Reeves, 1976), ulcers (Aleo & Nicassio, 1978), vaginismus (Shahar & Jaffe, 1978), and essential hypertension (Hughes & Cunningham, 1980).

COGNITIVE PROCEDURES

Conceptualization Training

It is assumed that the reader has had some professional training in behavior therapy or psychotherapy that will serve as the context within which cognitive behavioral procedures may be utilized. Conceptualization training has been delineated as an important component of cognitive behavior therapy (Jaremko, 1979; Meichenbaum, Turk, & Burstein, 1975). The objective is for the client and therapist to evolve a common conceptualization of the problem, and the treatment (Meichenbaum, 1976). It involves teaching the basic concepts relevant to understanding the therapy and its relationship to the target symptoms. To the extent this is accomplished, the client will be motivated to comply with the treatment procedures and thereby maximize the probability of successful results. Thus, the initial phases of conceptualization training necessitate the therapist obtaining information that may be utilized to understand the client's conceptualization of his problem, his expectation about treatment, and his attempts to formulate an understanding of his behavior. In other words, the focus is on perceptions, attributions, and appraisals. Conceptualization may be conducted in a manner similar to that presented in the chapter on biofeedback. Of course, the content of the material presented would be altered to include cognitive concepts and procedures. The following are some of the major points to be included: (1) physiological arousal is a chain of responses including thoughts and images that precede, accompany, and follow the physiological responses; (2) these covert responses may be such that they exacerbate the effects of external stress and facilitate increased physiological hyperarousal, or dampen excessive arousal and facilitate coping behaviors; (3) much of the internal dialogue involving self-evaluative statements are so habitual as to be experienced as automatic and more or less involuntary; (4) through training one can become aware of specific maladaptive automatic thoughts that occur in specified stress situations and learn adaptive self-statements appropriate to these situations; (5) through overt and covert rehearsal, home practice, and *in vivo* utilization with contingent covert and overt reinforcement, a behavioral repertoire of specific adaptive self-statements may be established concurrently with the reduction of maladaptive self-statements; and (6) as a result, coping self-control responses are facilitated, maladaptive physiological arousal and helplessness is reduced, and concomitant symptoms are alleviated. For additional information related to the content, which should be included in the conceptualization training, the reader is referred to articles by Coffman and Katz (1979), and Katz (1979).

Assessment

Psychophysiological assessment is not ordinarily considered to be a phase of cognitive behavior therapy; however, when utilized with behavioral medicine cases, it is indicated. In a larger sense, the authors advocate a multi-element therapeutic approach wherein behavior therapy, biofeedback training, relaxation training, and cognitive behavior therapy are integrated, and a self-management orientation is maximized (Hughes & Cunningham, 1980). The psychophysiological assessment procedures would be essentially those presented in the chapter on biofeedback training with the possible addition of procedures to assess automatic thoughts occuring during the assessment. The cognitive assessment components may be selected from the covert assessment procedures presented in this chapter.

The objective of cognitive behavioral assessment is to record and functionally analyze the client's internal dialogue as it relates to the presenting problem and associated antecedent and consequent events. Concomitant with assessment, there usually occurs a continuation of change in the client's conceptualization of the problem as the client explores his self-statement repertoire. The aspects of assessment presented in earlier chapters, such as careful specification of the overt response and overt antecedent and consequent events shall not be the primary focus in this chapter, although they would be a necessary part of a complete assessment. The cognitive portion of an assessment focuses on both adaptive and maladaptive self-statements. If a cognitive behavioral approach is indicated, one should find an appreciable quantity of maladaptive self-statements and a relative paucity of adaptive self-statements. There is likely to be an appreciable interdependence between the individual's cognitions and behavioral repertoire. The task is to determine which self-statement images, and associated circumstances, are contributing to the presenting problem and are interfering with adequate coping behavior (Meichenbaum, 1976).

Instructions to the client in cognitive assessment procedures for behavioral medicine problems require that the client describe the thoughts and images that precede, accompany, and follow relevant events. These events include stress situations, stress reactions, and occurrences of the target behavior. This interview procedure is utilized in the therapist's office in an individual or group situation. In addition to identifying relevant thoughts, the therapist explores the range of situations where the thoughts accompanying physiological arousal and/or target behavior occur. Later, the situations are simulated in the office setting by having the client imagine and role play critical incidents of the relevant events. Finally, the client self-monitors the thoughts and images in his life environment: home, work, and public settings. Generally, cognitive self-monitoring is implemented during specific time-limited intervals of 1 to 7 days occurring during baseline, treatment, and follow-up periods. Data may be recorded for, and at the end of specific time periods. Thus, one may record 30 minutes, 1 hour, or 1 day. A broad range of time intervals is available if one utilizes a portable auditory timer programmable from 1 second to 24-hour intervals. Cognitive self-monitoring may also be initiated upon the occurrence of specified events. Target symptoms, identified stress situations, and identified stress reactions are frequently utilized as discriminative stimuli for self-monitoring. Katz and Coffman (1979) consider environmental conditions, life changes, interpersonal conflict and loss to be the major sources of stress events. Examples of probable environmental sources of stress are time pressure, crowding, competition, work demands, financial problems, and drug problems. Marriage, divorce, pregnancy, vacation, moving, and loss of health are examples of life change stresses. Interpersonal conflict with a family member, roommate, employer, or social authority figures, such as a policeman, minister, or school teacher also exemplify sources of stress as does the loss of a person with whom one has a close interpersonal relationship. Here are a number of possible stress reactions often associated with stress events: forgetfulness, confusion, concentration problems, dizziness, fainting, ringing ears, visual disturbances, numbness, heightened sensitivity, itching, headache, pain, stiffness, restlessness, fatigue, clumsiness, immobilization, trembling, nervous mannerisms (tics, nail-biting, and the drumming of fingers), irritability, tearfulness, fever blisters, appetite abnormalities, stomach complaints, intestinal disturbances, diarrhea, constipation, urinary complaints, insomnia, excessive sleep, breathing difficulties, blushing, excessive sweating, palpitations, dry mouth, and cold hands and feet. In addition, prominent negative affective responses such as anger, hostility, hate, aggression, anxiety, fear, and depression are probably indicative of stress reactions.

Self-statements and images may be recorded in a systematic manner, utilizing forms and specific operational procedures or in a less systematic fashion, allowing the client to determine the specifics of what is to be recorded. Katz and Coffman (1979) utilized a progressive shaping procedure wherein clients gradually learned the various component self-monitoring responses. First they practiced self-monitoring symptoms and stress events.

At a later time they practiced self-monitoring symptoms, stress events, self-talk and associated beliefs. Maladaptive covert responses are the major focus of cognitive assessment and are characterized as being negative (self-defeating statements, i.e., "I can't," "I will fail"), evaluative ("I'm stupid," "They will think I'm stupid,"), and inaccurate. They are inaccurate according to Beck (1970) and Michenbaum (1976) due to distortions in logical thought processes such as: over-generalization (one failure is total incompetence), arbitrary inference (drawing a conclusion in the presence of insufficient or contrary information), magnification (exaggeration of the consequences of an event), cognitive deficiency (disregard of important data), personalization (interpreting events in terms of personal meaning) and polarization (construing events in terms of absolutes or dichotomies). The above distortions may often result in a negative and inaccurate evaluation of oneself and of past, present, and future life responses and events. Thought content may also be maladaptive as exemplified by the following ideas: one must have approval all the time from almost everyone; one's self-worth depends on the quality of one's performance and the approval of others; people and things should be better than they are, and it is awful and catastrophic if things do not go the way one would like them to go; and emotional distress comes from external events and one has little control over one's feelings. Additionally, fear of rejection by others, concern about competency or inadequacy, disturbance over being mistreated, and a desire to punish oneself or others are also frequently observed maladaptive ideational concerns (Ellis, 1962, 1977). Such thoughts are maladaptive in the sense that they are self-defeating and typically lead to frustration and disappointment (Ellis, 1962, 1977).

The specifics of exactly which covert responses should be recorded is, for the most part, a very individualized matter that varies as a function of circumstance, proclivities of the therapist, and the client's presenting problems. One records those thoughts and images that frequently precede, accompany, and follow stress situations, stress reactions, and target behaviors (*in vivo* or simulated through recall, imagery, or role playing) which appear to be relatively negative, evaluative, and inaccurate, and which, are therefore likely to be personally frustrating and self-defeating. The following are examples of maladaptive thoughts that would probably be recorded during self-monitoring:

> They will never forgive me if I . . . , I really need to have . . . , Oh God, what if I don't . . . , Damn, I'll never be able to . . . , God, am I stupid . . . , I bet they don't think I'm . . . , I wish they'd leave me alone . . . , Boy, do I hate this situation . . . , Oh no, I'm starting to do it again, and, I always do . . . , It's terrible, horrible, and catastrophic . . . , I can't stand it . . . , I must do better . . . , I have to hurry . . . , This is boring . . . , Things should be different . . . , This is dangerous . . . , I'm no good . . . , Nobody likes me . . . , He's no good . . . , Other people are so inconsiderate . . . , I knew it-I knew it . . . ,

> What if I can't . . . , I would be terrible if . . . , What should I do
> . . . , I'm making a fool of myself . . . , I'll never live it down . . . , He
> is taking advantage of me . . . , and I can't do anything right. (See also
> McMullin & Casey, 1975.)

In addition, one should monitor adaptive self-statements that appear to
be relatively positive and accurate, and are likely to lead to coping and
satisfaction. The following are examples of thought that are typically adaptive:

> So I might get tense . . . , I won't dwell on it as it doesn't help . . . ,
> Just slow down . . . , Relax for a few seconds . . . , You're in control
> . . . , Even if I don't do it this time there will be other chances . . . ,
> Let's see, I'll just concentrate on what I want to do . . . , Now just one
> step at a time, what's my first step . . . , There's plenty of time . . . ,
> I'm sure I'll be able to do this since I've done it before . . . , I'm ready
> to give it my best shot . . . , It wasn't as bad as I expected . . . , I'm
> doing better, and I'm pleased with my progress . . . , and, I can be proud
> of that . . . (Coffman & Katz, 1979).

The assessment of adaptive thoughts focuses on ascertaining their presence in the client's repertoire and whether they are being utilized in stress
situations related to the target symptoms. With maladaptive thoughts, the
focus is on identifying those that occur frequently and are functionally related
to stress reactions and target behaviors. In contrast with adaptive thoughts
one is concerned with their occuring infrequently and not occuring during
stress situations.

It should be noted that a discrimination training procedure is to a large
extent embedded in cognitive assessment. The client learns to discriminate
adaptive from maladaptive thoughts based on the guidelines presented by
the therapist (McMullin & Casey, 1975). Identified thoughts are then assessed
as to their functional relationship to stress reactions and target symptoms
resulting in further behaviorally-based discriminations for a given client.
Frequently, it is found that negative thoughts have some reinforcing consequences (secondary gain) such as attention from others or avoidance of
unpleasant events (i.e., social interactions that include the risk of failure).

Cognitive Skills Control Training

The primary objective of cognitive skills control training is to condition
adaptive self-statements. By this time in therapy the client has already
learned to identify and self-monitor negative and positive thoughts and images. The first phase of cognitive skills training involves generation of positive self-statements appropriate to the client's target symptoms. A list of
frequently occurring negative thoughts, that appear to be functionally related

to the client's stress reactions and target behaviors, will have been identified earlier in therapy. A modeling and shaping procedure is then utilized wherein each maladaptive thought is reviewed within the context of a specific situation, and the client is required to attempt, through reevaluation, to formulate one or more appropriate positive self-statements. For example, the client may be instructed to imagine responding to a situation exactly as it is, objectively without implicit negative interpretations. The therapist reinforces the client's verbalizations of thoughts as they more closely approximate desired coping responses. Once the client is able to generate adaptive reevaluative self-statements in the therapy setting, he is given a homework assignment designed to develop a positive self-statement for each negative thought recorded during self-monitoring. This process continues throughout treatment so that an appropriate list of functionally relevant maladaptive-adaptive self-statement pairs is generated and maintained.

The second phase of cognitive skills training involves conditioning acquisition of an adaptive coping self-statement repertoire, and the reduction (extinction, counter-conditioning) of the maladaptive thought repertoire. It should be noted that this is generally combined sequentially or concurrently with the conditioned acquisition of an adaptive behavioral (overt) and physiological repertoire. This skills conditioning procedure is somewhat continous with the generation of positive self-statement procedures, but the desired response is no longer writing thoughts and images. Now the focus is on performing the positive self-statements, and integrating them into the client's ongoing behavioral repertoire. Again, a modeling and shaping process is utilized in the therapy setting whereas the stress situation is simulated using overt and covert descriptions of stress situations and specific negative self-statements. Initially, overt-overt-rehearsal is utilized wherein the client overtly role plays his positive response to the simulation and overtly verbalizes his covert responses to allow the therapist to monitor the entire response-complex. The objective is to shape the client rapidly into performing the appropriate response so the inappropriate one is not practiced. The therapist provides appropriate instructions to initiate and maintain each rehearsal trial including instructions for the client to self-evaluate his performance at the end of each trial. At this point the therapist models evaluative feedback typically beginning with the preface, "What I liked about what you did was. . . ." (This emphasis on the positive is important since most clients are all too good at self-criticism). Of course, the therapist's feedback includes appropriate verbal positive reinforcement for successive approximation of the desired responses.

Once the client's performance reaches an acceptable level during the completely overt-rehearsal, each trial is lengthened so that it begins with a covert-covert-rehearsal. The completely covert rehearsal is essentially preparatory and involves the client's imagining that he is responding to the simulated stress overtly and covertly. The client should be instructed to include self-evaluation of his performance in his imagined covert responding. These combination rehearsals are practiced until the desired responses are attained, at which point the overt verbalizing of the covert self-statements fade.

The basic conditioning procedure presented so far involves modeling and shaping overt and verbalized covert responses with instructions to respond covertly in the same manner. That is, the desired covert behavior is first conditioned as an overt verbal response and then conditioned as a covert verbal response. This approach is essentially overt positive reinforcement followed by a combination of overt and covert positive reinforcement. Of course, covert negative reinforcement may also be employed. However, the positive reinforcement paradigm is the basic procedure utilized in the shaping of adaptive self-statements.

Cognitive Skills Transfer Training

The purpose of transfer training is to insure that the cognitive skills established in the office setting are reliably established in the client's life environment. Although training is continued in the office setting, the focus is shifted to home practice and *in vivo* utilization. Once the desired response has been attained in the office setting, the first phase of transfer training, home practice, is initiated. The client is instructed to practice at home one or more times each day, with a total practice time of approximately 15 minutes to an hour per day. For example, one might begin with one 15-minute practice session per day, later use two 10-minute sessions, and finally six 5-minute sessions. Refer to the biofeedback and self-management chapters for a more detailed consideration of home practice training and procedures.

It is desirable to formulate a set of written instructions for carrying out the home practice procedures including a list of stress situations, frequent negative thoughts, adaptive self-statements, and adaptive responses based on data from control training. Index cards may be utilized, with a stress situation or negative thought being written on one side and corresponding adaptive self-statements on the other. A typical home practice session would involve a number of the following procedures. A relevant physiological measure, such as blood pressure, skin temperature, or pulse rate may be taken at the beginning and end of the practice period. Stress situations are imagined and the vividness of the images may also be rated. The client covertly makes positive self-statements and imagines performing an adaptive overt coping response successfully. Positive reinforcing overt and covert events are imagined and an overt positive reinforcer may be delivered. The relevant physiological measure, the stress situation, the imagery rating, the covert reinforcer and the overt reinforcer are recorded on a self-monitoring form.

After these written instructions for the home practice procedure are developed in sufficient detail, the exercises are practiced in the therapist's office until the client is able to carry them out reliably and with sufficient ease. At this point, the client begins practicing at home utilizing the written instructions. Of course, any difficulties encountered during home practice are considered during the therapy sessions in the therapist's office. As practice progresses successfully, the client is instructed to utilize stress situations that are encountered daily for the content of the next home practice session, and begin to formulate new adaptive self-statements and coping responses during practice. Particular attention is then devoted to these self-management elaborations during subsequent therapy sessions.

When home practice appears to be firmly established, the second phase of transfer training begins and the client is instructed to utilize the learned skills *in vivo* as stress situations arise, and stress reactions and maladaptive thoughts are detected. Systematic ongoing practice is necessary to insure over-learning and to maximize treatment effects. At this point, careful attention should be directed to the client's ongoing self-monitoring data to ascertain whether there is an acceptable increase in the frequency of adaptive self-statements, and a decrease in the frequency of maladaptive thoughts. If these changes in self-statement behavior in the client's life environment occur for a sufficient period of time, focus is directed to assessing changes in the target symptoms in relation to baseline data. However, if the self-monitoring data indicates that the frequency of maladaptive thoughts have not decreased appreciably, then a decision is in order. The procedures being employed during skills training in the therapist's office and home practice could be continued for a longer period of time or the frequency of therapy sessions and home practice could be increased without appreciable alterations. Of course, the alternative is altering the procedures.

Usually, the conditioning of adaptive self-statements using positive reinforcement is maintained and other conditioning paradigms are added to condition a reduction in the frequency of maladaptive thoughts. The same basic procedures are utilized to condition the reduction in maladaptive thoughts except that a negative self-statement is substituted for the positive self-statement and an aversive or neutral stimulus is substituted for the positively reinforcing stimulus. Thus, extinction and punishment paradigms are employed. The basic home practice procedure is employed first in the therapist's office and then, if necessary, during home practice and *in vivo* utilization. Thus, the client imagines a stress situation, makes a negative self-statement, immediately imagines a neutral or aversive event and/or delivers a neutral or aversive overt event and records the situation, self-statement, covert reinforcer, and overt reinforcer.

It is necessary for the therapist to have available a number of covert and overt positive and negative reinforcers. Overt positive reinforcers are widely utilized and include attention (i.e., smiling) and positive verbal statements, (i.e., you did well, excellent) positive activities, (i.e., telephoning a friend, deep breathing, smoking, seeing a movie, watching T.V.) and edible reinforcers (i.e., raisins, candy, coffee, tea, soft drinks, other snacks). Overt aversive reinforcers include aversive verbal statements, aversive activities, and aversive stimuli (i.e., stop, no, serial 7s, cold pressor, holding one's breath, doing pushups, smelling unpleasant substances, popping oneself with a rubber band worn on the wrist). Covert reinforcers vary a great deal from person to person and include imagined experiencing of a great variety of events. Kroger and Fezler (1976) present 25 complete, structured images (i.e., scenes of beach, mountain cabin, garden, desert, space, farm, jungle, pool, arctic, bluebird, lake, thunder shower, mansion, scuba diving, picnic, Shangri-la, chalk cliff, volcano, cantina, hayloft, sandpit, mine, autumn) which may be utilized as covert reinforcers and used for practicing imaging. These structured images may also serve as models for construction of images individualized for the client. That is, information may be solicited from interviews and used to construct written images which are then presented to the client and successively altered, based on client feedback concerning the reinforcing properties of the image. Of course, some images are suggested by the client's symptom and its particular manifestation (i.e., natural consequences of the symptom or of the alleviation of the symptom). Images directed toward the induction of nausea and vomiting have been utilized frequently as a covert aversive stimulus.

There is no standardized approach to the usage of cognitive behavior therapy. Generally, it is conducted in individual sessions but it has also been carried out in a group format. The duration of a session is typically 50 minutes but has ranged from 30 to 120 minutes. Usually, 10 therapy sessions (3 to 20) are distributed over approximately 10 weeks but three sessions a week is not uncommon. Home practice procedures are almost always employed although the amount of structure varies. Two or three home practice sessions of about 15 minutes (1 to 30 minutes) are generally completed each day.

Although the therapy approach outlined here is relatively structured and specific, alterations may be made as needed by omitting specific portions of the procedures. The following references will provide a variety of approaches to, and examples of, cognitive behavior therapy: Barlow, Leitenberg, and Agras (1969), Barrow and Hetherington (1979), Beck (1970, 1976), Cautela (1967, 1977), Ellis (1962), Ellis and Harper (1975), Heppner (1978), Hollon and Kendall (1979), Kelly (1955), Lazarus (1971), Mahoney (1974), Marlatt (1979), Meichenbaum (1974, 1977), McMullin and Casey (1975), Novaco (1976, 1979), Rotter (1954), Turk and Genest (1979), Wolpe (1973), Wolpe and Lazarus (1966), and Zastrow (1979).

SUMMARY

Cognitive behavior therapy is concerned with the manipulation of operationally defined covert events in an attempt to alter covert and overt target behaviors. The utilization of biofeedback, relaxation and cognitive procedures in conjunction with behavior therapy conducted within a self-management context provides for an integrated and comprehensive multi-element approach that incorporates the three major sources of data—physiological, self-report, and behavioral observations. Two well-known types of cognitive behavior therapies are cognitive restructuring, which aspires to alter irrational beliefs and illogical thought processes and substitutes rational ones through Socratic dialogue and rational self-examination; and self-instructional training, which attempts to replace maladaptive self-statements with adaptive coping self-statements. A third major approach, the covert conditioning model assumes that cognitive stimuli and responses follow essentially the same principles as overt operants and thus utilize procedures analogous to operant conditioning procedures—covert positive reinforcement, covert negative reinforcement, covert extinction, and covert punishment. In practice these cognitive procedures are generally utilized in various combinations with simultaneous manipulation of both overt and covert stimuli and responses.

Conceptualization training is the first phase of cognitive therapy and the objective is for the client and therapist to develop a common view of the problem and the treatment. Assessment for cognitive techniques is oriented toward recording and analyzing the client's internal dialogue as it relates to the present problem and associated antecedent and consequent events. Covert events are self-monitored during psychophysiological assessment and in the client's life environment. Discrimination training is embedded in cognitive assessment as the client learns to differentiate adaptive self-statements from maladaptive self-statements which are associated with physiological arousal. The client learns to identify maladaptive covert responses that occur frequently and are functionally related to stress situations, stress reactions, and target symptoms. These cognitive events tend to be negative, judgmental, and inaccurate, and lead to self-defeating problem behavior, frustration, and negative affect. An attempt is also made to determine whether adaptive self-statements are present in the client's covert response repertoire and whether they are utilized in coping with stress situations.

Cognitive skills control training involves conditioning acquisition of an adaptive coping self-statement repertoire and extinction of the maladaptive thought repertoire. This procedure is combined concurrently with the conditioned acquisition of an adaptive behavioral (overt) and physiological repertoire. Cognitive skills training requires formulation of positive self-statements appropriate to the client's stress situations and target symptoms. These statements are modeled, shaped, and conditioned first as overt verbal responses and then as covert verbal responses, employing both overt and covert reinforcement. Finally cognitive skills transfer training is incorporated to insure generalization of the learned responses to the client's life environment. This phase of training primarily employs fading of the therapy conditions and establishing self-directed home practice.

REFERENCES

Aleo, S. & Nicassio, P. Auto-regulation of duodenal ulcer disease: A preliminary report of four cases. *Biofeedback and Self-Regulation,* 1978, **3,** 229.

Anderson, N.B., Lawrence, P.S., & Waldruff, D. A comparison of relaxation training and cognitive coping training in the treatment of headache pain. Paper presented at the meeting of the Society of Behavioral Medicine, San Francisco, December 1979.

Barlow, D.H., Leitenberg, H., & Agras, W.S. The experimental control of sexual deviation through manipulation of the noxious scenes in covert sensitization. *Journal of Abnormal Psychology,* 1969, **14,** 596–601.

Barrow, J. & Hetherington, C. Cognitive self-control procedures with socially anxious clients. Paper presented at the meeting of the American Psychological Association, New York, 1979.

Beck, A.T. Cognitive therapy: Nature and relation to behavior therapy. *Behavior Therapy,* 1970, **1,** 184–200.

Beck, A.T. *Cognitive therapy and the emotional disorders.* New York: International Universities Press, 1976.

Beck, A.T. & Emery, G. *Cognitive therapy of anxiety and phobic disorders.* Philadelphia: Center for Cognitive Therapy, 1979.

Bowen, W.F. & Turk, D.C. Cognitive-behavioral treatment of three medical conditions. Paper presented at the meeting of the Association for the Advancement of Behavior Therapy, San Francisco, December 1979.

Cautela, J.R. Treatment of compulsive behavior by covert sensitization. *Psychological Record,* 1966, **16,** 33–41.

Cautela, J.R. Covert sensitization. *Psychological Reports,* 1967, **20,** 459–468.

Cautela, J.R. The use of covert conditioning in modifying pain behavior. *Journal of Behavior Therapy and Experimental Psychiatry,* 1977, **8,** 45–52.

Coffman, D.A. & Katz, C. *Stress management: A structured group manual.* Austin, Tex.: Counseling-Psychological Services Center, University of Texas, 1979.

Daniels, L.K. Treatment of grand mal epilepsy by covert and operant conditioning techniques: A case study. *Psychosomatics,* 1975, **16,** 65–67.

Ellis, A. *Reason and emotion in psychotherapy.* New York: Lyle Stuart, 1962.

Ellis, A. Can we change thoughts by reinforcement? A reply to Howard Rachlin. *Behavior Therapy,* 1977, **8,** 666–672.

Ellis, A. & Harper, R.A. *A new guide to rational living.* Englewood Cliffs, N.J.: Prentice-Hall, 1975.

Follick, M.J. An outpatient-based behaviorally oriented approach to the management of chronic pain. Paper presented at the meeting of the American Psychological Association, New York, 1979.

Follick, M.J., Zitter, R., & Kulich, R. An outpatient based, behaviorally oriented, multidisciplinary team approach to management of chronic pain. Paper presented at the meeting of the Association for the Advancement of Behavior Therapy, San Francisco, December 1979.

Glenn, S. & Hughes, H. Imaginal response events in system-desensitization. *Journal of Biological Psychology,* 1978, **7,** 303–309.

Harrell, T.H. & Beiman, I. Cognitive-behavioral treatment of the irritable colon syndrome. *Cognitive Therapy and Research,* 1978, **2,** 371–375.

Heppner, P.O. The clinical alteration of covert thoughts: A critical review. *Behavior Therapy,* 1978, **9,** 717–734.

Holroyd, K.A. & Andrasik, F. Coping and the self-control of chronic tension headache. *Journal of Consulting and Clinical Psychology,* 1978, **46,** 1036–1045.

Holroyd, K.A., Andrasik, F., & Westbrook, T. Cognitive control of tension headache. *Cognitive Therapy and Research,* 1977, **1,** 121–133.

Hollon, S.D. & Kendall, P.C. Cognitive-behavioral interventions: Theory and procedure. In P.C. Kendall, & S.D. Hollon (Eds.) *Cognitive-behavioral interventions: Theory, research, and procedures.* New York: Academic Press, 1979.

Homme, L.E. Perspectives in psychology: XXIV control of covariants, the operants of the mind. *Psychological Record,* 1965, **15,** 501–511.

Huber, H.P. & Huber, D. Autogenic training and rational-emotive therapy for long-term migraine patients. An explorative study of a therapy. *Behavior Analysis and Modification,* 1979, **3,** 169–177.

Hughes, H. & Cunningham, D.P. Behavioral treatment of essential hypertension: Effect of multi-element and cognitive behavior self-regulation therapies. Unpublished manuscript, 1980.

Jaremko, M. A component analysis of stress inoculation: Review and prospectives. *Cognitive Therapy and Research,* 1979, **3,** 35–48.

Katz, C. Developing a stress management structured group for a college age population. Paper presented at the meeting of the American Psychological Association, New York, September 1979.

Kazdin, A.E. & Smith, G.A. Covert conditioning: A review and evaluation. *Advances in Behavior Research and Therapy,* 1979, **2,** 57–98.

Kelly, G.A. *The psychology of personal constructs.* New York: Norton, 1955.

Kroger, W.S. & Fezler, W.D. *Hypnosis and behavior modification: Imagery conditioning.* Philadelphia: Lippincott, 1976.

Lazarus, A.A. *Behavior therapy and beyond.* New York: McGraw-Hill, 1971.

Levendusky, P. & Pankratz, L. Self-control techniques as an alternative to pain medication. *Journal of Abnormal Psychology,* 1975, **84,** 165–168.

Lake, A., Rainey, J., & Papsdorf, J.D. Biofeedback and rational-emotive therapy in the management of migraine headache. *Journal of Applied Behavior Analysis,* 1979, **12,** 127–140.

Lowery, C.R., Denney, D.R., & Storms, M.D. Insomnia: A comparison of the effects of pill attributions and nonpejorative self-attributions. *Cognitive Therapy and Research,* 1979, **3,** 161–164.

Mahoney, M.J. *Cognition and behavior modification.* Cambridge, Mass: Ballinger, 1974.

Marlatt, G.A. Alcohol use and problem drinking: A cognitive-behavioral analysis.

In P.C. Kendall, & S.D. Hollon (Eds.) *Cognitive-behavioral interventions: Theory, research and procedures.* New York: Academic Press, 1979.

Meichenbaum, D.H. *Cognitive behavior modification.* Morristown, N.J.: General Learning Press, 1974.

Meichenbaum, D.H. Cognitive factors in biofeedback therapy. *Biofeedback and Self-Regulation,* 1976, **1,** 201–216.

Meichenbaum, D.H. *Cognitive-behavior modification.* New York: Plenum, 1977.

Meichenbaum, D.H., Turk, D., & Burstein, S. The nature of coping with stress. Paper presented at the NATO Conference on Dimensions of Anxiety and Stress, Oslo, 1975.

McMullin, R. & Casey, B. *Talk sense to yourself.* Lakewood, Colo.: Counseling Research Institute, 1975.

Mitchell, K.R. Behavioral treatment of presleep tension and intrusive cognitions in patients with severe predormital insomnia. *Journal of Behavioral Medicine,* 1979, **2,** 57–69.

Mitchell, K.R. & White, R.G. Self-management of severe predormital insomnia. *Journal of Behavior Therapy and Experimental Psychiatry,* 1977, **8,** 57–63. (a)

Mitchell, K.R. & White, R.G. Behavioral self-management: An application to the problem of migraine headaches. *Behavior Therapy,* 1977, **8,** 213–221. (b)

Navaco, R.W. Treatment of chronic anger through cognitive and relaxation controls. *Journal of Consulting and Clinical Psychology,* 1976, **44,** 681.

Navaco, R.W. The cognitive regulation of anger and stress. In P.C. Kendall & S.D. Hollon (Eds.) *Cognitive-behavioral interventions: Theory, research, and procedures.* New York: Academic Press, 1979.

Reeves, J.L. EMG-biofeedback reduction of tension headache: A cognitive skills-training approach. *Biofeedback and Self-Regulation,* 1976, **1,** 217–225.

Rotter, J.B. *Social learning and clinical psychology.* Englewood Cliffs, N.J.: Prentice-Hall, 1954.

Shahar, A. & Jaffe, Y. Behavior and cognitive therapy in the treatment of vaginismus: A case study. *Cognitive Therapy and Research,* 1978, **2,** 57–60.

Sobel, H.J. Coping, cognitive therapy and the cancer patient. Paper presented at the meeting of the Association for the Advancement of Behavior Therapy, Chicago, December 1878.

Stenn, P.G., Mothersill, K.J., & Brooke, R.I. Biofeedback and a cognitive behavioral approach to the treatment of myofacial pain dysfunction syndrome. *Behavior Therapy,* 1979, **10,** 29–36.

Turner, J., Heinrich, R., McCreary, C., & Dawson, E. Evaluation of two behavioral interventions for chronic low back pain. Paper presented at the meeting of the Society of Behavioral Medicine, San Francisco, December 1979.

Turk, D.C. & Genest, M. Regulation of pain: The application of cognitive and behavioral techniques for prevention and remediation. In P.C. Kendall & S.D. Hollon (Eds.) *Cognitive-behavioral Interventions: Theory, research and procedures.* New York: Academic Press, 1979.

Weisman, A.D. & Sobel, H.J. Coping with cancer through self-instruction: A hypothesis. *Journal of Human Stress,* 1979, **5,** 3–8.

Wolpe, J. *The practice of behavior therapy.* Oxford: Pergamon, 1969.

Wolpe, J. *The practice of behavior therapy,* 2nd ed. Oxford: Pergamon, 1973.

Wolpe, J. & Lazarus, A.A. *Behavior therapy techniques: A guide to the treatment of neuroses.* Oxford: Pergamon, 1966.

Zastrow, C. *Talk to yourself: Using the power of self-talk.* Englewood Cliffs, N.J.: Prentice-Hall, 1979.

CHAPTER 6

Self-Management Techniques

OVERVIEW

Self-management is particularly relevant to behavioral medicine if one considers the issue of responsibility for a person's health. The current U.S. health care system is primarily oriented toward physician assumption of responsibility for patient health during times of illness. There are, however, some exceptions such as public health immunization programs that involve physician assumption of responsibility for prevention of patient illness. Behavioral medicine seeks to broaden health care to include the client's assumption of individual responsibility for as much of the treatment of illness and maintenance of health as is possible. Self-management techniques, then, are an important means whereby an individual can modify behavior to maintain or restore health.

Life-style behaviors, such as smoking and over-eating, greatly affect health (Stachnik, 1980) and are most appropriately modified by self-management. In addition, self-management procedures have been utilized in the treatment of the following conditions, which include both physical disorders and behaviors related to physical disorders: abdominal pain (Levendusky & Pankratz, 1975); alcoholism (Miller, 1978; Miller & Munoz, 1976); anxiety (Deffenbacher & Michaels, 1979; Rathus & Nevid, 1977; Suinn & Richardson, 1977; Wenrich, Dawley, & General, 1976); assertive behavior (Dawley & Wenrich, 1976; Rehm, Fuchs, Roth, Dornblith, & Romano, 1979; Lazarus & Fay, 1975); asthma (Creer, 1979; Sirota, 1974); cancer (Hartman & Ainsworth, 1979; Weisman & Sobel, 1979); coronary-prone behavior pattern (Suinn, 1974); dysmenorrhea (Duson, 1977; Heczey, 1978); essential hypertension (Beiman, Graham, & Ciminero, 1978; Bradley & Hughes, 1979; Brady, Luborsky, & Kron, 1974; Hughes & Cunningham, 1980; Kristt & Engel, 1975); hyperactivity (Bornstein & Quevillon, 1976; Bugenthal, Collins, Collins, & Chaney, 1978; Friedling & O'Leary, 1979; Lupin, Braud, Braud, & Duer, 1976); insomnia (Alperson & Biglan, 1979; Coates & Thoresen, 1977; Hugonnet & Yates, 1979; Mitchell, 1979; Mitchell & White, 1977a; Rathus & Nevid, 1977; Weil & Goldfried, 1973); irritable bowel syndrome (Harrell & Beiman, 1978); ischemic heart pain (Hartman & Ainsworth, 1979; Roberts, Hughes, & Goldstrich, 1981); low back pain (Hartman & Ainsworth, 1979); obesity (Ferguson & Birchler, 1978; Glasgow & Rosen,

1978; Jeffrey & Katz, 1977; Rathus & Nevid, 1977; Stuart & Dairs, 1972; Yates & Hurley, 1979; Youdin & Hemmes, 1978); migraine headache (Hartman & Ainsworth, 1979; Mitchell, 1971; Mitchell & White, 1976); physical fitness (Cooper, 1970; Glasgow & Rosen, 1978; Maccoby & Farquhar, 1975; Turner, Polly, & Sherman, 1976); Raynaud's disease (Surwit, Pilon, & Fenton, 1978); relaxation (Benson, 1975; Brady, 1973; Goldfried & Trier, 1974; Reeves & Mealiea, 1975; Rosen, 1978; Wenrich, Dawley, & General, 1976); sexual dysfunction (Glasgow & Rosen, 1978; Heiman, LoPiccolo, & LoPiccolo, 1976; Rathus & Nevid, 1977; Zeiss & Zeiss, 1978); smoking (Danaher, Litchenstein, 1978; Glasgow & Rosen, 1978; Hurley & Yates, 1979; Lando, 1976; Pomerleau & Pomerleau, 1977; Rathus & Nevid, 1977); tension headache (Holroyd & Andrasik, 1978; Tasto & Hinkle, 1973); and ulcers (Aleo & Nicassio, 1978).

Skinner (1953) suggested that a person controls himself ". . . through the manipulation of variables of which behavior is a function." Goldiamond (1965) likewise agrees that self-control involves the organisms manipulating the environment in accordance with the principles of learning in order to alter one's own behavior. Thoresen and Coates (1976) offer a more cognitively oriented definition of self-control as "learnable cognitive processes used in generating controling responses, which, in turn, alter factors modifying behavior over time." These authors also distinguish between self-control with the focus on altering problematic behaviors (e.g., excessive tension, smoking) and self-regulation, which is involved in the maintenance of nonproblematic behavior.

Mahoney and Arnkoff (1979) feel that self-control behaviors are not topographically distinguishable from other behaviors. Rather, self-control is an attribution likely to be applied to human behavior in which immediate external consequences are not apparent, that do not have a high rate of occurrence, that are socially desirable and perceived to be motivated by social ideals, and that involve some degree of self-sacrifice. Finally, Cautela (1969) conceptualizes self-control in terms of a response repertoire wherein one responds in order to change the probability of a response perceived as injurious to oneself or to others.

A self-management approach offers certain advantages. First, there is the promise of reduced cost that would result if less professional time were required for a client, since a greater amount of conditioning occurs outside the therapy hour. There would be reduced cost if less formal educational preparation were required of the therapist, a trained "psychotherapist" (Ferguson & Birchler, 1978). Second, such an approach offers greater specificity of therapy procedures, thus enhancing uniformity of training and evaluation. Third, a self-management orientation sets forth the proper utilization of control that is client-centered as opposed to technique-centered (Karoly, 1977). Finally, these procedures would appear to enhance the probability of maintenance of therapy effects after contact with the therapist is ended (i.e., prevention of reconditioning of the maladaptive symptom by utilization *in vivo*) and to be particularly appropriate for the prevention of illness and the facilitation of compliance to other treatment regimens.

Self-management is based on conditioning principles and these principles may be presented as they apply to acquiring self-control without a focus on one specific problem area (Watson & Tharp, 1977). More typically the self-management literature focuses on somewhat homogenous populations of clients (i.e., smokers, clients with migraine headaches, obese clients). However similar the basic principles are and however similar the clients may appear to be, some individualization of treatment is often necessary. One approach to individualization involves the development of a basic self-management program with a constellation of subcomponent modules. The modules then may be utilized to allow for individualization (Miller, 1978; Wenrich, Dawley, & General, 1976).

Self-control can be conceptualized as varying along a continuum from its relative absence to a high level of self-regulation. Mahoney and Arnkoff (1979) consider two levels of self-control relevant to self-control techniques. First-order self-control limits the client's responsibilities to those of a technician carrying out specific procedures (i.e., data collection and intervention techniques) suggested by the therapist. Second-order self-control involves the therapist assisting the client in developing problem solving skills (i.e., problem identification, functional analysis, and generation of solutions) with the client having the responsibility of applying these skills to the presenting problems.

Additional information on self-control techniques is available (Goldfried & Merbaum, 1973; Mahoney & Thoresen, 1974; Thoresen & Mahoney, 1974; Thoresen & Coates, 1976; Karoly, 1977; and Mahoney & Arnkoff, 1978). Essentially the same behavioral principles and techniques are utilized in self-management as in other behavior therapies. The main differentiating factor is that they are applied to a larger degree by a different agent–the client as opposed to the therapist. The therapist teaches the client behavioral principles and self-management procedures and is involved otherwise only to the extent necessary to initiate the self-control program.

Self-management is most applicable to behaviors that involve a disparity between immediate and long-term consequences. Excessive eating, drinking, smoking, and emotional reactions may have immediate positive consequences but delayed negative consequences. There are, however, many behaviors that appear to persist with no obvious immediate positive reinforcement which may even be experienced as aversive (e.g., tics, nailbiting). Such behavior excesses are also appropriate targets for self-management. Although the above are singled out as appropriate for self-management, few behaviors could be definitely excluded (Bellack & Schwartz, 1976). In fact, limitations as to the application of self-management procedures may be related more to the client and the client's life situation. That is, it would generally appear to be necessary for the client to be cooperative and able to form a positive relationship with the therapist. It would also be necessary for the client's environment to be such that adequate control over potential antecedent and consequent stimuli could be exercised and the desired behavior could be practiced (Kanfer & Phillips, 1969).

Finally, it should be noted that biofeedback and relaxation essentially involve self-management of psychophysiological responses, and cognitive behavior therapy is focused on self-management of covert responses. Of course, a self-management approach may also be utilized for the overt behavioral aspects of biofeedback, relaxation, and cognitive approaches just as it may be utilized with the basic behavior therapies. The authors essentially recommend a comprehensive multi-element approach to behavioral medicine intervention wherein biofeedback, relaxation, cognitive and behavior components are integrated within a self-management framework.

SELF-MANAGEMENT PROCEDURES

Mahoney and Arnkoff (1979) identify five self-control strategies: (1) self-monitoring, (2) goal specification, (3) cueing strategies, (4)incentive modification, and (5) rehearsal. To these strategies the authors would add conceptualization training.

Conceptualization Training

Conceptualization training is concerned with teaching the client the concepts relevant to the therapy and its relation to the target symptoms. As discussed earlier, conceptualization training may be conducted in a manner similar to the procedures presented in the chapter on biofeedback training. The following are issues that should be included: individual responsibility for health care, reduced cost of treatment, specificity of procedures, enhanced maintenance of treatment effects, and focus on self-management as a continuous process involving specification of realistic goals, adequate implementation of selected means (self-management procedures), coping with problems of implementation, and assessment of goal attainment followed by a repetition of this cycle. Conceptualization training may be particularly important in self-management training since a clear understanding of basic principles of conditioning and behavior change may be helpful in facilitating generalization of the self-control skills learned in the treatment of a problem behavior to the solution of other problem behaviors.

Self-Monitoring Training

Self-monitoring was also presented in the previous chapters on biofeedback and relaxation. A system is devised to quantify the occurrence of target responses over relatively long periods of time (i.e., months, years). Additional data concerning antecedent stimuli, accompanying responses and consequent events (including those involved in intervention) are collected periodically over briefer periods of time (days, weeks). Data are also collected concerning the utilization of specific intervention procedures such as medication intake and home practice of relaxation. It is then necessary to determine where (home, work, or public places) and when (whenever the symptom occurs or during specified time intervals; during all or specific activities) self-monitoring is to occur.

Self-monitoring behaviors are learned, like any other behaviors, and thus should be shaped and reinforced, accordingly. First the client should receive a conceptual rationale as to the importance of the data to be collected. Next, sufficient instructions, materials (printed forms, written directions), apparatus (physiological and other measurement devices), and training are presented. To the extent that it is possible, simulation techniques should be utilized in the therapist's office to shape specific self-monitoring behaviors utilizing modeling and reinforced practice. If the self-monitoring task is relatively complex, it is desirable to introduce the procedures gradually as successive subcomponents. Consistent reinforcement of the client's self-monitoring behaviors is of extreme importance. Verbal reinforcement should occur at the beginning of each therapy session as soon as the self-monitoring data is presented to the therapist and again immediately after a quick perusal with appropriate feedback as to compliance with the procedures. In addition, self-monitoring data should be reliably transformed into a usable form, such as a graph and made available to therapist and client as soon as possible. Any disruption of the self-monitoring process should be accompanied by a shift of the therapeutic process focus to this issue. If necessary, specific tangible reinforcers should be utilized to insure attainment and maintenance of self-monitoring.

The accuracy of self-monitoring data is of great importance. The following are procedures that Mahoney and Arnkoff (1979) suggest to facilitate accuracy of self-monitoring: specification of target behavior, self-monitoring devices (counters, diaries), emphasis on the importance of accuracy and honesty in self-reports, demonstration of the self-monitoring strategy, supervised practice, agreement to include occasional unannounced checks on self-monitoring accuracy (laboratory tests of the presence of alcohol, nicotine or other drugs, or the ability to perform specified tasks), and use of additional outcome measures. In any event, one should not progress to the next phase of self-management training until adequate self-monitoring is achieved.

Goal Specification

Goal specification is a continuous process that should be initiated prior to the initiation of self-management procedures. It is important for goal setting to become explicit and to evolve from the level of implicit understanding or misunderstanding to the specification of realistic goals and possible means for their achievement. The cycle of specification of goals and means, adequate implementation of the means, and the assessment of goal attainment repeated as often as necessary, is the essence of self-management. Mahoney and Arnkoff (1979) suggest that goal attainment is facilitated by publicly stating goals (contracts), by stating goals in terms of behavior change (e.g., eating behavior rather than just weight loss), by specifying short range goals (rather than just distant ones), by graduated performance demands (small gradual behavior change) and by a focus on a coping model wherein one anticipates striving toward goals with some accompanying effort, difficulty, self-doubts, and distress, rather than the achievement of mastery with minimal effort, maximum self-confidence and no distress.

On the other hand, goal attainment is inhibited by dichotomous thinking and moralistic evaluations associated with perfective self-demands. In this context, one is either a saint who achieves relatively impossible goals instantly without effort or a sinner who is doomed to life-long failure with justified moralistic self-criticism and guilt. Goal specification then is an important process that should be thoroughly attended to before rushing into the self-management procedures, even though the average client is in a rush to get started. It should also be noted that self-monitoring training and goal specification are closely related and interactive.

Relevant information derived from behavioral interviews should be used to supplement the self-monitoring data (Martin & Pear, 1978). At some point during goal specification, adequate data must be accumulated and should be organized into a coherent picture, specifying each problem, when it occurs, where it occurs, and what consequences eventuate. The client and the therapist are then in a position to design a self-management program for the problem behavior specified as goals. A program generally involves a blend of stimulus control, contingency management, and repeated practice where antecedent stimuli and consequent stimuli are systematically altered over accumulating conditioning trials.

Cueing Strategies

A behavioral approach conceptualizes events in terms of the antecedents, the behavior, and the consequences of that behavior. Cueing strategies focus on antecendents to behavior. This approach to behavior change is commonly referred to as stimulus control, and involves gradual reduction and elimination of stimuli, which already have a high probability of eliciting undesirable behavior and increasing the occurrence of stimuli that are likely to elicit desirable behavior. Thus, stimulus control frequently involves instructions to restrict the place where the response can occur, the times it can occur, and what other responses are allowed to occur concomitantly. For example, the obese individual, the smoker, and the person suffering from insomnia respectively restricts eating, smoking and attempts to fall asleep to specified times and places while excluding other activities, such as watching television, reading, or worrying. Stimulus control may also involve discrimination conditioning trials wherein "new" stimuli acquire discriminative control of a response or whereby the discriminative control of "old" stimuli is extinguished. Thus, stopping for a traffic light may elicit the response of practicing relaxation exercises.

Finally, stimulus control may focus on response prevention. This may involve altering the stimulus environment at a time when controlling responses are highest. Thus, the client may avoid purchasing high caloric food or alcoholic beverages when shopping. Their availability in the home setting is then reduced, thereby altering the antecedent stimulus condition in such a manner as to decrease the probability of a maladaptive eating or drinking response.

Stimulus control procedures also focus on covert events, such as images or self-statements. Thus, a person's self-statements concerning the ability to successfully perform a self-management task (self-efficacy) may serve as a discriminative stimulus to elicit behavior in the direction of these expectations of performance. Accordingly, self-management procedures may focus on the stimulus control of self-statements as well as overt stimuli. The chapter of cognitive strategies considers procedures relevant to this issue.

It is important to determine when stimulus control procedures are indicated. This approach is most appropriate when the objective is to alter the frequency of a response rather than eliminate it, when the target response is under the control of inappropriate discriminative stimuli, and when appropriate discriminative stimuli currently fail to control the response (Bellack & Schwartz, 1976). Excessive alcohol intake exemplifies a problem for which the objective is frequently to alter response frequency. In this instance, stimulus control procedures are utilized to decrease the range of stimuli during which drinking is permitted. Sexual deviations and chronic back pain tend to involve behaviors under the control of inappropriate discriminative stimuli and thus suggest utilization of discrimination conditioning. Finally, insomnia and chronic constipation are examples of appropriate stimuli failing to control desired responses, which indicates that control procedures may be the treatment of choice.

Incentive Modification

Incentive modification in self-management involves contingency management through self-reinforcement and self-punishment. Thus, the client participates in the selection and/or presentation of the reinforcing contingencies. Mahoney and Arnkoff (1979) suggest that the effectiveness of self-reward is well established whereas the efficiency of self-punishment is still in question. Self-reinforcement involves the manipulation of both external reinforcers (money, interpersonal attention, coffee, coke, and candy) and covert reinforcers (self-statements and imagery). A large portion of the behavioral change literature has been concerned with the effects of therapist-directed contingency management, and a variety of procedures are available for utilization in an analogous manner for self-reinforcement.

The basic step in incentive modification is to identify potentially reinforcing events. Such a determination must be individualized and is initially based on the client's self-report during an interview concerned with his preferences as to reinforcers available in his life environment. Standardized questionnaires such as The Reinforcement Survey (Cautela & Kastenbaum, 1967) and The Pleasant Events Schedule (Lewinsohn, Munoz, Youngren, & Zeiss, 1978) may be used to supplement interviewing. Given that the client has identified and provided for the availability of reinforcing events, it is possible for appropriate self-reinforcing responses to occur. That is, the client learns to self-reinforce his self-monitored responses when they meet an explicitly stated criterion for reinforcement. Self-reinforcement of responses should not be assumed; rather, they should be self-monitored and shaped if they do not occur as a function of instructions. For example, problems arise when the client utilizes too stringent or too liberal a criterion for reinforcement. In fact, it is not uncommon to find that a client finds self-reinforcement to be childish and laborious. Additional conceptualization training is indicated in such cases before proceeding with more extensive shaping procedures.

The removal of reinforcers currently maintaining maladaptive behavior is equally as important as the programing of reinforcers to shape and maintain desirable new behaviors. Furthermore, maladaptive behaviors may persist in the absence of identifiable reinforcers. Such behaviors are frequently based on an avoidance paradigm and, in effect, are reinforced by anxiety reduction. Thus a client in chronic pain may persist in various pain behaviors despite such behaviors no longer resulting in inappropriate attention from a spouse. It may be that the pain behaviors allow the client to avoid attending social functions which elicit conditioned anxiety responses. Shaping procedures including self-directed systematic desensitization (Wenrich, Dawley, & General, 1976), self-directed assertive training (Dawley & Wenrich, 1976; Rehm, Fuchs, Roth, Kornblith, & Romano, 1979) and self-reinforcement for attending social functions may then result in extinction of the pain behaviors.

It may be necessary to incorporate externally controlled incentives into a self-management program. This may be accomplished by establishing behavioral contracts with significant persons in the client's environment. DeRisi and Butz (1975) present procedures for behavioral contracting. Essentially, a contract includes a clear statement of what client behaviors will be reinforced by specified others. Additionally, a contract includes details, such as a method for data collection, specification of the reinforcers to be employed, and scheduled times for review of the contract.

Rehearsal

Rehearsal focuses on the systematic practice of behaviors germane to self-management objectives. Rehearsal may be overt and involve a simulated or *in vivo* situation. Covert rehearsal that involves practicing via imagery may also be utilized (Mahoney & Arnkoff, 1979). Typically the levels of difficulty of rehearsal relative to the client's current functioning is graded to facilitate the emergence of new behaviors. The primary function of rehearsal is concerned with the shaping and strenghtening of desired responses. Thus, initially, the procedure serves an anticipatory function in preparation for *in vivo* utilization of the acquired behavior. Later, the focus shifts to the refinement of the skills in the target situation. A final phase involves repeated practice aimed toward over-learning in order to facilitate the establishment of the behaviors in the client's daily response repertoire.

In vivo rehearsal is the most important component of self-management training. Consequently all other aspects of training are designed to bring about the home practice objective, which is of central importance in self-control. Transfer of training is assured if this objective is attained. It is then of primary importance to develop a means of assessing *in vivo* rehearsal. It is desirable to employ multiple assessment methods, and systematic self-monitoring is almost always utilized. Behavioral observation by other persons in the client's environment is very useful, whenever possible. Generally this procedure is carried out by other persons, such as family members living with the client. It may be useful to have the observation occur relatively infrequently but with the client unaware as to exactly when it will occur. The idea is to increase the reliability of the client's self-monitoring by this and similar practices. Indirect observation may be utilized in many situations. For example, if the practice involves verbal behavior, the client may tape record all practices.

Of course, changes in target symptoms may be used as an indirect index of rehearsal, keeping in mind that a perfect correlation is not expected. Thus, if a hypertensive client's blood pressure readings taken in the therapist's office are consistently lower during the transfer training period of treatment, then the client's reports of home practice of relaxation are more credible. In some cases assessment in the therapist's office may serve as an index of home practice. Thus, if a client is practicing a prepared self-statement script several times a day he should be able to rapidly reproduce the script from memory during a therapy session. Likewise, if home practice involves practicing relaxation three times a day the client should be able to effect a significant reduction in his EMG level during self-directed relaxation in the therapist's office. It would also be expected that a client would show improvement on a cardiovascular stress test if he had been doing his home practice in physical exercise reliably.

Given that indices of *in vivo* rehearsal have been developed for the client, it is then possible to gradually formulate a training approach that would maximize attainment of home practice. Shelton and Levy (1979) have developed a procedure that would appear to be optimal for achieving the home practice objective. They utilize systematic behavioral assignments to enhance patient-management outside therapeutic activities. *In vivo* practice is then the primary focus of therapy and not an afterthought to be added to therapy if it appears to be necessary. Every therapy session is focused on preparing the client for the next behavioral assignment and involves joint therapist and client planning of assignments to be practiced outside the therapy hours.

A behavioral assignment typically involves a statement of what is to be done, what quantity is expected, what is to be recorded, what is to occur contingent upon the behaviors, and what is to be brought to the next therapy session. The assignment is specific and is written on no-carbon-required paper during the session as it is formulated and both therapist and client keep a copy. The therapist directly assesses whether the client has the skills necessary for carrying out each assignment. If the client does not have the skills, the therapist explains the importance of the necessary behaviors, models the behaviors, has the client covertly rehearse the behaviors, and then overtly rehearse them. The therapist provides feedback about the client's performance and coaches him while the client practices in the therapist's office until the skills are acquired. The therapist may telephone the client between sessions to assess progress, offer assistance, and reinforce practice. The client is generally instructed to complete each behavioral assignment before arranging for the next appointment.

The therapist's task is to assist the client in his efforts to learn the self-control techniques while shaping the client to assume more and more responsibility for carrying out the procedures. Although it is assumed that the optimal level of responsibility varies from client to client, the therapist objective is to maximize the client's self-control.

SUMMARY

Self-management is particularly relevant to behavioral medicine, which is oriented toward the client's assumption of responsibility for as much of the treatment of illness and maintenance of health as is possible. Self-management is part and parcel of all the therapy techniques presented in this book. Thus, biofeedback and relaxation involve self-management of physiological responses, and cognitive therapy is focused on the self-management of covert responses. A comprehensive multi-element approach wherein biofeedback, relaxation, cognitive and behavior components are integrated within a self-management framework, is advocated. Self-management techniques are concerned with training clients to manipulate the environment in accordance with the principles of learning in order to alter their own behavior. Self-control behaviors are not topographically distinguishable from other behaviors; rather self-control is an attribution most often applied to behavior for which immediate external consequences are not apparent, to behavior that does not have a high recent rate of occurrence, and to behavior that is socially desirable and that involves some degree of self-sacrifice.

A self-management approach offers advantages in reduced cost of therapy as less professional time may be required for problem behaviors associated with a disparity between immediate and long-term consequences. A self-management approach enhances the maintenance of therapy effects after contact with the therapist is ended, and establishes behavior designed to prevent illness. The degree of self-management employed may vary so that clients' responsibilities are increased to the maximum commensurate with their abilities and life situations. The first phase of self-management is conceptualization training, which includes presentation of the basic principles of conditioning and behavior change. During self-monitoring training, data is collected on the occurrence of target responses and their antecedent stimuli, accompanying responses and consequent events. Data concerning compliance with specific intervention procedures are also collected. Since self-monitoring behaviors are learned like any other behavior, they are thus shaped and reinforced accordingly.

Goal specification is a continuous process that is closely related to and interactive with self-monitoring. Goal attainment is facilitated by publicly stating goals, by stating goals in terms of measurable behavioral change, by specifying short-range intermediate goals, by graduated performance demands, and by striving toward goals with some accompanying effort, difficulty, self-doubt, and distress. It is necessary to continuously repeat a cycle of specification of goals and means, adequate implementation of means, and assessment of goal attainment. A self-management program generally involves a blend of stimulus control, contingency management, and repeated practice wherein antecedent and consequent stimuli are systematically altered over accumulating conditioning trials. Cueing strategies focus on the gradual elimination of both covert and overt stimuli, which currently have a high probability of eliciting undesirable behavior and increase the occurrence of stimuli that are likely to occasion desirable behavior. These stimulus control procedures are most appropriate when the objective is to alter the frequency of a response rather than eliminate it, and when the response is under the control of inappropriate discriminative stimuli.

Incentive modification involves contingency management through self-reinforcement and self-punishment, and includes behavioral contracting to provide for externally controlled incentives. The basic procedure is to identify reinforcing events and utilize them to self-reinforce one's self-monitored responses that meet an explicitly stated criterion for reinforcement. In addition, it is important to remove reinforcers currently maintaining maladaptive behavior. Rehearsal is the final training phase and focuses on systematic practice of behaviors germane to self-management objectives. Rehearsal typically involves overt and covert practice under simulated and *in vivo* conditions with shaping and fading to bring about the primary objective of successful practice and performance in the client's life environment. The major objective of the therapist is to assist the client in learning self-control skills while shaping the client to assume increasing responsibility for carrying out the procedures.

REFERENCES

Aleo, S. & Nicassio, P. Auto-regulation of duodenal ulcer disease: A preliminary report of four cases. *Biofeedback and Self-Regulation,* 1978, **3,** 229.

Alperson, J. & Biglan, A. Self-administered treatment of sleep onset insomnia and the importance of age. *Behavior Therapy,* 1979, **10,** 347–356.

Beiman, I., Graham, L.E., & Ciminero, A.R. Setting generality of blood pressure reductions and the psychological treatment of reactive hypertension. *Journal of Behavioral Medicine,* 1978, **1,** 445–453.

Bellack, A.S. & Schwartz, J.S. Assessment for self-control programs. In M. Hersen & A.S. Bellack (Eds.) *Behavioral assessment: A practical handbook.* New York: Pergamon Press, 1976.

Benson, H. *The relaxation response.* New York: William Morrow, 1975.

Bornstein, P.H. & Quevillon, R.P. The effects of a self-instructional package on overactive preschool boys. *Journal of Applied Behavior Analysis,* 1976, **9,** 179–188.

Bradley, R.W. & Hughes, H. Blood pressure biofeedback and relaxation training: The effects of home practice on reduction of blood pressure in persons with essential hypertension. Unpublished manuscript, 1979.

Brady, J.P. Metronome-conditioned relaxation: A new behavioral procedure. *British Journal of Psychiatry,* 1973, **122,** 729–730.

Brady, J.P., Luborsky, L., & Kron, R.E. Blood pressure reduction in patients with essential hypertension through metronome-conditioned relaxation: A preliminary report. *Behavior Therapy,* 1974, **5,** 203–209.

Bugenthal, D.B., Collings, S., Collins, L., & Chaney, L.A. Attributional and behavioral changes following two behavior management interventions with hyperactive boys: A follow-up study. *Child Development,* 1978, **49,** 247–250.

Cautela, J.R. Behavior therapy and self-control: Techniques and implications. In C.M. Franks (Ed.) *Behavior therapy: Appraisal and status.* New York: McGraw-Hill, 1969.

Cautela, J.R. & Kastenbaum, R.A. A reinforcement survey schedule for use in therapy, training, and research. *Psychological Reports,* 1967, **20,** 1115–1130.

Coates, T.J. & Thoresen, C.E. *How to sleep better: A drug-free program for overcoming insomnia.* Englewood Cliffs, N.J.: Prentice-Hall, 1977.

Cooper, K.H. *The new aerobics.* New York: Evans, 1970.

Creer, T.L. *Asthma therapy.* New York: Springer, 1979.

Danaher, B.G. & Litchenstein, E. *Become an ex-smoker.* Englewood Cliffs, N.J.: Prentice-Hall, 1978.

Dawley, H.H., Jr. & Wenrich, W.W. *Achieving assertive behavior: A guide to assertive training*. Monterey, Calif.: Brooks/Cole, 1976.

Deffenbacher, J.L. & Michaels, A.C. Two self-control procedures in the reduction of targeted and nontargeted anxieties—A year later. Paper presented at the meeting of the Association for Advancement of Behavior Therapy. San Francisco, December 1979.

De Rici, W.J. & Butz, G. Writing behavioral contracts: A case stimulation practice manual. Champaign, Ill.: 1975.

Duson, B.M. Effectiveness of relaxation-desensitization and cognitive restructuring in teaching the self-management of menstrual symptoms to college women. Dissertation Abstracts International, 1977, **37**, 6322B.

Ferguson, J.M. & Birchler, G.R. Therapeutic packages: Tools for change. In W.S. Agras (Ed.) *Behavior modification*. Boston: Little, Brown, 1978.

Friedling, C. & O'Leary, S.G. Effects of self-instructional training on second- and third-grade hyperactive children: A failure to replicate. *Journal of Applied Behavior Analysis,* 1979, **12**, 211–219.

Glasgow, R.E. & Rosen, G.M. Behavioral bibliotherapy: A review of self-help behavior therapy manuals. *Psychological Bulletin,* 1978, **85**, 1–23.

Goldfried, M.R. & Merbaum, M. (Eds.) *Behavior change through self-control*. New York: Holt, Rinehart, & Winston, 1973.

Goldfried, M.R. & Trier, C. Effectiveness of relaxation as an active coping skill. *Journal of Abnormal Psychology,* 1974, **83**, 348–355.

Goldiamond, I. Self-control procedures in personal behavior problems. *Psychological Reports,* 1965, **17**, 851–868.

Harrell, T.H. & Beiman, I. Cognitive-behavioral treatment of the irritable colon syndrome. *Cognitive Therapy and Research,* 1978, **2**, 371–375.

Hartman, L.M. & Ainsworth, K.D. The self-regulation of chronic pain: Preliminary empirical findings. Paper presented at the Association for Advancement of Behavior Therapy, San Francisco, December, 1979.

Heczey, M.D. *Woman to woman: On the menstrual experience*. Houston: Woman to Woman Books, 1978.

Heiman, J., LoPiccolo, L., & LoPiccolo, J. *Becoming orgasmic: A sexual growth program for women*. Englewood Cliffs, N.J.: Prentice-Hall, 1976.

Holroyd, K.A. & Andrasik, F. Coping and the self-control of chronic tension headache. *Journal of Consulting and Clinical Psychology,* 1978, **46**, 1036–1045.

Hughes, H. & Cunningham, D.P. Behavioral treatment of essential hypertension: Effect of multielement and cognitive behavior self-regulation therapies. Unpublished manuscript, 1980.

Hugonnet, M.H. & Yates, B.T. Mitigating insomnia with self-management bibliotherapy. In B.T. Yates, L.K. Hurley, & M.H. Hugonnet. Toward more cost-effective delivery systems in behavioral medicine: Self-management institute's obesity, insomnia and smoking divisions. Paper presented at the meeting of the Association for the Advancement of Behavior Therapy, San Francisco, December 1979.

Hurley, L.K. & Yates, B.T. Quitting smoking with plans to maintain abstinence. In B.T. Yates, L.K. Hurley, & M.H. Hugonnet, Toward more cost-effective delivery systems in behavioral medicine: Self-Management Institute's obesity, insomnia, and smoking divisions. Paper presented at the meeting of the Association for Advancement of Behavior Therapy, San Francisco, December 1979.

Jeffrey, D.B. & Katz, R.C. *Take it off and keep it off: A behavioral program for weight loss and healthy living.* Englewood Cliffs, N.J.: Prentice-Hall, 1977.

Kanfer, F.H. & Phillips, J.S. A survey of current behavior therapies and a proposal for classification. In C.M. Franks (Ed.) *Behavior therapy: Appraisal and status.* New York: McGraw-Hill, 1969.

Karoly, P. Behavioral self-management in children: Concepts, methods, issues and directions. In M. Hersen, R.M. Eisler, & P.M. Miller, (Eds.) *Progress in behavior modification,* Vol. 5. New York: Academic Press, 1977.

Kristt, D.A. & Engel, B.T. Learning control of blood pressure in patients with high blood pressure. *Circulation,* 1975, **51,** 370–378.

Lando, H.A. Manual for a broad-spectrum behavioral approach to cigarette smoking. *Catalog of Selected Documents in Psychology,* 1976, **6,** 113.

Lazarus, A. & Fay, A. *I can if I want to.* New York: Warner Books, 1975.

Levendusky, P. & Pankratz, L. Self-control techniques as an alternative to pain medication. *Journal of Abnormal Psychology,* 1975, **84,** 165–168.

Lewinsohn, P.M., Munoz, R.F., Youngren, M.A., & Zeiss, A.M. *Control your depression.* Englewood Cliffs, N.J.: Prentice-Hall, 1978.

Lupin, M., Braud, L.W., Braud, W., & Duer, W.F. Children, parents and relaxation tapes. *Academic Therapy,* 1976, **12,** 105–112.

Maccoby, N. & Farquhar, J.W. Communication for health: Unselling heart disease. *Journal of Communication,* 1975, **25,** 114–126.

Mahoney, M.J. & Arnkoff, D.B. Cognitive and self-control therapies. In S.L. Garfield & A.E. Bergin (Eds.) *Handbook of psychotherapy and behavior change.* New York: Wiley, 1978.

Mahoney, M.J. & Arnkoff, D.B. Self-management. In O.F. Pomerleau & J.P. Brady (Eds.) *Behavioral medicine: Theory and practice.* Baltimore: Williams & Wilkins, 1979.

Mahoney, M.J. & Thoresen, C.E. *Self-control: Power to the person.* Monterey, Calif.: Brooks/Cole, 1974.

Martin, G. & Pear, J. *Behavior modification: What it is and how to do it.* Englewood Cliffs, N.J.: Prentice-Hall, 1978.

Miller, W.R. Effectiveness of nonprescription therapies for problem drinkers. Paper presented at the meeting of the American Psychological Association, Toronto, August 1978.

Miller, W.R. & Munoz, R.F. *How to control your drinking.* Englewood Cliffs, N.J.: Prentice-Hall, 1976.

Mitchell, K.R. A psychological approach to the treatment of migraine with behavior therapy techniques. *British Journal of Psychiatry,* 1971, **119,** 533–534.

Mitchell, K.R. Behavioral treatment of presleep tension and intrusive cognitions in patients with severe predormital insomnia. *Journal of Behavioral Medicine,* 1979, **2,** 57–69.

Mitchell, K.R. & White, R.G. Behavioral self-management: An application to the problem of migraine headaches. *Behavior Therapy,* 1977, **8,** 213–221.

Mitchell, K.R. & White, R.G. Self-management of severe predormital insomnia. *Journal of Behavior Therapy and Experimental Psychiatry,* 1977, **8,** 57–63. (a)

Pomerleau, O.F. & Pomerleau, C.S. *Break the smoking habit: A behavioral program for giving up cigarettes.* Champaign, Ill.: Research Press, 1977.

Rathus, S.A. & Nevid, J.S. *Behavior therapy: Strategies for solving problems in living.* New York: Signet, 1977.

Reeves, J.L. & Mealiea, W.L. Biofeedback-assisted cue-controlled relaxation for the treatment of flight phobias. *Journal of Behavior Therapy and Experimental Psychiatry,* 1975, **6,** 105–109.

Rehm, L.P., Fuchs, C.Z., Roth, D.M., Dornblith, S.J., & Romano, J.M. A comparison of self-control and assertion skills treatments of depression. *Behavior Therapy,* 1979, **10,** 429–442.

Roberts, D., Hughes, H., & Goldstrich, J.D. Effect of autogenic relaxation training on angina pectoris: An N-1 design with a placebo control condition. Unpublished manuscript, 1980.

Rosen, G.R. *The relaxation book.* Englewood Cliffs, N.J.: Prentice-Hall, 1978.

Shelton, J.L. & Levy, R.L. Using systematic behavioral assignments in behavioral medicine regimens. Paper presented at the meeting of the Society of Behavioral Medicine, San Francisco, 1979.

Sirota, A.D. & Mahoney, M.J. Relaxing on cue: The self-regulation of asthma. *Journal of Behavior Therapy and Experimental Psychiatry,* 1974, **5,** 65–66.

Skinner, B.F. *Science and human behavior* New York: Macmillian, 1953.

Stachnik, T.J. Priorities for psychology in medical education and health care delivery. *American Psychologist,* 1980, **35,** 8–15.

Suinn, R.M. & Richardson, F. Anxiety management training: A nonspecific behavior therapy program for anxiety control. *Behavior Therapy,* 1977, **2,** 498–510.

Suinn, R.M. Behavior therapy for cardiac patients. *Behavior Therapy,* 1974, **5,** 569–571.

Surwit, R., Pilon, R., & Fenton, C. Behavioral treatment of Raynaud's disease. *Journal of Behavioral Medicine,* 1978, **1,** 323–335.

Tasto, D. & Hinkle, J.E. Muscle relaxation treatment for tension headaches. *Behavior Research and Therapy,* 1973, **11,** 347–349.

Thoresen, C.E. & Coates, T.J. Behavioral self-control: Some clinical concerns. In M. Hersen, R.M. Eisler, & P.M. Miller (Eds.) *Progress in behavior modification,* Vol. 2. New York: Academic Press, 1976.

Thoresen, C.E. & Mahoney, M.J. *Behavioral self-control.* New York: Holt, 1974.

Turner, R.D., Polly, S., & Sherman, A.R. A behavioral approach to individualized exercise programming. In J.D. Krumbotz & C.E. Thoresen (Eds.) *Counseling methods.* New York: Holt, Rinehart & Winston, 1976.

Watson, D.L. & Tharp, R.G. *Self-directed behavior. Self-modification for personal adjustment.* Monterey, Calif.: Brooks/Cole, 1977.

Weil, G. & Goldfried, M.R. Treatment of insomnia in an eleven-year old child through self-relaxation. *Behavior Therapy,* 1973, **4,** 282–294.

Weisman, A.D. & Sobel, H.J. Coping with cancer through self-instruction: A hypothesis. *Journal of Human Stress,* 1979, **5,** 3–8.

Wenrich, W., Dawley, H., & General, D. *Self-directed systematic desensitization.* Kalamazoo, Mich.: Behaviordelia, 1976.

Yates, B.T. & Hurley, L.K. Effectiveness and cost-effectiveness of cognitive, diet, and exercise bibliotherapies for obesity reduction. In B.T. Yates, L.K. Hurley, & M.H. Hugonnet (Eds.) Toward more cost-effective delivery systems in behavioral medicine: Self-Management Institute's obesity, insomnia, and smoking divisions. Paper presented at the meeting of the Association for Advancement of Behavior Therapy, San Francisco, December, 1979.

Youdin, R. & Hemmes, N.S. The urge to overeat—The initial link. *Behavior Therapy and Experimental Psychiatry,* 1978, **9,** 227–233.

Zeiss, R.A. & Zeiss, A. *Prolong your pleasure.* New York: Pocket Books, 1978.

PART TWO
Direct Applications

CHAPTER 7

Cardiovascular Disorders

OVERVIEW

Cardiovascular disease is the leading cause of death in this country, and since this fact has been widely publicized, cardiovascular disorders are disabling both intrinsically and by implication. The fear associated with heart disease is so widespread that it has been jingoistically labeled the "Number One Killer" in the United States.

In reviewing the apocrypha of cardiology, the nonorthodox literature on heart disease, a number of references are made to the important role which psychosocial or behavioral factors play in the emergence of cardiovascular disorders. Even as long ago as 130 A.D. Galen made reference to these interactions. In 1842, Tuke reviewed what was then known about psychosomatic links in cardiac disorders, and the neural mechanisms which might mediate those effects. White (1951) reviewed the cyclic trends in cardiology in relation to psychosomatic processes, but there is considerable evidence that contemporary cardiologists have been indifferent to the important role that psychological factors play in heart disease. For example, three of the major American textbooks on cardiology virtually ignore psychosocial or behavioral variables (Engel, 1977).

Almost everything written about behavioral factors in cardiac disease has been directed at the role such variables might play in triggering aberrant reactions. It has only been within the last 20 years, and the advent of behavioral medicine techniques, that the logical corollary of these morbid effects began to be considered: that it might be possible to prevent or treat abnormal cardiac responses through behavioral methods. With the advent of basic research in cardiology with humans as well as animal subjects, it became well documented that physiological responses under the control of the autonomic nervous system could be brought under voluntary control by the use of relaxation, biofeedback, and reinforcement.

Cardiovascular disorders for which behavioral treatment techniques have been most effective are divided into three categories: hypertension, cardiac arrhythmias, and Raynaud's disease.

HYPERTENSION

One of the most common diseases affecting the cardiovascular system and a major health problem is hypertension or high blood pressure. Hypertension is a pathological condition characterized by sustained elevation of diastolic and usually systolic blood pressure in the absence of demonstrable disease of the heart or blood vessels (Moriyama, Krueger, & Stamler, 1971).

Nationwide, it is a major cause of sickness, disability, and death among adults, afflicting an estimated 20 to 35 million persons (National Center of Health Statistics, 1975), and resulting in enormous human and economic costs. In 1966, 65,000 deaths were recorded as caused by hypertensive disease (Moriyama *et al.*, 1971) but this figure is probably a gross underestimate (Stamler, Schoenberger, Shekelle, & Stamler, 1974). Mortality statistics probably reflect only about 25% of the deaths in which hypertensive disease was a factor (Moriyama *et al.*, 1971). It is ranked as the most significant risk factor in the development of atherosclerotic diseases, kidney failure, congestive heart failure, coronary heart disease, heart attack, and stroke (Galton, 1973).

In addition to the cost in human lives, it is estimated that economic costs to the nation as a result of sickness, disability, and death were over 2.6 billion dollars in 1967 (National Heart and Lung Institute Task Force on Arteriosclerosis, 1972). The figure for the same period could be over nine billion dollars, if the contribution of hypertension to economic losses from heart attacks and strokes were included.

Since blood pressure occurs along a continuum with no clear line dividing normal pressure from elevated pressure, there is a lack of consensus on the point at which blood pressure becomes "high" (Pickering, 1968). Any dividing line between elevated and normal blood pressure is somewhat arbitrary. Although actuarial data indicate that longevity in adults is progressively reduced the more blood pressure exceeds 100 millimeters of mercury (mm Hg) systolic and/or 60 mm Hg diastolic (Engelman & Braunwold, 1977), the diagnosis of hypertension is usually given to people whose blood pressure is 160/95 mm Hg or above.

Persons having blood pressure of 140–159/90–94 mm Hg are usually labeled as having "borderline" hypertension (Smith, 1977a). "Mild" hypertension is a term sometimes used for the diastolic blood pressure range of 95–104 mm Hg. "Malignant" or "accelerating" hypertension is diagnosed if diastolic pressure is increasing rapidly in excess of 120–130 mm Hg. This constitutes a medical emergency, and such patients should be hospitalized (Agras & Jacob, 1979).

It is important to note that these values must be considered as general rules. What is considered normal blood pressure may vary with age, sex, and environmental factors (Pickering, 1968). A quantitative relationship has been shown to exist between blood pressure and risk of disability and death even in the normal range (Lew, 1967; Intersociety Commission for Heart Diesease Resources, 1970).

The existence of hypertensive disease can easily be recognized by means of indirect measurement with a sphygmomanometer, but determination of appropriate treatment requires that it be classified according to etiology. Hypertension is usually divided by etiology into two categories: primary or essential hypertension, in which the cause is unknown, and secondary hypertension, which results from an identifiable cause.

Secondary hypertension can be a result of any of the following disorders: renal disease; malfunction of certain endocrine organs, such as the adrenals or parathyroid glands; coarctation of the aorta, which is a constriction of the aortic arch; pregnancy; or oral contraceptive medication. While secondary hypertension may be treated through surgery or chemotherapy treatment, together they account for only a small percentage of the persons having hypertension (Agras & Jacob, 1979).

In the majority of cases of hypertensive disease, about 80% of the cases, no such cause can be found, and the diagnosis, by exclusion, is essential hypertension (Bech & Hilden, 1975). People with essential hypertension who display elevations of their blood pressure only temporarily are sometimes called "labile" hypertensives. Such lability often represents the beginning stages of the disorder (Agras & Jacob, 1979).

A substantial amount of research has failed to discover the cause(s) of essential hypertension, but there are presently three different theories pertaining to its etiology: genetic, hormonal, and central nervous system disorders. It is beyond the scope of this book to attempt to evaluate these theories, but it should be noted that the treatment of any disorder is not necessarily dictated by its etiology. Also, in addition to the lack of knowledge pertaining to the cause of essential hypertension, the presence of certain factors may increase the risk of its occurrence.

The development of hypertension seems to be related to a family history of hypertension. Children of hypertensive parents develop elevated blood pressure two to six times more often than those of normotensives, and the risk is greater when both parents have a history of hypertensive disease (Stamler, Stamler, & Pullman, 1967).

The results of a number of studies have pointed to a relationship between obesity and the risk of developing hypertension, with the risk of developing hypertension being two to three times greater (Chiang, Perlman, & Epstein, 1969; Kannel, Brand, Skinner, Dawber, & McNamara, 1967; Levy et al., 1945; and Stamler, 1967). There are also indications that hypertensive smokers are more likely than nonhypertensive smokers to develop premature vascular disease (Stamler, 1968). The findings of research on the role of serum cholesterol in hypertensive disease parallel those for smoking (Stamler, 1967; Stamler et al., 1967).

It has long been known that emotional stimuli have an elevating effect on blood pressure (Pickering, 1968; Wolf & Goodell, 1968). The cardiovascular response to stress is characterized by an increase in heart rate and vascular output, a widespread constriction of arterial vessels, and a subsequent increase in blood pressure. Prolonged periods of stressful events may eventually lead to an "upward resetting" of the pressure regulatory mechanisms, and the pressure remains permanently elevated (Wallace & Benson, 1972). While such research points to differences between hypertensives and nonhypertensives in their response to emotionally arousing events, it does not demonstrate the primacy of psychological factors in the etiology of hypertension, and must be considered only suggestive (Weiner, 1970).

In addition, data on morbidity and mortality demonstrate that the risk of developing hypertensive disease increases with age, at least through age 60–65 (Moriyama et al., 1971; Stamler, Stamler, Riedlinger, Algera, & Roberts, 1967). Also, the prevalence of hypertension in blacks is approximately twice as high as it is in the white population for any given age (Finnerty, Shaw, & Himmelsbach, 1973). Therefore, not only is the cause of essential hypertension still only speculative, a variety of other factors play a role, presently also unclear, in the development and prognosis of the disease.

At present, no specific treatment exists for essential hypertension, but recent collaborative studies have shown that pharmacotherapy leads to a significant reduction of certain complications of hypertension (Veterans Administration Cooperative Study Group on Antihypertensive Agents, 1967, 1970, 1972). These studies showed that the higher the pretreatment pressure, the larger the benefits from medication. However, patients with mild hypertension, unless they were over 50 years of age or already had cardiovascular or renal abnormalities, derived relatively little benefits from medication. This lower payoff for drug therapy for mild hypertension was confirmed in a recently completed 10-year controlled intervention study (Smith, 1977b).

It has also been shown that other factors relate to the lack of successful treatment in cases of mild hypertension, such as lack of motivation to continue a pharmacotherapy regime (Finnerty, 1974); cost of medication (Wilber, 1967); amount of time spent on clinic visits (Finnerty, Mattei, & Finnerty, 1973); and unpleasant side effects (V.A., 1972).

Some of the more common side effects occurring with the use of "milder" antihypertensive agents include elevation of blood sugar or decreased glucose tolerance associated with benzathiadiazine diuretics, drowsiness, lethargy, depression, and increased secretion of gastric acid may accompany the use of rauwolfia preparations. Side effects of the more potent antihypertensive drugs, the sympathetic blocking agents, include orthostatic hypotension, dizziness, reduced cardiac reserve, and disturbance of male sexual function (Herting & Hunter, 1967). It was partly the risk associated with these drugs that resulted in their initial restriction to treating only severe and malignant cases of hypertension (Stamler et al., 1974).

From the data reviewed, it can be seen that hypertensive disease is a large-scale health problem in this country, with essential hypertension making up the large majority of cases. Of particular concern is its association with cardiovascular mortality, which constitutes about 50% of the total mortality. Although lowering blood pressure to a satisfactory level has been shown to decrease the incidence of complications in persons with moderate and severe hypertension, only 50% of hypertensives are detected, and only in about half of these is blood pressure adequately controlled by antihypertensive drug treatment. For borderline hypertension, the data indicates that a favorable treatment for pharmacotherapy is even less clearly established. However, the overall mortality of these patients exceeds the age-adjusted mortality of the general population by at least 100% (Julius, 1977).

Therefore, a place may exist for the development of adjunctive or alternate treatments for hypertension for those in higher ranges who do not respond well to pharmacotherapy and for those in the borderline or mildly hypertensive range. For these reasons, much research has recently been directed toward finding effective behavioral treatments for essential hypertension.

Treatment

The behavioral treatment techniques used in the treatment of hypertension are relaxation and biofeedback strategies. The relaxation strategies used are progressive muscle relaxation, transcendental meditation, yoga, and autogenic training. The biofeedback techniques used are EMG biofeedback and blood pressure biofeedback. These strategies have been studied as treatments in themselves and in various combinations.

Progressive Muscle Relaxation

Several researchers have studied the effectiveness of progressive muscle relaxation (PMR) alone in treating hypertension. The first study was performed by Jacobson (1939) who had long maintained that high blood pressure can result in part from habitual tensions in the skeletal musculature, which can be progressively relaxed with a resultant hypotensive effect. Jacobson reported the blood pressure data on 10 normal and four hypertensive subjects before and during a relaxation session. The 10 normotensive subjects reduced both SBP and DBP approximately 8 mm Hg while hypertensive subjects obtained average reductions of 13 and 11.3 mm Hg. Although this early study suffered from a number of methodological inadequacies, it was truly a pioneer study for the field of behavioral medicine.

Brady, Luborsky, and Kron (1974), studying the effect of metronome-conditioned relaxation, was one of the first controlled studies of the effect of PMR on hypertension. Although significant results were reported, information regarding generalization of treatment effects showed blood pressure increased after PMR was discontinued. While this study effectively pinpointed one component of PMR, it did not control for expectation effects.

Taylor, Farquhar, Nelson, and Agras (1977) controlled for expectancy effects in subjects undergoing medical treatment for hypertension by randomly assigning them to one of three groups: relaxation, nonspecific therapy, and medical treatment alone. Results showed significantly lower SBP and somewhat lower DPB for the relaxation group than for the other two groups, and still lower BP at 6-month follow-up. Rici & Lawrence (1979) controlled for placebo effects and employed group training with hypertensives. Reductions in DBP were shown for the relaxation group, while no change was noted in attention or placebo groups.

Meditation

Several researchers studied the effects of transcendental meditation or the relaxation response as a form of relaxation in the treatment of hypertension (Benson, Rosner, Marzetta, & Klemchuk, 1974a & 1974b: Blackwell, Haneson, Bloomfield et al., 1976; Pollack, Weber, Case, & Larogh, 1977). Significant reductions were found by Benson et al., (1974a; 1974b) but mixed to nonsignificant results were found by Blackwell et al., (1976) and Pollack et al., (1977). Pollack et al., (1977) concluded that it was unlikely that TM contributed directly to lowering blood pressure. The authors speculate that the smaller effect seen in the latter studies compared to those by Benson and coworkers had some relationship to subject selection procedures.

Stone and DeLeo (1976) used a somewhat different method called "psychological relaxation" derived from Buddhist meditation in which after relaxation, the subject counted breath cycles in arithmetic progression. The treatment group exhibited a significant decline of both SBP and DBP pre- and post-treatment as compared to no change for controls. The authors concluded that reduction of peripheral adrenergic activity was an important contributor to the effect of relaxation therapy. However, a more recent study failed to replicate these findings (Brauer, Horlick, Nelson et al., 1978).

Relaxation Combinations

While the results of using relaxation alone have been relatively positive, the results of studies using meditation have been less successful. Several studies used various combinations of relaxation strategies.

One of the first large-scale applications of relaxation therapy to the treatment of hypertension employed a yoga exercise called "Shavasan" (Datey et al., 1969) which can be conceptualized as a combination of muscular relaxation and meditation, with mental focusing on the breathing movements and their associated sensations at the nostrils. Three groups were treated: those receiving no medication; those whose blood pressure was adequately controlled by medication; and those whose blood pressure was not adequately controlled by medication. For subjects not receiving medication, the average reduction in mean arterial pressure was 27 mm Hg, the largest reduction ever reported for a group of hypertensives treated with relaxation therapy. In the second group, 13 of 22 subjects were able to decrease medication, with an average reduction of 68%. Drug dosage was also reduced in 6 of 15 subjects in the third group, with an average reduction of 33%.

Byasse (1976) compared PMR, autogenic training, and "self-relaxation." All groups practiced at home and all procedures produced significant decreases in blood pressure but a 4-month follow-up showed reductions had failed to persist. Benson (1977) showed reductions in SBP and DBP in 22 unmedicated and 14 medicated hypertensive subjects using a combination of TM and progressive relaxation, while Dowdall (1977) combined three treatment strategies consisting of PMR, deep breathing exercises, and yoga exercises. This combined procedure produced reductions in blood pressure averaging from 158/85 to 142/76.

Redmond, Gaylor, McDonald, and Shapiro (1974) combined verbal instruction with PMR showing favorable results, and Beiman, Graham, and Ciminero (1978) combined PMR with systematic desensitization showing a reduction to nonhypertensive levels maintained 100 days after treatment. Although many of these studies used no controls and did not isolate treatment components, combined relaxation procedures were shown to be effective in reducing blood pressure for some subjects.

Biofeedback Assisted Relaxation

Many studies have attempted to measure the effectiveness of relaxation combined with EMG frontalis biofeedback in treating hypertensives. Moeller and Love (1975) combined relaxation, EMG feedback, and autogenic procedures resulting in significant decreases in both SBP and DBP. Love, Montgomery, and Moeller (1975) replicated the study using a control group and follow-up. Similar results were found for the treatment group with further decreases noted at 8-month follow-up. No change was found for controls.

Fray (1975) compared EMG feedback and autogenic training in reducing blood pressure and found both to be equally effective. Follow-up showed the group receiving autogenic training showed better maintenance of blood pressure reduction.

Patel and associates attempted to devise a treatment similar to that used by Datey et al., (1969) with additional biofeedback components added, and tested its efficacy in a series of studies (Patel, 1973, 1975a, 1975b; Patel & North, 1975; Patel & Datey, 1976; Patel & Carruthers, 1977). Techniques used to train subjects in relaxation included feedback of EMG, GSR, alpha brain waves, and instruction in passive yoga techniques and meditation. Results of the first study (Patel, 1973) showed reduction of blood pressure by 26/16 mm Hg from 159/100 mm Hg before treatment. Medication was reduced by 33 to 60% in seven patients and discontinued in five patients.

Patel (1975a) attempted to control for expectation or placebo effects by adding a comparison group. Training consisted of three half hour individual sessions per week over a 3-month period with a 12 month follow-up for treatment group and 9-month follow-up for control group who merely rested on a couch during "treatment." Results showed the treatment group reduced

SBP an average of 20.4 mm Hg and DBP an average of 14.2 mm Hg, both statistically significant, while the control group showed a small but nonsignificant decrease in SBP and DBP. During the 9 months of follow-up, the blood pressure level remained essentially at "pretreatment" level for controls while the treatment group maintained its gains throughout the 12 month period. This is the longest follow-up of relaxation therapy reported in the literature. A subsample of the patients underwent a series of stress tests. Treated patients had significantly shorter recovery times from their pressor response to the exercise and cold pressor test than controls (Patel, 1975b).

The third outcome study included treatment and control groups of 17 subjects each (Patel & North, 1975). Group assignment was random and medication was kept constant throughout the study. Treatment was the same with added features of group sessions before actual practice sessions. Results for treatment groups were of similar magnitude to those in the previous studies. After 6 months, the control group was given relaxation therapy identical to that given the treatment group resulting in a significant treatment effect, comparable to that in previous treatment groups.

The findings of Patel's earlier studies were again replicated by Patel and Carruthers (1977), focusing on coronary risk factor reduction with normotensive groups as well as hypertensives. In the latter, a reduction of 18.6/11.2 mm Hg from 164.5/101.1 mm Hg was noted.

From the studies reviewed, it can be seen that training in relaxation is generally effective in producing both statistically and clinically significant decreases in the blood pressure of hypertensives. Relaxation seems to work better for some than others, and individual decreases vary widely. When individuals are successful in decreasing blood pressure, there is some evidence for generalization of effects outside training and practice sessions (Blackwell et al., 1976; Taylor et al., 1977), but the majority of studies do not address this issue. The ability of subjects to maintain reductions once achieved seems to be dependent upon continued practice since blood pressure tends to return to baseline levels if practice is stopped.

Comparing the results of various relaxation modalities, it appears that studies utilizing combination treatments displayed the largest treatment effects, but also tended to have the largest pretreatment pressures. Thus, the effect of treatment modality is confounded with the effect of pretreatment values. Firm conclusions regarding the relative values of different relaxation modalities must be deferred until the results of studies comparing treatments on a randomized basis are available.

Blood Pressure Biofeedback

In blood pressure feedback, the measuring device most often used is a sphygmomanometer with a built in microphone. When the blood pressure cuff is placed around the upper arm, the microphone located over the brachial artery picks up the beat of the pulse (Korotkoff sounds), which can be heard when the cuff is inflated to a level between systolic and diastolic pressure.

To obtain frequent measurements, the cuff must be inflated quite often, about once per minute. An alternative to this method has been developed by Shapiro and colleagues (Shapiro, Tursky, Gershon, & Stern, 1969; Tursky, Shapiro, & Schwartz, 1972) and is known as the "constant cuff pressure procedure." The cuff is inflated to a predetermined pressure and left there for a set period of time. By using a stethescope or a transducer, the presence or absence of Korotkoff sounds can easily be determined. Thus, if the cuff is set at a pressure near or slightly below the average of a person's SBP, SBP below the cuff pressure will be signaled by the presence of Korotkoff sounds while SBP above cuff level will be signaled by the absence of sounds. Hence, by manipulating the preset cuff pressure and giving the individual feedback about the presence or absence of Korotkoff sounds, attempts can be made to alter the person's blood pressure. Recently, another measure of blood pressure has been developed in the measurement of pulse-wave velocity and will be described later (Walsh, Dale, & Anderson, 1977).

Although a few investigators have used diastolic feedback, most researchers have used systolic feedback. The first report of the reduction of blood pressure in hypertensives during feedback training was an uncontrolled study by Benson, Shapiro, Tursky et al. (1971). They attempted to lower SBP in seven subjects having moderate to severe essential hypertension who were seen daily for 5 to 16 control sessions, followed by 8 to 33 treatment sessions. With a moving criterion level using feedback tone and light plus slides and reminders of money earned, it was possible to shape successively larger decreases of SBP within treatment sessions. Results showed an overall decrease in SBP by 10%, an average of 16.6 mm Hg for the group with an individual range of 0.9 to 33.8 mm Hg.

Kristt and Engel (1975) devised a Korotkoff sound disappearing technique to be used as an adjunct to regular electronic feedback of blood pressure. The 3-week in-hospital training period consisted of learning to raise, lower, and alternate raising and lowering SBP by use of the electronic biofeedback. They also learned to use a blood pressure cuff at home to perform a blood pressure lowering technique which required them to make the Korotkoff sounds (KS) disappear while keeping the cuff pressure at the level of SBP. Cuff pressure was then released until KS again appeared, marking the lowered SBP level. Pre- and post-training blood pressure level comparisons found an average reduction in SBP of 18.2 mm Hg (11.2%) and in DBP of 7.5 mm Hg (7.2%). The result of the home practice was an average decrease in SBP of 15.8 mm Hg (11.5%). These are the most clinically significant results in the blood pressure feedback area to date.

Blanchard, Young, and Haynes (1975) used a somewhat different feedback system for decreasing SBP, by providing feedback of points plotted on a graph of SBP obtained at each trial which were displayed to the subject over closed-circuit television. Results showed all subjects to be successful in decreasing SBP, with the average decline being 17.4 mm Hg from 154.1 mm Hg baseline.

An interesting measure of generalization of treatment effect was reported in a series of studies (Goldman, Kleinman, Snow et al., 1974, 1975; and Kleinman, Goldman, Snow et al., 1977). After establishing an association between diastolic hypertension and brain dysfunction as measured by errors on the category subtest of the Halstead-Reitan Neuropsychological Test Battery for Adults (Goldman et al., 1974), two studies were conducted to see if test performance would improve when the hypertension was treated with feedback to systolic pressure (Goldman et al., 1975; Kleinman et al., 1977). Both studies reported statistically significant blood pressure reductions, as well as changes in the number of errors on the category test. A significant positive correlation was found between magnitude of systolic blood pressure improvement achieved during biofeedback training and improvement on the category test.

The studies so far presented did not provide adequate controls for confounding variables such as practice or expectation effects. These variables were addressed in a series of studies (Knust & Richter-Heinrich, 1975; Richter-Heinrich, Knust, Muller et al., 1975; Richter-Heinrich, Knust, Lori et al., 1977; Richter-Heinrich, Knust, & Lori, 1977). The control group received false feedback which was identical to true feedback given to the treatment group. Knust & Richter-Heinrich (1975) reported the feedback group, all hospitalized patients in the beginning stages of hypertensive disease, decreased SBP by 16 mm Hg from 145 mm Hg after four sessions. The treatment effect did not generalize outside treatment setting, however.

Although the majority of studies used systolic rather than diastolic feedback, several have used diastolic feedback. Schwartz and Shapiro (1973) found no decline of DBP over 10 biofeedback sessions. However, when diastolic feedback was combined with social reinforcement (Elder, Ruiz, Deabler et al., 1973; Elder & Eustis, 1975) positive results were obtained. Elder, Ruiz, Diabler et al., (1973) found that of three groups, control, feedback, and feedback plus praise, the feedback plus praise group showed significantly greater decrease of DBP than the other two groups. The feedback only group showed intermediate results.

Elder & Eustis (1975) used the same procedure and also attempted to define optimal scheduling of training, comparing massed versus spaced training. The massed-practice schedule involved 10 daily sessions, and the spaced schedule involved two sessions per week for 2 weeks, followed by one session per week for 2 weeks, two biweekly sessions, and a final session after 1 month. The overall reduction for both groups was 7.8/2.4 mm Hg and within-session measures showed subjects receiving massed practice had results superior to those receiving spaced practice.

The studies reviewed tend to support the belief that changes in blood pressure can be learned through operant conditioning techniques. Although most studies employing blood pressure biofeedback for hypertension have achieved statistically significant results, not all have demonstrated clinically important results, and several issues remain unresolved.

While some follow-up data indicate that subjects are able to maintain decreases in blood pressure after training, the support for this is limited by the brevity of many of the follow-up periods, the failure to control for intervening experience, and loss of subjects to follow-up. Related to this issue is the question of the ability of subjects to generalize control of blood pressure to nonlaboratory settings. The study reported by Kleinman et al., (1977) offers evidence of generalization outside the training session, while other studies suggest that such generalization may not be the norm. Generally, the evidence indicates that maintenance and generalization of blood pressure control may require continued home practice.

Another issue raised is the cost-effectiveness of blood pressure biofeedback in reducing blood pressure. Since the studies that have provided the most clinically significant results have studied hospitalized individuals for the treatment (Kristt & Engel, 1975; and Elder et al., 1973), the cost effectiveness of these procedures can be seriously questioned. Thus, additional studies demonstrating the efficacy of out-patient biofeedback approaches are needed. Some studies report such positive side effects as decreased drug requirements (Kristt & Engel, 1975) and improved cognitive functioning (Goldman et al., 1975; and Kleinman et al., 1977), but it is likely that these effects may also be generated by some relaxation methods that are relatively more cost effective (Datey et al., 1969; Patel, 1973, 1977; Surwit & Shapiro, 1977).

The final issue raised is the relative effectiveness of blood pressure biofeedback in reducing blood pressure when compared to relaxation training. The results of such comparisons tend to be mixed, with both approaches seeming to be equally effective. The question then arises whether the two techniques in combination may be more effective than either alone.

Blood Pressure Biofeedback Plus Relaxation

Several studies have attempted to address the issues of effectiveness of various treatments in relation to each other as well as in combination with each other. Shoemaker and Tasto (1975) compared the effectiveness of PMR and noncontinuous blood pressure feedback by assigning 15 subjects to one of three groups: PMR, biofeedback, or control. Results indicated that subjects in the relaxation group showed a significantly greater decline of blood pressure than the other two groups, both over treatment sessions and within session trials. Fidal (1975) in a similarly designed study found both relaxation and biofeedback groups decreased SBP equally but the biofeedback group decreased DBP an average of 15% whereas no decrease in DBP was shown in the relaxation group.

Russ (1974) reported no significant differences between relaxation plus EMG feedback, blood pressure feedback, or false feedback, although three of the five subjects in the relaxation group showed some improvement. Blanchard and Epstein (1978) compared blood pressure biofeedback and relaxation plus EMG biofeedback showing no significant differences among the three groups. Likewise, Surwit, Shapiro, and Good (1978) compared blood pressure biofeedback, EMG biofeedback, and meditation relaxation and found no significant difference among treatment conditions and no changes in blood pressure over the course of training.

Most of these comparative studies have shown little or no difference between effectiveness of biofeedback and relaxation. In an attempt to determine the effectiveness of them in combination, Sawyer (1977) trained hypertensives to reduce blood pressure using blood pressure feedback and MCR training. Sessions were 90 minutes long and consisted of three 30-minute periods: adaptation, MCR training, and biofeedback. Pre- to post-treatment decreases in SBP ranged from 27.3 to 35.4 mm Hg with an average reduction of 31.6 mm Hg. Unfortunately, the design of this study was such that it was not possible to assess the individual contributions of the treatment components.

Friedman and Taub (1977) compared SBP and DBP with hypnotic relaxation and with biofeedback and hypnosis combined. Hypnosis alone showed significantly larger reductions in DBP compared with the biofeedback-hypnosis combination, and that adding biofeedback detracted from rather than added to the effect of hypnosis.

Walsh et al., (1977) compared the effect of PMR with feedback of pulse wave velocity. Pulse wave velocity is a less obtrusive measure of blood pressure than the cuff method and is the pulse transit time (time required for the pulse to travel from the heart to a fixed peripheral point) divided by the arterial distance between points of transit. The feedback group showed a larger within-session decrease of DBP, but across sessions the two treatments were equally effective in reducing SBP and DBP. Combining the two treatments at a later time resulted in no further reductions in blood pressure.

Bradley and Hughes (1979) compared the relaxation response, blood pressure biofeedback, and the relaxation response and biofeedback in combination in the home setting. All subjects received all three treatments in various combinations. Significant reductions in blood pressure were attained during home treatment sessions for all types of treatment. This study points to the value of home practice per se rather than the type of treatment in effecting the relative success of blood pressure reduction. The results of these studies indicate that biofeedback and relaxation are not significantly different in effectiveness and that the combination of the two does not generally increase effectiveness.

Summary

Relaxation training and biofeedback have shown some effectiveness in the treatment of essential hypertension; however, the clinical impact or applicability of self-control treatments of hypertension has yet to be demonstrated to be uniformly or persistently effective. An additional problem relating to the mixed results of most of the hypertension studies is the difficulty presented in comparing studies. Studies vary in application of treatment modalities, length of training, use of follow-up data, and in method of data presentation offered. Further, the absence of standard subject selection makes comparisons across studies dubious.

Generally, with all the confounding variables considered, the data presented thus far show that relaxation strategies in combination have shown more positive results than a specific relaxation technique used alone. It has also been shown that there is no clear advantage for using biofeedback rather than relaxation and that the combination of the two does not seem to increase reductions in blood pressure. Home practice and continued practice after treatment seem to enhance results in both relaxation and biofeedback studies.

Relaxation training appears to be a simpler procedure and offers the advantage of not necessitating costly and complicated equipment. However, it is desirable to have patients self-monitor their blood pressure daily using relatively inexpensive portable devices. Furthermore, some biofeedback approaches have successfully utilized these devices for feedback (Kristt & Engel, 1975; Bradley & Hughes, 1979). There is no clear advantage in utilizing relaxation as opposed to the home based biofeedback training.

CARDIAC ARRHYTHMIAS

Cardiac arrhythmias are a function of abnormalities within the cardiac conduction system, and several different types of clinical disorders may arise, depending on the type of abnormality present. Cardiac arrhythmias are complex because they include abnormalities in the site of impulse formation, in the spread of impulses through the conduction system, in the rate at which the heart beats, or in the rhythm with which the heart beats (Engel, 1973). Furthermore, many patients will manifest more than one kind of arrhythmia, and these arrhythmias may interact or they may be independent.

This degree of complexity precludes any simple classification scheme. In general, however, cardiac arrhythmias can be considered in terms of three broad classes: ectopic rhythms, tachyarrhythmias, and conduction defects.

Ectopic Rhythms

Ectopic rhythms are characterized by a premature heart contraction. Ectopic beats take their name from the area of the premature depolarization: premature atrial contractions (PACs); junctional beats or the atrioventricular (AV) nodal-ventricular junction; and premature ventricular contractions (PVC).

The most common of these and the one receiving the most attention from behavioral intervention techniques is premature ventricular contractions. The reason for the focus on PVCs is that they are associated with sudden death and coronary artery disease (Chiang *et al.*, 1969; Lown & Wolf, 1971), and are often not suppressed by chemotherapy (Engel & Bleecker, 1974). Premature ventricular contractions are seen as premature, periodic depolarization and contraction of the heart ventricles. A PVC would thus appear in an electrocardiogram as a very quick heart beat followed by a long compensatory pause before the next beat.

Tachyarrhythmias

Tachyarrhythmias are characterized by rapid and repetitive beating of a heart region and are classified on the basis of the area of primary focus. Tachycardias are usually classified as: supraventricular, if the dominant focus is proximal to the ventricles; junctional, if the focus is in the AV nodal-ventricular junction; or ventricular, if the focus is in the ventricle (Engel & Bleecker, 1974).

Supraventricular tachycardias include: (1) sinus tachycardia in which atrial rates range from about 100 to 140 bpm, and in which each atrial depolarization leads to a ventricular depolarization; (2) atrial tachycardia in which atrial rates range from about 140 to 220 bpm, and is associated with one-to-one atrial-ventricular depolarization; (3) atrial flutter in which atrial rates range from about 220 to 300 bpm, at which rate ventricular rate no longer follows atrial rate on a beat-to-beat basis and the atrium is no longer capable of beating effectively; and, (4) atrial fibrillation in which atrial rate is in excess of 300 bpm, and atrial contraction and conduction patterns are totally disorganized. Atrial fibrillation is the most common cardiac arrhythmia. Ventricular tachycardia is a serious arrhythmia since it is incompatible with survival (Engel & Bleecker, 1974).

Conduction Defects

Conduction defects are characterized by an impairment in the transmission of impulses within the cardiac conduction system. The impairment may manifest itself in the electrocardiogram by a temporal prolongation of the conduction time between atrial and ventricular depolarization; in other words, by a prolonged P-R interval or by evidence of bundle branch block. A detailed discussion of all possible conduction defects is beyond the scope of this book; however, several subclasses of conduction defects will be briefly described.

Brady arrhythmia is the generic term for unusually slow rates in the heart beat, caused by defective impulse formation in the sino-atrial (SA) node or by a defect in impulse conduction (Rubenstein *et al.*, 1972). The Wolff-Parkinson-White (WPW) syndrome is characterized by preexcitation of the ventricles, and it is often associated with rapid tachycardias (James, 1970). It has been postulated that there are two conduction pathways to the heart in this disease (Wolferth & Wood, 1933). The two-pathway hypothesis postulates that one pathway mediates normal conduction through the atrio-ventricular node, and the second pathway mediates aberrant impulses that are transmitted from the sinus node to the ventricles.

Heart block includes three subcategories: first degree heart block, second degree heart block further divided into Mobitz type I and Mobitz type II, and third degree heart block. Third degree heart block is characterized by complete atrioventricular dissociation. The atria beat normally, about 75 bpm, whereas the ventricles beat abnormally slow, 40 bpm or slower, depending on the site of the ventricular focus (Engel & Bleecker, 1974).

Treatment

With the advent of certain behavioral treatment methods, specifically biofeedback, it became feasible to examine the possibility of treating abnormal cardiac responses through behavioral methods. Several cardiac conditioning studies with normal subjects had shown success (Engel & Chism, 1967; Engel & Hansen, 1966; and Levene, Engel, & Pearson, 1968), and Miller and his colleagues (1969) had shown that it was possible to operantly condition heart rate in the rat. Furthermore, extensive literature showed that the nervous system could play a major role in modulating the prevalence of cardiac arrhythmias (Scherf & Schott, 1953) and that temperamental variables affected the prevalence of many arrhythmias (Stevenson, Duncan, Wolf *et al.,* 1949). These data indicated that the nervous system exercised a significant role in cardiac function, and that at least some aspects of this nervous control were associated with volitional behavior. Therefore, subsequent research has centered around attempting to bring heart rate under voluntary control by use of operantly conditioned biofeedback techniques.

Although there are important variations in procedures, depending upon such factors as specific arrhythmia being treated, the patient's current stage of training, or his tolerance for long training sessions, there are also certain consistencies. Most patients have been trained in a series of sessions, during which they were required to learn to decrease the prevalence of their arrhythmias, to increase the prevalence of their arrhythmias, to clinically alternate between increasing and decreasing arrhythmias, and finally to decrease the prevalence of the arrhythmias without feedback. In addition to laboratory training, subjects in most of the studies have been hospitalized and their EEG's were monitored while on the ward.

Ectopic Rhythms

Biofeedback treatment has been more frequently attempted with premature ventricular contractions (PVCS) than with other types of ectopic rhythms. Engel and his associates (Engel & Bleecker, 1974; Weiss & Engel, 1971) have treated nine clients for PVCs in the four types of training previously described (increasing and decreasing heart rate, alternating, and maintaining heart rate within a present range). All of the subjects displayed some degree of heart rate control during at least one of the training conditions. Six clients showed some reductions in PVC rates during sessions, and five showed reduced extrasession PVC rates. Those five subjects continued to show infrequent PVCs during follow-up evaluations from 3 to 21 months. One client, followed for five years, discontinued antiarrhythmic medication and PVCs were rare. Another client learned to recognize PVC occurrences and was able to voluntarily decrease their frequency.

Engel and Bleecker (1974) noted that the four clients who did not exhibit improvements had the most severely disabled hearts. Thus, it appears that the clinical utility of biofeedback training with PVC clients decreases with increasing severity of disease. Pickering and Gorham (1975) treated a 31-year-old female who exhibited PVCs with a variable frequency correlating with being emotionally tense and having coffee or cigarettes. Over the course of 16 1-hour sessions during a 6-week period, the threshold above which the arrhythmia occurred increased from 79.1 bpm to 94.1 bpm. When arrhythmias did occur, she was able to decrease heart rate enough to stop arrhythmias. Pickering and Miller (1977) treated two PVC patients with similar results.

Weiss and Brady (cited in Weiss, 1977) applied biofeedback treatment to control premature atrial contractions in a 20-year-old client with a five year history of sinus tachycardia and premature atrial contractions. Biofeedback training for heart slowing was compared to relaxation training by alternating treatments over 20 training sessions. Biofeedback was found to be superior to relaxation, and at a 1 year follow-up the patient reported significant reductions in both tachycardia and premature atrial contractions.

Tachyarrhythmias

Among the tachyarrhythmias, sinus tachycardia has been the most extensively studied disorder (Engel & Bleecker, 1974; Scott, Blancard, Edmundson, & Young, 1973; Scott, Peters, Gillespie, Blanchard, Edmundson, & Young, 1973). However, biofeedback studies have also been conducted with clients who exhibited other supraventricular tachycardias (Engel & Bleecker, 1974), paroxysmal atrial tachycardia (Engel & Bleecker, 1974), and atrial fibrillation (Bleecker & Engel, 1973b; Engel & Bleecker, 1974; Weiss & Brady, cited in Weiss, 1977).

Biofeedback training in all of these cases was designed to teach the clients how to control their heart or ventricle rates. Two studies made biofeedback training contingent upon some type of reinforcement (either access to television or television plus money) in lowering heart rate levels of three clients with sinus tachycardia (Scott, Blanchard, Edmundson, & Young, 1973; and Scott, Peters, Gillespie, Blanchard, Edmundson, & Young, 1973). All of the clients were successful in decreasing their heart rates from a range of 87–97 bpm before training to a range of 71–84 bpm during training. Positive side effects were also noted for all clients: they felt less tense and anxious, made fewer requests for medication, and were able to participate in activities that had previously tired them.

Only one case of biofeedback treatment of supraventricular tachycardia has been reported (Engel & Bleecker, 1974) and one case in which biofeedback training was used in treating a patient having paroxysmal atrial tachycardia and episodes of sinus tachycardia was reported (Engel & Bleecker, 1974). Positive results were found in both cases with other positive side effects in addition. Although these results lack replication, they strongly suggest biofeedback treatment for these disorders should be further explored.

Bleecker and Engel (1973) also attempted to train six clients with histories of chronic atrial fibrillation and rheumatic heart disease. They were trained in ventrical rate control and ventrical rate range training. Although the clients were able to reduce ventricular rate variability while receiving biofeedback, no reduction in day-to-day variability was shown. Similarly, Weiss and Brady (cited in Weiss, 1977) failed to achieve a decrease in arrhythmia frequency with a client exhibiting paroxysmal atrial fibrillation. Thus, these results of biofeedback training for atrial fibrillation do not appear promising.

Conduction Disorders

Only three studies currently exist that have utilized biofeedback for the treatment of conduction disorders. Two of these studies (Bleecker & Engel, 1973a; and Weiss & Brady, cited in Weiss, 1977) treated clients with Wolff-Parkinson-White (WPW) syndrome, and the third report (Engel & Bleecker, 1974), although not designed as a clinical study, treated three individuals with third-degree heart block.

In the WPW studies, Engel and Bleecker (1974) trained the client, who also had supraventricular and sinus tachycardias, first in heart rate control, and then trained her to increase and decrease the frequency of abnormally conducted beats. Mean increase in normal conduction from baseline was 13%, and during a 10-week follow-up, the client retained the ability to differentially modify cardiac conduction. Weiss and Brady (Weiss, 1977) treated a client who not only had WPW syndrome, but supraventricular tachycardia. Relaxation training was initially provided. This was followed by biofeedback training for heart rate control and finally feedback training for abnormally-conducted ventricular beats. Although exact data are not provided, episodes of arrhythmia reportedly decreased in frequency during several months follow-up evaluations.

The three clients having third-degree heart blocks treated by Engel and Bleecker (1974) were given feedback of their ventricular rates. None of the clients were able to increase ventricular rate consistently. Although the data are too sparse to reach any conclusions regarding clinical efficacy, biofeedback treatment of third-degree heart block does not appear as promising as for other cardiac arrhythmias.

Summary

Several applications of biofeedback training with cardiac arrhythmias appear promising, while results with others have been relatively unsuccessful. Positive results have appeared in the treatment of the ectopic rhythms, specifically PVCs and PACs. Of the tachyarrhythmias, the supraventricular tachy-cardias being treated with relative success are sinus tachycardia and pa-roxysmal atrial tachycardia. The results reported for treating atrial fibrillation were not as promising. Of the conduction disorders, treatment of the WPW syndrome produced positive results, while treatment of clients having third-degree heart block was relatively unsuccessful.

The area in general suffers from a lack of research. In addition, given the lack of responsiveness to chemotherapy of some of these disorders, partic-ularly PVCs, applications of biofeedback treatment need further investiga-tion. If the clinical efficacy of biofeedback treatment for arrhythmias can be adequately documented, then it may prove to be a relatively cost-effective treatment procedure for these disorders.

RAYNAUD'S DISEASE

Raynaud's disease, like hypertension, is a functional disorder of the cardi-ovascular system, involving the digital arteries in the extremities. Symptoms consist of intermittent vasospasms in the small vessels in the hands, feet, and sometimes the face and tongue which can be elicited by cold stimulation and/or emotional stress (Allen, Barker, & Hines, 1972). Attacks may last for minutes or hours, and during an attack, the affected area goes through a three-stage color change: first blanching, then turning cyanotic blue, and finally becoming bright red as the vasospasm is relieved and reactive hy-peremia ensues. The attacks result in cold, numb hands that are frequently painful.

Simply stated, Raynaud's disease involves vasoconstriction and a reduc-tion of blood flow to the periphery. This vasoconstriction results in a drop in skin temperature of the affected part or parts. Visible symptoms are directly attributed to slowing of blood flow through the digital arterioles and subsequently, local capillaries and venules. Spasm of the arterioles and possibly the venules are responsible for observed digital pallor. At this stage, blood is not entering the capillaries. When cyanosis is observed, capillaries are dilated and blood within them is stagnant. There is also evidence that venules may be similarly dilated in cyanosis and that reflux may be taking place from venules to capillaries (Spittell, 1972).

In prolonged or chronic cases, the lack of blood flow may lead to discol-oration, ulceration, scleroderma, or gangrene (Sappington, Fiorito, & Bre-hony, 1979). In the progressive or advanced stages of the disease, the phe-nomenon may be so severe and frequent that it is disabling. While severe manifestations of this condition are not common, Lewis (1949) estimated that it affects approximately 20% of most young people in its mildest forms. Clinical Raynaud's disease is found to occur five times more often in women than in men (Allen, Barker, & Hines, 1972), with the time of onset occurring in the first and second decades of life (Blain, Coller, & Carver, 1951).

The etiology of Raynaud's disease is not completely understood. While

Raynaud himself (1862) attributed the malady to sympathetic overreactivity, Lewis (1949) maintained that the fault was primarily a local fault of the blood vessels. Other researchers have suggested modifications of these early theories. Cohen, Fisher, Lipschutz, Turner, Myers, and Schumacher (1972) suggest a common neurogenic association between Raynaud's syndrome and an esophageal abnormality. Similarly, Surwit (1973) distinguished between Raynaud's disease and Raynaud's phenomenon, the latter referring to symptoms resulting from known pathology.

While the role of environmental temperature as a stimulus to vasospastic episodes is not in question, there is considerable speculation about anxiety itself as a trigger stimulus. As early as 1932, Allen and Brown noted that changes in digit color may occur without physical stress, particularly when the person is under emotional stress. Mittlemann and Wolff (1939) demonstrated that emotional stress could reduce the digital blood flow as measured by skin temperature in both normals and Raynaud's disease patients. In Raynaud's patients, however, these changes in temperature were accompanied by the blanching-cyanotic-edemic color change and pain. They reported that temperature changes themselves were not a sufficient cause for the spasm; rather, the attacks occurred most reliably when emotional stress and low environmental temperature interacted. This theory was further substantiated by Graham (1955) and Graham, Stein, and Winokur (1958).

Data presented thus far clearly indicate that affective states are intimately related to the onset and duration of Raynaud's symptoms. Furthermore, even a purely organic etiology would not rule out direct behavioral intervention as an effective treatment. Traditional medical treatment involves the use of chemical or surgical procedures. Currently these techniques have not proven to be particularly effective in relieving this disorder. Sympathectomy offers inconsistent results and has the disadvantage of permanent side effects (Ruch, Patton, Woodbury, & Towe, 1965), and even when effective may be so only for a few months (Allen & Brown, 1932). Similarly, when vasodilators are effective, they, too, may result in side effects including low blood pressure, sinus difficulty, and subjective feelings of tiredness. Behavioral treatment strategies appear to be a useful addition to the therapies available without the unsatisfactory side effects produced by the traditional treatments.

Treatment

The behavioral treatment techniques that have been successfully used in the treatment of Raynaud's disease have centered around the patient learning voluntary control of the vasculature of the hands and fingers by use of skin temperature biofeedback. Relaxation procedures and autogenic training have often been used in conjunction with the skin temperature biofeedback.

In the early 1970s, temperature or photoplethysmographic feedback was employed to treat five published individual cases of Raynaud's disease in four different laboratories, two cases in one laboratory (Shapiro & Schwartz,

1972) and one case in three others (Jacobson, Hackett, Surman, & Silverberg, 1973; Peper, 1972; and Surwit, 1973). Each of the studies was undertaken on a pilot basis and therefore, the results provide only suggestive evidence. However, the report in each case was positive, and the work proved promising.

A review of the experimental literature produced only equivocal evidence for the ability of humans to learn to voluntarily vasodilate with the use of temperature feedback alone. While Taub and Emurian (1976) reported to be able to reliably elicit increases in skin temperature when skin temperature feedback was given from the web dorsum of the hand, Surwit, Shapiro, and Feld (1976), Lynch, Hama, Kohn, and Miller (1976) and Keefe (1975) were only able to produce minimal skin temperature increases when feedback was provided from the digit. Nevertheless, other investigators continue to report small numbers of cases in which biofeedback, often used in conjunction with autogenic training or some autohypnotic procedure produced clinical improvement in patients suffering from Raynaud's disease or Raynaud's phenomenon.

A study by Blanchard and Haynes (1975) represents one of the best methodological efforts to date. A 29-year-old female subject submitted to physiological recordings under three conditions: baseline, self-control without feedback, and feedback, each presented in a repeated sequence. The forehead/finger format was employed and results affirmed the superiority of feedback over both baseline and self control. The subject was, however, relatively successful at self-control following feedback training due to generalization of the feedback response.

A noteworthy phenomenon appeared in a study conducted by May and Weber (1976) in which they compared the performances of four primary Raynaud's patients to four with a diagnosis of Raynaud's phenomenon secondary to scleroderma, and a control group of three. The Raynaud's subjects appeared to have superior ability in learning the temperature control response, especially those who manifested the cold hands phenomenon secondary to the scleroderma. A significant relationship between success in training and remission of symptoms was also observed.

Freedman, Lynn, Ianni, and Hale (1978) also studied patients with primary and secondary Raynaud's disease. Results similar to the May and Weber (1976) study were found. In addition, Sappington (1977) successfully treated a 21-year-old woman with Raynaud's phenomenon secondary to systemic lupus erythromatosis. With positive response to skin-temperature-training in patients having Raynaud's secondary to a more serious disorder, the possible progression of the disease might be held in remission or stabilized.

Sedlacek (1976) and Stephenson (1976) both treated patients with advanced Raynaud's disease. Each produced positive results. The subject treated by Stephenson who had unhealed lesions and scattered necrosis of a finger was shown to be in complete remission at a 2 year follow-up. Although these studies have shown dramatic success in some cases, most of the studies lacked a no-treatment control condition and failed to differentiate the effects of feedback from auto-suggestion. Also, none of the early work established an objective method for indicating that voluntary vasomotor training was providing patients with increased resistance to cold-induced vasospasm.

Recently, Surwit, Pilon, and Fenton (1978) treated 30 patients with primary Raynaud's disease with either a combination of biofeedback and autogenic training or autogenic training alone. The subjects were trained in the laboratory or at home. All trained subjects demonstrated a significant ability to maintain digital skin temperature in the presence of a cold stress challenge and reported significant reductions in both frequency and intensity of vasospastic attacks. Interestingly, the addition of skin temperature feedback to autogenic training did not provide any additional clinical benefit. This study suggests the possibility that autogenic training alone may be as beneficial as the skin temperature feedback training.

In an attempt to study the effects of temperature biofeedback alone, Patterson (1979) treated three patients with medically refractory Raynaud's phenomenon. One patient failed to learn autodigital hyperthermia and two succeeded, with definite improvement in one and equivocal improvement in the other. These results suggest that biofeedback alone is helpful in the management of Raynaud's in some patients and exemplifies the need for further research to delineate its therapeutic contribution.

Summary

Thermal biofeedback and associated techniques have been shown to be very promising as a therapeutic approach to both Raynaud's disease and Raynaud's phenomenon. Medical treatments currently available for this disease are generally unsatisfactory, because of minimal effect, unpleasant side effects, or the radical nature of the procedure. In contrast, temperature self-regulation has two major advantages. First, long-term use has not been observed to have any secondary consequences, and certainly no undesirable side effects, in either normal subjects or Raynaud's disease patients. Second, since the vasospastic attacks are episodic, the patient need employ the technique only when attacks threaten to occur, and no continuous regimen is necessary. In addition, if, as several studies speculate, the control of Raynaud's syndrome can promote stabilization or remission of a more serious disorder to which it is secondary, then certainly it is worthy of attention as a useful alternative or adjunctive therapy for Raynaud's disease.

REFERENCES

Agras, S. & Jacob, R. Hypertension. In O.F. Pomerleau, & J.P. Brady (Eds.) *Behavioral medicine: Theory and practice.* Baltimore: Williams & Wilkins, 1979.

Allen, E.B., Barker, N.W., & Hines, E.A., Jr. *Peripheral vascular diseases,* 4th ed. Philadelphia: Saunders, 1972, Chap. 19.

Allen, E.V. & Brown, G.E. Raynaud's disease: A clinical study of one hundred and forty-seven cases. *Journal of the American Medical Association,* 1932, **99,** 1472–1478.

Bech, K. & Hilden, T. The frequency of secondary hypertension. *Acta Medica Scandinavica,* 1975, **197,** 65–69.

Beiman, I., Graham, L.E., & Ciminero, A.R. Setting generality of blood pressure reductions and the psychological treatment of reactive hypertension. *Journal of Behavioral Medicine,* 1978, **1,** 445–453.

Benson, H. Systemic hypertension and the relaxation response. *New England Journal of Medicine,* 1977, **296,** 1152–1156.

Benson, H., Rosner, B.A., Marzetta, B.R., & Klemchuk, H.P. Decreased blood pressure in borderline hypertensive subjects who practiced meditation. *Journal of Chronic Diseases,* 1974b, **27,** 163–169.

Benson, H., Rosner, B.A., Marzetta, B.R., & Klemchuck, H.M. Decreased blood pressure in pharmacologically treated hypertensive patients who regularly elicited the relaxation response. *Lancet,* 1974a, **1,** 289–291.

Benson, H., Shapiro, D., Tursky, B., & Schwartz, G.E. Decreased systolic blood pressure through operant conditioning techniques in patients with essential hypertension. *Science,* 1971, **173,** 740–742.

Blackwell, B., Bloomfield, S., Gartside, P., Robinson, A., Hanenson, I., Magenheim, H., Nidich, S., & Zigler, R. Transcendental meditation in hypotension: Individual response patterns. *Lancet,* 1976, **1,** 223–226.

Blain, A., Coller, F.A., & Carver, G.B. Raynaud's disease: A study of criteria for prognosis. *Surgery,* 1951, **29,** 387–397.

Blanchard, E.B. & Epstein , L.H. *A biofeedback primer.* Reading, Mass.: Addison-Wesley, 1978.

Blanchard, E.B. & Haynes, M.R. Biofeedback treatment of a case of Raynaud's disease. *Journal of Behavior Therapy and Experimental Psychiatry,* 1975, **6,** 230–234.

Blanchard, E.B., Young, L.D., & Haynes, M.R. A simple feedback system for the treatment of elevated blood pressure. *Behavior Therapy,* 1975, **6,** 241–245.

Bleecker, E.R. & Engel, B.T. Learned control of ventricular rate in patients with atrial fibrillation. *Psychosomatic Medicine,* 1973, **35,** 161–175.

Bleecker, E.R. & Engel, B.T. Learned control of cardiac rate and cardiac conduction in a patient with Wolff-Parkinson-White syndrome. *New England Journal of Medicine,* 1973, **288,** 560–562.

Bradley, R.W. & Hughes, H. Blood pressure biofeedback and relaxation training: The effects of home practice on reduction of blood pressure in persons with essential hypertension. Unpublished manuscript, 1979.

Brady, J.P., Luborsky, L., & Kron, R.E. Blood pressure reduction in patients with essential hypertension through metronome-conditioned relaxation: A preliminary report. *Behavior Therapy,* 1974, **5,** 203–209.

Brauer, A., Horlick, L., Nelson, E., Farguhar, J.F., & Agras, W.S. Relaxation therapy for essential hypertension: A VA outpatient study. Unpublished manuscript, Stanford University, 1978.

Byasse, J.E. Progressive relaxation and autogenic training in the treatment of essential hypertension. *Dissertation Abstracts International,* 1976, **37,** 452B. (University Microfilms No. 76-16, 329).

Chiang, B.N., Perlman, L.V., & Epstein, F.H. Overweight and hypertension: A review. *Circulation,* 1969, **39,** 403–421.

Chiang, B.N., Pealman, L.V., Ostander, L.D., Jr., & Epstein, F.H. Relationship of premature systoles to coronary heart disease and sudden death in the Tecumseh epidemiologic study. *Annals Internal Medicine,* 1969, **70,** 1159–1166.

Cohen, S., Fisher, R., Lipschutz, W., Turner, R., Myers, A., & Schumacher, R. The pathogenisis of esophageal dysfunction in scleroderma and Raynaud's disease. *Journal of Clinical Investigation,* 1972, **51,** 2663–2668.

Datey, K.K., Deshmukh, S.N., Dalvi, C.P., & Vinekar, S.L. "Shavasan": A yogic exercise in the management of hypertension. *Angiology,* 1969, **20,** 325–333.

Dowdall, S.A. Breathing techniques that help reduce hypertension. *Registered Nurse,* 1977, **40,** 73–74.

Elder, S.T. & Eustis, N.K. Instrumental blood pressure conditioning in out-patient hypertensives. *Behavior Research and Therapy,* 1975, **13,** 185–188.

Elder, S.T., Ruiz, R.Z., Deabler, H.J., & Dillenkoffer, R.L. Instrumental conditioning of diastolic blood pressure in essential hypertensive patients. *Journal of Applied Behavioral Analysis,* 1973, **6,** 377–382.

Engel, B.T. Clinical applications of operant conditioning techniques in the control of the cardiac arrhythmias. *Seminars in Psychiatry,* 1973, **5,** 433–438.

Engel, B.T. Cardiac Arrhythmias. In R.B. Williams, Jr. & W.D. Gentry (Eds.) *Behavioral approaches to medical treatment.* Cambridge, Mass.: Ballinger, 1977.

Engel, B.T. & Chism, R.A. Operant conditioning of heart rate speeding. *Psychophysiology,* 1967, **3,** 418–426.

Engel, B.T. & Hansen, S.P. Operant conditioning of heart rate slowing. *Psychophysiology,* 1966, **3,** 176–187.

Engelman, K. & Braunwald, E. Hypotension and the shock syndrome. In G.W. Thorn, R.D. Adams, E. Braunwald, K.J. Isselbacher, & R.G. Petersdorf (Eds.) *Harrison's principles of internal medicine,* 8th ed. New York: McGraw-Hill, 1977.

Fidel, E.A. The effectiveness of biofeedback and relaxation procedures in reducing high blood pressure (Doctoral dissertation, Texas Technological University, 1975). *Dissertation Abstracts International,* 1975, **36,** 3035B. (University Microfilms No. 75-26, 838)

Finnerty, F.A., Jr. Hypertension: New techniques for improving patient compliance. In *The hypertension handbook.* West Point, Penn.: Merck Sharp & Dohme, 1974.

Finnerty, F.A., Jr., Mattei, E.C., & Finnerty, F.A. III. Hypertension in the inner city, Part I: Analysis of clinic dropouts. *Circulation,* 1973, **47,** 73–79.

Finnerty, F.A., Jr., Shaw, L.W., & Himmelsbach, C.K. Hypertension in the inner city, Part II: Detection and follow up. *Circulation,* 1973, **46,** 76–81.

Fray, J.M. Implications of electromyographic feedback for essential hypertensive patients (Doctoral dissertation, Texas Technological University, 1975). *Dissertation Abstracts International,* 1975, **36,** 3036B. (University Microfilms No. 75–26, 839)

Freedman, R., Lynn, S.J., Ianni, P., & Hale, P. Biofeedback treatment of Raynaud's phenomenon. Paper presented at the meeting of the Biofeedback Society of America, Albuquerque, March, 1978.

Friedman, H. & Taub, H.A. The use of hypnosis and biofeedback procedures for essential hypertension. *The International Journal of Clinical and Experimental Hypnosis,* 1977, **25,** 335–347.

Galton, L. *The silent disease: Hypertension.* New York: Crown, 1973.

Goldman, H., Kleinman, K., Snow, M., Bidus, D., & Korol, B. Correlation of diastolic blood pressure and cognitive dysfunction in essential hypertension. *Diseases of the Nervous System,* 1974, **35,** 571–572.

Goldman, H., Kleinman, K.M., Snow, M.Y., Bidus, D.R., & Korol, B. Relationship between essential hypertension and cognitive functioning: Effects of biofeedback. *Psychophysiology,* 1975, **12,** 569–573.

Graham, D.T. Cutaneous vascular reactions in Raynaud's disease and in states of hostility, anxiety and depression. *Psychosomatic Medicine,* 1955, **17,** 201–207.

Graham, D.T., Stern, J.A., & Winokur, G. Experimental investigation of the specificity of the attitude hypothesis in psychosomatic disease. *Psychosomatic Medicine,* 1958, **20,** 446–457.

Herting, R.L. & Hunter, H.L. The physiologic and pharmacologic basis for the clinical treatment of hypertension. *Medical Clinics of North America,* 1967, **51,** 25–37.

Inter-society Commission for Heart Disease Resources. Primary prevention of the atherosclerotic diseases. *Circulation,* 1970, **42,** 55–67.

Jacobson, A.M., Hackett, L.P., Surman, O.A., & Silverberg, E.L. Raynaud phenomenon. *Journal of the American Medical Association,* 1973, **225,** 739–740.

Jacobson, E. Variation of blood pressure with skeletal muscle tension and relaxation. *Anals of Internal Medicine,* 1939, **12,** 1194–1212.

James, T.M. The Wolff-Parkinson-White syndrome: Evolving concepts of its pathogenesis. *Progress in Cardiovascular Diseases,* 1970, **13,** 159–180.

Julius, S. Borderline hypertension: An overview. *Medical Clinics of North America,* 1977, **61,** 495–411.

Kannel, W.R., Brand, R.R., Skinner, A., Dawber, P.L., & McNamara, J. The relation of adiposity to blood pressure and the development of hypertension. *Annals of Internal Medicine,* 1967, **67,** 48–59.

Keefe, F.V. Conditioning changes in differential skin temperature. *Perceptual and Motor Skills,* 1975, **40,** 283–288.

Kleinman, K.M., Goldman, H., Snow, M.Y., & Korol, B. Relationship between essential hypertension and cognitive functioning II: Effects of biofeedback training generalize to nonlaboratory environment. *Psychophysiology,* 1977, **14,** 192–197.

Kristt, D.A. & Engel, B.T. Learning control of blood pressure in patients with high blood pressure. *Circulation,* 1975, **51,** 370–378.

Knust, U. & Richter-Heinrich, E. Blutdrucksenkung durch instrumentell konditionierung bei arteriellen essentiellen hyperponikern. Duet. *Gesundheitswes.* 1975, **30**, 1014–1018.

Levene, H.T., Engel, B.T., & Pearson, J.A. Differential operant conditioning of heart rate. *Psychosomatic Medicine,* 1968, **30**, 837–845.

Levy, R.L., White, A.C., Stroud, M., & Hillman, H.E. Transient hypertension: The relative prognostic importance of various systolic and diastolic levels. *Journal of the American Medical Association,* 1945, **128**, 1059–1061.

Lew, E.A. Blood pressure and mortality: The life insurance experience. In J. Stamler, R. Stamler, & T.N. Pullman (Eds.) *The epidemiology of hypertension.* New York: Grune & Stratton, 1967.

Lewis, T. *Vascular disorders of the limbs: Described for practitioners and students.* London: Macmillan, 1949.

Love, W.A., Montgomery, D.D., & Moeller, T.A. Working paper number one. Unpublished research report, Nova University, 1975.

Lown, B. & Wolf, M. Approaches to sudden death. *Circulation,* 1971, **46**, 130–142.

Lynch, W.C., Hama, H., Kohn, S., & Miller, N.E. Instrumental control of peripheral vasomotor responses in children. *Psychophysiology,* 1976, **13**, 219–221.

May, D.S. & Weber, C.A. Temperature feedback training for symptom reduction in primary and secondary Raynaud's disease. *Biofeedback and Self-Regulation,* 1976, **1**, 317.

Miller, N.E. Learning of visceral and glandular responses. *Science,* 1969, **163**, 434–445.

Mittlemann, B. & Wolff, H.G. Affective states and skin temperature: Experimental study of subjects with "cold hands" and Raynaud's disease. *Psychosomatic Medicine,* 1939, **1**, 271–292.

Moeller, T.A. & Love, W.A. A method to reduce asterical hypertension through muscular relaxation. *Journal of Biofeedback,* 1975, **1**, 38–44.

Moriyama, I.M., Krueger, D.E., & Stamler, J. *Cardiovascular diseases in the United States.* Cambridge, Mass.: Harvard University Press, 1971.

National Center for Health Statistics. National health survey: Blood pressure of persons 18–74 years, United States, 1971–1972 (U.S. Department of Health Education, and Welfare, Series II. Publication No. 150). Washington, D.C.: U.S. Government Printing Office, 1975.

Patel, C. A 12-month follow-up of yoga and biofeedback in the management of hypertension. *Lancet,* 1975, **1**, 62–64.

Patel, C. Yoga and biofeedback in the management of hypertension. *Journal of Psychosomatic Research,* 1975, **19**, 355–360.

Patel, C.H. Yoga and biofeedback in the management of hypertension. *Lancet,* 1973, **2**, 1053–1055.

Patel, C. & Carruthers, M. Coronary risk factor reduction through biofeedback-aided relaxation and meditation. *Journal of the Royal College of General Practitioners,* 1977, **27**, 401–405.

Patel, C.H. & Datey, K.K. Relaxation and biofeedback techniques in the management of hypertension. *Angiology,* 1976, **27**, 106–113.

Patel, C.H. & North, W.R. Randomized control of yoga and biofeedback in management of hypertension. *Lancet*, 1975, **2**, 93–95.

Patterson, W.M. Treatment of Raynaud's phenomenon with temperature biofeedback. *American Journal of Clinical Biofeedback*, 1979, **2**, 19–21.

Peper, E. Case Report. Paper presented at the meeting of the Biofeedback Research Society, Boston, 1972.

Pickering, G. *High blood pressure*, 2nd ed. New York: Grune & Stratton, 1968.

Pickering, T. & Gorham, G. Learned heartrate control by a patient with a ventricular parasystolic rhythm. *Lancet*, 1975.

Pollack, A.A., Weber, M.A., Case, D.B., & Larogh, J.H. Limitations of transcendental meditation in the treatment of essential hypertension. *Lancet*, 1977, **1**(8002), 71.73.

Raynaud, A.G. *De l'asphyxie locale et de la gangrene symetiqice des extremites.* Paris: Reqout, 1862.

Redmond, D.P., Gaylor, M.S., McDonald, R.H., & Shapiro, A.P. Blood pressure and heart-rate response to verbal instruction and relaxation in hypertension. *Psychosomatic Medicine*, 1974, **36**, 285–297.

Richter-Heinrich, E., Knust, U., & Lori, M. Decrease in the blood pressure of patients with essential hypertension by instrumental conditioned reflexes with feedback. *Zhurnal Vysshei Nervoi Decatel Nosti*, 1977, **27**, 401–404.

Richter-Heinrich, E., Knust, U., Lori, M., & Sprung, H. Blood pressure control through biofeedback in arterial and essential hypertension. *Zeitschroift für Angewandte Psychologie*, 1977, **184**, 538–550.

Richter-Heinrich, E., Knust, B., Muller, W., Schmidt, K., & Sprung, H. Psychophysiological investigations in essential hypertensives. *Journal of Psychosomatic Research*, 1975, **19**, 251–258.

Rubenstein, J.J., Schulman, C.L., Yurchale, P.M., & DeSanctis, R.W. Clinical spectrum of the sick sinus syndrome. *Circulation*, 1972, **46**, 5–13.

Ruch, T.C., Patton, H.D., Woodbury, J.W. *et al.* (Eds.) *Neurophysiology* 2nd ed. Philadelphia: Saunders, 1965.

Russ, K.L. Effect of two different feedback paradigms on blood pressure levels of patients with essential hypertension. Proceedings of the Biofeedback Research Society Fifth Annual Meeting, Colorado Springs, 1974, 38.

Sappington, J.T. Operant conditioning of peripheral vasodilation in Raynaud's disease: A case study. Annual Meeting of the Southeastern Psychological Association, 1977.

Sappington, J.T., Fiorito, E.M., & Brehony, K.A. Biofeedback as therapy in Raynaud's disease. *Biofeedback and Self-Regulation*, 1979, **4**, 155–169.

Sawyer, J.E. The effects of muscle relaxation and biofeedback on blood pressure for essential hypertensives. *Dissertation Abstracts International*, 1977, **37**, 4164B. (University Microfilms No. 77-01, 432)

Scherf, D. & Schott, A. *Extrasystoles and allied arrhythmias.* New York: Grune & Stratton, 1953.

Schwartz, G.E. & Shapiro, D. Biofeedback and essential hypertension: Current findings and theoretical concerns. *Seminars in Psychiatry*, 1973, **5**, 493–503.

Scott, R.W., Blanchard, E.B., Edmundson, E.D., & Young, L.D. A shaping procedure for heart-rate control in chronic tachycardia. *Perceptual and Motor Skills*, 1973, **37**, 327–338.

Scott, R.W., Peters, R.C., Gillespie, W.J., Blanchard, E.B., Edmundson, E.D., & Young, L.D. The use of shaping and reinforcement in the operant acceleration and deceleration of heart rate. *Behavior Research and Therapy*, 1973, **11**, 179–185.

Sedlacek, K. EMG and thermal feedback as a treatment for Raynaud's disease. *Biofeedback and Self-Regulation*, 1976, **1**, 318.

Shapiro, P. & Schwartz, G.E. Biofeedback and visceral learning: Clinical application. *Seminars in Psychiatry*, 1972, **4**, 171–184.

Shapiro, D., Tursky, B., Gershon, E., & Stern, M. Effects of feedback and reinforcement on the control of human systolic blood pressure. *Science*, 1969, **163**, 588–590.

Shoemaker, J.E. & Tasto, D.L. The effects of muscle relaxation on blood pressure of essential hypertensives. *Behavior Research and Therapy*, 1975, **13**, 29–43.

Smith, W.M. Epidemiology of hypertension. *Medical Clinics of North America*, 1977a, **61**, 467–486.

Smith, W.M. Treatment of mild hypertension: Results of a 10-year intervention trial. *Circulation Research*, 1977b, **40**(Supplement 1), 98–105.

Spittell, J.A. Raynaud's phenomenon and allied vasospastic conditions. In J.F. Fairbairn, J.L. Juergens, & J.A. Spittell (Eds.) *Allen-Barker-Hines: Peripheral vascular diseases*. Philadelphia: Saunders, 1972.

Stamler, J. Cigarette smoking and atherosclerotic heart disease. *Bulletin of the New York Academy of Medicine*, 1968, **44**, 1476–1494.

Stamler, J. *Lectures on preventative cardiology*. New York: Grune & Stratton, 1967.

Stamler, J., Stamler, R., & Pullman, T.N. (Eds.) *The epidemiology of hypertension*. New York: Grune & Stratton, 1967.

Stamler, J., Schoenberger, J.A., Shekelle, R.B., & Stamler, R. Hypertension. The problem and the challenge. In *The hypertension handbook*. West Point, Penn.: Merck, Sharp, & Dohme, 1974.

Stamler, J., Stamler, R., Riedlinger, W.F., Algera, G., & Roberts, R.H. Hypertension screening of 1 million Americans: Community hypertension evaluation clinic (Check) program, 1973 through 1975. *Journal of the American Medical Association*, 1976, **235**, 2299–2306.

Stephenson, N.E. Two cases of successful treatment of Raynaud's disease with relaxation and biofeedback training and supportive psychotherapy. *Biofeedback and Self Regulation*, 1976, **1**, 318.

Stevenson, I.P., Duncan, C.H., Wolf, S. *et al.* Life situations, emotions, and extrasystoles. *Psychosomatic Medicine*, 1949, **11**, 257–272.

Stone, R.A. & DeLeo, J. Psychotherapeutic control of hypertension. *New England Journal of Medicine*, 1976, **294**, 80–84.

Surwit, R.S. Biofeedback: A possible treatment for Raynaud's disease. *Seminars in Psychiatry*, 1973, **5**, 483–490.

Surwit, B., Pilon, R., & Fenton, C. Behavioral treatment of Raynaud's disease. *Journal of Behavioral Medicine*, 1978, **1**, 323–335.

Surwit, R. & Shapiro, D. Biofeedback and meditation in the treatment of borderline hypertension. In J. Beatty & H. Legeure (Eds.) *Biofeedback and behavior*. New York: Plenum Press, 1977.

Surwit, R.S., Shapiro, D., & Feld, J.L. Digital temperature autoregulation and associated cardiovascular changes. *Psychophysiology*, 1976, **13**, 242–248.

Surwit, R.S., Shapiro, D., & Good, M.I. Comparison of cardiovascular biofeedback, neuromuscular biofeedback, and meditation in the treatment of borderline essential hypertension. Journal of Consulting and Clinical Psychology, 1978, **46**, 252–263.

Rici, D.M. & Lawrence, P.S. The effectiveness of group-administered relaxation training as an adjunctive therapy for essential hypertension. Paper presented at the meeting of the Association for the Advancement of Behavior Therapy, San Francisco, December, 1979.

Taub, E. & Emurian, C.S. Feedback aided self-regulation of skin temperature with a single feedback locus: I. Acquisition and reversal training. *Biofeedback and Self-Regulation*, 1976, **1**, 147–168.

Taylor, C.B., Farquhar, J.W., Nelson E., & Agras, W.S. Relaxation therapy and high blood pressure. *Archives of General Psychiatry*, 1977, **34**, 339–342.

Tursky, B., Shapiro, D., & Schwartz, G.E. Automated constant cuff pressure system to measure average systolic and diastolic blood pressure in man. *IEEE Transactions on Biomedical Engineering*, 1972, **19**, 271–276.

Veterans Administration Cooperative Study Group on Antihypertensive Agents. Effects of treatment on morbidity in hypertension: Influence of age, diastolic pressure, and prior cardiovascular diseases; further analysis of side effects. *Circulation*, 1972, **45**, 991–1004.

Veterans Administration Cooperative Study group on Antihypertensive Agents. Effects of treatment on morbidity in hypertension: Results in patients with diastolic blood pressures averaging 115 through 129 mm Hg. *Journal of the American Medical Association*, 1967, **202**, 1028–1034.

Veterans Administration Cooperative Study Group on Antihypertensive Agents. Effects of treatment on morbidity in hypertension: Results in patients with diastolic blood pressure averaging 90 through 114 mm Hg. *Journal of the American Medical Association*, 1970, **213**, 1143–1152.

Wallace, R.K. & Benson, H. The physiology of meditation. *Scientific American*, 1972, **226**, 84–90.

Walsh, P., Dale, A., & Anderson, D.E. Comparison of biofeedback pulse wave velocity and progressive relaxation in essential hypertensives. *Perceptual and Motor Skills*, 1977, **44**, 839–843.

Weiner, H. Psychosomatic research in essential hypertension: Retrospect and prospect. In M. Koster, H. Musaph, & P. Visser (Eds.) *Psychosomatics in essential hypertension*. New York: Karger, 1970.

Weiss, T. Biofeedback training for cardiovascular dysfunctions. *Medical Clinics of North America*, 1977, **61**, 913–928.

Weiss, T. & Engel, B.T. Operant conditioning of heart rate in patients with premature ventricular contractions. *Psychosomatic Medicine*, 1971, **33**, 301–321.

White, P.D. The psyche and the soma: The spiritual and physical attitudes of the heart. *Annals of Internal Medicine,* 1951, **35,** 1291–1305.

Wilber, J.A. Detection and control of hypertensive disease in Georgia, U.S.A. In J. Stamler, R. Stamler, & L.N. Pullman (Eds.) *The epidemology of hypertension.* New York: Grune & Stratton, 1967.

Wolf, S. & Goodell, H. *Stress and disease.* Springfield, Ill.: Charles C Thomas, 1968.

CHAPTER 8

Gastrointestinal Disorders

OVERVIEW

The gastrointestinal (GI) system, which consists of the stomach, the small and large intestines, and the anus, is instrumental in the digestion and absorption of food, and the elimination of solid waste material from the body. When any of these activities is disrupted, serious health problems may result. The gastrointestinal system, more so than any of the other bodily systems, is an astonishingly sensitive gauge of its owner's emotional state. A disturbance in an individual's emotional equilibrium, whether it is a surge of anger, the persistent penetration of anxiety, or even the excited anticipation of pleasure, commonly is registered by gastrointestinal symptoms: constipation, diarrhea, vomiting, nausea, indigestion, or loss of appetite. Many of the most frequently encountered gastrointestinal disorders, and some of the most intractable ones, can be explained etiologically in terms of stress.

Traditional medical management of these disorders has met with little success. The chronicity of these disorders, the life-threatening nature of some of them, and the underlying etiology of stress has led to the application of behavioral intervention techniques in treatment and alleviation of these disorders. The gastrointestinal disorders receiving attention in the behavioral medicine literature are: anorexia nervosa, chronic vomiting, encopresis and fecal incontinence, duodenal ulcers, and the irritable bowel syndrome, more commonly known as colitis.

ANOREXIA NERVOSA

Although identified in medical literature for many years, anorexia nervosa has only very recently come to the attention of the public at large. It is a relatively uncommon disorder in its more serious forms, but can pose a grave and sometimes life-threatening danger. Anorexia nervosa is described by Bruch (1970) as a self-imposed starvation and relentless pursuit of thinness leading to cachexia. It is characterized by refusal to consume food, and carries a rather alarming incidence of mortality, which may run as high as 15% (Stunkard, 1975). Extensive morbidity is also associated with anorexia and may include amenorrhea (loss of menstrual periods), and a variety of problems secondary to poor nutrition, such as electrolyte imbalance and avitaminosis. Weight loss is generally severe, and may be as great as 60% of normal body weight (Bachrach, Erwin, & Mohr, 1965).

The illness is most prevalent in young, 14–20 year old females, many of whom were overweight, or "perceived" themselves to be obese as children. Anorexia typically begins with self-imposed dieting in an attempt to loose only a few pounds, but develops into unrealistically low idealized weight goals. The intensity with which these patients pursue diets often borders on the obsessive. As the starvation progresses, the conflict between hunger and fear of gaining weight becomes more profound, often resulting in "binge" eating where vast amounts of normally prohibited foods are consumed. This act may be accompanied by self-induced vomiting and/or the ingestion of laxatives or diuretics. Often the person is embarrassed by this behavior, and will become isolated and avoid eating with other people.

The precise causes of anorexia nervosa are unclear but important physical, psychological, and environmental factors have been identified. All of these are affected by starvation and it is often difficult to differentiate the causes from the effect of the disorder. Explanations of the etiology of this disorder have included conflict over sexuality (Nemiah, 1963), fantasies of pregnancy, as well as a variety of other psychodynamic hypotheses (Bliss & Branch, 1960).

In the past, the treatment of anorexia has taken many forms, indicative of the difficulty in managing this disorder. Treatments have included intubation, high calorie diets, psychotherapy, chemotherapy (chlorpromazine), and one-to-one intensive nursing care. A variety of successful treatments have been reported in individual cases, but none have worked consistently (Bliss & Branch, 1960).

While these various methods are often useful in helping the patient gain weight, they have serious drawbacks: the risk of infection and death with tube feeding (Browning & Miller, 1968); the high incidence of bulimia and other undesirable effects following treatment with chlorpromazine (Dally & Sargant, 1966); and the very slow weight gain with psychotherapy (Blinder, Freeman, & Stunkard, 1970). In an attempt to overcome these drawbacks, a variety of behavior therapies have recently been introduced.

Treatment

One of the defining features of anorectic patients is that they display abnormally low rates of eating behavior. Viewing the intake of food as an operant, behavioral treatments have emphasized increasing eating by strict contingency management for caloric intake, food consumption, and weight gain. Extinction is frequently used as an adjunct to reinforcement and involves the removal of all potential reinforcement for activities incompatible with eating. Measures of weight and eating are taken regularly under standardized conditions, both as a dependent measure, and to arrange contingencies of reinforcement.

Most of the literature on anorexia nervosa consists of case studies with few subjects, usually only one. These case studies suggest that operant conditioning with positive reinforcement (Agras, Barlow, Chapin, Abel, & Leitenburg, 1974; Bachrach, Erwin, & Mohr, 1965; Bianco, 1972; and Neumann & Gaoni, 1975) and desensitization (Lang, 1965; and Schnurer, Rubin, & Roy, 1973) were effective. None of these studies, however, suggested how the practicing clinician was to decide which treatment approach was likely to be successful for a given patient.

Azerrad and Stafford (1969) used an A-B design in treating a 13-year-old hospitalized girl. Treatment consisted of a token system in which points were initially made contingent on weight gain, and later on amounts of food consumed. Points could be exchanged for various items. Weight gain was slow and variable but accelerated when reinforcement was switched from weight gain to actual food consumption. The girl gained 20 pounds and was released from the hospital. A 5-month follow-up indicated she was continuing to gain weight at the rate of one pound a month.

This study is noteworthy because it clearly emphasizes some of the obstacles frequently encountered in the treatment of anorexia. In this case the patient had been concealing heavy objects in her robe to produce initial weight gains and earn reinforcement surreptitiously. This study also illustrates that treatment of anorexia nervosa does not end when the patient leaves the hospital. The child's parents were involved and instructed in behavioral principles. The continuation of treatment procedures facilitated generalization of treatment effects to the home.

Leitenberg, Agras, and Thomson (1968) used reinforcement and extinction to treat anorexia in two adolescent girls. Praise and pleasurable activities were provided contingent on daily weight gain, resulting in weight gains of 23 and 22 pounds. Also, the persistent somatic complaints of one of the girls were eliminated by instructing ward staff to ignore them.

Blinder, Freeman, and Stunkard (1970), and Garfinkel, Kline, and Stancer (1973), used contingent positive reinforcement to produce weight gain in eight female patients. Blinder et al. (1970) used high activity levels of the patients as a reinforcer for weight gain by making periods of activity contingent on increases in weight. Garfinkel et al. (1973) used physical activity, off-ward socializing, passes, and other privileges contingent upon weight gain. Although rapid weight gain occurred in all of the patients after implementation of the reinforcement system, these studies also reflect the complexities of treating the severe anorectic: criteria for reinforcement must be easy for the patient to achieve and the patient must be closely monitored in order to eliminate the reinforcement of pseudo improvement and self-induced vomiting to offset required consumption. In addition, the ward environment must offer optimal control of reinforcing events, particularly staff attention, in order to avoid the inadvertent reinforcement of anorectic behaviors. These studies also make it clear that weight gain alone should not be considered as the only measure of a patient's total improvement. Often problems other than weight loss are present, each of which may require comprehensive assessment and treatment before therapeutic contact is terminated. This usually involves outpatient treatment after weight is restored and the patient has been discharged from the hospital.

Agras, Barlow, Chapin, Abel, and Leitenberg (1974) conducted the most carefully executed study to date, examining the effects of positive and negative reinforcement, informational feedback (knowledge of results), and meal size on the eating behavior of anorectics. Feedback, provided by having the patients monitor their daily weight, number of calories consumed, and amount of food eaten, exerted the greatest effect. That is, the largest increase in eating occurred with feedback. While patients ate more when served large meals instead of small ones, the magnitude of this effect was relatively small. The effects of contingent reinforcement were greater when used in combination with informal feedback. Presumably, having patients obtain feedback by self-observation serves to maintain eating, which is then further reinforced by weight gain.

Geller (1975) reproduced the design employed by Agras *et al.* (1974) adding psychotherapy and a 12-month follow-up. Similar results were obtained and maintained at follow-up.

Summary

Anorexia nervosa can be a very dangerous and life-threatening disorder if weight loss is substantial. Behavioral treatment has emphasized increasing eating by strict contingency management through use of positive reinforcement, extinction, and informal feedback for calorie intake, food consumption, and weight gain.

These studies should, however, be viewed as tentative due to several considerations: little experimental work, as opposed to case studies, has been conducted; most of the studies have little or no follow-up data; and a variety of different procedures will lead to immediate benefits, in terms of weight gain. Future efforts in the area of management of anorexia nervosa need to be directed at the collection of data on treatment effectiveness, both immediate and long term.

CHRONIC VOMITING

Chronic vomiting is another example of a debilitating and potentially dangerous gastrointestinal disorder, and is of considerable clinical significance in infants. Kanner (1957) defined chronic rumination as "bringing up food without nausea, retching, or disgust. The food is then ejected from the mouth (if liquid, allowed to run out) or reswallowed'' (p. 484). This behavior appears to be ''voluntary,'' that is, children actively engage in behaviors that induce the rumination. Infants have been observed to strain vigorously to bring food back to their mouth.

The incidence of rumination in the general population is unknown, since it is typically confused with food allergies, especially an allergy to milk. Serious clinical problems, such as malnutrition, dehydration, aspiration, pneumonia, and lowered resistance to infection, may prompt a life-threatening condition if significant amounts of food are lost. Kanner (1957) noted a 21% mortality rate for one group of 52 ruminating babies, and Gaddini and Gaddini (1959) reported death in one of six cases.

Recurrent vomiting can result from organic or psychological causes. Ruminating vomiting with an organic etiology is generally amenable to a variety of treatment techniques, including surgery, antinauseants, and antiemetics. If gastric, anatomical anomalies can be diagnosed, their surgical removal often proves to be the most effective treatment. However, as Hoyt and Stickler (1960) observed in their review of 44 children with persistent vomiting, the cause of the syndrome, while possibly psychogenic, is not known definitely.

When diagnosis excludes obvious, organic antecedents, both the etiology and treatment of the disorder appear less certain. Kanner (1957) noted treatments, other than those mentioned above, include the use of mechanical devices, such as chin straps or esophagus blocks, or special feedings of thickened farina, which have proven only minimally effective.

More positive results have been obtained with massive noncontingent attention, based on the psychoanalytic hypothesis that the syndrome results from a disruption in the mother-infant relationship (Richmond, Eddy, & Green, 1958). Typically, an adult is assigned to provide the ruminating child with his undivided attention for at least eight hours a day. Fullerton (1963), Gaddini and Gaddini (1959), Hollowell and Gardner (1965), Menking, Wagnitz, Burton, Coddington, and Sotos (1969), Richmond, Eddy, and Green (1958), and Stein, Rausen, and Blare (1959) reported reductions in rumination and increases in weight coincident with the onset of high levels of attention.

While this procedure appears to be somewhat successful, two major drawbacks exist: cessation of rumination is usually slow, and constant attention is usually required for at least eight hours per day. Since rumination is often life-threatening, a more rapid behavioral treatment has been sought.

Treatment

Punishment

According to behavioral principles, chronic vomiting involves a behavioral excess, vomiting, that should be rapidly suppressed. The choice treatment typically has been response-contingent punishment.

White and Taylor (1967) were the first researchers to use contingent electric shock for rumination. Although elimination was not completely successful, they concluded that shock did interfere with rumination. This study prompted several other researchers to use this approach. Bright and Whaley (1968) first attempted to eliminate regurgitation and vomiting in a 9-year-old retarded boy by administering Tabasco brand peppersauce contingent on rumination. The sauce was sprinkled on the vomitus which the child reconsumed. Some reduction in rumination was obtained, but complete cessation did not occur until contingent electric shock was administered. Luckey, Watson, and Musick (1968) and Galbraith, Byrick, and Rutledge (1970) reported cessation of vomiting and rumination within two to four days when shock was used.

One of the most dramatic cases in which chronic ruminative vomiting was successfully eliminated by contingent shock punishment was conducted by Lang and Melamed (1969) in the treatment of a 9-month-old child who was in danger of dying. Various medical procedures had proven unsuccessful and the youngster was in critical condition with a body weight of 12 pounds. The authors used an electromyograph to carefully monitor the child's vomiting response. At the first sign of reverse peristalsis, a brief, one second, shock was administered by electrodes attached to the child's calf. Three sessions were required to completely suppress the vomiting response. Subsequently, the child was described as more active, aware of his environment, and affectionate toward others. The child was continuing to gain weight and was healthy at a one-year follow-up.

Procedures similar to those used by Lang and Melamed (1969) have been used by Kohlenberg (1970), and Cunningham and Linscheid (1976). Kohlenberg made shock contingent on stomach contractions, a behavior that was detected visually and which reliably preceded vomiting. Results showed rapid suppression of vomiting along with a 10½ pounds weight gain during the 25 days after treatment. Cunningham and Linscheid (1976) made no attempt to punish antecedents to vomiting. Instead, shock was administered at the first visual sign of ruminative behavior. On the first day of treatment, ruminating decreased from a baseline of 36 to 4 occurrences. This was further reduced to one occurrence on each of the next 3 days of treatment. The child was discharged 2 weeks after treatment began, and a 6-month follow-up showed no recurrence of vomiting and a weight gain of 16 pounds. A significant feature of this study was the built-in effort to generalize treatment effects across observers, times, and treatment locations.

Because shock punishment is a controversial procedure, with potential risks and side effects, Sajwaj, Libet, and Agras (1974) used the contingent administration of lemon juice directly into the mouth to suppress vomiting in a 6-month-old infant. The inclusion of a brief reversal procedure suggested that the lemon juice was instrumental in reducing the vomiting. A 1-year follow-up showed continued improvement.

Becker, Turner, and Sajwaj (1978) replicated the study with a 36-month-old severely retarded girl who was treated as an outpatient. Not only was rumination suppressed and weight increased; but, in addition, several positive behaviors were noted: smiling, interactions, babbling, and object touching. Several negative behaviors, such as hand mannerism, rocking, head slap, and head weave increased also during treatment, but gradually disappeared or decreased in frequency.

Extinction

Wolf, Birnbrauer, Williams, and Lawler (1965) described another approach to ruminative vomiting involving extinction procedures in treating a 9-year-old retarded girl. The authors noted that the child's baseline rate of vomiting was increasing, and most of the vomiting occurred while the child was at school. It was suspected that being excused from class after vomiting was negatively reinforcing the vomiting. Treatment involved instructing the teacher to ignore the vomiting and detain the child until class was over. Rate reductions were slow and variable, but vomiting was completely eliminated within 30 days.

Duker and Seys (1977) used overcorrection procedures to greatly reduce vomiting in a 19-year-old profoundly retarded girl. Previous attempts to control the behavior by means of time-out, extinction combined with DRO, and aversive gustatory stimulation were unsuccessful. The overcorrection procedure consisted of verbal expressions of disapproval as results of vomiting were pointed out to the patient. The patient was then required to clean up the vomitus, clean the surrounding area, wash her face and hands, and put on clean clothes. A reversal design was used, and results showed a consistent reduction in vomiting each time overcorrection was instituted. A 2-month follow-up showed occasional episodes of vomiting, but at a greatly reduced rate.

Summary

Chronic ruminative vomiting can produce clinically significant problems as well as become a life-threatening condition, especially in infants and retarded youngsters. Since the vomiting behavior needs to be suppressed rapidly in life-threatening situations, response contingent punishment by use of an electric shock has proven successful in quickly eliminating the vomiting behavior. Using lemon juice instead of shock has also proven successful as a less aversive and controversial procedure. Extinction and over-correction procedures have proven successful in cases with older children in which environmental stimuli were believed to reinforce the vomiting behavior. Overall, the operant conditioning techniques have proven to be a reliable means of suppressing and eliminating the behavior of chronic ruminative vomiting.

ENCOPRESIS/FECAL INCONTINENCE

These two gastrointestinal disorders are both characterized by fecal soiling without regular bowel movements. The soiling is typically due to a lack of control of the anal sphincter. One of the major differences between the two is that diagnosis of encopresis is made on the basis of an absence of organic pathology, whereas fecal incontinence has an organic basis.

Encopresis is a disturbance in bowel control occurring after the age when such control is physiologically possible and should have been accomplished, usually between the ages of 2 and 3 years (Pierce, 1975). The disorder can take two forms: involuntary elimination (fecal soiling) or chronic constipation (fecal retention). It is known that encopresis is primarily a disorder of childhood, and that it seems to occur five times more often in boys than in girls (Pierce, 1975). Levine (1975) noted that 3% of the pediatric population reported encopresis.

Davidson (1958) was one of the first authors to break with the long standing tradition of attributing all encopresis to underlying psychopathology. He stated that encopresis almost never results from a single cause, but is the result of several factors including: a constitutional predisposition, dietary factors, difficulty with passage of hard stools because of failure to provide leverage, the influence of pain and voluntary resistance causing stool retention, and development of incontinence associated with fecal impaction. Both Wright (1975) and Levine (1975) report that 80% of their patients had fecal impaction accompanying their fecal incontinence at the time of the first visit to a clinic.

Fecal incontinence occurring in adults usually has an organic etiology characterized by a weak external anal sphincter (Alva, Mendeloff, & Schuster, 1967). This is most often the result of peripheral nerve injury secondary to pelvic surgery, disease, or alcoholism, but may also result from spinal cord injury or spinal cord defect.

Treatment

The emphasis in a majority of the studies in the behavioral treatment of encopresis have centered around contingency management. Essentially, the approach consists of frequent pants checks, ample reinforcement for clean pants or for defecation in the toilet, and mild aversive consequences for soiling. Parents often serve as the primary change agents, acting under the direction of a therapist. Several other researchers emphasize the use of medication, usually stool softeners, laxatives, or suppositories as part of a behavioral program.

Much success has been reported in the treatment of fecal incontinence with the use of a biofeedback training procedure in which balloons are used to detect changes in the external and internal anal sphincters. The patient is taught to contract the external anal sphincter whenever he perceives any pressure sensation in the rectum.

Contingency Management

Conger (1970) instructed the mother of a 9-year-old encopretic boy to ignore her son following incidents of soiling. The boy was required to take responsibility for cleaning himself. Soiling was reduced from a baseline level of one to four accidents daily after the first day of treatment. At 3-month follow-up only one additional soiling was noted. Also, Barrett (1969) and Edelman (1971) instructed parents in the use of contingent reinforcement and mild punishment consisting of brief seclusion time-out to eliminate encopresis in their children.

More recently, Doleys, McWhorter, Williams, and Gentry (1977) used an overcorrection procedure they called "full cleanliness training," combined with reinforcement for appropriate toileting to reduce encopresis in three children ranging in age from 4 to 9 years. Here also, the parents were taught to implement treatment in the home environment. In all three cases, encopresis was eliminated shortly after treatment was introduced, and continued improvement was noted at 12, 36, and 48 week follow-ups.

Ferinden and Van Handel (1970) and Pedrini and Pedrini (1971) also used behavioral methods to eliminate soiling in elementary school settings. Ferinden and Van Handel (1970) required the child to clean up the mess and make up lost time after school, while Pedrini and Pedrini (1971) used coupons exchangeable for backup reinforcers contingent on the child's pants being unsoiled.

Tomlinson (1970) and Lal and Lindley (1968) treated children with primary problems of bowel retention. Tomlinson (1970) describes the relative ease with which bowel retention of one year's duration in a 3-year-old boy was rapidly eliminated by giving him bubble gum contingent upon successful elimination in the toilet. Laxatives were required only twice to initiate the response. Normal, routine elimination had been established by the second week of therapy. A 2-week interval with the child's grandparents in which the contingency was removed, provided a natural reversal to show the efficacy of positive reinforcement in controlling appropriate bowel elimination patterns.

Lal and Lindsley (1968) treated a child with fecal retention by informing him that he could play in the bathtub with his toys as soon as he passed a stool. The mother was instructed to leave the bathroom and close the door. When the child indicated he had eliminated, the mother returned, checked for feces, praised him, and put him in the tub. Within 2 weeks, time spent on the toilet decreased from 2 hours to 15 minutes, at which time the child was actively requesting to use the toilet on his own.

Kohlenberg (1973) treated a 13-year-old boy who had suffered from Hirschpring's disease (a congenitally dilated colon) and who was being considered for a colostomy operation. Treatment designed to increase anal sphincter control consisted of reinforcing increases in anal sphincter pressure, first by visual feedback of the amount of pressure in the anal sphincter area, and then by monetary reinforcement. Direct and continuous measurement of sphincter pressure was achieved by inserting a fluid-filled balloon attached to a pressure indicator into the child's rectum. Training took place in a private room while the child was lying in bed positioned so that he could see how much pressure was present in his anal sphincter region. Results showed an increase in sphincter pressure during training, especially when monetary reinforcement was added. Further, these increases in sphincter pressure then occurred in settings other than the training environment.

Epstein and McCoy (1977) treated a 3-year-old girl with Hirshsprung's disease who had no control over bowel or bladder activity and experienced continuous diarrhea. Using a multifaceted toilet training approach, which consisted of: frequent pants checks, praise and edible reinforcers for cleanliness, giving the child responsibility for cleaning up messes, prompting correct use of the toilet, and retention control training after treatment, both urinary and bowel accidents decreased, and there were no accidents during the final 5 weeks of the study. The fact that these procedures can be carried out in the natural environment, without resorting to sophisticated and potentially traumatic instrumentation (at least for young children) would seem to offer distinct advantages over those of Kohlenberg.

Combined Medical Treatment and Contingency Management

At present, two major medical approaches to the management of encopresis are strikingly similar. Davidson (1958) and Levine and Barr (1978) both recommended cleaning out the child with enemas or laxatives and the daily use of mineral oil. Both studies call for a daily regimen of having the child sit on the toilet for one or two brief periods each day, and for the parent to monitor the child's bowel habits. Neither were specific on how this is to be done.

Wright (1973) and Wright and Walker (1977) prescribed glycerin suppositories in the morning before breakfast to regulate bowel movements to occur after breakfast. This was coupled with parental reinforcement for bowel movements in the toilet, and punishments, such as loss of TV privileges, for accidents.

Christopherson and Rainey (1976) used procedures similar to Wright (1973) but discouraged the use of punishment. Parents kept daily records of the child's bowel movements and had daily phone contact with the researchers to aid in maintaining treatment compliance. In a sequel to the Christopherson and Rainey study, Barnard (1978) describes a procedure for doing reliability checks on parental reports of soiling and cleanliness, which they believe is an essential component in studies on the effectiveness of treatment.

Although these studies are all case studies, collectively over 300 encopretic children have been treated with similar procedures. Since encopresis was treated rather than the underlying psychopathology, Levine, Mazonson, and

Bakon (1978) directly addressed the issue of symptom substitution and demonstrated clearly that it was not an issue of concern. These studies demonstrate that even when the physician develops an effective set of treatment procedures, the psychologist working in the medical setting (Wright, 1973; and Christopherson & Rainey, 1976) has expertise in areas of enhancing patient compliance and developing appropriate reward systems to encourage cooperation with the treatment procedures.

Biofeedback

One study, that was described earlier by Kohlenberg (1973) used a biofeedback technique for direct training of anal sphincter muscle pressure with a young boy having organically-based encopresis. This seems to be a less desirable treatment with children than the reinforcement procedures. However, with organically-based fecal incontinence in adults, this procedure has met with much success.

The use of biofeedback for fecal incontinence is reported by Schuster and colleagues (Engel, Nikoomanesh, & Schuster, 1974; Cerulli, Nikoomanesh, & Schuster, 1976) and summarized by Schuster (1977). Engel, Nikoomanesh, and Schuster (1974) taught seven persons with chronic fecal incontinence caused by external sphincter impairment to synchronize external sphincter contraction and internal sphincter relaxation. In an unspecified number of sessions, each lasting 2 hours, the patients were able to observe their anal sphincter pressure tracing as recorded by a rectal distention balloon and polygraph system. Training consisted of practice trials in which therapist-controlled rectal distention by balloon inflation signaled the patients to attempt external sphincter contraction. In addition to observing the continuous pressure tracings, patients were praised by the therapist for their success. Once this task was mastered, subjects were trained to synchronize internal and external sphincter activity by viewing their pressure tracings. Through gradual fading of the feedback, reliance on the machine was reduced.

Cerulli, Nikoomanesh, and Schuster (1976) report on 40 additional patients treated similarly. Incontinence in these patients was associated with prior anorectal surgery, laminectomy, or a variety of medical problems such as irritable bowel syndrome, diabetes, rectal prolapse or myelomeningocele. While undergoing two sessions of a training procedure similar to that described above, 28 of the 40 patients were able to achieve a 57% reduction in the threshold rectal distention needed to produce a rectosphincteric response and reduce the frequency of their incontinence by 90% or better. Over a 4-month to 8-year follow-up period, only two of the successful patients regressed, and this trend was reversed by a brief retraining.

Summary

Encopresis and fecal incontinence are both characterized by fecal soiling without regular bowel movements. Encopresis is primarily a disorder of young children usually with a psychopathologic etiology, whereas fecal incontinence typically results from an organically based weak external anal sphincter.

Much success in the treatment of encopresis has been seen with the use of contingency management with the parent being the primary change agent for the child's soiling behavior. Success has also been shown in a treatment program in which reinforcement is given for adherence to the medical regime. Biofeedback has shown to be successful in treating organically based encopresis but may not be as desirable as the contingency management treatments that can be carried out in the natural environment and may be less traumatic for the child. Biofeedback has, however, been successful in the treatment of organically based fecal incontinence.

Although the study of these gastrointestinal disorders has been dominated by case studies and has received less attention than other disorders, the studies conducted to date indicate that behavioral treatment techniques can be used as an effective treatment modality for encopresis and fecal incontinence.

ULCERS

A peptic ulcer is an erosion in the lining of the gastrointestinal tract caused by excess secretion of hydrochloric acid and pepsin. It can occur at any point in the tract where these gastric secretions come in contact with the lining, in the duodenum, in the stomach, or in rare instances, in the esophagus. Approximately 80% of these ulcers occur in the duodenum (Felton, Perkins, & Lewin, 1969).

Duodenal ulcers are three to six times more common in men than in women, and approximately 10% of the population develop peptic ulcers during their lifetime. There is a significant mortality, estimated to be as high as 10,000 deaths per year in the United States (Whitehead, 1978).

A substantial body of literature suggests that stress and anxiety contribute to the etiology of duodenal ulcers. In a limited number of instances, the stress may be physical: in severe burns, brain injury, or lung disease. More commonly, ulcers occur in persons vulnerable to psychological stress. Peptic ulcer is more prevalent in urban than in rural populations, and in wartime as compared to peacetime (Pflanz, 1971). Air traffic controllers whose job is psychologically stressful have an unusually high rate of peptic ulcer occurrences (Cobb & Rose, 1973; and Grayson, 1972). In an unpublished survey of a midwestern U.S. city, the author found that people with a history of peptic ulcer were more likely than the rest of the population to report to being anxious and depressed (Whitehead, 1978).

The classic ulcer symptom is pain in the upper abdomen when the stomach is empty and the gastric juices have no buffer between them and the involved area. This pain is relieved by the ingestion of food. Medical treatment includes drugs, which neutralize the gastric acids and reduce the motility of the gastrointestinal tract, and the prescription sedatives. Further, the intake of bland foods are a traditional part of the ulcer diet. Surgical treatment of an intractable ulcer may involve a gastric resection, or a vagatomy (since the vagus nerve controls secretion and motility) with enlargement of the pylorus (Felton, Perkins, & Lewin, 1969). Except for the treatment of complications, surgery is not routinely recommended in the management of ulcers because of the possibility of post-operative complications. Some interest has developed in the behavioral treatment of duodenal ulcers as an adjunct to traditional medical and dietary treatment.

Treatment

To date only five studies have been reported in the literature pertaining to the treatment of ulcers, and all refer to specifically treating duodenal ulcers. These five studies have each used different behavioral treatment modalities with varying success.

Biofeedback

Since several animal and normative studies have demonstrated learned control of gastric acid secretion, Welgan (1974) attempted to train increases in the ph of gastric acid secretions in peptic ulcer patients. A biofeedback technique was used in which patients swallowed a ph electrode connected to a meter giving visual feedback of acid secretion. The subjects were duodenal ulcer patients used to a nasogastric tube in the stomach. For two 15-minute periods, interrupted by a 15-minute rest period, the subjects watched an expanded meter recording ph and were reinforced by tones for producing the desired changes. In the presence of ph feedback, the 10 subjects showed significant increases in ph of gastric acid secretions, while acid concentration and volume of secretions significantly declined.

A second study then tested if initial changes following the basal period were experimental effects. Ten subjects were divided into two groups: one group received no feedback after a basal condition, while a second group received feedback after the basal condition. Results showed that significant increases in ph and decreases in acid concentration and volume occurred only after the onset of ph feedback. This preliminary work suggests that gastric acid secretions may be altered and controlled with the appropriate feedback.

While this biofeedback procedure is shown to be successful, it has not yet been utilized as a practical method of treating peptic ulcers. Behavioral procedures that attempt to modify the response of an anxious patient to situations which he perceives to be stressful have been shown to be successful.

Beaty (1976) used a multiple baseline design to examine the effectiveness of EMG feedback training and *in vivo* relaxation to specified stressors as intervention procedures for duodenal ulcers. Three patients with active ulcers rated stomach pain intensity every 2 hours and recorded frequency and dosage of medication prior to intervention. The intervention package consisted of several components: an initial placebo treatment phase, twice weekly frontalis EMG feedback training with daily relaxation practice, and the active use of relaxation in the presence of individually identified environmental stressors. Results suggested that the treatment package was associated with a reduction of recorded stomach pain intensity and medication usage. All three patients reported no stomach pain at the end of treatment and had discontinued medication. This improvement was maintained at 6-month follow-up.

Combinations

Aleo and Nicassio (1978) used similar procedures and added cognitive control procedures in the treatment of four duodenal ulcer patients. In the cognitive control phase, patients were taught to cope with stress by (1) changing negative self-statements concerning stressors, (2) diverting attention from the stressful situation by counting clothing while relaxing, (3) imaging their stomachs becoming relaxed, cool and dry, and their ulcers shrinking and healing. They then practiced the imagery *in vivo* in addition to practicing organ-specific imagery and stress-coping imagery twice daily with the aid of a tape. Results showed complete ulcer healing in three of the subjects with a sizeable reduction in the fourth.

Stambaugh (1977), in a case study, reported the use of two tape-recorded flooding scenarios in dealing with phobic responses accompanied by incapacitating somatic problems consisting of chest pain, shortness of breath, and gastric ulcers with abdominal pain. Remission of the somatic problems was accompanied by increased assertiveness and led to discontinuance of the antianxiety medications. Treatment gains were maintained at 1-month and 1-year follow-ups.

In the most recent study reported, Brooks and Richardson (1980) delivered an emotional skills training program to patients having duodenal ulcers. The program, consisting of anxiety management training and assertive training, was completed by 11 patients in eight 60–90-minute sessions over a 2–week period. Another similar 11 patients received an attention placebo treatment. Over a 60 day follow-up period, the treatment group reported less severe ulcer symptomatology, fewer days of symptomatic pain, reduced antacid medication, and reduced anxiety. A 3½ year follow-up revealed a significantly lower rate of ulcer recurrence in the treatment group.

Summary

The behavioral treatment of ulcers has received some attention to date. Of the procedures used in each of the five studies, all have shown some success. These include: biofeedback to directly reduce gastric acid secretion, EMG biofeedback and relaxation, cognitive control training, coping skills and assertiveness training, and flooding.

These preliminary studies show that peptic ulcers can be treated effectively with behavioral treatment techniques. These studies also point to a need for more indepth research with controlled and more refined designs and comparisons of treatment modalities in order to determine the effectiveness of each.

IRRITABLE BOWEL SYNDROME

The irritable bowel syndrome represents the most common problem encountered by gastroenterologists. It accounts for perhaps 50 to 70% of gastroenterologists' patients and a proportionately large group of patients seen by primary care physicians (Davis, 1978).

This disorder is a symptom complex with many names, perhaps reflecting its protean manifestations and lack of specificity. It is also known as the irritable colon syndrome, mucous colitis, spastic colon, functional colitis, nervous diarrhea, colon neurosis, and dysynergia of the colon (Alexander, 1950; Drossman, Powell, & Sessions, 1977; and Misiewicz, 1969). It is usually called the irritable bowel syndrome because there is evidence to suggest that the condition affects the small bowel as well as the large intestine, and may sometimes involve the entire digestive tube from esophagus to anus in producing symptoms.

This condition can be defined as a disturbed state of intestinal motility for which no anatomical cause can be found. It is characterized by altered bowel function with or without chronic abdominal pain and can be broadly divided into three clinical patterns: spastic colon, painless (nervous) diarrhea, and alternating diarrhea and constipation. Other symptoms are nonspecific and include complaints of dyspepsia, gas, bloating, nausea, vomiting, headache, flushing, fatigue, sighing respirations, hyperventilation, and dysuria (Drossman, Powell, & Sessions, 1977).

Often, manifestations of the condition can be related to life stresses and are seen to reflect the current emotional state (Lachman, 1972). Recent studies have emphasized the preponderance of psychoneurotic and depressive disorders associated with this syndrome (Hislop, 1971; Palmer, 1974; and Young, 1976). Studies have also revealed that such patients have higher scores for various sociocultural factors believed to represent life stresses than either the general population or patients with ulcerative colitis (Mendeloff, 1970).

Medical treatment has usually involved a program of physical exercise, bland diet, establishment of regular bowel habits, and antispasmodic medication. Antidepressants or mild sedatives are also beneficial. If persistent discomfort continues, often the physician refers the patient for psychotherapy. Recently, interest has developed in the behavioral treatment of patients having irritable bowel syndrome.

Treatment

Six studies have been reported that employed behavioral intervention techniques in the treatment of irritable bowel syndrome. Among the treatments used thus far are biofeedback, cognitive restructuring, and a multimodal approach utilizing several different behavioral treatment techniques.

Biofeedback

Furman (1973) utilized biofeedback for the treatment of functional diarrhea in five females ranging in age from 15 to 62 years with lifelong histories of bowel dysfunction. Subjects were treated in an unspecified number of individual half-hour sessions. The treatment consisted of audible feedback of bowel sounds (borborygmi) using an amplified electronic stethoscope placed upon the abdomen. In a relaxed setting, the patients were requested to increase and decrease bowel sounds and thus learn voluntary control of gastrointestinal peristalsis. Reductions in borborygmi were sought, for such reductions presumably represent a decrease in the activity of the bowel. The patients were praised by the therapist for evidence of control over the bowel sounds. Additionally, all patients were maintained on restrictive dietary regimens. Medication was maintained for four of the patients and the fifth was provided with systematic desensitization for relief of anxiety associated with GI dysfunction. While detailed results are not provided, all subjects demonstrated some degree of control over their intestinal motility during the biofeedback training, and reportedly were having normal bowel function.

Weinstock (1976) describes a successful attempt to control gastrointestinal hyperactivity. A technique of autonomic reconditioning was applied to 12 patients suffering from functional disorders of the lower intestinal tract. At first, an amplified electronic stethoscope was employed in a nonstressful therapy situation, coupled with verbal positive reinforcement for operant conditioning to achieve control of bowel activity. Response to treatment was sporadic, with three patients discontinuing treatment. The remaining nine patients were then subjected to a completely different treatment consisting of a golf counter to record each individual instance of bowel discomfort, daily charting of the same, EMG frontalis relaxation three times a week, and a relaxation tape to be played twice daily. Response to treatment was uniformly positive.

O'Connell and Russ (1978) in a case study compared the effectiveness of two biofeedback training procedures in the treatment of irritable bowel syndrome. One procedure involved training control of intestinal motility using acoustic recordings of abdominal sounds to provide feedback, and the other procedure consisted of relaxation training using EMG biofeedback. Results showed bowel-sound feedback was not effective with this subject. Voluntary increase and decrease in intestinal mobility was accomplished but without effect on pain experienced. Muscle relaxation, however, seemed to result in pain reduction.

Cognitive Restructuring

Youell and McCullough (1975) treated a young female who had one colitis attack per day at onset of treatment. A procedure was used in which antecedent stressful events appearing to precipitate attacks were labeled. The client was then taught a cognitive coping strategy to counter the stress events. There was subsequently a steady decline in attack frequency. No attacks were reported during a 43 week follow-up period.

Multimodal Approach

Harrell and Beiman (1978) treated a young man with a seven year history of gastrointestinal problems mediated by chronic anxiety in major life areas. Seven weeks of cognitive restructuring were followed by progressive relaxation and differential relaxation training. Systematic problem solving, socialization skills through behavioral rehearsal, and assertive training were also learned over a 6-month treatment period. As anxiety was reduced in major life areas, the gastrointestinal symptoms exhibited similar clinically significant reductions which were maintained at a 1-year follow-up.

Likewise, Briddell and Leiblum (1976) utilized a multimodal treatment approach in the treatment of a young man having spastic colitis and incapacitating anxiety. Treatment modalities consisted of desensitization, assertive training, relaxation and autogenic training, cognitive restructuring, imagery, implosion, fading, scheduling of reinforcing activities, and self-monitoring of undesirable behaviors. Colitis attacks continued to occur daily until the ninth session, at which time attacks fluctuated from one to two per week until the 16th session at which time they were nonexistent until treatment termination at session 18. His colitis appeared to be stabilized to one or two attacks every three or four weeks at 6- and 12-month follow-ups.

Summary

Irritable bowel syndrome, also known as colitis, or spastic colon, is the most common gastrointestinal disorder representing between 50 and 70% of all gastrointerology referrals. Surprisingly, however, this disorder has received little attention in the behavioral medicine literature. Biofeedback, cognitive restructuring, and multimodal approaches have been used with some success primarily in case studies. However, the actual clinical utility of these methods cannot be adequately assessed due to the lack of controlled studies and follow-up evaluations. Behavioral intervention for the irritable bowel syndrome seems promising and future research is warranted.

REFERENCES

Agras, S., Barlow, D., Chapin, H., Abel, G., & Leitenberg, H. Behavior modification of anorexia nervosa. *Archives of General Psychiatry*, 1974, **30**, 279–286.

Aleo, S. & Nicassio, P. Autoregulation of duodenal ulcer disease: A preliminary report of four cases. Proceedings of the Biofeedback Society of America, Ninth Annual Meeting, Denver, Biofeedback Society of America, 1978, 278–281.

Alexander, F. *Psychosomatic medicine.* New York: Norton, 1950.

Alva, J., Mendeloff, A.I., & Schuster, M.M. Reflex and electromyographic abnormalities associated with fecal incontinence. *Gastroenterology,* 1967, **53,** 101–106.

Azzerad, J. & Stafford, R. Restoration of eating behavior in anorexia nervosa through operant conditioning and environmental manipulation. *Behavior Research and Therapy,* 1969, **7,** 165–171.

Bachrach, A.J., Erwin, W.J., & Mohr, J.P. The control of eating behavior in an anorexic by operant conditioning techniques. In L.P. Ullman & L. Krasner (Eds.) *Case studies in behavior modification.* New York: Holt, Rinehart, & Winston, 1965.

Barnard, S.R. An experimental analysis of a parent-mediated behavioral treatment program for encopresis. Unpublished Masters thesis, University of Kansas, Lawrence, 1978.

Barrett, B. Behavior modification in the home: Parents adapt laboratory-developed tactics to bowel train a 5½ year old. *Psychotherapy: Theory, Research, and Practice,* 1969, **6,** 172–176.

Beaty, E.T. Feedback assisted relaxation training as a treatment for peptic ulcers. *Biofeedback and Self-Regulation,* 1976, **1,** 323–324.

Becker, J., Turner, S., & Sajwaj, T. Multiple behavioral effects of the use of lemon juice with a ruminating toddler-age child. *Behavior Modification,* 1978, **2,** 267–278.

Bianco, F.J. Rapid treatment of two cases of anorexia nervosa. *Journal of Behavior Therapy and Experimental Psychiatry,* 1972, **3,** 223–224.

Blinder, B.J., Freeman, D.M.A., & Stunkard, A.J. Behavior therapy of anorexia nervosa: Effectiveness of activity as a reinforcer of weight gain. *American Journal of Psychiatry,* 1970, **126,** 1093–1098.

Bliss, E. & Branch, C. *Anorexia nervosa.* New York: Paul B. Hocher, 1960.

Briddell, D.W. & Leiblum, S.R. Multimodal treatment of spastic colitis and incapacitating anxiety: A case study. In A.A. Lazarus (Ed.) *Multimodal behavior therapy.* New York: Springer, 1976.

Bright, G.O. & Whaley, D.L. Suppression of regurgitation and rumination with aversive events. Michigan Mental Health Research Bulletin, 1968, **11,** 17–20.

Brooks, G.R. & Richardson, F.C. Emotional skills training: A treatment program for duodenal ulcer. *Behavior Therapy,* 1980, **11,** 198–207.

Browning, C.H. & Miller, S.I. Anorexia nervosa: A study in prognosis and management. *American Journal of Psychiatry,* 1968, **124,** 1128–1132.

Bruch, H. Changing approachers to anorexia nervosa. *International Psychiatry Clinics,* 1970, **7,** 3–24.

Cerulli, M.A., Nikoomanesh, P., & Schuster, M.M. Progress in biofeedback conditioning for fecal incontinence. Unpublished manuscript. Abstract published in *Gastroenterology,* 1976, **70,** 869.

Christopherson, E.R. & Rainey, S. Management of encopresis through a pediatric out-patient clinic. *Journal of Pediatric Psychology,* 1976, **1,** 38–41.

Cobb, S. & Rose, R.M. Hypertension, peptic ulcer, and diabetes in air traffic controllers. *Journal of the American Medical Association,* 1973, **224,** 489–492.

Conger, J. The treatment of encopresis by the management of social consequences. *Behavior Therapy,* 1970, **1,** 386–390.

Cunningham, C. & Linscheid, T. Elimination of chronic infant ruminating by electric shock. *Behavior Therapy,* 1976, **7,** 231–234.

Dally, P.J. & Sargant, W. Treatment and outcome of anorexia nervosa. *British Medical Journal,* 1966, **2,** 793–795.

Davidson, M. Constipation and fecal incontinence. *Pediatrics Clinical of North America,* 1958, **5,** 749–757.

Davis, W.D. The irritable bowel syndrome—How to recognize and manage it. *Modern Medicine,* 1978, **46,** 62–65.

Doleys, D.M., McWhorter, A.Q., Williams, S.C., & Gentry, W.R. Encopresis: Its treatment relative to nocturnal enuresis. *Behavior Therapy,* 1977, **8,** 77–82.

Drossman, D.A., Powell, D.W., & Sessions, J.T. The irritable bowel syndrome. *Gastroenterology,* 1977, **73,** 811–822.

Duker, P. & Seys, D. Elimination of vomiting in a retarded female using restitutional overcorrection. *Behavior Therapy,* 1977, **8,** 255–257.

Edelman, R. Operant conditioning treatment of encopresis. *Journal of Behavior Therapy and Experimental Psychiatry,* 1971, **2,** 71–73.

Engel, B.T., Nikoomanesh, P., & Schuster, M.M. Operant conditioning of retrosphincteric responses in the treatment of fecal incontinence. *New England Journal of Medicine,* 1974, **290,** 646–649.

Epstein, L.H. & McCoy, J. Bowel control of Hirschsprung's disease. *Journal of Behavior Therapy and Experimental Psychiatry,* 1977, **8,** 97–99.

Felton, J.P., Perkins, D.C., & Lewin, M. A survey of medicine and medical practice for the rehabilitation counselor. U.S. Department of Health, Education, and Welfare, Washington, D.C., 1969.

Ferinden, W. & Van Handel, D. Elimination of soiling behavior in an elementary school child through the application of aversive techniques. *Journal of School Psychology,* 1970, **8,** 267–269.

Fullerton, D.T. Infantile rumination: A case report. *Archives of General Psychiatry,* 1963, **9,** 593–600.

Furman, S. Intestinal biofeedback in functional diarrhea: A preliminary report. *Journal of Behavior Therapy and Experimental Psychiatry,* 1973, **4,** 317–321.

Gaddini, R. & Gaddini, E. Rumination in infancy. In C. Jessner & E. Pavenstadt (Eds.) *Dynamic psychopathology in childhood.* New York: Grune & Stratton, 1959.

Galbraith, D., Byrick, R., & Rutledge, J.T. An aversive conditioning approach to the inhibition of chronic vomiting. *Canadian Pediatric Association Journal,* 1970, **15,** 311–313.

Garfinkel, P., Kline, S., & Stancer, H. Treatment of anorexia nervosa using operant conditioning techniques. *Journal of Nervous and Mental Disease,* 1973, **157,** 428–433.

Geller, J.L. Treatment of anorexia nervosa by the integration of behavior and psychotherapy. *Psychotherapy Psychosomatics,* 1975, **26,** 167–177.

Grayson, R.R. Air controllers syndrome: Peptic ulcers in air traffic controllers. *Illinois Medical Journal,* 1972, **142,** 111–115.

Harrell, T.H. & Beiman, I. Cognitive-behavioral treatment of the irritable colon syndrome. *Cognitive Therapy and Research,* 1978, **2,** 371–375.

Hislop, I.G. Psychological significance of the irritable colon syndrome. *Gut,* 1971, **12,** 452–457.

Hollowell, J.R. & Gardner, L.I. Rumination and growth failure in male fraternal twins: Association with disturbed family environment. *Pediatrics,* 1965, **36,** 565–571.

Hoyt, C. & Stickler, G. A study of forty-four children with the syndrome of recurrent (cyclia) vomiting. *Pediatrics,* 1960, **25,** 775–779.

Kanner, L. *Child Psychiatry.* Springfield, Ill.: Charles C Thomas, 1957.

Kohlenberg, R.J. Operant conditioning of human anal sphincter pressure. *Journal of Applied Behavior Analysis,* 1973, **6,** 201–208.

Kohlenberg, R.J. The punishment of persistent vomiting: A case study. *Journal of Applied Behavior Analysis,* 1970, **3,** 241–245.

Lackman, S.J. *Psychosomatic disorders: A behavioristic interpretation.* New York: Wiley, 1972.

Lal, H. & Lindley, O. Therapy of chronic constipation in a young child by rearranging social contingencies. *Behavior Therapy,* 1968, **6,** 484–485.

Lang, P.J. Behavior therapy with a case of nervous anorexia. In L.P. Ullmann & L. Krasner (Eds.) *Case studies in behavior modification.* New York: Holt, Rineholt, & Winston, 1965.

Lang, P.J. & Melamed, B.G. Avoidance conditioning therapy of an infant with chronic ruminative vomiting. *Journal of Abnormal Psychology,* 1969, **74,** 139–142.

Leitenberg, H., Agras, S., & Thomson, L. A sequential analysis of the effect of selective, positive reinforcement in modifying anorexia nervosa. *Behavior Research and Therapy,* 1968, **6,** 211–218.

Levine, M.D. Children with encopresis: A descriptive analysis. *Pediatrics,* 1975, **56,** 412–416.

Levine, M.D. & Barr, R.G. Clinical manual: Encopresis patient care data system. Unpublished manuscript, Children's Hospital Medical Center, Boston, 1978.

Levine, M.D., Mazonson, P., & Bakow, H. Behavioral symptom substitution in children cured of encopresis. Paper presented at the annual meeting of the Ambulatory Pediatric Association, New York, April, 1978.

Luckey, R.E., Watson, C.M., & Musick, J.K. Aversive conditioning as a means of inhibiting vomiting and rumination. *American Journal of Mental Deficiency,* 1968, **73,** 139–142.

Mendeloff, A.I. Illness experience and life stresses in patients with ulcerative colitis. *New England Journal of Medicine,* 1970, **282,** 14–17.

Menking, M., Wagnitz, J., Burton, J., Coddington, R.D., & Sotos, J. Rumination—A new fatal psychiatric disease of infancy. *The New England Journal of Medicine,* 1969, 281, 802, 804.

Misiewicz, J.J. The irritable colon syndrome. In B.C. Morson (Ed.) *Diseases of the colon, rectum, and anus.* New York: Appleton-Century-Crofts, 1969.

Nemiah, J. Emotions and gastrointestinal disease. In H. Lief, V.P. Lief, & R.N. Lief (Eds.) *The psychological basis of medical practice*. New York: Paul B. Hoeber, 1963.

Neumann, M. & Gaoni, B. Preferred food as the reinforcing agent in a case of anorexia nervosa. *Journal of Behavior Therapy and Experimental Psychiatry*, 1975, **6**, 331–333.

O'Connell, M.F. & Russ, K.L. A case report comparing two types of biofeedback in the treatment of irritable bowel syndrome. Paper presented at the meeting of the Biofeedback Society of America, Albuquerque, March 1978.

Palmer, R.L. Psychological characteristics of patients with the irritable bowel syndrome. *Postgraduate Medicine*, 1974, **50**, 416–419.

Pedrini, B. & Pedrini, D. Reinforcement procedures in the control of encopresis: A case study. *Psychological Reports*, 1971, **28**, 937–938.

Pflanz, M. Epidemiological and sociocultural factors in the etiology of duodenal ulcer. *Advances in Psychosomatic Medicine*, 1971, **6**, 121–151.

Pierce, D. Enuresis and Encopresis. In A. Freedman, H. Kaplan, & B. Sadock (Eds.) *Comprehensive textbook of psychiatry*, Vol. 2. Baltimore: Williams & Wilkins, 1975.

Richmond, J.B., Eddy, E., & Green, M. Rumination: A psychosomatic syndrome of infancy. *Pediatrics*, 1958, **22**, 29–55.

Sajwaj, T., Libet, J., & Agras, A. Lemon-juice therapy: The control of life-threatening rumination in a six-month-old infant. *Journal of Applied Behavior Analysis*, 1974, **7**, 557–566.

Schnurer, A.T., Rubin, R.R., & Roy, A. Systematic desensitization of anorexia nervosa seen as a weight phobia. *Journal of Behavior Therapy and Experimental Psychiatry*, 1973, **14**, 149–153.

Shuster, M.M. Biofeedback treatment of gastrointestinal dysfunction. *Medical Clinics of North America*, 1977, **61**, 907–912.

Stambaugh, E.E. Audio-taped flooding in outpatient treatment of somatic complaints. *Journal of Behavior Therapy and Experimental Psychiatry*, 1977, **8**, 173–176.

Stein, M.L., Rausen, A.R., & Blare, A. Psychotherapy of an infant with rumination. *Journal of the American Medical Association*, 1959, **171**, 2309–2312.

Stunkard, A.J. Anorexia nervosa. In J.P. Sanford (Ed.) *The science and practice of clinical medicine*. New York: Grune & Stratton, 1975.

Tomlinson, J.R. The treatment of bowel retention by operant procedures: A case study. *Journal of Behavior Therapy and Experimental Psychiatry*, 1970, **1**, 83–85.

Weinstock, S.A. The reestablishment of intestinal control in functional colitis. *Biofeedback and Self-Regulation*, 1976, **1**, 324.

Welgan, P.R. Learned control of gastric acid secretion in ulcer patients. *Psychosomatic Medicine*, 1974, **36**, 411–419.

White, J.C. & Taylor, J.D. Noxious conditioning as a treatment for rumination. *Mental Retardation*, 1967, **5**, 30–33.

Whitehead, W.E. Gastrointestinal disorders. *Behavioral Medicine Newsletter*, 1978, **1**, 6–9.

Wolf, M.M., Birnbrauer, J.S., Williams, T., & Lawler, J. A note on apparent behavior of a retarded child. In L.P. Ullman and L. Krasner (Eds.) *Case studies in behavior modification*. New York: Holt, Rinehart, & Winston, 1965.

Wright, L. Handling the encopretic child. *Professional Psychology*, 1973, **4**, 137–144.

Wright, L. Outcome of a standardized program for treating psychogenic encopresis. *Professional Psychology*, 1975, **6**, 453–456.

Wright, L. & Walker, E. Treatment of the child with psychogenic encopresis. *Clinical Pediatrics*, 1977, **16**, 1042–1045.

Youell, K.J. & McCullough, J.P. Behavioral treatment of mucous colitis. *Journal of Consulting and Clinical Psychology*, 1975, **43**, 740–745.

Young, S.J. Psychiatric illness and the irritable bowel syndrome. *Gastroenterology*, 1976, **70**, 162–166.

CHAPTER 9

Musculoskeletal Disorders

OVERVIEW

Since coordinated muscle activity is the *sine qua non* of behavior, it seems only logical that the modification of striate muscle system activity should be of great significance for behavioral medicine. This is for both practical and theoretical reasons. Since the striate musculature makes up almost 50% of body mass, it seems likely that it would have significant effects on the body as a whole. Also, it is obvious that the muscular activity is an inescapable part of adaptive behavior, and of response to stress. Without it, there is no behavior.

Disorders in the musculoskeletal system may be observed in poorly regulated muscles, as in spasmodic torticollis and tics; in muscle dysfunction secondary to central nervous system damage, such as in cerebral palsy resulting from brain damage usually at birth, or in paralysis after a stroke; and in muscle damage resulting from some sort of accident causing paralysis.

With the advent of behavioral medicine, there is a growing body of clinical evidence, much of it having been accumulated over the past several years, indicating that muscle alteration is a powerful variable and one which can be clinically useful in the treatment of various musculoskeletal disorders. The musculoskeletal disorders for which behavioral treatment techniques have proven most useful are spasmodic torticollis, tics, cerebral palsy, cerebrovascular accidents resulting in hemiplegia, and spinal cord injuries resulting in paraplegia or quadriplegia.

SPASMODIC TORTICOLLIS

Spasmodic torticollis is a disorder of the cervical muscles, particularly the sternocleidomastoid muscle, that results in abnormal movements of positioning of the head (Brierly, 1967). Also known as "wry neck," this condition is characterized by episodic spasms of the neck muscles which cause an involuntary and apparently uncontrollable twisting of the head to a distorted and uncomfortable position to either the right or left, depending upon the muscles involved. Insidious in onset, the twisting of the head in torticollis typically becomes more severe over a period of months, and then stabilizes.

Spontaneous remissions are rare but have been reported (Cleelend, 1973).

Despite advances in diagnostic sophistication and in pharmacologic research, the etiology of spasmodic torticollis remains obscure. One school of thought regards it as a consequence of basal ganglia dysfunction; others think the disorder is a conversion hysterical phenomenon.

One approach to treatment is surgical intervention, including rhizotomy (Sorenson & Hamby, 1966), or cryothalectomy (Cooper, 1964). These approaches are based on the assumption that the dyskinesia and excess muscle tone are secondary disorders of the basal ganglia. Cooper (1964) suggests it is caused by a disturbance of the impulses from the basal ganglia to the cortex. In several cases, a cryothalectomy was successful in providing relief of torticollis symptoms.

Eldredge (1970) reviewed another approach and suggested that spasmodic torticollis is a form of torsion dystonia. This prompted a number of investigators to pursue the problem as one of dopamine metabolism in the brain stem. However, chemical interventions are inconclusive. Barrett, Yahr, and Duvoisin (1970) reported no sustained improvement after levodopa treatments, while Gilbert (1972) described good responses to treatments involving either amantadine hydrochloride or haloperidol.

While the condition may be a symptom of disease of the extrapyramidal system, Brierly (1967) believes it may also have a hysterical origin. Distinction can usually be made as to whether it is an organic or hysterical disorder by considering the manner of its onset. In torticollis of the hysterical type, it is believed that the disorder follows an emotional trauma and presents with a relatively rapid onset, while an insidious onset indicates an organic problem (Brierly, 1967). Psychotherapy as a treatment of choice has met with infrequent success (Pattison, 1970). These unsuccessful conventional interventions prompted investigators to examine the potential application of behavioral techniques to relieve these symptoms.

Treatment

The majority of studies presented in the literature on the treatment of spasmodic torticollis has been in the use of biofeedback. Other researchers have used negative practice, aversive conditioning, and systematic desensitization.

Biofeedback

The first application of EMG biofeedback to the treatment of spasmodic torticollis was reported by Cleeland (1973). Auditory EMG feedback of sternocleidomastoid (SCM) muscle activity during relaxation of this muscle was combined with mild electric shock to the fingertips during spasm. During treatment 9 of the 10 subjects manifested 77% reduction in spasm frequency. At 18-month follow-up, six of these nine showed further improvement in spasm reductions.

Brudny and his colleagues presented findings in several publications (Brudny, Grynbaum, & Korein, 1974; Brudny et al., 1974; and Brudny et al., 1976), obtained using EMG feedback training with a series of torticollis patients. The most recent report (Brudny et al., 1976) summarizes results achieved in the treatment of 48 patients. The procedure included audiovisual EMG feedback of surface SCM activity, contra- and ipsilateral to the direction of head rotation, during rest and contraction practice. Nineteen (40%) of the patients were rated as showing moderate to major improvement. These patients could maintain a normal head position for prolonged periods of time without feedback and during daily activities.

Williams (1974) reported the use of a novel biofeedback strategy in a case study. Hypothesizing that the induction of heart rate slowing might produce decreased muscle activity, the patient was provided with visual feedback of her heart rate and instructed to use this feedback to help her learn to relax. Both within and across sessions, the patient was able to slow her heart rate and become more relaxed with a concomitant alleviation of torticollis as measured by EMG and clinical observation. This study is interesting to note because as the physiological symptoms improved, her psychological condition declined to the point of hospitalization. The clinician utilizing this approach should be prepared to manage any psychological complications should they occur.

The most recent study of the use of biofeedback was reported by Jankel (1978). Two experiments using A-B-A-B designs were conducted on a patient with spasmodic torticollis. In the first experiment, the subject was provided an analog tone as feedback for modifying the EMG levels of the left sternocleidomastoid to match those of the right sternocleidomastoid. In the second experiment, the subject was provided an analog tone as feedback for increasing or decreasing the muscle activity of both sternocleidomastoids in tandem. In both experiments, statistically significant changes in muscle activity were observed that resulted in a more vertical head position and relief from the torticollis symptoms.

The studies dealing with EMG feedback consist primarily of collections of individual clinical case reports with training procedures varying from case to case, and feedback often being combined with other interventions. The results are promising, but the failure to use appropriate control procedures renders it difficult to evaluate the role of EMG biofeedback training with spasmodic torticollis.

Operant Procedures

Agras and Marshall (1965) used negative practice in the treatment of two patients with spasmodic torticollis and reported success in one of them. This suggests that the ease with which the patient was able to make the return movement from the dystonic to tonic position is the distinguishing characteristic that would predict success in the use of negative practice. The patient reporting difficulty in moving the head back to normal position did not improve.

Brierly (1967) treated two torticollis patients using aversive conditioning. A specially designed head gear was used that administered a mild electric shock to the patients' wrists contingent upon the angle of their head and neck during training sessions. Both patients improved, with the improvement carrying over to their daily environment.

Bernhardt, Hersen, and Barlow (1972) used a combination of instructions and negative feedback with a design that allowed for assessment of the effectiveness of instructions, and of negative feedback by using video tapes separately as well as combined. Results showed that negative feedback alone was most effective in reducing torticollis. Further, Ericksen and Huber (1975) reported a patient regained complete voluntary control of head movements and remained symptom-free at 9-month follow-up after employing a procedure requiring the patient to make small head movements in syncronization with the beat of a metronome.

Systematic Desensitization

Meares (1973) postulated a model for the etiology of spasmodic torticollis based on the assumption that fortuitous head movements in the direction of the torticollis produce anxiety which the ensuing muscle spasm momentarily reduces. Therefore, the muscle spasms may become conditioned since they reduce anxiety. Systematic desensitization was employed with a 44-year-old-female, who had not been spasm-free while awake. Following treatment, she was spasm-free for hours at a time. Although success was shown in this case, desensitization may be limited for use to only those patients displaying accompanying anxiety.

Summary

Spasmodic torticollis is a disorder of the cervical muscles that results in abnormal movements or positioning of the head. The etiology of this condition has been debated and varying surgical, psychological, and behavioral techniques have been applied in relation to the etiological theories.

In comparison to other treatment procedures, EMG biofeedback appears to be among those most cost efficient. Surgical techniques such as rhizotomy and cryothalectomy involve considerable time, professional expertise, and patient expense, with limited and questionable long-term success (Meares, 1973). Although some of the operant conditioning treatments, such as aversive conditioning and negative practice have been successful in case studies, the results are inconsistent and equivocal. Therefore, even though the literature on EMG biofeedback represents a collection of uncontrolled anecdotal case reports, the promising comparative efficacy of the technique warrants further investigation.

TICS

A tic can be described as any spasmodic movement or twitching of a particular area of the body, the face for example, marked by quick sudden spasms that are identical with the movements of volitional intent. Tics occur in persons of neurotic tendency, are often hereditary, and usually develop in youth. Tics are also referred to as mimic spasm, habit spasm, and maladie des tics.

The syndrome of multiple tics that originates in childhood and consists of compulsive jerking of the voluntary musculature in the face, neck, or extremities combined with coprolalia, echolalia, or other spasmodic involuntary noises is known as the *maladie de Gilles de la Tourette* (Gilles de la Tourette, 1885). Many investigators have observed that these multiple tics are very frequently accompanied by so-called emotional disturbances, such as enuresis, phobias, and aggressiveness (Corbett *et al.*, 1969; Lucas, 1967; and Morphew & Sim, 1969).

The prognosis was originally thought to be poor, and many writers still describe pessimistic prospects. However, recent studies (Corbett *et al.*, 1969; and Lucus *et al.*, 1969) with long term follow-ups, suggest a more favorable prognosis.

The etiology of the syndrome is unknown. Although particular organic abnormalities have been found in some studies (Field *et al.*, 1966), other studies have failed to discover any consistent organic problem or history (Corbett *et al.*, 1969; Morphew & Sim, 1969). In addition to functional theories of origin (Ascher, 1948; Mahler, 1944 & 1945; and Morphew & Sim, 1969) there are explanations in terms of both functional and organic factors.

Stevens and Blachly (1966) have successfully treated this syndrome with the drug, haloperidol. This antipsychotic drug appears to be the most consistently effective drug, although success with it varies from complete, almost immediate relief of symptoms, to no discernible effect (Abuzzahab, 1970; Challas & Brauer, 1963; Connell *et al.*, 1967; Ford & Gottlieb, 1969; Lucas, 1967; Shapiro & Shapiro, 1968; and Stevens & Blachly, 1966). Recently, behavioral intervention strategies have been used to treat tics.

Treatment

The majority of emphasis in the treatment of tics has been with the use of massed practice, alone or in conjunction with time-out procedures or aversive conditioning. Self-monitoring has also been successfully used as well as a multiple component treatment.

Operant Procedures

One of the first trends in the treatment of tics was based on a theoretical formulation put forth by Yates (1958; 1970). According to his model, a tic is a drive-reducing conditioned response, a learned habit that has reached maximum habit strength. To extinguish this habit, it should be possible to build up an incompatible habit of not performing the tic. Massed practice involves instructing the patient repeatedly to perform the unwanted response until further repetitions become tiresome. The fatigue state produced by massed practice is aversive, and responses incompatible with the tic are assumed to be reinforced during a rest period by the avoidance of fatigue.

Since the initial work of Yates (1958), studies by Jones (1960), Lazarus (1960), Walton (1961, 1964), Raffi (1962), Clark (1966), Nicassio, Leiberman, Patterson, Rominez, and Sanders (1972) and Tophoff (1973) offer partial or strong support for both the theory and techniques. Rafi (1962) and Nicassio et al. (1972) report both positive and negative results. Feldman and Werry (1966) present the only results which clearly fail to support both the theory and treatment procedures.

Knepler and Sewall (1974) used a noxious olfactory stimulus (aromatic ammonia or "smelling salts") in conjunction with negative or massed practice to achieve rapid deceleration in a unilateral facial-eye-blink tic. After 80 minutes of massed practice paired with the smelling salts, the tic of 4-year duration declined significantly during voluntary evocation and in spontaneous occurrence. By the 6-month follow-up, almost total symptom remission had occurred.

Lahey, McNees, and McNees (1973) used brief seclusion time-out after massed practice to eliminate an obscene verbal tic in a child with Gilles de la Tourette's Syndrome. Massed practice resulted in a decrease in rate but not complete suppression of the response. Massed practice was also hard to administer in the child's classroom where the problem was particularly disruptive. Time-out quickly suppressed the verbal tic, and generalization to the home environment was also reported. Withdrawal and reimplementation of treatment were associated with increases and decreases in the rate of tic responses, demonstrating that response-contingent events exerted a powerful influence over supposedly involuntary acts.

Barrett (1962) used time-out from pleasant music to reduce multiple tics in a man having a lengthy history of tics. Barrett compared the effect of interruption from music to continuous noise and music. The marked reduction in tic rate was due to the contingencies associated with music interruption, not the availability of music itself.

Self-control Methods

Self-control methods have also been used in treating tics, and are useful because they enable implementation of treatment procedures in natural surroundings, as opposed to massed practice, which is restricted to the laboratory. Hutzell, Platzek, and Logue (1974) used self-monitoring to modify head and vocal tics. These responses were eliminated in succession utilizing a multiple-baseline design. The fact that each tic declined after the introduction of self-monitoring indicates a relationship between treatment and rate of the problem behavior. A 1-year follow-up showed continued improvement.

Thomas, Abrams, and Johnson (1977) treated an 18-year-old male with a long history of Gilles de la Tourette's Syndrome, whose symptoms had proven refractory to medical and psychiatric procedures. The treatment consisted of self-monitoring and systematic desensitization. A modified multiple-baseline design was used to assess treatment effects. Results showed that combined use of self-monitoring and desensitization reduced the rate of tics each time they were utilized to treat a new ticlike response. Although the long-term effectiveness of the treatment is unknown, results are encouraging and deserve continued exploration.

The most impressive data on the treatment of tics has been reported by Azrin and Nunn (1973) who used a multiple component approach. Their approach, called "habit reversal," is based on the assumption that tic-like disturbances begin as reactions to trauma or stress and persist because of limited personal or social awareness. Habit reversal is designed to (1) increase personal awareness of each occurrence of the unwanted habit, (2) strengthen antagonistic behavior, and (3) eliminate any social reinforcement (sympathy) that may maintain the habit. Several procedures were used, including self-monitoring, awareness training, competing response practice, habit inconvenience review, and social support procedures enlisting family and friends to promote and maintain desired behavior change in the natural setting. Azrin and Nunn (1973) present data on 12 clients with a variety of ticlike behavior and nervous habits. Dramatic results in rate reduction were achieved after a single session. The average percentage reduction below baseline after the first day of training was 95%. This increased to 99% after 3 weeks and remained at that level during a 5-month follow-up. Although these results are impressive, placebo and expectancy effects were not controlled for and data was obtained by self-report techniques.

Summary

Tics, or spasmodic movement or twitching of various parts of the body, have been treated with various methods. The most successful of these has been use of the drug haloperidol, even though results have been mixed with its use.

The literature on behavioral treatment of tics is sparse and most of the studies are uncontrolled case studies. These studies have shown some success, however, and warrant further investigation. The operant techniques of massed practice, time-out, and aversive conditioning have been used alone or in conjunction with one another in the reduction of tic behavior. Other treatment techniques showing reductions in tic behavior are self-monitoring and systematic desensitization as well as a multiple component treatment using many of the above strategies in combination. Due to the relative success of the behavioral treatment strategies as opposed to some of the more conventional treatments in modifying tic behavior, this area warrants further research.

CEREBRAL PALSY

Cerebral palsy is a disorder involving permanent impairment of sensori-motor functioning resulting from brain damage usually occurring before or during birth (Inglis, Campbell, & Donald, 1976). Among the factors which may precipitate such damage are faulty embryonic development, disease, or injury to the mother, particularly during the first trimester of pregnancy, disadvantageous blood factors between the mother and the developing infant, injury during birth, anoxia, or injury or infection after birth.

The damage may affect brain tissue in the motor areas of the cerebral cortex, the basal ganglia, or the cerebellum. Not infrequently, there are, in addition to motor dysfunction, evidences of mental retardation, impairment of hearing, vision, or speech, and behavioral dislocations. The characteristic motor patterns include: abnormal patterns of posture and gait; both spastic and flaccid paralysis; involuntary athetoid (twisting) movements and tremor.

Because of the inadequacies in testing methods and deficits in communication, many cerebral palsy children were considered to be of low intelligence. More skilled testing procedures have demonstrated mental competence, or even superior levels in a great number of children having cerebral palsy. An appreciable amount of improvement can be effected in the muscular disability of cerebral palsy children through prolonged rehabilitation.

Treatment

In recent years the use of biofeedback in the treatment of cerebral palsy has received some attention. Biofeedback procedures are typically employed to improve posture and gait and eliminate the athetoid movements.

One of the first attempts to develop a procedure for altering these characteristics in cerebral palsied children was developed by Harris, Spelman, and Hymer (1974). They developed a device for the control of head posture and another for assessing limb position in an attempt to restore or supplement defective proprioceptive feedback so as to normalize movements in their patients. The hypothesis used for the development of these devices was reported by Harris (1971) and it stated that a possible basis for the athetoid movements in cerebral palsy was "inapproprioception." This term refers to a faulty kinesthetic monitoring based on defective or disordered proprioceptive feedback. The aim of these researchers was to develop electronic sensory aides that would provide these children with external feedback that would carry correct information about their posture and movements.

Results showed that all of the 18 children using the head control device improved considerably in head stability. All of the children using the limb position monitor showed a decrease in tremor and improvement in the smoothness and accuracy of arm movements. Range of motion at the elbow joint also increased. In addition, there seemed to be considerable generalization of these improvements to other settings.

Wooldridge and Russell (1976) trained 12 cerebral palsied children with a wide range of IQs for correct head orientation. A tilt-activated mercury switch inside specially built head gear provided audiovisual information to the children regarding the spatial position of their heads. Feedback was provided when the head moved out of an upright, feedback-free area. Auxiliary feedback units used with some children included accumulated performance counters and clocks, cable cars, race tracks, record players, and television sets that were shut off when the head was positioned incorrectly. Training was conducted in a number of settings to maximize generalization. Training session number, duration, and activities varied among children according to their particular needs.

Clinical evaluation showed that three children showed minimal changes during feedback and no functional improvement. Six others showed consistent improvement during feedback and some functional change. Three other children maintained functional improvements during feedback and when feedback was removed. Follow-up on 10 of the 12 patients showed maintenance of these results at 3 months.

Another approach to cerebral palsy has utilized EMG feedback as a means of producing relaxation for the improvement of speech and motor functioning in cerebral palsied children. Finley, Niman, Stanley et al., (1976) attempted to use sensorimotor (SMR) feedback but noted that muscle activity of the head and face of these patients was at such a high level that it was not possible to detect SMR. Frontal EMG feedback was provided to one patient to reduce unwanted EMG activity before starting SMR training. Improvement in several aspects led the authors to proceed the same way with five other children. With the six patients, EMG levels decreased from an average of 28.9 to 13.0 microvolts. The patients improved in both fine and gross coordination, decreased tremor, and increased articulation of words.

Finley, Standler, and Wansley (1977) replicated the above study with a better controlled design in treating four children, each with a primary spastic component to the disease. They used a single case ABAB experimental design. Audiovisual feedback of EMG activity was provided twice weekly for 30 minutes over 10 weeks. Children were also provided with food and prize reinforcers, as well as redeemable tokens. Results showed decreases in EMG levels for all children during training sessions and increases in EMG levels during the no training sessions with decreases upon retraining. Some generalization of relaxation was evident in forearm muscles. Significant improvements in speech and motor functioning corresponded with EMG changes. Children showing the greatest decreases in EMG levels showed the most improvement in speech and motor functioning.

Summary

Cerebral palsy is an impairment of motor function resulting from brain damage incurred before or during birth. Traditional medical treatment has been aimed primarily at prolonged rehabilitation.

The application of biofeedback to cerebral palsy shows considerable significance and future promise. Biofeedback may be employed to correct the direct manifestations of the disorder, such as postural dysfunctions, and the speech and motor dysfunctions. Although most of the research in this area involves uncontrolled anecdotal case reports, the use of a single case A-B-A-B design by Finley *et al.* (1977), and the demonstration that changes in EMG levels and speech and motor functioning are correlated and contingent upon the treatment, strengthen the efficacy of using biofeedback for cerebral palsy.

CEREBROVASCULAR ACCIDENTS

Cerebrovascular accidents, also known as CVA or stroke, occur as a result of several different accidents: thrombosis, or occluding of a blood vessel in the brain causing collapse of the vessel; an aneurism, or ruptured blood vessel, causing an outflow of blood into the brain; bruising of brain tissue from trauma to the head; or damage caused by tumor excision. All of these accidents result in destruction of brain tissue which causes hemiplegia, impairment of voluntary movement on one side of the body with an ensuing paralysis. There are usually associated disturbances in muscle tone, sometimes reflected in spasticity or flaccidity on the effected side.

A substantial portion of the paralysis that manifests itself immediately after the accident is due, not to permanently damaged nerve tissue, but to edema. Once this subsides, a measure of spontaneous recovery can be expected. On the other hand, those functions controlled by the areas of the brain in which there has been actual destruction of tissue may possibly be restored through a prolonged program of rehabilitation. Most often, though, with tissue destruction, little return of function may be anticipated.

It has been shown in recent years that patients who have suffered a stroke can often regain voluntary control over previously spastic or flaccid muscle groups. Part of the problem lies in the inability of the patient to sense contraction of the muscles. A vital connection between the brain and the muscle seems to be lost. When the spastic hemiplegic attempts movement, the movement is resisted by the inappropriate response of spastic antagonist muscles. Biofeedback methods substitute for the inability to sense contraction, or the lack of proprioception.

Treatment

EMG biofeedback is the primary behavioral treatment technique used in the reeducation of voluntary control of muscles resulting from hemiplegia. The earliest report of EMG biofeedback in the rehabilitation of hemiplegia is by Marianacci and Horande (1960). EMG feedback was used with a 64-year-old male with left hemiplegia resulting from cerebral thrombosis. Needle electrodes were placed into paralyzed left deltoid muscles and no nerve impulse was apparent. The patient was taught to increase the strength of muscular contraction using raw EMG feedback. It was shown that the patient could generate muscle activity in 10–15% of the motor units with no previous activity, and that a 20% recovery of function in the paralyzed limb occurred in a single hour-long session.

Andrews (1964) reported use of EMG feedback with 20 hemiplegics in the biceps and triceps muscles to facilitate flexion and extension of the involved elbow. After 5 minutes of training 17 of the 20 displayed the ability to control muscular activity. The other three were able to attain such levels after 15 minutes of training.

Johnson and Garton (1973) examined the effectiveness of a combined laboratory and home EMG feedback training regimen with 11 hemiplegic patients having foot dorsiflection paralysis, or foot drop. Following three, 30-minute lab sessions with indwelling needle electrodes, daily home feedback training with a portable EMG unit was initiated. Results indicated three patients improved enough to be able to walk without short leg braces, four showed moderate improvement, and four failed to show much evidence of improvement.

Brudny and colleagues (Brudny, Kerein, Levidow, Grynbaum, Lieberman, and Friedman, 1974; Brudney, Korein, Grynbaum, Friedman, Weinstein, Sachs-Frankel, & Belandres, 1976) have treated hemiparesis by use of audio and visual EMG techniques. Brudny et al. (1976) summarized results with 45 patients using this technique. Thirty-nine of these patients had arm paralysis. Of these 39, 20 had retained significant gains in arm function at follow-up ranging from 3 months to 3 years. Of the six patients requiring lower extremity retraining, three were able to control ankle dorsiflection well enough to improve gait during ambulation. Both quadriparetic patients greatly improved their volitional control of upper extremity spasticity after 1½ and 3 years without functioning.

Basmajian, Kukulka, Narayan, and Takebe (1975) were the first researchers to use a control group and compared conventional physical therapy (PT) with a combined treatment of physical therapy and EMG biofeedback. The 20 subjects had dorsiflection paralysis and were randomly assigned to each group. The physical therapy group received exercise and gait training for 10 40-minute sessions. Patients in the combined group received 20 minutes of exercises and gait training followed by 20 minutes of audiovisual EMG biofeedback. Results indicated improvement in range of motion and strength for both groups. Patients in the combined PT and biofeedback group, however, showed increases twice as large as those in the PT only group. Gait improvement was noted in some, but no differences were found between groups. Further bioelectric analyses of these subjects by Takebe, Kukulka, Narayan, and Basmajian (1976) revealed no significant differences between groups in peroneal nerve conduction velocity or spasticity. The results of the Basmajian et al., (1975) study have been criticized on several methodological issues (Fish, Mayer, & Herman, 1976). Even with its problems, however, Basmajian *et al.*, (1975) stands as a benchmark study in the history of EMG biofeedback training in neuromuscular rehabilitation.

Another controlled group outcome study was reported by Mroczek, Halpern, and McHugh (1978) in which 9 patients having upper extremity hemiplegia for at least 1 year were trained for either greater contraction of the wrist extensors (seven patients), greater contraction of the biceps (one patient), or greater inhibition of the biceps (one patient). Following baseline of EMG and range of movement (ROM) pretreatment values, a "crossover" design was instituted with patients being randomly assigned to one of two groups. Group one (five patients) received 4 weeks of biofeedback followed by a 4-week period of PT. Group two (four patients) received the two treatments in the opposite order. Sessions were conducted three times per week for 30 minutes each. Measurements of EMG and active ROM were again made during sessions 4, 7, 10, and 12 of each 4-week period.

Pooled group analyses revealed no significant differences in either average EMG activity or active ROM between biofeedback and PT. Further, the treatments, individually or in combination, yielded significant improvements on both measures over baseline levels. Within groups, group one showed significant improvements in EMG levels during the first or biofeedback phase as compared to baseline. No further improvements were noted during the physical therapy phase. Group two, showed no such EMG improvements over baseline during either phase. The two groups also showed significant and equivocal improvements in active ROM over baseline levels.

Although the authors caution against direct comparison of the two treatments on the EMG-dependent measure, they conclude that biofeedback was effective in altering EMG activity and improving active ROM with less therapist contact than for PT. The methodological strength and level of results yielded by this study would have been greatly enhanced by the measurement of treatment-phase credibility and long term follow-up assessments. This study, however, is among the most methodologically advanced and theoretically heuristic in the area of neuromuscular rehabilitation.

Lee, Hill, Johnston, and Smiehorowski (1976) attempted to assess the specificity of EMG biofeedback effects in comparison to placebo feedback. Eighteen patients having varying grades of deltoid muscle power resulting from strokes were randomly assigned to the six possible orders of accurate (true), positive noncontingent (placebo), and no feedback conditions. Each patient received one session of each feedback condition, consisting of 20 isometric contractions of 5 seconds each with 10 seconds of intervening rest, on 3 consecutive days. Placebo feedback was derived from EMG activity of a hidden examiner who simultaneously contracted his deltoid muscle with each contraction of the patient.

Results showed no significant differences between treatment conditions regarding improvements in EMG amplitude over the 20 contractions in each condition. It was shown that older, poorly motivated patients benefited more from true feedback then the younger, more highly motivated patients. The groups did not differ in EMG activity during placebo or no-feedback conditions. The design of this study is a step toward understanding of placebo and nonspecific effects of biofeedback in neuromuscular rehabilitation, even though in this study, as with other studies, several methodological problems existed.

The most recent study in the use of biofeedback in muscular reeducation was conducted by Keefe and Trombly (1979) to determine whether EMG feedback training could enhance kinesthetic sensation, or the ability to judge limb position without the aid of a patient's eye watching. The patient was a 20-year-old male who had a CVA caused by an embolism from bacterial endocarditis in the mitral valve. He had regained use of his arm and leg with PT, but kinesthetic sensation was limited. An A-B-A-B withdrawal design was used with repeated measurements of accuracy of limb positioning being made on a 16-item functional task. Results showed that EMG feedback produced a dramatic improvement in performance relative to baseline. Over the course of the sessions performance improved, and evidence of generalization to functional tasks of daily living was obtained.

Summary

Considered as a whole, the studies that have used EMG biofeedback in the treatment of CVA patients appear to be lacking in methodological and statistical sophistication. The results, nevertheless, are impressive in view of the fact that virtually all patients in these studies had failed to respond to conventional forms of physical therapy and that for most patients, a number of years had passed since onset of CVA. In nearly every study patients have shown functional or cosmetic improvements that have been generally well maintained. These improvements have often come about in a shorter time span with less therapist contact than would be necessary for completion of a traditional physical therapy regimen.

Reports on the use of biofeedback with problems resulting from a stroke show that the technique possesses clinical efficacy and comparative cost effectiveness. Well-controlled studies with long term follow-up and appropriate statistical analyses are certainly warranted.

SPINAL CORD INJURIES

Both paraplegia and quadriplegia are caused by injury to the spinal cord; in most instances, there is no brain damage. The extent of the disability is determined by the level in the spinal cord at which the lesion occurs. If the lesion is high in the cord, in the region of the cervical vertebrae, all four extremities will be paralyzed, and this is called quadriplegia. Paraplegia is paralysis of the lower extremities as a result of injury to the cord in the thoracic or lumbar segments of the spine. In both types of paralysis, there is loss of voluntary movement and sensation; in both there is some trunk involvement, unless the injury is below L1; and in both there is some impairment of the functions, which are dependent upon the autonomic nerve fibers.

The most common cause of the two disabilities is trauma. Paraplegia may be the result of combat injury, a gunshot wound that transects the spinal cord, an accident in a motor vehicle, on the athletic field, or in an industrial setting, in which sudden and violent flexion or extension of the vertebrae column severs the cord. Injury to the cervical spine with resultant quadriplegia frequently occurs as the result of falling from great heights, of diving into shallow pools, of being thrown through the windshield of a car, of striking one's head or neck on a trampoline, and of injuries incurred in football and aquatic sports. Paraplegia is sometimes congenital, quadriplegia rarely so. Disease such as tuberculosis of the spine may create a transitory or permanent paraplegia.

Complications related to the injury sometimes include loss of bowel and bladder control, and frequently inpotence. The person is subject to urinary infection and formation of renal calcule. Decubitus ulcers form as a result of unrelieved pressure on the bony prominences of the body while the patient is bedridden, or later while sitting for prolonged periods in a wheelchair. The patient will be subject to all the deterioration associated with complete immobility such as muscle wasting, impaired circulation, and tissue breakdown because of interruption of the nutritional supply. Later, if the patient becomes ambulatory, pressure from braces, other supporting apparatus, and shoes may create ulceration, since he is unable to receive any warning signals of pain.

After medical treatment has stabilized the patient, he enters a prolonged program of rehabilitation to check further muscle and joint deterioration and to strengthen unimpaired muscles upon which, in the future, the patient will be inordinately dependent. As with the person having hemiplegia from a stroke, in spinal cord injuries biofeedback has been used to regain voluntary control over "paralyzed" muscles.

Treatment

EMG biofeedback is the primary behavioral treatment technique used in the reeducation of paralyzed muscles resulting from paraplegia or quadriplegia. Central to this use of EMG biofeedback is the assumption that some pathways still remain for the transmission of neural impulses. According to Fernando (1978), such patients can be evaluated for treatment by using EMG monitoring as a means of determining whether the lesion is complete or incomplete; in other words, whether there is any residual electromyographic activity left or not. Subsequently, EMG feedback can be used to enhance the EMG activity that remains. Not only can it be used to bring about desired movements, but also to inhibit spasticity, as is done with hemiplegia in persons having had a stroke.

Brudny and his colleagues (Brudny *et al.*, 1974; Brudny *et al.*, 1976) reported results achieved in biofeedback training of two patients who had suffered lesions of the spinal cord. Lesions were at C-5 and C-6 levels, and there was total paralysis of the lower extremities, and marked weakness with minimal functional movement in the upper extremities. Feedback training was limited to the upper extremities. One subject, a total care patient, was able with EMG feedback training to relax his right spastic biceps and pronate his forearm enough so that he could employ a wrist drive hand splint. Similar functional improvements occurred in the left arm although no feedback training was provided on this side. Follow-up 2-year post training revealed that the patient had maintained therapeutic gains and was able to use upper extremities in a variety of activities of daily living, such as feeding, grooming, and typing. Similar results were reported for the second spinal cord injured patient. These findings are impressive given the fact that neither of these patients had demonstrated progress after 3 and 1½ years, respectively, of conventional physical therapy.

Other case reports in the literature are those of Seymour and Bassler (1977), Fernando (1976), and Toomin and Johnson (1974). In these studies, EMG feedback was initially employed as a tool to determine which muscles were still innervated and was subsequently used to enhance activity in these muscles. Since, in these various studies, other therapeutic programs were used in addition to EMG feedback, it is difficult to evaluate precisely the results that were directly due to biofeedback. Nevertheless, it is worth noting that the EMG monitoring and feedback procedures helped both patients and therapists to locate target muscles which originally had not shown any signs of function.

Summary

Spinal cord injuries resulting in either paraplegia, or quadriplegia, depending on the level of the spinal cord at which the injury occurs, have recently been treated with EMG biofeedback. The biofeedback procedures helped to locate muscles having no previous function and in some cases aided in reeducating the muscles with some return of function.

Although only four case studies have been reported, this procedure is used quite often in rehabilitation settings. Further research, using controlled outcome studies, is warranted and should be pursued.

REFERENCES

Abuzzahab, F.S. Some uses of haloperidol in the treatment of psychiatric conditions, *Psychosomatics*, 1970, **11**, 188–193.

Agras, S. & Marshall, C. The application of negative practice to spasmodic torticollis. *American Journal of Psychiatry*, 1965, **122**, 579–582.

Andrews, J.M. Neuromuscular reeducation of the hemiplegic with the aid of the electrograph. *Archives of Physical Medicine and Rehabilitation,* 1964, **45,** 530–532.

Ascher, E. Psychodynamic considerations in *Gilles de la Tourette's* disease with a report of five cases and discussion of the literature. *American Journal of Psychiatry,* 1948, **105,** 267.

Azrin, N. & Nunn, R. Habit reversal: A method of eliminating nervous habits and tics. *Behavior Therapy,* 1972, **3,** 232–239.

Barrett, B.H. Reduction in rate of multiple tics by three operant conditioning methods. *The Journal of Nervous and Mental Disease,* 1962, **135,** 187–195.

Barrett, R.E., Yahr, M.D., & Duvoisin, R.C. Torsion dystonia and spasmodic torticollis—Results of treatment with 1-dopa. *Neurology,* 1970, **20,** 107–113.

Basmajian, J.V., Kukulka, C.G., Narayan, M.G., & Takebe, K. Biofeedback treatment of foot-drops after stroke compared with standard rehabilitation techniques: Effects on voluntary control and strength. *Archives of Physical Medicine and Rehabilitation,* 1975, **56,** 231–236.

Brierly, H. The treatment of hysterical spasmodic torticollis by behavior therapy. *Behavior Research and Therapy,* 1967, **5,** 139–142.

Brudny, J., Grynbaum, B.B., & Korein, J. Spasmodic torticollis: Treatment by feedback display of EMG. *Archives of Physical Medicine and Rehabilitation,* 1974, **55,** 403–408.

Brudny, J., Korein, J., Grynbaum, B.B., Friedmann, L.W., Weinstein, S., Sachs-Frankel, G., & Belandres, P.V. EMG feedback therapy: Review of treatment of 114 patients. *Archives of Physical Medicine and Rehabilitation,* 1976, **57,** 55–61.

Brudny, J., Korein, J., Levidow, L., Grynbaum, B.B., Leiberman, A., & Friedman, L.W. Sensory feedback therapy as a modality of treatment in central nervous system disorders of voluntary movement. *Neurology, 1974,* **24,** 925–932.

Brudny, J., Korein, J., Grynbaum, B.B., Friedman, L.W., Weinstein, S., Sachs-Frankel, G., & Belandres, P.B. EMG feedback therapy: Review of treatment of 114 patients. *Archives of Physical Medicine and Rehabilitation,* 1976, **57,** 55–61.

Challas, G. & Brauer, W. Tourette's disease: Relief of symptoms with R1625. *American Journal of Psychiatry,* 1963, **120,** 283.

Clark, D.F. Behavior therapy of *Gilles de la Tourette's syndrome, British Journal of Psychiatry,* 1966, **112,** 771–778.

Cleeland, C.S. Behavioral techniques in the modification of spasmodic torticollis. *Neurology,* 1973, **23,** 1241–1247.

Connell, P.H., Corbett, J.A., Horne, D.J., & Matthews, A.M. Drug treatment of adolescent ticquers—A double blind trial of diazepam and haloperidol. *British Journal of Psychiatry,* 1967, **113,** 375–381.

Cooper, I.A. Effect of thalamic lesions upon torticollis. *New England Journal of Medicine,* 1964, **270,** 967.

Corbett, J.A., Matthews, A.M., Connell, P.H., & Shapiro, D.A. *Tics and Gilles de la Tourette's syndome:* A follow-up study and critical review, *British Journal of Psychiatry,* 1969, **115,** 1229–1241.

Eldridge, R. The torsion dystonias: Literature review and genetic and clinical studies. *Neurology*, 1970, **20**, (Supplement), 1–78.

Ericksen, R.A. & Huber, H. Elimination of hysterical torticollis through the use of a metronome in an operant conditioning paradigm. *Behavior Therapy*, 1975, **6**, 405–406.

Feldman, R.B. & Werry, J.S. An unsuccessful attempt to treat a ticquer by massed practice. *Behavior Research and Therapy*, 1966, **4**, 111–117.

Fernando, C.K. Audio-visual reeducation in neuromuscular disorders. Paper presented at the meeting of the Biofeedback Research Society, Colorado Springs, February, 1976.

Fernando, C.K. The use of biofeedback in physical medicine and rehabilitation. Task Force study section report prepared for the Biofeedback Society of America, May, 1978.

Field, J.R., Corbin, K.B., Goldstein, N.P., & Klass, D.W. *Gilles de la Tourette's syndrome. Neurology*, 1966, **16**, 453–562.

Finley, W.W., Niman, C., Standler, J., & Ender, P. Frontal EMG biofeedback training of athetoid cerebral palsy patients: A report of six cases. *Biofeedback and Self-Regulation*, 1976, **1**, 169–182.

Finley, W.W., Niman, C.A., Standler, J., & Wansley, R.A. Electrophysiologic behavior modification of frontal EMG in cerebral-palsied children. *Biofeedback and Self-Regulation*, 1977, **2**, 59–79.

Fish, D., Mayer, N., & Herman, R. Letters to the editor: Biofeedback. *Archives of Physical Medicine and Rehabilitation*, 1976, **57**, 152.

Ford, C.V., & Gottlieb, F. An objective evaluation of haloperidol in *Gilles de la Tourette's Syndrome. Diseases of the Nervous System*, 1969, **30**, 328–332.

Gilles de la Tourette. Etude sur une affection nerveuse, caracterisée par de l'incoordination motrice accompagnie d'echolalie et de coprolalie. *Archives de Neurologie*, 1885, **9**, 159.

Harris, F.A. Inapproprioceptions: A possible sensory basis for athetoid movements. *Physical Therapy*, 1971, **51**, 761–770.

Harris, F.A., Spelman, F.A., & Hymer, J.W. Electronic sensory aids as treatment for cerebral-palsied children. *Physical Therapy*, 1974, **54**, 354–365.

Hutzell, R., Platzek, D., & Logue, P. Control of *Gilles de la Tourette's syndrome* by self-monitoring. *Journal of Behavior Therapy and Experimental Psychiatry*, 1974, **5**, 71–76.

Inglis, J., Campbell, D., & Donald, M.W. Electromyographic biofeedback and neuromuscular rehabilitation. *Canadian Journal of Behavioral Science*, 1976, **8**, 299–323.

Jankel, W.R. Electromyographic feedback in spasmodic torticollis. *American Journal of Clinical Biofeedback*. 1978, **1**, 28–29.

Jones, H.G. Continuation of Yate's treatment of a ticquer. In H.J. Eysenck (Ed.) *Behavior therapy and the neurosis*. Oxford: Pergamon, 1960.

Keefe, F.J. & Trombly, K. Impaired kinesthetic sensation: Can EMG feedback help? Paper presented at the American Association for Advancement of Behavior Therapy, San Francisco, December, 1979.

Knepler, K.N. & Sewall, S. Negative practice paired with smelling salts in the treatment of a tic. *Journal of Behavior Therapy and Experimental Psychiatry,* 1974, **5,** 189–192.

Lahey, B., McNees, P., & McKees, M. Control of an obscene "verbal tic" through timeout in an elementary school classroom. *Journal of Applied Behavior Analysis,* 1973, **6,** 101–104.

Lazarus, A.A. Objective psychotherapy in the treatment of dysphemia. *Journal of South African Logopedic Society,* 1960, **6,** 8–10.

Lee, K.H., Hill, E., Johnston, R., & Smichorowski, T. Myofeedback for muscle retraining in hemiplegia patients. *Archives of Physical Medicine and Rehabilitation,* 1976, **57,** 583–591.

Lucas, A.R. *Gilles de la Tourette's* disease in children: Treatment with haloperidal. *American Journal of Psychiatry,* 1967, **124,** 243–245.

Lucas, A.R., Kauffman, P.E., & Morris, E.M. *Gilles de la Tourette's* disease—A clinical study of fifteen cases. *Journal of American Academy of Child Psychiatry,* 1969, **6,** 700–722.

Mahler, M.S. Tics and impulsion in children: A study of motility, *Psychoanalytic Quarterly,* 1944, **13,** 430.

Mahler, M.S., Luke, J.A., & Daltoff, W. Clinical follow-up study of the tic syndrome in children. *American Journal of Orthopsychiatry,* 1945, **15,** 631.

Marianacci, A.A. & Horande, M. Electromyogram in neuromuscular reeducation. *Bulletin of the Los Angeles Neurological Society,* 1960, **25,** 57–71.

Meares, R.A. Behavior therapy and spasmodic torticollis. *Archives General Psychiatry,* 1973, **28,** 104–107.

Meares, A. *Hypnography.* Springfield: Charles C Thomas Publishers, 1957.

Morphew, J.A. & Sim, M. *Gilles de la Tourette's syndrome*—A clinical and psychopathological study. *British Journal of Medical Psychology,* 1969, **42,** 293–301.

Mroczek, N., Halpern, D., & McHugh, R. Electromyographic feedback and physical therapy for neuromuscular retraining in hemiplegia. *Archives of Physical Medicine and Rehabilitation,* 1978, **59,** 258–267.

Nicassio, F.J., Leiberman, R.P., Patterson, R.R., Raminez, R., & Sanders, N. The treatment of tics by negative practice. *Journal of Behavior Therapy and Experimental Psychiatry,* 1972, **3,** 281–287.

Pattison, E.M. The patient after psychotherapy. *American Journal of Psychotherapy,* 1970, **25,** 194.

Raffi, A.A. Learning theory and the treatment of tics. *Journal of Psychosomatic Research,* 1962 **6,** 71–76.

Seymour, R.J. & Bassler, C.R. Electromyographic biofeedback in the treatment of incomplete paraplegia. *Physical Therapy,* 1977, **57,** 1148–1150.

Shapiro, A.K. & Shapiro, E. Treatment of *Gilles de la Tourette's syndrome* with haliperidol. *Journal of Psychiatry,* 1968, **144,** 345–350.

Sorenson, B.F. & Hamby, W.B. Spasmodic torticollis: Results in 71 surgically treated patients. *Neurology,* 1966, **16,** 867–878.

Stevens, J.K. & Blachly, P.H. Successful treatment of *Maladie des Tics: Gilles de la Tourette's syndrome. American Journal of Diseases of Children,* 1966, **112,** 541–545.

Takebe, K., Kulkulka, C.G., Narayan, M.G., & Basmajian, J.V. Biofeedback treatment of foot-drop after stroke compared with standard rehabilitation technique. Part 2. Effects on nerve conduction velocity and spacticity. *Archives of Physical Medicine and Rehabilitation,* 1976, **57,** 9–11.

Thomas, E., Abrams, K., & Johnson, J. Self-monitoring and reciprocal inhibition in the modification of multiple tics of *Gilles de la Tourette's syndrome. Journal of Behavior Therapy and Experimental Psychiatry,* 1977, **2,** 159–171.

Toomin, H., Johnson, H.E. Biofeedback in neuromuscular reeducation. Unpublished manuscript, Biofeedback Research Institute, Los Angeles, 1974. Also presented at the meeting of the Biofeedback Research Society, Colorado Springs, Colorado, February, 1978.

Tophoff, M. Massed practice, relaxation and assertion training in the treatment of *Gilles de la Tourette's Syndrome. Journal of Behavior Therapy and Experimental Psychiatry.* 1973, **4,** 71–73.

Walton, D. Experimental psychology and the treatment of a ticquer. *Journal of Child Psychology and Psychiatry,* 1961, **112,** 148–155.

Walton, D. Massed practice and simultaneous reduction in drive level: Further evidence of the efficacy of this approach to the treatment of tics. In H. J. Eysenck (Ed.) *Experiments in behavior therapy.* London: Pergamon, 1964.

Williams, R.B. Heartrate feedback in the treatment of torticollis: A case report. Paper presented at the Annual Meeting for Psychophysiological Research, Salt Lake City, October, 1974.

Wooldridge, C.P. & Russell, G. Head position training with the cerebral palsied child: An application of biofeedback training. *Archives of Physical Medicine and Rehabilitation,* 1976, **57,** 407–414.

Yates, A.J. *Behavior therapy.* New York: Wiley, 1970.

Yates, A.J. The application of learning theory to the treatment of tics. *Journal of Abnormal Psychology,* 1958, **56,** 175–182.

CHAPTER 10

Nervous System Disorder

OVERVIEW

Traditionally, behavioral psychology has interacted with neurology through basic research in neurosciences, clinical research, and service in neuropsychology. New collaborations are now developing from behavioral medicine applications to neurological or nervous system disorders.

The nervous system disorder that has been the predominant target of behavioral procedures is epilepsy. Epilepsy has on various occasions been the subject of discussion as a neurological phenomenon, a psychological or psychiatric phenomenon, and more recently, a neuropsychological, psychosomatic, psychobiological, and behavioral-neurological problem (Mostofsky & Balaschak, 1977). Within these various discussions is imbedded the surfacing suggestion that environmental conditions external to the epileptogenic tissue may be a major source of potentiating or attenuating the seizure disorder.

Several million people in the United States suffer from one form of epilepsy or another. Barrow and Fabing (1966), assuming a 1% prevalence figure (two million epileptics), estimate that if each epileptic is a member of a family of four, over eight million people experience immediate effects of epilepsy.

The causes of epilepsy are diverse and include lesions, trauma, perinatal injury, infection, mental retardation, and metabolic disorders (Schmidt & Wilder, 1968). However, it has been estimated that in approximately 90% of patients with epilepsy the disorder is of unknown etiology; that is, the seizures are idiopathic in nature (Felton, Perkins, & Lewin, 1969).

Although chemotherapeutic advances have greatly added to the management and control of epilepsy, many individuals remain untouched by such treatment. Carter and Gold (1968) reported that 25% of children suffering seizure disorders benefited only partially from anticonvulsant medication, while an additional 25% did not respond at all. Thus, 50% of all children suffering from epilepsy have occasional seizures despite chemical efforts to control them. Although some investigators are more optimistic (Schmidt & Wilder, 1968), the fact remains that a significant percentage of seizures remain uncontrolled with chemotherapy alone.

It is becoming evident through a growing body of research that individuals having epilepsy display a hightened sensitivity to stress. In support of this thesis, anecdotal reports abound, which include descriptions of unusual circumstances under which seizures are triggered and of situations in which seizures rarely occur. A lesser but nonetheless impressive literature exists that provides descriptions of more careful observations of seizure states within the framework of a structured behavioral treatment program.

Investigators have begun to develop therapeutic procedures based on learning and conditioning principles for two reasons: chemotherapy alone has not been a sufficient treatment for a large percentage of epileptics (Carter & Gold, 1968) and clinicians frequently note the relationship between environmental events, anxiety, and epileptic attacks. These observations suggest that modification of stimuli that elicit or maintain the attack may be useful in treating epilepsy.

The ongoing collection of data on the frequency of symptom occurrence, associated or related response consequences, and antecedent stimulus conditions represents an important contribution of behavioral science to the field of medicine. This information may be used to supplement a patient's medical history, physical data, and laboratory findings in order to determine more accurately appropriate treatment plans.

EPILEPSY

Epilepsy may be defined as a paroxysmal disorder of the nervous system characterized by recurrent loss of consciousness, with or without convulsive muscular movement. To the observer, the seizure appears as an involuntary shift in muscular movement, either an abrupt increase or sudden cessation of motion. Seizures are associated with abnormal discharges of the electrical impulses in the brain (Baird, 1972; Puletti, 1969), and accordingly, the electroencephalograph plays a strategic role in diagnosis as well as some forms of treatment. Seizures are classified as either generalized or focal. They may involve the brain pervasively, or may be pinpointed to a specific portion of it. The generalized seizure types are grand mal and petit mal; the focalized seizure types are psychomotor and Jacksonian seizures.

Of the generalized seizures, the most dramatic and most severe is the *grand mal seizure*, in which all the neurons in the motor cortex discharge simultaneously and the patient experiences violent convulsions and complete loss of consciousness. The seizure typically consists of four phases. Initially the patient experiences an aura of premonitory sensations which may be visual, auditory, olfactory, or emotional. Examples would be dizziness, a ringing in the ears, or fear. Within moments, the tonic phase begins. The muscles of the body become suddenly rigid and the patient may stop breathing. After approximately a minute, the clonic phase begins, during which the muscles contract and relax. These violent convulsions, in which the tongue is often severely bitten, may be accompanied by loss of bladder and bowel control and the appearance of foamy saliva at the mouth. Finally, the patient passes into the coma phase. Recovery from unconsciousness is gradual; when the patient awakens, he has no memory of the episode. The patient will be confused and fatigued from the involuntary physical activity, and may require an abnormal amount of sleep (Felton, Perkin, & Lewin, 1969).

Petit mal attacks, by contrast, are much milder, often going unnoticed by the patient and those around him. Petit mal seizures usually manifest before the age of five. In this disorder, the patient presents neither an aura nor a convulsion. Typically, the patient simply stops what he is doing, his eyes roll up, his head nods, and he experiences loss of consciousness for a few seconds. Typically, there is nothing more than a momentary gap in his activities, with a related gap in memory. These episodes may occur in clusters during the day, or may be so infrequent and mild that they are scarcely noticed. Many children with this mild form of generalized epilepsy outgrow it after puberty. In some children, it progresses from petit mal to grand mal.

Among the epileptic seizures that result from a focal abnormality in electrical discharges in the brain, the most common is *psychomotor epilepsy*. It is assumed that the disordered response is localized in the temporal lobe, and the symptoms combine behavioral irregularities with some motor manifestations (Felton, Perkins, & Lewin, 1969). The patient suddenly begins to stare, may become either excessively pale or florid, engages in purposeless motor movements such as running around in a circle, and displays evidence of confusion and abnormal emotional behavior. He emerges from the episode with no memory of its occurence.

A disorder focused in the parietal lobe is called *Jacksonian epilepsy*. These seizures may produce sensory symptoms, such as numbness and tingling. If the abnormality is localized in the frontal cortex, there may be pronounced twitching, which is said to "march" or spread from one body sight to another. For example, the muscular spasm may spread from the hand to the arm, the shoulder, the trunk, and sometimes to the whole body. The attack may then resemble a grand mal seizure.

Convulsive disorders have a somewhat greater incidence among men than women (Bagley, 1971) with 90% of seizure disorders beginning before the age of 20 (Livingston, 1972). Since convulsions are much more common among children than adults, it has been hypothesized that as the brain matures, its resistance to seizures seems to increase (Robb, 1969). Although there is no evidence which definitely proves the role of hereditary factors in epilepsy (Livingston, 1972), many authorities feel that there may be transmission of a "convulsive predisposition," or a low seizure threshold, which may be expressed under physiological or emotional stress (Bagley, 1971). In the typical family history of an epileptic, an average of one parent and at least half of the patient's relatives show evidence of brain dysrhythmia, although they might not display full-blown seizures (Mostofsky, 1972).

Treatment

The three most prominent medical treatments of seizure disorder are drugs, diet, and surgery. Among anti-convulsant medications, phenobarbitol is widely used. Its sedative effects are said to dissipate after several days use, while its anticonvulsant effects accrue over a 7 to 10 day period (Baird, 1972). However, patients with high blood levels of anti-convulsants display a number of negative side effects, including psychomotor slowing, reduced intellectual functioning, and occasionally pathologic personality changes (Reynolds & Travers, 1974). Also, as was stated earlier, many patients still exhibit seizures while on medication.

Ketogenic diets have also been used for seizure control. In a hospital setting, all food is withheld from the patient until urine analysis reveals the presence of ketone bodies. The patient is then placed on a high fat, low carbohydrate diet, the weight of the fat content being four times the combined weight of carbohydrate and protein. Such a procedure is recommended only when drug management fails or produces unsatisfactory results. The limitations of the procedure include the fact that it is most effective in children between the ages of two and five, but is rarely successful with patients over 8 years of age (Livingston, 1972). Since it is difficult to adhere to such a diet, it cannot be used with children who have strong food preferences or whose parents are unlikely or unable to cooperate with the dietary demands (Baird, 1972).

When a focal injury to the brain is thought to be the cause of epilepsy, surgery may be considered as a last option (Bagley, 1971). It is never the treatment of choice unless the seizures are a symptom of a tumor, abscess, or hematoma (Livingston, 1972). Surgical treatment consists of removal of the neurons responsible for the abnormal electrical discharge. Therefore, the problem must be localized and in an accessible and expendable area of the cortex. Although the best therapeutic results are obtained in patients with psychomotor epilepsy who have resection of their temporal lobe, complete success is seldom found. At best, the usual result is a reduction in the frequency and severity of attacks.

As has been shown, medical management of seizure disorders has proven only partially successful. With the advent of the behavioral sciences and behavior therapy techniques, a new dimension to the treatment of epilepsy has emerged. Behavioral intervention techniques have been shown to produce clinically meaningful results where conventional treatment has had only limited success. Such instances are hardly isolated. One review of the literature reveals over 60 reports in which a variety of behavioral intervention techniques have provided seizure reduction in otherwise "refractory" patients (Mostofsky & Balaschak, 1977).

The various therapeutic strategies used to treat epilepsy can be classified into three broad categories: (1) behavior therapies based on respondent and operant conditioning methods used in control of seizure antecedents and consequences; (2) control methods, including relaxation and cognitive strategies, used in control of anxiety and cognitions as they become antecedents or consequences; and, (3) various forms of biofeedback, used in the control of seizure activity itself. Most treatment techniques can be seen to have features representative of several of these categories combined.

In the treatment of epilepsy a complete and accurate behavioral assessment is necessary in order to obtain the data needed to devise a treatment program best suited to an individual patient. Minimally, the therapist should develop a baseline of the patient's seizure problem, hour by hour over a 10-week period, or more if possible. Information pertaining to specific stressors, subjective experiences, and ability to exercise self-control should also be obtained (Mostofsky, 1978).

Much remains to be learned but whether one adopts a protocol from respondent or operant conditioning, self-control, or biofeedback, there is optimism for providing relief, even when drug intake has been ineffective.

Respondent and Operant Procedures

The procedures based on respondent conditioning approaches used in the treatment of reflex epilepsies include counterconditioning, extinction, flooding, fading, and desensitization. The procedures based on operant conditioning used primarily in the treatment of consequent events of seizure behavior include aversion therapy and various forms of contingency management with rewards and punishments involved.

Respondent Conditioning

"Sensory-evoked" or reflex epilepsy is a rare but often intractable form of epilepsy resulting from the presentation of specific environmental stimuli that stimulates physiological arousal and precipitates a seizure. Efron (1957) has reported using *counterconditioning* to reduce seizures reliably preceded by an olfactory cue, by sequentially replacing a competing olfactory stimulus with a visual cue and then a cognitive cue (see Chapter 2).

A remarkable amount of research on sensory-evoked epilepsy has been conducted by Forster (1969) and his associates. Among the various reflex epilepsies they have successfully treated with conditioning techniques include: stroboscopic-induced seizures (Forster, Booker, & Ansell, 1966; Forster & Campos, 1964; Forster, Ptacek, & Peterson, 1965; Forster et al., 1964); musicogenic epilepsy (Forster, Booker, & Gascon, 1967; Forster et al., 1965); reading epilepsy (Forster, 1975; Forster, Paulsen, & Baughman, 1969); acousticomotor or startle epilepsy (Booker, Forster, & Klove, 1965); voice-induced epilepsy (Forster et al., 1969); somatosensory or touch-evoked epilepsy (Forster & Cleeland, 1969); as well as pattern presentation and eye closure induced seizures (Forster, 1967). These researchers report that their procedures are derived from classical respondent conditioning, and treatment procedures are generally described in terms of *extinction,* although the treatment sometimes represents a conditioning process and not simply an extinction process.

Among the various strategies employed by Forster is the complete or partial avoidance of the evoking stimulus. Obviously in many cases such as musicogenic or stroboscopic epilepsy, total avoidance of the eliciting stimuli may not be feasible. In other instances, such as reading epilepsy, total avoidance of the provoking stimulus may be possible but not practical.

Another more practical approach consists of altering the evoking stimulus in such a way as to remove its seizure inducing qualities. The behavioral technique of *fading* has been used to increase stimulus tolerance by presenting the offending stimulus in a manner that will not elicit seizures. Gradually the intensity and/or duration of the stimulus is increased as long as seizures do not occur. For example, with the photosensitive patient in whom seizures are induced by stroboscopic stimulation, the experimental room is designed so that the strobe light can be presented with the ambient room light level at an intensity high enough to mask the strobe flash. Gradually the ambient light is decreased to where no seizure is induced. The procedure is continued until the patient is gradually conditioned to tolerate clearly discernable strobe light flashes. This technique has met with good success and has been computer automated to facilitate the speed and reliability of the treatment process (Forster, Booker, & Ansell, 1966). Essentially the same procedure has been successfully used with auditory stimuli (Forster, 1967).

Another method of altering the provoking stimulus is based upon the observation that some forms of reflex epilepsy do not result in a seizure when the sensory stimulation is unilateral in form. Thus, some photosensitive patients will not manifest seizures if the strobe light is presented to only one eye. In this way unilateral stimulation renders bilateral stimulation innocuous. It is important for the patient to continually employ home training sessions of unilateral stimulation to maintain the effectiveness of this procedure. For this reason Forster (1972) feels that the treatment procedure represents a conditioning process and not simply an extinction process.

To assist the generalization of the therapy process to the patient's environment, Forster has developed an ingeneous technique. Initially, innocuous strobe light flashes are associated with audible clicks, thereby developing a conditioned association between nonseizure inducing light flashes and a clicking sound. Specially designed glasses, incorporating a sensitive photoelectric cell and a miniature speaker then translate light flashes in the natural environment into clicking sounds that the patient can readily hear. In this way, strobe light flashes that are encountered in every day life produce a clicking sound that has previously been conditioned to be innocuous.

Still another method of rendering a provoking stimulus innocuous is to raise the threshold at which the patient responds to the stimulus. With musicogenic and voice induced epilepsy, this is done by continuing the stimulation of the patient throughout the induction of the seizure and into the postictal state. Reading epilepsy is not amenable to this approach, although a "vigilance method" has been effective. The patient maintains a vigilance for certain cues in the eliciting stimulus and responds to those cues in a specified way. For example, the patient might be told to slap his thigh or press his hands together at the sight of every "a" in the material he is reading. It is often necessary to change the target letter to maintain effectiveness.

For some patients the triggering stimuli for seizures may be feelings of stress or anxiety. Respondent conditioning techniques used to treat stress-induced seizures include *systematic desensitization* and *flooding*. Parrino (1971) used desensitization combined with deep muscle relaxation, producing an appreciable decrease in seizure activity over a 15-week period in the treatment of a 36-year-old male whose seizures were evoked by anxiety arousing situations in the environment. Ince (1976) similarly paired desensitization with cue-controlled relaxation used to abort a seizure in the treatment of a 12-year-old boy having petit mal and grand mal seizures. Pinto (1972) successfully treated a 31-year-old male with movement epilepsy and a generalized phobic response to being in public by having the patient listen to tape recorded accounts in which he was "flooded" with stories which dealt with his entering the phobic situation and developing a seizure with all of the feared embarrassments. Following each fantasy session, the patient experienced the situation *in vivo* without the seizure.

Operant Conditioning

Although it is unlikely that seizure disorders are learned, particularly in a response-consequence manner, a treatment strategy based on this paradigm may be useful in light of the emotional and/or manipulative aspects of epilepsy. An operant conditioning approach to seizure control might conceivably be designed to control the seizure by attending to the antecedents of seizures, the immediate consequences of seizures, or behaviors prior to the seizure and their consequences and antecedents (chaining).

A special application of antecedent control of seizures is provided in cases in which seizures are self-induced. These seizures usually are of the petit mal type and are self-induced by flashing light or hyperventilation. Statistically, these seizures are more common among females with low seizure thresholds and of below average intelligence (Katz & Zlutnick, 1974). Epileptics with self-induced seizures are the most difficult to help. In such cases it appears that the convulsion may serve a number of functions: as an escape from tension; as a manipulative social device; or most directly as a source of self-pleasure (Bagley, 1971). Thus, the behavior may be maintained by the positive reinforcement that presumably occurs in brief periods of clouding of the consciousness, or by negative reinforcement, such as the avoidance of unpleasant activities. For example, Fabisch and Darbyshire (1965) reported a case in which a shopgirl regularly induced seizures to escape from dealing with difficult customers. The need for a careful behavioral assessment, therefore, can be appreciated.

It is in this area that durg therapy is least effective because the usual dosage of anticonvulsant medication is too small to suppress the seizures, and the high dosage required to suppress the seizures could cause undesirable side effects. Self-induced seizures have most commonly been treated by *aversion therapy* and *punishment* (Katz & Zlutnick, 1974). Conditioning techniques have met with much more difficulty in attempting to moderate such seizures (Forster *et al.*, 1964). The reconditioning effect of a self-induced seizure proves troublesome when used in conjunction with aversion therapy. Conditioning depends upon a carefully monitored sensitivity threshold, and the reconditioning of induced seizures ruins the established threshold, so that a new one must be established. This is not only time-consuming but, in an attempt to establish a new threshold, the patient is again being reconditioned to seizures.

An example of unprogrammed punishment for self-induction was reported by Fabisch and Darbyshire (1965), whose young client induced seizures by hyperventilation, at an increasing frequency. One day, however, the child experienced three convulsive episodes which led to vomiting and prolonged stupor. These aversive consequences produced a 6-month period of abstention from hyperventilation and seizures.

Programmed punishment was used by Wright (1973) with a 5-year-old mentally retarded boy whose baseline rate of seizures was measured in hundreds of seizures each hour. The child induced seizures by waving his hands in front of his eyes or by rapid blinking. Hand waving was totally suppressed by five punishment sessions using shock to the child's leg. A subsequent course of shock sessions significantly reduced the blinking. At a 7-month follow-up, seizures remained at only 10% of the baseline rate.

Punishment was also used by Scholander (1972) in the treatment of an epileptic boy whose attacks were accompanied by painful twists of his head. Although the epilepsy responded somewhat favorably to medication, the boy had developed the habit of gripping and holding his neck with his hands, thereby precluding many normal activities. The patient was provided with portable shock equipment that automatically delivered a wrist shock whenever his hand got close to his neck. At a 6-month follow-up, not only was there significant improvement in the patient's general social behavior, but there was complete elimination of epileptic symptoms.

In some cases an examination of the typical environmental consequences of a convulsive episode may provide the key to control (Carter & Gold, 1968). It is not unusual to find that others in the patient's home environment have subtly shaped and maintained the seizures. Since the convulsive behaviors may be obviously distressing to family members, they usually respond immediately with solicitous caring. The importance of social attention to the understanding of a particular case may be discovered by taking seizure frequency counts when the patient knows he is being observed and when he thinks he is alone. The influence of modeling from the behavior of others may also commonly be seen in such cases. The most successful treatment in these cases is *contingency management* with various forms of positive reinforcement and punishment (Balaschak, 1976; Flannery, 1971; Flannery & Cautela, 1973; Gardner, 1967, 1973; Fowler, Niranjan, Lehmann, & Tindall, 1971; Iwata & Lorenson, 1976; and Richardson *et al.*, 1971).

Gardner (1967) in treating a 10-year-old whose seizures seemed to be maintained by parental attention, devised a plan of extinction for undesired behaviors and positive reinforcement (attention) for appropriate behaviors. The parents reported a rapid reduction in undesired behaviors. In a planned reversal, seizures reoccurred within 24 hours, but a return to contingency management rapidly eliminated the problem again. Gardner (1973) combined relaxation training, hypnosis, and positive reinforcement for nonseizure behavior in treating an 8-year-old girl whose seizure symptoms were identical to those of her older brother in response to parental attention he received.

Social support for "sick" behaviors may not only occur in home environments, but in school, work, and institutional settings. Balaschak (1976) engaged the aid of a child's teacher in the use of response consequences to control seizures in an 11-year-old girl. A tangible reinforcer was given for nonseizure behavior, and attempts were made to increase self-initiating behaviors and to teach the patient to cope with seizures.

Iwata and Lorentzson (1976) treated a 41-year-old institutionalized retarded male who displayed frequent "seizure-like" behavior. Treatment consisted of increasing his daily activities, receiving a reward every 20 minutes he was seizure-free, and placing him in a curtained off cubicle for a time-out period upon seizure occurrence. The use of a reversal design supported the effectiveness of the procedures, and as seizure control was established, the contingencies were gradually faded out.

A case of treatment in a medical hospital was reported by Fowler, Niranjan, Lehmann, and Tindall (1971). The patient was a 58-year-old woman whose spells of severe vertigo had increased to the point that she had remained bedridden for 13 months preceding treatment. She had received total support from husband, family, and friends and had escaped from demands of housekeeping and strenuous activity. Treatment in the hospital consisted of shaping with positive reinforcement (attention from family and staff) across various behaviors. Rest from exercises was also used as a reward, as well as graphic displays of progress which were posted on her bed. Sick behavior resulted in removal of rewards (visitors, food tray). At the end of 55 days, the patient was discharged, able to walk 1200 feet with a cane. One year later she could walk independently and perform household chores.

If the seizure is viewed as the end product of a longer chain of events, the identification of an aura may make it feasible to interrupt the chain at various points. Zlutnick, Mayville, and Moffat (1975) described five cases in which the seizure chain was broken by positively reinforcing incompatible behaviors and interrupting preseizure rituals. In four subjects, target behaviors were initiated by a "shake and startle" (interruption) procedure, in which, contingent upon the occurrence of a preseizure behavior, a teacher or parent shouted "no" loudly and shook the child briefly. In the fifth case, the child was differentially reinforced for not emitting particular preseizure behavior. Reduction in seizure frequency ranging from 40 to 100%, depending primarily on predictability of the target response was observed. A reversal procedure was used in all five cases, strengthening the credibility of the results.

Self-Control Methods

In stress-induced seizures, *relaxation training* is a useful procedure to use in treatment. If thoughts centering around the consequences of the seizures, such as social stigmatization, job discrimination, and denial of driver's license, produce fear or stress, thereby increasing the probability of further seizures or other behavior problems, *cognitive strategies* are useful in treatment.

There are only a few examples of seizures treated with relaxation therapy alone. In a report by Mostofsky and Vicks (1973), relaxation was the primary modality used with a 28-year-old retarded woman who suffered from both grand mal and petit mal seizures, averaging seven a day. Training in progressive relaxation took place at her home in one hour sessions for three weeks. The daily average for seizures for the entire three weeks of treatment was 3.14. Although a one year follow-up did not show complete remission, the patient remained improved. The study demonstrates the effectiveness of relaxation as well as the subtle reinforcements and praise, which may also have been beneficial (Mostofsky, 1975). However, it is possible that relaxation alone may effect seizure reduction.

Wells, Turner, Bellack, and Hersen (1978) conducted a well-controlled single-case analysis of cue-controlled relaxation in the treatment of a 22-year-old female with psychomotor seizures. After baseline rate of seizures and anxiety levels were collected, cue-controlled relaxation was implemented, withdrawn, and reimplemented. Seizure rates and anxiety level decreased when treatment was provided and increased when treatment was removed.

Many researchers have combined relaxation with one or more other procedures. Any study utilizing covert techniques or desensitization will also necessarily include some elements of training in progressive relaxation (Ince, 1976; Parrino, 1971). A combined EEG and EMG biofeedback relaxation training procedure reduced seizures in an adolescent female (Johnson & Meyer, 1974). Kaplan (1975) suggested that successful reductions in seizure rates with slow frequency EEG biofeedback training may have been due to reduced arousal or relaxation. Similarly, Kuhlman's (1976) therapeutic success with 12–15 Hz EEG biofeedback but lack of EEG and seizure correlations suggested a reduced arousal effect. Finally, a recently reported study with crossover design indicated that EEG biofeedback enhanced a relaxation-training effect (Cabral & Scott, 1976).

Occasionally, even when a patient responds favorably to pharmacologic control of his seizures, his fear of having another seizure may remain. Anthony and Edelstein (1975) treated a woman whose seizures had been completely controlled by medicine for 2 years, yet she continued to obsessively ruminate about the possibility that a seizure would occur. She had five to six severe anxiety attacks per week. The technique of *thought-stopping* was taught to the patient, phasing from therapist interruption of overt thoughts about having a seizure in a public place to patient covert interruption of covert thoughts. By the third week of practice, the anxiety attacks had disappeared. The patient reported the procedures had enabled her to identify and then eliminate the thoughts, which served as cues for the escalating ruminations. No further anxiety attacks were reported at a 6-month follow-up.

Perhaps the most striking report of a multifaceted approach is presented by Daniels (1975) who used a combination of covert and operant conditioning techniques, as well as relaxation in the treatment of a 22-year-old female with grand mal seizures. He combined covert extinction, covert reinforcement, overt reinforcement, denial of reward, deep muscle relaxation, and thought-stopping. The patient's seizure frequency dropped to zero, and she remained seizure free for 16 weeks. She obtained a job, but with the loss of her job and boyfriend, seizures recurred. Episodes leveled to one per month and remained so at a 6-month follow-up.

Biofeedback

In some cases of seizure, the patient may be able to identify internal premonitory symptoms such as an aura to the seizure itself. When this is possible, biofeedback may be clinically useful in helping the patient to control the attack (Johnson & Meyer, 1974). Using auditory or visual feedback with their EEG recordings, patients may be trained to control their slow rhythm (alpha) cortical activity or even to suppress their EEG seizure activity. Alpha waves reflect rhythmic activity in the cortex within a range of 8–13 Hz. The behavioral concomitant is a state of relaxed wakefulness, often subjectively described by the patient as a tranquil floating feeling. Several recent reports on alpha control have shown significant reductions in patient's seizure rates.

Johnson and Meyer (1974) reported the case of an 18-year-old girl with a 10-year history of grand mal seizures. Under medication, her seizures averaged three per month. The treatment included 2 weeks of relaxation training, seven half-hour sessions of EMG biofeedback, and 36 sessions of EEG training spaced over a 1 year period focusing upon production of alpha, alpha-theta, and finally, theta EEG patterns. The patient was also instructed to practice using the relaxation skills whenever she experienced a seizure aura. Results showed a 46% reduction in seizure frequency which was maintained over a 3-month follow-up. Although the patient could not terminate a seizure once it began, she could recognize the onset of a preseizure aura and reliably abort the seizure at that point.

Kuhlman (1976) used a reversal design to study the effect of alpha feedback. He met with five patients, two to three times a week, for 2 months, during which time only random EEG feedback was provided. Actual training then began, with biofeedback being given for cortical activity in the 9–12 Hz range. Three of the five patients responded with an average seizure reduction of 60%. A subsequent reversal to random biofeedback did not, however, lead to seizure increases. Kuhlman found significant increases in the amount of alpha activity seen in these patients, which he interpreted to mean that EEG biofeedback facilitated normal resting EEG pattern development. In other words, training may enable the epileptic patient to function at a lower level of arousal.

Sterman and his colleagues have reported work with feedback of slightly higher frequencies (12–16 Hz), which they termed Sensori-Motor Rhythm (SMR). They found that when SMR was conditioned in cats, they were resistant to seizures induced by convulsant drugs (Sterman, 1972). Relating these findings to humans suggests a clinical tool which might raise seizure thresholds of epileptics (Sterman, 1973; Sterman & Friar, 1972; Sterman, MacDonald, & Stone, 1974).

Treatment consists of multiple long-term biofeedback sessions in which the individual is given information about and incentives for the production of SMR EEG patterns. Feedback is usually provided in both visual and auditory modalities and incentive systems range from monetary rewards to presenting the patient with photo slides of pleasant scenes, contingent upon SMR performance. In some cases, a portable biofeedback EEG unit is provided for daily home use.

The results of intensive biofeedback training and well-controlled experimental procedures indicate that normal human subjects are able to produce significant increases in SMR activity. Clinically, there is a rather remarkable decrease in the incidence of major motor seizures when epileptics are given extensive SMR training. In some cases reductions of 67% have been noted, though change generally occurs slowly over several months of training. In some cases (Sterman, 1972) seizure reduction is accompanied by other positive personality changes and improved sleeping patterns, and Sterman (1973) noted marked academic improvement.

These results appear to be specific for the SMR training and are probably not simply due to placebo effects or generalized relaxation training since when SMR training is discontinued a number of patients revert to pretreatment seizure levels and biofeedback techniques must be reinstated. Thus, home practice and regular "booster" sessions are often necessary components in a total treatment plan.

More recent support for the effectiveness of SMR biofeedback has been presented by Finley, Smith, and Etherton (1975), Seifer and Lubar (1975), and Lubar and Bahler (1976). In summarizing the available biofeedback studies, the SMR procedures appear to be the technique that has proved to be of consistent value in the treatment of epilepsy.

In evaluating the overall effectiveness of biofeedback in the control of epilepsy, a number of points should be made. First, as Brown (1977) points out, the EEG is but a "faint mirror" of very complex events occurring within the brain, a far distance from the electrodes on the scalp. No one as yet is sure of the significance of the components of recorded brain wave activity or even of recurrent patterns of activity. Second, many failures to replicate positive findings have been reported, which may be attributable to differences in patient selection, length of training, or instrumentation. Third, the specific cortical activity under training is critical. Sterman found, for example, that biofeedback for lower frequency rates (6–9 Hz) worsened seizure frequency. Finally, although some patients do seem to be able to learn to abort attacks, once a seizure begins, control is often not possible. Overall, if biofeedback facilities are available, the research indicates that it may hold promise for help in the control of epilepsy. An important aspect of this new procedure may be the changed feeling of the patient that is associated with personal, internal control of his problem.

Summary

The empirical evidence, viewed even with the strongest conservatism, suggests much promise for the application of behavioral treatment protocols in epilepsy treatment. The greatest gain would be expected with those patients who experience many and severely disrupting seizures and for whom surgery is not possible and/or for whom pharmacological management has proven ineffective. It is quite likely that even among the more normative and "controlled" seizure patients, relief from seizures and potential reduction of anticonvulsant drug dependency may be realized by such adjunct treatment programs.

The various therapeutic strategies thus far used successfully to treat epilepsy include the behavior therapies based on respondent and operant conditioning principles, relaxation, cognitive strategies, and biofeedback. Most of these treatment techniques are used in various combinations, as certain treatments deal best with specific aspects of seizure activity. This is why a complete and accurate behavioral assessment is necessary in order to obtain the data needed to devise a treatment program best suited to an individual patient.

Respondent conditioning strategies are used mainly when dealing with the antecedent components of a seizure. Sensory-evoked or reflex epilepsy has most successfully been treated by counter conditioning (Efron, 1957), and extinction (Forster, 1969; Forster, Booker, & Ansell, 1966; Forster & Campos, 1964; Forster, Ptacek, & Peterson, 1965; Forster et al., 1964; Forster, Booker, & Gascon, 1967; Forster, 1975; Forster, Paulsen, & Baughman, 1969; Booker, Forster, & Klove, 1965; Forster & Cleeland, 1969). Stress-induced seizures have been successfully treated with systematic desensitization (Parrino, 1971) and flooding (Pinto, 1972).

Operant conditioning strategies not only deal with the antecedents of seizures, but also the immediate consequences of the seizure, and behaviors prior to the seizure and their consequences and antecedents (chaining). The use of aversion therapy has been somewhat successful in the treatment of self-induced seizures (Fabish & Darbyshire, 1965; Wright, 1973; Scholander, 1972). Conditioning techniques have met with difficulty, however, in attempting to moderate such seizures because the reconditioning effect of a self-induced seizure proves troublesome when used in conjunction with aversion therapy.

In cases where the environmental consequences to a convulsive episode are important contributors, contingency management with various forms of positive reinforcement and punishment is most successful (Balaschak, 1975; Flannery, 1971; Flannery & Cautela, 1973; Gardner, 1967, 1973; Fowler, Niranjan, Lehmann, & Tindall, 1971; Iwata & Lorentzson, 1976; and Richardson et al., 1971). If the seizure is viewed as the end product of a longer chain of events, interruption of the chain at various points by use of interruption of preseizure rituals, and positive reinforcing of incompatible behaviors has proven successful (Zlutnick, Mayville, & Moffat, 1975).

In addition to the respondent conditioning techniques used to treat stress-induced epilepsy, relaxation and cognitive strategies have also been successfully used. Relaxation has most often been used in conjunction with other treatment modalities, such as systematic desensitization and biofeedback. However, two studies using relaxation alone showed improvement in seizure activity (Mostofsky & Vick, 1973; and Wells, Turner, Bellack, & Hersen, 1978). If fear of seizure recurrence is involved, certain cognitive strategies such as thought-stopping have been used to identify and eliminate thoughts that serve as cues for seizure activity (Anthony & Edelstein, 1975).

If many of the factors thus far described are involved in promoting or maintaining seizure activity, a multi-faceted approach such as that used by Daniels (1975) warrants consideration. He combined covert extinction and reinforcement, overt reinforcement, denial of reward, deep muscle relaxation, and thought stopping.

In control of seizure activity itself, biofeedback has proven a useful tool. Training EEG activity, alpha waves within a range of 8–13 Hz, has shown some success (Johnson & Meyer, 1974; Kuhlman, 1976). However, the biofeedback procedures appearing to show the most consistently valuable results, are those which condition SMR activity, waves within a range of 12–16 Hz (Sterman, 1972, 1973; Sterman & Friar, 1972; Sterman, MacDonald, & Stone, 1974; Finley, Smith, & Etherton, 1975; Seifer & Lubar, 1975; and Lubar & Bahler, 1976).

Overall, behavioral treatments for seizure disorders are best conceived as a broad-spectrum set of treatment interventions which focus not only on the seizure itself, but also on the internal and external factors with which it interacts. The focus, therefore, is not merely on a symptom, but on the total patient as he interacts with his social environment. The history of behavioral approaches to the treatment of convulsive disorders is a short one, little more than 10 years long, and as such consists mainly of clinical reports of successful treatment. A great deal of future research is needed to clarify the effective treatment components, to increase prescriptive abilities, and better understand treatment failures. For the present, however, it appears that behavioral treatments have proven successful and hold considerable promise for the future.

REFERENCES

Antony, J. & Edelstein, B.A. Thought stopping treatment of anxiety attacks due to seizure-related obsessive ruminations. *Journal of Behavior Therapy and Experimental Psychiatry,* 1975, **6,** 343–344.

Bagley, C. *The social psychology of the epileptic child.* Coral Gables, Fla.: University of Miami Press, 1971.

Baird, H.W. *The child with convulsions.* New York: Grune and Stratton, 1972.

Balaschak, B.A. Teacher-implemented behavior modification in a case of organically based epilepsy. *Journal of Consulting and Clinical Psychology,* 1976, **44**(2), 218–223.

Barrow, R.L. & Fabing, H.G. *Epilepsy and the law.* New York: Harper & Row, 1966.

Booker, H.E., Forster, F.M., & Klove, H. Extinction factors in startle (acousticomotor) seizures. *Neurology,* 1965, **15,** 1095–1103.

Brown, B. *Stress and the art of biofeedback.* New York: Harper and Row, 1977.

Cabral, R.J. & Scott, D.F. Effects of two desensitization techniques, biofeedback and relaxation, on intractable epilepsy: Follow-up study. *Journal of Neurology, Neurosurgery, and Psychiatry,* 1976, **39,** 504–507.

Carter, S. & Gold, A. Convulsions in children. *New England Journal of Medicine,* 1968, **278,** 315–317.

Daniels, L.K. Treatment of grand mal epilepsy by covert and operant conditioning techniques: A case study. *Psychosomatics,* 1975, **16,** 65–67.

Efron, R. The effect of olfactory stimuli in arresting uncinate fits. *Brain,* 1957a, **79,** 267–281.

Efron, R. The conditioned inhibition of uncinate fits. *Brain,* 1957b, **80,** 251–262.

Fabisch, W. & Darbyshire, R. Report on an unusual case of self-induced epilepsy with comments on some psychological and therapeutic aspects. *Epilepsia,* 1965, **6,** 335–340.

Felton, J.S., Perkins, D.C., & Lewin, M. A Survey of Medicine and Medical Practice for the Rehabilitation Counselor. Washington, D. C.: U.S. Department of Health, Education, and Welfare, 1969.

Finley, W.W., Smith, H.A., & Etherton, M.D. Reduction of seizures and normalization of the EEG in a severe epileptic following sensorimotor biofeedback training: Preliminary study. *Biological Psychology,* 1975, **2,** 189–203.

Flannery, R.B., Jr. Behavior modification of "uncontrollable seizures" in an adult retardate trainee. Unpublished manuscript, 1971 (available from author, Somerville Mental Health Clinic, Somerville, Mass., 02144).

Flannery, R.B., Jr. & Cautela, J.R. Seizures: Controlling the uncontrollable. *Journal of Rehabilitation*, 1973, **39**, 34–36.

Forster, F.M. Conditioning of cerebral dysrhythmia induced by pattern presentation and eye closure. *Conditional Reflex*, 1967, **2**, 236–244.

Forster, F.M. Conditional reflexes and sensory-evoked epilepsy: The nature of the therapeutic process. *Conditional Reflex*, 1969, **4**, 103–114.

Forster, F.M. Reading epilepsy, musicogenic epilepsy, and related disorders. In H.R. Myklebust (Ed.) *Progress in learning disabilities*, Volume III. New York: Grune & Stratton, 1975.

Forster, F.M. & Campos, G.B. Conditioning factors in stroboscopic-induced seizures. *Epilepsia*, 1964, **5**, 156–165.

Forster, F.M. & Cleeland, C.S. Somatosensory evoked epilepsy. *Transactions of the American Neurological Association*, 1969, **94**, 268–269.

Forster, F.M., Booker, H.E., & Ansell, S. Computer automation of the conditioning therapy of stroboscopic induced seizures. *Transactions of the American Neurological Association*, 1966, **91**, 232–233.

Forster, F.M., Booker, H.E., & Gascon, G. Conditioning in musicogenic epilepsy. *Transactions of the American Neurological Association*, 1967, **92**, 236–237.

Forster, F.M., Paulsen, W., & Baughman, F. Clinical therapeutic conditioning in reading epilepsy. *Neurology*, 1969, **19**, 71–77.

Forster, F.M., Ptacek, L.J., & Peterson, W.G. Auditory clicks in extinction of stroboscope-induced seizures. *Epilepsia*, 1965, **6**, 217–225.

Forster, F.M., Klove, H., Peterson, W.G., & Bengzon, A.R.A. Modification of musicogenic epilepsy by extinction technique. *Transactions of the American Neurological Association*, 1965, **90**, 179–182.

Forster, F.M., Hansotia, P., Cleeland, C.S., & Ludwig, A. A case of voice-induced epilepsy treated by conditioning. *Neurology*, 1969, **19**, 319–325, 325–331.

Forster, F.M., Ptacek, L.J., Peterson, W.G., Chun, R.W.M., Bengzon, A.R.A., & Campos, G.B. Stroboscopic-induced seizure discharges: Modification by extinction techniques. *Archives of Neurology*, 1964, **11**, 603–608.

Fowler, Niranjan, Lehmann, & Lindall. An application of behavior therapy to a program of debilitating vertigo. *Behavior Therapy*, 1971, **2**, 589–591.

Gardner, G.G. Use of hypnosis for psychogenic epilepsy in a child. *American Journal of Clinical Hypnosis*, 1973, **15**, 166–169.

Gardner, J.E. Behavior therapy treatment approach to a psychogenic seizure case. *Journal of Consulting Psychology*, 1967, **31**, 209–212.

Ince, L.P. The use of relaxation training and a conditioned stimulus in the elimination of epileptic seizures in a child: A case study. *Journal of Behavior Therapy and Experimental Psychiatry*, 1976, **7**, 39–42.

Iwata, B.A. & Lorentzson, A.M. Operant control of seizure-like behavior in an institutionalized retarded adult. *Behavior Therapy*, 1976, **7**, 247–251.

Johnson, R.K. & Meyer, R.G. Phased biofeedback approach for epileptic seizure control. *Journal of Behavior Therapy and Experimental Psychiatry*, 1974, **5**, 185–187.

Kaplan, B.J. Biofeedback in epileptics: Equivocal relationships of reinforced EEG frequency to seizure reduction. *Epilepsia,* 1975, **16,** 477–485.

Katz, R. & Zlutnick, S. (Eds.) *Behavior therapy and health care: Principles and applications.* New York: Pergamon Press, 1974.

Kuhlman, W.N. EEG training in epileptic patients: Clinical and neurophysiological analysis. Paper presented at the meeting of the Biofeedback Research Society, Colorado Springs, March, 1976.

Livingston, S. Comprehensive management of epilepsy in infancy, childhood, and adolescence. Springfield, Ill: Charles C Thomas, 1972.

Lubar, J.F. & Bahler, W.W. Behavioral management of epileptic seizures following EEG biofeedback training of the sensorimotor rhythm. *Biofeedback and Self-Regulation,* 1976, **1,** 77–104.

Mostofsky, D.I. Behavior modification and the psychosomatic aspects of epilepsy. In D. Upper & D.S. Goodenough (Eds.). *Behavior modification with the individual patient.* Nutley, NJ: Roche Laboratories, 1972.

Mostofsky, D.I. Teaching the nervous system. *New York University Education Quarterly,* 1975, spring, 8–13.

Mostofsky, D.I. Epilepsy: Returning the ghost to psychology. *Professional Psychology,* 1978, **9,** 87–92.

Mostofsky, D.I. & Balaschak, B.A. Psychobiological control of seizures. *Psychological Bulletin,* 1977, **84,** 723–725.

Mostofsky, D.I. & Vicks, S.H. The therapeutic value of muscle relaxation in seizure control: A case study. Unpublished manuscript, 1973. (Available from senior author, Department of Psychology, Boston University, Boston, Mass. 02215)

Parrino, J.J. Reduction of seizures by desensitization. *Journal of Behavior Therapy and Experimental Psychiatry,* 1971, **2,** 215–218.

Pinto, R. A case of movement epilepsy with agoraphobia treated successfully by flooding. *British Journal of Psychiatry,* 1972, **121,** 287–288.

Puletti, F. Surgical treatment of epilepsy. *Wisconsin Medical Journal,* 1969, **68,** 285–288.

Reynolds, E.H. & Travers, R.D. Serum anticonvulsant concentration in epileptic patients with mental symptoms. *British Journal of Psychiatry,* 1974, **124,** 440–445.

Richardson, R., Lal, H., & Karkalas, Y. Manipulation of environmental contingencies in the control of epileptic seizures. Unpublished manuscript, 1971.

Robb, J.P. Clinical diagnosis in epilepsy. *Wisconsin Medical Journal,* 1969, **68,** 292–296.

Schmidt, R. & Wilder, B. *Epilepsy.* Philadelphia, Penn.: F.A. Davis, 1968.

Scholander, T. Treatment of an unusual case of compulsive behavior by aversive stimulation. *Behavior Therapy,* 1972, **3,** 290–293.

Seifert, A.R. & Lubar, J.F. Reduction of epileptic seizures through EEG biofeedback training. *Biological Psychology,* 1975, **3,** 157–184.

Sterman, M.B. Studies of EEG biofeedback training in man and cats. Highlights of 17th Annual Conference: V.A. Cooperative Studies in Mental Health and Behavioral Sciences, 1972.

Sterman, M.B. Neurophysiologic and clinical studies of sensorimotor EEG biofeedback training: Some effects on epilepsy. *Seminars in Psychiatry,* 1973, **5,** 507–524.

Sterman, M.B. & Friar, L. Suppression of seizures in an epileptic following sensorimotor EEG feedback training. *Electroencephalography and Clinical Neurophysiology,* 1972, **33,** 89–95.

Sterman, M.B., MacDonald, L.R., & Stone, R.K. Biofeedback training of the sensorimotor electroencephalogram rhythm in man: Effects on epilepsy. *Epilepsia,* 1974, **15,** 395–416.

Wells, K.C., Turner, S.M., Bellack, A.S., & Hersen, M. Effects of cue-controlled relaxation psychomotor seizures: An experimental analysis. *Behavior Research and Therapy,* 1978, **16,** 51–53.

Wright, L. Aversive conditioning of self-induced seizures. *Behavior Therapy,* 1973, **4,** 712–713.

Zlutnick, S., Mayville, W.J., & Moffat, S. Modification of seizure disorders: The interruption of behavioral chains. *Journal of Applied Behavioral Analysis,* 1975, **8,** 1–12.

CHAPTER 11

Respiratory Disorder

OVERVIEW

Chronic obstructive lung disease is a generic term used to designate those diseases in which bronchial obstruction to airflow is a principal feature. Chronic obstructive lung diseases includes asthma, chronic bronchitis, and emphysema. Synonyms for chronic obstructive lung diseases include: chronic airways obstruction (CAO), chronic obstructive pulmonary disease (COPD), chronic obstructive bronchopulmonary disease (COBPD), chronic aspecific respiratory affliction (CARA), and diffuse obstructive pulmonary syndrome (DOPS) (Mitchell, 1974).

ASTHMA

The respiratory disorder that has most often been the target of behavioral procedures is bronchial asthma. Based upon an average of several studies, Davis (1972) claimed that about 4% of American people are presently suffering from asthma and about 7% of the population reportedly have suffered from asthma at one time or another. This suggests that about 8.6 million Americans are handicapped by asthma and about 14 million either are or have been afflicted.

There are a number of reports suggesting that at least half of those having asthma are below the age of 15, and one estimate showed between 5 and 15% of American children have asthma (American Lung Association, 1975). Asthma is most frequent among boys younger than age 14 and men over 45, as well as in women between the ages of 15 and 45 (American Lung Association, 1975). Below the age of five, males are affected approximately two times as often as females. Between 5 and 9 years of age, the incidence in males and females is approximately the same. Thereafter, until age 60, women appear to exhibit a slightly greater incidence, and above 60, the onset of asthma is again more frequent in men than in women (Speizer, 1976).

Studies have indicated that the percentage of childhood asthma that persists into adulthood varies from 26 (Rackeman & Edwards, 1952) to 78% (Johnstone, 1968). In general, an earlier age of onset indicates a better prognosis, except when attacks begin at less than 2 years of age, and it also appears that the more severe cases of bronchial asthma tend to persist (Slavin, 1977).

According to studies cited by Davis (1972), asthma results in 27 million physician visits annually, 85 million days of restricted activity, 33 million sick days in bed, and 5 million lost work days. Asthma can further hinder the worker by limiting his choice of career or by preventing promotions (Creer, 1977). Asthma in children has become a leading contributor to school absenteeism (Schiffer & Hunt, 1963) and consequences of academic faltering and isolation from peers, sports activities, and the mainstream of community living have occurred.

In addition, asthma is an expensive condition. Besides the 27 million physician visits annually, asthma accounts for 75% of all admissions of patients with respiratory diseases to hospitals (American Lung Association, 1975). Cooper (1976) states that direct costs for physician services, hospital care, and drugs were estimated to be $850 million, and costs associated with morbidity were $440 million. Thus the total costs were estimated to be $1.3 billion for the year 1975 (Cooper, 1976).

Vance and Taylor (1971) indicated that asthma treatment consumed from 2 to 30% of a family's income when a member had childhood asthma, and in over half of the cases cited, 18% of the families income went for asthma treatment. Although the percentage is small, an increasing number of parents are finding that costs of childhood asthma are too great, and more and more youngsters with asthma are being treated in state-run medical facilities (Creer, 1977).

While asthma is not a major cause of death, Davis (1972) estimated that between 2000 and 4000 people die of asthma each year. Cooper (1976) determined that the cost of mortality in terms of lost productivity was $120 million in 1972. According to these statistics, asthma is a devastating disease in terms of economic and financial losses, as well as in impairment in development of normal family and individual functioning. The increased application of behavioral procedures in the treatment of asthma provides a relatively inexpensive, effective alternate or adjunctive treatment method to traditional medical care.

While references to asthma were made by Hippocrates (Rasenblatt, 1976), arriving at a definition has always sparked arguments and contentions. Asthma has been described in various ways and a composite definition will be attempted here. Asthma may be defined as an intermittent, variable, and reversible obstruction of bronchial airways (Chai, 1975), characterized by increased responsiveness of the trachea and bronchi to various stimuli (American Lung Association, 1975). It is caused by smooth muscle constriction, mucosal edema, and the retention of secretions, with resultant symptoms of respiratory insufficiency (Mathison, 1975).

The typical asthmatic attack is characterized by periods of labored breathing, shortness of breath, coughing, wheezing, and watery eyes. Attacks generally occur on an aperiodic basis: for example, a person could have several attacks in one week and remain asymptomatic for several months. Attacks vary in severity from extremely mild to life-threatening, and the severity of attacks by a particular patient usually varies from one episode to another. The condition can revert to normalcy either spontaneously or in response to adequate treatment. The reversible component differentiates asthma from other types of respiratory disorders, such as emphysema.

The inability to breathe—a hallmark of asthma   results from a narrowing of the large and/or small airways caused by muscle spasm, swelling of tissue, excessive mucus secretion, dried mucus plugs, or a combination of these factors (Creer, 1979). The exact proportions of each of these conditions vary from patient to patient and from attack to attack in the same patient (Snider, 1976). Smooth muscle spasm of large airways is an important feature in asthma. When unaccompanied by secretory plugging of small airways, it accounts for the dramatic occurrence and remission of attacks. If small airways obstruction has become widespread, the airways obstruction will undergo reversal much more slowly (Snider, 1976). During attacks the chest becomes overinflated, and exhalation is forced and prolonged (Ruth, 1975). During severe attacks, normal amounts of oxygen and carbon dioxide are not maintained in the blood or tissue (Creer, 1979).

It is worth noting that not all incidences of bronchospasm, wheezing, or intermittent airway obstruction are properly regarded as asthmatic responding (Frazer & Pare, 1970). A differential diagnosis requires ruling out bronchitis, obstructive emphysema, and congestive heart failure (Krupp & Chatton, 1976). Current somatic treatment for outpatients is pharmacological in the form of inhalation or oral bronchodilators with cromolyn sodium and/or corticosteroids in less responsive cases (Richerson, 1976). Acute attacks with status asthmaticus (failure to respond to emergency intravenous aminophylline and subcutaneous epinephrine treatment) require intensive inpatient care.

The pathophysiology of asthma is incompletely understood and there is as yet, no well accepted theory of etiology of the asthma syndrome (Weiss & Segal, 1976). Etiology may include such factors as allergy (Rowe & Rowe, 1963), respiratory infection (Forman, 1951), and psychophysiologic reactions to stress (Schneer, 1963). Persons who have attacks in response to specific allergens, such as pollen, dust, or animal danders, are said to have extrinsic or allergic asthma. Here, the triggering stimuli for attacks may be identified. Children and young adults are usually affected by this form of asthma. Attacks tend to be of sudden onset and brief duration, and the patient may be symptom-free between attacks. Persons having allergic asthma may have a history of both hay fever and eczema (Weiss, 1975).

When the etiology of a person's asthma cannot be specified, he is said to have intrinsic asthma. Infection is involved in many cases, it usually affects adults over 35, and prognosis is poorer than for allergic asthma. Mixed asthma refers to a combination of extrinsic and intrinsic factors in which allergies are a factor, but acute attacks may be initiated by infections (Weiss, 1975).

Psychological Factors

Historically, asthma has been considered to be a prime example of a psychosomatic disorder in which psychological variables were thought to play a crucial role in both the etiology and manifestation of the disorder. Four decades of increasingly careful and sophisticated research, has, however, begun to change these beliefs considerably. In more recent years, a number of authors have formulated conditioning theories (Turnbull, 1962; Yorkston, 1975; Dekker, Pleser, & Groen, 1957). Learning approaches generally emphasize one of two analyses: (1) classical conditioning in which antecedent stimuli have come to elicit asthmatic attacks, and (2) operant conditioning in which reinforcing stimuli serve to maintain or exacerbate attacks.

Through classical conditioning, asthma-like responses can be conditioned through the pairing of environmental stimuli with allergic substances and conditioned emotional responses associated with asthma attacks. Further, these conditions show generally that such stimuli along the same continuum also elicit attacks (Turnbull, 1962).

Chong (1977) reports that during wartime an army colonel developed asthma in Malta amid the extremely dusty conditions brought by bombing attacks. Years later, while standing on a ship's deck, he experienced an attack of asthma when one of the passengers said, "There's Malta."

Asthmatic symptoms, such as wheezing, chest constriction, coughing, labored breathing, are often severe enough to precipitate panic, fear, and anxiety. These symptoms become aversive stimuli. When the onset of an asthmatic attack is perceived by a patient, such stimuli serve as aversive cues for him and become conditioned stimuli for further anxiety. Before an attack begins, the patient experiences anxiety that serves to further exacerbate the onset of symptoms. This process can be described as the "vicious cycle" of asthma (Creer, 1979).

In some patients, the mere affording of a suggestion related to an asthma-eliciting stimulus serves as an aversive cue, or conditioned stimulus. For example, MacKenzie (1886) describes a female patient known to be allergic to roses. Exposure to an artificial rose that she believed to be a natural rose promptly precipitated an acute asthmatic attack.

From an operant point of view, principles such as shaping and reinforcement of asthma-like behavior are important, as symptoms may occur by the gradual shaping of breathing patterns, which are closer and closer approximations of asthmatic breathing (Turnbull, 1962), and reinforcing stimuli can serve to maintain asthma attacks (Creer, 1979). Creer (1979) cites the example of a young asthmatic boy who discovered that his "post-bedtime" attacks were reinforced by his mother's unfailing attention. Here again, is a disease entity that seems to be influenced by environmental factors. Because these factors may affect the patient's well-being, careful attention should be directed to their identification and control.

Treatment

With the advent of these theories and case studies, a number of investigators in the field of behavioral medicine has devised treatment methodologies based on respondent and operant conditioning. Behavioral intervention methods have been employed in the therapeutic management of asthma in three ways: (1) to alter the abnormal pulmonary functioning more or less directly by use of relaxation, biofeedback assisted relaxation, and operantly conditioned biofeedback, (2) to alter maladaptive emotional concomitants to asthma by use of relaxation and systematic desensitization, and (3) to alter maladaptive asthma-related behaviors and family patterns by use of the operant conditioning techniques.

Relaxation

Procedures based on anxiety reduction predominate in the behavioral control of asthma since it is often assumed that asthmatic responding is anxiety related. The literature presents several treatment paradigms employing relaxation such as progressive muscle relaxation, systematic desensitization, and EMG biofeedback assisted relaxation.

In one of the more straightforward demonstrations of the effectiveness of relaxation training on asthmatic responses, Alexander, Miklich, and Hershkoff (1972) compared Jacobsonian systematic relaxation training with sitting quietly at the onset of or during an asthmatic attack. They found that 20 minutes of relaxation training brought about a statistically significant, 11% improvement in peak expiratory flow rate (PEFR) immediately following relaxation in a group of severe chronic, asthmatic children, as contrasted to no change in a matched control group instructed to merely sit quietly.

These results were replicated by Alexander (1972) in another controlled study with a comparable sample of severely asthmatic children. A ten % PEFR improvement was found. Phillip, Wilde, and Day (1972) similarly found that 7 out of 10 subjects allowed 10 minutes in which to relax following previous relaxation training improved in forced expiratory volume (FEV) compared to controls, with the largest change reported as 20%. In addition, when the pre-post FEV training values were compared, the difference was also statistically significant. Similar results in children samples have been cited by Tal and Miklich (1976) who also used FEV.

A recent study by Alexander, Gerd, Cropp, and Chai (1979) used a three-phase experimental design with a group of 14 chronic asthmatic children who received treatment as follows: (1) phase one, consisting of three sessions of quiet rest, (2) phase two, consisting of five 30-minute sessions of relaxation training, and (3) phase three, consisting of three sessions of undirected relaxation. Pulmonary functioning (FVC), EMG and heart rate were assessed at pre- and post-session junctures. The results concluded that although EMG and HR did decrease following relaxation training, there was no clinically significant change in FVC noted.

Another study by Sirota and Mahoney (1974) attempted traditional relaxation training for a 41-year-old male with a 34-year history of asthma. A portable timer was used by the patient to set off a sound at varying time intervals. In this manner, the timer would sound at the end of a particular interval and the patient would then relax on cue. In addition, the patient was required to briefly postpone the use of a bronchodilator when the onset of symptoms was noticed, and set the timer for 3 to 4 minutes, during which time relaxation was practiced. When the timer sounded, the bronchodilator would be used only if needed. At the end of treatment, inhalation medication declined to zero, corticosteroid therapy terminated, bronchodilator use reduced by 80%, and all other asthmatic medications were reduced or eliminated.

The number of sessions in these studies range from three to six, with the length per session totaling 30 minutes, plus instructions for twice daily home practice. Relaxation training has rather consistently produced statistically significant improvement in subject's pulmonary function measures (PEFR, FEV, FVC), when compared to those subjects receiving no treatment (Alexander, 1972; Alexander et al., 1972; Davis et al., 1973; and Philip et al., 1972).

These results, though highly promising, presented several problems. First, the amount of change, averaging no more than a 10% increase in flow rate across studies, was of modest proportion. For clinical as opposed to statistical significance to be claimed, increases in flow rate should be substantially greater than 10 percent. The improvements found in the relaxation studies thus far would not necessarily be subjectively detectable by patients, nor do they approach the extent of lung function or subjective benefit obtainable from the most commonly used pharmacological alternatives for symptomatic relief.

Second, the highly effort-dependent forced expiratory flow rate measures that were employed tend to taint the relative significance that may be realistically placed on the findings of these studies. Such a measure is easily biased by therapist and patient expectancies. Furthermore, these measures are somewhat invalidated because they reflect predominantly large airway dynamics. Lung pathology in asthma occurs both in the larger airways as well as in the peripheral, smaller airways including the alveoli (McFadden & Ingram, 1976). Therefore, before any obtained effects of relaxation on pulmonary function could be accepted, more definitive and complete measurement of pulmonary physiology would have to be realized, involving measures of both large and small airways, as well as measures that are much less effort-dependent.

Third, with the exception of one of the more recent studies (Alexander *et al.,* 1979), the obtained effects of relaxation training on lung functioning had only been assessed immediately following relaxation. In order for a symptomatic treatment modality to be considered clinically efficacious, a beneficial influence capable of sustaining its effects for a prolonged period subsequent to the actual relaxation training would need to be demonstrated.

Relaxation and Desensitization

Several studies have reported improvement in asthma patients as a result of systematic desensitization designed to both promote relaxation and reduce anxiety (Cooper, 1964; Miklich, Renne, Creer, Alexander, Chai, Davis, Hoffman, & Danker-Brown, 1977; Moore, 1965; Sergeant & Yorkston, 1969; Walton, 1970; Yorkston, McHugh, Bradey, Serber, & Sergeant, 1974).

The various items in desensitization hierarchies have concerned asthmatic attacks per se (fighting for breath), stimuli which evoke attacks (a very hot day in a closed room), and idiosyncratic, psychologically stressful events (husband 30 minutes late coming home from work) (Sergeant & Yorkston, 1969). The number of sessions in these studies have ranged from six to ten, with duration of sessions varying from 30 to 60 minutes. When comparisons have been made between progressive relaxation training alone versus systematic desensitization, the latter method has invariably proven superior.

Yorkston, McHugh, Brody, Serber, and Sergeant (1974) compared the effects of verbal desensitization and relaxation in the control of FEV and subsequent use of medications. Fourteen adults with bronchial asthma were randomly assigned to two treatment groups: relaxation alone, and relaxation plus verbal desensitization. Patients trained in relaxation were taught to relax while sitting, standing, and in a variety of other positions. Patients in the desensitization group began by describing their symptoms of asthma by mentioning feelings, thoughts, and the circumstances in which attacks occurred. These descriptions were used to establish a list of hierarchies for the desensitization procedure. FEV was measured three times before and after each of the 6 half-hour sessions. While both groups reported feeling better after treatment sessions, only the group receiving desensitization showed significant improvement in pulmonary function. At a 2-year follow-up, the desensitization group continued to show the most improvement, including a reduced dosage of all medications. These subjects were also rated as more markedly improved clinically than those receiving relaxation alone.

Moore (1965) compared the effects of relaxation alone, relaxation plus hypnosis, and relaxation plus desensitization. The desensitization group included the use of three hierarchies for each subject: one for asthmatic attacks, another for allergic or infectious situations, and a third for psychological stress. Each hierarchy included ten steps. Maximum peak flow (MPF) was measured by the Wright Peak Flow Meter and subjective improvement was measured by the number of days during which asthma attacks occurred as recorded by the patient. Results indicated no differences between groups on subjective change, with all three groups reporting improvement in number of attacks. Changes on the objective measure (MPF) showed significant differences between relaxation plus desensitization, and both relaxation alone and relaxation plus suggestion. There were no differences between relaxation alone and relaxation plus suggestion and neither was as effective as relaxation plus desensitization.

The consensus among all of the studies employing desensitization primarily is that relaxation training when employed as a component of various modes of counterconditioning strategies can be of clinically significant value in the reduction of anxiety and fear responses to asthma itself. In so doing, symptomatology is reduced. However, a point to be emphasized is that such a treatment approach focuses on altering anxiety levels, and not necessarily on pulmonary function.

Relaxation and Biofeedback

A number of studies have employed EMG biofeedback assisted relaxation training to treat anxiety associated with asthma. Dependent variables have generally been various pulmonary functions (PEFR, FEV, or FVC) (Davis, Saunders, Creer, & Chai, 1973; Jayette, 1977; Kotses, Glaus, Crawford, Edwards, & Scherr, 1976; Kotses, Bricel, Edwards, & Crawford, 1978; Scherr, Crawford, Sergeant, & Scherr, 1975; and Scherr & Crawford, 1978).

The paradigms of the six reported EMG biofeedback-assisted relaxation training studies are as follows:

1. The comparison of EMG frontalis biofeedback assisted relaxation training versus relaxation alone, versus a no treatment control group (Davis *et al.*, 1973).
2. The combination of EMG frontalis biofeedback assisted relaxation training with Jacobsonian relaxation versus a no treatment control group (Scherr *et al.*, 1975).
3. EMG frontalis biofeedback assisted relaxation training using pre- and post-treatment comparisons (Jayette, 1977).
4. Comparison of EMG frontalis biofeedback assisted relaxation training, versus noncontingent EMG frontalis biofeedback versus a no-treatment control group (Kotses *et al.*, 1976; Scherr & Crawford, 1978).
5. Comparison of EMG frontalis biofeedback assisted relaxation training versus EMG brachio-radialis biofeedback assisted relaxation training versus a no treatment control group (Kotses *et al.*, 1978; Scherr & Crawford, 1978).

The outcomes of these studies all yielded favorable results with regard to improved pulmonary functioning except for the study by Jayette (1977). Although some studies reported statistically significant increases in lung functioning (Davis *et al.*, 1973; and Scherr *et al.*, 1975), these were not necessarily clinically significant. However, Scherr *et al.*, (1975) did report a statistically significant decrease in the number of asthmatic attacks for the treatment group.

Operantly Conditioned Biofeedback

The term "biofeedback" has been used to refer to both augmentation of relaxation training with EMG feedback, and feeding back an analog signal indicating level of respiratory resistance. While each procedure involves feedback, the use of respiratory resistance is an innovative technique (Knapp & Wells, 1978). Several studies have used this technique in an attempt to directly alter pulmonary function. These procedures have been described by the various authors as counterconditioning or biofeedback reinforcement (Kahn et al., 1974), instrumental conditioning (Danker et al., 1975), visceral learning (Vachon & Rich, 1976), and biofeedback training (Feldman, 1976). The first three techniques share the procedure of providing subjects with light on feedback during trials in which the respiratory measure equalled or exceeded a prescribed criterion. The later study presented subjects with an analogue feedback tone which varied as a logarithmic function of TRR. On occasion verbal praise (Kahn et al., 1974) or points without backup reinforcers (Danker et al., 1975) were added as consequences of obtaining the criterion.

Results show considerable variability among the studies. Kahn et al. (1974), Feldman (1976), and Vachon and Rich (1976) reported success at operantly shaping respiratory functions, while Danker et al. (1975) failed to find any evidence for conditioning. In the studies showing improvement, the degree of improvement was small. According to Vachon and Rich (1976), improvement was roughly equivalent to one inhalation of isoproterenol. Future research should be directed at producing larger effects, perhaps by increasing the reinforcement value, and reinforcing approximations in graded steps rather than a fixed criterion, and assessing generalization to the natural environment as well as long-term follow-up.

Operant Approaches

Operant approaches deal with treating maladaptive or undesirable asthma-related patterns of behavior. The operant techniques of positive reinforcement, extinction, time-out, response cost, shaping, modeling, and punishment have been utilized to treat a variety of behaviors associated with asthmatic children, such as hyperactivity (Gardner, 1968; Miklich, 1973), inappropriate behavior (Creer & Miklich, 1970), frequency and duration of hospitalization (Creer, 1970; Creer, Weinberg, & Molk, 1974), attending behavior (Creer & Yoches, 1971), and appropriate use of inhalation equipment (Renne & Creer, 1976).

Positive reinforcement and *extinction* have been used with much success in several studies. Gardner (1968) treated a 6-year-old male with hyperactivity and inappropriate behavior patterns by withdrawal of attention for inappropriate behaviors and reinforcement (tokens to exchange for toys) for slow rate and appropriate behaviors. He was also taught alternative responses to stress by modeling through story reading. Asthma attacks decreased to one or two per week and hyperactive and manipulative behavior remained nonexistent at 6-month follow-up.

Neisworth and Moore (1972) produced a dramatic reduction in the number of coughing episodes in an asthmatic child by instructing the parents to withhold the attention which the coughing had been eliciting. Renna and Creer (1976) used positive reinforcement to teach a young child to use properly an intermittent positive pressure breathing device. They rewarded more successively correct responses until the child had learned to use the device in its intended manners. They found that less follow-up medication was required as the child became more proficient at using his therapeutic apparatus.

Time out has been used in several studies. Creer (1970) used this procedure on two 10-year-old boys felt to be malingering. The boys requested unnecessary admissions to the hospital unit, usually to avoid social stress. Each time they were admitted, the usual pleasant time-passing items available there, such as comic books, games, television, were removed, and they had to spend their time recuperating in bed without them. A dramatic drop in frequency and duration of hospitalizations resulted with no increase in symptoms. Creer, Weinberg, and Molk (1974) replicated this study with another 10-year-old boy with similar results.

Creer and Yoches (1971) used the technique of *response cost* to increase the amount of time spent attending to classroom materials in two asthmatic children who had failed to develop these skills due to the amount of time lost from school because of illness. At the beginning of each classroom session, the children were given 40 points, from which one point was subtracted for each 30-second period spent not attending to classroom materials. Each subtraction was signaled. The children soon learned to retain the points which could be exchanged for gifts. As a result, academic performance improved.

Creer and Miklich (1970) treated a 10-year-old asthmatic boy engaging in oversleeping, tantrums, and inappropriate social behavior through *modeling*. The boy was afforded self-modeling by viewing a videotape of himself acting out the opposite behaviors to those in which there were complaints. The boy's behavior corresponded to that on the tape, and at a 6-month follow-up, appropriate behavior was maintained.

Alexander *et al.,* (1973) used *punishment* and a procedure called response suppression *shaping* in a case of coughing elicited by several specific stimuli. The boy being treated had to refrain from coughing for longer and longer periods following presentation of a precipitating stimulus in order to avoid a brief, mild electric shock to the forearm. He was able to reduce his tendency to cough in an ordinary fashion to each of the four precipitants of his coughing. Coughing had been maintained by contingent attention being paid to it by the boy's family. Three of the precipitants, the odor of cooking grease, the smell of hair spray, and the smell of hand soap, had required accommodations in the eating and toilet habits of the family, thus promoting constant stress. Behavioral intervention at the family level was required to alter reinforcement patterns so that the coughing was not reestablished once it had been eliminated by the suppression procedure.

This study points to one of the most important aspects of the total clinical management in chronic disorders, such as asthma. Even the most effective medical management regime can be subverted by inappropriate patterns of reacting to and dealing with asthma at the family level. The taking of medication, the assignment of responsibilities, and the ways in which the presence of symptoms are handled can have a profound effect on family life and the psychological development of the patient. Inappropriate response patterns can cause increased stress and can lay the foundation for psychological problems (Alexander, 1977). The outcome of these studies using operant techniques in the treatment of adjunct behavior problems associated with having asthma have been quite promising.

Summary

Asthma is a devastating disease both economically and emotionally. It may be defined as an intermittent, variable, and reversible obstruction of bronchial airways characterized by increased responsiveness of the trachea and bronchi to various stimuli caused by smooth muscle constriction, mucosal edema, and the retention of secretions, with resultant symptoms of respiratory insufficiency. The typical attack is characterized by periods of labored breathing, shortness of breath, coughing, wheezing, and watery eyes. Episodes can be triggered by many factors including allergens, infections, or any number of airway irritants. The significance of various stimulants and the specific manifestation of attacks can vary from person to person and from episode to episode in the same person. The pathophysiology of asthma is incompletely understood, and there is as yet no completely accepted theory of etiology of the asthma syndrome.

Historically, asthma was first viewed as a psychosomatic disorder in which psychological variables were thought to play an important role in both the etiology and manifestation of the disorder. Four decades of systematic research has begun to change those views. Learning theories based on classical and operant conditioning principles were developed and are the basis for much of the present research activity.

Currently, the prevailing attitude is that it is highly difficult, if not impossible, to be able to relate psychological variables to the etiology of asthma. Precipitation of actual asthma episodes by psychological variables in the laboratory has not been adequately shown.

Some investigators have been able to demonstrate small changes in lung functioning as a result of treatments involving relaxation, biofeedback, and desensitization. Although these changes have been statistically reliable, they are not necessarily clinically significant. It is necessary to emphasize that any positive claim of benefit to an asthmatic from any therapy, including psychological ones, must be substantiated by reliable pulmonary function measurement. Research has shown that assessment on any other basis can and has been deceivingly misinterpreted by clinicians and researchers not specifically familiar and experienced with this disorder.

At present, it may be concluded that psychological therapies do not prove effective as a cure for asthma. However, it is now believed that psychological difficulties can and do result from asthma. In this area, psychological treatment of anxiety and fear-related responses, which may precipitate an attack, or treatment of the maladaptive behavioral response patterns of the person having asthma or his family members, has proven quite successful. The treatment modalities of relaxation, desensitization, and biofeedback have shown success in reducing anxiety and fear-related responses which may exacerbate an attack. The operant conditioning therapies have proven quite successful in treating the maladaptive behavioral response patterns that maintain asthma-like behavior.

While, at present, under the research conditions thus far evidenced, attempts to alter lung function through psychological means has not been impressive. Nevertheless, the contribution of behavioral medicine specialists in the overall treatment efforts with asthmatics has proven effective as an adjunct treatment to traditional medical management and should continue in its development and expansion.

REFERENCES

Alexander, A.B. Systematic relaxation and flow rates in asthmatic children: Relationship to emotional participants and anxiety. *Journal of Psychosomatic Research*, 1972, **16**, 405–410.

Alexander, A.B. Behavioral methods in the clinical management of asthma. In W.D. Gentry & R.B. Williams (Eds.) *Behavioral approaches to medical practice*. Cambridge, Mass. Ballinger, 1977.

Alexander, A.B., Miklich, D.R., & Hershkoff, H. The immediate effects of systematic relaxation on peak expiratory flow rates in asthmatic children. *Psychosomatic Medicine*, 1972, **34**, 388–394.

Alexander, A.B., Chai, H., Creer, T.L., Miklich, D.R., Renee, C.M., & Cardoso, R. The elimination of chronic cough by response suppression shaping. *Journal of Behavior Therapy and Experimental Psychiatry*, 1973, **4**, 75–80.

Alexander, A.B., Gerd, J., Cropp, A., & Chai, H. Effects of relaxation training on pulmonary mechanics in children with asthma. *Journal of Applied Behavior Analysis*, 1979, **12**, 27–35.

American Lung Association. *Introduction to lung diseases*, 6th ed. 1975.

Chai, H. Management of severe chronic perennial asthma in children. *Advances in Asthma and Allergy*, 1975, **2**, 1–12.

Chong, T.M. The management of bronchial asthma. *Journal of Asthma Research,* 1977, **14,** 73–80.

Cooper, A.J. A case of bronchial asthma treated by behavior therapy. *Behavior Research and Therapy,* 1964, **1,** 351–356.

Cooper, B. The economic costs of selected respiratory diseases, 1972. Unpublished report prepared for the Division of Lung Diseases Task Force on Prevention, Control and Education in Respiratory Diseases, 1976.

Creer, T.L. The use of a time-out from positive reinforcement procedure with asthmatic children. *Journal of Psychosomatic Research,* 1970, **14,** 117–120.

Creer, T.L. Psychological impact of asthma. Unpublished report prepared for the Asthma Committee, Task Force on Asthma and Other Allergic Diseases, National Institute of Allergy and Infectious Diseases, 1977.

Creer, T.L. *Asthma therapy: A behavioral health care system for respiratory disorders.* New York: Springer, 1979.

Creer, T.L. & Miklich, D.R. The application of a selfmodeling procedure to modify inappropriate behavior: A preliminary report. *Behavior Research and Therapy,* 1970, **8,** 91–92.

Creer, T.L. & Yoches, C. The modification of an inappropriate behavioral pattern in asthmatic children. *Journal of Chronic Diseases,* 1971, **24,** 507–513.

Creer, T.L., Weinberg, E., & Molk, L. Managing a problem hospital behavior: Malingering. *Journal of Behavior Therapy and Experimental Psychiatry,* 1974, **5,** 259–262.

Danker, P.S., Miklich, D.R., Pratt, C., & Creer, T.L. An unsuccessful attempt to instrumentally condition peak expiratory flow rates in asthmatic children. *Journal of Psychosomatic Research,* 1975, **19,** 209–213.

Davis, D.J. NIAID initiatives in allergy research. *The Journal of Allergy and Clinical Immunology,* 1972, **49,** 323–328.

Davis, M.H., Saunders, D.R., Creer, T.L., & Chai, H. Relaxation training facilitated by biofeedback apparatus as a supplemental treatment in bronchial asthma. *Journal of Psychosomatic Research,* 1973, **17,** 121–128.

Dekker, E., Pelser, H.E., & Groen, J. Conditioning as a cause of asthmatic attacks. *Journal of Psychosomatic Research,* 1957, **2,** 97–108.

Feldman, G.M. The effect of biofeedback training on respiratory resistance of asthmatic children. *Psychosomatic Medicine,* 1976, **38,** 27–34.

Fraser, R.G. & Pare J.A. *Diagnosis of disease of the chest.* Philadelphia: Saunders, 1970.

Gardner, J.E. A blending of behavior therapy techniques in an approach to an asthmatic child. *Psychotherapy: Theory, Research, and Practice,* 1968, **5,** 46–49.

Jayette, B.A. The effect of EMG biofeedback training on selected physiological and personality variables in the adult asthma patient. Dissertation Abstracts International, 1977, 2419B.

Johnstone, D.E. A study of the natural history of bronchial asthma in children. *American Journal of Diseases in Children,* 1968, **115,** 213–216.

Kahn, A., Staerk, M., & Bonk, C. Role of counter-conditioning in the treatment of asthma. *Journal of Psychosomatic Research,* 1974, **18,** 89–92.

Knapp, T.J. & Wells, L.A. Behavior therapy for asthma: A review. *Behavior Research and Therapy*, 1978, **16**, 103–115.

Kotses, H., Glaus, K.D., Bricel, S.K., Edwards, J.E., & Crawford, P.L. Operant muscular relaxation and peak expiratory flow rate in asthmatic children. *Journal of Psychosomatic Research, 1978*, **22**, 17–23.

Kotses, H. Glaus, K.D., Crawford, P.L., Edwards, J.E., & Scherr, M.S. Operant reduction of frontalis EMG activity in the treatment of asthma in children. *Journal of Psychosomatic Research*, 1976, **20**, 453–459.

Krupp, M.A. & Chatton, M.J. *Current medical diagnosis and treatment.* Los Angeles: Lang Medical Publications, 1976.

MacKenzie, J.N. The production of "rose asthma" by an artificial rose. *American Journal of Medical Sciences*, 1886, **91**, 45–57.

Mathison, D.A. Asthma. In H.F. Conn (Ed.) *Current therapy.* Philadelphia: Saunders, 1975.

McFadden, E.R. & Ingram, R.H. Spirometry, lung volumes, and distribution of ventilation in asthma. In E.B. Weiss and M.S. Segal (Eds.) *Bronchial asthma: Its nature and management.* Boston: Little, Brown, 1976.

Miklich, D.R. Operant conditioning procedures with systematic desensitization in a hyperkinetic asthmatic boy. *Journal of Behavior Therapy and Experimental Psychiatry*, 1973, **4**, 177–182.

Miklich, D.R., Renne, C.M., Creer, T.L., Alexander, A.B., Chai, H., Davis, M.H., Hoffman, A., & Danker-Brown, P. The clinical utility of behavior therapy as an adjunctive treatment for asthma. *The Journal of Allergy and Clinical Immunology*, 1977, **60**, 285–294.

Mitchell, R.S. Chronic airways obstruction. In G.L. Baum (Ed.) *Textbook of pulmonary diseases,* 2nd ed. Boston: Little, Brown, 1974.

Moore, N. Behavior therapy in bronchial asthma: A controlled study. *Journal of Psychosomatic Research*, 1965, **9**, 257–276.

Neisworth, J.T. & Moore, F. Operant treatment of asthmatic responding with the parent as therapist. *Behavior Therapy*, 1972, **3**, 95–99.

Phillipp, R.L., Wilde, G.J.S., & Day, J.H. Suggestion and relaxation in asthmatics. *Journal of Psychosomatic Research*, 1972, **16**, 193–204.

Rackerman, F.M. & Edwards, M.C. Asthma in children. *New England Journal of Medicine*, 1952, **246**, 858–863.

Renne, C.M. & Creer, T.L. The effects of training on the use of inhalation therapy equipment by children with asthma. *Journal of Applied Behavior Analysis*, 1976, **9**, 1–11.

Richerson, H.B. Asthma in adults. In H.F. Conn (Ed.) *Current therapy.* Philadelphia: Saunders, 1976.

Rosenblatt, M.B. History of bronchial asthma. In E.B. Weiss & M.S. Segal (Eds.) *Bronchial asthma: Mechanisms and therapeutics.* Boston: Little, Brown, 1976.

Ruth, W.E. Examination of the chest, lungs, and pulmonary system. In M.H. Delp & R.T. Manning (Eds.) *Major's physical diagnosis, 8th ed.* Philadelphia: Saunders, 1975.

Scherr, M.S. & Crawford, P.L. Three-year evaluation of biofeedback techniques in the treatment of children with chronic asthma in a summer camp environment. *Annals of Allergy,* 1978, **41,** 288–292.

Scherr, M.S., Crawford, P.L., Sergent, C.B., & Scherr, C.A. Effect of biofeedback techniques on chronic asthma in a summer camp environment. *Annals of Allergy,* 1975, **35,** 289–295.

Schiffer, C.G. & Hunt, E.P. Illness among children. (Children's Bureau Publication No. 405). Washington, D.C.: U.S. Government Printing Office, 1963.

Schneer, N.I. *The asthmatic child: Psychosomatic approach to problems and treatment.* New York: Harper and Row, 1963.

Sergeant, H.G.S. & Yorkston, N.J. Verbal desensitization in the treatment of bronchial asthma. *Lancet,* 1969, **2,** 1321–1323.

Sirota, A.D. & Mahoney, M.J. Relaxing on cue: The self regulation of asthma. *Journal of Behavior Therapy and Experimental Psychiatry,* 1974, **5,** 65–66.

Slavin, R. Prognosis in bronchial asthma. Report prepared for the Asthma Committee, The Task Force on Asthma and Other Allergic Diseases, National Institute of Allergic and Infectious Diseases, 1977.

Snider, G.L. The interrelationships of asthma, chronic bronchitis, and emphysema. In E.B. Weiss & M.S. Segal (Eds.) *Bronchial asthma: Mechanisms and therapeutics.* Boston: Little, Brown, 1976.

Speizer, F.E. Epidemiology, prevalence, and mortality in asthma. In E.B. Weiss & M.S. Segal (Eds.) *Bronchial asthma: Mechanisms and therapeutics.* Boston: Little, Brown, 1976.

Tal, A & Miklich, D.R. Emotionally induced decreases in pulmonary flow rates in asthmatic children. *Psychosomatic Medicine,* 1976, **38,** 190–199.

Turnbull, J.W. Asthma conceived as a learned response. *Journal of Psychosomatic Research,* 1962, **6,** 59–70.

Vachon, L & Rich, E.S. Visceral learning in asthma. *Psychosomatic Medicine,* 1976, **38,** 122–130.

Vance, V.J. & Taylor, W.F. The financial cost of chronic childhood asthma. *Annals of Allergy,* 1971, **29,** 455–460.

Walton, D. The application of learning theory to the treatment of a case of bronchial asthma. In H.J. Eysenck (Ed.) *Behavior therapy and the neuroses.* New York: Pergamon Press, 1970.

Weiss, E.B. Bronchial asthma. *Clinical Symposia,* 1975, **27,** Nos. 1 and 2.

Weiss, E.B. & Segal, M.S. (Eds.) *Bronchial asthma: Mechanisms and therapeutics.* Boston: Little, Brown, 1976.

Yorkston, N.J. Behavior therapy in the treatment of bronchial asthma. In T. Thompson & W.S. Dockens (Eds.) *Applications of behavior modification.* New York: Academic Press, 1975.

Yorkston, N.J., McHugh, R.B., Brady, R., Serber, M., & Sergeant, H.G.S. Verbal desensitization in bronchial asthma. *Journal of Psychosomatic Research,* 1974, **18,** 371–376.

CHAPTER 12

Skin Disorders

OVERVIEW

In the era of psychosomatic medicine, and more recently behavioral medicine, a great deal of attention has been focused on skin disorders, and numerous clinical studies have related emotions to pathologic skin manifestations.

Although the skin is typically conceptualized as a mere outer coating of the body, it actually contains a wide variety of cells, including sense organs, that constantly react to pressure, temperature, and noxious stimulation from the outside world (Lackman, 1972). Further, the skin contains numerous glands, blood vessels, and smooth muscle elements, many of which come under autonomic nervous system control. Therefore, emotional stimuli are able to precipitate various skin reactions through autonomic arousal (Frankel, 1975).

Numerous accounts have cited the role of emotional factors in skin disorders (Dunbar, 1946; Feverman & Sandback, 1975; Grinker & Robbins, 1954; Harrison, 1977; Kellner, 1975; Musaph, 1977; Tan, 1970; and Wittkower & Lester, 1963). The autonomic nervous system mediates external and internal stimuli into experienced emotionality, affecting various cutaneous components, such as vascular blood flow and sweat glands. Some of the more common emotionally induced skin reactions include: blushing, a reddening of the skin surface of the face due to dilation of cutaneous blood vessels; pallor, a paling or whitening of the skin surface due to constriction of cutaneous blood vessels; and perspiration, the exudation of fluid by the sweat glands. It has been shown that perspiration directly affects the electrodermal response which is a change in resistance of the skin to the passage of an electric current. This phenomenon, the galvanic skin response (GSR) is considered to be an indicator of emotional activity (Lackman, 1972).

Why skin disorders occur, and vary from person to person, appearing and disappearing during the life span of the same person, is poorly understood (Frankel, 1975). Initially, research was based on the psychoanalytic theory of inner conflict, and hypnosis was generally used as the treatment modality (Fernandez, 1955; Mason, 1952; Schneck, 1954; Wink, 1961; Kidd, 1966; Zhukov, 1961).

Only recently have dermatologists, psychiatrists, and behavioral scientists begun to explore the psychophysiological mechanisms involved in skin disorders. With the advent of behavior therapy and psychophysiologic measuring devices and techniques, there has been a gradual shift in emphasis from speculations over the connection of psychic turmoil and dermatological lesions to emphasis on relevant psychophysiological processes.

The behavioral techniques used in the treatment of various skin disorders include: social reinforcement, assertive training, self-reinforcement, contingency contracting and token economies; cognitive strategies, such as thought-stopping; aversion therapy; systematic desensitization; and progressive relaxation. The various forms of biofeedback techniques used include: frontalis EMG training, temperature training, and GSR training. A brief description of each dermatological disorder will be given with a review of the behavioral strategies thus far used in its treatment.

NEURODERMATITIS

Neurodermatitis refers to any cutaneous eruption that is the result of emotional stimulation. Circumscribed neurodermatitis is also referred to as lichen simplex chronicus and lichenified dermatitis. It is characterized by circular, oval, or irregular patches of intensely pruritic, excessively furrowed and thickened shiny skin, except where covered by fine, grey scales (Allen, 1967). These lesions are commonly seen in one or more of several classic locations, such as the elbows, knees, inner thighs, nape of the neck, occipital area of the scalp, scrotum, vulva, the perianal region, eyelids, ears, and ankles. This disease begins with a small pruritic lesion or other minor irritation which incites a cycle of itching and scratching from which the chronic dermatosis develops. Secondary lesions include excoriations, lichenification, and in severe cases, marked verrucous thickening of the skin with pigmentary changes. In these severe cases, healing is usually followed by scarring.

The initial precipitating factor or factors of stasis dermatitis, tinea cruris, contact dermatitis, seborrheic dermatitis or psoriasis, may be very identifiable. It is commonly held that the chronicity of the disorder is perpetuated by the habit of scratching, thought to be brought on by stress and anxiety (Sauer, 1959). Other etiologies are thought to be antigen-antibody reactions, and external irritants. Determination of the specific causes are guided by the age of the patient, the season, and the local environment. Sensitization to foods and inhalants, in addition to bacterial and fungus stressors are all common in middle age. With older patients, the chief causes are focal infections, psychosomatic disorders, and metabolic abnormalities.

Atopic eczema is a specific type of neurodermatitis that occurs in two clinical forms: infantile and adult. The infantile form has blisters, oozing, and crusting with excoriation. Adult and adolescent forms have marked dryness, thickening, excoriation, and even scarring. The infantile form is distributed on the face, scalp, arms, and legs, or can be generalized. The adolescent or adult form is distributed on cubital and popliteal fossae and less commonly on dorsum of hands and feet, ears, or can be generalized.

The course varies from mild single episodes to severe, chronic, recurrent episodes. The infantile form usually becomes milder or disappears after the age of three or four. At puberty and in the late teens, flare-ups or new outbreaks can occur. Of patients with atopic eczema 30% eventually develop allergic asthma or hayfever. The family history is usually positive for one or more of the triad of allergic diseases. Atopic eczema is usually worse in winter due to decrease in home or office humidity. Wool and lanolin commonly irritate the skin, and food allergies can be a factor.

Medical treatment for neurodermatitis has usually involved antihistamine, calcium gluconate injections, specially prepared gauze compresses, and corticosteroids. These treatments are sometimes ineffective since they do not relieve the patient's tense emotional state, thereby failing to break the vicious cycle of tension-skin irritation-scratching-skin irritation-tension.

Treatment

A number of behavioral approaches have been utilized in the treatment of neurodermatitis, most of which are concerned with eliminating the scratching behaviors which maintain the skin condition. Several studies have focused on extinguishing the scratching behavior by reducing the reinforcing factors in scratching, which may have been attention from family members, and positively reinforcing nonscratching behavior.

The first study of this nature was reported by Walton (1960) who treated a 20-year-old woman with a 2-year history of neurodermatitis. It was assessed that attention from her family members and her fiance appeared to be powerful rewards for scratching behavior. Treatment was aimed at reducing these reinforcing factors by having the family extinguish these behaviors by refusing to discuss her skin problem and ignoring her scratching. Within 2 months, scratching was eliminated, and at 3 months, the condition of her skin was normal. A 4-year follow-up indicated that neurodermatitis had not returned.

Two later studies used similar strategies with children, but in addition to extinction, set up token economies to positively reinforce nonscratching behavior. Allan and Harris (1966) used behavior modification principles to train the mother of a 5-year-old girl with open sores and scabs in operant conditioning procedures, and Bar and Kuypers (1973) used the same procedures to train the mother of a 6-year-old girl with vulvar neurodermatitis. Both children were ignored when engaging in scratching behavior, and given rewards on prescribed, structured time intervals when scratching was absent. In both cases, after 6 weeks scratching was nearly eliminated, and the sores on the child with open wounds were completely healed. A 4-month follow-up done by Allan and Harris, and an 18-month follow-up done by Bar and Kuypers showed no recurrence.

Two similar studies used social reinforcement principles with older women to set up a self-modification program. Watson, Tharp, and Krisberg (1972) treated a 21-year-old woman with a 17-year history of dermatological problems. The woman taught herself to use behaviors incompatible with scratching, such as patting and rubbing. To control nocturnal scratching, she would wake herself up at specified intervals and scratch an unaffected area of her body. She also established a point system earning points to use for rewards, such as a bath. Twenty days of self-treatment eliminated all scratching, and a 6-month follow-up revealed stable improvement.

Dobes (1977) treated a 28-year-old female having a rash on the back of her neck. She kept a frequency chart on her scratching behavior and posted it visibly in her home. She attempted to decrease scratching each day by two or three instances and was to receive social reinforcement from her friends upon attainment of that goal. When weekly goals were met, her husband took her out to dinner. After 45 days of treatment, scratching was eliminated and a 2-year follow-up showed no recurrence.

Two studies cited in the literature used a combination of aversive conditioning and relaxation training in the treatment of longstanding dermatological problems. Ratliff and Stein (1968) treated a 22-year-old male with a 17-year history of dermatological problems that were progressively worsening during the 2 years prior to behavioral intervention. Bar and Kuypers (1975) treated a 33-year-old man with a 4-year history of severe lichen simplex on the scrotum, thighs, and ankles. In the Ratliff and Stein study, the client was seen once weekly for a total of nine 1-hour sessions. Treatment employed aversive conditioning consisting of a shock to the client's arm whenever he scratched. Shock was terminated when scratching stopped and the client said aloud "Don't scratch." Treatment also included instructions in progressive relaxation to be used whenever he felt the urge to scratch. After 5 weeks the scratching had been eliminated and the skin rash progressively diminished. After 6 months, the patient was still asymptomatic.

In the Bar and Kuypers study, the man was instructed to scratch, whereupon he received a shock on his hand. He also was instructed to say "Don't scratch" and was taught relaxation exercises. After 19 days of treatment, scratching had disappeared and improvement in the skin disorder was noted. A 13-month follow-up showed no further scratching.

There has been only one reported study thus far of the use of biofeedback in the treatment of neurodermatitis. Haynes, Wilson, Jaffe, and Britton (1979) treated eight persons with atopic eczema by using a combination of frontal EMG feedback and relaxation training. Treatment consisted of an initial interview and testing phase, a 2-week no treatment baseline phase, a placebo intervention phase consisting of two sessions per week for 2 weeks wherein subjects listened to an unchanging tone while EMG electrodes were attached to the forehead, and an EMG biofeedback/relaxation instruction phase of eight sessions for 4 weeks. In this treatment phase, subjects received EMG frontalis auditory biofeedback while listening to taped relaxation instructions for 20 minutes per session.

Overall results indicated 50% reductions in affected skin areas from photographic analyses, decreases in itching level within but not across treatment sessions, MMPI profiles to be within normal limits, low correlation between EMG/itching coefficients and response to treatment, and small within and between sessions effect with regard to EMG levels. Although dermatological problems did respond to the treatment package as a whole, it is not possible to ascertain which treatment components of the procedure were responsible for the improvement.

Brown and Bettley (1971) used a more broad-spectrum approach in treating 72 eczema patients. Subjects were randomly assigned to one of two treatment groups: those receiving dermatological treatment only; and those receiving identical dermatological treatment plus psychiatric treatment. Treatment lasted 4 months.

Dermatological treatment for all subjects consisted of elimination of all known allergens, application of steroid ointments, and antibiotics and/or antiseptics if needed. Psychiatric treatment for subjects in the second group was given on the basis of whether the patient demonstrated overt psychiatric symptoms and treatment consisted of identifying specific stressors in the patients' lives by facilitating awareness and ventilation of feelings of hostility and resentment. Progressive relaxation and hypnosis were used with the patients devoid of overt psychiatric symptoms.

It was concluded after a 14-month follow-up that short term psychiatric treatment when given unselectively did not significantly improve the eczema. With patients having overt psychiatric symptomatology and a willingness to undergo psychotherapy, the improvement of their eczema was significant.

URTICARIA

Synonymous with hives, this disorder is characterized by the appearance of whitish or reddish wheals, slightly elevated papules or welts which are usually surrounded by a halo and associated with itching, stinging, and prickling sensations (Andrews & Domonkos, 1963). The common areas affected are the trunk, buttocks, and chest. Acute cases may be mild or explosive, but usually disappear with or without treatment in a few hours or days. The chronic form has remissions and exacerbations for months or years.

Urticaria may have an allergic or nonallergic basis (Allen, 1967). Allergic causes are infection, food or drugs, inhaled pollens and dust, external contactants, and physical stressors, such as cold water, heat, and ultraviolet radiation. Nonallergic causes of what is termed "cholinergic urticaria" include psychogenic upsets, endocrinologic imbalance, exercise, and warming the body. Chronic urticaria is most difficult to treat. The removal of focal infections and emotional stress, in addition to the relief of fatigue are important procedures. Other medical treatments include a variety of internal pharmacologic remedies, tepid or cold tub baths, and ice-cold compresses. The use of local antipruritic lotions and drugs often give relief to the itching and stinging.

Treatment

There are three reported studies in the treatment of urticaria: one using various combinations of behavioral strategies, one using biofeedback, and one using a combination of behavioral strategies, antidepressant medication, and patient education. Daniels (1973) treated a 23-year-old female with urticaria covering her face and entire body who had interpersonal problems with her husband and in-laws. She was trained in deep muscle relaxation with accompanying anxiety hierarchies pertaining to her relationship with her husband and his family. A light hypnotic trance was used to reduce her anxiety. Covert reinforcement based on the woman's responses to a reinforcement survey schedule was used. She was also instructed how to use "thought stopping" as an emergency procedure to inhibit acute anxiety. She would utter "stop" subvocally, after which she would subvocally respond, "relax." She would then think a positive statement regarding the person or event which was at the root of her anxiety. Her hives disappeared after 12 weeks, and a 23-month follow-up revealed no recurrence.

Moan (1979) utilized GSR assisted relaxation training in treating a 28-year-old female's psychosomatic hives of 3 years duration that covered all portions of the body. During 2 months preceding treatment, the rashes occured and subsided twice daily, lasting from 1 to 2 hours, and were correlated with perceived levels of anxiety by the patient. Help consisted of eight weekly sessions of autogenic relaxation training with accompanying GSR audiovisual feedback. She also practiced relaxation at home on a daily basis without the aid of biofeedback. At termination of treatment, skin level conductivity had reduced from 12 microhms to four microhms. Anxiety levels were reportedly decreased, and no recurrence was seen during the final 5 weeks of treatment or at follow-up after 8 months.

Keegan (1976) utilized a combination of procedures in treating four patients with urticaria. Treatment involved utilization of a thorough medical history and physical assessment; patient education involving explanation of the various physical and emotional etiologies, and avoidance of specific allergens; use of antihistamines and Atarax, short-term use of minor tranquilizers and antidepressants for anxiety; and a combination of short-term problem oriented psychotherapy, family therapy, hypnosis, and relaxation training. Three of the four patients cited demonstrated complete remission of their hives.

PSORIASIS

A common chronic, recurrent, inflammatory disorder, this skin disease is characterized by rounded, circumscribed, dry scaling patches of varying sizes covered by grayish-white or silvery-white scales (Andrews & Domonkos, 1963). If the scales are removed by scraping or scratching, fine bleeding points occur. The lesions commonly appear on the scalp, elbows, knees, sacrol region, and under the nails. This disorder is found equally in men and women, but is rare in childhood (Allen, 1967). The condition is more prevalent in winter and in colder climates, and tends to improve in sunny climates. Etiology is unknown, although Andrews and Domonkos (1963) indicate a history of family incidences in 30% of the cases.

Hot starch or tar baths, local applications, and a low fat diet have been used for psoriasis treatment. The course of the disease can be chronic and recurrent. However, severe cases have been known to remit and not recur (Lever & Schaumburg-Lever, 1975).

Treatment

Psoriasis apparently involves what seems to be uncontrolled cell growth, with the number of cells in mitosis as much as 50 times greater than that of normal epidermis (Fry & McMinn, 1968; 1970). This disorder also results in increased vascularity and abnormal amounts of heat production (Herndon, 1975). The increased heat is accounted for by an increased metabolism as indicated by an elevated oxygen consumption at rest (Zoom & Mali, 1957). In addition, Baxter and Stoughton (1970) showed that vasoproliferation is crucial to cell growth and that occlusion alone was shown to decrease cellular mitosis. Therefore, the voluntary lowering of skin temperature at plaque sites, resulting from decreased peripheral blood flow in these areas, might serve to reduce psoriatic cell production.

Accordingly, Benoit and Harrell (1978) employed temperature biofeedback in treating three severe psoriatic patients. All three subjects had plaques on either the hand, forearm, lower leg, or foot, and had a plaque of equal size on a symmetrically identical area on the contralateral limb. One electrode was placed in the center portion of the experimental plaque, while the other electrode was placed on the contralateral plaque which served as a control. Both auditory and visual feedback of the experimental plaque's temperature were presented to the subjects. Training session duration was 30 minutes with seven such sessions over a 1-month time period.

The results demonstrated that biofeedback training was effective in decreasing the surface temperature of the psoriatic tissue. Although no photographs were taken, the authors report plaques of two subjects cleared completely, while the other subject showed great improvement. The authors further conclude, however, that the exact mechanism involved in the results cannot be ascertained because the subject who showed the greatest decrease in experimental plaque temperature, demonstrated the least plaque improvement. The fact did remain, however, that decreases in cellular proliferation did occur and seemed to be in some way related to temperature change achieved during biofeedback training.

Hughes, Goldsmith, and England (1979) employed temperature biofeedback and psychotherapy in the treatment of a 31-year-old psoriatic male. The skin disorder was severe and had been refractory to conventional dermatological treatment. Following a 3-week baseline period, 30 treatment sessions spanning 7 months were conducted. Each session consisted of skin temperature training for 20 minutes at the target plaque site and 15 minutes of supportive psychotherapy focusing on personal adjustment problems.

Results, obtained from blind ratings of photographs, showed a marked improvement of plaque areas, although reduction in skin temperature was not reliably attained. It was postulated that improvement may have been due to cognitive variables, such as expectancies and demand characteristics, and/or to stress reduction relating to the supportive psychotherapy. This study points out that stress reduction treatment approaches to the treatment of psoriasis symptoms deserves further consideration.

PRURIGO NODULARIS

This disorder is an uncommon, intractable disease occuring chiefly in women. The lesions are single or multiple itching nodules of skin in a linear arrangement located predominantly on the extremities, especially on the anterior surface of the thighs and legs (Andrews & Domonkos, 1963). The lesions are pea-sized or larger, firm, and brownish in color. The etiology is obscure, although bouts of extreme prurities occur when these patients are under emotional stress (Feverman & Sandbank, 1975; Greer, 1975; Tan, 1970). Medical treatments have included injections of triamcinolene suspension and corticosteroids (Andrews & Domonkos, 1963). Many patients show physical depletion and nervous exhaustion, pointing to the improvement of nutrition and rest as treatment procedures.

Treatment

Lamontagne (1978) treated a 61-year-old woman with a 25-year history of prurigo nodularis. Dermatological treatment had been ineffective in curing the condition. Insomnia was also a problem as a result of the itching, even though she was taking chlorpromazine and diazepam at bedtime, and trimeprazine three times daily.

Medication was continued and autogenic relaxation training along with auditory EMG frontalis biofeedback training were administered concurrently. Relaxation training consisted of listening to a relaxation tape in the laboratory and using it at home 30 minutes daily for 3 weeks. She decreased use of the tape as she learned to practice the relaxation response on her own from weeks 4 through 6. EMG biofeedback was utilized concurrently with home relaxation practice, and she received weekly laboratory sessions of 30 minutes each. Results showed muscular relaxation as measured by frontalis EMG improved, and both prurities and scratching decreased. An estimated 40% reduction in nodules was reported at the end of treatment and was maintained at a 6-month follow-up.

HYPERHIDROSIS

This disease is characterized by excessive perspiration, local or generalized, associated with physiologic activity, climatic conditions, emotional episodes, and the use of certain foods or drugs (Allen, 1967). Congenital factors pointing to organic or functional disturbances of the nervous system, dysfunctioning of the glands of internal secretion, obesity, sluggish circulation, and allergy have been shown to contribute to this disorder (Andrews & Domonkos, 1963). The sweating may be so extreme that it produces physical exhaustion. Certain individuals regularly experience sweating of the forehead, upper lip, circumoral region, or sternal region a few moments after eating spicy foods, chocolate, tomato sauce, or after drinking tea (Andrews & Domonkos, 1963). Medical treatment has involved reserpine, X-rays, a bland diet, moderate exercise, tonic baths containing sea salt or alum, and prepared lotions, creams, and dusting powders.

Treatment

Bar and Kuypers (1973) treated a 19-year-old female with severe palmar hyperhidrosis of several years duration. She had a history of feeling rejected and found it difficult to express negative feelings. Her low self-esteem produced anxiety in social situations which served to precipitate severe sweating which further produced more anxiety in anticipation of shaking hands with someone.

Assertive training and systematic desensitization were employed to help the patient feel more secure in social situations, and aided in remission of the hyperhidrosis. Although palmar sweating did not cease altogether, progress was made. A 12-month follow-up revealed no relapse of the former behavior pattern.

SUMMARY

Three types of skin disorders (neurodermatitis, urticaria, and hyperhidrosis) have been treated with various forms of behavior therapy. The behavior therapies used include: (1) social reinforcement, (2) systematic desensitization, (3) assertive training, (4) self-reinforcement, (5) token economies, (6) thought stopping, and (7) aversion therapy.

One characteristic of skin disorder studies employing behavior therapy is that two and often three distinct behavior therapy techniques were utilized concomitantly within the treatment plan. However, the use of social reinforcement was the specific technique demonstrated most frequently. This procedure was employed primarily to extinguish maladaptive scratching behaviors while at the same time reinforcing behaviors incompatible with scratching (Allen & Harris, 1966; Bar & Kuypers, 1973; Dobes, 1977; Walton, 1960; Sharp, & Krisberg, 1972).

The utility of the relaxation response was demonstrated in treating skin disorders apparently precipitated by anxiety (Bar & Kuypers, 1973; Daniels, 1973). In addition, progressive relaxation was found to be effective in competing with a patient's unpleasant state resulting from attempts to reduce his own scratching behavior (Ratliff & Stein, 1968). Biofeedback has been used in treating skin disorders. Two studies employed frontalis EMG training with auditory feedback (Haynes *et al.*, 1979; and Lamontagne, 1978). Two studies utilized temperature biofeedback training in treating psoriasis, one with auditory feedback (Hughes *et al.*, 1979) and another with combined auditory and visual feedback (Benoit & Harrell, 1978). A fifth study by Moan (1979) employed combined auditory and visual GSR training to treat hives.

The number of sessions utilized has ranged from seven to ten in all but one study (Hughes *et al.*, 1979) who used 30 sessions over a 6½-month period. The other four studies ranged from 4 to 10 weeks of either weekly or twice weekly sessions. Concerning length of actual biofeedback training per session, two studies reported 20 minute durations (Hayes *et al.*, 1979; Hughes *et al.*, 1979); two others utilized 30 minutes per trial (Benoit & Harrell, 1978; Lamontagne, 1978); while one study employed 45 minute laboratory sessions (Moan, 1979).

The use of relaxation training and specifically home relaxation practice in combination with biofeedback was reported in three studies (Haynes *et al.*, 1979; Lamontagne, 1978; and Moan, 1979). Hughes *et al.*, (1979) combined 15 minutes of supportive psychotherapy with each session of temperature training.

Analyzing the results of the five studies indicates that Moan (1979) achieved the most impressive outcome. Not only did the subject's hives disappear after 3 weeks of treatment, but skin conductivity was reduced from twelve to four microhms.

Several points of value to the private practitioner in behavioral medicine should be made. One would be the recommendation that a broad based, multicomponent approach be employed. The practitioner might do well to develop his own proficiency in the theory and techniques of behavior therapy, relaxation training, biofeedback training, as well as the utilization of general supportive psychotherapy. The literature has demonstrated the selective utility of all four of these modalities in the treatment of cutaneous disorders, especially in those cases refractory to medical treatment (Brown & Bettley, 1971; Daniels, 1973; Keegan, 1976; and Lamontagne, 1978).

Conceptualization training would appear to be extremely valuable in treating dermatological patients by psychological means. The client must realize the connection between anxiety, stress, and tension to skin disorders. He must also appreciate the role of relaxation training as an antithetical response to the effects of his own stressors. It is also helpful for the client to learn that biofeedback and relaxation training may enable him to regain control over whatever bodily processes he has given over to the mandate of various external variables. Effective modes of conceptualization might include: (1) verbal didacticism, (2) written handouts, (3) providing the client with reprints of representative treatment studies, and (4) a verbal question and answer interaction between client and clinician.

Another consideration to the clinician is how much emphasis should be placed on home practice of relaxation and biofeedback training where feasible. Several of the recent studies suggest the valuable utility of home practice accompanying either or both modes of training (Bar & Kuypers, 1973; Brown & Bettley, 1971; Daniels, 1973; Haynes *et al.*, 1979; Keegan, 1976; Lamontagne, 1978; Moan, 1979; and Ratliff & Stein, 1968). In addition to the research data supporting the use of home practice, it is hypothesized that in many cases the critical difference between patients realizing either no remission or little remission of symptoms and those achieving positive results might be the variable of home practice.

Another consideration is that most of the literature indicates usage of spaced practice of biofeedback and relaxation training (Hughes *et al.*, 1979; Lamontagne, 1978; and Moan, 1979). Although in some cases rather impressive results have ensued from using spaced sessions, the clinician might consider massed practice, which has been found to be effective with other disorders. At any rate, further research in such an approach to relaxation and biofeedback training is certainly warranted in the treatment of skin disorders.

Finally, the literature seems to point to the value of multicomponent approaches to the psychological treatment of skin disorders. Almost all research has utilized two or more approaches in combination. The most common combinations have been various forms of behavior therapy together, and biofeedback used with relaxation training. As different strategies are used in combination, perhaps the successful treatment of skin disorders will increase.

REFERENCES

Allen, A.C. *The Skin: A clinicopathological treatise.* London: Heinemann Medical, 1967.

Allen, K.E. & Harris, F.R. Elimination of a child's excessive scratching by training the mother in reinforcement procedures. *Behavior Research and Therapy,* 1966, **4,** 79–84.

Andrews, G.C. & Domonkos, A.N. *Diseases of the skin.* Philadelphia: Saunders, 1963.

Bar, L.H. & Kuypers, R.M. Behavior therapy in dermatological practice. *British Journal of Dermatology,* 1973, **88,** 591–598.

Baxter, D.L. & Stoughton, R.B. Mitotic index of psoriatic lesions treated with anthralin, glucorticosteroid and occlusion. *Journal of Investigative Dermatology,* 1970, **54,** 410–418.

Benoit, L.J. & Harrell, E.H. The effect of skin temperature control on cell proliferation in psoriasis. Presented at the 29th Southwestern Psychological Association, Ft. Worth, Texas, April 21–23, 1977.

Brown, D.G. & Bettley, F.R. Psychiatric treatment of eczema: A controlled trial. *British Medical Journal,* 1971, **2,** 729–734.

Daniels, L.K. Treatment of urticaria and severe headache by behavior therapy. *Psychosomatics,* 1973, **14,** 347–351.

Dobes, R.W. Amelioration of psychosomatic dermatosis by reinforced inhibition of scratching. *Journal of Behavior Therapy and Experimental Psychiatry,* 1977, **8,** 185–187.

Dunbar, H.R. *Emotions and bodily changes.* New York: Columbia University Press, 1946.

Fernandez, G.R. Hypnotism in the treatment of the stress factor in dermatological conditions. *British Journal of Medical Hypnotism,* 1955, **7,** 21–27.

Feverman, E. & Sandbank, M. Prurigo Nodularis. *Archives of Dermatology,* 1975, **111,** 1472–1477.

Frankel, F. Hypnosis as a treatment method in psychosomatic medicine. *International Journal of Psychiatry in Medicine,* 1975, **6,** 75–85.

Fry, L. & McMinn, R.M. Observations on mitosis in psoriatic epidermis. *British Journal of Dermatology,* 1970, **82,** 19–24.

Fry, L. & McMinn, R.M. The action of chemotherapeutic agents on psoriatic epidermis. *British Journal of Dermatology,* 1968, **80,** 373–379.

Grinker, R.R. & Robbins, F.P. *Psychosomatic case book.* New York: Blakiston, 1954.

Harrison, T. *Principles of internal medicine.* New York: McGraw-Hill, 1977.

Haynes, S.N., Wilson, C.C., Jaffe, P.G., & Britton, B.V. Biofeedback treatment of atopic dermatitis: Controlled case studies of eight cases. *Biofeedback and Self-Regulation,* 1979, **4,** 195–209.

Herndon, R. Medical complications of psoriasis. *Medical Grand Rounds,* Parkland Memorial Hospital, July 17, 1975.

Hughes, H.H., Goldsmith, D.A., and England, R. Biofeedback and psychotherapy treatment of psoriasis: A brief report. Unpublished research manuscript, 1979.

Keegan, D.L. Chronic urticaria: Clinical psychophysiological and therapeutic aspects. *Psychosomatics,* 1976, **17,** 160–163.

Kellner, R. Psychotherapy in psychosomatic disorders. *Archives of General Psychiatry,* 1975, **32,** 1021–1026.

Kidd, C. Congenital ichthyosiform erythroderma treated by hypnosis. *British Journal of Dermatology*, 1966, **78**, 101–105.

Lachman, S.J. *Psychosomatic disorders: A behavioristic interpretation*. New York: Wiley, 1972.

Lamontagne, Y. Treatment of prurigo nodularis by relaxation and EMG feedback training. *Behavioral Analysis and Modification*, 1978, 246–249.

Lever, W. & Schaumburg-Lever, G. *Histopathology of the skin*. Philadelphia: Lippincott, 1975.

Mason, A.A. Ichthyosis and hypnosis. *British Medical Journal*, 1955, **2**, 57–59.

Mason, A.A. A case of congenital ichthyosiform erythroderma of Brocq treated by hypnosis. *British Medical Journal*, 1952, **2**, 422–423.

Moan, E.R. GSR biofeedback assisted relaxation training and psychosomatic hives. *Journal of Behavior Therapy and Experimental Psychiatry*, 1979, **10**, 157–158.

Musaph, H. Anogenital pruritus. In E. Wihharver & H. Warnes (Eds.) *Psychosomatic medicine: Its clinical applications*. New York: Harper and Row, 1977.

Ratliff, R.G. & Stein, N.H. Treatment of neurodermatitis by behavior therapy: A case study. *Behavior Research and Therapy*, 1968, **6**, 397–399.

Sauer, G. *Manual of skin diseases*. Philadelphia: Lippincott, 1959.

Schneck, J. Ichthyosis treated with hypnosis. *Diseases of the Nervous System*, 1954, **15**, 211–213.

Tan, R. Prurigo nodularis. *British Journal of Dermatology*, 1970, **82**, 630–631.

Walton, D. The application of learning theory to the treatment of a case of neurodermatitis. In H.J. Eysenck (Ed.) *Behavior therapy and the neuroses*. Elmsford, N.Y.: Pergamon, 1960.

Watson, D.L., Tharp, R.G., & Krisberg, J. Case study in self-modification: Suppression of inflammatory scratching while awake and asleep. *Journal of Behavior Therapy and Experimental Psychiatry*, 1972, **3**, 213–215.

Wink, C. Congenital ichthyosiform erythroderma treated by hypnosis. *British Medical Journal*, 1961, **2**, 741–743.

Wittkower, E.D. & Lester, E.P. Emotions and skin disease. In H.I. Lief, V.F. Lief, & N.R. Lief (Eds.) *The psychological basis of medical practice*. New York: Harper and Row, 1963.

Zhukov, I.A. Hypnotherapy of dermatoses in resort treatment. In R.B. Winn (Ed.) *Psychotherapy in the Soviet Union*. New York: Philosophical Library, 1961.

Zoon, J.J. & Mali, J.W. The influence of erythroderma on the body. *Archives of Dermatology*, 1957, **75**, 573–578.

CHAPTER 13

Pain

OVERVIEW

Pain is undoubtedly the most significant and, perhaps, the most common problem with which the patient confronts the physician. Janzen (1970) has stated that "pain is for the doctor a *principium cognoscendi* and for the patient a *principium agendi*," which implies that pain has different meanings to different individuals. While the neurophysiologist sees pain as the firing of a particular kind of nerve ending in response to stimulation, or the transmission of specific spatial patterns of nerve impulses, the medical practitioner may see it as an indication of tissue damage. Likewise, the experimental psychologist may view pain as a threshold of sensation, while to a biochemist pain may represent metabolic changes in cell membranes. To the patient, pain may be perceived as an unpleasant physical sensation, an anxiety-evoking event, or a cause for despair.

A definite problem arises when attempting to define pain, and numerous authors have made reference to the puzzling complexities of pain (Weisenburg, 1977; Melzack, 1973; Sternbach, 1974). Most clinicians would agree with Sweet (1959) that the nature and range of the sensations covered by the word "pain" eludes precise definition.

Historically, the study of pain has evolved from studies of the nature of pain in human physiology. Von Frey proposed the specificity theory of pain in 1894, while at the same time Goldschneider, in his pattern theory of pain, hypothesized about pain in a supposedly contrasting and mutually exclusive way (Melzack & Wall, 1965). According to the specificity theory, specific receptors, which are free nerve endings, resulted in the sensation of pain when stimulated. Therefore, pain was believed to have its own central and peripheral mechanisms, similar to those of other specific bodily senses. Much research was generated in support of this theory (Bonica, 1953; Hill, Kornetsky, Flanery *et al.*, 1952).

The pattern theory contended that the sensations of pain experienced by an individual are primarily related to the transmission of nerve impulse patterns originating from and coded at the peripheral stimulation site. Therefore, it was believed that the pattern of stimulation resulting from a noxious event needed to be coded by the central nervous system, and this resulted in the experience of pain rather than a specific connection between pain receptors and the pain sites. Much research was generated in support of this theory also (Livingston, 1943; Noordenbos, 1959; Melzack & Wall, 1962). These studies showed that the pattern theory of pain allows for the existence of modulating or coding systems in the central nervous system, such as emotional state, prior experience, and alertness, which interact with the type of external stimulation to generate each person's pain experience.

The culmination of these theoretical trends appear to have occurred in the gate control theory (Melzack & Wall, 1965). An indepth description of this complex theory can be found in Melzack and Wall (1965). Basically, this theory proposes that pain phenomena are determined by the interaction of three specific systems in the central nervous system where effective closing of the gate results in pain not being experienced. The gate control theory has been extremely useful because it not only provided evidence suggesting specific types of pain receptors and the occurrence of patterns of sensations resulting from pain stimulation and transmission, but also allowed for the fact that central nervous system mediation is a significant factor in pain perception.

There are treatment strategies and tactics derived from the gate control theory that have an important role in pain management. The point is that this theory supports the following formulations, as stated by Fordyce and Steger (1979): (1) pain is not a specific or discrete entity but rather a complex set of phenomena, (2) there is a loose link between specific noxious stimulation, peripheral to the central nervous system, and the sensation assumed to result from this stimulation, even when viewed physiologically, and (3) central nervous system and cerebral mediation are important ingredients in the perception of, and response to pain, opening the door for systematic perusal of past experience, attitudinal set, and other cognitive-behavioral variables which might impinge upon the central nervous system, and thereby, interact with one's perceptions and sensations of pain (pp. 128–129).

All of the theories thus far described relate primarily to the sensations of pain and how these occur in man. There is little reference to what people do in response to their sensations of pain. How a person responds to pain sensations is an area of concern just as important as the specific mechanisms transmitting and generating pain experiences. Descriptions of pain based solely on physiological or neurological factors have proven inadequate in attempting to identify and account for all aspects of pain experiences. Traditional medical approaches have been relatively ineffective in many cases, low back pain and headaches, for example. This type of evidence, combined with the observation that placebo treatment alone can yield significant reduction in pain, has led investigators to formulate a more general and descriptive definition of pain that involves behavioral and psychological components as well as physiological sensations and mechanisms.

Weisenberg (1977) refers to pain as not only a sensation, but also an emotional-motivational phenomenon that leads to escape and avoidance behavior. Sternbach (1974) sees the word pain as an "abstraction used to refer to different feelings which have little in common except the quality of physical hurt . . . the injured or affected locus, or source of pain . . . a class of behaviors which operate to protect the organism from harm or to enlist aid in effecting relief'' (pp. 1–2). While this definition encompasses sensory, physiological, psychological, and behavioral variables, it still does not begin to reflect all of the complexities in the pain experience.

Many authors believe that there is no dependable relationship between the extent of physical injury and the pain experience (Beecher, 1956; Sternback, 1968; McGlashan, 1969). It is believed that pain is influenced by situational stimuli and prior experiences. Beecher's (1956) classical investigation, comparing requests for narcotics for pain relief for wounds suffered in combat with similar requests for narcotics for comparable surgical wounds in a hospital, illustrates this point. It was shown that only 25% of the combat-wounded soldiers requested narcotics, while over 80% of the hospital patients requested the medication. Beecher attributed the difference to the significance of the wound; in other words, the cognitive expectancy and emotional state. While the injured person was in the hospital in civilian life, the wound was threatening. On the battlefield, the wound signified a ticket to safety.

Beecher (1972) has also shown that clinical pain can be decreased with a placebo in about 35% of the cases and that certain drugs, such as morphine, work well for pain associated with anxiety, but fail to work as well for experimentally produced pain. Sternbach (1968) observed that pain tends to increase with anxiety, and Merskey and Spear (1967) noticed that depression and anxiety are often prevalent in patients reporting chronic pain.

In addition to the emotional state and cognitive set of the patient, studies have shown that epidemiological factors may also interact with the physiology of the impingement of the noxious stimulation on an organism. Tursky and Sternbach (1967) and Sternbach and Tursky (1965) showed significant differences in reactions to electric shock in Yankees, subjects of Irish descent, and Italians; and Christopherson (1966) reported that an Eskimo's response to pain is often laughter.

These studies and illustrations show that pain behavior or the response to pain can be influenced by a number of factors: mental set or cognitive expectancy, the personality or anxiety state of an individual, and by culturally conditioned response patterns.

Another aspect to be considered is pain termed as "psychogenic," in which no organic cause is found, and wherein emotional and psychological factors are assumed to be the primary cause of a patient's pain. Adding psychogenic considerations into the variables involved in the mechanisms of pain tends to complicate the issue further. It raises issues of "mind-body" concepts and still does little to establish whether there is a cause-effect relationship between cortical or centrally mediated functions and the sensations of pain. Sternbach and Fordyce (1975) have analyzed this tautology regarding pain as follows: "The essence of the problem lies in assuming that there are real mental and physical events which can and do interact. In fact, there are simply phenomena that we describe in physical language or mental language. We delude ourselves to believe that because we can impose both mental and physical concepts on such an abstraction as "pain" that in fact, such a causative sequence exists" (p. 122).

In an attempt to describe pain in a way by which diagnostic inferences and treatment judgements can be made, Fordyce (1976) defines pain in terms of behavior. In spite of arbitrary labeling and a complicated workup, what remains is the behavior of the patient reporting pain. Pain may be regarded as a set of responses communicated physiologically, verbally, or motivationally. In order for patients to communicate that they are in pain, they must behave in a certain way. Except in rare circumstances, the neurophysiological or biochemical events that may be a part of the pain experience cannot be seen. While one may be able to view tissue damage, it is the total, verbal, emotional, and psychomotor behavior of the patient that communicates to the environment, intentionally or not, the presence of pain.

The patient may signal the experience of pain verbally by describing the location, intensity, or quality of the pain, or by moaning or sighing. Nonverbal communication such as limping, grimacing, or massaging the painful body part are also communicated. This behavior serves simultaneously as a signal to the environment that the person is in pain, and a stimulus that elicits some action from the environment. Behavior may elicit medication from the physician, indicate to the spouse that sex is out of the question, or communicate to the boss that the person cannot perform the job effectively. Without the behavior, there would be no pain problem clinically, but only a private and personal sensation with no outward signs (Fordyce & Steger, 1979).

Opting to utilize this aspect of pain for a research or clinical definition, places the concept of pain within the observable, reproducible, and objective domain. As such, many recent studies consider "pain behavior" to be the direct target of therapeutic change (Fordyce, Fowler, & DeLateur, 1968; Fordyce, Fowler, Lehmann, DeLateur, Sand, & Treischman, 1973; Gottlieb et al., 1977). Consequently, pain viewed as behavior is subject to the laws of learning and conditioning as are other behaviors, and Fordyce (1976) believes this is the major variable differentiating acute from chronic pain.

CHRONIC PAIN

It is important to differentiate acute from chronic pain. However, the lack of definitional consistency is as apparent when considering the term "chronic" as when considering the term "pain."

Johnson (1977) notes that chronic pain may begin as an acute pain episode or may be more insidious, making it difficult to identify its onset. Furthermore, pain is considered chronic when it exists without a known time limit. Johnson states: "The pain may be continuous or intermittent, vary in intensity or remain the same while it becomes a constant companion, to be controlled if possible but always lived with. The source of pain may be recognized but an effective treatment is not available, or the source may be uncertain so that a diagnosis cannot be made'' (p. 141).

Le Shan (1964) states that chronic pain becomes not an event, but a state of existence in which the suffering patient is limited to bearing the pain. Fordyce and Steger (1979) differentiate acute from chronic pain on several dimensions. Acute pain, which is most often the result of actual or impending tissue damage, is usually relieved after specific treatment has been carried out. Chronic pain usually begins with an actue episode, in which professional advice, prolonged evaluation and treatment strategies have not resulted in significant reduction of pain.

Acute pain experiences are usually associated with increasing amounts of anxiety as pain intensity increases, followed by a reduction in this anxiety once proper diagnosis and treatment begins. Reduction in anxiety generally results in a decrease in the pain sensation which is further alleviated by proper treatment. With chronic pain patients, the initial anxiety associated with the pain experience persists and may eventually be replaced by hopelessness and despair.

Many chronic pain patients do not show all of the autonomic signs that typically accompany expression of pain behaviors in acute pain problems. The recently injured patient perspires, has tachycardia and rapid breathing, particularly when being examined and put through body motions likely to increase pain. The chronic pain patient displays only minimal autonomic responses, or none at all, when put through examination procedures likely to increase pain, but will exhibit facial grimaces or verbalizations. Thus, there is a separation of autonomic responses from pain-related behavior.

With chronic pain patients verbal behavior and nonverbal behavior are separate also, and what the patient does and what he says about the pain may differ. For example, the patient may claim to be incapable of sitting for more than 20 minutes, yet may sit and watch television for several hours.

Research definitions of chronicity are, more often than not, unstipulated (Mooney, Cairns, & Robertson, 1976). While operational definitions of chronicity exist, they lack interstudy concurrence. For example, while primarily studying low back pain patients, Fordyce et al. (1973) considered pain "chronic" when it was a clinical problem of several months' duration. Sternbach et al. (1973, 1974) defined the chronic patient as one whose pain had persisted for 6 months or longer. Gentry, Shows, and Thomas (1974) classified low back patients as chronic if they had received one or more spinal operations as well as other medical treatment and continued to experience pain and loss of function for a prolonged period of time. Finally, Cairns and Pasino (1977) defined the chronic low back pain patient by admission to a problem back treatment center where admission criteria were based on the recommendation of conservative rather than surgical treatment.

In summary, clinical and research definitions of "chronic" differ. It is, therefore, difficult to know whether previous research has included subjects from the same "chronic" population. This suggests a lack of homogeneity of patients studied making research with chronic patients less precise.

Chronic Low Back Pain

The majority of research conducted has centered on a particular type of chronic pain, namely, low back pain. Although patients having other types of chronic pain are included in many pain studies, low back pain is probably the most prevalent and debilitating. Beals and Hickman (1972) estimate that more than 1.25 million Americans injure their backs and 65,000 of these people are subsequently added to the list of persons considered permanently disabled. Billions of dollars are spent annually in the diagnosis and treatment of patients suffering from low back pain (Gottlieb *et al.*, 1977). Back-related disabilities, including chronic low back pain, are responsible for nearly 20% of all compensation payments made in a given year, and are considered the single most costly health problem in industry today (Pace, 1976; Sternbach, Wolf, Murphy, & Akeson, 1973).

Despite the pervasiveness of low back pain and the severe consequences of the disability, a large percentage of chronic back pain patients fail to respond to traditional treatment approaches (Gottlieb *et al.*, 1977). Traditionally, the relief of low back problems has been the domain of general practitioners and orthopedic surgeons (Cailliet, 1978). The treating physician has typically attempted to relieve low back pain either through conservative management, such as analgesics and other medication, bed rest, traction, corsets, exercises and massage, or surgical intervention (Gottlieb *et al.*, 1977).

In addition, chiropractic manipulation of the spinal column is often used to treat low back pain. According to Friedmann and Galton (1973), this form of treatment is based upon the assumption that "sublixations and dislocations of vertebrae cause pressure upon nerves, leading to diminished resistance to disease and to the appearance of abnormal conditions" (p. 133). Manipulation therapy is directed at stretching the tissues surrounding vertebrae joints, permitting the joint surfaces to return to their proper position, thus relieving nerve pressure and/or muscle spasm.

A large body of data reinforces the view that traditional medical and chiropractic treatment strategies are ineffective in rehabilitating a high proportion of chronic back pain patients (Gottlieb *et al.*, 1977). Sternbach *et al.* (1973) have consequently termed these treatment resistant patients "low-back losers" who have the following characteristics: complaints of back pain for 6 months or more; inability to work and are supported by social security, welfare, or disability payments; continual search for medical or surgical relief despite previous surgery.

Psychological Variables

The low-back loser most often experiences problems beyond the apparent pain experience. A large body of research suggests that these patients manifest concurrent psychological problems which interfere with successful treatment outcomes (Raskind & Glover, 1975). Kraus (1965) and Strite (1975) describe a "pain-tension-anxiety-cycle" stating that pain and psychological difficulties may arise from a number of sources, but once in evidence, the occurrence of one increases the likelihood that the others will develop. Thus, the chronic pain experience may increase problems of living, heightening psychological stress and its manifestations of anxiety and depression. This further decreases physiological efficiency creating muscle spasms, contractures, and tension, thereby maintaining or increasing pain perception. One representation of this model (Goldsmith, 1980) is presented in Figure 13.1. Similarly, the existence of psychological problems may increase the likeli-

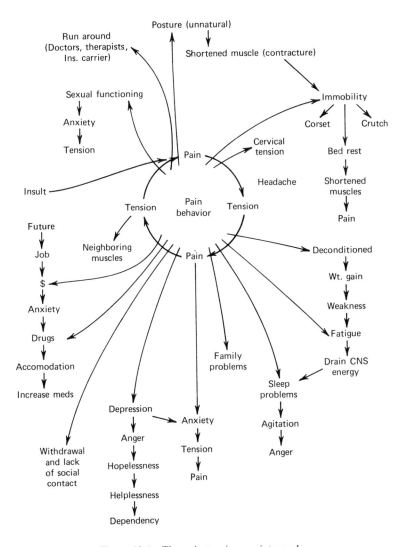

Figure 13.1 The pain-tension-anxiety cycle.

hood that pain experiences or pain behaviors will develop. Chronic low back patients frequently resort to a life-style of invalidism (Sternbach *et al.*, 1973) characterized by the loss of gainful employment (Beals & Hickman, 1972; Gentry *et al.*, 1974; Sarno, 1976; Shevick, 1975; Wolkind, 1974), or their performance as a homemaker or student (Raskind & Glover, 1975). Additionally, it has been noted that anxiety and depression are the most frequently evident psychological concomitants of chronic low back pain (Freeman, Calsyn, & Louks, 1976; Gentry *et al.*, 1974; Hanvik, 1951; Levine, 1971; Levit, 1973; McCreary, Turner, & Dawson, 1977).

Raskind and Glover (1975), among others, have reported that chronic low back pain patients often display a wide range of psychological difficulties including: insomnia, anorexia, sexual dysfunctions, obesity, irritability, and substance abuse. Studies using the Minnesota Multiphasic Personality Inventory (MMPI) indicated that both organic and psychogenic low back pain patients scored higher on the hysteria, depression, and hypochondriasis scales than "normals" (Freeman, Calsyn, & Louks, 1976; Gentry *et al.*, 1974; Hanvik, 1951). These studies have also confirmed the existence of severe anxiety in many chronic pain patients (Sternbach *et al.*, 1973b).

It has been suggested that the resistance to treatment evident in the "low-back loser" may be at least partially due to the reluctance of traditional medical strategies to address psychological and behavioral variables relevant to pain tolerance and/or responses to pain. Consideration of these variables has led to an interest in behavioral management of chronic pain and the development of new and innovative treatment strategies, particularly in the areas of viewing pain as learned behavior, and in breaking the pain-tension-anxiety cycle.

Treatment

Behavioral scientists have been utilizing behavioral treatment strategies in the treatment of chronic pain for nearly a decade. Due to the complexity of a pain problem for any given individual, most of the treatment strategies thus far utilized, have combined many of the behavioral strategies into a comprehensive multidisciplinary approach. The treatment modalities used in these pain centers involve all aspects of operant conditioning, relaxation and cognitive strategies, and biofeedback.

Operant Approaches

Much of the published work in the area of pain management has been reported by Fordyce and co-workers (Fordyce, Fowler, & De Lateur, 1968; Fordyce *et al.*, 1968; Fordyce & Steger, 1979) using an operant treatment model. Basically this learning theory model of chronic pain (Fordyce, 1974, 1976) emphasizes the role and importance of environmental factors in chronic pain states. In some patients pain behaviors occur as a result of environmental contingencies rather than from antecedent stimuli, such as tissue damage. Behaviors originally respondent in nature can become operant through learning. This is a result of pain behaviors receiving direct positive reinforcement, or being negatively reinforced because they lead to "time out" or avoidance of aversive situations, as well as nonreinforcement of activity related to "well behavior." The goal of this operant approach to pain management is not to directly modify pain, but to modify the maladaptive pain behaviors by extinction and to reinforce "well behavior."

Operant techniques have been most widely used for the inpatient treatment of chronic back pain behavior. Fordyce, Fowler, and De Lateur (1968) reported a case study of a woman who had experienced constant low back pain for nearly 20 years. The patient, previously having had four operations, stated that the pain was increasingly interfering with her homemaking activities. Medical evaluation revealed no neurological damage. Treatment consisted of : (1) providing medication on a time-contingent, rather than pain-contingent basis—that is, she received medication at specific time intervals, rather than when she experienced or complained of pain; (2) providing social reinforcement, such as staff or family attention and praise for improvement, and for nonpain behaviors such as increased ward activity and walking; (3) extinguishing pain behavior by ignoring such behavior as moaning, grimacing, and inactivity; (4) providing programmed rest periods as a reward for greater involvement in physical and occupational therapy. After 3 weeks of inpatient treatment and 22 weeks of outpatient treatment, the patient could remain physically active for up to 2 hours without complaining of pain or needing rest, and was able to function without pain medication entirely. She could walk further and faster than before, and was taking driving lessons to be able to resume an active mobile life.

Three additional case studies, using nearly identical treatment methods, were reported by Fordyce, Fowler, Lehmann, and De Lateur (1968). In all of the studies, the patients dramatically increased their daily activity from baseline levels during the treatment phase. Increased activity levels were apparently maintained during an outpatient follow-up period. The authors reported the generalization of positive effects, as nontargeted behaviors, such as grooming and medical adherence, were also improved.

Pain clinics utilizing a purely operant treatment approach can be found at the University of Washington, Department of Rehabilitation Medicine; University of Minnesota, Department of Rehabilitation Medicine; and Rancho Los Amigos Hospital in Downey, California. The University of Washington program involves a 4- to 8-week inpatient period designed to gradually increase general activity level and socialization, and to decrease medication usage and, ultimately, pain-related utilization of health services. This is accomplished through the use of quota systems of physical, occupational, and vocational activities and a pain-killing cocktail for medication usage, all of which are part of a contingency plan. Utilizing this approach, Fordyce et al., (1973) were able to obtain significant increases in out-of-bed time and activity level, and significant decreases in medication usage in the treatment of 36 chronic pain patients. On the average, the changes were maintained at a 22-month follow-up.

In a similar treatment program, the Pain Clinic at the University of Minnesota found treatment gains in 75–80% of the patients (Roberts, 1979), with the gains being maintained in most of the patients for 1 to 8 years. Rancho Los Amigos Hospital found that 70% of the chronic low back pain patients indicated reduction in pain or increase in activity level with analgesic medication reduced to zero by the end of treatment. The decrease in medication was maintained in 58% of the patients at a 10-month follow-up, with 74% not seeking further health care, and 75% working or in a vocational retraining program (Cairns, Thomas, Mooney, et al., 1976).

Although, in most cases, the post-treatment levels of functioning were significantly improved over the pretreatment levels, the above studies are limited by reliance upon subjective questionnaire data as the basis for follow-up evaluation. Mooney, Cairns, and Robertson (1976) and Cairns and Pasino (1977) improved upon the previous experimental methodology by using automated recording devices, isolating treatment components, and using a control group. The results of both studies concurred with previous findings. Operant techniques were effective in altering the pain behaviors of chronic back pain patients.

Multidisciplinary Approaches

Extensions of the techniques employed at pain centers utilizing operant approaches has included the addition of group exercises, organized group discussions, family therapy, biofeedback, and relaxation to augment physical and occupational therapy. This is the approach used at the Mayo Clinic. In this system, the average length of inpatient treatment is 3 weeks. The results of this treatment approach were that 27 out of 50 patients (54%) accepted into the program showed a moderate to marked improvement at post-treatment. At 6-month follow-up, only 50% of those completing the program had maintained their gains (Swanson, Floreen, & Swanson, 1976). As with many of the operant approach studies, criteria for outcome success are vague, subjective, and leave too much discretion to the raters to effectively determine actual outcome.

Another similar multidisciplinary approach has been evaluated by Newman, Seres, Yospe, et al. (1978). This treatment program lasts 3 weeks and it was demonstrated that significant gains were maintained for chronic low-back pain patients in the reduction of analgesics and on four measures of physical functioning. Follow-up occurred at 8 weeks and was done in the hospital by direct evaluation, minimizing the effects of biased verbal reports. This study found, as did those conducted by Fordyce et al. (1973) and Hilgard and Hilgard (1975), that patient's verbalizations of pain did not change over the course of treatment, even though other behaviors showed improvement.

Greenshoot and Sternbach (1974) evaluated another multidisciplinary approach lasting 4 weeks, which is situated on a neurological service. This treatment program employs operant approaches, physical rehabilitation, and work-related procedures as well as group transactional and gestalt techniques. Evaluation of treatment outcome for 62 chronic pain patients indicated that significant improvements were made in pain reports, medication use, and activity levels. As seen in many of the other studies, at a 6-month follow-up only medication use remained at the post-treatment level. Subjective pain reports and activity levels regressed toward pretreatment levels, although some improvement was still in evidence. Again questionnaire data was used for follow-up evaluation.

At the Chronic Back Pain Management Program, Casa Colina Hospital for Rehabilitation in Pomona, California, low-back pain patients are treated for an average of 6½ weeks with a variety of treatment modalities centered around self-regulation. The treatment approach is similar to the one at the Mayo Clinic as it uses biofeedback for muscle tension reduction, group discussions among patients, and occupational and physical therapy. In addition, self regulation techniques are taught using psychological counseling for stress management and assertive training, patient-regulated medication programs and didactic presentations. A vocational planning service as well as individual and marital counseling are also provided. At the end of treatment, 57 of the 72 low-back pain patients demonstrated unimpaired physical movement, and 59 of the 72 were functioning successfully in vocational activities (Gottlieb, Strike, Koller, *et al.*, 1977). Using a more operationalized outcome criteria involving a clinical rating system based on physical functioning, clinical judgement, and vocational restoration, about 66% showed significant improvement at one-month follow-up.

Wooley, Blackwell, and Winget (1978) have reported the treatment of over 300 patients referred to a "psychosomatic" inpatient unit using a program involving contingency management, social skills and assertive training, and family therapy. The treatment lasted one month and focused upon the role of the patient's interpersonal behaviors which may elicit caretaking responses and increase dependency on others. Efforts were made to involve the family unit in developing and maintaining independent patient behaviors. The authors concluded that the factor most predictive of maintenance of progress or continuing improvement was return to an intact family.

It is difficult to compare the effectiveness of these different pain clinics or treatment centers for several reasons. First, the populations are not the same for all centers. Some treat persons having different types of chronic pain, while others specifically treat low-back pain. The word "chronic" is not uniformly or operationally defined, as was discussed earlier. Second, most of the studies have employed clinical case study designs with no control groups and no placebo-control methodology. In addition, these studies have rarely separated different treatment elements, often combining several techniques in one package. This makes it impossible to separate the essential ingredients to make determinations about the more effective components of a given program. Finally, outcome criteria are not operationally defined so as to allow comparison with other programs with respect to the same variables. Further operationalization of different outcome variables will be necessary if important psychological indicators are to be compared across treatment modalities and settings.

Relaxation and Cognitive Strategies

While inpatient pain clinics focus primarily on operant approaches to pain, some researchers are investigating the feasibility of outpatient treatment centers. A recent and promising outpatient treatment strategy for chronic pain is labeled "cognitive-behavioral" (Turk, 1978). This approach is designed to reduce anxiety and covert self-statements concerning pain. In this way, it is hoped that indirect modification of pain perception and tolerance will occur and allow the patient to increase activity levels and decrease medication use.

Levendusky and Pankratz (1975) treated a 65-year-old male with chronic abdominal pain in self-control techniques to be used as an alternative to pain medication. The patient was taught progressive relaxation and imagery. Since the patient was an engineer he imaged his pain as a tight steel band unwinding. Drug withdrawal was put on a time-contingent plan and the man was to relax and image his pain at specific times of the day. After 6 months of treatment, he was socially active, had resumed teaching activities, and was teaching his wife the self-control techniques for her migraine headaches.

Turner, Heinrich, McCreary, and Dawson (1979) compared the effects of progressive relaxation and cognitive behavior therapy in the treatment of chronic low back pain patients. Treatment was conducted in an outpatient setting and lasted for 5 weeks. Subjects were randomly selected to be in one of three groups: those receiving progressive relaxation instructions, those receiving cognitive behavior training to identify events associated with pain, learn coping skills such as relaxation, imagery, and positive statements concerning their reaction to pain; and those acting as a control on a waiting list. Subjective ratings at 1-month follow-up showed both groups having improved with the cognitive behavior therapy group showing more improvement than the group receiving progressive relaxation alone.

Follick (1979), used a multidimensional approach to the treatment of chronic pain in an outpatient clinic. The treatment program lasted 10 weeks and consisted of a 2-week self-monitored baseline period, 1 week of formal evaluation, 6 weeks of actual treatment and 1 week of post-treatment evaluation. Treatment consisted of contingency management of pain behaviors and medication usage, physical therapy three times a week, marital therapy once a week in which both patient and spouse learned cognitive restructuring of pain perceptions and behaviors. Results showed improvement along several dimensions: increased activity level, decrease in report of pain level and medication usage, and marital adjustment. Although research is sparse in regard to the use of cognitive behavioral approaches, there seems to be evidence that cognitive strategies appear to have much potential for use with chronic pain.

Biofeedback

Biofeedback procedures have been used in the chronic pain clinics in conjunction with other treatment modalities, but application of the biofeedback
procedures alone to relieve chronic pain is a very limited area of research.

Handler *et al.* (1977) reported on the treatment of 13 patients having
chronic pain. Under the rationale that anxiety reduction and decreases in
pain perception are functionally related, and that EMG biofeedback serves
to reduce subjective anxiety, the subjects were provided with audiovisual
feedback of frontalis EMG activity and trained in the relaxation of this
muscle. Before and after each of the five 1-hour sessions conducted during
1 week, the patients completed a pain questionnaire. Only 2 of the 13 subjects
could alter the EMG feedback by tensing the muscle group affected by the
pain. Only one of these two subjects obtained subjective pain relief from
the procedure. Overall, 6 of the 13 subjects reported less pain on at least
four of the five days after EMG biofeedback. The six subjects who had
obtained relief were using their own biofeedback equipment and maintaining
the pain relief 1 month following training. However, the ability to control
the EMG feedback for all but one subject was independent of the achievement of pain relief.

Fowler (1975) combined frontalis EMG biofeedback with various relaxation strategies. The relaxation techniques used in assisting a patient to lower
EMG activity included: making the "mind" blank, focusing on breathing,
covertly saying "relax" to oneself, and counting backwards from 300 and
repeating "relax" after each number. Along with the biofeedback training,
relaxation training includes both autogenic phrases and progressive relaxation exercises. In two clinical case studies reported, lowered EMG level
and subjective pain level were noted after 10 sessions.

Nouwen and Solinger (1979) trained 18 patients with chronic low back
pain (of muscle tension origin) in EMG biofeedback. Compared to seven
controls, they showed a significant decrease during training in muscle tension
and subsequently in pain reduction. However, at follow-up, EMG levels
returned to the initial high level. Pain scores of patients with high pain
decrements during training showed further improvement during follow-up,
which was not the case with patients showing less substantial improvement.
The authors conclude that the past hypothesis showing no significant relation
between high or low pain decrements, and the relapse in muscle tension
between post session and follow-up gives evidence for the idea that other
factors, operating independent of muscle tension, must be considered. As
self-control could not be demonstrated in most cases, it seems plausible that
a feeling of self control, rather than actual control of physiological functions
is crucial for further pain reductions.

These findings suggest the distinct possibility that biofeedback works for
other than purely informational and reinforcing reasons. On the basis of the
results of biofeedback studies thus far reviewed, it can be concluded that
biofeedback per se is not a clinically useful procedure for the reduction of

chronic pain, but when used in conjunction with operant approaches, relaxation and/or cognitive strategies, it may aid in the reduction of anxiety thus reducing the pain-tension-anxiety cycle.

Summary

Chronic pain is not uniformly defined by researchers. Therefore, it is difficult to say whether the same "chronic" population has been studied. The most widely used definition of chronic pain looks at pain in terms of behavior; how the person behaves and communicates his pain to others. This learning theory model of chronic pain emphasizes the importance of environmental contingencies in chronic pain states, and focuses on modifying maladaptive pain behaviors by operant approaches, such as extinction and positive reinforcement.

The operant approaches to treating chronic pain on an inpatient pain unit are the most widely used and clinically successful. Combining operant approaches with other treatments, such as physical and occupational therapy, relaxation and biofeedback, group discussions, and family therapy have also met with relative success. The use of relaxation, cognitive strategies or biofeedback alone does not seem to be the most effective treatment. Any of these strategies used in combination with one or more other approach does seem to be effective in treating chronic pain, however.

Although many problems exist in the research designs of most of the chronic pain studies, evidence does appear to indicate that behavioral treatment strategies are successful when applied to chronic pain patients. Behavioral treatment strategies are aimed not at curing the patient's pain directly; but rather, it is intended to teach the patient to be more functional in his environment despite his pain experience, which itself decreases significantly as a result of change in pain behavior or reduced levels of muscle tension.

Behavioral treatment methods are not competitive with more traditional medical and surgical treatment programs, but simply represent an alternative means of treating the pain behaviors exhibited in response to the pain experience. These methods should be considered when the more traditional methods fail to remedy the pain experience, particularly in cases where the evidence for an organic etiology for the pain is not sufficient to warrant surgical procedures, and with patients evidencing a chronic pain syndrome, whose pain persists despite all attempts to treat it over a long period of time.

HEADACHES

Headache is the most common pain symptom afflicting man, with 90% of the population being affected at one time or another. The most frequently experienced types of headaches, classified by the Ad Hoc Committee on the

Classification of Headaches includes: (1) vascular, commonly known as migraine, in which the cranial arteries are painfully dilated and distended; (2) muscle contraction, or tension headache, in which there is sustained contraction of the muscles of the face, scalp, and neck; (3) the combined vascular and muscle contraction headache; and (4) the conversion, or hypocondriacal headache, in which there is no specific neurological change. There are at least 10 other categories of headaches of biogenic etiologies. Many medical scientists tend to believe that the more common headache types are stress-induced in clients having predisposed psychophysiologic characteristics (Bakal, 1975).

Ninety percent of all headaches are either of the vascular or muscle-contraction type. Within that 90%, those headaches secondary to increased muscle tension form the greatest proportion. The true proportion, however, is difficult to estimate, since most patients with migraines also have muscle contraction headaches at some time in conjunction with their vascular headache.

Traditional medical treatments for these common headaches have included the use of ergotomines, analgesics, antidepressants, or other drugs for symptom alleviation. However, recently developed behavioral treatment approaches have made possible a significant improvement in the treatment of this common medical problem.

Much of the research has progressed with the assumption that a specific type of treatment should be used for treating a specific headache type. This assumption is based on popular ideas concerning the specific etiologies of migraine and tension headache pain. It is therefore important to differentiate between migraine and tension headaches in order to select the treatment strategy or combination of strategies which will most successfully alleviate the headache.

The following characteristics are helpful in differentiating among vascular, muscular, and other types of headaches.

Migraine

The classical concept of vascular or migraine headache is that of a paroxysmal, episodic disturbance of cerebral function associated with unilateral headache and vomiting. Although headache is the most prominent feature of migraine, the diagnosis is made on the basis of the occurrence in an individual of several of the following symptoms as described by Frazier (1969): (1) temporal visual disorders preceding the attack, (2) recurrent throbbing headaches, usually unilateral at onset, (3) nausea, vomiting, constipation or diarrhea, and irritability commonly occurring at the height of the attack, (4) dizziness, sweating, and other vasomotor disorders during an attack, (5) duration commonly from 2 to 8 hours, (6) history of migraine in the immediate family, and (7) response to ergotamine tartrate if administered early.

The pain commonly starts in one temple or on one side of the forehead, but it can progress and become generalized. The quality of the pain can go from throbbing to steady, probably a result of extreme distension and stiffening of the arterial walls. The pathophysiology of vascular headache appears to involve an initial phase of vasoconstriction, which is followed, perhaps secondarily, by smooth muscle fatigue, and, finally, a vasodilatory phase. This latter phase is associated with the throbbing pain, presumably secondary to stretching of the arterial coat. The initial vasoconstrictor phase can be associated with typical prodromal symptoms, such as scotoma (depressed vision surrounded by normal vision), visual field defect, and even hemiplegia. These occur regularly in only 10–15% of the cases, however, and are of no real help in diagnosis. Diagnosis must depend on the presence of the typical overall clinical picture (Williams, 1977).

Tension

In contrast to the unilateral, throbbing pain of vascular headaches, muscle contraction, or tension, headaches are usually symmetrical in distribution and are characterized by a steady, nonpulsatile ache. The pain is bilateral and often described as dull or "bandlike."

This type of headache, also known as "psychogenic," or "nervous" headache, is likely to arise at times of emotional conflict or psychological stress. The immediate cause of pain, as demonstrated in the experiments by Wolff (1963) and his associates, is thought to be the sustained contraction of muscles in the forehead, scalp, and neck. The onset of pain is gradual and its duration can vary from hours to weeks. In contrast to migraine headaches, neither scotoma nor nausea is present.

Most, but not all investigators, have noted elevated frontal EMG levels in tension headache patients. Sainsbury and Gibson (1954) reported that the resting level of frontal EMG activity was higher in tension headache patients than in headache-free individuals. Similarly, Budzynski, Stoyva, Adler, *et al.* (1973), found that resting EMG levels in the patient group appeared to be at least twice those observed in nonheadache volunteers. More recently, Haynes, Griffin, Mooney, *et al.* (1975), Hutchins and Reinking (1976), and Phillips (1977) all found frontal EMG levels to be significantly higher in persons with tension headaches than in nonheadache controls.

There is also evidence of a vasoconstriction component in tension headache. Dalessio (1972a, 1972b), in summarizing several studies, states that a moderate amount of vasoconstriction by itself does not lead to pain. However, if vasoconstriction occurs in a contracted muscle, pain can occur. Dalessio further stated that sustained muscle contraction by itself can be painful, but if, in addition, there is vasoconstriction of the relevant nutrient arteries, the resultant pain from muscle contraction may be much greater.

Other Types

Despite the low incidence of causes of headache other than tension or migraine, these other causes are potentially of great danger, and the history and physical examination of the patient should be carried out meticulously to search for signs or symptoms which would raise the possibility of other causes. Clearly, any focal neurological signs or symptoms would be indications to obtain skull X-rays, brain scan, EEG and neurological consultation, to evaluate the possibility of an intracranial process. Where sinus headaches are suspected, there invariably will be found engorgement and inflammation of the nasal turbinates. The headache associated with high blood pressure is often indistinguishable from a typical muscle tension headache, and if the blood pressure is found to be elevated, appropriate diagnostic and treatment measures should be undertaken.

Psychological factors

The psychological characteristics of patients with frequent headaches and the life setting in which the headaches occur are important considerations in any discussion of headache. The early descriptions by Wolff (1937), Kolb (1963), and Selinsky (1939) of characteristics common to migraine patients applies nearly as well to many patients with muscle contraction headache. This could stem from a common role of psychophysiological factors in the etiology of both vascular and muscular headache pain.

According to these early studies, migraine sufferers are usually sensitive, worrisome and perfectionistic individuals, often chronically tense, apprehensive, and preoccupied with achievement and success. The key word described in most studies is a need to be in "control." Although later studies have shown no consistent relationship between personality factors and headache (Adams, 1979), the "control" theory remains throughout the studies.

The setting in which the headaches occur is often one in which a period of high stress is followed by a period of planned relaxation during which the headache begins, leading the patient to question that stress is the cause. Adams (1979) calls this phenomenon "release pressure." One theory advanced by Williams (1977) is that this letdown phenomenon may result from discomfort with a setting in which inactivity is the requirement, since the patient's characteristic style is one of controlling the world through activity.

It is therefore important during the assessment phase of working with a patient to obtain not only a measure of type, frequency and duration of headache, but also a measure of environmental antecedent and consequent events which act as stressors, and a measure of settings in which the headache occurs. Consideration of these variables aid in determining which combination of treatment strategies is best suited for a particular patient.

Treatment

Generally, most of the patients who will seek medical attention are those in whom the initial self-prescribed pharmacologic approaches have failed. Further analgesic medication has been shown to provide only temporary relief during an acute attack. Physiological procedures such as dieting, tranquilizers, antidepressants, drugs, histamine desensitization, and manipulative and surgical operations have been tried but the results have been inconsistent and disappointing (Mitchell & Mitchell, 1971). At present the medical management of migraine, in particular, still depends on pharmacotherapy (Lance, 1969). Preparations such as ergotamine tartrate and its derivations afford most migraine sufferers relief from the intensity of an acute attack, but are by no means preventative. Daily prophylactic pharmacotherapy is perhaps the most effective type of medication available for the treatment of migraine, though many patients are unable to tolerate the side effects. Ergot preparations have definitive dangers in use with patients having cardiovascular disease because possible side effects could include hypertension, tachycardia, or bradycardia. Methylsergide preparations have serious side effects, such as retroperitoneal fibrosis. Further, dependency upon the physician and the medications prescribed often threaten the patient's need to be in control, resulting in frustration to both patient and physician.

If properly introduced and carried out, behavioral approaches circumvent many of the problems inherent in the traditional medical management of the patient with headache. Unlike the pharmacologic approach to headache, which is often aimed primarily at relieving the symptom, the behavioral approach proceeds from assumptions concerning the pathogenesis of the headache and attempts to correct the initiating pathophysiological situation itself. Basically this approach assumes that the headache results from sustained high levels of vascular or muscular response in persons whose behavioral attempts to satisfy high needs for control are not successful in their current life situation. This is sufficient to initiate the events in blood vessels and/or muscles which result in a headache.

All of the behavioral approaches might be considered as having two central goals. First, the patient must learn to reverse the basic pathophysiological process. This involves either reducing the vasospasm which precedes the painful vasodilation of a migraine, or relaxing the tense muscles of a tension headache. This can be accomplished with a variety of techniques used singly, or in combination. Second, the patient must apply his newly acquired skills on a regular basis so that when he recognizes the onset of the pathophysiologic events, he will be able to reverse them, or prevent them from preceding to the point of causing a headache.

The types of behavior therapy that have been used in the treatment of headache include systematic desensitization and assertive training. Progressive relaxation training and various cognitive strategies have also been reported as being effective as well as certain self management techniques. The psychophysiological technique used in treating headache is biofeedback. In practice, most centers with extensive experience in treating headaches use a combination of these techniques.

Some of the earlier studies have reported the efficacy of using combined behavioral techniques in the treatment of migraine headaches. Mitchell and Mitchell (1971) compared certain single-model and combined behavior therapy programs in the treatment of migraine. Results indicated that the combined program of relaxation, desensitization and assertive training was superior to single-model approaches, obtaining significant reductions in migraine attack frequency and duration. In a similar study, Mitchell and Mitchell (1971) compared single-model and combined behavior therapy programs with persons having previous pharmacotherapy treatment and those with no previous pharmacotherapy treatment. Again the two groups receiving combined therapies showed significant reduction in headache frequency and duration with the group having no previous pharmacotherapy treatment responding more favorably than those having pharmacological treatment.

Biofeedback has also proven to be successful in treating both migraine and tension headaches. Since tension headache is thought to result from forehead muscle tension, Budzynski et al. (1970, 1973) proposed frontalis EMG feedback as the most efficacious treatment for tension headaches. Sargent et al. (1973) suggested that skin temperature feedback might be the most effective treatment for migraines, since the lowering of sympathetic nervous system arousal may be a precursor to the lessening of dilation in cranial arteries. However, Phillips (1978) suggests that the diverse tension and migraine headache pain patterns reflect a continuum of symptom severity of a single headache disorder.

The true etiology of headache pain is nebulously understood at best with theories ranging from a strictly physiological etiology to a strictly psychodynamic etiology. The earlier assumptions that EMG feedback is best for tension headaches and skin temperature feedback is best for migraines has not been sustained. Feurstein and Adams (1977) have speculated that cranial vasomotor feedback is likely to be the most logical treatment for migraines. This feedback acts directly to reduce blood flow in the cranial arteries since dilation of the cranial arteries is commonly associated with migraine pain.

Substantial research has shown that EMG feedback is as effective as skin temperature feedback in mitigating migraine pain (Bakal & Kagnov, 1977; Blanchard et al., 1978; Feurstein & Adams, 1977; Phillips, 1977; Lake, et al., 1979). However, no studies of skin temperature feedback applied to tension headaches have been reported.

Biofeedback and Relaxation

In regard to *tension* headaches, many studies have compared the use of verbal-instruction relaxation, EMG feedback, placebo medication, and false EMG feedback (Wickramasekera, 1972, 1973; Hutchings & Reinking, 1976; Phillips, 1977; Cram, 1978; Epstein & Abel, 1977; Haynes et al., 1975; Chesney & Shelton, 1976; and Cox, Freundlich, & Meyer, 1975). It was generally concluded in these studies that false EMG feedback and placebo medication did not significantly reduce headache duration, frequency or severity. Both verbal relaxation and EMG feedback significantly reduced headache duration and frequency with EMG feedback reducing duration and frequency more significantly than verbal relaxation. Biofeedback also proved superior in producing reduction in medication intake. Combined procedures of verbal relaxation used in conjunction with EMG feedback also proved successful in reducing headache duration and frequency, and proved superior to either verbal relaxation or EMG feedback alone in reducing headache severity.

In regard to *migraine* headaches, several studies have compared the use of relaxation procedures with the use of biofeedback training. There have been numerous reports on the efficacy of temperature feedback combined with autogenic training (Andreychuk & Shriver, 1975; Mitch, McGrady, & Iannone, 1976; Sargent, Green, & Walters, 1972, 1973) and on the efficacy of temperature biofeedback alone (Mullinix, Norton, Hack, & Fishman, 1978; Reading & Mohr, 1976; Turin & Johnson, 1976; Wickramasekera, 1973). There have also been reports on the efficacy of relaxation training alone in the treatment of migraine (Paulley & Haskell, 1975; Warner & Lance, 1975). Few of these studies have shown systematic findings beyond a 3-month follow-up, and of those only two reported sufficient follow-up data to allow an adequate evaluation of the findings. Medina, Diamond, and Franklin (1976), in a retrospective survey, reported favorable results with temperature feedback, and Warner and Lance (1975) reported good results with relaxation training.

Blanchard, Theobald, Williamson, Silver, and Brown (1978) completed a prospective, controlled comparison of temperature biofeedback with autogenic training, progressive relaxation, and a waiting list group who monitored headaches. At the end of the initial 6 weeks of treatment, subjects from the waiting list were randomly assigned to either the relaxation training or the temperature biofeedback and autogenic training group. For the final week of training, patients in the relaxation group were significantly better than those in the biofeedback group. However, follow-up data obtained at 1, 2, and 3 months showed no difference between the two treatment groups on any dependent measures.

In a subsequent follow-up study (Silver, Blanchard, Williamson, Theobald, & Brown, 1979) the findings indicated a maintenance of treatment gains for members of both groups at a 1-year follow-up. With the exception of medication consumption, for which relaxation training led to better long-term results, the 1-year follow-up data revealed no differential effectiveness for temperature biofeedback or progressive relaxation in treating migraine headaches.

In summarizing the available studies, the data clearly demonstrates the usefulness of relaxation training in headache treatment, either by use of verbally instructed relaxation, or by use of EMG or temperature biofeedback. There is still generally no consistent basis on which to choose one treatment over the other.

Verbal methods of inducing relaxation are probably more cost-effective than biofeedback since they do not involve expensive electronic equipment and readily lend themselves to group training techniques. However, without physiological monitoring, it is more difficult for both the therapist as well as the patient to determine if relaxation is being learned. The biofeedback studies serve to standardize relaxation training, and increase its reliability. The feedback instruments are important also as assessment devices. Whenever possible, the use of relaxation and biofeedback in combination is optimal.

Although combined procedures of relaxation and biofeedback techniques have been the central focus in the literature, other combinations of strategies have been successfully employed. Recent studies have addressed the effectiveness of cognitive variables in both migraine and tension headache treatment.

Biofeedback and Cognitive Strategies

Reeves (1976) successfully combined EMG biofeedback training of *tension* headache pain with a cognitive skills training course focusing on identification of negative self-statements related to stressors and training of the replacement of these negative self-statements with coping self-instructions. Also in treating tension headaches, Steger and Harper (1977) demonstrated that biofeedback combined with "stress inoculation" was significantly more effective in reducing pain and general feelings of anxiety and distress than self-monitored relaxation. The stress inoculation technique combined didactic discussion about stress reactions, generalization of alternative self-statements about one's ability to cope with stress, specific relaxation training, and *in vivo* applications of newly learned stress coping skills.

In the treatment of *migraine* headache, Huber and Huber (1979) successfully treated patients who had been unsuccessfully pretreated with medication as well as with relaxation and biofeedback training. It was shown that a "rational-emotive enriched" autogenic training in a group setting resulted in the reduction of headache duration and disappearance of the hyperemetic attacks.

Relaxation and Cognitive Strategies

Several researchers have combined relaxation training with cognitive strategies in treating *tension* headache. Anderson, Lawrence, and Olson (1979) compared the use of relaxation training alone, cognitive coping training alone, and a combination of both techniques. Results showed that both relaxation and coping skills training used alone were effective in reducing headache pain. It also appeared that in some instances, the additive effects of both treatments facilitated this reduction. Bowen and Turk (1979) used a two-part cognitive-behavioral program designed to provide symptom control and facilitate adaptive life changes through cognitive restructuring and coping skills training. The first phase of treatment was comprised of the self-monitoring of target behaviors and a sequential imagery relaxation exercise. Imagery was combined with relaxation to enhance generalization and persistence of treatment effects. The second phase consisted of cognitive restructuring that focused on identification of appraisals, attributions and self-evaluations, and on the recognition of self-statements and images generated prior to, accompanying, and following symptom manifestation. This phase was also designed to stimulate generalization of alternative coping skills and the practice of cognitive reappraisal. Significant decreases in symptoms were obtained following 24 weekly hour-long sessions, and were maintained at a 6-month follow-up. The rapid decline in frequency and intensity of target behaviors was followed by a gradual rise in personally and socially rewarding activities as constructive coping behaviors replaced maladaptive ones.

Self-Management Combinations

Several studies have also combined certain treatment strategies with self-management techniques. Holroyd and Andrasik (1978) treated *tension* headaches by combining cognitive training skills with self-control training.

Subjects were assigned to one of two self-control treatment groups, a headache discussion group, or a symptom-monitoring group. Participants in the self-control groups and the discussion group were taught to monitor their cognitive responses to stress-eliciting situations. Participants in the self-control groups were also taught either cognitive or both cognitive and relaxation coping skills for controlling headaches. The headache discussion group was led in a discussion of the historical roots of symptoms. Both the self-control treatment groups and the discussion group produced substantial reductions in headaches, which were maintained at a 6-week follow-up. No change was shown in the symptom-monitoring control group.

Mitchell and White (1977) evaluated the effects of self-management techniques on *migraine* headaches. Self-recordings of headaches, self-monitoring of environmental stress events, and two stages of self-management skill acquisition served as the treatment component. The first skill acquisition stage included training in cue-controlled muscle relaxation, mental and differential relaxation, and self-desensitization. The second stage included training in identifying stress and the events which precipitate stress and provided training in a series of 13 self-change techniques. The treatment procedures were implemented over a 48-week period for 12 patients in a sequential dismantling strategy, in which all 12 subjects were provided self-recordings. Nine of these were subsequently provided self-monitoring, six of these later received Skills Package I, and finally three also received Skills Package II. Results showed the entire package (self-recording, self-monitoring, Skill Phases I and II) produced the best effects. Subjects provided only Skills Phase I had fewer headaches than subjects given only self-recording or self-monitoring, who did not improve. Positive effects were maintained over a 12-week follow-up.

Other Variables

The literature reflects relatively successful outcomes in treating both tension and migraine headaches with combinations of behavior therapy, relaxation training, biofeedback training, cognitive training, and self-management training. In addition to the type of treatment strategy used, other variables are involved, which may be of use to the practitioner. In the successful studies employing adequate controls, there has been a great deal of variation in the length and distribution of treatment in both EMG biofeedback (Budzynski et al., 1970; Cox et al., 1975; Haynes et al., 1975; Hutchings et al., 1975; Chesney & Shelton, 1976; Kundo & Carter, 1977; Phillips, 1977; and Cram, 1978), and in skin temperature feedback studies (Sargent et al., 1973; Blanchard et al., 1977; Turin & Johnson, 1976; and Largen et al., 1979). However, in general, these studies have included two feedback sessions per week lasting between 30 and 60 minutes. The duration of treatment ranged from 2 to 8 weeks of training for the EMG studies and from 8 to 16 weeks for the skin temperature studies. The mean treatment length for the EMG studies was 4 weeks and for the skin temperature studies 12 weeks.

The steps for the implementation of biofeedback training may include: assessment and self-monitoring of duration, intensity, and frequency of headaches, as well as antecedent and consequent environmental events, control training, discrimination training, and generalization of skills into the home setting.

In assessment, consideration of the pretreatment EMG or temperature levels should be noted. If pretreatment feedback indicates that EMG is already low or skin temperature is already high, substantial reductions of EMG or increases of skin temperature are unlikely, and therapeutic effects are hypothesized not to result with feedback.

Cox (1979) suggests that if feedback changes do not occur in the first few sessions, feedback training should be discontinued. Research has shown that if some feedback changes do not occur in the first few sessions, feedback changes in later therapy are unlikely to occur.

Self monitoring should be continuous throughout the baseline and control training phases of treatment but does not appear to be an active ingredient in headache reduction. Discrimination training has been shown to increase the efficacy of the biofeedback intervention for some clients (Budzynski, 1970; Gainer, 1978). Studies demonstrate that the identification of particular stressors in vivo facilitates headache reduction. When stressors are actively discriminated through the identification of elevated muscle tension in vivo, they may function as a cue for the implementation of psychophysiologic skills, and headache reduction is greater than when this discrimination training has not occurred. In the generalization phase, the lowering of muscle tension learned from EMG feedback or the raising of skin temperature in temperature feedback, are practiced at home. The home setting rehearsal of the acquired psychophysiological skills has most often been prescribed twice daily for 10- to 20-minute practice sessions (Budzynski et al., 1973; Cox et al., 1975; Hutchings et al., 1975; Johnson & Turin, 1975; Diamond & Franklin, 1976; Turin & Johnson, 1970; Peek & Kraft, 1977; Russ et al., 1977; Diamond et al., 1978; and Lake et al., 1979). Some researchers prescribed home practice at symptom onset or at the time of self-discriminated physiological arousal in addition to the twice scheduled daily practice sessions, while others simply prescribed practice at the onset of headache symptoms. Most studies have demonstrated that the continuation of home practice after self-control and generalization training is an important component in maintaining long-term treatment effects (Budzynski *et al.*, 1973: Reinking *et al.*, 1976; and Blanchard *et al.*, 1977).

Typically, throughout the feedback training, patients continue to take prescribed medications. Diamond *et al.* (1978), reports that patients habituated to medication prior to feedback treatment will show less of a trend towards long-term improvement than nonhabituated patients. Habituation to drugs for headache treatment prior to any psychological intervention seems to impede treatment effects, as was cited earlier (Mitchell & Mitchell, 1971). In this study, patients with previous pharmacological treatment did not respond as well to verbal relaxation or combined relaxation therapies as those who had not had such medication.

Several therapeutic tactics may be implemented to increase the success of feedback, relaxation training, or other psychophysiologic interventions with habituated patients. One approach might be simply to have the client discontinue medication for several weeks prior to treatment. In this way, patients receiving placebo effects from the medication might notice similar patterns of headache without the medication as with it. The likelihood is that they would be more receptive to feedback training and less inclined to fall back into habituation after termination of treatment.

Fordyce (1976) has devised a more systematic method of breaking patterns of habituation. In his approach, the therapist or physician controls the medication so that both prescribed medication and placebo medication are randomly given to the patient. The patient is unaware of which pill he is receiving, and he charts the effectiveness of the pills. The patient is ultimately able to compare the effects of the analgesics to the placebo pills, and often finds their effectiveness comparable.

A final approach to prevent return to medication usage after psychological intervention is to extend the training period past those in reported studies. It may be postulated that return to medication usage might be a result of discontinuing treatment before overlearning of the training has occurred. By increasing the length of training, the possibility of achieving overlearning becomes more likely and would possibly offset the tendencies of patients to become rehabituated to medication.

Summary

The most common types of headache experienced are migraine and tension. Migraine headaches are usually unilateral, throbbing headaches accompanied often by temporal visual disorders, nausea, vomiting, and irritability, each of which lasts usually from 2 to 8 hours. Tension headaches are usually symmetrical in distribution, characterized as "bandlike," with a steady, nonpulsatile ache which can last from hours to weeks.

After differentiation of headache type, it is important to consider specific environmental stimuli, be they antecedent or consequent events, that act as stressors and relate to headache onset, duration, severity, and frequency. Generally, most studies show persons having headaches to have a strong desire to be in control, and that headaches most often occur during a period of planned relaxation after a period of high stress.

Traditional medical treatment has primarily included many forms of pharmacotherapy which aid in relieving symptoms during an acute attack. These medications do produce side effects and are not, to a large extent, preventative. Behavioral approaches often circumvent many of the medical management problems and have proven to be relatively successful in correcting the initiating pathophysiological situation.

Relaxation, desensitization, and assertive therapy combined seem to be more successfully employed in the alleviation of headache symptoms than either of the treatment strategies used singularly. These treatment strategies combined also are more successful with patients having no previous pharmacological treatment than those having had previous pharmacotherapy.

Biofeedback has proven relatively successful in treating headache pain. Tension headaches are usually treated with frontalis EMG feedback. Migraines are usually treated with either skin temperature feedback, EMG feedback, or cranial artery vasomotor feedback. Both relaxation training and biofeedback training have been shown to be relatively comparable in effectiveness when used singularly. However, combined procedures of verbal relaxation and EMG feedback have proven superior to either procedure alone in reducing headache severity. Cognitive coping strategies used alone, or in combination with relaxation training or biofeedback training appear to aid in the reduction of headache symptoms. Self-management techniques used alone or in combination with relaxation training or cognitive-coping skills training has also resulted in alleviation of headache pain.

Other variables involved relating to treatment outcome, particularly in regard to biofeedback training are worth noting. Biofeedback training usually involves two sessions per week ranging from 30 to 60 minutes each with an average of 4 weeks duration for the EMG training and 12 weeks for the skin temperature training. It has also been shown that optimal results occur when discrimination training and generalization of skills into the home setting has occurred.

Patients not habituated to medication usually respond more favorably to either the verbal relaxation procedures, biofeedback, or a combination of both than do persons currently on medication. Therefore, it is usually optimal to attempt to reduce medication intake prior to or during treatment. This can be done by either discontinuing medication intake altogether, or receiving placebo medication randomly with prescribed medication. Return to medication use may be reduced by extending training periods until over-learning of the process has occurred.

Overall, behavioral approaches seem to be effective techniques for the control of headache pain without the side effects and difficulties associated with traditional pharmacotherapy. These approaches not only relieve the symptom, but also identify certain environmental stressors, and attempt to teach the patient himself how to correct the initiating pathophysiological situation so as to alleviate or prevent the headache recurrence.

REFERENCES

Adams, H. Migraine headache: Theory and modification. Paper presented at the Ecological and Behavioral Medicine Conference, Dallas, Texas, November 1979.

Anderson, N.B., Lawrence, P.S., & Olsen, T. A comparison of relaxation training and cognitive coping training in the treatment of headache pain. Presented at meetings of the Association for the Advancement of Behavior Therapy. San Francisco, 1979.

Andreychuk, T. & Shriver, C. Hypnosis and biofeedback in the treatment of migraine headache. *The International Journal of Clinical and Experimental Hypnosis,* 1975, **13** (3), 172–183.

Bakal, D.A. Headache: A biopsychological perspective. *Psychological Bulletin,* 1975, **82** (3), 369–382.

Bakal, D.A. & Kaganov, J.A. Muscle contraction and migraine headache: Psychophysiologic comparison. *Headache,* 1977, **17**, 208–215.

Beals, R.K. & Hickman, N.W. Industrial injuries of back and extremities: Comprehensive evaluation—An aid in prognosis and treatment. *Journal of Bone and Joint Surgery,* 1972, **54** (15), 93–1611.

Beecher, H.K. Relationship of significance of wound to the pain experienced. *Journal of the American Medical Association,* 1956, **161**, 1609–1613.

Beecher, H.K. The placebo effect as a nonspecific force surrounding disease and the treatment of disease. In R. Janzen, W.D. Keidel, A. Henz, C. Steichele, J.P. Payne, & R.A. Burt (Eds.) *Pain: Basic principles, pharmacology, therapy.* Stuttgart, West Germany: Georg Thieme, 1972.

Blanchard, E.B., Theobald, D.E., Williamson, D.A., Silver, B.V., & Brown, D.A. Temperature biofeedback in the treatment of migraine headaches: A controlled evaluation. *Archives of General Psychiatry,* 1978, **35**, 581–588.

Bonica, J.J. *The management of pain.* Philadelphia: Lea & Febiger, 1953.

Bowen, W.F., & Turk, D.C. Cognitive-behavioral treatment of three medical conditions. Paper presented at the Association for the Advancement of Behavior Therapy, San Francisco, 1979.

Budzynski, T.H., Stoyva, J.M., & Adler, C.S. EMG biofeedback and tension headache: A controlled outcome study. *Psychosomantic Medicine,* 1973, **35** (6), 484–496.

Budzynski, T.H., Stoyva, J.M., & Adler, C.A. Feedback-induced muscle relaxation: Application to tension headache. *Journal of Behavior Therapy and Experimental Psychiatry,* 1970, **1**, 205–211.

Cailliet, R. *Soft tissue pain and disability.* Philadelphia: F.A. Davis, 1978.

Cairns, D., Thomas, L., Mooney, V., & Pau, J.B. A comprehensive treatment approach to chronic low back pain. *Pain,* 1976, **2** (3), 301–308.

Cairns, D. & Pasino, J. Comparison of verbal reinforcement and feedback in the operant treatment of disability due to chronic low back pain. *Behavior Therapy,* 1977, **8,** 621–630.

Chesney, M.A. & Shelton, J.L. A comparison of muscle relaxation and electromyogram biofeedback treatment for muscle contraction headache. *Journal of Behavior Therapy and Experimental Psychiatry,* 1976, **7,** 221–225.

Christophenson, V. Sociocultural correlates of pain response. Final report of Project No. 1390, Vocational Rehabilitation Administration. Washington, D.C.: United States Department of Health, Education, and Welfare, 1966.

Cox, D.J. Nonpharmacological integrated treatment approach to headaches. *Behavioral Medicine Update,* 1979, **1,** 14–19.

Cox, P.J., Freundlich, A., & Meyer, R.G. Differential effectiveness of electromyograph feedback, verbal relaxation, instructions, and medication placebo with tension headaches. *Journal of Consulting and Clinical Psychology,* 1975, **43** (6), 892–898.

Cram, J.R. EMG biofeedback and the treatment of tension headaches: A systematic analysis of treatment components. *Proceedings of the Biofeedback Society of America,* 1978, **9,** 49–51.

Dalessio, D.J. Headache. In C.G. Costello (Ed.) *Symptoms of psychopathology.* New York: Wiley, 1972(a).

Dalessio, D.J. *Wolff's headache and other head pain,* 3rd ed. New York: Oxford University Press, 1972(b).

Diamond, S. & Frankling, M. Clinical application of biofeedback training. *Archives of General Psychiatry,* 1974, **30,** 573–589.

Diamond, S. & Medinu, J.L. Value of biofeedback in the treatment of chronic headache: The patients' opinion. In A.P. Friedman, M.E. Granger, & M. Critchley (Eds.) *Research and Clinical Studies in Headache,* Vol. 6, Basel, Switzerland: S. Karger, 1978.

Epstein, L.H. & Abel, G.G. An analysis of biofeedback training effects for tension headache patients. *Behavior Therapy,* 1977, **8,** 37–47.

Feurstein, M. & Adams, H.E. Cephalic vasomotor feedback in the modification of migraine headache. *Biofeedback and Self-regulation,* 1977, **2** (3), 241–253.

Follick, M.J. An outpatient based behaviorally oriented approach to the management of chronic pain. Paper presented at the meeting of the American Psychological Association, New York, 1979.

Fordyce, W. Pain viewed as learned behavior. In J.J. Bonica (Ed.) *Advances in neurology.* New York: Raven, 1974, 415–422.(a)

Fordyce, W. Treating chronic pain by contingency management. In J.J. Bonica (Ed.) *Advances in neurology,* Vol. 4, New York: Raven, 1974, pp. 538–589.(b)

Fordyce, W.E. *Behavioral methods for chronic pain and illness.* Saint Louis: C. V. Mosby, 1976.

Fordyce, W.E., Fowler, R.S., & DeLateur, B. An application of behavior modification technique to a problem of chronic pain. *Behavior Research and Therapy,* 1968, **6,** 105–107.

Fordyce, W.E., Fowler, R.S., Lehmann, J.F., DeLateur, B.J., Sand, D.L., & Treischman, R.B. Operant conditioning in the treatment of chronic pain. *Archives of Physical Medicine and Rehabilitation,* 1973, **54,** 399–408.

Fordyce, W.E., & Steger, J.C. Chronic Pain In O.F. Pomerleau & J.P. Brady (Eds). *Behavioral Medicine: Theory & Practice*. Baltimore: Williams & Wilkins, 1979.

Fowler, R.S. Biofeedback in the treatment of chronic pain. In J.J. Bonica (Ed.) *The management of pain*. Philadelphia: Lea & Febiger, 1975.

Frazier, S.H. The psychotherapy of headache. In A.P. Friedman (Ed.) *Research and clinical studies in headache*. Basel, Switzerland: Karger, 1969.

Freeman, C., Calsyn, D., & Louks, J. The use of the Minnesota Multiphasic Personality Inventory with low back pain patients. *Journal of Clinical Psychology*, 1976, **32**, 294–298.

Friedmann, L.W. & Galton, L. *Freedom from backaches*. New York: Simon & Schuster, 1973.

Gainer, J.C. Temperature discrimination training in the biofeedback treatment of migraine headache. *Journal of Behavior Therapy and Experimental Psychiatry*, 1978, **9**, 185–188.

Gannon, L. & Sternback, R.A. Alpha enhancement or a treatment for pain: A case study. *Journal of Behavior Therapy and Experimental Psychiatry*, 1971, **2**, 209l–213.

Gentry, W.D., Shows, W.D., & Thomas, M. Chronic low back pain: A psychological profile. *Psychosomatics*, 1974, **15**, 174–177.

Goldsmith, D.A. A multielement psychological management program for chronic low back pain. Unpublished doctoral dissertation. North Texas State University, 1980.

Gottlieb, H., Strite, L., Koller, R., Madnsky, A., Hocksmith, V., Kleeman, M., & Wagner, J. Comprehensive rehabilitation of patients having chronic low back pain. *Archives of Physical Medicine and Rehabilitation*, 1977, **58**, 101–108.

Greenhoot, J. & Sternbach, R. Conjoint treatment of chronic pain. *Advances in Neurology*, 1974, **4**, 595–603.

Hanvik, L.J. MMPI profiles in patients with low back pain. *Journal of Consulting Psychology*, 1951, **15**, 350–353.

Haynes, S.N., Griffin, P., Mooney, Dean, & Parise, M. Electromyographic biofeedback and relaxation instructions in the treatment of muscle contraction headaches. *Behavior Therapy*, 1975, **6**, 672–678.

Handler, N., Derogatesh, H., Avella, J., & Long, D. EMG feedback in patients with chronic pain. *Diseases of the Nervous System*, 1977, **38**, 505–509.

Hilgard, E.R. & Hilgard, J.R. *Hypnosis in the relief of pain*. Los Altos, Calif.: William Kaufman, 1975.

Hill, H.E., Kornetsky, C.G., Flanary, H.G., & Wilder, A. Effects of anxiety and morphine on the discrimination of intensities of pain. *Journal of Clinical Investigation*, 1952, **31**, 373–480.

Holroyd, K.A. & Andrasik, F. Coping and the self-control of chronic tension headache. *Journal of Consulting and Clinical Psychology*, 1978, **46**, 1036–1045.

Huber, H.P. & Huber, D. Autogenic training and rational-emotive therapy for long-term migraine patients–An explorative study of a therapy. *Behavior Analysis and Modification*, 1979, **3**, 169–177.

Hutchings, O.F. & Reinking, R.H. Tension headaches. What form of therapy is most effective? *Biofeedback and Self-Regulation*, 1976, **1**, 183–190.

Hutchings, D., Reinking, R., & Margret, M. Tension Headaches: What type of therapy is most effective? Biofeedback Research Society, Sixth Annual Proceedings, 1975.

Janzen, R. *Pain analysis: A guide to diagnosis.* Bristol, England: J. Wright & Sons, 1970.

Johnson, M. Assessment of clinical pain. In A.K. Jacox (Ed.) *Pain: A sourcebook for nurses and other health professionals.* Boston: Little, Brown, 1977.

Johnson, W.G. & Turin, A. Biofeedback treatment of migraine headache: A systematic cast study. *Behavior Therapy,* 1975, **6,** 394–397.

Kolb, L.C. Psychiatric aspects of the treatment of migraine. *Neurology,* 1963,**13,** 34.

Kundo, C. & Carter, A. True and false feedback: Effect on tension headache. *Journal of Abnormal Psychology,* 1977, **86** (1), 93–95.

Kraus, H. *The cause, prevention, and treatment of backache stress and tension.* New York: Simon & Schuster, 1965.

Lake, A., Rainey, J., & Papsdorf, J.D. Biofeedback and rational-emotive therapy in the management of migraine headache. *Journal of Applied Behavior Analysis,* 1979, **12,** 127–140.

Lance, J.W. *The mechanism and management of headache.* London: Butterworths, 1969.

Largen, J.W., Mathew, R.J., Dobbins, K., Meyer, J.S., Sakai, F., & Claghorn, J.L. The effect of direction of skin temperature self-regulation on migraine activity and regional cerebral blood flow. Unpublished manuscript, 1979.

Le Shan, L. The world of the patient in severe pain of long duration. *Journal of Chronic Diseases,* 1964, **17,** 119.

Levendusky, P. & Pankratz, L. Self-control techniques as an alternative to pain medication. *Journal of Abnormal Psychology,* 1975, **84,** 165–168.

Levine, M.E. Depression, back pain, and disc protrusion. Relationships and proposed psychophysiological mechanisms. *Diseases of the Nervous System,* 1971, **32,** 41–45.

Levit, H.I. Depression, back pain, and hypnosis. *American Journal of Hypnosis,* 1973, **15,** 266–269.

Livingston, W.K. *Pain mechanisms.* New York: Macmillan, 1943.

McCreary, C., Turner, D., & Dawson, E. Differences between functional versus organic low back pain patients. *Pain,* 1977, **4,** 73–78.

McGlashan, T.H., Evans, F.J., & Orne, M.T. The nature of hypnotic analgesia and placebo response for experimental pain. *Psychosomatic Medicine,* 1969, **31,** 227–246.

Medina, J.L., Diamond, S., & Frankling, M.A. Biofeedback therapy for migraine. *Headache,* 1976, **16,** 115–118.

Meichenbaum, D.H. & Turk, D.C. The cognitive-behavioral management of anxiety, anger, and pain. In P. Davidson (Ed.) *The behavioral management of anxiety, depression, and pain.* New York: Brunner/Mazel, 1976.

Melzack, R. & Wall, P.D. On the nature of cutaneous sensory mechanisms. *Brain,* 1962, **85,** 331–356.

Melzack, R. & Wall, P. Pain mechanisms, a new theory. *Science,* 1965, **150,** 971.

Melzack, P. *The puzzle of pain.* New York: Basic Books, 1973.

Merskey, H. & Spear, F.G. *Pain: Psychological and psychiatric aspects.* London: Bailliere, Tindall & Cassell, 1967.

Mitch, P.S., McGrady, A., & Iannone, A. Autogenic feedback training in migraine: A treatment report. *Headache,* 1976, **15,** 267–270.

Mitchell, K.R. & Mitchell, D.M. Migraine: An exploratory treatment application of programmed behavior therapy techniques. *Journal of Psychosomatic Research,* 1971, **15,** 137–157.

Mitchell, K.R. & White, R.G. Behavioral self-management: An application to the problem of migraine headaches. *Behavior Therapy,* 1977, **8,** 213–221.

Mooney, V., Cairns, D., & Robertson, J. A system for evaluating and treating chronic back disability. *Western Journal of Medicine,* 1976, **124,** 370–376.

Mullinix, J.M., Norton, B.J., Hack, S., & Fishman, M.A. Skin temperature biofeedback and migraine. *Headache,* 1978, **17,** 242–244.

Newman, R., Seres, J., Yospe, L., & Garlington, B. Mutlidisciplinary treatment of chronic pain: Long-term follow-up of low-back pain patients. *Pain,* 1978, **4,** 283–292.

Noordenbos, W. *Pain.* New York: American Elsevier, 1959.

Nouwen, A. & Solinger, M.W. The effectiveness of EMG biofeedback training in low back pain. *Biofeedback and Self-Regulation,* 1979, **4,** 103–111.

Pace, J.B. *Pain: A personal experience.* Chicago: Nelson–Hall, 1976.

Paulley, J.W. & Haskell, D.A.L. The treatment of migraine without drugs. *Journal of Psychosomatic Research,* 1975, **19,** 367–374.

Peek, C.L. & Kraft, G.H. Electromyographic biofeedback for pain related to muscle tension. *Archives of Surgery,* 1977, **112,** 889–895.

Philips, C. The modification of tension headache pain using EMG biofeedback. *Behavior Research and Therapy,* 1977, **15,** 119–129.

Philips, C. Tension headache: Theoretical problems. *Behavior Research and Therapy,* 1978, **16** (4), 249–262.

Raskind, R. & Glover, M.B. Profile of a low back derelict. *Journal of Occupational Medicine,* 1975, **17,** 258–259.

Reading, C. & Mohr, P.D. Biofeedback control of migraine: A pilot study. *British Journal of Social and Clinical Psychology* 1976, **15,** 429–433.

Reeves, J.L. EMG-biofeedback reduction of tension headache: A cognitive skills-training approach. *Biofeedback and Self-Regulation,* 1976, **1,** 217–225.

Roberts, A. The behavioral treatment of pain. In J.M Ferguson & C.B. Taylor (Eds.) *A comprehensive handbook of behavioral medicine.* New York: Spectrum, 1979.

Russ, K.L., Hammen, R.L., & Adderton, M. Clinical follow-up: Treatment and outcome of functional headache patients treated with biofeedback. *Biofeedback and Self-Regulation,* 1977, **2,** 298.

Sainsbury, P. & Gibson, J.G. Symptoms of anxiety and tension and the accompanying physiological charger in the muscular system. *Journal of Neurology, Neurosurgery, and Psychiatry,* 1954, **17,** 216–224.

Sargent, J.D., Green, E.E., & Walters, P.E. The use of autogenic feedback training in a pilot study of migraine and tension headaches. *Headache,* 1972, **12,** 120–124.

Sargent, J.D., Green, E.E., & Walters, P.E. Preliminary report on the use of autogenic feedback training in the treatment of migraine, and tension headaches. *Psychosomatic Medicine*, 1973, **35** (2), 129–135.

Sarno, J.E. Chronic back pain and psychic conflict. *Scandinavian Journal of Rehabilitation Medicine*, 1976, **8**, 143–153.

Selensky, H. Psychological study of the migraine syndrome. *Bulletin of the New York Academy of Medicine*, 1939, **15**, 757.

Shevick, B.H. A symposium on the chronic pain syndrome in problem low back cases: Introduction case presentation. *Journal of Occupational Medicine*, 1975, **17**, 654–655.

Silver, B.V., Blanchard, E.B., Williamson, D.A., Theobald, D.E., & Brown, D.A. Temperature biofeedback and relaxation training in the treatment of migraine headache—One year follow-up. *Biofeedback and Self-Regulation*, 1979, **4** (4), 359–366.

Steger, J. & Harper, R. EMG Biofeedback versus *in vivo* self-monitored relaxation in the treatment of tension headaches. Paper presented at the meeting of the Western Psychological Association, Seattle, April 1977.

Sternbach, R.A. *Pain: A psychophysiological analysis*. New York: Academic Press, 1968.

Sternbach, R.A. *Pain patients: Traits and treatment*. New York: Academic Press, 1974.

Sternbach, R.A. & Tursky, B. Ethnic differences among housewives in psychophysiological and skin potential responses for electric shock. *Psychophysiology*, 1965, **1**, 241–246.

Sternbach, R.A., Wolf, S.R., Murphy, R.W., & Akeson, W.H. Traits of pain patients: The low-back "loser." *Psychosomatics*, 1973, **14**, 226–229. (a)

Sternbach, R.A., Wolf, S.R., Murphy, R.W., & Akeson, W.H. Aspects of chronic low back pain. *Psychosomatics*, 1973, **14**, 52–56. (b)

Sternbach, R.A. & Fordyce, W. Psychogenic pain. In J.J. Bonica (Ed.). *The management of pain*, 2nd ed. Philadelphia: Lea & Febiger, 1975.

Strite, L.C. Overview of the patient treatment in the chronic back pain management program. Paper presented at the meeting of the American Psychological Association, Chicago, 1975.

Swanson, D., Floreen, A., & Swanson, W. Program for managing chronic pain: Short for results. *Mayo Clinic Proceedings*, 1976, **51**, 409–411.

Sweet, W.H. Pain. In J. Field, H.W. Magoun, & V.E. Hall (Eds.) *Handbook of Physiology*. American Physiological Society, Washington, D.C., 1959, Vol I., 459–506.

Turin, A. & Johnson, W.G. Biofeedback therapy for migraine headaches. *Archives of General Psychiatry*, 1976, **33**, 517–519.

Turk, D. Cognitive-behavioral techniques in the management of pain. In J. Foreyt & D. Rathjen (Eds.) *Cognitive behavior therapy: Research and applications*. New York: Plenum, 1978.

Turner, J., Heinrich, R., McCreary, C., & Dawson, E. Evaluation of two behavioral interventions for chronic low back pain. Paper presented at the meeting of the Society of Behavioral Medicine, San Francisco, December 1979.

Tursky, B. & Sternbach, R. Futher physiological correlation of ethnic differences in responses to shock. *Psychophysiology,* 1967, **4,** 67–74.

Warner, G. & Lance, J.W. Relaxation therapy in migraine and chronic tension headache. *The Medical Journal of Australia,* 1975, **1,** 298–301.

Weisenberg, M. Pain and pain control. *Psychological Bulletin,* 1977, **84,** 1008–1044.

Wickramasekera, I.E. Electromyographic feedback training and tension headache: Preliminary observations. *The American Journal of Clinical Hypnosis,* 1972, **15** (2), 83–85.

Wickramasekera, I.E. Temperature feedback for the control of migraine. *Journal of Behavior Therapy and Experimental Psychiatry,* 1973, **4,** 343–345.

Williams, R.B., Jr. Headache. In R.B. Williams, Jr., & W.D. Gentry (Eds.) *Behavioral approaches to medical treatment.* Cambridge, Mass.: Ballinger, 1977.

Wolff, H.G. Personality features and reactions of subjects with migraine. *Archives of Neurology and Psychiatry,* 1937, **37,** 895–921.

Wolff, H.G. *Headache and other head pain.* New York: Oxford University Press, 1963.

Wolkind, S.N. Psychiatric aspects of low back pain. *Physiotherapy,* 1974, **60,** 75–77.

Wooley, S.C., Blackwell, B., & Winget, C. A learning theory model of chronic illness behavior: Theory, treatment, and research. *Psychosomatic Medicine,* 1978, **40,** 379–401.

CHAPTER 14

Other Disorders

OVERVIEW

In this, the final chapter, the behavioral treatments of insomnia, diabetes mellitus, dysmenorrhea, dental disorders, and cancer will be discussed. These disorders have been grouped under the rather nebulous category of "other" because they, in contrast to the earlier groupings, do not contain maladies which have a biologic, etiologic or other convenient categorical commonality. They are, nevertheless, disorders of obvious importance both to the physician and the practitioner of behavioral medicine.

INSOMNIA

Insomnia has been an area of concern for many years, yet the application of behavioral intervention strategies to the treatment of insomnia has a relatively recent history. This disorder has the capacity to seriously interfere with normal functioning.

Hauri (1977) states that between 12 and 15% of all people living in industrialized countries have serious sleep problems. In a survey of health characteristics, Karacan *et al.* (1973) found substantially more than half of 1,645 randomly selected individuals, 16 years of age or older, complained about sleeping too little or too much. Based upon these data, it was estimated that at least 30 million people in the United States have sleep disturbances. Hammond (1964) noted that death rates were lowest in individuals who habitually slept 6 hours, and dramatically elevated for those who habitually slept 4 hours or less, or 10 hours or more. In a national survey by Kales (1974), of selected symptoms or mental stress, sleep disturbances were reported among 32.4% of the population and were second only to anxiety among "mental" symptoms. Research during the past several years has demonstrated the efficacy of certain behavioral procedures for the amelioration of certain types of sleep related problems.

Most investigators would agree that insomnia involves sleep difficulties. Defining this disorder, however, is apparently a more difficult task. Kleitman (1963) has defined three types of insomnia according to the time of occurrence. The first type, latency insomnia, is characterized by an inability to initially fall asleep. The second type, interrupted sleep, is characterized by frequent awakenings during the night. The third type, terminal insomnia, involves early morning awakenings, often at an intolerable hour. While the first type is the most common, and the third type is seen more frequently in older people, insomniacs often complain of a combination of these problems.

An insomniac is commonly defined as anyone who complains of too little sleep (Dement, 1974). It is clear that insomnia is a relative term, as the person's report of dissatisfaction with his/her sleep patterns represents a prime criterion for determining the presence of a sleeping problem.

Behavioral research has focused on the most common of the complaints, latency insomnia. Researchers have either not measured the occurrence of the other symptoms, or have failed to demonstrate significant changes in those problems after treatment. While studies vary in the criteria used to assess the presence of insomnia, the most commonly used criteria is a latency of 30 minutes or longer before one finally goes to sleep.

Insomnia has been attributed to a variety of causes. During the earlier part of this century, improper diet, indigestion, impure air, extreme temperatures, medical problems, demoralizing thoughts, fear of nightmares, anxiety, trauma, and grief were all thought to be causes of insomnia (Bruce, 1915; Collins, 1930; Millet, 1938).

Sleep laboratory research over the past decade has indicated very clearly the contribution of biological factors to disordered sleep. In the cases of known biological etiology, behavioral treatment is not the treatment of choice, and thus far, there is no evidence that behavioral treatment has any impact on insomnia which is mediated by biologic factors. Therefore, determination of the suitability of behavioral approaches for a given patient is very important.

There are several biological causes for insomnia of which the most prevalent is drug dependency. Frequently, insomnia is maintained by the very drugs prescribed for the treatment of the insomniac. Initially, with the use of hypnotics, a patient's sleep time increases, but within 1 to 2 weeks, total sleep will decline, and a higher dosage of medication is needed. Tolerance to the medication occurs and the patient may develop drug dependency, with a return of the original sleeping problem and a disordered sleep pattern. The solution is gradual elimination of the medication. Dement (1972) reports that withdrawal has led to greatly improved sleep in every patient so treated. Behavioral treatment may then be indicated, but unless the medication has been eliminated, behavioral intervention is unlikely to have any effect.

Another biological cause of insomnia is sleep apnea, or sleep-induced respiratory impairment. In diaphragmatic apnea the diaphragm stops moving during sleep. In obstructive or upper-airway sleep apnea, the upper airway becomes obstructed and air cannot move in or out. With either of these syndromes, the patient may awaken hundreds of times at night gasping for air. Disturbed sleep or frequent awakenings is recalled by the patient, but the respiration problem is not. As yet, there is no known simple form of treatment, but behavioral procedures would be contraindicated (Borkovec, 1977).

Dement (1975) has found a subset of sleep-disturbed patients who display rhythmic leg twitches. Leg jerks periodically awaken the patient, who is usually unaware of the movements, but complains of insomnia. Kleitman (1963), Aschoff (1969), and Webb and Agnew (1974) have identified another subset of sleep disorders termed circadian rhythm disturbances. Phase shifts in circadian rhythm may be responsible for disordered sleep, with the well-known jet lag syndrome being an example of this malady.

Many cases of insomnia do not clearly involve any of the biological factors reviewed, but, rather, appear to be caused by psychological or environmental factors, and are quite amenable to behavioral intervention. There are several distinctions to be made regarding persons having insomnia of a nonbiologic etiology. The most important distinction is between insomnia in the absence of obvious environmental stress, and complaints of insomnia from persons with specific environmental problems. The former is called "primary insomnia," and a fairly direct application of behavioral strategies is indicated. The latter is termed "secondary insomnia" and a more simple behavioral intervention may be useful as an adjunct to other interventions depending upon the nature of the environmental stress.

Insomnia may be secondary to a number of stressful situations, or to psychiatric disturbances. Kales (1976) found that over 80% of 200 insomniac patients had one or more clinical scales in the pathologic range on the Minnesota Multiphasic Personality Inventory (MMPI). Estimates vary from 30 to 85%, but emotional and psychiatric disturbances are the underlying cause of the complaint of insomnia in a significant number of patients. Disordered sleep stemming from life problems or emotional disturbances contribute more stress and its amelioration through behavioral intervention may help the patient resolve the problems without sleep loss.

Another important distinction to be made is between those patients who actually do show a significant sleep deficit and those who complain of sleep deficit but actually have normal sleep recordings. Dement (1972) has termed the former as idiopathic insomniacs and the latter as pseudoinsomniacs. The diagnosis of idiopathic insomnia is applied to patients who sleep 6 hours or less and complain of daytime drowsiness. The diagnosis of pseudoinsomnia is applied to patients who sleep 6 hours or more, and in whom no cause can be established for the complaint, including insomnia secondary to illness or chronic pain. Patients having pseudoinsomnia usually respond positively to the knowledge that their sleep is normal, and sleep-inducing medication is likely to compound the problem and therefore is contraindicated as a treatment procedure. Data suggests that both idiopathic and pseudoinsomniacs benefit from behavioral intervention strategies.

Treatment

Montgomery *et al.* (1975) noted that there has been an increase of interest in nondrug treatments for insomnia in the past 10 years. A basic therapeutic factor common to all behavioral treatments of insomnia is anxiety reduction. In addition, these techniques attempt to provide the individual with some degree of self-control over the problem behavior.

In general, a variety of behavioral techniques have been investigated. These include variants of systematic desensitization, autogenic training, progressive relaxation, stimulus control, and biofeedback. The results of these studies were generally positive and suggest that these techniques can be effectively used to treat insomnia.

Systematic Desensitization and Autogenic Training

Geer and Katkin (1966) successfully applied a modified form of systematic desensitization in the treatment of a 29-year-old female insomniac. Kahn, Baker, and Weiss (1968), in their group study using autogenic training, found significant improvement on self-report measures and median estimates of decreased sleep onset compared with pretreatment reports. Both of these studies suggest the possibility that relaxation alone might be equally as effective as relaxation plus desensitization or relaxation with autogenic training.

Relaxation Techniques

Relaxation training has consistently produced improvement in the treatment of insomnia, as pointed out in a review of the literature by Montgomery, Perkins, and Wise (1975). Evidence in support of this statement is available from case studies (French & Tupin, 1974; Hinkle & Lutker, 1972; Kahn, Baker, & Weiss, 1968; Weil & Goldfried, 1973) and from controlled outcome research (Borkovec & Fowles, 1973; Borkovec, Steinmark, & Nau, 1973; Gershman & Clouser, 1974; Steinmark & Borkovec, 1974; Nicassio & Bootzin, 1974; Haynes, Woodward, Moran, & Alexander, 1974; Borkovec, Kaloupek, & Salma, 1975; Lick & Heffler, 1977; and Borkovec, Grayson, O'Brien, & Weerts, 1979).

Borkovec and Fowles (1973) showed relaxation procedures to be more effective than no treatment for persons with moderate insomnia, and Borkovec, Steinmark, and Nau (1973) suggested that group relaxation training may be efficacious. It should be noted that neither study contained a follow-up and while treatment effects were statistically significant, they did not present dramatic declines in latency to sleep.

It has also been suggested that the use of a group setting and automated relaxation procedures may be effective in treating insomnia (Gershman & Clouser, 1974; Haynes, Woodward, Moran, & Alexander, 1974; and Nicassio & Bootzin, 1974). Gershman and Clouser (1974) exposed insomniacs to group relaxation or group desensitization treatments via automated tape recorded directions. Both treatment groups showed significant improvement, while two control groups showed no changes. Haynes *et al.* (1974) compared group relaxation and placebo therapy. Both groups demonstrated significant improvement with the relaxation group showing more improvement than the placebo group. Nicassio and Bootzin (1974) compared progressive relaxation, autogenic training, self-relaxation, and no treatment. Relaxation and autogenic training were found to be equally effective and superior to both control groups. It is important to note, however, that the subjects in these studies were not sleeping as well after treatment as the average noninsomniac.

Two studies attempted to control for the effects of demand characteristics. The first study compared active relaxation and placebo treatments under counter-demand and positive demand instructions (Steinmark & Borkovec, 1974). Subjects were told that improvement would not occur until after completion of a fourth session. Although all treatment groups showed significant improvement after the fourth session, only the active treatment group showed significant improvement during the counterdemand period. These results were maintained at follow-up.

Using a similar design, Borkovec, Kaloupek, and Salma (1975) investigated the effects of muscle-tension-release in the relaxation treatment of insomnia. Only the group that used muscle-tension-release showed significant improvement during the counterdemand period. However, the difference in latency between the two experimental groups after the third session was less than 3 minutes. The lack of statistical significance for the improved latency time of the relaxation group that did not use muscle-tension-release may reflect an effect of differing pretreatment latencies rather than differential treatment effects.

The severity of the insomnia may also have an interactive effect and this interaction may partially explain the discrepant results of the Borkovec and Fowles (1973) and the Nicassio and Bootzin (1974) investigations. The latter study found relaxation training to be more effective than self-relaxation with severe insomniacs, whereas Borkovec and Fowles found these two procedures equally effective with moderate insomniacs. These data imply that research findings obtained with subjects having mild to moderate insomnia may not generalize to severe insomniacs.

Lick and Heffler (1977) compared the effectiveness of progressive relaxation with and without a supplementary relaxation tape and an attention placebo manipulation in the modification of severe insomnia. Results indicated relaxation procedures were more effective than placebo and no treatment in modifying sleeping behavior, in reducing medication intake, and in influencing a self-report anxiety measure. The supplementary tape did not increase relaxation effectiveness and there was no difference in the efficacy of placebo and no treatment conditions.

Borkovec, Grayson, O'Brien, and Weerts (1979) compared tension-release relaxation, no tension-release relaxation, and no treatment with idiopathic and pseudoinsomniacs. Tension-release relaxation was more effective than the other two conditions regardless of insomnia subtype on subjective measures, and only for idiopathic insomniacs on objective measures.

Stimulus Control

Stimulus control procedures have been successfully applied in several insomnia investigations. Jason (1975) treated a 24-year-old graduate student and found substantial improvement at the tenth and final session with maintenance at 6-month follow-up. Haynes, Price, and Simons (1975) trained three subjects in the modification of the stimulus properties of their bedroom. The results showed a significant decrease in latency to sleep at post-treatment with maintenance at 9 month follow-up.

Alperson and Boglan (1979) examined the effects of self-administered manuals on relaxation and stimulus control treatments using self-monitoring records. Subjects under age 55 received either relaxation or stimulus control manuals or a manual on exercise. Another group used self-monitoring only. Subjects above age 55 received either relaxation or stimulus control manuals. Both treatment groups of younger subjects showed significant improvement over the no treatment groups at four weeks, but at 12 weeks there was no differences among any groups. Older subjects improved less than younger subjects and failed to improve significantly during treatment or at follow-up.

Biofeedback

Raskin, Johnson, and Rondestvedt (1973) in treating anxiety patients, found that subjects complaining of insomnia received sporadic benefits from biofeedback training. Budzynski (1973) trained 11 sleep onset insomnia patients with EMG biofeedback followed by EEG (theta) feedback and found that 6 of the 11 improved, and 3 of the 11 improved dramatically. Freedman and Papsdorf (1976) compared the effects of EMG biofeedback, progressive relaxation training, and a placebo set of relaxation exercises on 18 subjects. Sleep-onset time was significantly reduced in the two experimental groups with no significant differences between groups. However, sleep changes did not correlate with EMG changes.

Hughes and Hughes (1978) compared EMG biofeedback, pseudobiofeedback, relaxation, and stimulus control training in the treatment of 36 insomnia subjects. Results showed sleep latency to be reduced significantly in all four groups, yet EMG levels were not significantly reduced.

In an attempt to evaluate different biofeedback modalities as treatments for insomnia, Hauri (1978) compared frontalis EMG biofeedback, EMG and theta biofeedback, sensorimotor training, and no treatment. Results showed EMG biofeedback yielded significant improvements in total sleep and sleep latency according to home logs, but little change in laboratory sleep. EMG/theta feedback produced no significant sleep changes. SMR feedback showed significant improvements in sleep latency according to home logs and in sleep efficiency according to lab measurements. Controls showed no changes. The author concluded that EMG and SMR feedback seem useful in the treatment of some forms of insomnia. SMR is difficult to administer, however, and EMG feedback does not appear to show objective (laboratory measures) improvement.

Summary

To date, the relative contribution of elements critical to the treatment of insomnia have not been clearly ascertained. The behavioral treatments, which generally involve some form of relaxation and concomitant anxiety reduction, or stimulus control procedures, appear to be a promising type of treatment for insomnia at this point. While this type of treatment has a number of advantages, its efficacy has not yet been shown to generalize beyond a relatively young population with mild, primary insomnia. Future research might do well to address potentially confounding variables such as age, sex, social class, and psychiatric history, as well as the influences of factors, such as sleep-incompatible cognitive activity, expectancy and stimulus properties which may be functionally related to insomnia.

DIABETES

It has long been speculated that stress and emotional factors play an important role in the etiology and maintenance of diabetes mellitus. As the field of behavioral medicine continues to develop, treatment of the stress-factors involved in this disease will undoubtedly become more useful, particularly in areas of adherence to medical regimen and self-management.

The prevalence of diabetes mellitus is difficult to estimate due to the different standards of diagnosis. Cull and Hardy (1974) estimate that approximately 4.4 million persons in the United States have the disease, with approximately 562,000 experiencing some interference in normal functioning, and approximately 168,000 entirely unable to perform their major activities. Because diabetes in its mild form may be asymptomatic, it has been estimated that approximately half of the cases of diabetes have not been diagnosed. Approximately 70,000 new patients become known each year (Felton, Perkins, & Lewin, 1969).

Diabetes mellitus is a chronic disease of metabolism characterized by an excess of glucose in the blood (hyperglycemia), usually by sugar in the urine (glycosuria), and frequently by the elevated fatty acid content in the blood. It thus represents a generalized disorder of the body's ability to adequately utilize not only carbohydrates, but proteins and fats as well. Symptoms may include abnormal thirst, hunger, increased urination, genital itching, and loss of weight and strength. Complications are numerous and varied, affecting the entire homeostatic system of the body. Prior to the advent of insulin therapy, most diabetics experienced such shortened life spans that generalized systemic complications were precluded. With the increased duration of life brought about with insulin therapy, chronic vascular, nervous system, and skin conditions have emerged. Acute complications include ketoacidosis and coma, and increased risk of infection and hypoglycemia due to insulin reactions. Any of these complications may lead to death if untreated.

Diabetes mellitus is generally considered to be an inherited disorder of pancreatic functioning. Although the disease is classified as hereditary, it is not transmitted as a fully developed disease; rather, the tendency to develop it is inherited. It is approximately two to three times more prevalent among Jewish persons than among the general population (Felton, Perkins, & Lewin, 1969).

Hereditary diabetics are usually classified into two categories according to age of onset. Juvenile or growth-onset diabetes is arbitrarily defined as developing prior to the age of 15 (Assal & Martin, 1974) and as developing prior to the age of 20 (Knowles, 1964; Cull & Hardy, 1974). Frequently the term "brittle diabetic" is applied to this category of diabetics, referring to insulin-dependent diabetics with such fragile control that frequent fluctuations between hyperglycemia and insulin reactions occur (Woodyatt, 1938). The second category of hereditary diabetics is called adult or maturity-onset diabetes, in which clinical hyperglycemia occurs later in life, especially in old age. In general, the prognosis is improved with later onset (Pyke, Oakley, & Taylor, 1968).

Given the popular attribution of the etiology to genetic factors, the question still remains as to the precipitating factors involved in expression of the disease symptom in a given patient. Pyke (1968) cites six factors in addition to heredity that appear to play a role in the onset of diabetes: obesity, age, sex, parity, occupation, and diet. For a review of suspected etiological factors see Oakley, Pyke, and Taylor (1968).

An additional causative factor in the expression of diabetes mellitus which has received widespread support from current research endeavors is that emotional stress serves as a triggering mechanism to set off or exacerbate diabetes in the constitutionally predisposed individual (Cannon, Shohl, & Wright, 1911; Folin, Dennis, & Smillie, 1914; Menninger, 1935; Daniels, 1936; Dunbar, 1943; Meyer, Ballmeyer, & Alexander, 1945; Hinkle & Wolf, 1952; Vandenbergh, Sussman, & Titus, 1966; Vandenbergh, Sussman, & Vaughan, 1967; Slauson et al., 1963; Hong & Holmes, 1973; Grant, Kyle, Teichman, & Mendels, 1974; Holmes & Rahe, 1967; Simon & Minsky, 1953; Benton, 1953; and Treuting, 1962).

The contemporary treatment for diabetes follows three different treatment modalities used singularly or in combination depending upon the severity of the disorder. These are diet regulation, exercise, and oral hypoglycemic agents or insulin therapy. A high percentage of patients can be treated successfully by dietary restriction alone, and all diabetics must follow certain dietary limitations. Since strict dietary, exercise, and medical regimens are prescribed, it would also seem plausible that factors involved in adhering to these medical regimes would add to either stabilization or exacerbation of the disease process. This is an area of concern which warrants further investigation. Many of the early studies relating stress to the etiology of diabetes failed to control for altered or abandoned therapeutic regimes, which led Rosen and Lidz (1949) to dismiss such claims as secondary to medication-diet-exercise management.

With the advent of increased use of behavioral interventions in the treatment of medical disorders, the factors of stress reactions, and adherence to medical regime seem to be viable avenues for research and treatment with diabetes mellitus.

Treatment

To date, the literature has focused on two areas of concern in the treatment of diabetes mellitus: operant techniques in addressing the issue of adherence to therapeutic regime, and stress management in addressing the issue of etiological factors of stress.

Operant Procedures

One recent study (Lowe & Lutzker, 1979) addressed the issue of noncompliance to medical regime with a juvenile diabetic. Using a multiple baseline design, the effects of written instructions (memos) and a point system were examined. Three behaviors, compliance to foot care, dieting, and urine testing, were selected from the subject's prescribed medical regime. Compliance increased to nearly 100% and remained consistent when the point system was introduced after baseline. Compliance to diet was sporadic during baseline, but was increased and maintained at a consistently high level during the memo condition. This study shows that medical regimen can be improved with juveniles by using simple contingency management procedures.

Stress Management

The group therapy treatment for the diabetics themselves and family members has received some attention. Stephens and Marble (1951) used a systematic group intervention strategy in summer camps for diabetic children. Here the opportunities in such group living situations afforded close observation, management, and education of the diabetic child, for engendering attitudes of self-reliance, peer-associations, and community sharing, as well as for escape from harassing or over-protective parents. Similar reports have been made by Hooker (1960), Pond and Oakley (1968), Tattersall (1977), and White (1974). Although these programs teach stress management, no reports of their effectiveness are mentioned.

A similar approach is reported by Frizzell (1968) working with diabetic mental patients. Problems of self-control, self-awareness, and self-concept were addressed. Patients were also taught data collection and recording of blood-sugar levels. Results showed an overall decrease in blood-sugar levels for the 12 male patients over the 6 months of group therapy. No control group was used in this study.

Since obesity appears to play a major role in the etiology and course of diabetes, several authors encourage group therapy for the obese diabetic patient (Allen, 1962). Knox (1955) and Treuting (1962) feel that group therapy for obesity is the choice treatment and holds the greatest promise for success in symptom management. None of these authors report research data to support their claims, however.

Rosenbaum (1963) has asserted that the most critical environmental stress for most patients lies within the family. Assal and Martin (1974) have asserted that when diabetes goes out of control repeatedly in a child, the parent-child relationship needs investigation. These authors alert the practitioner to four categories of parental behavior that are counterproductive to good self-management by the child: overanxiety, overindulgence, perfectionism, and indifference. Stearns (1953, 1959), McArthur, Tomm, and Leahey (1976), and Tattersall (1977) have called for a defusing of the stressful environment by family counseling. No research has been conducted in this area, however.

The close relationship between blood glucose levels and arousal has been known for a number of years (Dunbar, 1954). Consequently, practitioners have endeavored to lower blood sugar via induced relaxation. Most of the early studies reported have used hypnotic induced relaxation to lower blood level (Mohr, 1925; Gigon, Aigner, & Bauch, 1926; Stein, see Dunbar, 1954, p. 291).

Bauch (1935) presents seven cases of diabetes treated by autogenic training in deep muscle relaxation. Each patient showed a significant decrease in blood sugar levels and a 10 to 60 unit decrease in exogenous insulin requirements after becoming proficient in relaxation acquisition.

Fowler, Budzynski, and Vandenberg (1976) utilized massed EMG biofeedback and taped relaxation training for one college semester in a single case study endeavoring to lower insulin requirements. Results indicated a decrease in daily insulin from 85 units to 59 units during training, with 1 week of 44 units per day during stressful college exams. Follow-up 6 months later found insulin maintained at 52 units per day.

Although the body of research is small, these studies indicate that some aspect of relaxation training, whether the style be hypnosis, direct relaxation training, or biofeedback relaxation training, has an effect on blood glucose levels and on required daily insulin.

Summary

Diabetes mellitus is a hereditary disease with a number of precipitating factors involved in expression of the disease symptom, one of which is stress. A review of the published studies of psychological treatment modalities for diabetes reveals a number of treatment alternatives. Indications show that stress management techniques such as group therapy, family therapy, and hypnotic, autogenic, and biofeedback approaches to relaxation do relate to decreased blood sugar levels, and that contingency management aids in problems of adherence to the dietary, exercise, or medical regime prescribed by the physician. It is hoped that future research will include studies comparing the various behavioral approaches to treatment.

DYSMENORRHEA

One of the most frequent complaints encountered in medicine and in gynecology is that of pain accompanying menstruation or dysmenorrhea (Novak, Jones, & Jones, 1965; Ogden, Wade, Anderson, & Davis, 1970). The incidence of this disorder ranges from 21 to 80% in women of childbearing age (Heald, Masland, & Sturgis, 1956; Stone & Warshaw, 1960; Pennington, 1957; Doster, McNiff, Lampe, & Corliss, 1961; Kessel & 1963; Smith, 1971; Moos, 1968).

Dalton (1964) investigated the effect of premenstrual and menstrual changes on job and life problems. He found these changes to coincide with high rates of absenteeism, psychiatric illness, accidents, and criminal offenses by women.

There are two major classifications of dysmenorrhea. Primary, or idiopathic, dysmenorrhea is pain occurring in the absence of gross pathological conditions in the pelvic organs. The pain experienced in primary dysmenorrhea is described as either short episodes of acute cramplike abdominal pain or prolonged dull aching pains throughout the body. These pains may be accompanied by nausea, headache, irritability, and gastrointestinal disturbances. Secondary, or acquired, dysmenorrhea is menstrual pain resulting from organic, pelvic disorders. Primary dysmenorrhea is the type dealt with in the behavior therapy literature.

The etiology of dysmenorrhea is obscure and research findings have presented contradictory explanations. It is the general consensus that a combined physiological and psychological approach should be taken (Paulson & Wood, 1966) in part because of the cultural, social, and emotional taboos linked to menstruation (Israel, 1967). Dalton (1969) claimed that there are two types of primary dysmenorrhea—spasmodic and congestive, which could explain previous contradictory findings.

Dalton states that spasmodic dysmenorrhea is pain beginning on the first day of menstruation, which is felt as spasms of acute pain sometimes causing vomiting and fainting. The pain is limited to the body parts controlled by uterine or ovarian nerves, such as the back, inner sides of the thighs, and lower abdomen. Congestive dysmenorrhea is a part or variation of the premenstrual syndrome. Advanced warning of menstruation is felt for several days with feelings of heaviness and a dull, aching pain in the lower abdomen and sometimes breasts and ankles. This pain may be accompanied by other symptoms such as lethargy, depression, and irritability.

Dalton proposed both types of dysmenorrhea are related to an hormonal imbalance between the circulating ovarian hormones estrogen and progesterone. Women with higher levels of progesterone than estrogen are more likely to have spasmodic dysmenorrhea. Conversely, women with higher estrogen levels than progesterone are likely to have congestive dysmenorrhea. Determination of type is important because hormonal treatment should be different. If the wrong hormone is administered, symptoms are likely to increase.

Hormone therapy is one of the most frequently used treatments. However, certain side effects, such as pulmonary embolism, thrombophlebitis, cerebral thrombosis, and neuro-ocular lesions may occur. In addition, weight gain, nausea, and breast changes have been noted (Tyler, 1973). Other treatments are being explored since these side effects and nuisances are prevalent with the use of hormones.

Treatment

Several different types of behavioral interventions have recently been applied in the treatment of dysmenorrhea with relative success. These include systematic desensitization, relaxation procedures, cognitive restructuring and self-management, and biofeedback.

Systematic Desensitization and Relaxation

Mullen (1968) treated a 31-year-old woman having severe dysmenorrhea for 21 years. She was seen for 16 sessions over a period of 6 months, and treatment consisted of muscle relaxation training and development of an anxiety hierarchy for use in systematic desensitization. Results indicated that the patient became free of pain and anxiety during normal menstruation and this improvement was maintained at 6-month follow-up.

Mullen (1971) extended this treatment program into a controlled experiment and found that systematic desensitization of individually constructed anxiety hierarchies using imagery could be effectively utilized. A no-treatment control group showed no significant reductions in symptoms. Likewise, Cox and Meyer (1978) successfully treated 14 women with primary dysmenorrhea using systematic desensitization.

Tasto and Chesney (1974) investigated a group procedure for treatment of primary dysmenorrhea. Patients were taught relaxation exercises to images of reduced menstrual pain with the purpose of transferring relaxation training to the actual onset of menstrual pain, and thus mitigating its occurrence. Results suggested these treatment approaches can be effective, and the simplicity of the group approach suggests that less therapy time is involved, and that other paraprofessionals can be easily trained to administer the procedures.

Chesney and Tasto (1975) used similar procedures of relaxation and imagery with groups of women differentiated as having either spasmodic or congestive dysmenorrhea. The major finding of clinical significance was that the treatment procedure was highly effective in reducing symptomatology of women having spasmodic dysmenorrhea, whereas this approach was not effective in reducing symptomatology of women having congestive dysmenorrhea. These results point to the need to differentiate type of dysmenorrhea before proceeding with this type of treatment.

Duson (1977) studied the effectiveness of relaxation-desensitization and cognitive restructuring in teaching the self-management of menstrual symptoms. Both groups showed significant reductions in symptomatology with a control group showing no improvement. Both groups showed maintenance at 1 month follow-up. Additional analyses indicated the relaxation-desensitization training to be more effective with patients having spasmodic dysmenorrhea as opposed to congestive dysmenorrhea. No such differences were found for the cognitive restructuring treatment.

Biofeedback

In several cases patients receiving biofeedback training for hypertension and migraine headache noticed simultaneous cessation of dysmenorrhea. One explanation of this is to postulate that vasodilation learned by the temperature training was transferred to the body, particularly to the uterus.

Tubbs and Carnahan (1976) administered EMG and temperature training to 10 volunteers for nine sessions. One subject showed dramatic improvement with sporadic results shown by the other nine subjects. Sedlacek and Heczey (1977) noted in using EMG and temperature biofeedback that reduction of symptoms appeared to be associated with learned changes in vaginal temperature. Twenty-four patients were treated with EMG training and vaginal-uterine temperature training. Autogenic phrases were used in conjunction with a vaginal-uterine placement of the thermister with visual feedback. It was found that 83% of the subjects achieved significant reduction in dysmenorrhea.

Mathew, Claghorn, Largen, and Dobbins (1979) treated 12 patients, manifesting premenstrual tension syndrome or congestive dysmenorrhea, using skin temperature control. Subjects were divided randomly into two groups taught to either raise or lower skin temperature of the hands via temperature biofeedback techniques. Although there was considerable between-subject variability in symptom topography and change, generalized factors independent of temperature control per se appeared to be responsible for a majority of symptom improvement or decline. Only the "arousal" symptom factor showed a consistent temperature related alteration.

Summary

The behavioral treatment of primary dysmenorrhea, particularly the spasmodic subtype, seems to show promise and offers a viable alternative to hormonal therapy. Systematic desensitization and relaxation seem to reduce symptomatology significantly in patients having spasmodic dysmenorrhea. Vaginal-uterine temperature training and cognitive restructuring also seems to hold promise as a useful treatment technique. These studies point to the need for differentiation among subtypes before treatment, as in most cases, the subtype of spasmodic dysmenorrhea responded more favorably to behavioral intervention. Future research should focus on more refined methods of treating both subtypes of dysmenorrhea.

DENTAL DISORDERS

Recently there has been much interest in research examining the relationship of emotional stress and dental disease. Relatively strong experimental evidence now indicates that emotional factors are related to bruxism, temporomandibular joint disorders, myofascial pain, some forms of denture soreness, and periodontal disease (Rugh, Perlis, & Disraeli, 1977). This has led to the development of some theories which maintain that emotional, behavioral, and personality factors are the primary causes of several disorders. Other theories maintain, however, that structural, occlusal, and systemic factors are more important. Debate over etiology of specific disorders will no doubt continue. A likely outcome of this debate will probably be an acknowledgement that each disorder is a result of multiple factors. At present, there is sufficient evidence relating stress and dental disorders to warrant the use of stress control therapies in dentistry (Davis & Jenkins, 1962; DeMarco, 1976; Rugh & Solberg, 1974, 1975, 1976; Yemm, 1969, 1972, 1976; Eraskus & Laskin, 1972).

Muscle activity in the form of bruxism, the nonfunctional gnashing and grinding of the teeth that usually occurs while sleeping, is undoubtedly one of the most important causes of dental disease (Cannistraci, 1975). Excessive tension of the masticatory muscles is known to aggravate or even cause many common disorders. The component parts of the oral cavity are the teeth, gums, alveolar bone, temporomandibular joint (jaws), and the masticatory muscles. Prolonged and excessive clenching, grinding, or clicking of the teeth will cause breakdown of the weakest of these components.

In some individuals the teeth exhibit excessive wear, while in others, the teeth are strong but the alveolar bone which holds the teeth deteriorates, causing periodontal disease. Finally, if the teeth, alveolar bone, jaw, and gums are all strong, then the masticatory activity can cause spasm of the muscles surrounding the temporomandibular joint causing the temporomandibular joint syndrome (TMJ).

TMJ disorders can be categorized broadly into five major groups: spontaneous dislocation, traumatic joint, chronic mandibular hypomobility, temporomandibular arthritis, and temporomandibular pain-dysfunction syndrome, also called myofascial pain dysfunction syndrome (MPDS) (Bell, 1969). There is little difficulty in determining what constitutes spontaneous dislocation or traumatic effects, and chronic mandibular hypomobility is a painless restriction of jaw movement. This leaves only the need to differentiate between myofascial pain, which is primarily a masticatory muscle problem, and temporomandibular arthritis, which is a true joint disease. Both exhibit chronic pain and hypomobility of the mandible, but they differ according to which of these is the primary or secondary symptom. Ineffective therapy or prompt relapse should alert one to the likelihood that an incorrect diagnosis has been made. For an indepth review of differential diagnoses of TMJ disorders, see Bell (1969).

Bruxism is almost universally accepted as the precursor of myofascial pain, but many diverse theories have been proposed to account for the etiology of these disorders. Psychodynamic theories, personality trait correlates, perceptual styles, attitudes, emotional states, and learning theories have all been proposed but not empirically supported (Rugh & Solberg, 1976).

Traditionally, dentists believed that improper occlusion of the teeth led to a displacement of the mandible, with a compression of the retrocondylar connective tissue, causing pain (Granger, 1958). Treatment has consisted of adjusting the occlusion or repositioning the mandible manually, injecting the muscles with local anesthetics, spraying the muscles with ethyl chloride, or prescribing muscle relaxants and tranquilizers. In many cases these techniques are successful, but they more often provide incomplete or temporary relief. Most patients remain unable to cope with tension and stress, continue to clench and grind, and therefore maintain the muscle spasms and pain (Cannistraci, 1975).

A current, widely accepted theory proposes that stress leads to bruxing, which in turn produces spasm in one or more of the masticatory muscles. This leads to pain and limitation of movement, and also produces a change in jaw position so that the teeth do not occlude properly. If the abnormal jaw position persists for a few days, the teeth shift to accommodate the new position. If the muscle spasms are relieved, the teeth again do not occlude properly (Laskin, 1969). Assuming that the stress theory of TMJ disorders holds merit, treatment would consist of stress reduction techniques in combination with dental reconstruction of the teeth or repositioning of the mandible where necessary.

Treatment

The most commonly used form of behavioral intervention in treating bruxism and myofascial pain has been EMG biofeedback. In addition, several studies report relative success in treating these disorders with aversive conditioning, relaxation procedures, and cognitive strategies.

Aversive Conditioning

An automated aversive conditioning procedure was developed by Heller and Strange (1973) in the treatment of a 24-year-old graduate student having bruxism. Upon retiring at night, the patient set up an apparatus constructed to emit a loud noise upon the patient's bruxing at a certain criterion level. The patient's bruxism was significantly reduced, although not eliminated.

Biofeedback

Rugh and Solberg (1972) treated 15 persons having bruxism and myofascial pain. Each were provided with a portable EMG unit that emitted a signal when masseter muscle activity exceeded a preset threshold. Subjects were instructed to attempt to learn new behaviors to cope with stressful situations and the EMG device was to show how well they were doing. Although no specific evaluation criteria was given, 10 of the 15 significantly improved.

Rugh and Solberg (1975) treated bruxism with three treatment modalities: biofeedback during sleep, splint therapy (wearing a mouthguard during sleep), and massed negative practice (clenching 600 times a day to produce fatigue). None of the treatments showed lasting effects.

Kardachi and Clark (1977) treated nine nocturnal bruxists employing a grinding warning system. The audible tone varied in frequency with the intensity of masseter and frontalis muscles, and did not awaken subjects but altered their levels of sleep from Stage B (where bruxism tends to occur) to Stage A. Seven of nine subjects showed 70% reduction in grinding frequency.

Cannistraci (1979) treated 18 subjects having bruxism. EMG recordings were obtained while subjects practiced relaxation techniques such as hypnosis, progressive relaxation, autogenic training, and meditation. At 3-month follow-up, the nine clients who practiced relaxation daily had complete remission of symptoms, the eight clients who practiced only upon symptom occurrence had satisfactory results, and the one client who did not practice was again in great pain.

The clinical efficacy of biofeedback treatment for bruxism has yet to be adequately evaluated. Most reports are at a pre-experimental stage with lack of control groups or long-term follow-up. Biofeedback in the treatment of myofascial pain has been more successfully used.

Carlson *et al.* (1975) treated a 21-year-old myofascial pain patient who had already received traditional dental treatments without pain relief. Following 18 EMG biofeedback sessions using discrimination, control, and transfer training, the patient was pain free for 6 months. Sixteen myofascial pain subjects received auditory EMG feedback from their masseter muscles in a study by Dohrmann and Laskin (1976). No further treatment was required for 75% of the subjects. A similar study with similar results was conducted by Carlson and Gale (1977). One of their findings directly challenged the conclusion that treatment effects were due to biofeedback per se. No correlation was found between success in establishing muscular relaxation and symptom relief. The two treatment failures were the best relaxers. These findings point to the need for future research designed to isolate and evaluate treatment components and nonspecific factors.

Dohrmann and Laskin (1978) randomly assigned 24 outpatients with myofascial pain to two groups: a control group and a group receiving auditory feedback of masseter EMG activity with gradual shaping to reduce EMG levels. All patients were provided with instructions for twice daily, 20-minute, home relaxation sessions. Over the treatment course and 12-month follow-up, 75% of the biofeedback patients and 25% of the control patients needed no additional treatment. Several confounding variables in this study again pointed to the need to evaluate and control nonspecific factors.

If, as was suggested in the previous studies, there is no correlation between the bioelectrical responses being modified and the clinical relief of symptoms, the basis for biofeedback treatment may be questioned. Stenn, Mothersill, and Brooke (1979) investigated the use of biofeedback and cognitive behavior therapy in the treatment of 11 myofascial pain patients. During the first half of a session, all subjects were "hooked" to EMG masseter electrodes and given relaxation instructions, but only half received feedback. During the last 30 minutes of a session, each client received individualized cognitive behavior therapy. Both groups reduced EMG levels equally, but the biofeedback group reported less pain. Stenn challenged the assumption that muscle tension is involved in the etiology of myofascial pain and states that cognitive variables need further investigation.

Summary

Although psychological factors are an important etiological factor in producing and perpetuating bruxism and TMJ disorders, the problem may best be understood through the concept of multifactorial etiology, with emotionally induced muscle tension being one component. Despite reports of reducing bruxism and myofascial pain from biofeedback training, research tends to point to other nonspecific factors involved in treatment effect. Biofeedback appears at least to be equal in efficacy to the more expensive dental treatments. Treatment involving simultaneous dental and psychological strategies appears to be more promising than either approach alone.

CANCER

As the field of behavioral medicine develops as a distinct discipline, it is evident that participation in the care of the cancer patient by researchers and behaviorally-oriented clinicians will become more prevalent. Current epidemiological studies show that one out of every four Americans will have some form of neoplastic disease during their lifetime. Cancer is still surrounded by many unknowns, and despite recent dramatic advances in treatment and research, the cause of cancer is not clearly understood. The course of the disease varies extremely from organ to organ, from individual to individual. The prognosis, although always guarded, now carries a hope for longer and longer, but uncertain, survival time.

Given the fact that more and more people are contracting cancer and survival rates are longer, problems of dealing with a chronic, often disabling, and sometimes terminal illness arises. This implies that health professionals, other than oncologists and primary medical caretakers, will be called upon to provide psychosocial evaluation and care (Sobel, 1979). Psychologists are finding themselves in a unique position to offer their research, diagnostic, and clinical skills in this area.

Up to now, a great deal of attention has been given to psychobiological or psychosomatic investigations of tumor incidence and growth (Achterberg, Lawlis, Simonton, & Simonton, 1977; Bahnson & Bahnson, 1966; Greer & Morris, 1975; Kissen, 1963; Kissen & LeShan, 1964; LeShan, 1969; Watson & Schuld, 1977). Although psychobiological research remains potentially useful for primary prevention, the actual stresses of the disease require that psychologists also address issues pertaining to psychosocial adaptation and coping (Brown, 1966; Monat & Lazarus, 1977; Worden & Sobel, 1978). This seems to be a crucial area for behavioral medicine, and one that demands more attention.

One major problem in facilitating coping has been that factors involved in the urgency of the illness often seem to demand immediate professional attention, including practical, short-term intervention. This has led to the application of various "improvement packages" (Deitz, 1978) without first analyzing whether all medical patients do in fact manifest coping deficits that require intervention. Prior research has shown that assumptions of coping homogeneity among cancer patients are fallacious, often leading to unwarranted or premature clinical prescriptions (Cromes & Pinkerton, 1976; Weisman & Worden, 1975, 1976, 1977; Worden & Sobel, 1978; Worden & Weisman, 1977).

Cancer patients cope in different ways, reveal varying patterns of adaptation, and experience many different illness-related concerns. In a survey of 150 patients having various forms of cancer (Cromes & Pinkerton, 1976) 50% showed no signs of psychological distress and appeared to be coping well. Of those expressing illness-related concerns they were categorized as follows: 50% of the problems were family related; 15% were fear of cancer or death; 10% were problems concerning appearance; 10% were sleep related; 10% were pain related; and 5% were problems related to sexual difficulties.

Generalized notions about cancer patients and cancer-related problems have hindered the understanding of the specificity of problems and coping responses. These factors point to the need for a sequential "process" approach to the cancer patient prior to blind application of behavioral intervention techniques (Lazarus, 1978; Turk, Sobel, Follick, & Youkilis, 1978). It is neither empirically or clinically sound to assume that all cancer patients, because they have cancer, suffer anxiety, depression, or general coping deficiencies. Such generalizations obscure the benefits of specificity in cognitive behavioral research, and reinforce "uniformity myths" (Kiesler, 1971).

It is not within the scope of this chapter to describe cancer as a disease process in that it can affect any area of the body or a combination of body parts. Problems relating to the body part affected, the severity of the cancer, and disability or life-style alterations are also specific to various cancer types. It will suffice to say that in general, cancer and cancer-related problems, including ramifications of medical treatments such as radiation and chemotherapy, do present some patients having cancer with serious coping and adjustment problems. In its very broadest sense, psychosocial cancer care, or psycho-oncological work (Garfield, 1978), will focus on the understanding, prediction, modification, and teaching of the coping process during the course of the illness.

Treatment

Two treatment strategies have been primarily used in cancer care. Cognitive coping strategies have been used relatively successfully in dealing with the problems cancer patients experience as a result of their disease, and progressive relaxation has been found to help the cancer patient cope with side effects of chemotherapeutic drugs.

Cognitive Strategies

In a 5-year-longitudinal study, Sobel (1979) studied how cancer patients cope or fail to cope with their illness, its treatment, and psychosocial ramifications. Recent findings indicate that there are significant differences between patients who cope well, and those who experience more emotional distress (Weisman & Worden, 1976; Weisman, 1972; Weisman & Worden, 1975; Worden & Weisman, 1977; Worden & Sobel, 1978). Furthermore, it was found that these differences cannot be accounted for solely on the basis of physical status. That is, some patients with advanced cancer cope better than other patients, whom, after treatment, have no evidence of disease.

Sobel found the most effective copers confronted their problems directly and tended to redefine salient issues and immediate concerns in solvable terms. While independent and self-reliant, they did not hesitate to use other resources when needed. Good copers were cooperative but not passively compliant. By resourceful shifting from one strategy to another, good copers were able to correct themselves. It was concluded that coping well is a continuous process which uses several strategies and is not a closed or permanent state of well-being.

In a case study Weisman and Sobel (1979) observed a 67-year-old postmastectomy patient's coping style. She had innumerable family and financial problems in addition to her cancer yet seemed to cope extremely well. It was shown that she used positive self-reinforcement, means-end thinking, monitored assessment of progress, and external attribution of task difficulty not only on administered tests but customarily as problems arose. This anecdotal account emphasizes the self-management paradigm instead of the medical model which views a patient as the passive victim of forces beyond control. Self-management theory has made viable the possibility that some medical patients can observe their own behavior, control contingencies, and practice appropriate coping responses. One aspect of cognitive self-control is covert self instruction, which also includes "vigilant information processing" (Janis & Mann, 1977).

Several problem-solving steps were identified in working with cancer patients within a cognitive-behavioral intervention model: (1) identifying the primary effect, (2) defining the primary problem and subsidiary concerns, (3) generating alternative solutions, (4) considering pros and cons of each possible solution, (5) ranking in order possible solutions, (6) selecting the most acceptable and feasible solution, and (7) reexamining and redefining the original problem in light of this assessment. The patient should be encouraged to interact more explicitly with the clinician in verbalizing the process; therefore, covert instruction is modeled, taught, and reinforced as a means of self-control.

Cromes and Pinkerton (1976) report the successful use of cognitive behavioral strategies in the treatment of specific problems in two cancer patients. A 44-year-old post-mastectomy patient had two basic beliefs which presented marital problems and interfered with the treatment process. She believed her cancer was contracted through sexual intercourse and she would not allow herself any contact with her husband. Through cognitive restructuring, she changed this belief and resumed normal sexual relations with her husband. Another belief was that radiation would injure her and that if she did not follow-up with recommended treatment, she would be better off. Cognitive restructuring also proved beneficial and she resumed treatment with an excellent prognosis.

Certain maladaptive beliefs of a 28-year-old male having terminal testicular cancer were also dealt with successfully through cognitive restructuring. This young man had to quit work and was unable to have normal sexual activities with his wife. He believed he was an invalid and worthless, divorced his wife and attempted suicide. Through use of a problem solving technique, and cognitive restructuring, he became "a happy housewife" as he termed it, and reunited with his wife for the 4 months before his death. It should be noted that psychotherapy over a 1-year period was used in conjunction with the behavioral strategies.

Relaxation

One study (Burish & Lyles, 1979) reported the use of progressive relaxation in reducing the aversiveness of chemotherapy in the treatment of cancer. In a design including therapist-directed relaxation and patient-directed relaxation, results indicated that during the therapist-directed phases and one or both of the patient-directed phases, the patient showed reductions in negative affect, frequency of vomiting, and post-session physiological arousal. It was concluded that progressive muscle-relaxation training may be an effective procedure for reducing the adverse side effects of cancer chemotherapy and possibly aid in weight gain which further improves the general health of the patient.

Operant Procedures

Cairns and Altman (1979) used positive reinforcement, access to play activities and a token system to reverse weight loss in the successful treatment of cancer-related anorexia in an 11-year-old female having a history of frequent hospitalizations for treatment of malignant hemangiopericytoma.

Summary

While the research is sparse, and mainly anecdotal at this point, the use of behavioral treatment strategies in coping with the psychosocial or physiological problems that occur as a result of having cancer or its treatment seem promising. Future research should address itself to more controlled studies using cognitive coping strategies, progressive relaxation and reinforcement in determining avenues by which to alter these problems.

REFERENCES

Achterberg, J., Lawlis, G., Simonton, O., & Simonton, S. Psychological factors and blood chemistries as disease outcome predictions for cancer patients. *Multivariate Experimental Clinical Research*, 1977, **3**, 107–122.

Allen, F.M. A personal view of therapy of diabetes mellitus. *Diabetes*, 1962, **11**, 336.

Alperson, J. & Boglan, A. Self-administered treatment of sleep onset insomnia and the importance of age. *Behavior Therapy*, 1979, **10**, 347–356.

Aschoff, J. Desynchronization and resynchronization of human circadian rhythms. *Aerospace Medicine*, 1969, **40**, 844–849.

Assal, J. & Martin, D.B. Management of juvenile diabetes mellitus. In J.G. Cull & R.E. Hardy (Eds.) *Counseling and rehabilitating the diabetic*. Springfield, Ill.: Charles C Thomas, 1974.

Bahnson, C. & Bahnson, M. Role of the ego defenses: Denial and repression in the etiology of malignant neoplasms. *Annals of the New York Academy of Science*, 1966, **125**, 827–845.

Bauch, M. Beeinflessing des diabetes mellitus durch psychophysche entspannungsubungen. *Deutsches Archiv fuer Klinische Medizin*, 1935, **178**, 149–166.

Bell, W.H. Nonsurgical management of the pain-dysfunction syndrome. *Journal of American Dental Association*, 1969, **79**, 161–163.

Benton, P.C. The emotional aspects of diabetes mellitus. *Journal of the Oklahoma Medical Association*, 1953, **46**, 11.

Borkovec, T.D. Insomnia. In R. Williams & W.D. Gentry (Eds.) *Behavioral approaches to medical treatment*. Cambridge, Mass.: Ballinger, 1977.

Borkovec, T.C. & Fowles, D.C. Controlled investigation of the effects of progressive and hypnotic relaxation on insomnia. *Journal of Abnormal Psychology*, 1973, **82**, 153–158.

Borkovec, T.D., Grayson, J.B., O'Brien, G.T., & Weerts, T.C. Relaxation treatment of pseudoinsomnia and idiopathic insomnia: An electroencephalographic evaluation. *Journal of Applied Behavior Analysis,* 1979, **12**, 37–54.

Borkovec, T.D., Kaloupek, D.G., & Salma, K.M. The facilitative effect of muscle tension-release in the relaxation treatment of sleep disturbance. *Behavior Therapy,* 1975, **6**, 301–09.

Borkovec, T.D., Steinmark, S.W., & Nau, S.D. Relaxation training and single-item desensitization in the group treatment of insomnia. *Journal of Behavior Therapy and Experimental Psychiatry,* 1973, **4**, 401–403.

Brown, F. The relationship between cancer and personality. *Annals of the New York Academy of Science,* 1966, **125**, 865–873.

Bruce, H.A. *Sleep and sleeplessness.* Boston: Little, Brown, 1915.

Budzynski, T.H. Biofeedback procedures in the clinic. *Seminars in Psychiatry,* 1973, **5**, 537–547.

Burish, T.G. & Lyles, J.N. Effectiveness of relaxation training in reducing the aversiveness of chemotherapy in the treatment of cancer. *Journal of Behavior Therapy and Experimental Psychiatry,* 1979, **10**, 357–361.

Cairns, G.F. & Altman, K. Behavioral treatment of cancer-related anorexia. *Journal of Behavior Therapy and Experimental Psychiatry,* 1979, **10**, 353–356.

Cannistraci, A.J. Biofeedback—The treatment of stress-induced muscle activity. In Harold Gelb (Ed.) *Clinical management of head, neck, and TMJ pain and dysfunction.* Philadelphia: Saunders, 1979.

Cannistraci, A.J. Procedures for voluntary stress release and behavior therapy in the treatment of clenching and bruxism. New York: Biomonitoring Applications, Inc., Cassette Tape T13, 1975.

Cannon, W.B., Shohl, A.T., & Wright, W.W. Emotional glycosuria. *American Journal of Physiology,* 1911, **29**, 280.

Carlson, S.G. & Gale, M. Biofeedback in the treatment of long-term temporomandibular joint pain. *Biofeedback and Self-Regulation,* 1977, **2**, 161–171.

Carlson, S.G., Gale, E.M., & Ohman, A. Treatment of temporomandibular joint syndrome with biofeedback training. *Journal of American Dental Association,* 1975, **91**, 602–605.

Chesney, M.A. & Tasto, D.L. The effectiveness of behavior modification with spasmodic and congestive dysmenorrhea. *Behavior Research and Therapy,* 1975, **13**, 245–253.

Collins, J. *Insomnia: How to combat it.* New York: Appleton, 1930.

Cox, D.J. & Meyer, R.G. Behavioral treatment parameters with primary dysmenorrhea. *Journal of Behavioral Medicine,* 1978, **1**, 297–300.

Cromes, G.F. & Pinkerton, S.S. Rational counseling in cancer rehabilitation. Paper presented at the Annual Convention of Physical Medicine and Rehabilitation, 1976.

Cull, J.G. & Hardy, R.E. *Counseling and rehabilitating the diabetic.* Springfield, Ill.: Charles C Thomas, 1974.

Dalton, K. *The menstrual cycle.* New York: Pantheon Books, 1969.

Daniels, G.E. Emotional and instinctual factors in diabetes mellitus. *American Journal of Psychiatry,* 1936, **93**, 711.

Davis, C.H. & Jenkins, C.D. Mental stress and oral diseases. *Journal of Dental Research,* 1962, **41,** 1045–1049.

Deitz, S. Current status of applied behavior analysis: Science versus technology. *American Psychologist,* 1978, **33,** 805–814.

DeMarco, T.J. Peridontal emotional stress syndrome. *Journal of Periodontology,* 1976, **47,** 67–68.

Dement, W. Daytime sleep recordings in narcoleptics and hypersomniacs. *Sleep Research,* 1972, **1.**

Dement, W.C. *Some must watch while some must sleep.* San Francisco: W.H. Freeman, 1974.

Dement, W., Guillemnault, C. & Zarcone, V. The pathologies of sleep: A case series approach. In D.B. Tower (Ed.) *The nervous system.* Vol. 2, *The clinical neurosciences.* New York: Raven Press, 1975.

Dohrmann, R.J. & Laskin, D.M. An evaluation of electromyographic biofeedback in the treatment of myofascial pain-dysfunction syndrome. *Journal of the American Dental Association,* 1978, **96,** 656–662.

Dohrmann, R.J. & Laskin, D.M. Treatment of myofascial pain dysfunction syndrome with EMG biofeedback. IADR Abstracts, *Journal of Dental Research,* 1976, **55,** B249.

Dolster, M.E., McNiff, A.L., Lampe, J.M., & Corliss, L.M. A survey of menstrual function among 1668 secondary school girls and 720 women employees of the Denver Public Schools. *American Journal of Public Health and the Nation's Health,* 1961, **51,** 1841–1846.

Dunbar, F. *Emotions and bodily changes.* New York: Columbia University Press, 1954.

Dunbar, H.F. *Psychosomatic diagnosis.* New York, London: Paul B. Holber, 1943.

Duson, B.M. Effectiveness of relaxation-desensitization and cognitive restructuring in teaching the self-management of menstrual symptoms to college women. Dissertation Abstracts International, 1977, **37,** 6322B.

Eraskus, D.S. & Laskin, D.M. A biochemical measure of stress in patients with myofascial pain dysfunction syndrome. *Journal of Dental Research,* 1972, **51,** 1464–1466.

Felton, J.S., Perkins, D.C., & Lewin, M. Survey of medicine and medical practice for the rehabilitation counselor. Washington D.C.: U.S. Department of Health Education and Welfare, 1969.

Folin, O., Dennis, W., & Smillie, W.G. Some observations on emotional glycosuria in man. *Journal of Biological Chemistry,* 1914, **17,** 519.

Fowler, J.E., Budzynski, T.H., & Vandenbergh, R.L. Effects of an EMG biofeedback relaxation program on the control of diabetes. *Biofeedback and Self-Regulation,* 1976, **1**(1), 105–112.

Freedman, R. & Papsdorf, J.D. Biofeedback and progressive relaxation treatment of sleep-onset insomnia: A controlled, all-night investigation. *Biofeedback and Self-Regulation,* 1976, **1,** 253–271.

French, A.D. & Tupin, J.P. Therapeutic application of a simple relaxation method. *American Journal of Psychotherapy,* 1974, **28,** 282–287.

Frizell, M.K. Group therapy for diabetes mellitus patients. *Hospital and Community Psychiatry,* 1968, 47–48.

Garfield, C. *Psychosocial care of the dying patient.* New York: McGraw–Hill, 1978.

Geer, J.H. & Katkin, E.S. Treatment of insomnia using a variant of systematic desensitization: A case report. *Journal of Abnormal Psychology,* 1966, **71,** 161–164.

Gershman, L. & Clouser, R.A. Treating insomnia with relaxation and desensitization in a group setting by an automated approach. *Journal of Behavior Therapy and Experimental Psychiatry,* 1974, **5,** 31–35.

Gigon, A., Aigner, E., & Bauch, W. Ueber den einfluss der psyche aut korperliche vorgange: Hypnose and blutzucker. *Schweizerische Mediginische Wochenschrift,* 1926, **56,** 749–750.

Granger, E.R. Occlusion in temporomandibular joint pain. *Journal of the American Dental Association,* 1958, **56,** 659.

Grant, I., Kyles, G.C., Teichman, B.A., & Mendels, J. Recent life events and diabetes in adults. *Psychosomatic Medicine,* 1974, **36,** 121–128.

Greer, S. & Morris, T. Psychological attitudes of women who develop breast cancer: A controlled study. *Journal of Psychosomatic Research,* 1975, **19,** 147–153.

Hammond, E. Some preliminary findings on physical complaints from a prospective study of 1,064,004 men and women. *American Journal of Public Health,* 1964, **54,** 11–22.

Hauri, P. Biofeedback techniques in the treatment of serious, chronic insomniacs. *Proceedings of the Biofeedback Society of America,* 1978, **9,** 206–208.

Hauri, P. Sleep disorders in current concepts. Kalamazoo, Mich.: Upjohn, MS-5595, 1977.

Haynes, S.N., Price, M.G., & Simons, J.P. Stimulus control treatment of insomnia. *Journal of Behavior Therapy and Experimental Psychiatry,* 1975, **6,** 279–282.

Haynes, S.N., Woodward, S., Moran, R., & Alexander, D. Relaxation treatment of insomnia. *Behavior Therapy,* 1974, **5,** 555–558.

Heald, F.P., Masland, R.P., Sturgis, S.H., & Galeagher, J.R. Dysmenorrhea in adolescence. *Pediatrics,* 1956, **20,** 121.

Heller, R.Z. & Strange, H.R. Controlling bruxism through automated aversive conditioning. *Behavior Research and Therapy,* 1973, **11,** 327.

Hinkle, J. & Lutker, E. Insomnia: A new approach. *Psychotherapy: Theory, Research and Practice,* 1972, **9,** 236–237.

Hinkle, L.E. & Wolf, S. A summary of experimental evidence as relating life stress to diabetes mellitus. *Journal of the Mount Sinai Hospital,* 1952, **19**(4), 537–570.

Holmes, T.H. & Rahe, R.H. The social readjustment rating. *Journal of Psychosomatic Research,* 1967, **11,** 213–218.

Hong, M. & Holmes, T.H. Transient diabetes mellitus associated with culture change. *General Psychiatry,* 1973, **29,** 683–687.

Hooker, A.D. Camping and the diabetic child. *Journal of the American Diabetic Association,* 1960, **37,** 143.

Hughes, R.C. & Hughes, H.H. Insomnia: Effects of EMG biofeedback, relaxation training and stimulus control. *Behavioral Engineering*, 1978, **5**, 67–72.

Israel, S.L. *Diagnosis and treatment of menstrual disorders and sterility*. New York: Harper & Row, 1967.

Janis, I. & Mann, J. *Decision making: A psychological analysis of conflict, choice, and commitment*. New York: Macmillan, 1977.

Jason, L. Rapid improvement in insomnia following self-monitoring. *Journal of Behavior Therapy and Experimental Psychiatry*, 1975, **6**, 349–350.

Kahn, H., Baker, B.L., & Weiss, J.M. Treatment of insomnia by relaxation training. *Journal of Abnormal Psychology*, 1968, **73**, 556–558.

Kales, A. Incidence of insomnia in the Los Angeles metropolitan area. *Sleep Research*, 1974, **3**, 139.

Kales, A., Caldwell, A.B., Preston, T.A., Healey, S., & Kales, J.D. Personality patterns in insomnia. *Archives of General Psychiatry*, 1976, **33**, 1128–1134.

Kales, A. & Kales, J.D. Sleep disorders: Recent findings in the diagnosis and treatment of disturbed sleep. *New England Journal of Medicine*, 1974, **290**, 487–499.

Karacan, I., Salis, P.J., & Williams, R.L. Clinical disorders of sleep. *Psychosomatics*, 1973, **14**, 77–88.

Kardachi, B.J. & Clarke, N.G. The use of biofeedback to control bruxism. *Journal of Period*, 1977, **10**, 639–642.

Kessel, N. & Coppen, A. The prevalence of common menstrual symptoms. *Lancet*, 1963, **61**, 1961–1964.

Kiesler, D. Experimental design in psychotherapy research. In A. Bergin & S. Gerfield (Eds.) *Handbook of psychotherapy and behavior change*. New York: Wiley, 1971.

Kissen, D. Personality characteristics in males conducive to lung cancer. *British Journal of Medical Psychology*, 1963, **36**, 27–36.

Kissen, D. & LeShan, L. (Eds.) *Psychosomatic aspects of neoplastic disease*. Philadelphia: Lippincott, 1964.

Kleitman, N. *Sleep and wakefulness*, rev. ed. Chicago: University of Chicago Press, 1963.

Knowles, H.C. Brittle diabetes. In T.S. Danowski (Ed.) *Diabetes mellitus: Diagnosis and treatment*. New York: American Diabetes Association, 1964.

Knox, K.R. Management of the overweight diabetic patient. *Medical Clinics of North America*, 1955, **39**, 1599.

Laskin, D.M. Etiology of the pain-dysfunction syndrome. *Journal of American Dental Association*, 1969, **79**, 147.

Lazarus, R. Strategy for research in hypertension. *Journal of Human Stress*, 1978, **4**, 34–39.

Le Shan, L. An emotional life-history pattern associated with neoplastic disease. *Annals of the New York Academy of Science*, 1969, **164**, 546–557.

Lick, J.R. & Haffler, D. Relaxation training and attention placebo in the treatment of severe insomnia. *Journal of Consulting and Clinical Psychology*, 1977, **45**, 153, 161.

Lowe, K. & Lutzker, J.R. Increasing compliance to a medical regimen with a juvenile diabetic. *Behavior Therapy,* 1979, **10,** 57–64.

Mathew, R.J., Claghorn, J.L., Largen, J.W., & Dobbins, K. Skin temperature control for premenstrual tension syndrome: A pilot study. *American Journal of Clinical Biofeedback,* 1979, **2,** 7–10.

McArthur, P.B., Tomm, K.M., & Leahey, M.D. Management of diabetes mellitus in children. *CMA Journal,* 1976, **114,** 783–787.

Menninger, W.C. Psychological factors in the etiology of diabetes mellitus. *Journal of Nervous and Mental Disorders,* 1935, **81,** 1.

Meyer, A., Bollmeyer, L.N., & Alexander, F. Correlations between emotions and carbohydrate metabolism in two cases of diabetes mellitus. *Psychosomatic Medicine,* 1945, **7,** 335–341.

Millet, J.A.P. *Insomnia: Its causes and treatment.* New York: Greenberg Publisher, 1938.

Mohr, F. *Psychophysiche behandlungsmethoden.* Leipzig, Germany: Hirzel, 1925.

Monat, A. & Lazarus, R. *Stress and coping: An anthology.* New York: Columbia University Press, 1972.

Montgomery, I., Perkins, G., & Wise, D. A review of behavioral treatments for insomnia. *Journal of Behavior Therapy and Experimental Psychiatry,* 1975, **6,** 93–100.

Moos, R.H. The development of a menstrual distress questionnaire. *Psychosomatic Medicine,* 1968, **30,** 853–867.

Mullen, F.G. The treatment of a case of dysmenorrhea by behavior therapy techniques. *Journal of Nervous and Mental Disease.* 1968, **147,** 371–376.

Nicassio, P. & Bootzin, R. A comparison of progressive relaxation and autogenic training as treatments for insomnia. *Journal of Abnormal Psychology,* 1974, **83,** 253–260.

Novak, E.R., Jones, G.S., & Jones, H.W., Jr. *Novak's textbook of gynecology,* 7th ed. Baltimore: Williams & Wilkins, 1965, 653–661.

Oakley, W.G. Treatment management in clinical diabetes and its biochemical basis. In W.G. Oakley, D.A. Pyke, & K.W. Taylor (Eds.) *Clinical diabetes and its biochemical basis.* Oxford: Blackwell Science Publications, 1968, 360.

Oakley, W.G., Pyke, D.A., & Taylor, K.W. *Clinical diabetes and its biochemical basis.* Oxford: Alden Press, 1968.

Ogden, J., Wade, M.E., Anderson, G., & Davis, C.D. Treatment of dysmenorrhea. *American Journal of Obstetrics and Gynecology,* 1970, **106,** 838–842.

Paulson, M.J. & Wood, K.R. Perceptions of emotional correlates of dysmenorrhea. *American Journal of Obstetrics and Gynecology,* 1966, **95,** 991–996.

Pennington, V.M. Meprobomate (Miltown) in premenstrual tension. *Journal of the American Medical Association,* 1957, **164,** 638–640.

Pond, H. & Oakley, W.G. Diabetes in children. In W.G. Oakley, D.A. Pyke, & K.M. Taylor (Eds.) *Clinical diabetes and its biochemical basis.* Oxford: Alden Press, 1968.

Pyke, D.A. Aetiological factors. In W.G. Oakley, D.A. Pyke, & K.W. Taylor (Eds.) *Clinical diabetes and its biochemical basis.* Oxford: Alden Press, 1968.

Raskin, M., Johnson, G., & Rondestvedt, J. Chronic anxiety treated by biofeedback induced muscle relaxation: A pilot study. *Archives of General Psychiatry*, 1973, **28**, 263–267.

Rosen, H. & Lidz, T. Emotional factors in the precipitation of recurrent diabetic acidosis. *Psychosomatic Medicine*, 1949, **11**, 211.

Rosenbaum, M. Treatment of psychometric disorders. In H.I. Lief & V.F. Lief (Eds.) *The psychological basis of medical practice*. New York: Harper & Row, 1963.

Rugh, J.D., Perlis, D.B., & Disraeli, R.I. Biofeedback in dentistry: Research and clinical applications. *Biofeedback in Dentistry*, 1977.

Rugh, J.D. & Solberg, W.K. Electromyographic studies of bruxist behavior before and during treatment. *Journal of California Dental Association*, 1975, **3**, 56–59.

Rugh, J.D. & Solberg, W.K. Psychological implications in temporomandibular pain and dysfunction. *Oral Sciences Reviews*, 1976, **7**, 3–30.

Rugh, J.D. & Solberg, W.K. The identification of stressful stimuli in natural environments using a portable biofeedback unit. Proceedings of the Biofeedback Research Society, 5th Annual Meeting, Colorado Springs, 1974.

Sedlacek, K. & Heczey, M. A specific treatment for dysmenorrhea. Proceedings of the Biofeedback Society of America, 1977, **8**, 26.

Simon, N.M. & Minsky, S. The roles of emotional stress and diet in the etiology of diabetes mellitus. *Quarterly Bulletin of Northwestern University Medical School*, 1953, **27**, 2.

Slauson, P.F., Flynn, W.R., & Kollar, E.J. Psychological factors associated with the onset of diabetes mellitus. *Journal of the American Medical Association*, 1963, **185**, 96–100.

Smith, M.A. Menstrual disorders: Incidence and relationship to attitudes, manifest needs and school achievement in college freshman women. Doctoral dissertation, University of Denver, 1971.

Sobel, H.J. Coping with physical illness—Cancer. *Behavioral Medicine Newsletter*, 1979, **1**, 6–9.

Stearns, S. Self-destructive behavior in young patients with diabetes mellitus. *Diabetes*, 1959, **8**, 379.

Stearns, S. Some emotional aspects of the treatment of diabetes mellitus and the role of the physician. *New England Journal of Medicine*, 1953, **249**, 471–476.

Steinmark, S.W. & Borkovec, T.D. Active and placebo treatment effects on moderate insomnia under counter-demand and positive demand instructions. *Journal of Abnormal Psychology*, 1974, **83**, 157–163.

Stenn, P.G., Mothersill, K.J., & Brooke, R.I. Biofeedback and a cognitive behavioral approach to treatment of myofascial pain dysfunction syndrome. *Behavior Therapy*, 1979, **10**, 29–36.

Stephens, J.W. & Marbel, A. Place and value of summer camps in management of juvenile diabetes, observations and a report of activities at a camp for diabetic boys in 1950. *American Journal of Diseases of Children*, 1951, **82**, 3.

Stone, M.L. & Warshaw, L.J. Dysmenorrhea. *Journal of Occupational Medicine,* 1960, **2,** 278.

Tasto, D.L. & Chesney, M.A. Muscle relaxation for primary dysmenorrhea. *Behavioral Therapy,* 1974, **5,** 668–672.

Tattersall, R. Brittle diabetes. *Clinics in Endocrinology and Metabolism,* 1977, **6**(2), 403–419.

Treuting, T.F. The role of emotional factors in the etiology course of diabetes mellitus: A review of the recent literature. *Journal of Medical Science,* 1962, **244,** 93–110.

Tubbs, W. & Carnahan, C. Clinical biofeedback for primary dysmenorrhea. *Proceedings of the Biofeedback Research Society,* 1976, **1,** 85.

Turk, D., Sobel, H., Follick, M., & Youkilis, H. A method of sequential criterion analysis for assessing coping. Paper presented at the 12th Annual Meeting of AABT, Chicago, 1978.

Tyler, E.T. Contraceptive control: The pill is best for most. In D.P. Lauler (Ed.) *Reproductive endocrinology.* New York: Medcom, 1973.

Vandenbergh, R.L., Sussman, K.E., & Vaughan, G.D. Effects of combined physical-anticipatory stress on carbohydrate-lipid metabolism in patients with diabetes mellitus. *Psychosomatics,* 1967, **3,** 16–19.

Vandenbergh, R.L., Sussman, K.E., & Titus, C.C. Effects of hypnotically induced acute emotional stress on carbohydrate and lipid metabolism in patients with diabetes mellitus, *Psychosomatic Medicine,* 1966, **28,** 382–389.

Watson, C. & Schuld, D. Psychosomatic factors in the etiology of neoplasms. *Journal of Consulting and Clinical Psychology,* 1977, **45,** 455–461.

Webb, W. & Agnew, H. Sleep and walking in a time-free environment. *Aerospace Medicine,* 1974, **45,** 617–622.

Weil, G. & Goldfried, M.R. Treatment of insomnia in an eleven-year old child through self-relaxation. *Behavior Therapy,* 1973, **4,** 282–294.

Weisman, A.D. *On dying and denying.* New York: Behavioral Publications, 1972.

Weisman, A.D. & Sobel, H.J. Coping with cancer through self-instruction: A hypothesis. *Journal of Human Stress,* March 1979, 3–8.

Weisman, A.D. & Worden, J.W. Psychosocial analysis of cancer deaths. *Omega,* 1975, **6,** 61–75.

Weisman, A.D. & Worden, J.W. The existential plight in cancer. Significance of the first 100 days. *International Journal of Psychiatry in Medicine,* 1976, **7,** 1–15.

White, P. Programs for the child with diabetes. In J.G. Cull & R.E. Hardy (Eds.) *Counseling and rehabilitating the diabetic.* Springfield, Ill.: Charles C Thomas, 1974.

Woodyatt, R.T. Diabetes mellitus. In R. Cecil (Ed.) *A textbook of medicine,* 4th ed. Philadelphia: Saunders, 1938.

Worden, J.W. & Sobel, H. Ego strength and psychosocial adaptation to cancer. *Psychosomatic Medicine,* 1978, **40,** 32-35.

Worden, J.W. & Weisman, A.D. The fallacy in post mastectomy depression. *American Journal of the Medical Sciences,* 1977, **273,** 169–175.

Yemm, R. Neurophysiologic studies of temporomandibular joint dysfunction. *Oral Science Reviews,* 1976, **7,** 31–53.

Yemm, R. Stress-induced muscle activity: A possible etiologic factor in denture soreness. *Journal of Prosthetic Dentistry,* 1972, **28,** 133.

Yemm, R. Variations in the electrical activity of the human masseter muscle occurring in association with emotional stress. *Archives of Oral Biology,* 1969, **14,** 873–878.

Concluding Remarks

Throughout this book, our primary intention was to demonstrate the manner in which behavioral psychology has manifested its scientific orientation and its technology in a new domain, behavioral medicine. Part 1 presented an overview of behavior therapy and its techniques as they relate to the amelioration of problems once regarded as primarily medical. Part 2, the crux and *raison d'être* of this book, demonstrated the efficacy of behavior therapy techniques in their direct service application to a wide variety of maladies which included hypertension, Raynaud's disease, ulcers, irritable bowel syndrome, strokes, spinal cord injuries, epilepsy, asthma, psoriasis, pain, headaches, cancer, and insomnia.

Every day, innovations in behavior therapy techniques are being made and are being applied to an ever increasing variety of malady. As this final page is being written, greater sophistication in theory, technique, research, and practice is promoting advances in behavioral medicine.

It should also be noted that this increased sophistication bears not only on direct service applications, but also on two other very important facets of behavioral medicine. These facets pertain to the modification of inadequate or inconsistent adherence to a medical regime and, of equal importance, to modifying behaviors that constitute risk factors for health. Our forthcoming volume will address these facets of behavioral medicine as well as some of the more tangential, but no less important, aspects of this domain, such as orthomolecular medicine, holistic medicine, and clinical ecology.

In conclusion, we believe this book represents a current and comprehensive account of behavioral medicine as it relates to direct service applications, and demonstrates some of the ways in which behavioral psychology and medicine have formed an alliance in the delivery of health services.

Appendix

BIOFEEDBACK INSTRUMENTATION

An overview of biofeedback instrumentation is presented as preparatory to a more adequate appreciation of biofeedback procedures. It is useful to make a distinction between two types of biofeedback units: self-contained and modular. A self-contained unit includes its own power supply, generally either batteries or a 110 VAC line. Modular units share a DC (5-, 12-, or 28-volt) power supply system which is itself powered by a 110 VAC line. Almost all the major biofeedback equipment companies market self-contained units, and this type would appear to be the most frequently utilized instrument. Self-contained units offer several advantages. First, the initial cost is lower, given that one or two response modalities, such as EMG and skin temperature are desired. Second, each system can be used independently either with a single client simultaneously or two different clients simultaneously in different places. Finally, they require little or no programming; that is, the electrical circuits are fixed with the exception of a few switches and dials.

In contrast, modular units have a higher initial cost since they include one power supply that is large enough to allow for addition of modules at a later time. Generally speaking, this type of unit does not allow for simultaneous utilization for two different clients. Modular units require initial programming and subsequent programming is necessary to fully utilize the adaptive capacities of the system. The major advantage of a modular system is its adaptability, which allows for the addition of modules that improve and extend system capabilities. Thus, modular systems have a greater likelihood of keeping abreast of technological advances and expansion of capabilities.

Before considering the instrumentation for the various physiological responses, we will consider the instrumentation employed in data acquisition. Conceivably, biofeedback training can occur with little or no data acquisition. However, as mentioned previously, it is our opinion that the continuous recording of objectively quantified information concerning physiological responses is one of the major contributions of biofeedback methods. It is desirable to have a data acquisition system that insures the availability of the maximum amount of utilizable information about a given physiological response as well as the maximum number of possible physiological responses.

Simultaneous recordings of a number of physiological responses are limited by the practicalities of the situation, such as the cost and availability of equipment and the capacity for automatic recording of the data. A multichannel strip chart recording of the output of the biofeedback equipment is most frequently utilized. Its advantage is the retention of the maximum amount of raw data. The disadvantage is the necessity of transforming the raw data (lines on chart paper) into the data utilized clinically (numerical data such as skin temperature in degrees Fahrenheit or muscle potential in average microvolt seconds over successive temporal units). In addition, chart recorders often require additional skills and time to set-up and calebrate. An alternative is to utilize a multichannel printer to record the output in a numerical and clinically useful form. Data transformation problems are eliminated and the additional skills and time are obviated; however, the raw data is no longer available for retrospective analysis. At this point in time, the printer, interfaced with biofeedback equipment, would appear to be the best solution to data recording requirements. Of course, a strip chart and printer recording can be utilized simultaneously. In addition, microprocessor interfaced with computers results in increases in the possible transformation and recording of data as well as sophisticated programmed presentation of stimulus conditions. Such a system is likely to be practical as production increases and costs are reduced. Finally, data recording can be accomplished semiautomatically by man-machine interface. That is, the therapist or biofeedback technician may record by hand the output of apparatus that transforms data and presents it in numerical form by light-emitting diodes. There are, of course, limitations to this procedure, as either the number of different physiological responses or the frequency of recording is limited.

In general, most of the instrumentally measured physiological responses have application as an objective, quantifiable measure of physiological arousal subject to response specificity limitations; that is, specific stereotype responses or response patterns may be identified as valid indices of arousal for specific individuals, but as a specific response index across individuals it does not appear to be valid.

Electromyograph

The EMG detects the amount of electrical potential in microvolts emanating from the muscle units in proximity to the recording electrodes, thus muscle contraction and relaxation is assessed. At this time, EMG appears to be the most widely used biofeedback instrument. It has been utilized in neuromuscular reeducation, e.g., spasticity, dorsiflexion, torticollis, facial paralysis, stroke-paralysis, cerebral palsy, dysteria, hemiplegia, and fecal incontinence. It has also been used in lowered-arousal, or relaxation-related biofeedback training in the amelioration of hypertension, tension headache, migraine headache, Raynaud's disease, arthritis, bruxism, myofascial pain syndrome, temperomandibular joint syndrome, low back pain, blepharospasm, and dysphagia.

The electrical activity recorded by an EMG is produced when muscle fibers contract. Muscle fibers are grouped into motor units, wherein the fibers contract almost simultaneously. The amount of contraction of a muscle is a function of the number of motor units in that muscle that are activated at a given time. The electrical activity of a single motor unit may be recorded; this is generally accomplished through the utilization of needle electrodes that are placed directly in the muscle (Basmajian, 1974). It appears that an individual is able to learn specific discriminative control of a single motor unit in a very short period of time (Basmajian, 1963; Hefferline & Perera, 1963). However, for most biofeedback applications surface electrodes are placed on the skin directly over the muscle or muscles of interest. Whether the activity recorded by an EMG is localized and thus specific to one muscle or motor unit, or is more generalized thus including several muscles, is a function of the size and placement of the electrodes.

EMG's record electrical activity of certain frequencies is referred to as the band pass. Typically, the band pass width is from 30 to 95 to 1000 cycles per second (cps). Usually, the band pass for a particular instrument is fixed but some models allow for adjustment of the band pass width. In general, the wider the band pass the greater the muscular activity recorded, other things being equal. Thus, if one is attempting to make a comparison of the EMG levels of a client with those reported in the literature, one should be sure to use the same band pass width. Units frequently have 60 cps and 95 or 100 cps filters to eliminate interference from household current and heartbeats, respectively. An integrator is necessary for quantification of the EMG signal. This instrument summates the raw signal and represents it as a quantified average over some unit of time, usually from 10 to 120 seconds. However, integrators vary with respect to the type of average employed; i.e., root mean square, average, peak to peak. Although formulas may be utilized to transform one type of averaging into another, this variation in equipment along with differences in band pass and other differences such as muscle development, fat tissue and skin electrode impedance, make comparison of EMG values across studies difficult. In addition to quantifying muscle activity in microvolt units for specified time periods, quantification may take the form of the number of time units during which muscular activity is above or below a selected microvolt level (Rugh & Solberg, 1975). It may also be noted that biofeedback equipment in general, including EMG, should have a shock hazard safety feature. This involves optical isolation of any line-powered (nonbattery powered) units.

Selection of the body site for electrode placement is, of course, dependent on the purpose of the recording. Precise placement and sometimes small electrodes (approximately .5 cm diameter) are necessary if one wishes to record the activity of specific muscles, as is generally done in neuromuscular reeducation (Owen, Toomin, & Taylor, 1975). This is particularly the case with smaller muscles, such as those involved in facial expressions, which have been utilized in the study of depression (Schwartz, Fair, Salt *et al.,* 1976) and bruxism (Rugh, Perlis, & Diseralli, 1977). Basmajian (1974), and Owen, Toomin and Taylor (1975) provide additional information about anatomy and muscular function relevant for specific muscle applications.

In most cases, however, muscle tension of a large number of muscles from an area of the body is recorded rather than that of specific muscles. This approach results in a better index of general muscle tension. For this purpose, average-sized electrodes (approximately 1 cm in diameter) are generally placed over the frontalis muscle. Such a placement is widely used and has the advantage of being readily assessible because it is not covered by clothing or hair. EMG recordings taken in this manner do not represent specific activity of the frontalis muscle, rather they reflect activity from the muscles of the face, head, and neck down to about the first rib, and includes sensitivity to activities such as swallowing, breathing, and movements of the jaws, tongue, lips, eyelids, and eyeballs (Basmajian, 1976).

Next to the frontalis placement, forearm extension and trapezius placements have been most frequently employed. Procedurally, it would be possible, though somewhat less than practical, to utilize multiple sets of electrodes located at different sites that may involve the frontalis, forearm, trapezius, and leg. Utilizing a switching device, one EMG can be utilized to record for 10 seconds from all four sites as they are sequentially and repetitively scanned every minute. Still another approach to the recording of general muscle activity is the wrist-to-wrist placement which purports to measure upper body tension (Gregg, 1979). Similarly, an ankle-to-ankle placement can be utilized for lower body tension (Fuller, 1977).

Once the placement site is determined, the electrodes are usually affixed in a row or triangular pattern with the ground equidistant from the recording electrodes. It should be observed that in order to avoid excessive impedance, placement over scar tissue, tattoos, skin blemishes, edema spots, or pulsatile arteries should be avoided (Adkins, 1978). It is generally desirable to locate the exact site where each electrode is to be placed and mark the site with a skin-marking pencil. A ruler may be helpful in accomplishing this and the electrodes are generally placed 1½ to 2 inches apart, less distance for the smaller muscles. Cap type silver/silver chloride electrodes are most commonly used. Preparation of the placement site is critical to achieving electrical contact, and the area should be washed with an abrasive soap or an abrasive cleansing cream and rinsed with water (preferably with distilled water). An alternative is to rub the placement area briskly with a cottonball saturated with alcohol or acetone. For placement on areas such as the arm, neck, or leg, it may be necessary to gently abraid the skin with fine sandpaper, cosmetic pumice stone, or an ink eraser (Adkins, 1978). While the area is drying, one side of a double-face adhesive collar (washer) should be attached to the already clean electrode. This is done by peeling off the paper covering and pressing the exposed adhesive surface to the bottom of the plastic cup of the electrode, taking care to align the centers of the collar and the electrode.

Next, the electrode cup should be filled with electrode cream. The cup should be filled in such a manner that there are no air spaces or air bubbles, and the electrode cream rises just above the plastic rim of the electrode cup as viewed from the side. If too much electrode cream has been applied, use the paper covering you peeled off the adhesive collar to remove the excess. Too little electrode cream generally results in poor electrical contact. On the other hand, excess electrode cream runs underneath the adhesive disk when it is applied to the skin. This may result in other problems, such as the electrode coming loose or falling off during the session, or the cream from two electrodes may come into contact and cause a signal short-circuit. At this point, it may be desirable to relocate and re-mark the placement site for each electrode and to apply a small amount of electrode cream to each site and rub it into the skin with a cottonball or cotton swab.

Next, the paper covering should be peeled away from the other side of the adhesive collar and each electrode affixed to the prepared site. As soon as this is done, the impedance between all possible pairs of the three electrodes should be checked either with an ohmmeter or an electrode check function built into the biofeedback equipment. Essentially, electrical resistance is being measured across the wires leading from sets of two electrodes, thereby assessing each time the electrical contact at the skin of two electrodes. Each manufacturer specifies the acceptable resistance levels for equipment. In general, the resistance should not exceed 50,000 ohms, and the difference between any pairs of electrodes should not exceed 10,000 to 20,000 ohms. If these criterion are achieved, the ends of the electrode wires should then be attached to the electrode cable and the directions provided in the manufacturers manual should be followed for operation of the apparatus. Practice in attaching electrodes is necessary and should be continued until one is able to reliably attain good electrical contact. It should be noted that electrodes may also be attached to the client by utilizing an elastic (rubber) band, the diameter of which is adjustable. Finally, an alternative approach to electrode attachment, which provides very low impedance in minimal time and in difficult placements, is presented by Gans (1979).

Vasomoter Responses

The peripheral vasomotor response is the constriction or dilation of the smooth muscles surrounding the small arterioles near the surface of the skin. This response controls the amount of blood flow through the peripheral vessels. Skin temperature may be utilized as an index of the vasomotor response, given relatively constant internal body temperature and environmental temperature. Blood flow and, hence, vasomotor responding may also be measured by a photoplethysmograph, which is based on the amount of light transmitted, or the amount and wavelength of light reflected by the body tissue. A photoplethysmographic index of blood flow may be used to measure the peripheral vasomotor response (e.g., of the finger; Friar & Beatty, 1976) or the cephalic vasomotor response (e.g., of the temporal artery; Koppman, McDonald, & Kunzel, 1974; Feurstein, Adams, & Beiman, 1976).

Peripheral vasoconstrictin results from sympathetic nervous system arousal and is, thus, influenced by environmental and emotional stress in many clients as well as by environmental substances, such as alcohol, tobacco, and carbon dioxide. Thus, in general, vasodilation and increased peripheral blood flow reflect lowered arousal.

The peripheral vasomotor response has been employed primarily in the treatment of migraine headache and Raynaud's disease, with some initial application to hypertension, psoriasis, menstrual cramps, arthritis, pain, and asthma (Fuller, 1977; Green & Green, 1979). It also has applications in the assessment of sympathetic arousal and sexual arousal. The cephalic vasomotor response appears to have been utilized almost exclusively with migraine headache.

A photoplethysmographic approach to measurement of vasomotor responding possesses several advantages. It may be utilized to measure either peripheral or cephalic response and, simultaneously, it provides a measure of pulse rate. The difficulty with this measure is the relative absence of research on its application relative to those employing a skin temperature measure. There is, thus, less information available as to normative data and clinical procedures. In addition, the necessary equipment is at the present time less readily available. This measurement approach yields two components quantified in units of millivolts per selected unit of time (i.e., 30 seconds). Blood volume pulse represents relative changes in blood flow and vessel diameter with each heartbeat. Blood volume level indicates that level upon which the blood volume pulses are superimposed (Feurstein & Adams, 1977). The photoelectric transducer may be positioned over the right or left zygomaticofacial branch of the superficial temporal artery (forehead) or the ventral surface of the index finger. It may be held in place by an elastic band or micropose tape with care being taken not to occlude blood flow. The light history of the transducer should be controlled by ensuring that it is not excessively exposed to light prior to placement. Additional references concerning photoplethysmography are: Brown, 1967; Cook, 1974; Novelly, Perona, & Ax, 1973; and Weinman, 1967.

A skin temperature approach to measurement of the vasomotor response has been widely employed. This response is relatively slow changing and can be recorded at 1- to 5-minute intervals by hand if necessary. The type of thermometer used is relatively easy to operate, inexpensive, and somewhat free of movement artifacts. An additional advantage results from the possibility of utilizing this device to record respiration rate (Gunderson, 1971). The thermister is easily and quickly attached relative to the placement of EMG electrodes. It may be attached by an elastic band, velcro band, or micropore tape, again taking care not to occlude blood flow. A common error involves fastening one or more layers of micropore tape tightly around the finger circumference. This should be avoided by using a single layer of tape applied with light pressure. The placement site most generally employed is the distal digit of the dominant hand, although placement may be varied (i.e., any of the other 19 digits on the hands and toes) within or between sessions if a more generalized response is desired. In addition, a number of conditions are necessary to minimize artifacts. Room temperature should be recorded at the beginning and the end of the session. For optimum results, room temperature should be held constant, ideally around 75°, and room temperature stability should be checked periodically. Whenever possible, it is desirable to record room and skin temperature simultaneously. If room temperature variations of more than 1.5°F occur during a session, steps such as reducing drafts should be taken to correct the situation. It is also recommended that outside temperature be recorded.

A client habituation period of 30 minutes in the biofeedback room (perhaps encouraging the client to read or listen to music) should help to mitigate the effects of differences in outside temperature and other factors such as vigorous exercise (e.g., the client running up the stairs because he is late). An alternative is to utilize a stability criterion such as four consecutive minutes of no variation greater than 0.25°F (Taub & School, 1978). It is also suggested that extreme changes in the clothing worn by the client be avoided in order to further stabilize conditions of the session. For instance, tight clothing or jewelry effect blood flow. Also, during feedback per se, the position of the hand relative to the body should likewise be constant, generally resting on the arm of a reclined chair or on a framed screen lapboard. The thermister and its point of contact with the finger is kept in contact with air, that is, it does not touch anything else that results in an insulation effect. Instructions to move as little as possible (especially the hands) and to avoid changing normal breathing patterns are also helpful. In summary, all the conditions and parameters related to the biologic systems being measured must be held as constant as possible if reliable measurement is to be obtained.

Blood Pressure

The pressure in the blood vessels is continually varying. As the left ventricle of the heart contracts, the maximum or systolic pressure is attained, and, conversely, as it relaxes the minimum or diastolic pressure occurs. Blood pressure valves are expressed in millimeters of mercury as a ratio-systolic/diastolic. Readings in excess of 140/90 mm Hg are considered hypertensive. The mechanisms involved in the regulation of blood pressure are relatively complex (Shapiro & Surwit, 1976). In general, blood pressure is a function of cardiac output (the heart) and total peripheral resistance (the vasculature). Cardiac output is primarily a function of the amount of blood pumped (stroke volume) and the rate of contraction of the left ventricle (heart rate). Peripheral resistance is primarily a function of the degree of constriction of dilation of the tiny blood vessels (arterioles). Both cardiac output and peripheral resistance are to some extent controlled by the autonomic nervous system. Increased sympathetic arousal may lead to higher blood pressure, and decreased sympathetic arousal to lower blood pressure (Blanchard & Epstein, 1978). Hyperarousal of the sympathetic nervous system may be a major factor in the elevation of blood pressure in the early stages of essential hypertension, particularly in individuals susceptible as a function of factors, such as genetic, constitutional, obesity, smoking, or particular emotional-behavioral patterns (Shapiro & Surwit, 1976).

The measurement of blood pressure has its primary application in the assessment and treatment of essential hypertension. Blood pressure is not easily monitored on a continuous basis as would be desirable for biofeedback purposes. A number of relatively expensive and complex automated blood pressure biofeedback systems have been devised for research purposes. Generally, such systems are not available as a complete unit from a commercial source; however, this may not be the case in the future assuming a more satisfactory system is developed. Schneider (1978) has reviewed these blood pressure biofeedback systems and concluded that their major shortcoming was a failure to provide near continuous feedback. That is, relatively large periods (30 to 120 seconds per inflation trial) of blood pressure cuff deflation, during which biofeedback information is not available, are necessary. Consequently 30 to 50% or more of the biofeedback session is lost. Elder, Longacre, Welsh, and McAfee (1977) were able to overcome this problem by utilizing two blood pressure cuffs, one on each arm; however, an additional difficulty arises in attaining exact microphone placement in both arms.

The second major shortcoming of these systems is the requirement of relatively high cuff pressures during the major portion of their inflation periods. This increases the probability that the client will experience pain or discomfort during the procedure. Another shortcoming is that most of these systems are limited to binary feedback as to whether the client's blood pressure has increased or decreased in contrast to analogue feedback, which also provides information as to the absolute blood pressure. Schneider (1978) presented a new method that appears to mitigate these shortcomings. In his procedure, the blood pressure cuff is automatically inflated and deflated, as is generally done, but the inflation-deflation cycle is rapid (3 to 6 seconds) when compared to other techniques. Visual analogue feedback is accomplished employing two mercury columns that give the absolute blood pressure for the preceding and current measurement. With auditory feedback added, this system would appear to hold great promise. However, currently, it is relatively untried.

At the present time, we suggest the use of a manual sphygnomanometer (similar to those used in a general practioner's office) for clinical applications of blood pressure biofeedback. Typically, a blood pressure cuff is wrapped around the upper arm and inflated by manually squeezing a rubber bulb to a pressure of 200 mm Hg or 30 mm Hg above the client's last systolic blood pressure reading. At this point, the cuff pressure occludes the flow of blood through the brachial artery. The cuff is then deflated slowly until the first regularly (with each heart beat) appearing Korotkoff sound appears as indicated by a beeping tone and a flashing light (the typical sphygmomanometer utilizes a stethoscope to monitor K sounds). The K sound results upon each heart beat as the blood just begins to flow through the artery. The systolic blood pressure is read from the pressure gauge at this point. Deflation is then continued until the K sounds first cease. Blood flow is no longer restricted as the cuff pressure is equal to the resting pressure of the artery. The diastolic blood pressure is then read from the pressure gauge.

In closing this section, it may be mentioned that a small portable sphygmomanometer has been successfully employed for self-monitoring blood pressure (Beiman, Graham, & Ciminero, 1978; Kleinman, Goldman, Snow, & Korol, 1977; Krist & Engel, 1975) and for blood pressure biofeedback in the client's home environment (Krist & Engel, 1975). A written procedure for blood pressure self-monitoring and self-directed blood pressure biofeedback training using a portable sphygmomanometer is presented here because of its great potential for use in behavioral medicine applications.

Blood Pressure Self-Monitoring Procedure

Introduction

The following procedure is intended as a standardized procedure for measuring your own blood pressure. There are several variables which affect the blood pressure readings that you get, such as the position of your arm and amount of time since physical exertion (e.g., climbing stairs). For research purposes and for your own efforts to control your blood pressure, it is important that these factors be held constant so that you will know and the researchers will know that any changes in the blood pressure readings obtained are the result of real changes in your blood pressure and are not due simply to differences in the procedure used in obtaining the blood pressure readings. Therefore, the procedure outlined below should be followed exactly throughout the duration of your participation in the research project and in your continued efforts to control your blood pressure.

Time

Throughout your participation in this research project you will be asked to take your blood pressure on three occasions each day and obtain three readings of both systolic and diastolic pressure on each occasion. The suggested times for obtaining these readings are (a) shortly after awakening in the morning and preferably after voiding, (b) shortly before eating lunch, and (c) shortly before going to sleep at night.

Preparation

When you are ready to begin measuring your blood pressure, sit quietly with a minimum of physical exertion for at least 15 minutes in order to eliminate the chance of obtaining abnormally high readings due to recent physical activity. During this resting period, record on the data card provided the exact time that you began this procedure. Also, during the resting period, avoid drinking coffee, tea, or soft drinks containing caffeine and avoid smoking.

Assume a seated position at a desk or table, where you can rest your nondominant arm at about the same level as your heart. It is important that you be able to rest this arm with the palm turned upward and the arm extended so that it will rest almost perfectly still while blood pressure readings are being taken because movements of the arm may cause false readings. It is also important that you assume as closely as possible the same position each time you take your blood pressure. The position you assume must, therefore, be comfortable, particularly since the measurement procedure may require several minutes to complete. It is also recommended that the same physical arrangement be utilized as regularly as possible in taking your blood pressure readings so that you will be in approximately the same posture and environment from one day to the next when readings are taken. Thus, it may be necessary for you to develop a standardized setting for each of the three blood pressure monitoring occasions that occur each day. For example, you might have one standard setting for before-lunch measurement and another standard setting for after-waking measurement or you might develop a standard setting for taking your blood pressure at home and another for taking your blood pressure at work and a third for taking it in your car. You will probably need to try out several different arrangements in order to find the ones which are most comfortable and convenient for you.

Fitting the Equipment

While resting quietly, remove the blood pressure cuff from its carrying case. Before attaching the cuff to the pressure gauge unit (unless they are permanently fixed together), slide the cuff up your left arm making sure that no clothing is between the cuff and your arm. The hoses which go to the pressure gauge and the inflation bulb should be on the side of the cuff toward your hand. Pull the loose end of the cuff through the metal "D" ring until the cuff is snug around your arm but will slide up or down, then wrap the loose end of the cuff back under and around your arm and press together the velcro tape to secure the cuff in position. To facilitate future use of the cuff, once the circumference of the cuff is adjusted properly, a dab of fingernail polish or a red felt tip pen can be used to mark the distance the end of the cuff extends around the body of the cuff. In the future the velcro tape can be secured using these marks and the cuff simply slid over the hand and up the arm.

When the cuff has been secured around the arm snugly, rotate the cuff and slide it either up or down until the dot on the cuff—just above where the rubber hoses go into the cuff—is on the inside of your arm over the large artery near the hollow of your elbow where your arm bends. This artery can be found by feeling for the pulse of the artery. Straighten your arm completely and use the index finger of the other hand. The artery is located with the arm outstretched and palm up, about ½ inch to the bodyside of the center of the arm just above the hollow of the elbow. When the cuff has been properly positioned, attach the air hose to the pressure gauge and plug the microphone jack into the receptacle at the bottom of the gauge unit. Rotate the air flow valve screw on the bulb clockwise in order to close the air flow valve. The valve does not have to be closed very tightly in order to prevent air from escaping the cuff. Place the pressure gauge in a convenient location where the sphygmomanometer dial can be easily read. *Do not turn on the power switch.*

Taking Your Blood Pressure

Inflate the cuff quickly by repeatedly squeezing the bulb with your free hand. Raise the pressure in the cuff to about 30 mm above your last systolic pressure reading or 200 mm Hg. The systolic pressure is the larger of the two blood pressure readings (usually above 110 mm) and indicates the amount of pressure required to just close off the artery. Move the sphygmomanometer power switch to the "on" position. You will generally get an immediate "beep" sound and the light on the gauge will flash. If the unit continues to "beep" and the light continues to flash for more than 5 seconds and you feel sure that your arm is not moving, deflate the cut by turning the air flow valve screw in a counterclockwise direction. Wait 15 to 30 seconds (count i.e., 1001, 1002) after the cuff is completely deflated and then repeat the procedure raising the cuff pressure an additional 30 mm. *Be sure to move the power switch to the "off" position during inflation.*

When the cuff has been inflated and unit turned on, if the unit is not continuously "beeping" and flashing", begin decreasing the pressure in the cuff by turning the air flow valve screw slightly in a counter-clockwise direction so that the needle of the sphygmomanometer is falling at the rate of about 2 to 4 mm per second (1 to 2 marks). Continue decreasing the pressure in the cuff, keeping your arm as stationary as possible, until the unit "beeps" and "flashes." Immediately close the air flow valve by turning the screw clockwise. The unit should continue "beeping" and "flashing" in a regular manner corresponding to your pulse rate. If this is indeed occurring, read your systolic blood pressure from the sphygmomanometer dial and *record the reading on the form provided.* If the unit does not continue to "beep" and "flash" regularly, you probably have a false reading and should continue to decrease the pressure in the cuff as before until you get another "beep" and "flash." Shut the air flow valve immediately as before to see if you are getting regular "beeps" and "flashes." If so, it is your systolic blood pressure. Record the reading from the sphygmomanometer dial. If the unit is still not "beeping" and "flashing" in a regular manner, continue decreasing the pressure following the same procedure until regularly spaced "beeps" and "flashes" occur. If after these three efforts regularly spaced "beeps" and "flashes" are not obtained, deflate the cuff completely, wait 30 seconds, and begin the procedure again.

After your systolic pressure has been obtained and recorded according to the above procedure, again begin to reduce the cuff pressure by turning the air flow valve screw counterclockwise slightly so that the needle of the sphygmonometer falls at the rate of about 2 to 4 mm per second (1 to 2 marks). Continue decreasing the cuff pressure until the unit stops "beeping" and "flashing". Close the air flow valve *immediately* by turning the screw in a clockwise direction. At this point the unit should not be "beeping" and flashing" or should at least "beep" only very infrequently. This is your diastolic pressure. If the unit begins "beeping" and "flashing" at regular intervals within a few seconds, again reduce the cuff pressure until the regular "beeping" and "flashing" ceases while the cuff pressure is held stable for 5 seconds. Record the sphygmomanometer reading at this point.

Decrease the cuff pressure to zero. Wait at least 30 seconds (count) and repeat the entire procedure. Continue until you have taken and recorded both blood pressure readings three times.

Blood Pressure Self-Monitoring Procedure Checklist

Before Starting

Follow the directions in the "preparation" paragraph of instructions.
Have the Home Record Form or postcard handy to record your readings.

Preparing the Equipment

Connect the microphone plug to the gauge unit (if necessary).
Be sure the unit is turned off.
Slide the cuff on your nondominant arm and adjust to fit (at the bottom of the cuff).
Find the brachial artery and make sure the dot on the cuff is over it.

Taking the Blood Pressure

Hold or place the gauge so you can easily read it.
Turn the air valve clockwise to close it (Not too tight).
Inflate the cuff to about 30 mm above your last systolic pressure or 200 mm.
Turn the switch on.

Slowly release air pressure by turning the air valve counterclockwise.

Watch the light, not the gauge needle.

When the light comes on, close the air valve (the unit should be beeping and flashing regularly).

Read your systolic pressure on the gauge and record it.

Release air pressure again.

Watch the light.

When the light goes out and the beeping stops, close the air valve (the unit should not beep and flash) and record your diastolic pressure.

Open the air valve completely by turning it counterclockwise.

Turn the unit off.

Wait 30 seconds and repeat the procedure.

Take three blood pressure readings and record them each time you take your pressure.

Putting the Equipment Away

Be sure the unit is turned off.

Cuff should be completely deflated.

Care of the Blood Pressure Unit

Don't drop or shake.

Avoid hitting things against the unit.

Keep away from heat or strong sunlight.

Avoid getting the cuff or gauge wet.

Store carefully when not in use.

Blood Pressure Biofeedback Training Procedure

Introduction

During this training period, you will be practicing biofeedback techniques for lowering blood pressure. The place you choose should be suitable for both recording and practice. Record your blood pressure before practice in the usual manner, then follow the instructions for biofeedback practice. When you have completed 15 minutes of biofeedback, record your blood pressure again. Record your blood pressure and practice the biofeedback procedure three times each day.

Biofeedback Procedure

You have been monitoring your blood pressure for some time now and should be completely familiar with the blood pressure monitoring procedure. You are now ready to begin the biofeedback training period of this study where you will learn to control your systolic blood pressure. To a large extent, this is a trial and error process. Even people who have learned to control their blood pressure very effectively cannot satisfactorily explain how they do it. It seems to be similar to trying to tell someone how to wiggle his ears: the learning is very individualized.

What works for one person will not necessarily work for someone else, so you will need to find the way that works for you. Whatever strategy you choose to try, it is particularly important to assume a passive attitude, that is, be attentive, but just let it happen without trying to *make* anything happen. Don't try to force yourself to make your blood pressure go down; instead, *let* it go down. While you are learning to control blood pressure, try to avoid becoming discouraged if you don't succeed right away. Learning to control bodily processes frequently seems slow, but if you continue to practice reductions will eventually occur. The blood pressure instrument you have been using to monitor your blood pressure can and will be used as a biofeedback device to provide you with information regarding your systolic blood pressure.

Begin biofeedback practice by utilizing the same procedure you have been employing to record your blood pressure; however, immediately upon detection of your systolic blood pressure, hold the cuff pressure constant by turning the air flow valve off. Then close your eyes and let the "beeping" and the "flashing" go away. When these signals stop or decrease in frequency, you have reduced your blood pressure below the level indicated on the gauge. Decreases in systolic pressure are almost always accompanied by proportional decreases in diastolic pressure. Whether or not the signals go away, at the end of the trial, release the cuff pressure and rest. Each training trial will last approximately 30 seconds, and there will be a 30-second break between trials. The cassette tape has recorded tones to signal the beginning and end of biofeedback trials. Before beginning a practice session, be sure the tape is completely rewound. You will continue to record your blood pressure three times each day, taking three readings each time. Immediately after you have finished recording your pressure, begin the cassette tape with instructions for blood pressure biofeedback training. A 15-minute interval with tone signals every 30 seconds for practice is recorded on the tape.

Blood Pressure Biofeedback Procedure Checklist

1. Prior to carrying out the procedure, set up the tape recorder, with rewound cassette in place, nearby where you can turn it on and off without getting up.
2. Complete the blood pressure monitoring procedures, as previously instructed.
3. After completing the blood pressure monitoring procedure, leave the cuff in place but completely deflate and rest for approximately 30 seconds.

4. Turn on the tape recorder.
5. At the sound of the first tone, inflate the cuff to about 30 mm above your last self-monitored systolic reading.
6. Turn the gauge unit power switch to "on" and reduce the pressure in the cuff until the unit *just* begins "beeping" and "flashing" at regular intervals. Immediately close the air flow valve.
7. Close your eyes and begin practicing whatever strategy you have chosen to employ to allow the "beeping" and "flashing" stop. If it does, continue with whatever strategy you are employing until the next tone occurs. If it does not stop or slow, continue without becoming discouraged.
8. The second tone signals the end of the trial. Open the air flow valve and let pressure in the cuff drop to zero.
9. At the sound of the next tone, inflate the cuff and repeat the procedure above. Continue repeating this procedure for 15 minutes.
10. Complete the self-monitoring procedure a second time.

Heart Rate

A heartbeat is the successive muscle contraction and relaxation of the atria and ventricles of the heart. Although the heartbeat originates in the heart muscle itself and is not directly dependent on the nervous system, there is some nerve control over heart action. The heart is connected to the central nervous system by nerve fibers from both branches of the autonomic nervous system. In general, parasympathetic stimulation slows heartbeat and sympathetic stimulation increases it. Of course, such influences on heart rate are superimposed on a homeostatic regulatory system, this system is based on a control center located in the medulla that is under continual influence of vasomotor reflex activity, which includes sensory receptors located in the heart and other portions of the circulatory system (i.e., carotid sinus) that are sensitive to abnormal levels of heart rate and blood pressure (Grollman, 1978).

Heart rate measures have found application with cardiac arrhythmias (generally done in an inpatient coronary care unit) and tachycardia with some initial attempts in utilization as a component in the treatment of essential hypertension. Heartbeats may be self-monitored manually at major vessels, such as the radial artery at the wrist. Of course, heart rate may be monitored in a similar manner utilizing a photoplethysmographic index, an acoustic index (K sounds during blood pressure measurement), or an electrical index. In its simplest form, heart rate may be quantified by counting and recording the number of beats that occur over successive 1-minute intervals. However, heart rate may be determined more rapidly (on a beat-by-beat basis) if the length of time between successive heartbeats (interbeat interval) is measured; heart rate is the reciprocal of this value (Blanchard & Epstein, 1978). The basic instrument for measuring heart rate is a cardiotachometer. Heart rate is also recorded as a portion of the complex of information gathered during an electrocardiogram (ECG). The electrical index of heartbeat, which is the basis of the ECG, has been most frequently employed in the measurement of heart rate. The electrical potential associated with each heartbeat is relatively large compared to other measurable biopotentials such as EMG, and is thus relatively easily recorded over a wide surface area of the body. Consequently, heart rate evidences few artifacts but is a possible artifact for other physiological measures based on the recording of electrical potentials. Although skin preparation is not a major consideration, proper electrode contact utilizing electrode cream is necessary. Standard ECG electrodes may be utilized and a variety of electrode sites is possible. A frequently utilized site involves placement of the recording electrode on the chest to the left of the sternum between the third and fourth ribs, the reference electrode on the left side midway between the front and back of the body between two ribs, and the ground electrode on the arm or leg (Gaarder & Montgomery, 1977). Another frequently used site requires placement of electrodes on both ankles and the right wrist. The attachment of photoplethysmographic transducers to placement sites (previously discussed under the section on vasomotor responses) is relatively easier than bioelectric transducers (electrodes). They also offer the additional advantage of providing information concerning blood flow.

Electrodermal Response

Electrodermal responding may be assessed in two different ways. The Galvonic Skin Response (GSR) is a measure of changes in resistance of the skin to an external (generated by the apparatus) current. The Skin Potential Response (SPR) is a measure of the changes in electrical potential of the skin (no external current is applied). The electrodermal response is directly related to the activity of the sweat glands, which is related to sympathetic nervous system arousal hypothesized in many cases to be indicative of emotional arousal. Different behavioral and emotional states (e.g., orienting response, startle response, fear, anger, arousing thoughts) produce similar or no electrodermal responses. In general, decreased skin resistance and increased skin potential is a reflection of increased sympathetic arousal.

It is necessary to hold room temperature relatively constant as skin resistance increases appreciably with decreases in temperature. Electrodes are generally placed on the fingers or palm approximately 2 cm apart. Silver-silver chloride electrodes (2 cm^{2+}) are utilized with electrode cream or silver impregnated cloth electrodes without cream (Fuller, 1977). The medial and lateral hypomalleolar areas of the ankle are an alternative recording site (Rickles & Day, 1968). GSR is frequently expressed in terms of conductance (mho), the reciprocal of resistance (ohm) and ranges between 10,000 and 800,000 ohms cm^2. SPR is measured as the electrical potential difference between the electrodes and varies up to 50 or 60 millivolts. Electrodermal responses have typically been quantified utilizing strip chart recording, and SPR may be quantified through the use of an integrator analogous to those used with an EMG.

Generally, two response measures of electrodermal activity are recorded. Response amplitude changes level with relative slowness and is considered to be indicative of general arousal. In contrast, response frequency is a relatively fast change in level, evidencing a latency of approximately 1.5 to 2 seconds (0.5-5 seconds) with a recovery to preresponse levels in 1 to 30 seconds (Edelberg, 1972). These phasic changes are considered to be in response to short-term stimuli such as thoughts, sounds, and other events. They are referred to as spontaneous GSR or SPR frequency and are the response characteristic typically used for electrodermal biofeedback. The criterion for a spontaneous GSR is 550 ohms or greater (Edleberg, 1967) within approximately 1.5 seconds. Spontaneous SPR has been defined as a change of 0.25 millivolt or greater within a time period of 3 seconds (Shapiro & Watanabe, 1971).

There appear to be no studies that demonstrate the clinical efficacy of electrodermal biofeedback for any specific disorder (Steiner & Arkin, 1978). Electrodermal measures have been utilized as an adjunct to psychotherapy and behavior therapy to facilitate awareness of internal arousal and con- committant stress stimuli (Toomin & Toomin, 1975; Wolpe, 1967; Wolpe & Flood, 1970). In this respect, it may be useful as an introduction to biofeedback to demonstrate mind-body interactions experientially (Fuller, 1977). Electrodermal responses have been utilized as a treatment component in the treatment of hypertension (Datey, 1977; Patel, 1973; Patel & North, 1975) hyperhidrosis (Fuller, 1977) asthma (Fuller, 1977), and childbirth pain (Gregg, 1979).

Electroencephalogram

The EEG is a product of the electrochemical activity of brain cells and reflects an average signal from the relatively synchronous firing of thousands of cortical neurons (Blanchard & Epstein, 1978). The recorded signals are typically of low voltage (less than 20 microvolts) with a frequency range from 0.5 to 50 cycles per second (Hz). Classically, four EEG rhythms are identified: delta (0.5-3 Hz) seen with deep dreamless sleep; theta (4-7Hz) seen in sleep onset and associated with twilight imagery; alpha (8-13 Hz, amplitude of 25-100 microvolts) monitored when a person is relaxed, drowsy, calm, and engaged in unfocused passive attention; and beta (14-30 + Hz), which is observed during focused attention, a high level of mental arousal, and active concentration (Fuller, 1977; Steiner & Arkin, 1978). Additionally, Sterman identified a sensorimotor rhythm (SMR) (12-14 Hz, 3-6 microvolts at operant level) associated with voluntary suppression of movement.

The major successful application of EEG is in the treatment of seizure disorders utilizing SMR biofeedback (Sterman, 1977), or normalization of EEG through biofeedback to suppress abnormally low frequency EEG activity, or to enhance alpha rhythm (Kuhlman, 1979). Although the validity of other applications is unclear at this time, several investigators have attempted to utilize alpha biofeedback in the treatment of headache or chronic pain (Gannon & Sternbach, 1971; McKenzie, Ehrisman, Montgomery, & Barnes, 1974; and Melzack & Perry, 1975). It has also been suggested that alpha biofeedback is useful in achieving mental relaxation with reduction of intrusive cognitions in cases of insomnia (Fuller, 1977).

EEG electrodes are generally flat disc or cup shaped and are not necessarily contained within a plastic holder. The metal surface may then be applied directly against the scalp. Skin preparation and electrode application is similar to that utilized with EMG electrodes. Although seldom used, sterile pin electrodes are an alternative. The pin electrodes may be easily and rapidly inserted through the alcohol moistened, raised, loose skin with only momentary pain experienced by the client. While sterile pin electrodes are advantageous in terms of ease of application, it appears that most patients prefer the disc or cup electrodes.

The ground electrode is generally placed on the ear lobe, or the bony mastoid area behind the ears, which are electrically quiet sites (Gaarder & Montgomery, 1977). The active and reference electrodes should be placed on either the left or the right hemisphere. Alpha is generally recorded from the occipital area although it is also present in the parietal area. The active electrode may be located one inch up and one inch to the left or right of the external occipital protuberance, which is the most prominent point directly above the center of the back of the neck. The reference electrode may be placed 2 inches to the left or right of the vertex. The vertex is a point on top of the head where two imaginary lines cross: one line goes from the nose across the top of the head to the external occipital protuberance, and the other goes from one external auditory meatus (hole in the ear) across the top of the head to the other. As with EMG signals, EEG signals may be integrated to form a resultant integrated amplitude measure. A percentage of time within the rhythm above and/or below a selected amplitude may also be employed.

Theta rhythm is generally recorded at a frontal-temporal site and beta rhythm at a frontal or central site. SMR is recorded over the sensorimotor area which is located in a band across the top of the head between the ears. One electrode is placed 10% of the interaural distance to the left or the right of vertex on the medial lateral plane and the second is placed approximately 20% below the first. In closing this section on measurement of the electrochemical activity of the brain, it is worth stressing the fact that many artifacts can effect one's results. For instance, alpha is subject to disturbance by a large variety of influences including general movements and eyes tensed in a position away from center (Gaarder & Montgomery, 1977). As a cautionary note, it should be remembered that considerable care must be taken to modulate or obviate all artifacts if valid measurements are to be obtained.

Other Physiological Responses

This section will make reference to a number of physiological response measures and instruments of importance in biofeedback, though used less frequently than those already described. Welgan (1974) and Whitehead, Renault and Golddiamond (1975) developed methods to monitor the stomach acid pH, which may be useful in the treatment of ulcers. Nikoomanesh, Wells, and Schuster (1973) were able to measure the pressure exerted by the lower esophageal sphincter in patients with esophageal reflex disorders. This method may also be applicable to pyloric sphincter dysfunction, which may be related to duodenal ulcers. Engel, Nikoomanesh, and Schuster (1974) utilized pressure transducers to measure contraction of the rectal sphincters and thereby employed biofeedback to successfully treat fecal incontinence. Furman (1973) utilized an electronic stethoscope to amplify bowel sounds (borborygmi) which are presumably related to intestinal motility, and biofeedback of bowel sounds was used in treating patients with irritable bowel syndrome. Hölzl (1979) also recorded gastrointestinal motility indirectly utilizing an electrogastrogram and a magnetogastrogram.

Barlow, Becker, Leitenberg, and Agras (1970) utilized a mechanical strain gauge to measure degree of penile circumference and therefore degree of penile erection. This approach has resulted in successful clinical applications to male sexual disorders, such as deviant sexual arousal and impotence (Abel & Blanchard, 1976). Blood flow measures (temperature, plethysmographic) may be used to assess sexual arousal in both females and males with potential applications similar to those just mentioned. A more complete consideration of instrumentation and application is given by Haynes (1978).

Blood alcohol level can be measured by breath analysis (Sobell & Sobell, 1973, 1975), with alcohol content being a function of the level of alcohol in the capillaries of the lungs. This measure has been utilized in conditioning blood alcohol level discrimination (Maisto & Adesso, 1977). It would appear that as the practice of biofeedback continues, new and varied instrumentation and techniques of measurement will be developed.

RELAXATION TRAINING INSTRUCTIONS

The first step in beginning relaxation training is to find a quiet place to practice. Since you will also be recording your measurements of some physiological response(s) (in this case your blood pressure) before and after practice, and using the tape recorder, try to find a place where you can complete the procedure and practice relaxation without having to move about. You should begin relaxation practice by sitting quietly in a comfortable position with your eyes closed. Deeply relax all your muscles, beginning at your feet and progressing to the top of your head. Allow each part of your body to become deeply relaxed. Breathe easily and freely through your nose. Become aware of your breathing. As you breathe out, say the word "one" silently to yourself. For example, breathe in, out "one"; in, out "one"; and continue this for 15 minutes as designated by the tone on the tape. Don't worry about whether you are successful in achieving a deep level of relaxation. Maintain a passive attitude and permit relaxation to occur at its own pace. Expect other thoughts to intrude. When these distracting thoughts occur, ignore them by thinking "oh well" and continue repeating "one." With practice, the response will come with less and less effort. Practice this technique three times each day, at your usual blood pressure recording times. At the end of the relaxation practice, mentally count from one to five and then open your eyes. This count from one to five is a brief awakening or transition time. It takes you from a relaxed state to an operational state. Remember to record blood pressure (or your measurements of other physiological responses) before and after each practice session. These instructions are taken from Hughes and Cunningham (1980) and are similar to those utilized by Benson (1975).

AUTOGENIC TRAINING

In autogenic training, we take advantage of the relationship between the activity of the nervous system and the blood flow in your fingers and toes. The procedure involves three important elements:

(1) Teaching you to relax, causing the sympathetic nervous system to slow down its activity and allow the blood vessels to open;

(2) Focusing your attention on the sensations that come from increases in blood flow—that is, warmth and pulsation, and

(3) Having you learn this response in the most favorable situation; then gradually teaching you to generalize the response to more difficult environments (colder).

A small thermometer gives you information about your success in controlling the temperature of your fingers. You are to use a thermometer when practicing with the autogenic tape. Place the base of the thermometer on the underside of the end of the middle finger of your dominant hand. Allow the other side of the base of the thermometer to remain open to the air. Leave the thermometer on your finger for about 2 minutes before taking a reading.

Every day you are to spend two 15-minute periods in a quiet room where the temperature is 75–80°F (no colder). In order to learn the technique, it is important that you practice where it is easier to raise your hand temperature. When you have mastered the technique, you can begin practicing in cooler places. If you have difficulty finding a room that is warm enough, you may want to practice in the bathroom after showering or warm a small room with a space heater.

Sit in a comfortable chair and allow yourself to relax with your arms resting on your knees and your head bending slightly forward. This position will assist you in increasing the blood flow in your hands. You should assume this position during your practices until you are getting increases in your finger temperature during each practice session (or at least 1 week). You may then sit in a more comfortable chair, resting your arms on the chair. Be sure that your fingers are not touching each other or the chair during your practice sessions.

Before you begin, put the thermometer on the middle finger of your dominant hand in the manner previously described. After about 2 minutes, take a temperature reading and record this temperature on a record sheet as "beginning temperature." Sit in the position previously described, play one side of the autogenic tape or utilize the autogenic scripts in written form and follow the instructions.

Script for Autogenic Tape, Side One

I feel quite quiet.

I am beginning to feel quite relaxed.

My right foot feels heavy and relaxed.

My left foot feels heavy and relaxed.

My ankles, knees, and hips feel heavy, relaxed and comfortable.

My abdomen and chest feel heavy and relaxed.

My neck, jaw, and forehead feel completely relaxed.

They feel comfortable and smooth.

My right arm feels heavy and relaxed.

My left arm feels heavy and relaxed.

My right hand feels heavy and relaxed.

My left hand feels heavy and relaxed.

Both of my hands feel heavy and relaxed.

Then, repeat to yourself, "My hands feel heavy and relaxed." Approximately every 15 seconds you will hear the tone. When you hear the tone, repeat to yourself, "My hands feel heavy and relaxed." Sound a tone every 15 seconds.

Script for Autogenic Tape, Side Two

I feel quite quiet.

My whole body is relaxed and comfortable.

My right arm is heavy and warm.

My left arm is heavy and warm.

My right hand is becoming warmer.

My left hand is becoming warmer.

Warmth is flowing into my hands.

They are warm.

I can feel the warmth flowing down into my right hand.

It is warm and relaxed.

I can feel the warmth flowing down into my left hand.

It is warm and relaxed.

My hands are warm and heavy.

Then, repeat to yourself, "My hands are warm and heavy." Approximately every 15 seconds you will hear a tone. When you hear the tone, repeat to yourself, "My hands are warm and heavy. My hands are warm and heavy." Sound a tone every 15 seconds. Notice sensations of pulsation growing in strength. Sometimes these feelings occur before you actually feel warm. They occur as your blood flow increases. During the tape, you may wish to occasionally glance at the thermometer. Some people find this helpful and others find it distracting. You will want to experiment and decide which way works best for you.

At the end of the tape, open your eyes and reorient to the room. This signals the end of your practice session. At this time, look down at your thermometer and record this temperature on your record sheet as "end temperature."

By the third week of the program, you should be able to produce consistent increases in the temperature of your fingers when you practice the autogenic training techniques in a warm room. For this to be useful to you, however, you must learn to produce skin temperature increases in the more demanding situations that you will encounter outside your home. We have found that the best way to accomplish this is for you to develop the habit of practicing briefly many times throughout the day.

We have previously described the connection between your emotions, the activity of your nervous system, and the blood flow in your fingers. Consequently, it is to be expected that any emotional stress will make hand temperature control more difficult. Therefore, we ask you to use stressful situations as cues to remind you to practice relaxing. Specifically, we would like for you to develop the habit of practicing relaxation each time you find yourself becoming annoyed.

Each time you encounter an annoying situation, such as a traffic jam, a long line in the supermarket, a busy signal on the telephone when you are trying to make an important call, stop yourself, take a long deep breath, slowly exhale, and while you are doing so, concentrate on the sensations of warmth and pulsation in your fingertips. No matter what you are doing, the trick is to stop for approximately 30 seconds and allow yourself to relax and focus on the sensations of increased blood flow to your fingers and toes. After 30 seconds have passed, go about your business regardless of how well you succeed in achieving relaxation. You will find that as you practice these brief relaxations (mini-practices), you will become better and better at producing increases in hand temperature in a short period of time. You should never extend a mini-practice session beyond 1 minute. If you do not feel relaxed, continue what you were doing and stop yourself the next time an annoying situation reminds you to practice. Learning to increase your skin temperature quickly is similar to learning to shoot at a target or hit a baseball. *Frequent practice is the key!* As the target shooter becomes more accurate or the baseball player a better hitter, you will find that you will be able to feel increases in skin temperature more reliably each time you practice.

Our experience has shown that most people notice minor annoyances many times during the day. Your goal should be to do approximately 30 mini-practices a day using a counter to keep a record of how many times you practice relaxation. At the end of the day, record on your record sheet the number of times you have practiced; and try to increase that number the next day. By the time you are practicing relaxation 30 times a day for 30 seconds, you will have developed the habit of keeping your body relaxed to the point where your hands will stay warmer more of the time.

When you have mastered the mini-practice techniques, you will find that your hands will be warmer even in cold weather. If you anticipate going into a cold environment (for instance, going out to your car on a cold day), stop and practice warming your hands before you leave the house. We have found that the technique is more useful when used to prevent the problem rather than to relieve a problem which has already developed. Once the body is chilled, it becomes more difficult to voluntarily produce temperature increases. Therefore, you should always practice relaxation to warm your hands before entering a cold environment.

WEEK 1

Sit in a comfortable chair in a warm room. Place the thermometer on the middle finger of your dominant hand. After 2 minutes, take a temperature reading, and record this temperature on your record sheet as "beginning temp." Sit in the described position, play Side One of the autogenic tape and follow the instructions. When the tape ends, take a temperature reading and record it on your record sheet as "end temp." Your finger temperature may sometimes decrease when you practice, especially while you are learning the technique. This is *not* unusual. Continue practicing regularly and you will begin to see temperature increases. Practice with Side One of the autogenic tape for 3 days this week, and then practice with Side Two of the autogenic tape. Remember, relax and maintain a passive attitude while letting your body follow the instructions you are giving it.

WEEK 2

Continue practicing with Side Two of the autogenic tape *twice daily* this week and follow the same procedures outlined for Week one.

WEEK 3

Continue practicing with Side Two of the autogenic tape twice daily this week and follow the same procedures outlined for Week 1. In addition, you will start mini-practice sessions this week. Remember, warm your hands voluntarily before you are exposed to the cold. Autogenic training works best as a prevention. These instructions are adapted from an unpublished manuscript, Autogenic Training Manual by Richard S. Surwit, that was utilized by Surwit, Pilon, and Fenton (1978).

REFERENCES

Abel, G.G. & Blanchard, E.B. The measurement and generation of sexual arousal in male sexual deviates. In M. Hersen, R.M. Eisler, & P.M. Miller, (Eds.) *Progress in behavior modification,* Vol. 2. New York: Academic Press, 1976.

Adkins, J.M. Electrodes. *Response,* 1978 Nos. 51 (March) and 52 (April). Leigh Valley, Penn.: Coulbourn Instruments Newsletter.

Barlow, D.H. Becker, R., Leitenberg, H., & Agras, W.S. A mechanical strain gauge for recording penile circumference change. *Journal of Applied Behavior Analysis,* 1970, **3,** 73–76.

Basmajian, J.V. Control and training of individual motor units. *Science,* 1963, **141,** 440–441.

Basmajian, M.V. *Muscles alive.* Baltimore: Williams & Wilkins, 1974.

Basmajian, J.V. Facts and myths in EMG biofeedback. *Biofeedback and Self-Regulation,* 1976, **1,** 369–371.

Beiman, I., Graham, L.E., & Ciminero, A.R. Setting generality of blood pressure reductions and the psychological treatment of reactive hypertension. *Journal of Behavioral Medicine,* 1978, **1,** 445–453.

Benson, H. *The relaxation response.* New York: William Morrow, 1975.

Blanchard, E.B. & Epstein, L.H. *A biofeedback primer.* Reading, Mass.: Addison-Weley, 1978.

Brown, C.C. The techniques of plethysmography. In C.C. Brown (Ed.) *Methods in psychophysiology.* Baltimore: Williams & Wilkins, 1967.

Cook, M.R. Psychophysiology of peripheral vascular changes. In P.A. Obrist, A.H. Black, J. Brenner, & L.V. Dicara (Eds.) *Cardiovascular psychophysiology: Current issues in response mechanisms, biofeedback, and methodology.* Chicago: Aldine, 1974.

Edelberg, R. Electrical properties of the skin. In C.C. Brown (Ed.) *Methods in psychophysiology.* Baltimore: Williams & Wilns, 1967.

Edelberg, R. Electrical activity of the skin: Its measurement and uses in psychophysiology. In N.S. Greenfield & R.A. Sternbach (Eds.) *Handbook of psychophysiology.* New York: Holt, Rinehart & Winston, 1972.

Elder, S.T., Longacre, A., Jr., Welsh, D.M. & McAfee, R.D. Apparatus and procedure for training subjects to control their blood pressure, *Psychophysiology,* 1977, **14,** 68–72.

Engel, B.T., Nikoomanesh, P., & Schuster, M.M. Operant conditioning of recto-sphincteric responses in the treatment of fecal incontinence. *New England Journal of Medicine,* 1974, **290,** 646–649.

Feurstein, M. & Adams, H.E. Cephalic vasomotor feedback in the modification of migraine headache. *Biofeedback and Self-Regulation,* 1977, **2,** 241–254.

Feurstein, M., Adams, H.H., & Beiman, I. Cephalic vasomotor and electromyographic feedback in the treatment of combined muscle contraction and migraine headaches in a geriatric case. *Headache,* 1976, **16,** 232–237.

Friar, L.R. & Beatty, J. Migraine: Management by trained control of vasoconstriction. *Journal of Consulting and Clinical Psychology,* 1976, **44,** 46–53.

Fuller, G.D. *Biofeedback: Methods and procedures in clinical practice.* San Francisco: Biofeedback Press, 1977.

Furman, S. Intestinal biofeedback in functional diarrhea: A preliminary report. *Journal of Behavior Therapy and Experimental Psychiatry,* 1973, **4,** 317–321.

Gaarder, K.R. & Montgomery, P.S. *Clinical biofeedback.* Baltimore: William & Wilkins, 1977.

Gannon, L. & Sternbach, R.A. Alpha enhancement as a treatment for pain: A case study. *Behavior Therapy and Experimental Psychiatry,* 1971, **2,** 209–213.

Gans, G.E. A highly efficient method of constructing and attaching biomonitoring electrodes. Proceedings of the Biofeedback Society of America Tenth Annual Meeting, 1979, 255.

Gregg, R.H. Biofeedback and biophysical monitoring during pregnancy and labor. In J.V. Basmajian (Ed.) *Biofeedback—Principles and practice for clinicians.* Baltimore: Williams & Wilkins, 1979.

Grollman, S. *The human body: Its structure and function.* New York: Macmillan, 1978.

Gunderson, J. Graphic recording of breathing rate using a simple thermocouple system. *Biomedical Engineering,* 1971, **6,** 208, 210.

Haynes, S.N. *Principles of behavioral assessment.* New York: Gardner Press, 1978.

Hefferline, R.F. & Perera, T.B. Proprioceptive discrimination of a covert operant without its observation by the subject. *Science,* 1963, **139,** 834–835.

Holzl, R. Indirect gastrointestinal motility measurement for use in experimental psychosomatics: A new method and some data. *Behavior Analysis and Modification,* 1979, **3,** 77–97.

Hughes, H. & Cunningham, D.P. Behavioral treatment of essential hypertension: Effect of multi-element and cognitive behavior self-regulation therapies. Unpublished manuscript, 1980.

Kleinman, K.M., Goldman, H., Snow, M.Y., & Korol, B. Relationship between essential hypertension and cognitive functioning II: Effects of biofeedback training generalize to nonlaboratory environment. *Psychophysiology,* 1977, **14,** 192–197.

Koppman, J.W., McDonald, R.D., & Kunzel, N.G. Voluntary regulation of temporal artery diameter by migraine patients. *Headache,* 1974, **10,** 133–138.

Krist, D.A. & Engel, B.T. Learning control of blood pressure in patients with high blood pressure. *Circulation,* 1975, **51,** 370–378.

Kuhlman, W.N. EEG feedback training in the treatment of seizures: Mechanisms and maintenance of effect. *Proceedings of the Biofeedback Society of America,* 1979, **10,** 123–124.

Maisto, A. & Adesso, V.J. Effect of instructions and feedback on blood alcohol level discrimination training in nonalcoholic drinkers. *Journal of Consulting and Clinical Psychology,* 1977, **45,** 625–636.

Melzack, R. & Perry, C. Self-regulation of pain: The use of alpha feedback and hypnotic training for the control of pain. *Experimental Neurology,* 1975, **46,** 452–469.

McKenzie, R.E., Ehrisman, W.J., Montgomery, P.S., & Barnes, R.H. The treatment of headaches by means of electroencephalographic biofeedback. *Headache,* 1974, **13,** 164–172.

Nikoomanesh, P., Wells, D., & Shuster, M.M. Biofeedback control of lower esophageal sphincter contraction. *Clinical Research* 1973, **21,** 521.

Novelly, R.A., Perona, P.J., & Ax, A.F. Photoplethysmography: System calibration and light history effects. *Psychophysiology,* 1973, **10,** 67–73.

Owen, S., Toomin, H., & Taylor, L. *Biofeedback in neuromuscular rehabilitation.* Los Angeles: Biofeedback Research Institute, 1975.

Rickles, W.H., Jr., & Day, J.L. Electrical activity in nonpalmar skin sites. *Psychophysiology,* 1968, **4,** 421–435.

Rugh, J.D. & Schwitzgabel, R.L. Instrumentation for behavioral assessment. In A.R. Ciminero, K.S. Calhoun, & H.E. Adams (Eds.) *Handbook for behavioral assessment.* New York: Wiley, 1976.

Rugh, J.D., Perlis, D.B., & Disraeli, R.I. *Biofeedback in dentistry: Research and clinical applications.* Phoenix: Semantodontics, 1976.

Schneider, J.A. Rapid absolute blood pressure: Introducing a new method of providing blood pressure feedback. Paper presented at the annual meeting of the American Psychological Association, Toronto, 1978.

Schwartz, G.E., Fair, P.L., Salt, P., Mandel, M.R., & Klerman, G.L. Facial expression and imagery in depression: An electromyographic study. *Psychosomatic Medicine,* 1976, **38,** 337–347.

Shapiro, D. & Surwit, R.S. Learned control of physiological function and disease. In H. Leitenberg (Ed.) *Handbook of behavior modification and behavior therapy.* Englewood Cliffs, N.J.: Prentice-Hall, 1976.

Shapiro, D. & Watamabe, T. Timing characteristics of operant electrodermal modification: Fixed-interval effects. *Japanese Psychological Research,* 1971, **13,** 123–130.

Sobell, M.B. & Sobell, L.C. A brief technical report on the MOBAT: An inexpensive portable test for determining blood alcohol concentration. *Journal of Applied Behavior Analysis,* 1975, **8,** 117–120.

Steiner, S.S. & Arkin, A.M. Biofeedback in the treatment of medical illness. In T.B. Karasu & R.I. Steinmuller (Eds.) *Psychotherapeutics in medicine.* New York: Grune and Stratton, 1978.

Sterman, M.B. Effects of sensorimotor EEG feedback training on sleep and clinical manifestations of epilepsy. In J. Beatty & H. Legewie (Eds.) *Biofeedback and behavior.* New York: Plenum Press, 1977.

Surwit, R., Pilon, R., & Fenton, C. Behavioral treatment of Raynaud's disease. *Journal of Behavioral Medicine,* 1978, **1,** 323–335.

Taub, E. & School, P.J. Some methodological considerations in thermal biofeedback training. *Behavior Research Methods and Instrumentation,* 1978, **10,** 617–622.

Toomin, M. & Toomin, H. GSR feedback in psychotherapy: Some clinical observations. *Psychotherapy: Theory, Research, and Practice,* 1975, **12,** 33–38.

Weinman, J. Photoplethysmography. In P.H. Venables & I Martin (Eds.). *A manual of psychophysiological methods.* Amsterdam: North Holland Publishing Com pany, 1967.

Welgan, P.R. Learned control of gastric acid secretions in ulcer patients. *Psychosomatic Medicine,* 1974, **36,** 411–419.

Whitehead, W.E., Renault, P.F., & Golddiamond, I. Modification of human acid secretion with operant conditioning procedures. *Journal of Applied Behavior Analysis,* 1975, **8,** 147–156.

Wolpe, J. & Flood, J. The effects of relaxation on the GSR to repeated phobic stimuli in ascending order. *Journal of Behavior Therapy and Experimental Psychiatry,* 1970, **1,** 195–200.

Author Index

Abel, G. G., 91, 176, 177, 279
Abrams, K., 202
Abuzzahab, F. S., 200
Achterberg, J., 60, 91, 310
Adams, H., 277
Adams, H. E., 59, 279, 328
Adams, H. H., 328
Adesso, V. J., 73
Adkins, J. M., 326
Adler, C. S., 62, 70, 80, 276
Agnew, H., 295
Agras, A., 179
Agras, S., 146, 147, 176, 177, 198
Agras, W. S., 92, 97, 120, 150
Aigner, E., 302
Ainsworth, K. D., 126, 127
Akeson, W. H., 266
Aleo, S., 112, 127, 187
Alexander, A. B., 237–239, 242, 243
Alexander, D., 296
Alexander, F., 188, 300
Algera, G., 148
Allen, A. C., 249, 252, 254, 256
Allen, E. B., 162
Allen, E. V., 163
Allen, F. M., 302
Allen, K. E., 250, 251, 257
Alperson, J., 120, 298
Altman, K., 313
Alva, J., 181
Anderson, D. E., 153
Anderson, G., 303
Anderson, N. B., 112, 281
Andrasik, F., 112, 127, 282
Andrews, G. C., 252, 254, 256
Andrews, J. M., 206
Andreychuk, T., 280
Ansell, S., 219, 220, 227
Anthony, J., 225, 228
Arkin, A. M., 339
Arnkoff, D. B., 127–132, 134

Ascher, E., 200
Aschoff, J., 295
Assal, J., 300, 302
Avenci, C. A., 60, 91
Ax, A. F., 328
Ayllon, T., 45
Azerrad, J., 176
Azrin, N., 43–45, 202

Bachrach, A. J., 175, 176
Baer, D., 2
Bagley, C., 217, 218, 221
Bahler, W. W., 226, 228
Bahnson, C., 310
Bahnson, M., 310
Baird, H. W., 216, 218
Bakal, D. A., 275, 279
Baker, B. L., 296
Bakon, H., 184
Balaschak, B. A., 215, 218, 223, 228
Ballmeyer, L. N., 300
Bandura, A., 41, 44
Bar, L. H., 250, 251, 256–258
Barber, T. X., 60, 90
Barker, N. W., 162
Barlow, D., 176, 177, 199
Barlow, D. H., 120
Barnard, S. R., 183
Barnes, R. A., 340
Barr, R. G., 183
Barrett, B., 182
Barrett, B. H., 201
Barrett, R. E., 197
Barrow, J., 120
Barrow, R. L., 215
Basmajian, J. V., 206, 207, 325, 326
Basmajian, M. V., 325, 326
Bassler, C. R., 210
Bauch, M., 302
Bauch, W., 302
Baughman, F., 219, 227

Baxter, D. L., 254
Beals, R. K., 266, 268
Beary, J. F., 60, 90
Beatty, J., 328
Beaty, E. T., 186
Bech, K., 147
Beck, A. T., 15, 107, 115, 120
Becker, J., 180
Beecher, H. K., 263
Beiman, I., 62, 73, 80, 112, 126, 151, 190, 328, 331
Belandres, P. V., 206
Bell, W. H., 306, 307
Bellack, A. S., 17, 28, 128, 132, 224, 228
Benoit, L. J., 254, 257
Bensen, H., 60, 90
Benson, H., 60, 90, 97, 98, 127, 148, 150, 151, 153, 342
Benton, P. C., 300
Bernstein, D. A., 60, 90–92, 95, 98, 100
Bettley, F. R., 252, 258
Bianco, F. J., 176
Biglan, A., 126
Birchler, G. R., 126, 127
Birnbrauer, J. S., 180
Blachly, P. H., 200
Black, J. L., 17
Blackwell, B., 150, 152, 271
Blain, A., 162
Blanchard, E. B., 51, 52, 62, 69, 70, 71, 80, 153, 155, 160, 164, 279, 280, 283, 284, 330, 337, 339
Blare, A., 178
Blatt, S. J., 15
Bleecker, E. R., 158–161
Blinder, B. J., 175, 176
Bliss, E., 175
Bloomfield, S., 150
Boglan, A., 298
Bonica, J. J., 261
Booker, H. E., 219, 220, 227
Bootzin, R., 296, 297
Borkovec, T. D., 60, 90–92, 95, 98–100, 295–297
Bornstein, P. H., 120
Bortnichak, E., 67, 72
Bowen, W. F., 112, 281
Bradley, B. W., 126
Bradley, R. W., 62, 73, 77, 80, 82, 98, 99, 156, 157
Brady, J. P., 3, 7, 60, 67, 72, 90, 100, 126, 127, 149, 160, 161
Brady, R., 239
Branch, C., 175

Braud, L. W., 126
Braud, R. R., 147
Braud, W., 126
Brauer, A., 150
Brauer, W., 200
Braunwold, E., 146
Brehony, K. A., 162
Brener, J., 73
Bricel, S. K., 240
Briddell, D. W., 190
Brierly, H., 196, 197, 199
Bright, G. O., 179
Britton, B. T., 62
Britton, B. V., 251
Broden, M., 17
Brooke, R. I., 112, 309
Brooks, G. R., 187
Brown, B., 70, 80, 227
Brown, C. C., 328
Brown, D. A., 280
Brown, D. G., 252, 258
Brown, F., 310
Brown, G. E., 163
Browning, C. H., 175
Bruce, H. A., 294
Bruch, H., 174
Brudny, J., 198, 206, 210
Budzynski, T. H., 56, 59, 62, 69, 70, 75, 77, 78, 80, 81, 101, 276, 279, 283, 284, 298, 302
Bugenthal, D. B., 126
Burish, T. G., 312
Burstein, S., 112
Burton, J., 178
Butz, G., 133
Byasse, J. E., 151
Bykov, K. M., 26
Byrick, R., 179

Cabral, R. J., 224
Cailliet, R., 266
Cairns, D., 265, 270
Cairns, G. F., 313
Calsyn, D., 268
Campbell, D., 203
Campos, G. B., 219, 227
Cannistraci, A. J., 306–308
Cannon, W. B., 300
Carlson, S. G., 308
Carnahan, C., 305
Carol, M. P., 60, 90
Carruthers, M., 151, 152
Carter, A., 283
Carter, S., 215, 216, 222

Carver, G. B., 162
Case, D. B., 150
Casey, B., 116, 120
Cautela, J. R., 15, 39, 40, 110, 120, 127, 133, 223, 228
Cerulli, M. A., 184
Chai, H., 234, 237, 239, 240
Challas, G., 200
Chaney, L. A., 126
Chapin, II., 176, 177
Chesney, M. A., 91, 279, 283, 304
Chiang, B. N., 147, 158
Chism, R. A., 159
Chong, T. M., 236
Christopherson, E. R., 183, 184
Christopherson, V., 263
Ciminero, A. R., 62, 72, 80, 126, 151, 331
Cinciripini, P. M., 73
Claghorn, J. L., 305
Clark, D. F., 201
Clark, E. G., 67
Clarke, N. G., 308
Cleeland, C. S., 197, 219, 227
Clifton, R. K., 26
Clouser, R. A., 296
Coates, T. J., 126–128
Cobb, S., 185
Coddington, R. D., 178
Coffman, D. A., 113, 114, 116
Cohen, S., 163
Coller, F. A., 162
Collins, J., 294
Collins, L., 126
Collins, S., 126
Conger, J., 182
Connell, P. H., 200
Cook, M. R., 328
Cooper, A. J., 239
Cooper, B., 234
Cooper, I. A., 197
Cooper, K. H., 127
Corbett, J. A., 200
Corliss, L. M., 303
Cox, D. J., 60, 90, 283, 304
Cox, P. J., 279, 283
Coyne, L., 27
Cram, J. R., 279, 283
Crawford, P. L., 240
Creer, T. L., 120, 234–236, 239–242
Cromes, G. F., 310, 312
Cropp, A., 237
Cull, J. G., 299, 300
Cunningham, C., 179

Cunningham, D. P., 62, 73, 80, 82, 98, 112, 113, 126, 342
Cutter, H. S. G., 60, 91

Dale, A., 153
Dalessio, D. J., 276
Dally, P. J., 175
Dalton, K., 303, 304
Dalvi, C. P., 60
Danaher, B. G., 127
Daniels, G. E., 300
Daniels, L. K., 225, 228, 253, 257, 258
Danker, P. S., 241
Danker-Brown, P., 239
Darbyshire, R., 221, 222, 228
Datey, K. K., 60, 90, 150, 151, 155, 339
Davidson, M., 181, 183
Davis, C. D., 303
Davis, C. H., 306
Davis, D. J., 233, 234
Davis, M. H., 238, 239, 240
Davis, R., 58
Davis, W. D., 188
Dawber, P. L., 147
Dawley, H., 126–128, 133
Dawley, H. H., Jr., 41, 126, 133
Dawson, E., 268, 272
Day, J. H., 237
Day, J. L., 338
Deabler, H. J., 77, 154
Deffenbacher, J. L., 91, 96, 126
Deitz, S., 310
Dekker, E., 236
DeLateur, B. J., 264, 268, 269
DeLeo, J., 150
DeMarco, T. J., 306
Dement, W. C., 294, 295
Denney, D. R., 112
Dennis, W., 300
DeRisi, W. J., 133
Deshmukh, S. N., 60
Dial, M. H., 100
Diamond, S., 280, 283, 284
Dickey, L. D., 59
Dillenkoffer, R. L., 77
Disraeli, R. I., 306, 326
Dobbins, K., 305
Dobes, R. W., 251, 257
Dohrmann, R. J., 308
Doleys, D. M., 182
Dolster, M. E., 303
Domonkos, A. N., 252, 254–256
Donald, M. W., 203
Dornblith, S. J., 126, 133

Dowdall, S. A., 151
Driscoll, R., 60, 91
Drossman, D. A., 188
DuBois, K. E., 81
Duer, W. F., 126
Duker, P., 180
Dunbar, F., 302, 382
Dunbar, H. F., 300
Dunbar, H. R., 248
Dunbar, J., 6
Duncon, C. H., 159
Duson, B. M., 126, 305
Duvoisin, R. C., 197
Dykman, R. A., 26

Eddy, E., 178
Edelberg, R., 27, 339
Edelman, R., 182
Edelstein, B. A., 225, 228
Edmundson, E. D., 160
Edwards, J. E., 240
Edwards, M. C., 233
Efron, R., 34, 219, 227
Ehrisman, W. J., 340
Elder, S. T., 77, 154, 155, 330
Eldredge, R., 197
Ellis, A., 107, 115, 120
Emery, G., 107
Emurian, C. S., 75, 164
Endler, N. S., 15
Engel, B. T., 52, 62, 73, 74, 77, 80, 82, 126, 145, 153, 155, 157–161, 184, 331
Engelman, K., 146
England, R., 62, 255
Epstein, F. H., 147, 155
Epstein, L. H., 51, 69, 70, 71, 73, 91, 183, 279, 330, 337, 339
Eraskus, D. S., 306
Eriksen, R. A., 199
Erwin, R., 81
Erwin, W. J., 175, 176
Etherton, M. D., 226, 228
Eustis, N. K., 154
Ewing, J., 59, 77, 79

Fabing, H. F., 215
Fabisch, W., 221, 222, 228
Fair, P. L., 326
Farquhar, J. W., 92, 127, 150
Fay, A., 126
Feld, J. L., 164
Feldman, G. M., 241
Feldman, R. B., 201
Felton, J. P., 185, 186

Felton, J. S., 215, 217, 299, 300
Fenton, C., 59, 60, 62, 73, 80, 82, 91, 98, 127, 165, 346
Ferguson, J. M., 126, 127
Ferinden, W., 182
Fernandez, G. R., 248
Fernando, C. K., 209, 210
Feurstein, M., 56, 279, 328
Feverman, E., 248, 255
Fezler, W. D., 109, 120
Fidel, E. A., 155
Field, J. R., 200
Finley, W. W., 204, 205, 226, 228
Finnerty, F. A., Jr., 148
Finnerty, F. A., III, 148
Fiorito, E. M., 162
Fish, D., 206
Fisher, R., 163
Fishman, M. A., 280
Flanery, H. G., 261
Flannery, R. B., Jr., 223, 228
Flood, J., 339
Floreen, A., 270
Folin, O., 300
Follick, M., 310
Follick, M. J., 112, 272
Ford, C. V., 200
Fordyce, W. E., 42, 68, 262–265, 268–270, 284
Forster, F. M., 219, 220, 222, 227
Fowler, J. E., 80, 302
Fowler, R. S., 264, 268, 269, 273
Fowles, D. C., 90, 296, 297
Fowles, D. S., 60
Frankel, F., 248
Franklin, M. A., 280, 283
Fray, J. M., 151
Frazer, R. G., 235
Frazier, L. M., 62
Frazier, S. H., 275
Freedman, R., 164, 298
Freeman, C., 268
Freeman, D. M. A., 175, 176
French, A. D., 296
Freundlich, A., 60, 90, 279
Friar, L., 226, 228
Friar, L. R., 328
Friedling, C., 126
Friedman, H., 156
Friedman, L. W., 206, 266
Frizzell, M. K., 301
Fry, L., 254
Fuchs, C. Z., 126, 133

Fuller, G. D., 56, 59, 60, 78, 92, 326, 328, 338–340
Fullerton, D. T., 178
Furman, S., 189

Gaarder, K. R., 56, 69, 78, 83, 92, 338, 340
Gaddini, E., 178
Gaddini, R., 178
Gainer, J. C., 70, 72, 283
Galbraith, D., 179
Gale, E. M., 308
Galen, 145
Galton, L., 146, 266
Gambrill, E. D., 15
Gannon, L., 340
Gans, G. E., 327
Gantt, W. H., 26
Gaoni, B., 176
Gardner, G. G., 223, 228
Gardner, J. E., 223, 228, 241
Gardner, L. I., 178
Garfield, C., 311
Garfinkel, P., 176
Garton, 206
Gascon, G., 219, 227
Gavira, B., 27
Gaylor, M., 73
Gaylor, M. S., 151
Geer, J. H., 296
Geller, J. L., 177
General, D., 126–128, 133
Genest, M., 120
Gentry, W. D., 265, 268
Gentry, W. R., 182
Gerd, J., 237
Gershman, L., 296
Gershon, E., 153
Gibb, J. D., 60
Gibson, J. G., 276
Gigon, A., 302
Gilles de la Tourette, 200
Gillespie, W. J., 160
Glasgow, R. E., 126, 127
Glaus, K. D., 240
Glenn, S., 109
Glock, C. Y., 67
Glover, M. B., 267, 268
Gold, A., 215, 216, 222
Goldfried, M. R., 91, 126–128, 296
Goldiamond, I., 127
Goldman, H., 62, 154, 155, 331
Goldman, M. P., 79
Goldman, M. S., 72
Goldsmith, D. A., 62, 255, 267

Goldstein, I. B., 60
Goldstrich, J. D., 73, 126
Good, M. I., 156
Goodell, H., 148
Gordon, S. B., 28
Gorham, G., 160
Gottlieb, F., 200
Gottlieb, H., 264, 266, 271
Graham, D. T., 163
Graham, F. K., 26
Graham, L. E., 62, 73, 80, 126, 151, 331
Granger, E. R., 307
Grant, I., 300
Grayson, J. B., 296, 297
Grayson, R. R., 185
Green, E. E., 280
Green, M., 178
Greenshoot, J., 270
Greer, S., 255, 310
Gregg, R. H., 62, 326, 339
Griffin, P., 24, 276
Grinker, R. R., 60, 248
Groen, J., 236
Grollman, S., 337
Grynbaum, B. B., 198, 206
Gunderson, J., 92, 328
Gunn, C. G., 26
Guyton, A. C., 56

Hack, S., 280
Hackett, L. P., 163
Hahn, K. W., 60, 90
Hall, P., 164
Halpern, D., 207
Hama, H., 164
Hamby, W. B., 197
Hammer, C. L., 17
Hammond, E., 293
Handler, N., 273
Hannum, J. W., 17
Hanenson, I., 150
Hansen, S. P., 159
Hanvick, L. J., 268
Hardy, R. E., 299, 300
Harper, R., 281
Harper, R. A., 120
Harrell, E. H., 254, 257
Harrell, T. H., 112, 126, 190
Harris, F. A., 203
Harris, F. R., 250, 251, 257
Harrison, T., 240
Hartman, L. M., 126, 127
Haskell, D. A. L., 280
Hastings, J. E., 74

Hauri, P., 293, 298
Haynes, M. R., 153, 164
Haynes, S. N., 12, 15, 17, 18, 24, 28, 62,
    91, 251, 257, 258, 276, 279, 283, 296–298
Heald, F. P., 303
Heath, H. A., 60
Heczey, M., 305
Heczey, M. D., 126
Hefferline, R. F., 325
Heffler, D., 296, 297
Heiman, J., 127
Heinrich, R., 272
Heller, R. Z., 307
Hemmes, N. S., 127
Henry, D., 77, 81, 101
Heppner, P. O., 120
Herman, R., 44, 206
Herndon, R., 254
Hersen, M., 28, 199, 224, 228
Hershkoff, H., 237
Herting,.R. L., 148
Hetherington, C., 120
Hickman, N. W., 266, 268
Hilden, T., 147
Hilgard, E. R., 59, 270
Hilgard, J. R., 270
Hill, E., 207
Hill, H. E., 261
Himmelsbach, C. K., 148
Hines, E. A., Jr., 162
Hinkle, J., 296
Hinkle, J. E., 127
Hinkle, L. E., 300
Hippocrates, 234
Hislop, J. G., 188
Hoffman, A., 239
Hollon, S. D., 120
Hollowell, J. R., 178
Holmes, T. H., 300
Holroyd, K. A., 112, 127, 282
Holz, W., 43, 45
Homme, L. E., 15, 100
Hong, M., 300
Hooker, A. D., 301
Horande, M., 205
Horlick, L., 150
Hoyt, C., 178
Hubbard, D. R., Jr., 17
Huber, D., 112, 281
Huber, H., 199
Huber, H. P., 112, 281
Hughes, A., 77, 81, 101
Hughes, H., 58, 59, 62, 73, 77, 79, 80–82,
    98–101, 109, 112, 113, 126, 156, 157, 342

Hughes, H. H., 255, 257, 258, 298
Hughes, R. C., 298
Hugonnet, M. H., 126
Hunt, E. P., 234
Hunt, J. McV., 15
Hunter, H. L., 148
Hurley, L. K., 127
Hutchings, D., 283
Hutchings, O. F., 276, 279
Hutzell, R., 201
Hymer, J. W., 203

Ianni, P., 164
Iannone, A., 280
Ince, L. P., 221, 224
Inglis, J., 203
Ingram, R. H., 238
Israel, S. L., 303
Iwata, B. A., 223, 228

Jackson, K., 81
Jacob, R., 146, 147
Jacob, R. G., 97
Jacobson, A. M., 164
Jacobson, E., 25, 60, 90, 91, 95, 96, 98, 149
Jaffe, P. G., 62, 251
Jaffe, Y., 112
Jakubowski, P., 41
James, T. M., 158
Janis, I., 312
Jankel, W. R., 198
Janzen, R., 261
Jaremko, M. A., 112
Jason, L., 298
Jaytte, B. A., 240
Jeffrey, D. B., 127
Jenkins, C. D., 306
Johnson, G., 298
Johnson, H. E., 210
Johnson, J., 202
Johnson, M., 264
Johnson, R. K., 224, 225, 228
Johnson, W. G., 280, 283
Johnston, R., 207
Johnstone, D. E., 233
Jones, G. S., 303
Jones, H. G., 201
Jones, H. W., Jr., 303
Jones, J. M., 73
Julius, S., 149

Kaganov, J. A., 279
Kahn, A., 241
Kahn, H., 296

Kales, A., 293, 295
Kallman, N. N., 56
Kaloupek, D. G., 296, 297
Kanfer, F. H., 4, 129
Kannel, W. R., 147
Kanner, L., 178
Kaplan, B. J., 224
Karacan, I., 293
Kardachi, B. J., 308
Karoly, P., 127, 128
Kastenbaum, P., 39
Kastenbaum, R. A., 15, 133
Katkin, E. S., 296
Katz, C., 113, 114, 116
Katz, R., 40, 44, 221, 222
Katz, R. C., 127
Kazdin, A., 45
Kazdin, A. E., 17, 108–110
Keefe, F. J., 28, 208
Keefe, F. V., 164
Keegan, D. L., 253, 258
Kellner, R., 248
Kelly, G. A., 120
Kendall, P. C., 120
Kessel, N., 303
Kidd, C., 248
Kiesler, D., 310
Kimble, G., 38
Kissen, D., 310
Kleinman, K. M., 62, 154, 155, 331
Kleitman, N., 293, 295
Klemchuck, H. M., 60, 90, 150
Kline, S., 176
Klove, H., 227, 229
Knapp, T. J., 241
Knepler, K. N., 201
Knowler, H. C., 300
Knox, K. R., 302
Knust, B., 154
Knust, U., 154
Kohlenberg, R. J., 179, 182, 184
Kohn, S., 164
Kolb, L. C., 277
Koller, R., 271
Kopel, S. A., 28
Koppman, J. W., 328
Korein, J., 198, 206
Korol, B., 62, 331
Kornetsky, C. G., 261
Kotses, H., 240
Kraemer, H. C., 97
Kraft, G. H., 283
Kraus, H., 267
Krisberg, J., 251, 257

Kristt, D. A., 62, 73, 74, 77, 80, 82, 126, 153, 155, 157, 331
Kroger, W. S., 109, 120
Kron, R. E., 60, 67, 72, 90, 100, 126, 149
Krueger, D. E., 146
Krupp, M. A., 235
Kuhlman, W. N., 224, 226, 228, 340
Kukulka, C. G., 206
Kulich, R., 112
Kundo, C., 283
Kanzel, N. G., 328
Kunzelmann, H. D., 17
Kuypers, R. M., 250, 251, 256–258
Kyle, G. C., 300

Lacey, J. I., 56
Lachman, S., 35
Lachman, S. J., 188, 248
Lahey, B., 201
Lake, A., 112, 279, 283
Lal, H., 182
Lamontagne, Y., 255, 257, 258
Lampe, J. M., 303
Lance, J. W., 278, 280
Lando, H. A., 127
Lang, P. J., 26, 44, 74, 176, 179
Lange, A. F., 59
Lange, A. J., 41
Lansky, D., 73
Largen, J. W., 283, 305
Laragh, J. H., 150
Laskin, D. M., 306–308
Lawler, J., 180
Lawlis, G., 60, 310
Lawlis, G. F., 91
Lawrence, P. S., 112, 150, 281
Lawson, D. M., 73
Layne, C. C., 17
Lazarus, A. A., 58, 60, 90, 95, 98, 120, 126, 201
Lazarus, R., 310
Leahey, M. D., 302
Lee, K. H., 207
Lee, R. M., 72
Lehmann, J. F., 223, 228, 264, 269
Leiberman, A., 206
Leiberman, R. P., 201
Leiblum, S. R., 190
Leitenberg, H., 120, 176, 177
Lenox, J. R., 59
LeShan, L., 265, 310
Lester, E. P., 248
Levendusky, P., 112, 126, 272
Levene, H. T., 159

Levidow, L., 206
Levine, M. D., 181, 183
Levine, M. E., 268
Levit, H. I., 268
Levitz, L., 67, 72
Levy, R. L., 135, 147
Lew, E. A., 147
Lewin, M., 185, 186, 215, 217, 299, 300
Lewinsohn, P. M., 15, 133
Lewis, T., 162, 163
Libet, J., 179
Lick, J. R., 296, 297
Lidz, T., 301
Lindley, O., 182
Lindsley, O., 17
Linscheid, T., 179
Lipinski, D. P., 17
Lipschutz, W., 163
Litchenstein, E., 127
Livingston, S., 217, 218
Livingston, W. K., 262
Logue, P., 201
Longacre, A., Jr., 330
LoPiccolo, J., 127
LoPiccolo, L., 127
Lorentson, A. M., 223, 228
Lori, M., 154
Louks, J., 268
Love, W. A., 151
Lowe, K., 301
Lowenstein, T. J., 99
Lowery, C. R., 112
Lown, B., 158
Lubar, J. F., 226, 228
Lubin, B., 15
Luborsky, L., 60, 67, 72, 90, 100, 126, 149
Lucas, A. R., 200
Luckey, R. E., 179
Luiselli, J. K., 93
Lupin, M., 126
Luthe, W., 60, 90, 98
Luther, E., 296
Lutzker, J. R., 301
Lyles, J. N., 312
Lynch, W. C., 164
Lynn, S. J., 164

McAfee, R. D., 330
McArthur, P. B., 302
McClintoch, M., 67, 72
Maccoby, N., 127
McCoy, J., 183
McCoy, J. F., 73
McCowan, W. T., 91

McCreary, C., 268, 272
McCullough, J. P., 190
McCutcheon, B. A., 59
MacDonald, H., 59
MacDonald, L. R., 226, 228
McDonald, R. D., 328
McDonald, R. H., 73, 151
McFadden, E. R., 238
McFall, R. M., 17
McGlashan, T. H., 263
McGrady, A., 280
McHugh, R., 207
McHugh, R. B., 239
MacKenzie, J. N., 236
McKenzie, R. E., 340
McMinn, R. M., 254
McMullin, R., 116, 120
McNamara, J., 147
McNees, M., 201
McNees, P., 201
McNiff, A. L., 303
McWhorter, A. Q., 182
Mahler, M. S., 200
Mahoney, M. J., 17, 120, 127–132, 134, 238
Maisto, A., 73
Maletzky, B. M., 17
Mali, J. W., 254
Mann, J., 312
Mann, R. A., 42
Marble, A., 301
Marholin, D., 93
Marianacci, A. A., 205
Marlatt, G. A., 120
Marshall, C., 198
Marshall, G. D., 59
Marshall, W. R., 73
Martin, D. B., 300, 302
Martin, G., 131
Martin, J. E., 73
Marzetta, B. R., 60, 90, 100
Masland, R. P., 303
Mason, A. A., 248
Mathew, R. J., 305
Mathison, D. A., 234
Mattei, E. C., 148
May, D. S., 164
Mayer, N., 206
Mayville, W. J., 223, 228
Mealiea, W. L., 60, 79, 90, 127
Meares, R. A., 199
Medina, J. L., 280
Meichenbaum, D. H., 107, 112, 113, 115, 120
Melamed, B. G., 44, 179

Melzack, P., 261
Melzack, R., 261, 262, 340
Mendeloff, A. I., 181, 188
Mendels, J., 300
Meninger, W. C., 300
Menking, M., 178
Merbaum, M., 128
Merskey, H., 263
Meyer, A., 300
Meyer, R. G., 60, 90, 224, 225, 228, 279, 304
Michaels, A. C., 91, 126
Miklich, D. R., 237, 239, 241, 242
Mikulas, W. L., 43
Miller, N., 38
Miller, N. E., 159, 160, 164
Miller, S. I., 175
Miller, W. R., 126, 128
Millet, J. A. P., 294
Minsky, S., 300
Misiewicz, J. J., 188
Mitch, P. S., 280
Mitchell, D. M., 278, 279, 284
Mitchell, K. R., 58, 92, 99, 112, 126, 127, 278, 279, 282, 284
Mitchell, R. S., 233
Mittleman, B., 163
Moan, E. R., 253, 257, 258
Moeller, T. A., 151
Moffat, S., 228
Mohr, F., 302
Mohr, J. P., 175, 176
Mohr, P. D., 280
Molk, L., 241, 242
Monat, A., 310
Montgomery, D. D., 151
Montgomery, I., 296
Montgomery, P. S., 56, 69, 78, 83, 92, 338, 340
Mooney, D., 24, 276
Mooney, V., 265, 270
Moore, F., 242
Moore, N., 239
Moos, R. H., 303
Moran, R., 296
Morgan, A. H., 59
Moriyama, I. M., 146, 148
Morphew, J. A., 200
Morris, T., 310
Moseley, D., 91
Mostofsky, D. I., 215, 217–219, 224, 228
Mothersill, K. J., 112, 309
Mozonson, P., 183
Mroczek, J. A., 207

Mullen, F. G., 304
Muller, W., 154
Mullhaney, D., 62, 70, 80
Mullinix, J. M., 280
Munoz, R. F., 126, 133
Murphy, R. W., 266
Musaph, H., 248
Musick, J. K., 179
Myers, A., 163

Narayan, N. G., 206
Nathan, P. E., 73
Nau, S. D., 296
Navaco, R. W., 120
Neisworth, J. T., 242
Nelson, E., 92, 150
Nelson, R. O., 17
Nemiah, J., 175
Nesbit, R. A., 62
Neumann, M., 176
Nevid, J. S., 126, 127
Newman, R., 270
Nicassio, F. J., 201
Nicassio, P., 112, 127, 187, 296, 297
Nikoomanesh, P., 52, 184
Niman, C. A., 204
Noordenbos, W., 262
North, W. R., 60, 90, 92, 151, 152, 339
Norton, B. J., 280
Nouwen, A., 273
Novak, E. R., 303
Novelly, R. A., 328
Nunn, R., 202

Oakley, W. G., 300, 301
O'Brien, G. T., 296, 297
O'Connell, M. F., 189
Ogden, J., 303
O'Leary, S. G., 126
Olsen, D., 60
Olson, T., 281
Owen, S., 326

Pace, J. B., 266
Pall, M., 24
Palmer, R. L., 188
Pankratz, L., 112, 126, 272
Papsdorf, J. D., 112, 298
Pare, J. A., 235
Parise, M., 24
Parrino, J. J., 221, 224, 227
Pasino, J., 265, 270
Patel, C. H., 60, 90, 92, 151, 152, 155, 338
Patterson, R. R., 201

Patterson, W. M., 165
Pattison, E. M., 197
Patton, H. D., 163
Paul, G. L., 60, 90, 92, 99, 100
Paulley, J. W., 280
Paulsen, W., 219, 227
Paulson, M. J., 303
Payne, D. M., 96
Pear, J., 131
Pearson, J. A., 159
Pedrini, B., 182
Pedrini, D., 182
Peek, C. L., 283
Pennington, V. M., 303
Peper, E., 164
Perera, T. B., 325
Perkins, D. C., 185, 186, 215, 217, 299, 300
Perkins, G., 296
Perlis, D. B., 306, 326
Perlman, L. V., 147
Perona, P. J., 328
Perry, C., 340
Peters, R. C., 160
Peterson, W. G., 219, 227
Pflanz, M., 185
Philip, R. L., 237, 238
Phillips, C., 279, 283
Phillips, J. S., 129
Pickering, G., 146, 148
Pickering, T., 160
Pierce, D., 181
Pilon, R., 59, 60, 62, 73, 80, 82, 91, 98,
    127, 165, 346
Pinkerton, S. S., 310, 312
Pinto, R., 221, 227
Platzek, D., 201
Pleser, H. E., 236
Pollack, A. A., 150
Pollack, M. H., 62, 73, 80
Polly, S., 127
Pomerleau, C. S., 127
Pomerleau, O. F., 3, 7, 127
Pond, H., 301
Powell, D. W., 188
Premack, D., 40, 70
Price, M. G., 298
Ptacek, L. J., 219, 227
Puletti, F., 216
Pullman, T. N., 147
Pyke, D. A., 300

Quevillon, R. P., 126

Rackeman, F. M., 233
Raffi, A. A., 201

Rahe, R. H., 300
Rainey, J., 112
Rainey, S., 183, 184
Raskin, M., 298
Raskind, R., 267, 268
Rathus, S. A., 15, 126, 127
Ratlift, R. G., 251, 257, 258
Rausen, A. R., 178
Raynaud, A. G., 27, 163
Reading, C., 280
Redmond, D. P., 73, 151
Reeves, J. L., 60, 79, 90, 105, 112, 127, 281
Rehm, L. P., 126, 133
Reinking, R., 80
Reinking, R. H., 276, 279, 284
Renne, C. M., 239, 241, 242
Reynolds, E. H., 218
Rich, E. S., 241
Richardson, F., 126
Richardson, F. C., 187
Richardson, R., 223, 228
Richerson, H. B., 235
Richey, C. A., 15
Richmond, J. B., 178
Richter-Heinrich, E., 154
Rici, D. M., 150
Rickles, W. H., Jr., 338
Riedlinger, W. F., 148
Rinn, R. C., 59
Risley, T., 2
Robb, J. P., 217
Robbins, F. P., 248
Roberts, A., 270
Roberts, D., 73, 126
Robertson, J., 265, 270
Roberts, R. H., 148
Rogers, G. S., 62, 80
Rohm, C. E. T., Jr., 60
Romanczyk, R. G., 17
Romano, J. M., 126, 133
Rominez, T., 201
Rondestvedt, J., 298
Rose, R. M., 185
Rosen, G. M., 98, 126, 127
Rosen, G. R., 127
Rosen, H., 301
Rosenbaum, M., 302
Rosenblatt, M. B., 234
Rosenstein, A. J., 15
Rosner, B. A., 150
Rosser, B. A., 60, 90
Roth, D. M., 126, 133
Rotter, J. B., 15, 120
Roy, A., 176
Rubenstein, J. J., 158

Rubin, R. R., 176
Ruch, T. C., 163
Rugh, J. D., 62, 64, 73, 80, 91, 306–308, 325, 326
Ruiz, R. Z., 77, 154
Russ, K. L., 155, 189, 283
Russell, G., 204
Russell, H. L., 59
Russell, R. K., 60, 79, 90, 100
Ruth, W. E., 235
Rutledge, J. T., 179

Sachs, L. B., 59
Sachs-Frankel, G., 206
Sainsbury, P., 276
Sajwaj, T., 179, 180
Salma, K. M., 296, 297
Salt, P., 326
Sand, D. L., 264
Sandbank, M., 248, 255
Sanders, N., 201
Sappington, J. T., 162, 164
Sargant, W., 175
Sargent, J. D., 279, 280, 283
Sarno, J. E., 268
Sauer, G., 249
Saunders, D. R., 240
Sawyer, J. E., 156
Schaumurg-Lever, G., 254
Scherf, D., 159
Scherr, C. A., 240
Scherr, M. S., 240
Schiffer, C. G., 234
Schmidt, R., 215
Schmitzer, M. D., 67
Schneck, J., 248
Schneer, N. I., 235
Schneider, J. A., 330
Schneider, R. A., 80
Schnurer, A. T., 176
Scholander, T., 222, 228
School, P. J., 329
Schott, A., 159
Schuld, D., 310
Schultz, J., 90
Schultz, J. H., 60
Schumacher, R., 163
Schuster, M. M., 52, 181, 184
Schwartz, G., 3, 38
Schwartz, G. E., 153, 154, 163, 326
Schwartz, J. S., 128, 132
Schwitzgebel, R. L., 62, 73, 80
Scott, D. F., 224
Scott, R. W., 160
Sedlacek, K., 164, 305

Segal, M. S., 235
Seifert, A. R., 226, 228
Selensky, H., 277
Serber, M., 239
Seres, J., 270
Sergeant, H. G. S., 239
Sergent, C. B., 240
Sessions, J. T., 188
Sewall, S., 201
Seymour, R. J., 210
Seys, D., 180
Shahar, A., 112
Shapiro, A. K., 200
Shapiro, A. P., 73, 151
Shapiro, D., 38, 153–156, 164, 329, 330, 339
Shapiro, E., 200
Shapiro, P., 163
Shaw, L. W., 148
Shekelle, R. B., 146
Shelton, J. L., 91, 135, 279, 283
Sherman, A. R., 127
Shevick, B. H., 268
Shipman, W. G., 60
Shoemaker, J. E., 155
Shoenberger, J. A., 146
Shohl, A. T., 300
Shows, W. D., 265
Shriver, C., 280
Sides, J. K., 99
Silver, B. V., 52, 70, 80, 280
Silverberg, E. L., 164
Sim, M., 200
Simon, N. M., 300
Simons, J. P., 298
Simonton, O., 310
Simonton, S., 310
Sipich, J. F., 90, 100
Sipich, J. R., 60, 79
Sipprelle, C. N., 92
Sirota, A. D., 126, 238
Skinner, A., 147
Skinner, B. F., 51, 127
Slauson, P. F., 300
Slavin, R., 234
Smiehorowski, T., 207
Smillie, W. G., 300
Smith, F. J., 59
Smith, G. A., 108–110
Smith, H. A., 226, 228
Smith, M. A., 303
Smith, W. M., 146, 148
Snider, G. L., 235
Snow, M., 154
Snow, M. Y., 62, 154, 331
Snyder, A. L., 96

Sobel, H., 310, 311
Sobel, H. J., 112, 126, 310, 311
Solberg, W. K., 62, 64, 73, 80, 91, 306–308, 325
Solinger, M. W., 273
Sorenson, B. F., 197
Sotos, J., 178
Spear, F. G., 263
Speilberger, C. D., 15
Speizer, F. E., 233
Spelman, F. A., 203
Spiegel, D., 60
Spiegel, H., 60
Spittell, J. A., 162
Stachnik, T. J., 126
Stafford, R., 176
Stambaugh, E. E., 187
Stamler, J., 146–148
Stamler, R., 146–148
Stancer, H., 176
Standler, J., 204
Stearn, S., 302
Steger, J., 268, 281
Steger, J. C., 262, 264, 265
Stein, D. B., 73
Stein, J. A., 163
Stein, M. L., 178
Stein, N. H., 251, 257, 258
Steiner, S. S., 339
Steinman, D., 93
Steinman, W. M., 93
Steinmark, S. W., 296, 297
Stenn, P. G., 112, 309
Stephan, E., 60
Stephens, J. W., 301
Stephenson, N. E., 164
Sterman, M. B., 69, 226–228, 339, 340
Stern, M., 153
Sternbach, R., 270
Sternbach, R. A., 261–263, 265, 266, 268, 340
Stevens, J. K., 200
Stevenson, I. P., 159
Stickler, G., 178
Stone, M. L., 303
Stone, R. A., 150
Stone, R. K., 226, 228
Storms, M. D., 112
Stoughton, R. B., 254
Stoyva, J. M., 56, 59, 62, 70, 75–77, 80, 98, 101, 276
Strange, H. R., 307
Striefel, S., 91, 99
Strite, L. C., 267, 271

Stroebel, C. F., 91, 100
Stroufe, L. A., 74
Stunkard, A. J., 6, 174–176
Sturgis, S. H., 303
Suinn, R. M., 126
Surman, O. A., 164
Surwit, B., 156, 165
Surwit, R., 59, 60, 62, 73, 80, 82, 98, 127, 155
Surwit, R. S., 163, 164, 329, 330, 346
Sussman, K. E., 300
Swanson, D., 270
Swanson, W., 270
Sweet, W. H., 261
Switzgebel, R. L., 91

Takebe, K., 206
Tal, A., 237
Tan, R., 248, 255
Tanner, B. A., 59
Tasto, D. L., 304
Tattersoll, R., 301, 302
Taub, E., 75, 164, 329
Taub, H. A., 156
Taylor, C. B., 90–93, 97, 150, 152
Taylor, J. D., 179
Taylor, K. W., 300
Taylor, L., 326
Taylor, W. F., 324
Teichman, B. A., 300
Tentoni, S. C., 60, 91
Terdall, L. G., 28
Tharp, R. G., 127, 251
Theobald, D. E., 70, 80, 280
Thetford, P. E., 27
Thomas, E., 202
Thomas, L., 270
Thomas, M., 265
Thomson, L., 176
Thoreson, C. E., 17, 126–128
Titus, C. C., 300
Tomlinson, J. R., 182
Tomm, K. M., 302
Toomin, H., 210, 326, 339
Toomin, M., 339
Tophoff, M., 201
Travers, R. D., 218
Treischman, R. B., 264
Treuting, T. F., 300, 302
Trier, C., 91, 127
Trimble, R. W., 99
Trombly, K., 208
Tubbs, W., 305
Tupin, J. P., 296

Turin, A., 280, 283
Turk, D., 112, 272, 310
Turk, D. C., 112, 120, 281
Turnbull, J. W., 236
Turner, D., 268
Turner, J., 272
Turner, R., 163
Turner, R. D., 127
Turner, S., 180
Turner, S. M., 224, 228
Tursky, B., 153, 263
Twentyman, C. T., 26
Tyler, E. T., 304

Vachon, L., 241
Vance, V. J., 234
Vandenbergh, R. L., 80, 300, 302
VanHandel, D., 182
Vaughan, G. D., 300
Vaughn, R., 24
Vaught, R. L., 67
Vicks, S. H., 224, 228
Vidergar, L. J., 72
Vinekar, S. L., 60

Wade, M. E., 303
Wagnitz, J., 178
Waldruff, D., 112
Walk, R. D., 58
Walker, E., 183
Wall, P., 261, 262
Wallace, R. K., 148
Walsh, P., 153, 156
Walters, P. E., 280
Walton, D., 201, 239, 250, 257
Wansley, R. A., 204
Warner, G., 280
Warshaw, L. J., 303
Watanabe, T., 339
Watson, C., 310
Watson, C. M., 179
Watson, D. L., 128, 251
Webb, W., 295
Weber, C. A., 164
Weber, M. A., 150
Webster, J. S., 91
Weerts, T. C., 296, 297
Weiher, R. G., 91, 99
Weil, G., 126, 296
Weinberg, E., 241, 242
Weiner, H., 1, 148
Weinman, J., 328
Weinsenburg, M., 261, 262
Weinstein, S., 206

Weinstock, S. A., 189
Weisman, A. D., 112, 126, 310, 311
Weiss, E. B., 235, 236
Weiss, J. M., 296
Weiss, S., 3
Weiss, T., 7, 159–161
Welgan, P. R., 186
Wells, K. C., 224, 228
Wells, L. A., 241
Welsh, D. M., 330
Wenger, M. A., 56
Wenrich, W. W., 41, 126–128, 133
Werry, J. S., 201
Westbrook, T., 112
Whaley, D. L., 179
White, J. C., 179
White, P. D., 145
White, R. G., 58, 92, 99, 112, 126, 127, 282
Whitehead, W. E., 185
Wickramaskera, I. E., 58, 78, 279, 280
Wilber, J. A., 148
Wilde, G. J. S., 237
Wilder, B., 215
Williams, R. B., 198
Williams, R. B., Jr., 276, 277
Williams, S. C., 182
Williams, T., 180
Williamson, D., 70, 80, 280
Wilson, A. E., 59
Wilson, C. C., 62, 251
Winget, C., 271
Wink, C., 248
Winokur, G., 163
Wise, D., 296
Wittkower, E. D., 248
Wolf, M., 158
Wolf, M. M., 180
Wolf, S., 148, 159, 300
Wolf, S. R., 266
Wolferth, 158
Wolff, F. G., 163, 276, 277
Wolkind, S. N., 268
Wolpe, J., 2, 36, 58, 60, 90, 95, 98, 110, 120, 339
Wood, K. R., 158, 303
Woodbury, J. W., 163
Woodward, S., 296
Woodyatt, R. T., 300
Wooldridge, C. P., 204
Wooley, S. C., 271
Worden, J. W., 310, 311
Wright, L., 181, 183, 184, 222, 228
Wright, W. W., 300

Yohr, M. D., 197
Yates, A. J., 200, 201
Yates, B. T., 126, 127
Yemm, R., 306
Yoches, C., 241, 242
Yorkston, N. J., 236, 239
Yospe, L., 270
Youdin, R., 127
Youell, K. J., 190
Youkilis, H., 310
Young, L. D., 153, 160
Young, S. J., 188
Youngren, M. A., 133

Zastrow, C., 120
Zeiler, M., 59
Zeiner, A. R., 62, 73, 80
Zeiss, A. M., 127, 133
Zeiss, R. A., 127
Zhukov, I. A., 248
Zimmerman, J., 17
Zitter, R., 112
Zlutnick, S., 40, 221–223, 228
Zoon, J. J., 254
Zuckerman, M., 15

Subject Index

Abdominal pain:
  cognitive behavior therapy for, 112
  self-management of, 126
Accelerating hypertension, 146. *See also*
  Hypertension
Acousticomotor epilepsy, 219
Active coping skill, relaxation as, 90–91
Actometer motoric movement, hyperactivity
  and, 62
Adherence, prescribed medical regime, 5–6
Age, hypertensive disease and, 148
Alcohol intake, stimulus control and, 132
Alcoholism, self-management of, 126
Allergic asthma, 235. *See also* Asthma
Aneurism, *see* Cerebrovascular accidents
Anginal pain, psychophysiological assessment,
  57
Anorexia nervosa, 174–175
  treatment, 175–177
Anxiety:
  hierarchies, construction of, 36–37
  lower back pain and, 268
  questionnaires for, 15
  self-management of, 126
Arbitrary inference, cognitive behavior
  therapy, 115
Arousal, biofeedback control training and,
  76
Arrhythmias, *see* Cardiac arrhythmias
Arthritis, psychophysiological assessment,
  57
Assertion inventory, 15
Assertiveness:
  questionnaire for, 15
  self-management of, 126
Assertiveness training, 41
  headaches and, 278–279
  for hyperhidrosis, 256
  self-management and, 133
  social skills biofeedback and, 83
  ulcers and, 187

Assessment:
  cognitive behavior therapy, 113–116. *See
    also* Psychophysiological assessment
  function of, 11–12
  interview, 12–14
  observation, 18–22
    in natural environment, 18–20
    in structural settings, 20–22
  psychophysiological, biofeedback and, 56–61
  psychophysiological measurement, 22–28
    cardiovascular measures, 25–27
    electrodermal activity, 27
    electromyography, 24–25
    see also specific measures
  questionnaires, 14–16. *See also specific
    questionnaires*
  self-monitoring, 16–18
  significance of, 4
Asthma:
  description, 233–236
  desensitization for, 37
  psychological factors, 236–237
  psychophysiological assessment, 57
  self-management of, 126
  treatment, 237
    operant approaches, 241–243
    operantly conditioned biofeedback, 241
    relaxation biofeedback, 240–241
    relaxation and desensitization, 239–240
    relaxation training, 237–239
Atopic dermatitis, pictures of, 62
Atopic eczema, *see* Eczema
Atrial fibrillation, 158, 161
Atrial flutter, 158
Audio tape:
  biofeedback control training and, 75
  observation and, 19
  relaxation training and, 99
Autogenic relaxation training:
  prurigo nodularis, 255–256
  urticaria, 253

Autogenic training, 60, 90, 98
  biofeedback and, 83
  hypertension and, 151
  instructions, 90–91, 342–346
  insomnia and, 296
Autonomic nervous system (ANS),
    electromyography for, 24
Aversion therapy, self-induced seizures and,
    222
Aversive conditioning:
  bruxism and, 307–308
  control of physiological variables and, 23
  relaxation training, and skin disorders, 251
  for spasmodic torticollis, 199
Aversive counterconditioning, 37

Back pain, *see* Lower back pain
Beck Depression Inventory, 15
Behavioral assessment, *see* Assessment
Behavioral medicine:
  applications, 5–7. *See also specific
    applications*
  definition, 1–4
  treatment interventions, 4–5. *See also
    specific treatments*
Behavioral observation, *see* Assessment
Behavioral modification, 250
Behavior therapy, 107
  definition, 2
  see also Cognitive behavior therapy
Biofeedback, 23, 25, 51–52
  asthma and:
      operantly conditioned biofeedback and,
        241
      relaxation and, 240–241
  blood pressure, hypertension and, 152–155
  for bruxism, 308–309
  cardiac abnormalities, 159
    conduction disorders, 161
    ectopic rhythms, 159–160
    tachyarrhythmias, 160–161
  cerebral palsy and, 203–204
  for cerebrovascular accidents, 205–208
  chronic pain and, 270, 271, 273–274
  colitis and, 189
  conceptualization theory, 53–56
  dysmenorrhea and, 305
  encopresis/fecal incontinence and, 184
  epilepsy and, 225–227
  goal setting, 61–62
  headaches and, 23, 24, 278–279, 281. *See
    also* Biofeedback, migraine headache
  heart rate for assessing, 26
  insomnia and, 298–299

instrumentation, 53, 323–324
  blood pressure, 329–331
  blood pressure procedure checklist,
    336–337
  blood pressure self-monitoring, 331–335
  blood pressure training procedure,
    335–336
  electrodermal response, 338–339
  electroencephalogram(EEG), 339–340
  electromyograph, 324–327
  heart rate, 337–338
  vasomotor response, 327–329
migraine headache, 279–281, 283–284
  cognitive behavior therapy and, 281
  relaxation training, 279–281
for myofascial pain, 308–309
neurodermatitis and, 251–252
prurigo nodularis, 255–256
psychophysical assessment, 56–61
relaxation, hypertension and, 151–152
relaxation training:
  chronic pain and, 273
  epilepsy and, 224–225
for spasmodic torticollis, 197–198
for spinal cord injuries, 209–210
temperature:
  for psoriasis, 254–255
  Raynaud's disease, 163
tension headache, 281
thermal, Raynaud's disease, 163–165
  blood pressure for assessing, 26
  control, 73–78
  discrimination, 69–73
  self-monitoring, 62–69
  transfer, 78–83
ulcers and, 186–187
urticaria and, 253
Blacks, hypertension in, 148
Blood alcohol level, 341
  for biofeedback, 53
  discrimination with, 73
Blood flow, 26–27, 53
  biofeedback equipment, 68
Blood pressure, 26
  biofeedback, 53, 68, 69, 77, 329–331
    procedure checklist, 336–337
    self-monitoring and, 331–335
    training procedures, 335–336
  completed biofeedback control training for,
    77
  cuff, for biofeedback, 68
  discrimination with, 73
  feedback, hypertension and, 152–155
  headache, 277

home measurement of, 75
home practice and, 82
high, *see* Hypertension
hypertension and, 62
for relaxation training, 92
Borderline hypertension, 146. *See also*
    Hypertension
Brady arrhythmia, 158
Breathing:
    biofeedback and, 83
    exercise, 60
Bronchial asthma, *see* Asthma
Bruxism, 306, 307
    aversive conditioning for, 307–308
    biofeedback for, 308–309
    electromyograph for, 62
    psychophysiological assessment, 57
Bowel sounds, for biofeedback, 53

Cancer:
    cognitive behavior therapy for, 112,
        311–312
    coping with, 309–312
        operant procedures, 313
        relaxation training, 312–313
    self-management of, 126
Cardiac arrhythmias, 157
    conduction defects, 158–159
        treatment, 161
    ectopic rhythms and, 157–158
        treatment, 159–160
    heart rate for assessing, 26
    psychophysiological assessment, 57
    tachyarrhythmias, 158
        treatment, 160–161
Cardiotachometer, 25–26
Cardiovascular disorders, 145. *See also*
        Cardiac arrhythmias; Hypertension;
        Raynaud's disease
Cardiovascular measures, 25–27. *See also*
        specific measures
Causalgia, psychophysiological assessment,
        57
Cerebral palsy, 203
    treatment, 203–204
Cerebrovascular accidents (CVA), 205
    treatment, 205–208
Childbirth pain:
    electromyograph for, 62
    psychophysiological assessment, 57
    skin temperature for, 62
Children, biofeedback control training and, 77.
        See also Vomiting
Cholesterol, hypertension and, 147

Cholinergic urticaria, 252–253. *See also*
        Urticaria
Chronic airways obstruction (CAO), 233. *See*
        also Asthma
Chronic aspecific respirator affliction (CARA),
        233. *See also* Asthma
Chronic back pain, stimulus control and, 132,
        133
Chronic lower back pain, *see* Lower back pain
Chronic obstructive bronchopulmonary disease
        (COBPD), 233. *See also* Asthma
Chronic obstructive lung disease, 233. *See*
        also Asthma
Chronic obstructive pulmonary disease
        (COPD), 233. *See also* Asthma
Chronic pain, *see* Pain
Chronic vomiting, *see* Vomiting, chronic
Classical conditioning, asthma and, 236–
        237
Cognitive behavior therapy, 107–108
    advantages of, 111–112
    assessment, 113–116
    cancer and, 311–312
    chronic pain and, 272
    conceptualization training, 112–113
    control training, 116–118
    covert conditioning procedures, 119–120
        combinations, 110–112
        extinction, 109–110
        negative reinforcement, 109
        positive reinforcement, 108–109
        punishment, 110
    headache:
        biofeedback, 281
        relaxation training, 281–282
        self-control training, 282
    for lower back pain, 272
    transfer training, 118–120
Cognitive control training, ulcers and, 187
Cognitive deficiency, cognitive behavior
        therapy and, 115
Cognitive focusing, as relaxation training
        component, 97–98
Cognitive restructuring, colitis and, 190
Cognitive strategies, for stress-induced
        seizures, 224
Cognitive stressors, 59–60
Colitis, 188
    cognitive behavior therapy for, 112
    psychophysiological assessment, 57
    self-management of, 126
    treatment, 189
        biofeedback, 189
        bowel sounds, 341

cognitive restructuring, 190
multimodal approach, 190
Concentration exercises, biofeedback and, 83
Conceptualization training:
biofeedback and, 53–56
cognitive behavior therapy and, 112–113
relaxation and, 92
as self-management technique, 129
Conditioned response, 34
Conditioned stimulus, 34
Conditioning, *see* Operant techniques;
Respondent techniques
Conduction defects, *see* Cardiac arrhythmias
Congestive dysmenorrhea, 303. *See also*
Dysmenorrhea
Constipation, stimulus control and, 132, 133
Contact dermatitis, 249
Contingency contracting, 42–43
Contingency management:
chronic pain, 269, 272
encopresis/fecal incontinence and, 182–183
epilepsy and, 223
medical treatment combined with, 183–184
Contracting, 42–43
Controlled breathing, 90–91
Control training, 95–99
biofeedback, 73–78
cognitive skills, 116–118
Convulsive disorders, *see* Epilepsy
Coping skills:
relaxation as active, 90–91
ulcers and, 187
Coronary-prone behavior, self-management of, 126
Counterconditioning, 36–38. *See also* Aversive
counterconditioning; Relaxation
training; Systematic desensitization
epilepsy and, 219
Counting, relaxation training and, 100
Covert conditioning:
procedures, *see* Cognitive behavior therapy
techniques, 25
Covert-covert-rehearsal, cognitive behavior
therapy and, 117
Covert extinction, 109–110
Covert modeling, 110
Covert negative reinforcement, 109
Covert positive reinforcement, 108–109
Covert punishment, 110
Covert reinforcement, 40
Covert response cost, 110
Covert sensitization, 23

Covert techniques, progressive relaxation for
epilepsy, 224
Cue-controlled relaxation, 60, 90, 100
for psychomotor seizures, 224
Cue-controlled training:
fading of sensory restriction conditions and, 81
transfer training and, 79
Cueing strategies, self-management and, 131–132
CVA, *see* Cerebrovascular accidents

Deep muscle relaxation method, 36
Dental disorders, 306–307. *See also* Bruxism;
Myofascial pain dysfunction syndrome;
Temporomandibular joint syndrome
Depression:
low back pain and, 268
questionnaire for, 15
Dermatitis, psychophysiological assessment, 57
Dermatological problems, *see* Skin disorders
Dermatological and psychiatric treatment for
eczema, 252
Desensitization:
progressive relaxation for epilepsy, 224
relaxation, asthma and, 239–240
see also Systematic desensitization
Desirable behavior, increasing, *see* Operant
techniques
Diabetes, 299–301
psychophysiological assessment, 57
treatment, 301–302
Diastolic blood pressure, 26
Diastolic feedback, hypertension and, 153–154
Differential reinforcement, 46
Differential relaxation, 90–91
Diffuse obstructive pulmonary syndrome
(DOPS), 233. *See also* Asthma
Direct patient service, 5
Discrimination learning, 41
Discrimination training, 283
biofeedback and, 69–73
relaxation training and, 94–96
Duodenal ulcers, 185
Dysmenorrhea, 303–304
psychophysiological assessment, 57
self-management of, 126
treatment:
biofeedback, 305
systematic desensitization and relaxation, 304–305

Ectopic rhythms, *see* Cardiac arrhythmias
Eczema:
  atopic, 249–250. *See also* Neurodermatitis
  dermatological and psychiatric treatment for,
    252
  epilepsy and, 219–220
Electrodermal, for relaxation training, 92
Electrodermal response (galvanic skin
    response), 27
  for biofeedback, 53
  description, 338–339
  eruptive childbirth pain and, 62
Electroencephalography (EEG), 27
  for biofeedback, 53
  description, 339–340
  epilepsy and, 227
  psychophysiological assessment, 56, 57
  for relation training, 92
Electrograph, 68
  biofeedback and, 69
Electromyography (EMG), 24–25
  for biofeedback, 53. *See also* Biofeedback
  completed biofeedback control training for,
    77
  home measurement of, 73
  psychophysiological assessment, 56, 57
  relaxation and, 91
  relaxation training and, 95
  transfer training and, 79
  use of, 324–327
Electromyograph feedback, hypertension and,
    151–152
EMG biofeedback, *see* Biofeedback
Encopresis/fecal incontinence, 181
  treatment, 181–182
    biofeedback, 184
    contingency management, 182–183
    medical management with contingency
      management, 183–184
Environmental stressors, 59
Epilepsy, 215–216
  description, 216–217
  desensitization for, 37
  psychophysiological assessment, 57
  respondent conditioning and, 34
  self-induced seizures, 221–222
  touch-evoked, 219
  treatment, 218–219
    biofeedback, 225–227
    operant conditioning, 221–224
    respondent conditioning, 219–221
    self-control measures, 224–225
Essential hypertension, *see* Hypertension

Estimated baseline arousal condition, 58
Evaluative responses, cognitive behavior
    therapy and, 115
Exercise physiology, biofeedback and, 83
Extinction, 35–36, 44–46
  anorexia nervosa and, 175–176
  asthma and, 241–242
  chronic pain and, 269
  chronic vomiting and, 180
  covert, 109–110
  neurodermatitis and, 250
Eye closure, 219

Fading, 47
  epilepsy and, 220
  relaxation training, 101
  of sensory restriction conditions, 81
  see also Prompting
Family interactions, observations, 21
Family therapy, chronic pain and, 270, 271
Fecal incontinence, psychophysiological
    assessment, 57. *See also* Encopresis/
    fecal incontinence
Fecal retention, *see* Encopresis/fecal
    incontinence
Fecal soiling, *see* Encopresis/fecal
    incontinence
Feedback:
  anorexia nervosa and, 177
  cognitive behavior therapy and, 117
Finger temperature, completed biofeedback
    control training for, 77
Flooding, 35
  epilepsy and, 221
  ulcers and, 187

Galvanic Skin Response (GSR), 27, 338
  completed biofeedback control training for,
    77
  psychophysiological assessment, 56, 57
Gastrointestinal activity, 27
Gastrointestinal disorders, 174. *See also*
    Anorexia nervosa; Colitis; Duodenal
    ulcers; Encopresis/fecal incontinence;
    incontinence; Vomiting, chronic
Gastrointestinal motility, for biofeedback, 53
Gate control theory of pain, 262
Gestalt techniques, chronic pain and, 271
Gilles de la Tourette's syndrome, 201, 202.
    See also Tics
Goals:
  biofeedback and, 61–62
  self-management and, 130–131

Grand mal seizure, 216–217. *See also*
    Epilepsy
"Grandma's Rule," 40
Group discussions, chronic pain and, 270, 271
Group format, relaxation training and, 99

Habit reversal, Tics and, 202
Habit spasm, *see* Tics
Headache, 274–275
    biofeedback for, 23, 24
    migraine, 112, 275–276
        biofeedback for, 279, 280–281, 283–284
            with cognitive behavior therapy, 281
        blood flow for assessing, 27, 68
        combined behavior therapy for, 278–279
        hourly recording, 62–63
        medical treatment, 278
        peripheral vasomotor response, 328
        psychological factors, 277
        relaxation training, 280–281
        self-control training and, 282
        self-management of, 127
    muscle-contraction, electromyography for,
        23, 24–25
    psychological factors and, 277
    psychophysiological assessment of, 22–23
    relaxation training for, 23, 24
    self-reported ratings, 67
        biofeedback for, 279–280, 283–284
            with cognitive behavior therapy, 281
    tension, 276
        cognitive behavior therapy for, 112
        hourly recording, 62–63
        relaxation training with cognitive behavior
            therapy, 281–282
        self-control training with cognitive
            behavior therapy, 282
        self-management of, 127
        verbal relaxation, 279–280
    treatment, 277–284
Heart block, 159
Heart rate:
    assessing, 25–26
    for biofeedback, 53
    description, 337–338
    discrimination with, 73
    for relaxation training, 92
Hemiplegia, *see* Cerebrovascular accidents
High-probability behavior, as reinforcer, 40
Hirschsprung's disease, contingency training
    for, 182–183
Hives, *see* Urticaria
Home measurement, objective, 73

Home practice:
    cognitive behavior therapy, 118–119
    epilepsy and, 220
    relaxation training and, 100–101, 102
    self-management and, 134
    transfer training and, 80–82
Homosexuality, psychophysiological
    assessment, 57
Hospital, observations in, 21
Hyperactivity:
    actometer motoric movement, 62
    psychophysiological assessment, 57
    self-management of, 126
Hyperhidrosis, 256
    treatment, 256
Hypertension, 146–149
    blood pressure biofeedback for, 152–155
        relaxation and, 155–156
    blood pressure cuff recordings for, 62
    completed biofeedback control training for,
        77
    discrimination training and, 94
    essential, 147
        assessment, 22
        blood flow for assessing, 27
        blood pressure for assessing, 26
        cognitive behavior therapy for, 112
        electromyography for, 25
        etiology, 147, 148
        heart rate for assessing, 26
        self-management and, 126
        treatment, 148
    psychophysiological assessment, 57
    relaxation for:
        biofeedback assisted, 151–152
        blood pressure feedback and, 155–156
        combinations, 150–151
        meditation, 150
        progressive muscle, 149–150
    secondary, 147
Hypnosis, 60, 90, 253
    biofeedback and, 83

Ideopathic insomnia, 295. *See also* Insomnia
Imagery, 60, 90–91
    biofeedback and, 83
    chronic pain, 272
    covert positive reinforcement and, 109
Imitation, *see* Modeling
Impotence, psychophysiological assessment,
    57
Inapproprioception, cerebral palsy and, 203
Incentive modification, self-management, 132

Individualization, relaxation training and, 99
Infants, *see* Vomiting, chronic
Insomnia, 293–296
  cognitive behavior therapy for, 112
  psychophysiological assessment, 57
  stimulus control for, 47, 131–132, 133
  stimulus generalization for, 47
  self-management of, 126
  treatment, 296
    biofeedback, 298–299
    relaxation training, 296–298
    stimulus control and, 298
    systematic desensitization and autogenic
      training, 296
Instructional set component, 97
Interview, 12–14
Intrinsic asthma, 235. *See also* Asthma
Irritable bowel syndrome, *see* Colitis
Ischemic, self-management of, 126

Jacksonian epilepsy, 217. *See also* Epilepsy

"Labile" hypertensives, 147. *See also*
  Hypertension
Laboratory, structured observation, 21–22
Letdown phenomenon, migraine and, 277
Lichenified dermatitis, 249. *See also*
  Neurodermatitis
Lichen simplex, 251
Lichen simplex chronicus, 249. *See also*
  Neurodermatitis
Life-style behaviors, 126. *See also* Self-
  management techniques
Low arousal procedures, biofeedback and, 83
Lower back pain, 266
  psychological variables, 266–268
  psychophysiological assessment, 57
  self-management of, 126
  treatment:
    cognitive behavior therapy and, 272
    operant approach, 270
    progressive relaxation, 272
    self regulation, 271
Lowered arousal exercises,
  psychophysiological assessment, 60
Low probability behavior, 40
Lung disease, chronic obstructive, 233. *See
  also* Asthma

Magnification, cognitive behavior therapy and,
  115
Maladie de Gilles de la Tourette, 200. *See
  also* Tics

Maladie des tics, *see* Tics
Manipulation therapy, biofeedback and, 83
Marital therapy, chronic pain, 272
Medical psychology, behavioral medicine
  differentiated from, 2
Medication:
  for hypertension, 148, 150
  intake, biofeedback and, 67–68, 74
Meditation:
  biofeedback and, 83
  intake, relaxation and, 94
  relaxation skills and, 60, 96
Menstruation, pain accompanying, *see*
  Dysmenorrhea
Metronome-conditioned relaxation, 60, 90,
  100, 149
Migraine, psychophysiological assessment, 57
Migraine headaches, *see* Headaches
Mimic spasm, *see* Tics
Mini-relaxation, 90–91
Minnesota Multiphasic Personality Inventory
  (MMPI), lower back pain for, 268
Mixed asthma, 235–236. *See also* Asthma
Modeling, 40–41
  cognitive behavior therapy and, 117
  covert, 110
  see also Assertiveness training
Money, as reinforcer, 39
Multimodal approach, colitis and, 190
Multiple Affect Adjective Checklist, 15
Muscle-contraction headaches, *see* Headaches
Muscle quietude, as relaxation training
  component, 97
Muscle tension/relaxation, discrimination
  training for, 95
Musculoskeletal disorders, 196. *See also*
  Cerebral palsy; Cerebrovascular
  accidents; Spasmodic torticollis; Spinal
  cord injuries; Tics
Musicogenic epilepsy, 219, 220–221
Myofascial pain dysfunction syndrome
  (MPDS), 306–307
  biofeedback for, 308–309
Myofascial pain syndrome, cognitive behavior
  therapy for, 112

Negative responses, cognitive behavior therapy, 115
Nervous (tension) headache, *see* Headache
Nervous system disorder, *see* Epilepsy
Neurodermatitis, 248–250
  treatment, 250–252
  see also specific types of neurodermatitis
Nonverbal behaviors, assertiveness training, 41

Obesity:
  hypertension and, 147
  self-management of, 126
  stimulus control and, 131–132
Observations, relaxation training assessment,
    92–93. *See also* Assessment
Operant approaches:
  asthma and, 241–243
  chronic pain and, 268–270
  see also specific approaches
Operant conditioning, epilepsy and, 221–224
Operantly conditioned biofeedback, asthma
    and, 241
Operant procedures:
  cancer and, 313
  diabetes and, 301
  for spasmodic torticollis, 198–199
  for tics, 200–201
Operant techniques, 38–39
  decreasing undesirable behavior, 43
    differential reinforcement of other
      behavior, 46
    extinction, 44–46
    punishment, 43–44
  increasing desirable behavior:
    assertiveness training, 41
    contingency contracting, 42–43
    modeling, 40–41
    positive reinforcement, 39–43
    prompting, 40
    shaping, 40
  stimulus control, 46–47
Overcorrection procedure:
  chronic vomiting, 180
  encopresis/fecal incontinence and, 182
Over-eating, self-management of, 126
Over-generalization, cognitive behavior
    therapy and, 115
Overt aversive reinforcers, 119–120
Overt-overt-rehearsal, cognitive behavior
    therapy and, 117
Overt positive reinforcers, 119

Pain:
  chronic, 264–266. *See also* Lower back pain
  description, 261–264
  treatment, 268
    biofeedback, 273–274
    multidisciplinary approaches, 270–272
    operant approaches, 268–270
    relaxation and cognitive strategies, 272
  see also Headache
Paraplegia, *see* Spinal cord injuries
Passive mental relaxation, 60

Passive relaxation, 90–91
  biofeedback and, 83
Pattern theory of pain, 261–262
Pedophilia, psychophysiological assessment,
    57
Peptic ulcer, 185. *See also* Ulcers
Perspiration, see Hyperhidrosis
Petit mal attacks, 217. *See also* Epilepsy
Peripheral blood flow, 26–27, 53
Personalization, cognitive behavior therapy,
    115
Photoplethysmograph, 327–328
  for biofeedback, 53
Physical exercise, 90–91
Physical fitness, self-management of, 127
Physical rehabilitation, chronic pain and,
    271
Physical therapy:
  biofeedback and, 83
  chronic pain, 272
Physiological relaxation, 97
Pictures, skin disorders and, 62
Pink noise, 60, 90–91
Pleasant events schedule, 15
  self-management and, 133
Pneumographs, relaxation and, 91–92
Polarization, cognitive behavior therapy and,
    115
Positive reinforcement, *see* Reinforcement
Practice, relaxation training and, 97, 98. *See
    also* Home practice
Praise, as reinforcer, 39
Premack principle, 40
  relaxation control training and, 95
Premature ventricular contractions (PVC), 157,
    159–160
Pressure traducers, 27
Prevention of disease, 6
Primary dysmenorrhea, 303. *See also*
    Dysmenorrhea
Primary insomnia, 295. *See also* Insomnia
Progressive muscle relaxation (PMR), for
    hypertension, 149–150
Progressive relaxation, 90, 95, 98
  biofeedback and, 83
  chronic pain, 272
  for lower back pain, 272
Progressive physical tension relaxation, 60
Prompting, 40
  fading, 40
Prurigo nodularis, 255
  psychophysiological assessment, 57
  treatment, 255–256
Pseudoinsomniacs, 295. *See also* Insomnia

Psoriasis, 249, 254
    psychophysiological assessment, 57
    treatment, 254–255
Psychogenic pain, 263–264
Psychogenic (tension) headache, *see* Headache
Psychological relaxation, hypertension and,
    150
Psychomotor epilepsy, 217. *See also* Epilepsy
Psychophysiological assessment:
    biofeedback and, 56–61
    relaxation training and, 92–93
Psychophysiological measurement, 22–24. *See
    also* Assessment
Psychosocial stressors, 59
Psychosomatic medicine, behavioral medicine
    differentiated from, 1
Punishment, 43–44
    asthma and, 242–243
    chronic vomiting and, 178–180
    covert, 110
    self-induced seizures and, 222
Pupillometry, 27

Quadriplegia, *see* Spinal cord injuries
Questionnaires, 14–16. *See also specific
    questionnaires*
"Quiet," as relaxation training component, 97

Rapid relaxation, 90–91
Raynaud's disease, 162–163
    blood flow for assessing, 27
    peripheral vasomotor responses for, 328
    psychophysiological assessment, 57
    self-management of, 127
    skin temperature for, 62
    treatment, 163–165
Reading epilepsy, 219, 221
Rebreathing, biofeedback and, 83
Recall, relaxation training and, 100
Reflex epilepsy, 219, 220
Rehearsal, self-management and, 134
Reinforcement, 100
    anorexia nervosa and, 175–177
    aversive, overt, 119–120
    covert, 40
        urticaria, 253
    differential, 46
    of home practice, 80
    positive, 39–43
        asthma and, 241–242
        covert, 108–109
        overt, 119
        punishment and, 43–44
        time-out from, 45

    negative, covert, 109
    questionnaires measuring sources of, 15
    relaxation training and, 98
    self-, 40
    self-management and, 132–133
    for self-monitoring, 67
    social, chronic pain and, 269
Reinforcement Menu, 15
Reinforcement survey, self-management and,
    133
Reinforcement Survey Schedule, 15, 39
Relaxation, 60
    biofeedback control training and, 76
    blood pressure for assessing, 26
    dysmenorrhea and, 304–305
    exercises, 95
    headache and, 23
    metronome-controlled, 60
    passive mental, 60
    Raynaud's disease, 163
    self-management of, 127
    see also Hypertension
Relaxation response, 90, 98
    hypertension and, 150
Relaxation training, 23, 25, 36, 90–91
    asthma and, 237–239
        biofeedback and, 240–241
        desensitization and, 239–240
    aversive conditioning, skin disorders and, 251
    biofeedback, chronic pain and, 273
    cancer and, 312–313
    chronic pain and, 270, 271, 272
    conceptualization training, 92
    control training, 96–99
    discrimination training, 94–96
    headaches and, 24, 278–282
    heart rate for assessing, 26
    hypnosis, 253
    insomnia and, 296–298
    instructions, 341–342
    instrumentation, 91–92
    migraine headache, 280–281
    positive:
        epilepsy and, 221
        neurodermatitis and, 250
    prurigo nodularis and, 255–256
    psychophysiological assessment, 92
    self-directed, biofeedback, 58–59
    self-monitoring training, 93–94
    social, neurodermatitis and, 251
    for stress-induced seizures, 224
    tension headache, 279–280
        cognitive behavior therapy, 281–282
    transfer training, 99–102

Release pressure, migraine and, 277
Respiration, for biofeedback, 53
Respiratory disorder, 233. *See also* Asthma
Respondent conditioning, 34–35
    epilepsy and, 219–221
Respondent techniques, 33–34
    counterconditioning, 36–38. *See also*
        Aversive counterconditioning;
        Relaxation; Systematic desensitization
    extinction, 35–36
    respondent conditioning, 34–35
Response-contingent punishment, chronic
    vomiting and, 178–180
Response cost, 45
    asthma and, 242
    covert, 110
Response suppression shaping, asthma and,
    242–243
Rheumatic heart disease, 161
Rothus Assertiveness Inventory, 15
Rotter I-E Scale, 15
Rumination, *see* Vomiting

Scratching, 44. *See also* Skin disorders
Seborrheic dermatitis, 249
Secondary hypertension, 147. *See also*
    Hypertension
Secondary insomnia, 295. *See also* Insomnia
Seizures, 57
    self-induced, 221–222
    stroboscopic-induced, 219
    see also Epilepsy
Self-control behaviors, 127. *See also* Self-
    management techniques
Self-control methods:
    for epilepsy, 224–225
    for tics, 201–202
Self-control techniques, chronic pain, 272
Self-detection, self-monitoring through, 62–63
Self-induced seizures, 221–222
Self-instructional training, 108
Self-managed relaxation, 90–91
Self-management techniques, 126–129
    conceptualization training, 129
    cueing strategies, 131–132
    goal specification, 130–131
    headaches and, 278–279, 282
    incentive modification, 132–133
    rehearsal, 134–135
    self-monitoring training, 129–130
Self-modification, neurodermatitis and, 251
Self-monitoring, 16–18
    blood pressure, 331–335
    headaches and, 283

Self-monitoring training:
    biofeedback and, 62–69
    relaxation training and, 93–94
    self-management and, 129–130
Self-punishment, self-management and, 132
Self-ratings, relaxation training assessment, 92
Self regulation techniques, chronic pain and,
    271
Self-reinforcement, 40
    aversive counterconditioning for, 37
    self-management and, 132
Sensori-Motor Rhythm, epilepsy and, 226
Sensory-evoked epilepsy, 219
Sensory restriction baseline arousal condition,
    58
Sensory restriction conditions, relaxation
    training and, 101
Sexual arousal, for biofeedback, 53
Sexual deviations:
    male, 341
    stimulus control and, 132
Sexual dysfunction, self-management of, 127
Shaping, 40
    procedures, self-management and, 133
    response suppression, asthma and, 242–243
Shock, neurodermatitis, 251
Shock punishment, chronic vomiting and, 179
Sinus headaches, 277
Skin, *see* Electrodermal response
Skin disorders, 248–249. *See also*
    Hyperhidrosis; Neurodermatitis;
    Urticaria
Skin Potential Response (SPR), 338
Skin temperature:
    biofeedback, 68, 69
        Raynaud's disease, 163
    home measurement of, 73
    home practice and, 82
    measurement, for biofeedback, 68
    Raynaud's disease and, 62
    thermometers, for relaxation training, 92
    vasomotor response measurement and,
        328–329
Sleep, 293
    biofeedback control training and, 76
    relaxation training and, 98
    see also Insomnia
Smoking, 147
    self-management of, 126, 127
    stimulus control and, 131–132
Social factors, muscle-contraction headaches,
    24
Social skills training, biofeedback and, 83
Soiling, *see* Encopresis/fecal incontinence

Somatosensory epilepsy, 219
Spasmodic dysmenorrhea, 303. *See also*
    Dysmenorrhea
Spasmodic torticollis, 196–197
    treatment, 197
        biofeedback, 197–198
        operant procedures, 198–199
        systematic desensitization, 199
Spasms, *see* Tics
Specificity theory of pain, 261
Sphincter activity, for biofeedback, 53
Spinal cord injuries, 208–209
    treatment, 209–210
S-R Inventory of Anxiousness, 15
Startle epilepsy, 219
Stasis dermatitis, 249
State Trait Anxiety Inventory, 15
Stimulation generalization, 47
Stimulus control:
    insomnia and, 298
    self-management and, 131–132
Stomach acid pH, for biofeedback, 53
Stress, 174
    arousal, psychophysiological assessment,
        58–60
    cardiovascular response to, 148
    epilepsy and, 215–216
    management:
        conceptualization training and, 54–56
        diabetes and, 301–302
    migraine and, 277
    questionnaires for, 15
    reactions, cognitive behavior therapy, 114
    stimulus, transfer training and, 81–82
    see also Gastrointestinal disorders
Stroboscopic epilepsy, 220
Stroboscopic-induced seizures, 219
Stroke, *see* Cerebrovascular accidents
Structured interviews, 12–13, 14
Stuttering, psychophysiological assessment, 57
Successive approximation, *see* Shaping
Supraventricular tachycardias, 158, 160
Surgery, extinguishing fear response in child
    and, 35
Systematic desensitization, 36–37
    dysmenorrhea and, 304–305
    epilepsy and, 221
    headaches and, 278–279
    for hyperhidrosis, 256
    insomnia and, 296
    modification, 23
    monitoring, electromyography and, 25
    self-management and, 133
    for spasmodic torticollis, 199

Systolic blood pressure, 26
Systolic feedback, hypertension and, 153–154

Tachyarrhythmias, *see* Cardiac arrhythmias
Tachycardias, 158, 160
Tardive dyskinesia, psychophysiological
    assessment, 57
Teeth, improper occlusion of, 307. *See also*
    Dental disorders
Temperature biofeedback, psoriasis and,
    254–255
Tempomandibular joint, myofascial pain-
    dysfunction, psychophysiological
    assessment, 57
Temporomandibular joint syndrome (TMJ),
    306
Temporomandibular pain-dysfunction
    syndrome, *see* Myofascial pain
    dysfunction syndrome
Tension headaches, *see* Headaches
Tension/muscle contraction headache,
    psychophysiological assessment, 57
Thermal biofeedback, Raynaud's disease and,
    163–165
Thought-stopping, 253
    epilepsy and, 225
Thrombosis, *see* Cerebrovascular accidents
Tics, 200
    treatment, 200
        operant procedures, 200–201
        self-control methods, 201–202
Time out:
    asthma and, 242
    from positive reinforcement, 45
Tinea cruris, 249
Tinnitus, psychophysiological assessment, 57
Token economies, 42, 250
Token system, anorexia nervosa and, 176
Torticollis, psychophysiological assessment,
    57. *See also* Spasmodic torticollis
Touch-evoked epilepsy, 219
Transcendental meditation, 60, 90
    hypertension and, 150
Transfer training:
    biofeedback and, 78–83
    cognitive skills, 118–120
    monitoring during, 65, 66
    relaxation training and, 99–102

Ulcers, 185–186
    psychophysiological assessment, 57
    self-management of, 127
    stomach acid pH in treatment of, 341
    treatment, 186–187

biofeedback, 186–187
  combinations, 187
Undesirable behavior, decreasing, *see* Operant
  techniques
Unstructured interview, 13
Urticaria, 252–253
  psychophysiological assessment, 57
  treatment, 253

Vasomotor, for relaxation training, 92
Vasomotor responses, description, 327–329
Verbal feedback, relaxation training and, 98
Videotape:
  biofeedback control training and, 75
  observation and, 19
Video-tape relaxation, 90–91
  training, 99
Vigilance method, epilepsy and, 221
Visualization, biofeedback and, 83

Voice-induced epilepsy, 219, 220–221
Vomiting, chronic, 177–178
  aversive counterconditioning for, 37
  punishment used for, 44
  treatment:
    extinction, 180
    punishment, 178–180

Wolff-Parkinson-White (WPW) syndrome,
  158, 161
Wrist counter self-monitored behaviors
  recorded by, 17
Wry neck, *see* Spasmodic torticollis

Yoga, 90
  biofeedback, 83
  exercises, 60
  hypertension and, 150–151